American Indians at Risk

Volume 2

Jeffrey Ian Ross

AN IMPRINT OF ABC-CLIO, LLC
Santa Barbara, California • Denver, Colorado • Oxford, England

Library of Congress Cataloging-in-Publication Data

Ross, Jeffrey Ian.
American Indians at risk / Jeffrey Ian Ross.
pages cm
Includes bibliographical references and index.
ISBN 978-0-313-39764-6 (hardcover : alk. paper) — ISBN 978-0-313-39765-3 (ebook)
1. Indians of North America—Criminal justice system. 2. Indians of North America—Social conditions. 3. Indians of North America—Government relations. I. Title.
E98.C87R67 2014
323.1197 -dc23 2013012802

ISBN: 978-0-313-39764-6
EISBN: 978-0-313-39765-3

18 17 16 15 14 1 2 3 4 5

This book is also available on the World Wide Web as an eBook.
Visit www.abc-clio.com for details.

Greenwood
An Imprint of ABC-CLIO, LLC

ABC-CLIO, LLC
130 Cremona Drive, P.O. Box 1911
Santa Barbara, California 93116-1911

This book is printed on acid-free paper ♾
Manufactured in the United States of America

Dedicated to
Kine Monteros Serano, la madre de mi esposa, la abuela de mis hijos, y mi suegra.
I'm forever grateful for your love and commitment to my family and me.

Contents

American Indian and Alaskan Native Mental Health Issues

Favian Alejandro Martín

Recent Census statistics suggest that there are 5.2 American Indians and Alaskan Natives (AI/NA) in the United States (Norris, Vines, and Hoeffel 2012) comprising about 1.7 percent of the total population. Although the AI/NA population has grown from previous years (Ogunwole 2006), they continue to confront many challenges ranging from high rates of poverty to substance abuse; the most pertinent of these being mental health issues. Current research reveals that AI/NAs are more likely to suffer from mental health issues than the general U.S. population (Johnson and Cameron, 2001; Zahran et al. 2004). In fact, over 20 percent of the total AI/NA population experiences a mental health issue (Duran, Sanders, Skipper, Waitzkin, Malcoe, Paine, and Yager 2004). More importantly, AI/NA mental health problems are further exacerbated by barriers and obstacles that impede their ability to receive adequate treatment to overcome their illness. Although the prevalence of mental health issues among AI/NAs is high, the problem continues to be neglected by the medical field (U.S. Department of Health & Human Services 2001; Manson and Altschul 2004). This chapter provides an overview of AI/NA mental health issues as well as of the barriers and obstacles that obstruct their access to treatment. Before discussing these challenges, a brief analysis of colonialism, as it relates to AI/NA mental health issues, is provided, followed by a general discussion of this problem among these individuals.

COLONIALISM

Scholars suggest that the social ills of colonialism contribute to the social pathology of the AI/NA population (Snipp 1992). Brave Heart and Debruyn (1998, 60) assert that many of the social problems experienced by the AI/NA population (i.e., mental health issues and substance abuse) are "primarily the product of a legacy of chronic trauma and unresolved grief across generations." For instance, prior to the colonialism of the Americas an estimated 8 to 12 million indigenous individuals inhabited the North American continent (Sale 1990); however, by the late 1890s the population was substantially reduced to 250,000 (Healey 2003). The significant decline in the indigenous population was caused by the European conquest for territory and exposure to diseases (Smedley, Stith, and Nelson 2003). In the aftermath of colonialism, the indigenous population experienced historical trauma and cultural oppression, which has been linked to their contemporary mental health issues (Kirmayer, Simpson, and Cargo 2003; Duran 2006; Gone 2007). For example, an earlier study, examining AI/NA mental health issues, found that a large percentage of Navajo Nation tribal members experience depression due to unresolved grief stemming from the effects of colonialism (Miller and Schoenfeld 1973). Likewise, Kleinfeld and Bloom (1977) found that nearly 50 percent of Native Alaskan former Indian boarding students were suffering from emotional and social adjustment problems. Similarly, a substantial portion of the Coastal Salish Indian tribe in the Pacific Northwest reported feelings of depression, which was largely attributed to the loss of their cultural identity and acculturation policies (Jilek 1974). Due to the effects of colonialism, many AI/ NAs continue to experience mental health issues.

AI/NA MENTAL HEALTH ISSUES

Research on AI/NA mental health issues is severely limited (Gone 2003; Manson and Altschul 2004), but available studies suggest that this segment of the population experiences high rates of psychological distress, suicide, and other mental health issues compared to the general U.S. population (Zahran et al. 2004; Indian Health Service 2005). More recently, the American Indian Service Utilization, Psychiatric Epidemiology, Risk and Protective Factors Project (AI-SUPERPFP) was initiated to understand the prevalence of mental health issues within two reservation communities (Beals et al. 2005). Their findings suggest that tribal members from both reservation communities suffered from a lifetime prevalence of substance abuse and posttraumatic stress disorder (PTSD). Upon comparing the data from the AI-SUPERPFP with the National Comorbidity Survey (NCS), the researchers found that AI/NAs experienced higher rates of lifetime PTSD and lifetime alcohol dependence compared to the general population. Aside from the AI-SUPERPFP study, other research has found that AI/NAs experience high rates of behavioral and mood disorders as well as suicide (Gone and Alcántara 2007). Similarly, researchers found that depression within three American Indian tribes was linked to alcoholism and hallucinations (Shore et al. 1987). While studies have examined the prevalence of AI/NA mental health issues, other research has focused on these problems experienced by Native war veterans.

AMERICAN INDIAN VIETNAM WAR VETERANS AND MENTAL HEALTH ISSUES

To address the needs of Vietnam War veterans, the federal government created a series of initiatives to treat veterans suffering from PTSD and other adjustment problems. One such program was specifically directed towards the AI/NA population, the American Indian Vietnam Veterans Project (AIVVP), which examined mental health problems among AI/NA individuals. Scholars argue that AI/NAs were exposed to more dangerous situations than their white counterparts. The AIVVP found that PTSD was a common occurrence for AI/NA Vietnam War veterans. For instance, in a survey of Indian Vietnam War veterans living in two reservations—one located in the Southwest and the other in the northern plains—57 percent and 45 percent (respectively) reported to be suffering from a lifetime prevalence of PTSD (National Center for Post-Traumatic Stress Disorder and the National Center for American Indian and Alaska Native Mental Health Research [NCPTSD/NCAIANMHR] 1996). Similarly, AI/NA Vietnam War veterans are more likely to experience current and lifetime episodes of PTSD at a higher rate than whites (Gurley et al. 2001; Beals et al. 2002). As Holm (1995, 83) notes, "Some of their commanders, clinging to the stereotype of Indians as natural practitioners of woodcraft, ordered Native soldiers to walk point more than others and assigned them to long range reconnaissance patrols, thereby increasing their chances of becoming causalities." Given the harsh realities of war, many AI/NA veterans experience a series of mental health issues.

AI/NA YOUTH MENTAL HEALTH ISSUES

AI/NA youth experience high rates of mental health problems. These challenges are widespread, considering that AI/NA youth are more likely than their non-AI/NA counterparts to experience a mental health problem such as anxiety disorder, mood disorder, conduct and oppositional defiant disorder, disruptive behavior disorder, and separation anxiety disorder (Novins et al. 1996; Beals et al.1997; Costello et al.1997; Duclos et al. 1998). Moreover, older AI/NA youth (14–16 years) are more likely to suffer from higher rates of disorder than non-AI/NA juveniles (Beals et al. 1997). A limited number of studies have focused on the prevalence of mental health issues among Native youth in their reservation communities; however, these studies suggest that these youth are experiencing mental health issues at higher rates. For example, over 60 percent of the northern plains tribal youth were diagnosed with a depressive disorder (U.S. Department of Health & Human Services 2001). Similarly, Native Alaskan youth seeking treatment at a mental health clinic have been reported to be suffering from substance abuse and/or attempted suicide due to their illness (Aoun and Gregory 1998). AI/NA mental health issues (both adult and juvenile) are linked to several factors that range from living in poor conditions to experiencing a traumatic event. This includes historical as well as contemporary traumatic events. Consider the role of boarding schools.

Traumatic experiences at Indian boarding schools have contributed to a myriad of mental health issues within the AI/NA population (Fuchs and Havighurst 1972; Kleinfled and Bloom 1977). In an attempt to assimilate the Native population into the Anglo society, these institutions were utilized to immerse the AI/NA youth in the values and culture of the Anglo culture (Irwin and Roll 1995; Kunitz et al. 1999). The immersion process proved to be traumatic for individuals attending these schools. For instance, these youths were forcibly removed from their parents and ancestral homes and placed in institutions hundreds of miles away (Churchill 2004). Upon their arrival, they were given a new "Anglo" identity, which required them to adopt an English name and wear European-style clothing. The youth were restricted from practicing their Native culture and religion; instead, they were required to embrace Christianity and speak the English language. As part of a strict regimen, the youth were required to accomplish grueling chores, and failure to complete the tasks often resulted in severe forms of abuse. Moreover, many reported being mentally, physically, and sexually abused by Indian boarding school faculty and staff (Smith 2005). As a result of Indian boarding schools, many former students were found to be suffering from several mental health issues that include anxiety, depression, suicidal behavior, and substance abuse (Novins, Beals, Roberts, and Manson 1999). With generations of AI/NAs being enrolled in Indian boarding schools, it is not surprising that many of these former students and their families continue to experience a host of mental health issues.

FACTORS AFFECTING MENTAL HEALTH ISSUES

Currently, a substantial percentage of the AI/NA population lives in a stressful environment that is conducive to negative mental health issues (Evans and English 2002; Evans, Wells, and Moch 2003). Federal policies of forced relocation and isolation have continuously caused this segment of the population to suffer from economic deprivation and social exclusion. Recent poverty statistics paint a grim situation for the AI/NA population: this segment of the population has the highest rate of poverty (28.4 percent), which is almost two times higher than the national average (14.2 percent) (U.S. Census 2010). In order to survive, nearly half of all reservation residents rely on federal assistance in the form of food stamps and welfare checks as a form of sustenance (Feagin and Feagin 2008). Another problem for reservation residents is that a significant percentage of these individuals do not have electricity, running water, or sewage facilities. In fact, about 12 percent of the total AI/NA population residing on a reservation do not have access to adequate water supplies or sewage facilities (Pickering 2000). Given these conditions, many AI/NAs experience negative mental health issues (Manson, Shore, and Bloom 1985). Research has shown that there is a correlation between low socioeconomic status and mental health issues (Barrett and Turner 2005). Although living in a stressful environment can cause mental health issues, experiencing a traumatic event can also exacerbate this problem.

TRAUMATIC EVENTS

Traumatic experiences can greatly impact the cognitive, emotional, physical, and social development of individuals (O'Brien 1998). As a result, traumatic experiences can lead to several mental health issues including conduct, dissociative, and posttraumatic stress disorders (O'Brien 1998; Perry and Pollard 1998). In general, the AI/NA population experiences more traumatic events (directly or indirectly) than any other group in the United States (Manson et al. 2005; Boyd-Ball et al. 2006). However, Native youth are more likely to be impacted by these events than AI/NA adults. For instance, when an American Indian child reaches the age of nine years, they have already had three to five people who were close to them pass away (Bad Wound 2000). Due to the interconnectedness of tribal communities, a traumatic event resulting in a serious injury or death of a tribal member can greatly impact the behaviors of AI/NA individuals, especially Native youth (Robin, Long, Rasmussen, Albaugh, and Goldman 1998). Over 60 percent of northern plain youth reported that they have experienced a traumatic event (*American Indian and Alaska Native Resource Manual* [NAMI] 2003). For many AI/NAs, another source of trauma comes from being victims of a violent crime. Recent statistics from the Bureau of Justice suggest that AI/NAs are more likely to be victims of a violent crime than any other group in the United States; one in ten AI/NAs is likely to experience a violent crime in their lifetime (Perry 2004). These rates are especially high for AI/NA women. For example, AI/NA women experience higher rates of violent victimization than other women in the U.S. population (Greenfield and Smith 1999; Perry 2004). AI/NA women are two and a half times more likely to be a victim of rape or sexual assault than other women (Perry 2004). In addition, both AI/NA males and females are subjected to physical and sexual abuse by family members at a higher rate than the general population (Fairchild, Fairchild, and Stoner 1998; Vernon and Bubar 2001; Bohn 2002; Malley-Morrison and Hines 2004). In fact, between 1992 and 1996 one in six AI/NAs was violently victimized by a family member (Greenfeld and Smith 1999). Bachmann (1992, 95) notes that "family members are often the scapegoats of the aggression that results from everyday stressors." Given that a large percentage of the AI/NA population experiences financial and social hardships, many are susceptible to family violence. Research has shown that the exposure to such traumatic events is related to negative mental health issues such as PSTD, anger, and depression (Kessler et al. 1995). Given the pervasiveness of mental health issues among AI/NAs, this group of individuals also experience high rates of suicide.

SUICIDE

Research suggests that over 90 percent of individuals who have committed suicide were suffering from a psychiatric disorder (Ghosh and Victor 1999; Maris et al. 2000). Given that AI/NAs experience high rates of mental health issues, this segment of the population also has the highest rates of suicide in the country (Centers for Disease Control and Prevention [CDC] 2008). In fact, suicide is the eighth leading cause of death of AI/NAs in all age groups (Indian Health Service 1996; Peters, Martin, Ventura, and Maurer 1997). Furthermore, the suicide rate among Native youth has risen substantially in recent years. It is the second leading cause of death for those 15 to 24 years (CDC 2003), and Native youth experience a suicide rate that is two times higher than their non-Native peers (CDC 2005). Several studies found that 14 percent to 30 percent of Native high-school students have attempted suicide (Blum et al. 1992; Borowsky et al.1999; Freedenthal and Stiffman 2004). This is extremely high, considering that 4 percent to 10 percent of non-Native high-school students have attempted suicide (Substance Abuse and Mental Health Services Administration 2002). Native juveniles living in urban areas are more likely to commit suicide. These juveniles are geographically removed from their ancestral communities, but also any entitlement to Indian health programs in the Indian reservation that may prevent suicide. As Johnson and Tomren (1999, 298) note, "risk factors for American Indian suicide including stress, rapid economic and cultural change, acculturation and loss of culture, isolation and lack of strong identity are increased among American Indian youth in urban areas." Although the AI/NA population experience high rates of suicide, another problem that is correlated with mental health issues is alcohol and illegal drug consumption.

Fort Peck Tribal Judge Roxanne Gourneau talks about her son's suicide in 2010, while her nieces display poster boards with pictures of her dead son, during U.S. Senate Committee on Indian Affairs hearing on August 9, 2011 in Poplar, Montana. The rash of suicides in Poplar shocked the community and prompted the U.S. Public Health Service to send emergency teams to provide counseling and mental health services in Fort Peck in 2010. (AP Photo/Richard Peterson)

SUBSTANCE ABUSE

Research has shown that chronic drug users (alcohol and illegal drugs) often suffer from mental health issues (Mueser, Drake, and Noordsy 1998). Moreover, recent statistics suggest that over 20 percent of individuals suffering from depression were dependent on alcohol or an illegal drug (Office of Applied Studies 2009). Historically, AI/NAs have struggled with alcohol and illegal drug problems.

A National Survey on Drug Use and Health (NSDUH) (2011) found that AI/NA adults experience higher rates of alcohol binges (and illegal drug use) than the general population. The report found that 9.6 percent of the total AI/NA population received treatment for their substance abuse, which is higher than the national average of 18 percent. The high rates of alcohol and illegal drug consumption also transcend into the Native juvenile population. The National Institute on Drug Abuse (NIDA) (2003) report found that Native juveniles are over two times more likely to use alcohol than other juveniles. Moreover, Native juveniles begin consuming alcohol at an earlier age than non-Natives (Barnes, Welte, and Hoffman 2002). The risk for alcohol consumption and illegal drug use is greater for those living on Indian reservations (NIDA 2003), and consequently these young people are more likely to drop out of school. Other individuals also consume other illegal drugs. In recent years, the total AI/NA population has seen an increase in illegal drug use such as marijuana, cocaine, and methamphetamine (National Congress of American Indians [NCAI] 2006). The Navajo Nation reported a 100 percent increase in methamphetamine use within recent years (Vigil 2006). This drug has devastated AI/NA families. According to the Californian Indian Services, whenever a Native child is taken out of their home, either one or both parents are methamphetamine addicts (NCAI 2006). Despite the high prevalence of mental health issues and its related problems (i.e., suicide and substance abuse), AI/NAs are eligible for treatment; however, this, too, is limited.

Hiawatha Insane Asylum for indians in Cranton, South Dakota, ca. 1903. (Sioux Valley News)

Given the prevalence of general health and mental health issues among AI/NAs, the federal government has implemented programs and policies to assist these individuals to overcome their afflictions. Historically, AI/NAs believed that health issues were caused by demonic entities, which could only be cured through the help of a medicine man or shaman. All too often, the Native healer would perform a healing prayer or give the individual a mixture of herbs to cure them of their affliction (Alexander 2005). The first institution created to treat AI/NAs for mental health issues was founded in 1889; the Hiawatha Asylum for Insane Indians in Canton, South Dakota (Yellow Bird 2001), was the only federal-sponsored mental health institution with the sole purpose of treating those suffering from mental health issues. The creation of this institution was due to the belief that a "separate institution for Native Americans was needed because they had unique mental health afflictions" (Bhatara, Gupta, and Brokenleg 1999, 767). Similar to Indian boarding schools, the Hiawatha Asylum provided poor care, and there were a high number of mistreated patients. The mental health facility lacked indoor plumbing and electricity; the hospital staff lacked basic medical training. Problems were further exacerbated by the use of physical force to control the individuals. For the hospital staff, force and abuse served as means to control the patients. An investigation of the facility found that many of the patients were not suffering from mental health issues. In fact, many were alcoholics or were confined for opposing the federal government (Yellow Bird 2001). It was not until 1934 that the mental health facility was closed. However, the need to treat AI/NAs for general health and mental health issues led the federal government to establish the Indian Health Service in 1955, and all tribal members of federally recognized AI/NA tribes are entitled to access health care at any of the Indian Health Service hospitals or clinics (Gone 2003; Pevar 2004). Despite access to health care, many AI/NAs suffering from mental health issues often confront obstacles that impede their ability to receive adequate treatment.

BARRIERS TO MENTAL HEALTH TREATMENT

Given the legacy of the federal government's assimilation policies (i.e., Indian boarding schools and forced relocation) as well as other atrocities (the Hiawatha Asylum for Insane Indians), many AI/NAs are distrustful about receiving treatment from government-sponsored clinics (*American Indian and Alaska Native Resource Manual* [NAMI] 2003). In general, many AI/NA individuals suffering from mental health issues refuse to seek professional treatment because such services represent the "white man's" culture (Gone 2004; Grandbois 2005). AI/NA culture can serve as a barrier: Native languages can impede the ability of receiving mental health treatment. Recent statistics suggest that about 18 percent of the entire AI/NA population speaks a language other than English (Ogunwole 2006), more specifically older Natives. However, the Navajo Nation has the highest rate (25 percent) of tribal members speaking their Native language rather than English. With such a substantial portion of the AI/NA population speaking their Native language, many physicians and clinicians have difficulty in diagnosing mental health issues. Native languages do not have words such as *depressed* or *anxious,* which provides difficulties in diagnosing mental health issues (Manson, Shore, and Bloom 1985). The absence of such words from Native languages can lead to the misdiagnosis of several depressive disorders. Therefore, it is important that clinicians carefully examine AI/NA individuals to determine the extent of their mental health infliction. Aside from cultural ideology and feelings of embarrassment, structural conditions also serve as a barrier in receiving adequate treatment.

Many Indian Health Service (IHS) clinics are ill-equipped to meet the needs of AI/NAs due to budgetary constraints, limited personnel, and a lack of emergency care (Henson et al. 2005). Only about 7 percent of the entire IHS budget is directed toward mental health and substance abuse programs and treatment (Gone 2004). Moreover, due to government budget constraints several Indian health centers had to operate on a substantially low allocation of funds and in some cases had to close to meet budget shortfalls (Avant 2012). AI/NAs not living in Indian Country experience additional difficulties in receiving treatment. The IHS is a tribal-based health and social service provider, which is only available to AI/NAs living in Indian Country. AI/NAs living in urban areas are ineligible to receive treatment from IHS and in most cases do not have the resources to obtain a health care provider (Gone 2003; Pevar 2004).

CONCLUSION

Given the difficulty of the IHS in treating AI/NAs with their mental health issues, many scholars and activists argue that tribal governments need to have greater control in providing their tribal members with adequate access to treatment. As Henson et al. (2007, 225) assert, "given the rising rates of chronic diseases and the significant role of social, economic, behavioral, lifestyle, and community factors in the changing health status of American Indians and Alaskan Natives, a more community-orientated, public health approach appears to be the key to improving health in Indian communities." That is, the federal government needs to enhance policies of Indian self-determination and self-government in order to meet the mental health needs of AI/NAs. In order to improve mental health treatment initiatives and programs, organizations such as Inter-Tribal Voices of Children and Families have created a network of AI/NA families across several different tribes to raise concerns about mental health issues and pressure government officials into substantially changing the IHS behavioral treatment program (Slaton 2000). Such efforts led the federal government to realize the mental health problems contributed to other social problems such as delinquency and suicide. As a result, the federal government has increased funding for the IHS. President Obama's 2012 FY budget request for the IHS is $4.6 billion, which is a 14 percent increase ($571.4 million) from the 2010 fiscal year budget. The increased funds would assist in improving mental health treatment programs for many AI/NAs.

AI/NAs continue to suffer from mental health issues that stem from a combination of historical trauma and cultural oppression. While it is not possible to rewrite the sociohistorical suffering of this group of individuals, it is important to address current AI/NA social problems such as poverty and substance abuse, which facilitate their mental health issues. Such problems continue to leave the AI/NA community in a fragile state in an overpowering Anglo-dominant society. The failure to assist these individuals in overcoming their social problems will cripple the future legacy of AI/NA culture. Although great strides have been made to meet the mental health needs of AI/NAs, a substantial amount of progress still needs to be made to ensure that generations of AI/NAs can live in health and secure tribal communities.

◀ FURTHER INVESTIGATIONS ▶

Several questions have emerged from the current chapter on mental health issues. First, if given the opportunity, can tribal governments effectively implement a community-orientated public health initiative to address mental health issues? Second, does the ethnic background of the mental health-care provider impact the cooperation of the AI/NA patient? Lastly, how does a nongovernmental organization such as Inter-Tribal Voices of Children and Families build a collaborative relationship among culturally distinctive reservation communities?

Although the U.S. government has increasingly enhanced tribal sovereignty, tribal governments continue to rely on federal funding for programs and initiatives. Unfortunately, AI/NAs consistently find federal appropriations for mental health and general health treatment programs have been substantially reduced in recent years. As a result, AI/NAs do not have the quality of care that is needed to address their mental health issues. Coupled with lack of federal funding and reservation economic deprivation, the possibility of implementing tribal government community-orientated public mental health initiative remains bleak.

Unfortunately, the ethnic composition of social service providers is not representative of the AI/NA population. Given the historical mistreatment of AI/NA mental health sufferers at the hands of Anglo caregivers, it is not surprising that these individuals are reluctant to seek treatment. The lack of AI/NA caregivers is the product of the "brain drain" effect that is occurring

within many reservation communities as many tribal members leave their ancestral homes for economic and social reasons. This, too, exacerbates problems for AI/NAs suffering from mental health issues.

While many nongovernmental organizations realize the need to care for and educate AI/NAs, such entities must be cognizant of the cultural distinctiveness of the various Native cultures in the United States. These organizations are well positioned to assist AI/NAs with mental health problems; however, they are also in a critical position in which the organization has to treat the individual while simultaneously respecting their ancestral culture. More importantly, one mental health program tailored for one tribal community may not be effective for another. With that being said, it is important to continually change mental health programs that not only treat the individual, but also honors their Native culture.

References

Alcántara, Carmela, and Joseph P. Gone. 2007. "Reviewing Suicide in Native American Communities: Situating Risk and Protective Factors within a Transactional–Ecological Framework." *Death Studies* 31: 457–77.

Alexander, Harltey Burr. 2005. *Native American Mythology.* Mineola, NY: Dover Publications.

American Indian and Alaska Native Resource Manual (NAMI) 2003.

Aoun, Suzanne L., and Robert J. Gregory. 1998. "Mental Disorders of Eskimos Seen at a Community Mental Health Center in Western Alaska. " *Psychiatric Services* 49: 1485–87.

Avant, Lydia Seabol. 2012. "Director Braces for Cuts in Budget." *Tuscaloosa News,* 1–2.

Bachman, Ronet. 1992. *Death and Violence on the Reservation: Homicide, Family Violence, and Suicide in American Indian Population.* New York City: Auburn House.

Bad Wound, Barbara. 2000. "American Indian Youth Outnumber Others in Justice System." Indian Country Today.

Barnes, Grace M., John W. Welte, and Joseph H. Hoffman. 2002. "Relationship of Alcohol Use to Delinquency and Illicit Drug Use in Adolescents: Gender, Age, and Racial/Ethnic Differences." *Journal of Drug Issues* 32: 153–78.

Barrett, Anne E., and R. Jay Turner. 2005. "Family Structure and Mental Health: The Mediating Effects of Socioeconomic Status, Family Process, and Social Stress." *Journal of Health and Social Behavior* 46: 156–69.

Beals, Janette, Spero M. Manson, Christina M. Mitchell, Paul Spicer, and AI-SUPERPFP Team. 2003. "Cultural Specificity and Comparison in Psychiatric Epidemiology: Walking the Tightrope in American Indian Research." *Culture, Medicine and Psychiatry* 27: 259–89.

Beals, Janette, Spero M. Manson, James H. Shore, Matthew Friedman, Marie Ashcraft, John A. Fairbank, and William E. Schlenger. 2002. "The Prevalence of Posttraumatic Stress Disorder among American Indian Vietnam Veterans: Disparities and Context." *Journal of Traumatic Stress* 15: 89–97.

Beals, Janette, Spero M. Manson, Nancy R. Whitesell, Paul Spicer, Douglas K. Novins, and Christina M. Mitchell. 2005. "Prevalence of DSM-IV Disorders and Attendant Help-Seeking in 2 American Indian Reservation Populations." *Archives of General Psychiatry* 62: 99–108.

Beals, Janette, Douglas Novins, Christina Mitchell, James Shore, and Spero Manson. 2002. "Comorbidity between Alcohol Abuse/Dependence and Psychiatric Disorders: Prevalence, Treatment Implications, and New Directions for Research among American Indian Populations." In *Alcohol Use among American Indians and Alaska Natives: Multiple Perspectives on a Complex Problem: Cultural Specificity and Comparison in Psychiatric Epidemiology,* edited by Patricia Mail, Suzanne Heurtin-Roberts, Susan Martin and Jan Howard. 371–410. Bethesda, MD: U.S. Department of Health and Human Services.

Beals, Janette, Joan Piasecki, Scott Nelson, Monica Jones, Ellen Keane, Paul Dauphinais, Roy Red Shirt, William H. Sack, and Spero M. Manson. 1997. "Psychiatric Disorder among American Indian Adolescents: Prevalence in Northern Plains Youth." *Journal of the American Academy of Child & Adolescent Psychiatry* 36: 1252–59.

Bhatara, V. S., A. Gupta, and M. Brokenleg. 1999. "The Hiawatha Asylum for Insane Indians: The First Federal Mental Hospital for an Ethnic Group." *The American Journal of Psychiatry* 156: 767.

Blum, R., Harmon, B., Harris, L., Bergeisen, L., and Resnick, M. 1992. "American Indian-Alaska Native Youth Health." *Journal of the American Medical Association.* 267: 1637–1644.

Bohn, Diane. 2002. "Lifetime and Current Abuse, Pregnancy Risks, and Outcomes among Native American Women." *Journal of Health Care for the Poor and Underserved* 13: 184–97.

Borowsky, Iris Wagman, Michael D. Resnick, Marjorie Ireland, and Robert W. Blum. 1999. "Suicide Attempts among American Indian and Alaska Native Youth: Risk and Protective Factors." *Arch Pediatric Adolescent Med* 153: 573–80.

Boyd-Ball, Alison J., Spero M. Manson, Carolyn Noonan, and Janette Beals. 2006. "Traumatic Events and Alcohol Use Disorders among American Indian Adolescents and Young Adults." *Journal of Traumatic Stress* 19: 937–47.

Brave Heart, M. Y., and L. M. DeBruyn. 1998. "The American Indian Holocaust: Healing Historical Unresolved Grief." *American Indian and Alaska Native Mental Health Research Journal of the National Center* 8: 56–78.

Centers for Disease Control and Prevention, National Center for Injury Prevention and Control. 2003. *Injury Mortality among American Indians & Alaska Native Children and Youth—United States, 1989–1998.*

Centers for Disease Control and Prevention, National Center for Injury Prevention and Control. 2005. *Web-Based Injury Statistics Query and Reporting System.*

Centers for Disease Control and Prevention, National Center for Injury Prevention and Control. 2008. *Suicide Prevention: Youth Suicide.*

Churchill, Ward. 2004. *Kill the Indian, Save the Man: The Genocidal Impact of American Indian Residential Schools.* San Francisco: City Lights Books.

Costello, E. J., E. M. Farmer, A. Angold, B. J. Burns, and A. Erkanli. 1997. "Psychiatric Disorders among American Indian and White Youth in Appalachia: The Great Smoky Mountains Study." *American Journal of Public Health* 87: 827–32.

Duclos, Christine Wilson, Janette Beals, Douglas K. Novins, Cheryl Martin, Chastity S. Jewett, and Spero M. Manson. 1998. "Prevalence of Common Psychiatric Disorders among American Indian Adolescent Detainees." *Journal of the American Academy of Child and Adolescent Psychiatry* 37: 866–73.

Duran, Bonnie, Margaret Sanders, Betty Skipper, Howard Waitzkin, Lorraine Halinka Malcoe, Susan Paine, and Joel Yager. 2004. "Prevalence and Correlates of Mental Disorders among Native American Women in Primary Care." *American Journal of Public Health* 94: 71–77.

Duran, Eduardo. 2006. *Healing the Soul Wound: Counseling with American Indians and Other Native Peoples.* Multicultural Foundations of Psychology and Counseling Series. New York: Teachers College Press.

Elias, Brenda, Javier Mignone, Madelyn Hall, Say P. Hong, Lyna Hart, and Jitender Sareen. 2012. "Trauma and Suicide Behavior Histories among a Canadian Indigenous Population: An Empirical Exploration of the Potential Role of Canada's Residential School System." *Social Science & Medicine* 74: 1560–69.

Evans, Gary W., and Kimberly English. 2002. "The Environment of Poverty: Multiple Stressor Exposure, Psychophysiological Stress, and Socioemotional Adjustment." *Child Development* 73: 1238–48.

Evans, Gary W., Nancy M. Wells, and Annie Moch. 2003. "Housing and Mental Health: A Review of the Evidence and a Methodological and Conceptual Critique." *Journal of Social Issues* 59: 475–500.

Fairchild, David G., Molly Wilson Fairchild, and Shirley Stoner. 1998. "Prevalence of Adult Domestic Violence among Women Seeking Routine Care in a Native American Health Care Facility." *American Journal of Public Health* 88: 1515–17.

Feagin, J. R., and C. B. Feagin. 2008. *Racial and Ethnic Relations.* 8th ed. Upper Saddle River, NJ: Pearson.

Freedenthal, Stacey, and Arlene Rubin Stiffman. 2004. "Suicidal Behavior in Urban American Indian Adolescents: A Comparison with Reservation Youth in a Southwestern State." *Suicide and Life-Threatening Behavior* 34: 160–71.

Fuchs, E., and R. J. Havighurst. 1972. *To Live on This Earth: American Indian Education.* Garden City, NY: Doubleday.

Ghosh, T. B., and B. S. Victor. 1999. "Suicide." In The *American Psychiatric Press Textbook of Psychiatry.* 3rd ed., edited by R. E. Hales, S. C. Yudofsky, and J. A. Talbott. 1383–404. Washington, D.C.: American Psychiatric Press.

Gone, J. P. 2003. "American Indian Mental Health Service Delivery: Persistent Challenges and Future Prospects." In *Culturally Diverse Mental Health: The Challenges of Research and Resistance,* edited by J. S. Mio and G. Y. Iwamasa, 211–29. New York: Brunner-Routledge.

Gone, J. P. 2004. "Mental Health Services for Native Americans in the 21st Century United States." *Professional Psychology: Research and Practice* 35: 10–18.

Gone, J. P. 2007. 'We Never Was Happy Living Like a Whiteman' : Mental Health Disparities and the Postcolonial Predicament in American Indian Communities." *American Journal of Community Psychology* 40: 290–300.

Gone, Joseph P., and Carmela Alcántara. 2007. "Identifying Effective Mental Health Interventions for American Indians and Alaska Natives: A Review of the Literature." *Cultural Diversity and Ethnic Minority Psychology* 13: 356–63.

Grandbois, Donna. 2005. "Stigma of Mental Illness among American Indian and Alaska Native Nations: Historical and Contemporary Perspectives." *Issues in Mental Health Nursing* 26: 1001–24.

Greenfeld, Lawrence A., and Steven K. Smith. 1999. American Indians and Crime.

Washington, D.C.: U.S. Department of Justice, Bureau of Justice Statistics.

Gurley, Diana, Douglas Novins, Monica Jones, Janette Beals, James Shore, and Spero Manson. 2001. "Comparative Use of Biomedical Services and Traditional Healing Options by American Indian Veterans." *Psychiatric Services* 52: 68–74.

Haraldson, Sixten S. R. 1988. "Health and Health Services among the Navajo Indians." *Journal of Community Health* 13: 129–42.

Healey, Joseph F. 2003. *Race, Ethnicity, Gender, and Class: The Sociology of Group Conflict and Change.* Thousand Oaks, CA: Pine Forge Press.

Henson Eric C., Jonathan B. Taylor, Catherine E. A. Curtis, Stephen Cornell, Kenneth W. Grant, Miriam R. Jorgensen, Joseph P. Kalt, Andrew J. Lee. 2007. *The Harvard Project on American Indian Economic Development. The State of the Native Nations Conditions under U.S. Policies of Self-Determination.* New York: Oxford University Press.

Holm, Tom. 1995. "PTSD in Native American Vietnam Veterans: A Reassessment." *Wicazo Sa Review* 11: 83–86.

Horwitz, Allan V., Cathy Spatz Widom, Julie McLaughlin, and Helene Raskin White. 2001. "The Impact of Childhood Abuse and Neglect on Adult Mental Health: A Prospective Study." *Journal of Health and Social Behavior* 42: 184–201.

Indian Health Service. 1996. *Indian Health Service, Office of Planning, Evaluation, and Legislation.* Rockville, MD: Department of Health and Human Services.

Indian Health Service. 2005. "Facts on Indian Health Disparities."

Jilek, W. G. 1974. *Salish Indian Mental Health and Culture Change.* Toronto: Holt, Rinehart and Winston.

Irwin, M. H., and S. Roll. 1995. The Psychological Impact of Sexual Abuse of Native American Boarding School Children. *Journal of the American Academy of Psychoanalysis* 23 (3): 461–473.

Johnson, Jeannette L., and Mark C. Cameron. 2001."Barriers to Providing Effective Mental Health Services to American Indians." *Mental Health Services Research* 3: 215–23.

Johnson, T., and Holly Tomren. 2001. "Helplessness, Hopelessness, and Despair: Identifying the Precursors to Indian Youth Suicide." In *Medicine Ways: Disease, Health, and Survival among Native Americans,* edited by C. Trafzer and D. Weiner, 234–50. Walnut Creek, CA: AltaMira Press.

Kessler, Ronald C., Amanda Sonnega, Evelyn Bromet, Michael Hughes, and Christopher B. Nelson. 1995. "Posttraumatic Stress Disorder in the National Comorbidity Survey." *Archives of General Psychiatry* 52 (12): 1048–60.

Kirmayer, Laurence, Cori Simpson, and Margaret Cargo. 2003. "Healing Traditions: Culture, Community and Mental Health Promotion with Canadian Aboriginal Peoples." *Australasian Psychiatry* 11:15–23.

Kleinfeld, Judith, and Joseph Bloom. 1977. "Boarding Schools: Effects on the Mental Health of Eskimo Adolescents." *The American Journal of Psychiatry* 134: 411–17.

Kunitz, S. J., K. R. Gabriel, J. E. Levy, E. Henderson, K. Lampert, J. McCloskey, G. Quintero, S. Russell, and A. Vince. 1999. "Risk Factors for Conduct Disorder among

Navajo Indian Men and Women." *Social Psychiatry and Psychiatric Epidemiology* 34:180–89.

Malley-Morrison, Kathleen, and Denise A. Hines. 2004. *Family Violence in a Cultural Perspective: Defining, Understanding, and Combating Abuse.* Thousand Oaks, CA: Sage.

Manson, S. M., and D. B. Altschul. 2004. "Cultural Diversity Series: Meeting the Mental Health Needs of American Indians and Alaska Natives," edited by and National Association of State Mental Health Program Directors National Technical Assistance Center for State Mental Health Planning. Washington, D.C.

Manson, Spero, James Shore, and Joseph Bloom. 1985. "The Depressive Experience in American Indian Communities: A Challenge for Psychiatric Theory and Diagnosis." In *Culture and Depression: Studies in the Anthropology and Cross-Cultural Psychiatry of Affect and Disorder,* edited by Arthur Kleinman and Byron J. Good, 331–68. Berkeley: University of California Press.

Manson, Spero M., Janette Beals, Suzell A. Klein, and Calvin D. Croy. 2005. "Social Epidemiology of Trauma among 2 American Indian Reservation Populations." *American Journal of Public Health* 95: 851–59.

Maris, Ronald W., Alan Lee Berman, Morton M. Silverman, and Bruce Michael Bongar. 2000. *Comprehensive Textbook of Suicidology.* New York City: Guilford Publications, Inc.

Miller, Sheldon I., and Lawrence Schoenfeld. 1973. "Grief in the Navajo: Psychodynamics and Culture." *International Journal of Social Psychiatry* 19: 187–91.

Mueser, Rim T., Robert E. Drake, and Douglas L. Noordsy. 1998. "Integrated Mental Health and Substance Abuse Treatment for Severe Psychiatric Disorders." *Journal of Psychiatric Practice* 4: 129–39.

National Congress of American Indians [NCAI]. 2006. *Law Enforcement and Tribal Courts 2001–2006.*

National Center for Post-Traumatic Stress Disorder and the National Center for American Indian and Alaska Native Mental Health Research. 1996. White River Junction, VT: Matsunaga Vietnam Veterans Project.

National Institute of Drug Abuse (NIDA). 2003. *Epidemiologic Trends in Drug Abuse.* Community Epidemiology Work Group.

Norris, Tina, Paula L. Vines, and Elizabeth M. Hoeffel. 2012. *The American Indian and Alaska Native Population: 2010,* edited by U.S. Census Bureau. Washington, D.C.

Novins, Douglas K., Janette Beals, Robert E. Roberts, and Spero M. Manson. 1999. "Factors Associated with Suicide Ideation among American Indian Adolescents: Does Culture Matter?" *Suicide and Life-Threatening Behavior* 29: 332–46.

Novins, Douglas K., Cathleen Patrick Harman, Christina M. Mitchell, and Spero M. Manson. 1996. "Factors Associated with the Receipt of Alcohol Treatment Services among American Indian Adolescents." *Journal of the American Academy of Child & Adolescent Psychiatry* 35: 110–17.

O'Brien, L. Stephen. 1998. *Traumatic Events and Mental Health.* Cambridge: Cambridge University Press.

Office of Applied Studies. 2009. *Results from the 2008 National Survey on Drug Use and Health: National Findings.* Rockville, MD: Substance Abuse and Mental Health Services Administration.

Ogunwole, Stella. 2006. *We the People: American Indians and Alaska Natives in the United States.* U.S. Census Bureau. Washington, D.C.

Perry, B. D., and R. Pollard. 1998. "Homeostasis, Stress, Trauma, and Adaptation: A Neurodevelopmental View of Childhood Trauma." *Child and Adolescent Psychiatric Clinics of North America* 7: 33–51.

Perry, Steven W. 2004. *American Indians and Crime.* Bureau of Justice Statistics U.S. Department of Justice. Washington, D.C.

Peters, K. D., J. A. Martin, S. J. Ventura, and J. D. Maurer. 1997. "Births and Deaths: United States." *Monthly Vital Statistics Report* 45: 5–30.

Pevar, Stephen. 2004. *The Rights of Indians and Tribes: The American Civil Liberties Union.* Carbondale: Southern Illinois University Press.

Pickering, Kathleen. 2000. "Alternative Economic Strategies in Low-Income Rural Communities: Tanf, Labor Migration, and the Case of the Pine Ridge Indian Reservation*." *Rural Sociology* 65: 148–67.

Robin, Robert W., Jeffrey C. Long, Jolene K. Rasmussen, Bernard Albaugh, and David Goldman. 1998. "Relationship of Binge Drinking to Alcohol Dependence, Other Psychiatric Disorders, and Behavioral Problems in an American Indian Tribe." *Alcoholism: Clinical and Experimental Research* 22: 518–23.

Sale, Kirkpatrick. 1990. *The Conquest of Paradise: Christopher Columbus and the Columbian Legacy* New York: Knopf.

Shore, J. H., S. M. Manson, J. D. Bloom, G. Keepers, and G. Neligh. 1987. "A Pilot Study of Depression among American Indian Patients with Research Diagnostic Criteria." *American Indian and Alaska Native Mental Health Research* 1: 4–15.

Slaton, Elaine. 2000. "Offering Technical Assistance to Native Families: Clues from a Focus Group." Federation of Families for Children's Mental Health.

Smedley, B. D., A.Y. Stith, and A.R. Nelson. 2003. Institute of Medicine. Committee on Understanding and Eliminating Racial and Ethnic Disparities in Health Care. *Unequal Treatment: What Health Care Providers Need to Know about Racial and Ethnic Disparities in Health Care. Institute of Medicine.* Washington, D.C.: National Academy Press.

Smith, Andrea. 2005. *Conquest: Sexual Violence and American Indian Genocide.* Cambridge, MA: South End Press.

Snipp, Matthew C. 1992. "Sociological Perspectives on American Indians." *Annual Review of Sociology* 18:351–71.

Substance Abuse and Mental Health Services Administration. 2002. *Report to Congress on the Prevention and Treatment of Co-occurring Substance Abuse Disorders and Mental Disorder.* Washington, D.C.

Substance Abuse and Mental Health Services Administration. 2011. *Results from the 2010 National Survey on Drug Use and Health: Summary of National Findings.* Rockville, MD: Substance Abuse and Mental Health Services Administration.

U.S. Census Bureau 2010.

U.S. Department of Health and Human Services. 2001. *Mental Health: Culture, Race, and Ethnicity—A Supplement to Mental Health: A Report of the Surgeon General,* edited by Substance Abuse and Mental Health Services Administration, U.S. Department of Health and Human Services, Center for Medical Health Services. Rockville, MD.

Vernon, Irene S., and Roe Bubar. 2001. "Child Sexual Abuse and HIV/AIDS in Indian Country." *Wicazo Sa Review* 16: 47–63.

Vigil, Donna. 2006. Oral Testimony Offered to the U.S. Senate Committee on Indian Affairs. Division of Health Programs, White Mountain Apache Tribe. "Hearing: Indian Youth Suicide."

Yellow Bird, P. 2001. "Wild Indians: Native Perspective on the Hiawatha Asylum for Insane Indians." http://www.mindfreedom.org/.

Zahran, Hatice S., Rosemarie Kobau, David G. Moriarty, Matthew M. Zack, James Holt, and Ralph Donehoo. 2004. "Self-Reported Frequent Mental Distress among Adults—United States, 1993–2001." *Morbidity and Mortality Weekly Report* 53: 963–66.

Native Americans and the Abuse of Alcohol and Drugs

M. George Eichenberg

While alcoholism and drug abuse among Native Americans and Alaskan Natives is often considered by both whites and American Indians to be well documented as a major, chronic problem, the reality of what that means is not quite so simple. Some Native American activists see substance abuse as the major problem confronting American Indians and the foundational problem of all other problems faced. Other activists point to research indicating the problem is no worse than among whites of similar socioeconomic status, assuming any group of whites and Indians can ever be considered of similar socioeconomic status. Perhaps the middle view is that although substance abuse is not greater among Native Americans, it does disparately negatively impact them, for numerous social and cultural reasons. At least one writer implies substance abuse is mainly a negative, racist stereotype, in effect, a social construction (Quintero 2001). This discussion will examine substance use and abuse among Native Americans historically, the scope and nature of the problem in contemporary society as presented from an often limited research perspective, and mitigation policy issues raised by research, and conclude with a brief examination of treatment programming.

The specter of the "drunken Indian" is a well-established cliché. It is a stereotype that invariably invades the discussion of the problems facing American Indians. Even if the issue of alcohol and drugs is unspoken, the image is doubtless there, haunting the conversation. It is a ghost so deeply entrenched into our societies, red and white, as to have entered American folklore and art. The Firewater Myth, based in racism, has served as a basis of the white perspective of Native Americans for some 400 years (French 2000; Quintero 2001, Davis 1991). The alleged susceptibility of Native Americans to the most negative individual and social effects of alcohol consumption has been featured as a subplot by generations of novelists, scriptwriters, and others. For example, the reader may remember Johnny Cash singing "The Ballad of Ira Hayes." For those unfamiliar with the lyrics, the implication of the song is that even if an Indian is a war hero he is still likely to end as just another drunken Indian. If the drunken Indian stereotype with all its negative effects has served as a basis for the white view of Native Americans, it has done infinitely more damage to the view Native Americans have of themselves, leaving them with feelings of powerlessness and low self-esteem, and for some even the ingrained belief that it is criminal merely to be Native American (Holmes and Antell 2001; Ross 1998).

In reviewing the fairly extensive literature on Native Americans and alcohol, one is left with the impression that substance use has pretty much destroyed the tribes as social and cultural entities. Or that the problem is at least somewhat overblown. We are confronted by two opposing belief systems, almost theologies, of the historical and contemporary effects of alcohol and drug abuse among Indians. The use of the term *theology* here is analogous to Walker's (2005) concept of "Crime Control Theology" implying that in matters related to government policy as in religion, personal belief is more important than objective fact.

The first belief system, or theology if you will, states that regardless of negative stereotype, substance abuse, abuse of alcohol in particular, has been the bane of Native America for hundreds of years and is largely responsible for most of the problems on modern reservations and for urban Indians as well (Young and Joe 2009; Lamarine 1988). System, or theology, two, an admittedly minority voice, states that alcohol and drug abuse as a particularly American Indian problem, represented by the Firewater Myth, is merely a racist stereotype intended to keep Native Americans in a position of inferiority and dependency (La Marr 2003; Quintero 2001). There is a third belief system (at least)—that both of the other systems are true. Both have a supportable basis in research and, in terms of fact and application to policy development, they need not be considered as mutually exclusive (Holmes and Antell 2001). Regardless of objective reality, the popular conception of Indians and alcohol and drug abuse is of vital importance to the majority culture's understanding of American Indians' understanding of themselves, where they are, and how they arrived to that point. Beyond the simple need to understand the problem, tribal and federal policy in terms of resource allocation have been based on the perception, more so than reality, of the problem and are likely to remain so. Resources once allocated to solve the problem based on one or the other system of understanding are unlikely, or at least not easily, reallocated; and resources for Native Americans have never been generous.

HISTORY OF THE PROBLEM

Potable alcohol is not particularly problematic to make; one need only water, yeast, some form of sugar to feed the yeast, and time for fermentation to occur. It is generally accepted among anthropologists and archeologists that pre-Colombian Native Americans made beer and wine, of sorts, both with a much lower alcohol content than the European version of these beverages (French 2000). It is also widely known that peyote and marijuana use were part of at least a few Native cultures.

Generally, pre-Columbian use of intoxicating substances is portrayed as being part of a well-regulated system of formal religious ceremonies. The recreational use of alcohol or other substances purely for the pleasures of intoxication are presented as rare if not unheard of. While there is some evidence of the recreational use of alcohol, there is a lack of evidence of a "culture of recreational intoxication" prior to contact with Europeans.

In contrast, alcohol use was pervasive in early modern Europe with adults and children consuming, by modern standards, vast amounts of beer and wine (Rose and Cherpital 2011). Distilled spirits, notably brandy and later rum, became increasingly common after about 1600, notably coinciding with the early years of the European conquest. Much of the beer and wine consumption in early modern Europe was due to the widespread unavailability of potable water, especially in urban areas. Contaminating drinking water was a "skill" Europeans brought with them to North America thus necessitating or at least excusing heavy consumption of alcohol by Europeans in the New World. Additionally, alcohol supplied an efficient source of calories to a society based in strenuous manual labor, and alcohol kept well without refrigeration. However, the use of alcohol for its intoxicating effects is well documented as is the fact Europeans brought their culture of heavy recreational use of alcohol to America.

In addition to the pleasures and nutritional value of alcoholic beverages, early European immigrants found alcohol to be a convenient item for trade with Native Americans (French 2000; Sheehan 1973). It was cheap to make, relatively portable, and had a long shelf life. For the trading program to work, Europeans needed to create a recreational drinking culture among Native Americans. The intoxicating effects of alcohol were doubtless an easy sell to Native Americans as they have been to diverse cultures throughout the world. Doubly utilitarian, alcohol was used not only as an item of trade, but was used to "lubricate" the trade process, thus enabling Europeans to gain advantage through its debilitating effects (Gould 2006).

Alcohol also served a less direct, though far more insidious role in the European conquest than merely simplifying a stilted commercial process. Europeans widely viewed Native Americans as their cultural and biological inferiors (Ross and Gould 2006). European colonists claimed as partial evidence of this alleged biological inferiority to have noted a particular susceptibility among Native Americans to the more negative effects of alcohol consumption (Gould 2006; Sheehan 1973; 1980). Whereas a drunken white man was often considered as demonstrating his masculinity through alcohol consumption, a drunken Indian was demonstrating his inferiority through his inability to "hold his liquor." That this was contradictory was irrelevant. The goal was proof of the alleged racial inferiority of Native Americans. Since racist ideology was a major assumption on which the conquest rested, observations, however contradictory, were used merely to support the preexisting conclusion (Ross and Gould 2006). That said, when reading European and later European-American accounts of Indians and alcohol, the modern reader should consider that much of the alleged hypersusceptibility of Indians to the negative effects of strong drink were likely based in racism (Davis 1991; Sheehan 1980). That is, Indians were portrayed as more susceptible than Europeans to intoxication and more likely to exercise poor judgment when intoxicated not because it was so, but to support European claims Indians were physically and mentally inferior to whites. This racist speculation among early European colonists may be an important factor in the development of the persistent, negative stereotypy surrounding Native Americans and alcohol (Quintero 2001). Regardless of the facts, bad things do happen when people (regardless of race and/or ethnicity) consume large quantities of alcohol. In the short term, there is an increased likelihood of interpersonal violence and accidental injuries, among other problems; and in the long term, heavy alcohol consumption leads to a breakdown of individual and societal health.

Given the foundational racism of the European conquest of America, it was predictable that Europeans would tend to overlook the deleterious effects of alcohol among themselves while taking special note of it among those they wished to displace (Sheehan 1973; 1980). Thus, the Firewater Myth developed in support of the racist notion of the inferiority of the Indian to the European. In time, this myth became as much a weapon of conquest as the firearm (La Marr 2003; Quintero 2001). The Firewater Myth simply put is the belief that something in the biological makeup of Indians makes them especially susceptible to alcoholism. Once introduced to alcohol, they become obsessive consumers and are quite vulnerable to all the worst effects of the substance.

The idea that Indians and alcohol were inevitably a bad combination (only for American Indians, but not for the foreigners who took advantage of them) became basis for official government policy beginning in 1832, when a clause of the Indian Intercourse Act banned sale to or possession of alcohol by Indians (Quintero 2001). The law was rarely enforced, however, and thus largely ignored. Wherever whites went, they took their culture of alcohol consumption-to-intoxication with them and generously shared the substance and the culture with their Indian neighbors. It may be argued that alcohol made the European conquest of North America possible or at least expedited it through its use to demoralize and dissipate the tribes across the continent. When Frederick Jackson Turner delivered his famous thesis in 1893 that the age of the frontier had passed, the European conquest of the Native American was accomplished fact by more than a few years (http://nationalhumanitiescenter.org/pds/gilded/empire/text1/turner.pdf). Native Americans were largely relegated to reservations in remote, rural areas, out of sight and out of mind. Alcohol was no longer a factor in treaty negotiations although it was doubtless used in trade, both as an item of sale as well as part of the negotiation process preceding other commercial activity.

When the dust obscuring the knowledge of Indians held by most whites cleared from the Indian Wars and the Wild West Shows by the early years of the

20th century, one of the few enduring images of the Indian was that of the drunk (La Marr 2003; Davis, 1991). Alongside the literary device of the Noble Savage, the Ignoble Savage, and the Mighty Warrior was that of the Drunken Indian. In fact, by the early 20th century, the Savage and the Warrior were portrayed as part of a romantic past, and the drunk became the contemporary image. While the Savage, noble or not, and the Warrior might inspire whites to awe or perhaps even a grudging respect, the Drunken Indian as modern folklore was to be scorned or pitied.

Why the Drunken Indian?

It may be argued that the stereotypical view of Indians and alcohol served and serves as a control mechanism keeping Native peoples in a state of perpetual inferiority (Quintero 2001). It may also be argued that whites, coming from a "hard-drinking" culture, served as role models, teaching their bad habits to the conquered by example and that the habits, good and bad, of the newly dominant culture became desirable for Native Americans to imitate because of their association with the conquerors (French 2000). It may also be argued that Indians took to alcohol consumption as a means of coping with the anomie resulting from the destruction of their cultures (Young 1992). It may also be argued that drinking became a coping mechanism for dealing with "historical trauma," a concept stating that when culturally destructive trauma occurs to a culture, descendants of that culture will continue to reenact the pain and grief of the historical culture wounding, in this case the European conquest, as if it were happening to them; alcohol serves as an escape, however temporary (Brave Heart 1995; Bubar and Jumper-Thurman 2004). It has also been argued that Native Americans have some genetic predisposition to alcoholism, some biological flaw that makes them more susceptible to alcoholism and the most negative health effects of alcohol (La Marr 2003; Caetano, Clark, and Tam 1998). This is more than just a modern reprise of the Firewater Myth because there is "scientific evidence" from biology and genetics to bolster it and make it look less racist. It may also be argued that all of the above statements are true and that all are merely social constructions. But there must be something here beyond racism, literary devices, and supposition.

ALCOHOL USE AMONG NATIVE AMERICANS

John Adams famously said, "Facts are stubborn things," meaning they are unalterable regardless of our preference (McCullough 2001). Adams, being a rationalist, would likely concede that interpretation and understanding of the facts is not always quite so straightforward. The facts do not speak for themselves; they speak only with the voices we give them. Perhaps this is no more so than when attempting to quantify and understand Native Americans and substance use and abuse. It is important to remember that the research material available is of limited generalizability as each of the First Nations has a unique culture, history, and experience with substances. Additionally, some of the research material readily available is seemingly out of date. Some research suffers from questionable methodology. The result is a necessarily incomplete picture, and an incomplete picture is susceptible to misinterpretation and distortion. Yet one must work with what one has.

Much of the older data on alcohol and drug use among Native Americans came from official records, notably arrest records; other law enforcement data (including suicide reports which may have underreported the problem); and hospital release records containing alcohol or drug abuse references in their diagnoses (Lamarine 1988). Questions concerning accuracy and completeness of police records have long been the bane of researchers. While medical records may be more accurate, they may be no more complete. Additionally, for either police or medical records to exist there must have been a problem severe enough at some point to warrant some type of intervention. It is problematic to accurately estimate the prevalence of any social problem based solely on intervention records. Purely scholarly research on Indians and drugs and alcohol has traditionally been limited by the difficulty in obtaining access to subject populations due to their often remote residence and the reluctance of many tribal governments to grant access to study more sensitive problems, especially those problems involving intercultural understanding. These difficulties have in many respects been overcome by numerous, diligent researchers so that much of the more recent scholarship has been based in self-report surveys and case studies. As a result, we have a body of work based on official records, scholarship, or both. While doubtless still incomplete and perhaps distorted as viewed through a cultural lens, it does give at least an approximation of reality.

It must be understood by non-Indians that it is inaccurate to speak in terms of alcohol and drug use among Native Americans as if there were any uniformity in attitudes toward and the actual use and abuse of alcohol and drugs among American Indians. Just as the tribes vary culturally in other aspects of life, they vary in these respects as well. Within groups, there is also often great variation in use and attitudes; men often having different views of substance use than women and younger people having attitudes differing from those who are older.

Patterns of Alcohol Use

Young (1992) identified four patterns of alcohol use among Native Americans, abstinence, social, recreational, and anxiety. As they age, Indians become more likely to become abstainers, far more likely in fact, than whites. Social drinking among Native Americans is similar to social drinking in the general population. It is often associated with festive social events. It is used as a means of social bonding, particularly among same-sex relatives and peers. Social drinking should be differentiated from recreational drinking. Social drinking is intended to promote social relationships; intoxication during such drinking may or may not be frowned upon, but either way, intoxication is not really the goal. Recreational drinking, closely associated with binge drinking, is primarily intended for intoxication even when engaged in in a social setting. Such recreational drinking in groups of peers is often regarded as a "rite of passage" among Indians as well as other racial and ethnic groups. Anxiety drinking is the use of alcohol as a coping mechanism during times of stress. It should be noted that drinking may be the foundational source of that stress or may become so.

Reviewing past studies, Young (1992) reported that among the Navajo, 30–42 percent of adults reported using alcohol at least occasionally, compared to 69 percent of Standing Rock Sioux of South Dakota, 80 percent of the Igacio Ute of Colorado, and 84 percent of the Ojibwa on Canada's Brokenhead reserve. By comparison, about 75 percent of Americans other than Indians admit to at least

A group of Native Americans on the streets of Whiteclay, Nebraska, on June 7, 2003. The Oglala Sioux Tribe announced in February 2012, that it will file a $500 million federal lawsuit against some of the nation's largest beer distributors, alleging that they knowingly contributed to the chronic alcoholism, health problems and other social ills on the Pine Ridge Indian Reservation. The lawsuit also targets the four beer stores in Whiteclay, a Nebraska town with population of 11, on the South Dakota border that sells about 5 million cans of beer per year. (Associated Press)

having used alcohol in the past if not currently, so one could argue that Indians as a group are about as abstemious as the general population, if not more so. Members of southwestern tribes are less likely to drink; members of northern plains tribes are more likely. Urban dwellers are more likely to drink than reservation dwellers (O'Connell, Novins, Beals, and Spicer 2005). Particularly in the latter case, this may be due to greater availability of alcohol in urban areas as many reservations are legally "dry."

In terms of the *general population,* that is all races and ethnicities other than Native American, 60 percent of males versus 39 percent of females are current drinkers (O'Connell et al. 2005) while 20 percent of males and 39 percent of females claim to be lifetime abstainers. For Native Americans as a group, 56 percent of males and 33 percent of females admit to being current drinkers with 15 percent of males and 41 percent of females being lifelong abstainers. By regions, 62 percent of northern plains males and 48 percent of northern plains women reported being drinkers with 25 percent and 33 percent respectively being lifetime abstainers. Among southwestern reservation dwellers, 48 percent of males and 22 percent of females were current drinkers with abstainers making up 32 percent and 62 percent of the population, respectively. The missing percentages within each group were those who were former drinkers.

Binge drinking (generally in survey research, this means five or more drinks in any one day according to O'Connell et al. 2005) is reported at 9–24 percent for the Standing Rock Sioux, 26 percent for the Ute, and 42 percent for the Ojibwa, compared to 9–18 percent for the general population, suggesting that while fewer Indians may use alcohol as compared to other groups, those who do use it tend to use more of it in one sitting than Americans in general (Quintero 2001). It should be noted that a higher percentage of both male and female Indians were more likely to binge drink and to report being drunk at least once in the past year than females and males in the general population (O'Connell et al. 2005). Among the U.S. population of current drinkers, 67 percent of males and 47 percent of females admitted to binge drinking at least once and 55 percent of males and 46 percent of females to being drunk the year (2004) of the O'Connell et al. survey. By comparison, 76 percent of Indian males and 66 percent of females who were current drinkers reported at least one binge with 73 percent and 69 percent respectively reporting being drunk at least once. Other researchers have noted this phenomenon as well; while Indians as a group were not much more likely to drink than non-Indians, Indians were much more likely to binge drink (Young and Joe 2009). This seems to be more so for reservation dwellers than urban Indians and as previously noted may be the result of the relative difficulty in accessing alcohol on the reservation. Many reservations are dry, transportation to dealers is limited, and money is always tight. Perhaps because of the inconvenience there is a tendency to purchase and consume large amounts at a time when money and other resources are available.

However, it has been noted that at least some, perhaps most, of the difference in heavy drinking between Native Americans and the general population disappears when socioeconomic status, including rural residency, is controlled for.

The Indian Health Service (1977) found that drinking was most prevalent among 25- to 44-year-olds of both sexes, although alcohol consumption begins dropping sharply after age 40. Quintero (2000) found that among the Navajo, drinking peaked about age 20, then rapidly declined. Young and Joe (2009) found that for Native Americans in general, the highest rates of alcohol use and dependency occurred among those between 18 and 29 years of age, with a sharp drop for the 30–44 year age group, and another sharp drop after age 45. Alcohol use among 18- to 29-year-old whites was similar, but dropped much more precipitously after age 30. Alcohol use tends to begin early in life, particularly among males (Spillane and Smith 2007). An early 1960s study found that among the Sioux, at least 60 percent of males were regular drinkers by age 15 as were 40 percent of the females (Weibel-Orlando 1984). Among those who became lifetime users of alcohol, use among Indians was likely to begin at about the eighth grade (13–14 years of age) with non-reservation Indian youth most likely to begin drinking during this stage of life, followed by reservation youth; white eighth graders were least likely (Beauvais 1992). A more recent study found Native American adolescents were about twice as likely to report drinking and being drunk within the 30 days prior to being surveyed than their white age-mates (Beauvais, Jumper-Thurman, Helm, Plested, and Burnside 2004). Drinking among Native Americans peaked between ages 20 and 29 for both men *and* women (Young and Joe 2009; Weibel-Orlando 1984). The pattern of Indian drinking seems similar across tribes with an early onset (sometimes as early as preteen), peak use in the 20s, a gradual discontinuance after age 30, and a sharp drop at 40 years of age (Young and Joe 2009; Beauvais et al. 2004; Lamarine 1988). Binge drinking seems to peak between ages 20 and 25. Those Native American men and women who continued to drink past age 40 reported rates of alcohol dependence at about twice the rate for whites in the same age groups (Young and Joe 2009). In short, while the number of people who drink and overall alcohol consumption may not vary a great deal between Indians as a whole and the general population, Indians who do drink tend to start at an earlier age, binge drink more often, report being drunk more often, and are alcohol dependent at a greater rate. It may be concluded that the *pattern* of drinking rather than the overall *amount* of alcohol consumed over time may be a major factor in the greater deleterious effects of alcohol on American Indians as compared to American society as a whole.

The sudden drop in consumption of alcohol at about age 40 may be related to the "aging out phenomenon" associated with criminality and other forms of deviance. For reasons not clearly accounted for by most theories of criminality and deviance, as people age they tend to normalize their behavior with even once high-rate offenders tapering off or discontinuing deviant behaviors beginning at about age 25. It is also possible that there are strong cultural controls at work here as well. For example, among the Navajo it is quite simply unacceptable for women over 30 to drink (Young and Joe 2009).

Social and Individual Effects of Alcohol

Alcohol has been hard on Native Peoples, and it is difficult to spin the facts to indicate any other conclusion. While some researchers dispute this conclusion as being merely a social construct (Quintero 2001; Tompkins n.d.), numerous studies indicate otherwise (Frank, Moore, and Ames 2000; May and Gossage 2001; Spillane and Smith 2007). It has been estimated that up to 75 percent of Native American deaths are directly or indirectly related to alcohol (Young 1992). According to Andre (1979), during the 1970s 5 of the 10 leading causes of death among Native Americans were directly alcohol related. These were accidents, cirrhosis of the liver, alcoholism (in general), suicide, and homicide, in that order. Recent research indicates little change over time (May and Gossage 2001; Young and Joe 2009). The Indian Health Service (1997) reported a death rate from alcoholism and alcohol-related cirrhosis at 48.7/100,000 compared to 7.3/100,000 for the general U.S. population. Other studies confirm the alcoholism-related death rate for Native Americans as a group tends to be several times higher than that of other racial/ethnic groups and the population as a whole (Spillane and Smith 2007). The Indian death rate for cirrhosis and other alcohol-associated liver conditions is five times that of whites.

Native American men are more likely to die of alcohol-related problems than Native American women (Spillane and Smith 2007). This holds true specifically for alcohol-related health problems including cirrhosis and other liver ailments, diabetes, and heart disease. Although alcohol use peaks among the 20-something crowd, deaths from alcohol-related health problems rarely becomes an issue until people reach their 40s. Younger people tend to die of alcohol-related accidents and violence; older people of alcohol-related health problems, some of which trace back to heavy alcohol use when they were young. Native American deaths related to alcohol-related health issues peak between ages 45 and 54 then gradually taper off, although remaining higher than for the general population. This may be explained in part by the availability of reservation health care or a cultural reluctance to seek treatment. Tobacco use is likely a factor here as well, as alcohol use and tobacco use are closely associated, and both are closely associated with diseases of the liver, heart, and lungs (Shiffman and Balabanis 1995). However, no studies could be found of interactional effects of alcohol and tobacco use and health among Native Americans. Likewise, no studies could be found of a relationship between death rates, alcohol, and diet as related to Native Americans, leaving a grossly incomplete picture of any possible interactional effects of these variables for this population.

Another serious health issue related to drinking is fetal alcohol syndrome (FAS). May, McCloskey, and Gossage (2002) found a great deal of variation in FAS rates among American Indians, with rates ranging from a low 1/1,000 to a high of 120/1,000. They determined an average rate of 7.86 incidents of FAS per 1,000 live births among Native Americans; this compares to a rate of 3/1,000 for the general population and 3.4/1,000 for African Americans, the next highest group. As noted, although Indian women in general are less likely to drink than their white counterparts, those who do drink are more likely to binge drink and become intoxicated. Although rates of FAS tend to be more prevalent among American Indians than among the population as a whole, no research could be identified regarding the specific phenomenon of alcohol consumption among Native American women during pregnancy. Additionally, there is little clear documentation as to what the Indian Health Service or tribal governments are doing in terms of preventive education. During fetal development, FAS causes permanent damage to the central nervous system and is associated with attention deficit disorder in children and adult survivors as well as impulsivity and poor judgment. Adult FAS survivors are also more prone to mental health issues in general, as well as drug and alcohol addiction than is the general population (Guerri 2002). As a result, the problem would tend to be self-perpetuating as one generation produces another generation prone to alcohol abuse.

According to the Center for Disease Control, unintentional injuries are the leading cause of death among Native Americans, of both sexes, between the ages of 1 and 44. An estimated 75 percent of these accidental deaths among Native Americans are alcohol related. This includes drunk driving accidents as well as falls, drownings, and firearms-related accidents (Lamarine 1988). Seventy-five percent of Native American *driver* fatalities are alcohol related, compared to 46 percent for the general population (Loyola n.d.). Eighty percent of pedestrian fatalities with Native American victims are alcohol related. Mothers Against Drunk Driving reports, "More than 50 percent of Native American child pedestrian (6-15 years-old) fatalities are alcohol related, and half of those fatalities involve children who have been drinking" (http://www.thetennesseeautoaccidentattorney.com/minority-populations-face-highest-traffic-fatality-rates/). The *overall* death rate from traffic accidents for Indians is 4.4 times that of the general population and 50 to 65 percent of all traffic fatalities among Native Americans are alcohol related. At least some of the high death rate for drunk driving accidents may be an unintended consequence of most reservations being "dry" thus necessitating often long drives to secure alcohol. It was once claimed the stretch of Nebraska Highway 87 between the Pine Ridge Reservation and Whiteclay, Nebraska, the nearest source of alcohol to the reservation, was the deadliest stretch of road in America due to the number of alcohol-related fatalities between the two points. Another factor is the rural location of reservations; it can take a very long time to get emergency medical services to the site of a rural accident followed by a long run to the nearest trauma center.

The Indian suicide rate is approximately 10.84/100,000, compared to a general population rate of 10.75 (CDC n.d.). Suicide is ranked by the CDC as the eighth leading cause of death among Native Americans of all age groups; it is the second highest cause of death for males 10–34 years of age. It is believed that 80 percent of Indian suicides are in some way alcohol or substance driven. The suicide rate among American Indian/Alaska Native males 15–24 years of age is 28/100,000 compared to 18/100,000 for whites and 13/100,000 for African Americans in that age group. If the estimate is accurate, the substance use–related suicide rate for Indians is just over 22/100,000, well over the total suicide rate for youth of other ethnicities.

Perry (2004), using data collected by the Bureau of Justice Statistics, stated 62 percent of crimes reported on reservations were alcohol related. This compares to 42 percent for reported crime nationally. In terms of violent crime involving Indians, in cases where the sobriety status of the offender was known, 71 percent were under the influence of alcohol and/or illegal drugs, roughly twice the rate for the general population.

In a random sample of nearly 1,400 adult Indians from four reservations, Grobsmith (1994) found 47 percent of the men and 25 percent of the women reported at least one alcohol-related arrest. He also interviewed the 45 Native American inmates serving time in Nebraska's state prison system, and all reported addiction to alcohol and/or drugs. These inmates nearly always stated their crimes were related to their substance abuse. In a study by Bachman (1992), all but one of 30 reservation Indians serving time for some level of homicide reported being intoxicated on drugs or alcohol at the time of the offense. A 1974 study by Levy and Kunitz estimated 90 percent of reservation homicides were directly attributable to alcohol consumption by perpetrator, victim, or both.

DRUGS OTHER THAN ALCOHOL

Perhaps few people regard tobacco as a consciousness-altering drug; anyone who has inhaled deeply of a non-filter cigarette or while smoking a cigar may dispute that idea, having dealt with the "buzz," dizziness, nausea, or perhaps a vision of their own impending death after a few deep drags. Many Native Peoples used tobacco as a psychoactive agent during religious rituals and often as a means of binding participants during social rituals long before the Conquest, and in some cases continue to do so (Laurence 2000). As tobacco smoke rose it symbolized humankind's link to "Father Sky." It was also chewed and may have been so used in combination with other plant substances to induce a trancelike state. Also used by some tribes in religious ritual was mescaline, one of the alkaloids present in the peyote cactus. Its use among Native Americans has been documented from Venezuela to the northern plains. While a controlled substance today, members of the Native American Church may legally use it during carefully prescribed religious ceremonies. The Cherokee, prior to removal, prepared the "black drink" for purification ceremonies. Made from black snakeroot, a member of the morning glory family, black drink stimulated the nervous system and induced sweating and vomiting. It could also cause hallucinations. There were numerous mushrooms, herbs, and other plant substances used by Native Americans for spiritual purposes; sometimes to promote spiritual cleansing, sometimes to aid visions. According to Laurence, there is little evidence they were used for recreation.

Prior to passage of the Pure Food and Drug Act of 1904 and other laws, there was little difficulty for most Americans, including Native Americans, in obtaining opiates, cocaine and other stimulants, or most other drugs now carefully controlled due to their propensity for abuse. Peyote was one of the drugs banned during the early 20th century. Because of its association with religious ritual, this led to years of civil litigation ending in passage of the American Indian Religious Freedom Act of 1994. There is no evidence that the carefully controlled use of substances during religious ritual has ever been a social problem among the American Indians nor is it so now. This is not to suggest that drugs other than alcohol have not been the source of considerable trouble on the "Rez." The trouble is there are limited studies of drug use, other than alcohol, by Indians (Young and Joe 2009).

After alcohol, marijuana is the most used drug by Native Americans (and the general population) (Young and Joe 2009). The rate of Indians reporting any use of marijuana at any time during their lives is 49 percent, compared to 40 percent for the general population. Marijuana use is most prevalent among the southwestern tribes and least prevalent among northern plains and Canadian tribes. The rate of regular marijuana use is also slightly higher for Indians at about 9 percent, compared to 6 percent for the general population. Cocaine use rates, stated as any use during one's life, were 19.1 percent for Indians and 14.2 percent for the population as a whole. Hallucinogen use was roughly a third higher for Indians (22.5 percent versus 14.3 percent), although recreational use was not differentiated from religious use so that may not be an entirely fair comparison.

Inhalants have their adherents among Native Americans, most especially adolescents (Young and Lawson 1986). Spray paint, certain adhesives, even gasoline may be utilized for their psychoactive properties. They are cheap, readily obtained, and produce rapid intoxication. They have the additional advantage of being legal, so long as not misused, thus making possession less problematic than alcohol or more controlled substances. It is estimated that among the general population 11 percent of adolescents have used inhalants for their intoxicating effects. According to Young (1992) the rate for Native youth is twice that, 22 percent. A more recent study by

Navajo Police Officer Gilbert Yazzie speaks with self-proclaimed members of the All-Star Krew gang while patrolling, March 21, 2006 on the Navajo Reservation in Ft. Defiance, Arizona. Yazzie, a member of the Navajo Police drug enforcement unit, pursues methamphetamine use on the Reservation. The highly addictive stimulant continues to be a scourge on the Navajo Reservation despite a push by tribal lawmakers to criminalize the drug. (Associated Press)

Young and Joe (2009) showed a rate of inhalant abuse of 9.5 percent for the general population as opposed to 19.6 percent for Native Americans. This may represent a decline, but the rate is still much higher for Indians than the general population. Arguably, inhalants are one of the more dangerous substances available for recreational use, associated with sudden cardiac arrest, asphyxia, and self-destructive behavior. Long-term use is associated with a variety of cancers and other serious health problems.

Methamphetamine use hit rural America hard during the 1990s and has become, after alcohol, the leading chronic drug problem in rural areas. The reservations did not escape. Meth is cheap, easy to make, and readily available. It is estimated that 1.7 percent of Native Americans have used meth, compared to .7 percent of whites and .1 percent of African Americans (Young and Joe 2009). Although the numbers may seem small, meth has a well-deserved reputation for being disproportionately destructive with its introduction to an area strongly correlated with an increase in a host of social problems including violent crime, child abuse and neglect, and suicide.

In summation, the mortality rates associated with drugs other than alcohol are higher for Indians than for whites and the general population (Indian Health Service 1997). Drug-related mortality among Native Americans increased 300 percent between 1979 and 1998 (Young and Joe 2009). Drug and alcohol use are also associated with chronic health problems and fatal and nonfatal accidents. Substance abuse has also further impoverished an already desperately poor people and has undoubtedly sapped much of the initiative needed to improve life on the reservations, in particular. In urban areas, substance abuse has likewise further debilitated people suffering from racism and blocked opportunity. While drug and alcohol abuse are problems across American society, it has disproportionately harmed American Indians.

SOLUTIONS

The first proposed solution to the problem of Indians and substance abuse was prohibition. While proposed by Jefferson during the early 19th century, the previously mentioned clause of an 1832 federal law banned sale of alcohol to Indians and their possession of it. This law was later determined to violate the equal protection clause of the 14th Amendment to the Constitution, and liquor control was delegated to tribal authorities on the reservations. While exact numbers are unavailable, it appears the majority of reservations are "dry" (May 1975; French 2000). Prohibition has not worked as well as anticipated and may be responsible in part for higher levels of binge drinking and alcohol-related traffic fatalities as people return to the reservation after an often long drive to the nearest source of alcohol (May 1975; Johansen 1999).

With the failure of prohibition, four major treatment philosophies or approaches have developed (French 2000). These are tradition or nativistically based; Fundamentalist or Evangelical Christianity based; those based in the so-called "medical model"; and those based in a traditional, holistic philosophy. The traditional or nativistic model is based in the Native American mystical tradition. It emphasizes a return to traditional values and practices as a precursor to a day of restoration for individuals as well as Native cultures. While these traditions may permit the use of peyote as part of worship within the Native American Church, use of drugs or alcohol for social or recreational purposes is forbidden as these practices will delay the restoration. The number of practitioners of this system or its effectiveness in healing individuals or tribes is unknown; perhaps unknowable.

Christian missionaries on reservations are almost a cliché, having been a fixture of reservation life for nearly 150 years and the missionization of the Indians going back to first contact. Fundamentalist Christianity in particular places a great emphasis, perhaps value, on the "crisis conversion." Similar to the basis of Alcoholics Anonymous, this relies on the individual reaching a crisis in life. Unlike AA, Christianity believes that faith in Jesus will save the individual spiritually, thus negating the need to drink or use drugs. Further, through prayers and support of other Christians, the individual will be brought safely through further crises. Christian groups claim a high success rate in assisting people in leaving drug and alcohol addiction, but the empirical support is sparse. What evidence exists suggest these programs are successful for some individuals (French 2000).

The medical model of drug and alcohol treatment has been a mainstay of such treatment in general society and among American Indians since the early years of the 20th century. The Indian Health Service estimates that up to 70 percent of the services they offer are related to alcohol. The percentage of these services that are specific to treatment of addiction is unclear. Quintero (2001) states most tribes operate some form of substance abuse treatment for their members, and most of these programs seem to be based in non-Indian practices, specifically, modern, "Western" medicine and psychiatry. In some cases, these programs have become a tribal industry, making a profit by bringing in outside money and creating a class of paid counselors and administrators. Alcoholics Anonymous may be included as falling under this model. The AA program, like the intensive, often in-patient based treatment programs used by the Indian Health Service and tribal groups, were developed from a white perspective, which may not translate well into Indian understanding (Lamarine 2003; French 2000). These programs are more successful among non-reservation Indians who are more fully acculturated into the mainstream of American society.

Due to the limited success of the aforementioned treatment modalities, a fourth approach began to develop: the more traditional, holistic, group-based approach. Rejecting much of the Fundamentalist Christian and medical model as un-Indian and thus unlikely to work, it takes a more practical approach than the mystically based nativistic approach. These programs are premised in the idea that alcohol and drug abuse are tribal problems affecting all members of the tribe and thus requiring participation by all tribal members (French 2000). The idea is to treat the individual as a member of society rather than as an individual. There is a heavy reliance on Native American traditional healing practices including the sweat lodge. For non-reservation dwellers, including prison inmates, there is a strong effort to create links to the tribe and to Indian mentors and organizations.

Recently, a new approach has developed, but not one of treating the individual or really, the tribe. This approach is to demand responsibility to the tribes for those who provide alcohol to tribal members. In February 2012, the Oglala Sioux of the Pine Ridge Agency filed a $500 million suit in Federal Court against the four largest brewing corporations in the United States and against the four beer stores in Whiteclay, Nebraska. Citing the damage done to Oglala society, the tribal government is demanding the manufacturers and distributers, who they claim knowingly contributed to the alcohol-related problems of Pine Ridge, do something to alleviate those problems through financing alcohol treatment programs and other programming. It is likely they intend to bankrupt the beer dealers in Whiteclay as well and thus remove what is perceived as the immediate source of the problem. The lawsuit, which will have far-reaching consequences for all American Indians, will undoubtedly take several years to settle.

CONCLUSION

Although drug and alcohol use were known to Native Americans prior to contact with Europeans, the recreational use of these substances was not. Whites made careful use of alcohol in particular as a means to manipulate and control Indians as part of the European conquest, both the conquest and the means of conquest having long-term devastating effects to the spirit and the society of American Indians. Whites have long ignored their role in introducing and maintaining a culture of drug and alcohol use among Indians. While rates of substance consumption between Indians, whites, and the population in general are roughly comparable, especially after controlling for socioeconomic status, the negative effects of substance use have disproportionately damaged Native America. In part, this is due to anomie wrought by cultural destruction or marginalization. Some blame must be placed on the failure of whites to accept responsibility or at the least to express regret and act to mitigate the damage created. However, there is a lack of interest or concern among the general populations toward Indians who are often hidden on remote reservations or acculturated into urban residency, and thus largely invisible. Until, and unless, Native Americans can be incorporated into the general society and yet retain cultural identity, the problem may well be unresolvable.

◀ FURTHER INVESTIGATIONS ▶

Social problems are always difficult to unravel; the problem is to determine which phenomenon is the cause and which the effect. Although the culture of recreational substance use and abuse was introduced into Indian society by whites, what followed over the next few hundred years is not quite so easy to identify as the pathogen or merely a symptom. One can argue that substance abuse among Native Americans is the result of high unemployment, poverty, the boredom of reservation life, lack of opportunity, historical trauma, and/or some genetic predisposition to crave intoxicants.

And yet, the same argument can be made to explain the same phenomenon among other racial and socioeconomic groups—groups that have not been so stereotypically identified with substance abuse. Additionally, although research suggests Native Americans are more likely to binge drink than other racial/ethnic groups, they are no more likely to drink or abuse alcohol and other drugs than other groups. As a result, one could argue that the actual problem is not rampant substance abuse among Native Americans, but rather the racist stereotype of rampant substance abuse among Native Americans.

One can argue that whites introduced the culture of substance abuse to Native Americans as both an economic ploy and a means of social control, that culture has been maintained by whites for the same reason. It can be further argued that stereotypes serve as social controls; if one believes something to be real, it is real in its effects. Whatever the reality, substance abuse is a problem seemingly inextricably wound into all other problems affecting Native America, magnifying and compounding all the others. As a result, attempts to treat substance abuse as a problem separate from all others are bound to fail. Rather, the problems affecting Native Americans must be treated as a whole, something that would seem compatible with the traditional Native American worldview.

References

Andre, J. M. 1979. *The Epidemiology of Alcoholism among American Indians and Alaska Natives.* Albuquerque, NM: U.S. Indian Health Services.

Bachman, Ronet. 1992. *Death and Violence on the Reservation.* New York: Auburn House.

Beauvais, Fred. 1992. "Comparison of Drug Use Rates for Reservation Indian, Non-reservation Indian, and Anglo Youth." *American Indian and Alaska Native Mental Health Research* 5: 13–31.

Beauvais, Fred, Pamela J. Jumper-Thurman, H. Helm, B. Plested, and M. Burnside. 2004. "Surveillance of Drug Use among American Indian Adolescents: Patterns over 25 Years." *Journal of Adolescent Health* 34: 493–500.

Brave Heart, Marie. 1995 "The Return to the Sacred Path: Healing from Historical Unresolved Grief among the Lakota and Dakota." PhD diss., Smith College, Northampton, MA.

Bubar, Roe, and Pamela Jumper-Thurman. 2004. "Violence against Native Women." *Social Justice* 31 (4): 70–86.

Caetano, Raul, C. L. Clark, and Tammy Tam. 1998. "Alcohol Consumption among Racial/Ethnic Minorities." *Alcohol Health & Research World* 22: 233–41.

Centers for Disease Control (n.d). www.cdc.gov.

Davis, Randall C. 1991. "Firewater Myths: Alcohol and Portrayals of Native Americans in American Literature." PhD diss., Ohio State University. ProQuest Dissertations & Theses (PQDT).

Frank, John W., Roland S. Moore, and Genevieve M. Ames. 2000. "Historical and Cultural Roots of Drinking Problems among American Indians." *American Journal of Public Health* 90: 344–51.

French, Laurence A. 2000. *Addiction and Native Americans.* Westport, CT: Praeger.

Grobsmith, Elizabeth S. 1994. *Indians in Prison.* Lincoln: University of Nebraska Press.

Guerri, Consuelo. 2002. "Mechanisms Involved in Central Nervous System Dysfunctions Induced by Prenatal Ethanol Exposure." *Neurotoxicity Research* 4 (4): 327–35.

Gould, Larry. 2006. "Alcoholism, Colonialism, and Crime." In *Native Americans and the Criminal Justice System,* edited by Jeffrey Ian Ross and Larry Gould, 87–102. Boulder, CO: Paradigm Publisher.

Holmes, Malcolm D., and Judith A. Antell. 2001. "The Social Construction of American Indian Drinking: Perceptions of American Indian and White Officials." *The Sociological Quarterly* 42 (2): 151–73.

Indian Health Services. 1977. *Alcoholism: A High Priority Health Problem.* Washington, D.C.: U.S. Department of Health and Human Services.

Indian Health Services. 1997. *Trends in Indian Health.* Rockville, MD.

Johansen, Bruce E. 1999. "Whiteclay, Nebraska: The Town That Booze Built." *Native Americas Journal,* January 28.

French, Laurence A., 2000. *Addictions and Native Americans.* Westport, CT: Praeger Publishers.

Lamarine, Roland J. 1988. "Alcohol Abuse among Native Americans." *Journal of Community Health* 13 (3): 143–55.

La Marr, Claudette J. 2003. "'Firewater Myth': Fact, Fantasy or Self-Fulfilling Prophecy." PhD diss., University of Washington. ProQuest Dissertations & Theses (PQDT).

Levy, Jerold E., and Stephen J. Kunitz., 1974. *Indian Drinking: Navajo Practices and Anglo-American Theories.* New York: John Wiley and Sons.

Loyola University Health System. n.d. "Alcohol and Non-Alcohol Fatalities by Ethnic Group." http://www.stritch.luc.edu/depts/injprev/Transprt/tran1-06.htm#Alcohol and Non-Alcohol Fatalities by Ethnic Group.

May, Phillip A., and J. Phillip Gossage. 2001. "New Data on the Epidemiology of Adult Drinking and Substance Abuse among American Indians of the Northern States: Male and Female Data on Prevalence, Patterns, and Consequences." *American Indian and Alaska Native Mental Health Research* 10: 1–25.

May, Phillip A., Joanne McClosky, and J. Phillip Gossage. 2002. "Fetal Alcohol Syndrome among American Indians. Epidemiology, Issues, and Research." In *Alcohol Use among American Indians: Multiple Perspectives on a Complex Problem.* National Institute on Alcohol Abuse and Alcoholism Research Monograph No. 37, edited by P. D. Mail, S. Heurtin/Roberts, S. E. Martin, and J. Howard. Bethesda, MD: National Institute on Alcohol Abuse and Alcoholism.

McCullough, David G. 2001. *John Adams.* NY: Simon & Schuster.

O'Connell, Joan M., Douglas K. Novins, Janette Beals, and Paul Spicer. 2005. "Disparities in Patterns of Alcohol Use among Reservation-Based and Geographically Dispersed American Indian Populations." *Alcoholism: Clinical and Experimental Research* 29 (1): 107–16.

Perry, Stephen W. 2004. *American Indians and Crime.* ABJS Statistical Profile, 1992–2002. Office of Justice Programs: U.S. Department of Justice.

Quintero, Gilbert. 2000. "The Lizard in the Green Bottle: 'Aging Out' of Problem Drinking among Navajo Men." *Social Sciences & Medicine* 51: 1031–45.

Quintero, Gilbert. 2001. "Making the Indian: Colonial Knowledge, Alcohol, and Native Americans." *American Indian Culture and Research Journal* 25 (4): 57–71.

Rose, Mark E., and Cheryle J. Cherpital. 2011. *Alcohol: Its History, Pharmacology, and Treatment.* Hazelden, MN: Hazelden Foundation.

Ross, Jeffrey I., and Larry Gould. 2006. "Native Americans, Criminal Justice, Criminological Theory, and Policy Development." In *Native Americans and the Criminal Justice System,* edited by Jeffrey Ian Ross and Larry Gould, 3–14. Boulder, CO: Paradigm Publisher.

Ross, Luana. 1998. *Inventing the Savage.* Austin: University of Texas Press.

Sheehan, Bernard W. 1973. *Seeds of Extinction: Jeffersonian Philanthropy and the American Indian.* Chapel Hill: University of North Carolina Press.

Sheehan, Bernard W. 1980. *Savagism and Civility: Indians and Englishmen in Colonial Virginia.* Cambridge: Cambridge University Press.

Shiffman, S., and M. Balabanis. 1995. "Associations between Alcohol and Tobacco." In *Alcohol and Tobacco: From Basic Science to Clinical Practice.* NIAAA Research Monograph No. 30. NIH Pub. No. 95-3931, edited by J. B. Fertig, and J. P. Allen. Washington, D..C.: Supt. of Docs., U.S. Government Printing Office.

Spillane, Nichea S., and Gregory T. Smith. 2007. "A Theory of Reservation-dwelling American Indian Alcohol Use Risk." *Psychological Bulletin* 133 (3): 395–418.

Tompkins, Jane. n.d. “Indians: Textualism, Morality, and the Problem of History.” http://www.public.asu.edu/~jvanasu/Indians.html.

Turner, Frederick J. 1893. “The Significance of the Frontier in American History.” http://nationalhumanitiescenter.org/pds/gilded/empire/text1/turner.pdf.

Walker, Sam. 2005. *Sense and Nonsense about Crime and Drugs: A Policy Guide.* 6th ed. Belmont, CA: Wadsworth.

Weibel-Orlando, Joan. 1984. “Substance Abuse among Native American Youth; A Continuing Crisis.” *Journal of Drug Issues* 14: 313–33.

Young, Thomas J. 1992. “Native Americans and Substance Abuse.” In *Handbook for Assessing and Treating Addictive Disorders,* edited by Chris Stout, John Levitt, and Douglas Ruben, 203–13. Westport, CT: Greenwood Press.

Young, Thomas J., and Gary Lawson. 1986. “Voluntary Inhalation of Volatile Substances: A Clinical Review.” *Corrective and Social Psychiatry* 32: 49–54.

Young, Robert S., and Jennie R. Joe. 2009. “Some Thoughts about the Epidemiology of Alcohol and Drug Use among American Indian/Alaska Native Populations.” *Journal of Ethnicity in Substance Abuse* 8: 223–41.

Native Americans, Environmental Harms, and Justice

Michael J. Lynch and Paul B. Stretesky

Native Americans occupy a unique place in American society. Yet, like other minority groups, they have been discriminated against since the European conquest (Brooks 1998). This chapter examines the patterns and consequences of environmental injustice for Native Americans and its link to the economic treadmill of production. Environmental injustice involves (1) the disproportionate burden that Native Americans face from environmental hazards and (2) the ecologically unsustainable production practices that create those hazards.

In her cancer study, Weaver (2010) suggested that Native American populations have the poorest health among U.S. population subgroups. Medical researchers often attribute health difference to individual factors and choices such as smoking, alcohol use, and diet (Paltoo and Chu 2004). Weaver rejects these explanations and instead focuses on political and economic factors. For example, Native American disease rates may be tied to toxins found on reservations (e.g., uranium, PCBs). Contemporary Native American health is, in short, the product of a long historical process that laid the foundations for the isolation and impoverishment of Native Americans and to unequal treatment that has subjected them to pollution. Evidence reviewed below supports this view. These observations are also consistent with Brooks's (1998, 105) perspective that environmental injustices represent "a new form of genocide"

> against Native Americans . . . in modern times with modern techniques. In the past, buffalo were slaughtered or corn crops were burned . . . threatening local native populations; now the government and large corporations . . . create toxic, lethal threats to human health. . . . this type of genocide . . . is the consequence of activities . . . carried out on and near the reservations with reckless disregard for the lives of Native Americans.

We use treadmill of production theory developed by Schnaiberg in 1980 to explain why Native Americans are targets for environmental destruction, and examine three common environmental hazards Native populations face: (1) PCBs, (2) nuclear waste, and (3) oil, using case studies among the Akwesasne, the upper western territories of the Cheyenne, the western territories of the Navajo, and Native Alaskans.

TREADMILL OF PRODUCTION

Schnaiberg (1980) developed treadmill of production theory during the 1970s to explain why environmental degradation was steadily increasing. In treadmill theory (Gould, Pellow, and Schnaiberg 2008) environmental destruction is an efficiency outcome associated with enhancing profit through energy and chemical intensive production practices, which decreases the need for human labor, promotes increased raw material extraction, and contributes to escalating land, air, and water pollution and ecosystem disruption.

This theory can be applied to Native American lands, which often contain oil, minerals, and precious metal deposits. As explained below, the extraction of these resources has severe health impacts for Native Americans. Thus, one aspect of the treadmill is increased oppression of Native Americans through unfair land and lease agreements that facilitate natural resource extraction. In the process of extracting resources profitably, Native American health and well-being are placed at risk.

Another aspect of the treadmill is increased social inequality (Gould, Pellow, and Schnaiberg 2008). This often results by exporting raw material extraction to nations with fewer environmental regulations and lower labor costs, but this process can also be seen within the United States when local populations are entrenched in poverty (e.g., Appalachian coal mining). As the treadmill process displaces U.S. workers with toxic technology, they are exposed to unsustainable, toxic production practices at work and at home. The proximity of low income and racial minorities to hazardous waste sites has been well documented (Mohai et al. 2009).

Native American Environmental Injustice. Treadmill of production theory has implications for examining environmental justice and the disproportionate exposure of Native Americans to environmental hazards as reservations became dumping grounds for dangerous chemicals used in production or as raw material extraction sites. During the 1980s–1990s, the federal government and the commercial waste industry targeted Native lands as "the new dumping grounds" for toxic wastes, as nuclear landfills, and for commercial toxic waste and garbage incineration because of the relative powerlessness of Native Americans (Bullard et al. 2007, 95).

Economic conditions combine with Native American culture to produce devastating effects, making Native American communities a clear example of treadmill of production effects. For example, exploitation of Native lands combines with Native diets (e.g., a reliance on local fish and game) to produce amplified health effects. Schell et al. (2004), for example, discovered elevated levels of organochlorines, lead, and mercury among Native American youth. Difference in toxic exposure levels linked to diets reflects a structural condition of life for Native

Skull Valley nuclear waste sign riddled by shotgun blasts, stands along the highway leading to the Goshute Indian Tribe Reservation. Skull Valley, Utah, May 3, 2006. (AP Photo/Douglas C. Pizac)

American populations that represent the intersection between traditional food acquisition methods and the modern treadmill of production effects.

A key issue is whether Native American toxin exposure patterns are different than those for other racial and ethnic groups. This question illustrates distributional environmental justice; that is, whether toxic exposure is equally or unequally distributed across subgroups within a population as a consequence of their racial or class locations. A brief review of relevant studies follows.

Orr et al. (2002) addressed this issue by documenting the effects of living in proximity to hazardous waste sites on birth defects across racial and ethnic groups in California (1983–1988; N = 28,401). They found the strongest effects for Native American populations. Other research indicates that soil and lead dust pollution from mining waste poses a more significant health concern for Native Americans (Malcoe et al. 2002). Anderton (1997) found that Native Americans were more likely to live in close proximity to Superfund sites (i.e., toxic waste sites that pose a significant risk to human health and are designated to receive federal cleanup funds), while Bullard et al. (2007) found them 1.8 times more likely to reside near a commercial toxic waste facility. Gowda and Easterling (2000) discovered that environmental injustice extended to the planning stages of hazardous waste sites and that Native lands were targeted for nuclear waste disposal sites, an outcome consistent with the treadmill of production, wherein the most economically disadvantaged populations are targeted for exploitation.

Treadmill of production research has focused on the economics of ecological destruction. In the case of American Indians, however, political institutions also play a role. Hooks and Smith (2004) found an association between Native American populations, military sites locations, and dangerous conditions presented by the presence of unexploded military ordnance. They draw upon treadmill of production theory to argue that Native Americans have been unequally exposed to military waste produced by the Cold War's toxic legacy. In the same way that manufacturing left behind a toxic legacy in central cities, the military left behind the toxic remnants of war on reservations.

Natural Resource Extraction. Consistent with treadmill theory, lands granted to Native Americans have been targeted for expanded natural resource extraction. While treadmill of production theory emphasizes effects on "ecosystems outside our bioregions" (Gould, Pellow, and Schnaiberg 2008), American Indian reservations hold significant coal, oil, natural gas, and uranium reserves, making them resource extraction targets, producing both extraction (environmental destruction) and pollution effects.

To gain access to natural resources on Native reservations, reservation land grants (that transferred lands to Native Americans) have been voided to benefit corporate and governmental interests. The Papago of Arizona lost control of lands granted them because they contain extensive copper deposits (Churchill and LaDuke 1992, 242), and to the U.S., "Department of Defense (for a bombing range), to the National Park Service (Organ Pipe Cactus National Monument) and the many white corporations . . . allowed to remove mineral resources with only nominal payment" (Forbes 1979, 9). Papago lands in Arizona were taken in violation of the Papago-Apache Treaty of 1853, and since the mid-1940s, it has "been the policy of the United States to 'pay off' all Indian land claims by means of cash awards from the Indian Claims Commission" (Forbes 1979, 9). Forced resource extraction has also been implemented to access the Fort Union coal deposit in Wyoming, Montana, and North Dakota, reclaimed in violation of the Fort Laramie Treaty of 1868 (Churchill and LaDuke 1992, 242). Through processes such as Native reservation land reclamation, by the 1990s Native land holdings had shrunk to 2.5 percent of the land originally granted them under treaties (Churchill and LaDuke 1992, 243).

Natural resource extraction on reservations was accelerated by centralizing the control of Native lands under the Indian Reorganization Act of 1934 (IRA)—a period in U.S. history explained by political and economic conditions. Under this act, the federal government imposed tribal council governments on reservations that replaced traditional Native governance. The tribal council system not only undermined traditional Native governance, they were charged with new responsibilities such as central economic control over mineral rights and lease contracts. Consistent with treadmill of production theory, Churchill and LaDuke point out that in this way, a neocolonial government that owed allegiance to the federal government rather than to Native populations was created. The tribal governance system was reinforced with federal subsistence allowances or Native welfare programs that met only minimal lifestyle costs (Churchill and LaDuke 1992). In effect, the IRA enforced new tribal governance, expanded poverty among Native populations, and enhanced efforts of the U.S. government to reclaim Native lands, a process that has accelerated since the 1970s energy crisis (Churchill and LaDuke 1992, 245).

The extraction of natural resources from Native American lands is often crafted by outsiders. Consistent with treadmill of production theory, Native peoples are physically destroyed by adding toxic pollutants to the local environment for external economic gain. The value of these lands to U.S. energy policy has promoted the undermining of Native rights and treaties and the dislocation of Native populations from lands granted them by the U.S. government. In order to better understand the effect of toxic waste on American Indian populations, five case studies are reviewed.

CASE STUDIES IN NATIVE AMERICAN ENVIRONMENTAL INJUSTICE

In this section, we examine studies of environmental harms in three regions employing three categories of toxic waste found to impact Native American health. These studies illustrate how the treadmill produces environmental injustice.

Akwesasne Nation Studies. The Akwesasne Mohawks reside in upper eastern New York State and the southern parts of the Canadian Provinces of Quebec and Ontario along the St. Lawrence, St. Regis, and Raquette Rivers. Though divided by international borders, the Akwesasne consider themselves a single community of approximately 12,000 members.

A series of studies facilitated by the Akwesasne Task Force on the Environment provides an in-depth look at the polychlorinated biphenyls (PCB) problem. PCBs are dangerous chemicals that were used to help increase manufacturing production because they had ideal insulating properties needed to help run large industrial electrical equipment. Consistent with the notion of treadmill of production theory, PCBs were used extensively after World War II and were finally banned in the United States in 1976 (Burns, Lynch, and Stretesky 2008). Many industrial manufacturers released large quantities of PCBs into the environment. Significant industrial presence in the Akwesasne region contributes to high levels of PCB exposure (including hexachlorobenzene, HCB, and -dichlorophenyldichloroethylene, DDE; Manning 2005). Studies suggest that rates of exposure to toxins are higher among the Akwesasne than the general population (Haase et al. 2009), and in particular for Akwesasne women and infants (Fitzgerald et al. 1998, 2004; Hwang, Fitzgerald, and Bush 1996). These exposure concerns begin with the accumulation of toxins in the food chain, and elevated PCB levels sufficient to cause developmental problems in turtles (Ashpole, Bishop, and Brooks 1996) have been found in Akwesasne wild snapping turtle eggs (de Solla et al. 2000; Bishop et al. 1996).

Organic pollutants have important health consequences. PCBs are classified as probable carcinogens by the U.S. Environmental Protection Agency and as reasonably likely carcinogens by the National Toxicological Program, and have been linked to cancers of the liver, gall bladder, gastrointestinal tract, brain, and possibly breasts and melanomas (Johnson et al. 1999). Pregnant women exposed to PCBs give birth to children with significant neurological and motor skill deficiencies, low IQ, poor short-term memory, low birth weight, and reduced head size (Jacobson and Jacobson 1996). PCBs act as hormone mimics that disrupt the normal functioning of the hormonal system, including the thyroid, and impair immune system functions (Schell et al. 2003), and have been related to coronary heart disease (Sergeev and Carpenter 2005). Organochlorine pesticide exposure, a widespread problem in the Akwesasne region, is associated with numerous negative health consequences including: pancreatic cancer; non-Hodgkins lymphoma; breast cancer; thyroid disruption; preterm births; neurological effects; and memory, attention, and verbal skills deficits in children (Garabrant et al. 1992; Cantor et al. 1992; Cohn et al. 2007; Jurewicz and Hanke 2008; Korrick and Sagiv 2008; Longnecker et al. 2001; Chevrier et al. 2008; Rathore et al. 2002).

Research has examined the direct effects of persistent organic pollutants on the Akwesasne (DeCaprio et al. 2005; Kinney et al. 1997). For example, evidence of an association between PCB exposure and elevated anti-thyroid levels (TPOAb) in young Akwesasne adults and in breast-fed youth and infants (Schell et al. 2009) and between PCBs and serum triglycerides and cholesterol levels among Akwesasne adults (Goncharov et al. 2008) have been discovered. Two important studies by Newman et al. (2006, 2009) addressed the effects of PCB exposure on cognitive functioning. Newman et al. suggest that Mohawk adolescents are exposed to PCBs in quantities sufficient to produce measureable declines in cognitive functioning, including long-term memory, comprehension, and knowledge (2006). The researchers believe that this association "provide[s] evidence of subtle negative effects of PCB exposure."

Four PCB variants with potential estrogenic effects were found to correlate with age of first menstruation among a sample of Akwesasne females (Denham et al. 2005; see also Schell and Gallo 2010). PCB exposure has also been linked to lower serum testosterone levels among Akwesasne men (Goncharov et al. 2009), to diabetes (Codru et al. 2007), and thyroid disease (Sukdolová et al. 2000; Schell et al. 2004).

Exposure to PCBs among the Akwesasne in relation to fish eating has been widely examined (Fitzgerald et al. 1996, 1999, 2005). Fitzgerald et al. (2007) examined Mohawk men occupationally exposed to PCBs and compared them to those without occupational PCB exposure for the appearance of PCB serum congeners. Occupational exposed men had higher serum (i.e., the clear body fluid that can be separated from the blood) PCBs controlling for fish eating. Indeed, when fish consumption decreases, exposure levels also decrease (Fitzgerald et al. 1998). PCB exposure for pregnant and breast-feeding women is especially troubling since PCB contamination can be passed from mother to child during pregnancy and in breast milk. Fitzgerald et al. (1995) found higher PCB and fish-eating behaviors among Akwesasne women compared to Caucasian women, in a sample (N=111) of pregnant Akwesasne women (Fitzgerald et al. 2004), and when comparing breast milk samples between Akwesasne and Caucasian women (Fitzgerald et al. 1998). These findings also extend to fish eating and p,p'-DDE and mirex (a pesticide) levels among Akwesasne women compared to a control group of Caucasian women (Fitzgerald et al. 2010). These differences were not evident among Akwesasne women who ate less fish.

The Church Rock Nuclear Spill. On July 16, 1979, one of the largest (1,100 tons and 95 million gallons of nuclear waste water) yet not widely acknowledged nuclear accidents in U.S. history occurred at the United Nuclear Corporation facility in Church Rock, New Mexico (Brugge, deLemos, and Bui 2007). The spill was caused by a failure in the earthen dam system used to contain nuclear mine waste constructed on a geologically unstable site, as acknowledged in United Nuclear's internal documents and federal and state reports (Brugge, deLemos and Bui 2007, 1598).

Church Rock is a small Navajo community on the Puerco River with a 1980 U.S. Census population of 1,633. Approximately 12 percent (200 local Navajo) of the population were employed in uranium mining. Given the low income of the community and its dependence on the Puerco River as a water source, and the extensive groundwater contamination produced by the incident, the Church Rock spill had many severe consequences for the Navajo, even prior to the spill (Brugge, deLemos, and Bui 2007).

Following the spill, United Nuclear claimed financial hardship, petitioned the federal government to resume operations, and was granted this request despite the damaged retention and burrow pits that contained mine tailings. The continued use of these unlined retention areas produced extensive groundwater contamination, and by 1983, Church Rock was added to the Environmental Protection Agency's National Priorities list as a Superfund site. In 1982, United Nuclear announced a temporary suspension of work at the facility, which never reopened, leading to immediate, long-term unemployment for the community.

Signs along the Rio Puerco warning residents in three languages to avoid the water in Church Rock, New Mexico after a uranium tailings spill by the United Nuclear Corporation in 1975. A Native American group appealed in 2011 to the Inter-American Commission on Human Rights for help in stopping a planned uranium leach mining operation on lands bordered by the sprawling Navajo reservation. The petition alleged human rights violations were committed when the Nuclear Regulatory Commission granted Hydro Resources Inc. a license to mine near the Navajo communities of Church Rock and Crownpoint in western New Mexico. (Associated Press)

Recent studies by deLemos et al. (2009) detail potential concerns associated with the spill including elevated rates of kidney disease, a condition caused by uranium exposure, among the Navajo three times higher than the age-adjusted rate for the U.S. population. Several conditions that exist in the local Navajo community related to the spill may be responsible. For example, between 50 and 80 percent of local Navajo obtained water from unregulated sources, while deLemos et al. also note that some Navajo live within a few hundred feet of uranium mining waste, and that there is contamination in the Navajos' food chain, including livestock.

Church Rock is one of the more serious uranium mining accidents on American Indian lands. However, according to Quartaroli (2002) the U.S. Nuclear Regulatory Commission acknowledges that at least ten additional incidents occurred in this region between 1959 and 1977. In 1984, for instance, a flash flood caused four tons of high-grade uranium ore to wash into the Colorado River and Kanab Creek. In Moab, Utah, the 130-acre mine tailing site left by Atlas Mining leaks 57,000 gallons of radioactive contamination into the Colorado River daily. And Shiprock, New Mexico, is the site of a 72 acre, 2.7 million ton pile of mine tailings.

The health consequences of exposure to uranium in general are well known. Research among Native Americans occupationally exposed to uranium links exposure to elevated rates of lung cancer (Brugge and Goble 2002), while research examining radiation exposure among Native Americans in nuclear test areas confirms these and other serious consequences (Frohmberg et al. 2000; Dawson and Madsen 1995; Eichstaedt 1994; Shields et al. 1992; US EPA 2006).

Four Corners Region Uranium Mining. Nuclear accidents are not the only uranium exposure pathway for Native Americans. The four corners region of the United States (southwest Colorado, northwest New Mexico, northeast Arizona, and southeast Utah) was the site of the largest uranium mining endeavors. Mining began toward the end of World War I, and on Navajo lands in 1920. "Boomtown" mining from the 1940s through the 1960s, facilitated by new mining methods and government incentives for uranium prospecting and discoveries, and guaranteed minimum ore prices expanded mining and promoted environmental destruction and pollution (Quartaroli 2002). Little is known about the effects of early uranium mining on the Navajo people, but this began to change in the 1950s.

The Navajo probably understood little about uranium mining and its effects. As Brugge and Goble (2002, 1411) note, the Navajo lived in relative isolation, and many spoke Native languages that did not contain a word for *radiation.* In the early 1960s, the first cases of lung cancer among Navajo uranium miners surfaced (Brugge and Goble 2002, 1415; Brugge, Benally, and Yazzie-Lewis 2006). Studies illustrate the consequences of environmental exposure among Native Americans working in the uranium extraction industry (Gottlieb and Husen 1982; Dawson 1992; Roscoe et al. 1995; Gilliland et al. 2000). Dawson interviewed fifty-five Navajo uranium workers in Arizona and New Mexico, and discovered interviewees were uninformed about the dangers of radiation exposure. In hindsight, respondents noted that the lack of information lead them to feel betrayed by the government. They emphasized that they were unable to make rational decisions about employment opportunities or their health because of the withholding of relevant health and safety information. As evidence of the extent of this problem consider Roscoe et al.'s (1995) postmortality examination of 757 Navajo uranium miners from the Colorado Plateau, which revealed elevated rates of lung cancer, tuberculosis, pneumoconiosis, and other respiratory diseases. Nearly 25 years after their last occupational exposure, Navajo miners faced excessive mortality risks from these diseases (Roscoe et al. 1995).

Anaconda's uranium mine in Laguna Pueblo, New Mexico, opened in the early 1950s, became the world's largest uranium strip mine, over five miles long (LaDuke 1979), posing significant health risks to local Native populations. In addition to health effects, Navajo miners were prohibited from joining or forming unions by the Federal Bureau of Indian Affairs, and were paid two-thirds the wage given to whites (LaDuke 1979). Thus, not only were Native American miners exposed to unsafe working conditions, their labor was supcrexploited.

In addition to direct health consequences for workers, the mining processes employed at the site produced "yellow cake," or enriched uranium extracts that result from digging out and discarding low grade ore, a process that creates extensive mine waste (tailings) since it takes one ton of uranium ore to produce 2.24 ounces of yellow cake (LaDuke 1979). In Shiprock, the Kerr McGee mine left behind 72 *acres* of mine tailings which retain 85 percent of their radioactivity and sat only 60 feet from the San Juan River, posing other environmental and health consequences in Navajo territories (LaDuke 1979). The legality of the uranium mining process has also been questioned. In 1977, for example, the Department of the Interior waived thirteen protective regulations to grant Exxon a mining lease on 625 square miles of the Navajo reservation (LaDuke 1979).

In their study, Raymond-Whish et al. (2007) found that uranium possessed endocrine disruption effects, and related these results to the health of Native Americans in the Four Corners region (i.e., Arizona, Colorado, New Mexico, Utah), where an estimated 1,300 abandoned uranium mines exist. Unremediated uranium mine waste sites pollute the air, water, soil and food chain, and the effects can be extensive (Brugge and Goble 2002). As Raymond-Whish et al. point out, Oak Ridge National Laboratories estimated that 10,000 gallons of uranium-laced water leaks into the Colorado River daily. Of 226 water sources tested in the region, 90 were contaminated with uranium in excess of EPA standards, some with concentration 38 times higher than standards allow. At least one-half of Navajo obtain drinking water from unregulated, non-municipal water systems (Raymond-Whish et al. 2007).

Prior research on health effects among the Navajo in this region support Raymond-Whish et al.'s contentions. Shields et al. (1992) examined birth defects, still-births, and other adverse pregnancy outcomes among 13,329 Navajos born in Ship Rock (1964–1981) and discovered 320 different congenital defects among the sample. Through interviews with 226 matched pairs of children and parent, Shields et al. discovered significant relationships between birth defects and mother's proximity to mine dumps and tailings, father's mine work histories, and parent's employment at the Ship Rock electronic plant (on psychological effects, see Markstrom and Charley 2003).

Uranium Mining in Upper Western Native Lands. The effects of uranium mining have been noted among Native Americans in South and North Dakota, Wyoming, and Montana who live on reservations established by the Fort Laramie Treaties of 1851 and 1868. In recent years, Native populations have collected and posted data on the extent of the uranium problem (Face n.d.). In Cave Hill, South Dakota, the Grand River is affected by mine runoff from 89 abandoned mines. At one mine, the radioactivity level is 120,000 times above regional background levels. Mine runoff also impacts the Cheyenne River Indian Reservation, the Morreau River, and several Pine Ridge Indian Reservation water sources. Drug net studies of the Cheyenne River confirm the effects of radiation on local wildlife, and lead to the posting of radioactivity warming signs along the river near Hermosa, South Dakota (Defenders of the Black Hills n.d.; Environmental Nightmares 2007). According to the South Dakota Cancer Report (2003), Pine Ridge residents have a "significantly higher rate of cancer, diabetes, and infant mortality than the SD state average," and cancers have been declining for white residents but increasing for Native Americans (Censored News 2007; for water assessment data see, Bureau of Reclamation n.d.; Heakin, 1999). Native Americans suggest that President Nixon's 1972 secret Executive Order declaring this four-state area a "National Sacrifice Area" is responsible for the problems (Defenders of the Black Hills n.d.).

***Valdez* Oil Spill and Native Americans.** As suggested by treadmill of production theory, a significant environmental justice issue is the extraction of coal and oil from Native-owned lands, and the pollution produced by transporting, cleaning, and burning of coal in electric facilities located near Native lands (Grahame and Sisk 2002). While Native populations receive royalties from extracting coal and oil, the processes are, nevertheless, destructive. Oil extraction has contaminated Native American water sources, exposing local populations to a variety of chemicals associated with oil extraction techniques. Coal extraction has also depleted Native American water tables since electrical generation plants need large amounts of water (Grahame and Sisk 2002). The production of coal creates coal slurry, which once impounded can be spilled and cause groundwater contamination. Moreover, even though Native Americans sell coal to help produce electricity, many lack basic access to electricity (Grahame and Sisk 2002). Besides coal and oil extraction, the transportation of oil has become a serious concern.

In March 1989, the largest shipping oil spill in U.S. history—258,000 barrels or 10.8 million gallons—occurred when the Exxon *Valdez* ran aground in Prince William Sound, Alaska. The spill affected 1,200 miles of coastline, and drifted nearly 500 miles. Some twenty communities, many Native Alaskan (15 Alutiiq communities), were impacted (Davis 2010). Unlike other environmental problems faced by Native Americans, relatively few studies have examined health effect outcomes of the spill (e.g., U.S. Department of the Interior 1990).

Palinkas et al. (1993, 2004; Palinkas, Peterson, and Downs 1993) examined spill effects upon community residents from various racial and ethnic groups. Of particular importance to Native Alaskans was the spill's effect on subsistence-based economic activity, such as gathering food, and physical and mental health (e.g., Picou and Gill 1996; Picou et al. 1992; Dyer, Gill, and Picou 1992). These studies also indicate a decline in traditional social relationships due to the spill, increases in drug and alcohol use, and declining mental health.

Dyer (1993) suggests mental health issues were related to the long-term consequences of the spill on local traditions, a decline in subsistence activities, and eroded traditional and social support networks. Palinkas et al. (2004) found that elevated indicators of posttraumatic stress disorder one year after the spill were associated with low levels of family support, participation in spill cleanup activities, and a decline in subsistence activities.

At the time of the spill, a study of social life in the Alaskan villages in the Prince William Sound area underway since 1986 was expanded to examine the effects of the spill (McNabb 1992). The study revealed that residents perceived a significant decline in the availability and quality of natural resources, and that these perceptions were related to proximity to the spill and the extent to which communities relied on local natural resources for subsistence and their livelihoods. Of particular concern was the effect of the spill on employment in the fishing industry.

Fishing industry effects were explored by Fall and Field (1996: Fall et al. 2001) among 2,200 Alaskan Natives in 10 of 15 affected communities. They found that fishing catches declined up to 77 percent after the oil spill, and that the decline was linked to fears concerning the effect of the oil spill on the health and safety of local fish populations. Following the release of a three-year study by an oil spill task force that found fish but not invertebrates safe to eat, Native Alaskan reliance on subsistence fishing increased despite continued fears. These fears appear be well founded: more than a decade after the Exxon *Valdez* spill, evidence of the spill remains both on beach surfaces where weathered or hardened oil can be found, and below beach surfaces where liquid oil deposits are located, waiting to be unearthed by erosion (Short, Rice, and Lindeberg 2002).

CONCLUSION

The distribution of toxic chemicals is a serious issue for Native Americans. We have described the state of the environmental conditions that many Native Americans face, as well as potential explanations for this inequality. As noted, the negative health effects of toxic chemicals on Native American populations are not private troubles but public issues shaped by social and economic forces. For example, the difference in cancer and other disease rates between Native Americans and other groups can be described using treadmill of production theory, which emphasizes that environmental injustice is linked to production institutions.

Importantly, many Native Americans occupy more traditional, "underdeveloped" and "less desirable" lands, and given extensive unemployment on reservations, Native American communities are susceptible to offers of economic incentives for allowing the waste streams associated with accelerated production to be disposed of on their lands.

Also, important to the study of Native American environmental justice is the role of culture. Rates of specific diseases in Native American communities are tied to economic exploitation and the role Native cultures (e.g., subsistence hunting and fishing, water collection) plays in exposing Native American populations to the consequences of toxic hazards on Native American territories. This chapter has explored how contemporary Native American health and environmental justice is the product of a long historical process that laid the foundations for the isolation and impoverishment of Native Americans on reservations.

◀ FURTHER INVESTIGATIONS ▶

The historical relationship between the U.S. government and Native American populations has been characterized by government domination, usury, and neglect. This history began with various wars, enslavement, germ warfare, imprisonment, and the reservation system. When the land given Native Americans, however, proved valuable (e.g., contain natural resources) or when these isolated otherwise worthless areas were needed as sites for disposing waste, such as military waste or for military testing, those lands were (and are) used at the expense of Native American health and culture. We outline three policy approaches that could attenuate the problems identified in this chapter along with the drawbacks to those approaches.

First, to reduce future environmental harms, policy approaches should extend reservation rights or lands to include upstream water supplies and other important proximate natural resources that are critical to American Indian health and well-being. These policies are not without controversy. Natural resources are valuable and transferring land and/or natural resource rights (lakes, streams, forests, etc.) to tribal governments would be difficult at best and involve popular opposition and legal challenges. Moreover, it could be argued that it would not be fair to ask people to give up the use of these natural resources. Such policy approaches are needed, however, because Native American health is threatened by production practices that occur upstream from reservations and are therefore currently beyond the ability of tribal governments to control.

The U.S. government must dedicate, second, additional financial resources to clean up Native American lands. These funds could be managed by tribal governments whose people suffer from the health impacts of environmental hazards. Again, there is controversy in such an approach because of the large financial cost and because there are sometimes charges of political corruption or inefficiency among Native American leaders. Moreover, opponents of such an approach might argue that the U.S. government could do a better job managing those large operations to clean up the environment. However, from a historical standpoint, interactions between the U.S. government and Native peoples tend to favor the U.S. government. Thus, allowing Native Americans to manage their lands may increase the likelihood that hazards will be removed and dealt with appropriately.

Third, because the health effects of ecological destruction are geographically widespread, the treadmill of production itself must be reversed. There is little doubt that Native Americans face health threats as corporations pursue production and the U.S. government seeks to develop its military might. As a result, American Indian social movement organizations have formed to protest treadmill institutions. Movement organizations are important because it is unlikely that U.S. policy will address the institutional arrangements causing ecological destruction in any serious way without widespread public mobilization. As a result, social change must be sought from outside those institutions that maintain the treadmill and must include both Native and non-Native organizations. If successful, such widespread mobilization would not only improve the health of Native Americans, but of all people who are impacted by treadmill policies and institutions.

References

Anderton, Douglas. 1997. "Environmental Equity in Superfund: Demographics of the Discovery and Prioritization of Abandoned Toxic Sites." *Evaluation Review* 21: 3–26.

Ashpole, S., C. Bishop, and R. Brooks. 2004. "Contaminant Residues in Snapping Turtle (Chelydra S. Serpentina) Eggs from the Great Lakes-St. Lawrence River Basin (1999 to 2000)." *Archives of Environmental Contamination and Toxicology* 47: 240–52.

Bishop, C., P. Ng, K. Pettit, S. Kennedy, J. Stegeman, R. Norstrom, and R. Brooks. 1996. "Environmental Contamination and Developmental Abnormalities in Eggs and Hatchlings of the Common Snapping Turtle (Chelydra Serpentina Serpentina) from the Great Lakes-St Lawrence River Basin (1989–1991)." *Environmental Pollution* 101: 143–56.

Brooks, Daniel. 1998. "Environmental Genocide: Native Americans and Toxic Waste." *The American Journal of Economics and Sociology* 57: 105–13.

Brugge, Doug, and Rob Goble. 2002. "The History of Uranium Mining and the Navajo People." *American Journal of Public Health* 92: 1410–19.

Brugge, Doug, Timothy Benally, and Esther Yazzie-Lewis. 2006. *The Navajo People and Uranium Mining.* Albuquerque: University of New Mexico Press.

Brugge, Doug, Jamie deLemos, and Cat Bui. 2007. "The Sequoyah Corporation Fuels Release and the Church Rock Spill: Unpublicized Nuclear Releases in American Indian Communities." *American Journal of Public Health* 97: 1595–600.

Bullard, Robert, Paul Mohai, Robin Saha, and Beverly Wright. 2007. "Toxic Wastes and Race at Twenty: 1987–2007. Grassroots Struggles to Dismantle Environmental Racism in the United States." http://www.ejnet.org/ej/twart.pdf [accessed Feb. 19, 2010].

Bureau of Reclamation. n.d. "Sediment at Angostura Reservoir." U.S. Department of the Interior. Technical Services Center. http://www.usbr.gov/pmts/wquality_land/assessments/yahnke/sed-rep1.htm [accessed July 16, 2012].

Burns, Ronald, Michael J. Lynch, and Paul Stretesky. 2008. *Environmental Law, Crime, and Justice: An Introduction.* New York: LFB Scholarly Publishing.

Cantor, Kenneth, Aaron Blair, George Everett, Robert Gibson, Leon Burmeister, Linda Brown, Leonard Schuman, and Fred Dick. 1992. "Pesticides and Other Agricultural Risk Factors for Non-Hodgkin's Lymphoma among Men in Iowa and Minnesota." *Cancer Research* 52: 2447–55.

Censored News. 2007. "Uranium Mining, the Oglala Lakota People and Mni Wakan (Sacred Water)." Censored News Special Edition. http://censored-news.blogspot.com/2007/08/uranium-mining-oglala-lakota-people-and.html [accessed July 16, 2012].

Chevrier, Jonathan, Brenda Eskenazi, Nina Holland, Asa Bradman, and Dana Barr. 2008. "Effects of Exposure to Polychlorinated Biphenyls and Organochlorine Pesticides on Thyroid Function during Pregnancy." *American Journal of Epidemiology* 168: 298–310.

Churchill, Ward, and Winona LaDuke. 1992. "Native North America: The Political Economy of Radioactive Colonialism." In *State of Native America: Genocide, Colonization and Resistance,* edited by Annette Jaimes, 241–66. Cambridge, MA: South End Press.

Codru, Neculai, Maria Schymura, Serban Negoita, Robert Rej, and David Carpenter. 2007. "Diabetes in Relation to Serum Levels of Polychlorinated Biphenyls and Chlorinated Pesticides in Adult Native Americans." *Environmental Health Perspectives* 115: 1442–47.

Cohn, Barbara, Mary Wolff, Piera Cirillo, and Robert Sholtz. 2007. "DDT and Breast Cancer in Young Women." *Environmental Health Perspectives* 115: 1410–14.

Davis, Nancy. 2010. "The Exxon Valdez Oil Spill, Alaska." In *The Long Road to Recovery: Community Responses to Industrial Disaster,* edited by James K. Mitchell, 231–72. New York: United Nations University Press.

Dawson, Susan. 1992. "Navajo Uranium Workers and the Effects of Occupational Illnesses: A Case Study." *Human Organization* 51: 389–97.

Dawson, Susan, and Gary Madsen. 1995. "American Indian Uranium Mill Workers: A Study of the Perceived Effects of Occupational Exposure." *Journal of Health & Social Policy* 7: 19–31.

DeCaprio, Anthony, Glenn Johnson, Alice Tarbell, David Carpenter, Jeffrey Chiarenzelli, Gayle Morse, Azara Santiago-Rivera, and Maria J. Schymura. 2005. "Polychlorinated Biphenyl (PCB) Exposure Assessment by Multivariate Statistical Analysis of Serum Congener Profiles in an Adult Native American Population." *Environmental Research* 98: 284–302.

Defenders of the Black Hills. n.d. "Uranium Cheyenne River." http://www.defendblackhills.org/index.php?option=com_content&view=article&id=143:uraniumcheyenneriver&catid=16:uranium&Itemid=27 [accessed July 16, 2012].

de Lemos, Jamie L., Doug Brugge, Miranda Cajero, Mallery Downs, John L. Durant, Christine M. George, Sarah Henio-Adeky, Teddy Nez, Thomas Manning, Tommy Rock, Bess Seschillie, Chris Shuey, and Johnnye Lewis. 2009. "Development of Risk Maps to Minimize Uranium Exposures in the Navajo Churchrock Mining District." *Environmental Health* 8: 29–44.

Denham, Melinda, Lawrence Schell, Glenn Deane, Mia Gallo, Julia Ravenscroft, and, Anthony DeCaprio. 2005. "Relationship of Lead, Mercury, Mirex, DDE, HCB, and PCBs to Age at Menarche among Akwesasne Mohawk Girls." *Pediatrics* 115: 125–34. DOI:10.1542/peds.2004-1161 [accessed May 7, 2011].

de Solla, S., C. Bishop, H. Lickers, and K. Jock. 2000. "Organochlorine Pesticides, PCBs, Dibenzodioxin, and Furan Concentrations in Common Snapping Turtle Eggs

(Chelydra Serpentina Serpentina) in Akwesasne, Mohawk Territory, Ontario, Canada." *Archives of Environmental Contamination and Toxicology* 40: 410–17.

Dyer, Christopher. 1993. "Traditional Loss as Secondary Disaster: Long-Term Cultural Impacts of the Exxon Valdez Oil Spill." *Sociological Spectrum* 13: 65–88.

Dyer, Christopher, Duane A. Gill, and Steven Picou. 1992. "Social Disruption and the Valdez Oil Spill: Alaskan Natives in a Natural Resource Community." *Sociological Spectrum* 12: 105–26.

Eichstaedt, Peter. 1994. *If You Poison Us: Uranium and Native Americans.* Santa Fe, NM: Red Crane Books.

Environmental Nightmares. 2007. "Radiation Warning Signs Placed on Cheyenne River." http://www.environmentalnightmares.com/2007/07/radiation-warning-signs-placed-on.html [accessed July 16, 2012].

Face, White. n.d. "America's Secret Chernobyl: Fact Sheet." http://www.eaglerocktradingpost.com/uranium.htm [accessed July 13, 2012].

Fall, J., and L. Field. 1996. "Subsistence Uses of Fish and Wildlife before and after the Exxon Valdez Oil Spill." *American Fisheries Symposium* 18: 819–36.

Fall, James, Rita Miraglia, William Simeone, Charles Utermohle, and Robert Wolfe. 2001. *Long-Term Consequences of the Exxon Valdez Oil Spill for Costal Communities of Southcentral Alaska.* Technical paper #264. Division of Subsistence, Alaskan Department of Fish and Game: Juneau, Alaska. http://www.subsistence.adfg.state.ak.us/TechPap/tp264.pdf [accessed May 7, 2011].

Fitzgerald, Edward, Synian Hwang, Kelley Brix, Brian Bush, and Priscilla Worswick. 1995. "Fish PCB Concentrations and Consumption Patterns among Mohawk Women at Akwesasne." *Journal of Exposure Analysis and Environmental Epidemiology* 5: 1–19.

Fitzgerald, Edward, Synian Hwang, Brian Bush, Katsi Cook, and Priscilla Worswick. 1998. "Fish Consumption and Breast Milk PCB Concentrations among Mohawk Women at Akwesasne." *American Journal of Epidemiology* 148: 164–72.

Fitzgerald, Edward, Synian Hwang, George Lambert, Marta Gomez, and Alice Tarbell. 2005. "PCB Exposure and in Vivo CYP1A2 Activity among Native Americans." *Environmental Health Perspectives* 113: 272–7.

Fitzgerald, Edward, Kelley Brix, Debra Deres, Synian Hwang, Brian Bush, George Lambert, and Alice Tarbell. 1996. "Polychlorinated Biphenyl (PCB) and Dichlorodiphenyl Dichloroethylene (DDE) Exposure among Native American Men from Contaminated Great Lakes Fish and Wildlife." *Toxicology and Industrial Health* 12: 361–68.

Fitzgerald, Edward, Synian Hwang, Marta Gomez, Brian Bush, Bao-Zhu Yang, and Alice Tarbell. 1999. "Local Fish Consumption and Serum PCB Concentrations among Mohawk Men at Akwesasne." *Environmental Research* 80: s97–s103.

Fitzgerald, Edward, Synian Hwang, Marta Gomez, Brian Bush, Bao-Zhu Yang, and Alice Tarbell. 2007. "Environmental and Occupational Exposures and Serum PCB Concentrations and Patterns among Mohawk Men at Akwesasne." *Journal of Exposure Analysis and Environmental Epidemiology* 17: 269–78.

Fitzgerald, Edward, Synian Hwang, Karyn Langguth, Michael Cayo, Bao-Zhu Yang, Brian Bush, Priscilla Worswick, and Trudy Lauzon. 2001. "The Association between Local Fish Consumption and DDE, Mirex, and HCB Concentrations in the Breast Milk of Mohawk Women at Akwesasne." *Journal of Exposure Analysis and Environmental Epidemiology* 11: 381–88.

Fitzgerald, Edward, Synian Hwang, Karyn Langguth, Michael Cayo, Bao-Zhu Yang, Brian Bush, Priscilla Worswick, and Trudy Lauzon. 2004. "Fish Consumption and Other Environmental Exposures and Their Associations with Serum PCB Concentrations among Mohawk Women at Akwesasne." *Environmental Research* 94: 160–70.

Forbes, Jack. 1979. *The Papago-Apache Treaty of 1853: Property Rights and Religious Liberties of the 'O'odham, Maricopa and Other Native Peoples.* Davis: University of California.

Frohmberg, Eric, Robert Goble, Virginia Sanchez, and Dianne Quigley. 2000. "The Assessment of Radiation Exposures in Native American Communities from Nuclear Weapons Testing in Nevada." *Risk Analysis* 20: 101–11.

Garabrant, David, Janetta Held, Bryan Langholz, John Peters, and Thomas Mack. 1992. "DDT and Related Compounds and Risk of Pancreatic Cancer." *Journal of the National Cancer Institute* 84: 764–71.

Gilliland, Frank, William Hunt, Marla Pardilla, and Charles Key. 2000. "Uranium Mining and Lung Cancer among Navajo Men in New Mexico and Arizona, 1969–1993." *Journal of Occupational & Environmental Medicine* 42: 278–83.

Goncharov, Alexey, Richard Haase, Azara Santiago-Rivera, Gayle Morse, Robert McCaffrey, Robert Rej, and David Carpenter. 2008. "High Serum PCBs are Associated with Elevation of Serum Lipids and Cardiovascular Disease in a Native American Population." *Environmental Research* 106: 226–39.

Goncharov, Alexey, Robert Rej, Serban Negoita, Maria Schymura, Azara Santiago-Rivera, Gayle Morse, the Akwesasne Task Force on the Environment, and David Carpenter. 2009. "Lower Serum Testosterone Associated with Elevated Polychlorinated Biphenyl Concentrations in Native American Men." *Environmental Health Perspectives* 117: 1454–60.

Gottlieb, L.S., and L. A. Husan. 1982. "Lung Cancer among Navajo Uranium Miners, *Chest* 81, 4: 449–452.

Gould, Kenneth, David Pellow, and Allan Schnaiberg. 2008. *The Treadmill of Production: Injustice and Unsustainability in the Global Economy.* Boulder, CO: Paradigm.

Gowda, Rajeev, and Doug Easterling. 2000. "Voluntary Siting and Equity: The MRS Facility Experience in Native America." *Risk Analysis* 20: 917–30.

Grahame, John, and Thomas Sisk. 2002. *Canyons, Cultures and Environmental Change: An Introduction to the Land-Use History of the Colorado Plateau.* http://www.cpluhna.nau.edu [accessed Sept. 7, 2011].

Haase, Richard, Robert McCaffrey, Azara Santiago-Rivera, Gayle Morse, and Alice Tarbell. 2009. "Evidence of an Age-Related Threshold Effect of Polychlorinated Biphenyls (PCBs) on Neuropsychological Functioning in a Native American Population." *Environmental Research* 109: 73–85.

Heakin, Allen. 1999. *Water Quality of Selected Springs and Public-Supply Wells, Pine Ridge Indian Reservation, 1992–1997.* U.S. Geological Survey. Water-Resources Investigations Report 99-4063. http://pubs.usgs.gov/wri/wri994063/ [accessed Sept. 1, 2011].

Hooks, Gregory, and Chad Smith. 2004. "The Treadmill of Destruction: National Sacrifice Areas and Native Americans." *American Sociological Review* 69: 558–75.

Hwang, Synian, Edward Fitzgerald, and Brian Bush. 1996. "Exposure to PCB's from Hazardous Waste among Mohawk Women and Infants at Akwesasne." *Technology Journal of the Franklin Institute* 333A: 17–23.

Jacobson, Joseph, and Sandra Jacobson. 1996. "Intellectual Impairment in Children Exposed to Polychlorinated Biphenyls in Utero." *New England Journal of Medicine* 335: 783–89.

Johnson, Barry, Heraline Hicks, William Cibulas, Obaid Faroon, Annette Ashizawa, and Christopher De Rosa. 1999. "Public Health Implications of Exposure to Polychlorinated Biphenyls (PCBs)." Agency for Toxic Substances and Disease Registry. http://www.atsdr.cdc.gov/DT/pcb007.html [accessed Aug. 15, 2011].

Jurewicz, Joanna, and Woiciech Hanke. 2008. "Prenatal and Childhood Exposure to Pesticides and Neurobehavioral Development: Review of Epidemiological Studies." *International Journal of Occupational Medical and Environmental Health* 21: 121–32.

Kinney, Andrea, Edward Fitzgerald, Synian Hwang, Brian Bush, and Alice Tarbell. 1997. "Human Exposure to PCBs: Modeling and Assessment of Environmental Concentrations on the Akwesasne Reservation." *Drug Chemistry and Toxicology* 20: 313–28.

Korrick, Susan, and Sharon Sagiv. 2008. "Polychlorinated Biphenyls, Organochlorine Pesticides and Neurodevelopment." *Current Opinion in Pediatrics* 20: 198–204.

LaDuke, Winona 1979. "Uranium Mines on Native Land: The New Indian Wars." *The Harvard Crimson,* May 2. http://pubs.usgs.gov/wri/wri994063/ [accessed May 22, 2011].

Longnecker, Matthew, Mark Klebanoff, Haibo Zhou, and John Brock. 2001. "Association between Maternal Serum Concentration of the DDT Metabolite DDE and Preterm and Small-for-Gestational-age Babies at Birth." *The Lancet* 358: 110–114.

Malcoe, L., R. Lynch, M. Keger, and V. Skaggs. 2002. "Lead Sources, Behaviors, and Socioeconomic Factors in Relation to Blood Lead of Native American and White Children." *Environmental Health Perspectives* 110: s2: 221–31.

Manning, Jennifer. 2005. "PCBs (Polychlorinated Biphenyls) in New York's Hudson River." http://EnvironmentalChemistry.com/yogi/environmental/200510hudsonriverpcbs.html [accessed May 22, 2011].

Markstrom, Carol, and Perry Charley. 2003. "Psychological Effects of Human Caused Environmental Disasters: Examination of the Navajo and Uranium." *American Indian and Alaska Native Mental Health Research* 11: 19–45.

McNabb, Steven. 1992. " Native Claims in Alaska: A Twenty-Year Review." *Études/Inuit/Studies* 16 (1–2): 85–95.

Mohai, Paul, Paula Lantz, Jeffrey Morenoff, James House, and Richard Mero. 2009. "Racial and Socioeconomic Disparities in Residential Proximity to Polluting Industrial Facilities." *American Journal of Public Health* 99: s3: 649–66.

Newman, Joan, Amy Aucompaugh, Lawrence Schell, Melinda Denham, Anthony DeCaprio, Mia Gallo, Julia Ravenscroft, Chin-Cheng Kao, Mary Ellen Rougas Hannover, Dawn David, Agnes Jacobs, Alice Tarbell, Priscilla Worswick, and Akwesasne Task Force on the Environment. 2006. "PCBs and Cognitive Functioning of Mohawk Adolescents." *Neurotoxicology and Teratology* 28: 439–45.

Newman Joan, Mia Gallo, Lawrence Schell, Anthony DeCaprio, Melinda Denham, Glenn Deane, and the Akwesasne Task Force on the Environment. 2009. "Analysis of PCB Congeners Related to Cognitive Functioning in Adolescents." *Neurotoxicology* 30: 686–96.

Orr, Maureen, Frank Bove, Wendy Kaye, and Melanie Stone. 2002. "Elevated Birth Defects in Racial or Ethnic Minority Children of Women Living near Hazardous Waste Sites." *International Journal of Hygiene and Environmental Health* 205: 19–27.

Palinkas, Lawrence, John Peterson, and Michelle Downs. 1993. "Community Patterns of Psychiatric after the Exxon Valdez Oil Spill." *American Journal of Psychiatry* 150: 1517–23.

Palinkas, Lawrence, Michelle Downs, John Peterson, and John Russell. 1993. "Social, Cultural and Psychological Consequences of the Exxon Valdez Oil Spill." *Human Organization* 52: 1–13.

Palinkas, Lawrence, John Peterson, John Russell, and Michelle Downs. 2004. "Ethnic Differences in Symptoms of Post-Traumatic Stress after the Exxon Valdez Oil Spill." *Prehospital and Disaster Medicine* 19: 102–12.

Palinkas, Lawrence, John Russell, Michelle Downs, and John Peterson. 1992. "Ethnic Differences in Stress, Coping and Depressive Symptoms after the Exxon Valdez Oil Spill." *The Journal of Nervous and Mental Disease* 180: 287–95.

Paltoo, Dina, and Kenneth Chu. 2004. "Patterns in Cancer Incidence among American Indians/Alaska Natives, United States, 1992–1999." *Public Health Reports* 119: 443–51.

Picou, Steven, and Duane Gill. 1996. "The Exxon Valdez Oil Spill and Chronic Psychological Stress." *American Fisheries Society Symposium* 18: 879–93.

Picou, Steven, Duane Gill, Christopher Dyer, and Evans Curry. 1992. "Disruption and Stress in an Alaskan Fishing Community: Initial and Continuing Impacts of the Exxon Valdez Oil Spill." *Industrial Crisis Quarterly* 6: 235–57.

Quartaroli, MaryLynne. 2002. "Leetso, The Yellow Monster: Uranium Mining on the Colorado Plateau." In *Canyons, Cultures and Environmental Change,* edited by John Grahame and Thomas Sisk. http://www.cpluhna.nau.edu/ [accessed Sept. 7, 2010].

Rathore, Minakshi, Pradeep Bhatnagar, D. Mathur, and G. Saxena. 2002. "Burden of Organochlorine Pesticides in Blood and its Effect on Thyroid Hormones in Women." *The Science of the Total Environment* 295: 207–15.

Raymond-Whish, Stefanie, Loretta Mayer, Tamara O'Neal, Alisyn Martinez, Marilee Sellers, Patricia Christian, Samuel Marion, Carlyle Begay, Catherine Propper, Patricia Hoyer, and Cheryl Dyer. 2007. "Drinking Water with Uranium below the U.S. EPA Water Standard Causes Estrogen Receptor–Dependent Responses in Female Mice." *Environmental Health Perspectives* 115: 1711–16.

Roscoe, Robert, James Deddens, Alberto Salvan, and Teresa Schnorr. 1995. "Mortality among Navajo Uranium Miners." *American Journal of Public Health* 85: 535–40.

Schell, Lawrence, and Mia Gallo. 2010. "Relationships of Putative Endocrine Distruptors to Human Sexual Maturation and Thyroid Activity in Youth." *Physiology and Behavior* 99: 246–53.

Schell, Lawrence, Mia Gallo, Julia Ravenscroft, and Anthony DeCaprio. 2009. "Persistent Organic Pollutants and Anti-Thyroid Peroxidase Levels in Akwesasne Mohawk Young Adults." *Environmental Research* 109: 86–92.

Schell, Lawrence, Mia Gallo, Anthony DeCaprio, Lech Hubicki, Melinda Denham, Julia Ravenscroft, and The Akwesasne Task Force on the Environment. 2004. "Thyroid Function in Relation to Burden of Polychlorinated Biphenyls (PCB's), p,p'-DDE, HCB, Mirex, and Lead among Akwesasne Mohawk Youth: A Preliminary Study." *Environmental Toxicology and Pharmacology* 18: 91–99.

Schell, Lawrence, Lech Hubicki, Anthony DeCaprio, Mia Gallo, Julia Ravenscroft, Alice Tarbell, Agnes Jacobs, Dawn David, Priscilla Worswick, and The Akwesasne Task Force on the Environment. 2003. "Organochlorines, Lead, and Mercury in Akwesasne Mohawk Youth." *Environmental Health Perspective* 111: 954–61.

Schnailberg, Allan. 1980. *The Environment: From Surplus to Scarcity.* New York: Oxford.

Sergeev, Alexander, and David Carpenter. 2005. "Hospitalization Rates for Coronary Heart Disease in Relation to Residence Near Areas Contaminated with Persistent Organic Pollutants and Other Pollutants." *Environmental Health Perspectives* 113: 756–61.

Shields, L., W. Wiese, B. Skipper, B. Charley, and L. Banally. 1992. "Navajo Birth Outcomes in the Shiprock Uranium Mining Area." *Health Physics* 63: 542–51.

Short, Jeff, Stanley Rice, and Mandy Lindeberg. 2002. "The Exxon Valdez Oil Spill: How Much Oil Remains?" Alaska Fisheries Science Center. http://www.afsc.noaa.gov/Quarterly/jas2001/feature_jas01.htm [accessed July 16, 2012].

Sukdolová, V., S. Negoita, L. Hubicki, A. DeCaprio, and D. Carpenter. 2000. "The Assessment of Risk to Acquired Hypothyroidism from Exposure to PCBs: A Study among Akwesasne Mohawk Women." *Central European Journal of Public Health* 8:167–68.

U.S. Department of the Interior. 1990. "Impact of Potential Oil Spills in the Arctic Ocean on Alaska Natives." *Federal Register* 55Q27: 43144.

U.S. Environmental Protection Agency. 2006. *Abandoned Uranium Mines (AUM) on the Navajo Nation: Eastern AUM Screening Assessment Report.* San Francisco: U.S. EPA.

Weaver, Hilary. 2010. "Native Americans and Cancer Risks: Moving toward Multifaceted Solutions." *Social Work in Public Health* 25: 272–85.

Physical Activity, Nutrition, and Obesity in American Indians and Alaska Native Children and Families

Paul Spicer

American Indian and Alaska Native communities have rates of obesity that are significantly higher than national averages, often the highest in the nation, placing them at risk for a broad range of disabilities and premature mortality (Barnes, Adams, and Powell-Griner 2005; Denny, Holtzman, and Cobb 2003). American Indian and Alaska Native communities are not unique in confronting these problems, which have become a focus of national attention, especially for children (Institute of Medicine 2005), but the levels of obesity, coupled with the additional challenges that many American Indian and Alaska Native communities confront, make this a potentially quite difficult situation.

This chapter places the challenge of American Indian and Alaska Native obesity in a broad context, in the hopes of pointing the way toward potential solutions at multiple levels. As will become clear in the course of this review, obesity is a problem with political, environmental, economic, cultural, and psychological dimensions. A comprehensive solution will address the problem at many of these levels, but interventions can begin at almost any of them. There is much work to be done in this area and multiple ways to contribute. The focus here is on literature specific to American Indian and Alaska Native children and families, which was not possible previously (e.g., Spicer and Moore 2007). Recent research has changed this situation significantly, which is an encouraging development. This chapter also focuses on social and behavioral research, since the clinical utility of biological knowledge has, to date, been negligible (Lewis et al. 2012). Obesity is a physical problem with clear connections to multiple chronic diseases, but there can be little doubt that physical activity and nutrition remain the most significant factors in shaping the patterns of physical growth seen in American Indian and Alaska Native communities (Schell and Gallo 2012). This chapter begins with a brief review of the data on the prevalence and consequences of obesity in American Indian and Alaska Native communities, but devotes the bulk of its attention to the correlates and opportunities for intervention. This perspective on possible solutions is vital in the context of the overall theme of risk that shapes the current volume.

PREVALENCE

Data on the prevalence of obesity consistently points to higher prevalence in American Indian and Alaska Native communities, especially in the context of childhood obesity where better data is available. While most national reports do not include specific data on American Indian and Alaska Native populations (e.g., National Health And Nutrition Examination Survey), a recent report from the Early Childhood Longitudinal Survey found that American Indian and Alaska Native children had the highest rates of obesity of any racial and ethnic group in the United States at 31.2 percent, which was over 50 percent higher than the U.S. average of 18.4 percent and nearly 100 percent higher than the rate of 15.9 percent for U.S. non-Hispanic white children (Anderson and Whitaker 2009). Although it is not clear what parts of Indian Country were included in this national sample, reports from specific regions of the country also consistently emphasize these patterns (e.g., in the Aberdeen area, which includes North and South Dakota, Nebraska, and Iowa—Zephier et al. 2006) and in the baseline data from the Pathways study in Arizona, New Mexico, and South Dakota (Caballero et al. 2003). In an explicit comparative study, Janitz and colleagues examined American Indian and white students from the same rural school district in Oklahoma between 2005 and 2009, observing persistently higher prevalence of overweight and obesity for the American Indian students (Janitz et al. 2012). This last study is particularly significant since the students lived in the same communities and the analyses controlled for socioeconomic differences.

CONSEQUENCES

Obesity is a known risk factor for multiple chronic diseases, many of which affect American Indian and Alaska Native communities disproportionately. Most notable is diabetes. Over the decade from 1994 to 2004, there has been a 68 percent increase in the prevalence of type II diabetes in American Indian and Alaska Native adolescents (Centers for Disease Control and Prevention 2006). Obesity also has direct links to risk for cardiovascular disease, which continues to impact American Indian and Alaska Native communities at high rates, especially among diabetics (Xu et al. 2012). Associations with multiple forms of cancer have also been documented (Spicer and Moore 2007), but these often have less clear biological links to disease and require ongoing investigation. One obvious connection between obesity and all forms of chronic disease, including cancer, is that it often provides an index of inactivity and poor nutrition, which have associations with multiple causes of premature morbidity and mortality in and of themselves.

CORRELATES

There has been considerable enthusiasm in recent years for biological (and especially genetic) research into obesity and chronic disease, but there are solid indications that trends in obesity in American Indian and Alaska Native communities are recent, with reports from midcentury emphasizing underweight as a much more significant problem in American Indian and Alaska Native communities (Schell and Gallo 2012). This pattern suggests that environmental and behavioral causes are likely the most significant in understanding the rise in obesity in Native North America since environments have changed much more than genes over this period. Analyses of risks for, and protection from, obesity focus on the environments for eating and activity, which are shaped by policy, and individual choices within these contexts. Research also increasingly calls attention to the impact of stress, both as a risk factor for obesity and as a moderating factor for any intervention that directly targets physical activity and nutrition.

Policy, systems, and environment have been the target of special attention, especially by the Centers for Disease Prevention and Control. These approaches emphasize the aspects of contemporary environments that promote obesity. Available evidence suggests that American Indian and Alaska Native communities may be especially vulnerable in this regard, with poor access to healthy food and opportunities for activity. In an analysis of the availability of food in Washington State, for example, O'Connell and her colleagues found few supermarkets and poor availability of fruits and vegetables in multiple American Indian reservations (O'Connell, Buchwald, and Duncan 2012). With regard to activity, work with the Cherokee Nation in Oklahoma identified a lack of access to recreational and community facilities that could safely support physical activity and neighborhood and community design that discouraged active transportation (Spicer 2011). This small body of work, when linked to the broader inquiry into the environmental determinants of obesity (Ding et al. 2011; Taylor et al. 2006; Story et al. 2008), underscores the significant limitations that many tribal communities confront when attempting to improve physical activity and nutrition.

These environmental factors, in turn, shape lifestyles that promote obesity. As Jim Hill and his colleagues remind us, the fundamental contribution to weight gain in our society is the growing excess of what we consume over what we expend (Hill et al. 2003), and this balance is shaped, in fundamental ways, by behavioral choices with regard to food and activity. Analyses of the Youth Risk Behavioral Survey by Everett Jones and colleagues (2011) found that American Indian and Alaska Native youth were less likely than white youth to engage in sufficient vigorous activity or play in an organized sport and were more likely to watch at least three hours of TV per day (one form of what is commonly discussed as screen time). Unfortunately, this research does not control for what are likely very different environments of American Indian and white youth. But an analysis of risk factors for urban American Indian and Alaska Native youth in the same dataset found significant differences in sedentary activity and eating in that subset of youth who lived in urban contexts (distinguished from suburban and rural): Urban American Indian and Alaska Native youth were more likely than urban white youth to watch more than 3 hours of television a day (45.1 vs. 31.7 percent) and less likely to have had a green salad in the prior week (60.2 vs. 70.1 percent; Rutman et al. 2008). These differences within the urban context suggest important behavioral determinants that may be at least partially separable from the environment.

Data from the Wisconsin Nutrition and Growth Study underscore the importance of early risk factors for obesity, especially weight gain during pregnancy, high birth weight, and early termination of breastfeeding. Indeed, these risk factors, all manifest before the end of the first year of life, largely explain overweight in the preschool years in this American Indian cohort (Lindberg, Adams, and Prince 2012). The importance of breastfeeding here echoes an earlier report from the Phoenix Indian Medical Center that found that American Indian and Alaska Native children who were breastfed exclusively for the first six months of life experienced an overweight and obesity rate of 23 percent at the ages of three and four years, as compared with an overweight and obesity rate of 64 percent in children who were exclusively fed formula (Thomas and Cook 2005).

Data from preschool, also from the Wisconsin Nutrition and Growth Study, noted the importance of outdoor play as the most significant physical activity correlate of overweight in the preschool years. Interestingly, associations of obesity with screen time were not significant (Adams and Prince 2010), perhaps because these effects are shown in outdoor activity rather than screen time (screen time and outdoor activity are unlikely to be engaged in at the same time). Baseline data from intervention research by the Wisconsin team found significant differences between overweight and normal weight children in sweetened beverage intake and television viewing, suggesting that these may be important determinants to obesity. Furthermore, all children in the trial were engaged in moderate to vigorous physical activity less than 20 minutes per day and consumed more added sugar and less than recommended amounts of fruits and vegetables, suggesting higher levels of risk even for those not yet overweight (LaRowe et al. 2010). Polley and colleagues (2005) observed strong correlations between parent and grandparent obesity and sedentary activity and children's television viewing in both African American and American Indian families in Oklahoma, pointing, as well, to the influence of the family environment in shaping children's lifestyles.

An important result from research by Arcan and colleagues in South Dakota provides evidence for a point made in Spicer and Moore (2007) based on the broader literature: American Indian parents may underestimate the extent of their children's overweight. American Indian–specific research was not available at that time (2007), but Arcan and colleagues have recently confirmed these findings in an American Indian context: parents of overweight American Indian children in South Dakota were much more likely to under- rather than overestimate their children's weight status. Underestimation of weight was also significantly associated with parents' own overweight/obesity (Arcan et al. 2012). These differences in perception may raise unique challenges in public health messages if parents are not motivated to address their children's obesity because they do not perceive it.

Stress has been a topic of intense interest and focus in broader discussions of American Indian and Alaska Native health, especially in the context of historical trauma (e.g., Brave Heart and DeBruyn 1998), but little empirical research currently links these phenomena to obesity in American Indian and Alaska Native communities. This is especially surprising given the ways in which obesity may be rooted in disrupted aboriginal life ways (with respect to both food and activity). There are also known connections between adverse childhood experiences and obesity in the more general primary care population. Indeed, as Felitti and Anda (2010) present it, the origins of the Adverse Childhood Experiences study are to be found in their experiences running a medical weight loss clinic, where they realized that many of the individuals who dropped out of the program after successfully losing weight had had experiences of childhood abuse. The Adverse Childhood Experiences study subsequently confirmed this linkage (Williamson et al. 2002). The literature also delineates more general links between stress, obesity, and chronic disease (e.g., Stringhini et al. 2012; Tamashiro 2012), and poverty is known to subject children and families to increased stress in biologically measurable ways (Blair at al. 2011). These risk factors undoubtedly work to increase the prevalence of obesity in multiple populations who are at risk for adverse childhood experiences and subject to ongoing chronic stress in their lives, including American Indian and Alaska Native communities. These dynamics are likely exacerbated by the historical disruptions experienced in so many American Indian and Alaska Native communities.

Stress may also complicate efforts to change physical activity and nutrition. This is perhaps most evident in the context of depression. Physical activity has a known impact upon mood, but this has yet to translate into interventions with any demonstrable impact (Mead et al. 2009). In no small part, this is likely due to the difficulty of engaging depressed patients in activity. This has been much less appreciated in the literature on obesity prevention, however, which regularly assumes motivation and capacity to improve health behavior. Indeed, none of the interventions in the published literature on American Indian and Alaska Native childhood obesity engage maternal mental health in any significant way. Most focus simply on education without explicitly addressing questions of motivation at all.

This is especially troubling because available data suggests high levels of substance abuse and mental health problems in some American Indian communities (Beals et al. 2005) and rates of American Indian and Alaska Native youth suicide consistently lead the nation (CDC 2009). Efforts to address physical activity and nutrition in American Indian and Alaska Native communities must obviously at least be cognizant of mental health issues, which can complicate any effort to change health behavior.

This review of the risk factors for obesity in American Indian and Alaska Native children and families emphasizes the importance of environmental factors, shaped by policy, as well as individual behavior, which is shaped by complex cultural and psychological factors. Intervention is possible at any of these levels. As will be seen next, there is a small but growing body of work that has begun to point the way to what works.

INTERVENTIONS

At the level of environmental interventions, Blue Bird Jernigan and her colleagues (2012) describe a community-based participatory approach on the Round Valley Indian Reservation in northern California that led to the development of community-supported agriculture and the use of this produce in school lunches. In addition, the effort was successful in creating the option to use electronic benefits transfer cards at local farmers' markets and for improved display of local produce at retailers. The Mvskoke Food Sovereignty Initiative (http://www.mvskokefood.org/), which strives to improve the food environment in eastern Oklahoma, is also notable in this regard. They publish a monthly newsletter and foster a range of community action. Both of these initiatives point to the very real possibility of community mobilization for environmental change, especially with regard to healthy eating.

A persistent concern about environmental interventions, especially those that can promote active living, is the cost of these changes. Many of the most successful environmental interventions capitalize on new community planning initiatives, e.g., community redevelopment, new housing developments. In efforts like these, large public investments permit the development of neighborhoods that are more supportive of active transportation (e.g., walking and biking) and higher levels of physical activity more generally (e.g., parks). Zoning can also create resources for healthy eating in walking distance from housing. The opportunity for such large-scale efforts in community redesign has been, unfortunately, quite rare in Indian Country. This is ironic given the substantial government involvement in most reservation housing construction. An effort by the Winnebago tribe in Nebraska to create a village that supports more active living does, however, represent an exciting example of innovative thinking in this area (http://activelivingbydesign.org/communities/profiles/winnebago-ne). The availability of tribal resources from gaming and other economic development may promote additional efforts in at least some communities. It is important to remember, however, that the majority of tribes fail to realize economic benefits from gaming (Spicer and Sarche 2012).

The largest trial of a preventive obesity intervention in American Indian communities to date has been the Pathways study (Byers 2003; Caballero et al. 2003). This randomized, controlled, school-based trial involved 1,704 children in 41 schools and was conducted from the third to fifth grades, in schools serving American Indian communities in Arizona, New Mexico, and South Dakota. The trial's objective was to evaluate the effectiveness of a school-based, multicomponent intervention for reducing percentage of body fat. The intervention had four components: 1) change in dietary intake; 2) increase in physical activity; 3) a classroom curriculum focused on healthy eating and lifestyle; and 4) a family-involvement program. Unfortunately, the intervention resulted in no significant reduction in percentage of body fat, which was the primary hoped-for outcome. The percentage of energy from fat and total energy intake (by 24-hour dietary recall) were significantly reduced in the intervention schools, but the intervention had no effect on directly measured energy intake (Himes et al. 2003) or actual activity levels (Going et al. 2003). Some knowledge, attitudes, and behaviors were, however, positively and significantly changed by the intervention (Stevens et al. 2003).

In their preschool intervention in Wisconsin, LaRowe et al. (2007) describe the development of intervention materials to support four behavioral objectives: 1) increasing fruit and vegetable intake; 2) increasing physical activity; 3) decreasing consumption of candy, soda, and other sweetened beverages; and 4) decreasing television viewing time. While results of the trial have not yet been published, it was designed in partnership with Native communities and the curriculum uses explicit messages about traditional tribal physical activity and nutrition in presenting the lessons underscoring the importance of these issues in tribal communities and the possibilities for collaborative intervention development and research.

The need for the earliest possible intervention is supported by recent findings from Lindberg, Adams, and Prince (2012), which suggest that risk factors in pregnancy and immediately postpartum may be especially significant—including weight gain in pregnancy, high birth weight, and early termination of breastfeeding. Interventions that begin in pregnancy have received recently renewed attention in the Maternal, Infant, and Early Childhood Home Visiting Program, which was funded under the Affordable Care Act. While this initiative does not explicitly target obesity as an outcome, it does work to engage women in preconception and prenatal care as well as to promote regular participation in well-child visits. These approaches could easily be expanded to include explicit attention to feeding, sleep, and activity. But engaging maternal health behavior in pregnancy requires change in maternal self-care, which may be underdeveloped given the traumatic histories of mothers and may be complicated by ongoing depression. These deficits in self-care in parents obviously compromise their ability to care for the newborn child as well. Interventions that support the development of preconception health in young women offer one possibility for intervention prior to the birth of the child, but the evidence base for these interventions is extremely limited, both generally (Whitworth and Dowswell 2009) and in the more specific case of diabetic women (Tieu, Middleton, and Crowther 2010). To date none of these approaches has been subjected to rigorous research in American Indian or Alaska Native communities. Emerging evidence does, however, suggest that interventions that focus on stress in the perinatal period can have a significant effect on mothers (e.g., Urizar and Munoz 2011). These approaches may point the way toward alternative intervention points, with an explicit focus on the mental health needs of new parents. Recalling the manifold ways that stress can compromise efforts to address obesity discussed above, these early results warrant much more careful study in American Indian and Alaska Native communities.

CONCLUSION

Obesity is rooted in a series of profound and very disruptive changes in American Indian and Alaska Native communities. The immediate causes of these problems are clear—there is an excess of caloric intake over what is expended in activity—but recent research on these issues underscores how difficult solutions to these problems may be. It is not sufficient to simply recommend healthy eating and activity. Effective obesity prevention requires environments that can support healthy eating and activity, which require community action and resources. It also requires motivation to engage in healthy behaviors, which may be compromised by high levels of poverty and stress. Unfortunately, the results from the Pathways study confirm more general conclusions about school-based interventions: we cannot simply engineer healthier school environments and expect them to work without the participation of families and communities. This work requires a comprehensive approach addressing community and family environments as well as schools and other institutions, e.g., Head Starts, child care, etc.

At the same time, the risk factors for obesity, and especially dietary change, are potent symbols in Indian Country. Obesity prevention and intervention creates exciting possibilities for community mobilization, as the example from Jernigan et al. (2011)

illustrates. Ongoing community consultation in Native communities consistently emphasizes the importance of dietary change as a community concern and a well-established consensus in communities that contemporary diets are literally making people sick (Lewis et al. 2012). All of this suggests exciting opportunities for public education and social marketing with regard to healthier lifestyles that may be uniquely motivating in Native communities.

And individual change is possible. The Diabetes Prevention Program has demonstrated the possibility of making lifestyle change in preventing diabetes (Diabetes Prevention Program Research Group 2002), and it has since been extended in a series of demonstration projects in 38 different American Indian and Alaska Native communities. This program emphasizes the value of simple changes in diet and activity that can literally reverse what once appeared to be an inevitable diagnosis of diabetes in people at risk for the disorder. An emerging science of behavioral change, much of it derived from work in addiction, can and should also be harnessed to promote changes in physical activity and nutrition insofar as these are consonant with community priorities and planning. Motivational interviewing (Miller and Rollnick 2002) and contingency management (Higgins et al. 2008) represent approaches that might be profitably applied in obesity prevention in tribal communities.

The question of the ways in which obesity is rooted in unresolved mental health problems is, potentially, the most troubling, given the level of need and lack of adequate mental health care in Indian Country more generally (Gone and Trimble 2012). Yet, here, too, there are some interesting approaches. While potentially far from our immediate concern with obesity, interventions in the area of fetal alcohol syndrome, especially the Parent Child Assistance Project run by the University of Washington, point to the very real possibility of engaging even high-risk mothers through paraprofessional intervention (Ernst et al. 1999). This approach does not require a suite of licensed professionals and is currently being implemented in a number of tribal communities. Approaches like this can and should be extended in tribal communities that often need to rely on paraprofessional workforces (e.g., Spicer et al. 2012).

As this overview of obesity in American Indian and Alaska Native communities makes clear, these are problems that will require concerted attention across multiple levels. Given the connections between these problems and the history of American Indian and Alaska Native communities, there are powerful incentives to address these challenges as part of community renewal. But given the multiple ways in which risk interacts to shape contemporary patterns of obesity, it is clear that there remain significant challenges as communities move forward. This chapter was designed to serve as an orientation toward the most reasonable places to begin to address these challenges.

FURTHER INVESTIGATIONS

There are four major promising areas for research based on the literature reviewed in this chapter:

1. **There is a need for much better analyses of the ways in which stress impacts peoples' abilities to make changes in physical activity and nutrition. Research and intervention efforts should make better use of available approaches to support behavioral change.**
2. **Approaches to mental health need to be much better integrated with those to physical health. These problems appear to be closely related and would likely benefit from an integrated approach.**
3. **Interventions that support family change are needed in addition to those that can promote individual change. Especially for childhood obesity, interventions should be able to reach and engage everyone involved in shaping the child's home environment and supporting healthy choices for physical activity and nutrition in the household as a whole.**
4. **Community mobilization matters for promoting advocacy for healthy eating and active living at a broader level. Exciting opportunities for social marketing that draw on tribal traditions exist.**

References

Adams, A., and R. Prince. 2010. "Correlates of Physical Activity in Young American Indian Children: Lessons Learned from the Wisconsin Nutrition and Growth Study." *Journal of Public Health Management Practice* 16 (5): 394–400.

Anderson, S. E., and R. C. Whitaker. 2009. "Prevalence of Obesity among Preschool Children in Different Racial and Ethnic Groups." *Archives of Pediatric and Adolescent Medicine* 163 (4): 344–48.

Arcan, C., P. J. Hannan, J. H. Himes, J. A. Fulkerson, B. Holy Rock, M. Smyth, and M. Story. 2012. "American Indian Parents' Assessment of and Concern about Their Kindergarten Child's Weight Status, South Dakota, 2005–2006." Preventing Chronic Disease 2012; 9:110215. DOI: http://dx.doi.org/10.5888/pcd9.110215.

Barnes, P. M., P. F. Adams, and E. Powell-Griner. 2005. *Health Characteristics of the American Indian and Alaska Native Adult Population: United States, 1999–2003.* Advanced Data from Vital and Health Statistics, no. 356. Hyattsville, MD: National Center for Health Statistics.

Beals J., D. K. Novins, N. R. Whitesell, P. Spicer, C. M. Mitchell, S. M. Manson, and the AI-SUPERPFP Team. 2005. "Mental Health Disparities: Prevalence of Mental Disorders and Attendant Service Utilization of Two American Indian Reservation Populations in a National Context." *American Journal of Psychiatry* 162: 1723–32.

Blair, C., C. C. Raver, D. Granger, R. Mills-Koonce, and L. Hibel. 2011. "Allostasis and Allostatic Load in the Context of Poverty in Early Childhood." *Development and Psychopathology* 23 (3): 845–57.

Blue Bird Jernigan, V., A.L. Salvatore, D. M. Styne, and M. Winkleby. 2012. "Addressing Food Insecurity in a Native American Reservation Using Community-Based Participatory Research." *Health Education Research* 27: 645–55.

Brave Heart, M. Yellow Horse, and L. M. DeBruyn. 1998. "The American Indian Holocaust: Healing Historical Unresolved Grief." *American Indian and Alaska Native Mental Health Research* 8 (2): 60–82.

Byers, T. 2003. "On the Hazards of Seeing the World through Intervention-Colored Glasses." *American Journal of Clinical Nutrition* 78: 904–5.

Caballero, B., T. Clay, S. M. Davis, B. Ethelbah, B. Holy Rock, T. Lohman, et al. 2003. "Pathways: A School-Based, Randomized Controlled Trial for the Prevention of Obesity in American Indian Schoolchildren." *American Journal of Clinical Nutrition* 78: 1030–38.

Caballero, B., J. H. Hime, T. Lohman, S. M. Davis, J. Stevens, M. Evans, S. Going, and J. Pablo for the Pathways Study Research Group. 2003. "Body Composition and Overweight Prevalence in 1704 Schoolchildren from 7 American Indian Communities." *American Journal of Clinical Nutrition* 78 (2): 308–12.

Centers for Disease Control and Prevention. 2006. "Diagnosed Diabetes among American Indians and Alaska Natives aged < 35 Years—United States, 1994–2004." *MMWR,* 55 (44): 1201–3.

Centers for Disease Control and Prevention. 2009. *Suicide Rates among Persons Ages 10–24 Years, by Race/Ethnicity and Sex, United States, 2002–2006.* September 30. http://www.cdc.gov/violenceprevention/suicide/statistics/rates03.html [accessed Jan. 20, 2012].

Denny, C. H., D. Holtzman, and N. Cobb 2003. "Surveillance for Health Behaviors of American Indians and Alaska Natives: Findings from the Behavioral Risk Factor Surveillance System, 1997–2000." *MMWR Surveillance* 52 (7): 1–13.

Diabetes Prevention Program Research Group. 2002. "Reduction in the Incidence of Type 2 Diabetes with Lifestyle Intervention or Metformin." *New England Journal of Medicine* 346: 393–403.

Ding, D., J. F. Sallis, J. Kerr, S. Lee, and D. E. Rosenberg. 2011. "Neighborhood Environment and Physical Activity among Youth: A Review." *American Journal of Preventive Medicine* 41: 442–55.

Ernst, C. C., T. M. Grant, A. P. Streissguth, and P. D. Sampson. 1999. "Intervention with High-Risk Alcohol and Drug Abusing Mothers: II. Three-Year Findings from the Seattle Model of Paraprofessional Advocacy." *Journal of Community Psychology* 27 (1): 19–38.

Everett Jones, S., K. Anderson, R. Lowry, H. Conner. 2011. "Risks to Health among American Indian/Alaska Native High School Students in the United States." *Preventing Chronic Disease* 8 (4): A76. http://www.cdc.gov/pcd/issues/2011/jul/10_0193.htm.

Felitti, V.J. and R. J. Anda. 2010. "The Relationship of Adverse Childhood Experiences to Adult Medical Disease, Psychiatric Disorders, and Sexual Behavior: Implications for Health Care." In *The Impact of Early Life Trauma on Health and Disease: The Hidden Epidemic,* edited by R.A. Lanius, E. Vermetten, and C. Pain, 77–87. Cambridge: Cambridge University Press.

Going, S. B., J. Thompson, S. Cano, D. Stewart, E. Stone, L. Harnack, et al. 2003. "The Effects of the Pathways Obesity Prevention Program on Physical Activity in American Indian Children." *Journal of Preventive Medicine* 37 (1): S62–S69.

Gone, J. P ., and J. E. Trimble. 2012. "American Indian and Alaska Native Mental Health: Diverse Perspectives on Enduring Disparities." *Annual Review of Clinical Psychology* 8: 131–60.

Higgins, S. T., K. Silverman, S. H. Heil, and J. V. Brady. 2008. *Contingency Management in Substance Abuse Treatment.* New York: Guilford.

Hill, J. O., H. R. Wyatt, G. W. Ree, and J. C. Peters. 2003. "Obesity and the Environment: Where Do We Go from Here?" *Science,* 299, 853–55.

Himes, J. H., K. Ring, J. Gittelsohn, L. Cunningham-Sabo, J. L. Weber, J. Thompson, et al. 2003. "Impact of the Pathways Intervention on Dietary Intakes of American Indian Schoolchildren." *Preventive Medicine,* 37, S55–S61.

Institute of Medicine. 2005. *Preventing Childhood Obesity: Health in the Balance.* Washington, D.C.: Institute of Medicine.

Janitz, A. E., W. E. Moore, A. L. Stephens, K. E. Abbott, and J. E. Eichner. 2012. "Weight Status of American Indian and White Elementary School Students Living in the Same Rural Environment, Oklahoma, 2005–2009." *Preventing Chronic Disease* 9: 110223. DOI: http://dx.doi.org/10.5888/pcd9.110233.

LaRowe, T. L., A. K. Adams, J. E. Jobe, K. A. Cronin, S. M. Vannatter, and R. J. Prince. 2010. "Dietary Intakes and Physical Activity among Preschool-Aged Children Living in Rural American Indian Communities before a Family-Based Healthy Lifestyle Intervention." *Journal of the American Dietetic Association* 110: 1049–57.

LaRowe, T. L., D. P. Wubben, K. A. Cronin, S. M. Vannatter, and A. K. Adams. 2007. "Development of a Culturally Appropriate, Home-based Nutrition and Physical Activity Curriculum for Wisconsin American Indian families." *Preventing Chronic Disease* 4 (4). http://www.cdc.gov/pcd/issues/2007/oct/07_0018.htm.

Lewis, C. M., A. Obregon-Tito, R. Y. Tito, M. W. Foster, and P. G. Spicer. 2012. "The Human Microbiome Project: Lessons from Human Genomics." *Trends in Microbiology* 20: 1–4.

Lindberg, S. M., A. K. Adams, and R. J. Prince. 2012. "Early Predictors of Obesity and Cardiovascular Risk among American Indian Children." *Maternal and Child Health Journal* DOI 10.1007/s10995-012-1024-9.

Mead, G. E., M. Morley, P. Campbell, C. A. Greig, M. McMurdo, and D. A. Lawlor. 2009. "Exercise for Depression." *Cochrane Database of Systematic Reviews* 2009, Issue 3. Art: CD004366. DOI: 10.1002/14651858.CD004366.pub4.

Miller, W. R., and S. Rollnick. 2002 *Motivational Interviewing, Second Edition: Preparing People for Change.* New York: Guilford.

Moore, K. 2010. "Youth-Onset Type 2 Diabetes among American Indians and Alaska Natives." *Journal of Public Health Management and Practice* 16 (5): 388–93.

O'Connell, M., D. S. Buchwald, G. E. Duncan. 2012. "Food Access and Cost in American Indian Communities in Washington State." *Journal of the American Dietetic Association* 111: 1375–79.

Polley, D. C., M. T. Spicer, A. P. Knight, and B. L. Hartley. 2005. "Intrafamilial Correlates of Overweight and Obesity in African-American and Native-American Grandparents,

Parents, and Children in Rural Oklahoma." *Journal of the American Dietetic Association* 105 (2): 262–65.

Rutman, S., A. Park, M. Castor, M. Taualii, and R. M. Forquera. 2008. "Urban American Indian and Alaska Native Youth: Youth Risk Behavior Survey 1997–2003." *Maternal and Child Health Journal* 12 (S1): S76–S81.

Schell, L. M., and M. V. Gallo. 2012. "Overweight and Obesity among North American Indian Infants, Children, and Youth." *American Journal of Human Biology* 24: 302–13.

Spicer, P. 2011. Active Living in Oklahoma. Webinar presented for Active Living Research and the Association of American Indian Physicians. June.

Spicer, P., and K. Moore. 2007. "Responding to the Epidemic of American Indian and Alaska Native Childhood Obesity." In *Obesity in America. Volume 2: Development and Prevention,* edited by Hiram E. Fitzgerald and Vasiliki Mousouli, 143–66. Westport CT: Praeger.

Spicer, P., and M. C. Sarche. 2012. "Poverty and Possibility in the Lives of American Indian and Alaska Native Children and Families." *The Oxford Handbook of Poverty and Child Development,* 480–88. Oxford: Oxford University Press.

Spicer., P, D. S. Bigfoot, B. Funderburk, and D. K. Novins. 2012. "Evidence-Based Practice and Early Childhood Intervention in American Indian and Alaska Native Communities." *Zero To Three* March 2012, 19–24.

Stevens, J., M. Story, K. Ring, D. M. Murray, C. E. Cornell, Juhaeri, et al. 2003. "The Impact of the Pathways Intervention on Psychosocial Variables Related to Diet and Physical Activity in American Indian Schoolchildren." *Journal of Preventive Medicine* 37 (1): S70–S79.

Story, M., K. M. Kaphingst, R. Robinson-O'Brien, and K. Glanz. 2008. "Creating Healthy Food and Eating Environments: Policy and Environmental Approaches. *Annual Review of Public Health* 29: 253–72.

Stringhini, S., A. G. Tabak, T. N. Akbaraly, S. Sabia, M. J. Shipley, M. G. Marmot, E. J. Brunner, G. D. Batty, P. Bovet, M. Kivimäki. 2012. "Contribution of Modifiable Risk Factors to Social Inequalities in Type 2 Diabetes: Prospective Whitehall II Cohort Study." *British Medical Journal* 345: e5452 DOI: 10.1136/bmj.e5452.

Tamashiro, K. L. K. 2012. "Metabolic Syndrome: Links to Social Stress and Socioeconomic Status." *Annals of the New York Academy of Sciences* 1231: 46–55.

Taylor, W. C., W. S. C. Poston, L. Jones, and M. K. Kraft. 2006. "Environmental Justice: Obesity, Physical Activity, and Healthy Eating." *Journal of Physical Activity and Health* 3, Suppl 1: S30–S54.

Thomas, S. L., and D. Cook. 2005. Breastfeeding Duration and Prevalence of Overweight among 4- and 5-Year Olds." *The IHS Primary Care Provider* 30 (4): 100–2.

Tieu J, P. Middleton, C.A. Crowther. 2010. "Preconception Care for Diabetic Women for Improving Maternal and Infant Health." *Cochrane Database of Systematic Reviews* 2010, Issue 12. Art. No.: CD007776. DOI: 10.1002/14651858.CD007776.pub2.

Urizar, G. G., and R. F. Munoz. 2011. "Impact of a Prenatal Cognitive-Behavioral Stress Management Intervention on Salivary Cortisol Levels in Low-income Mothers and Their Infants." *Psychoneuroendocrinology* 36 (10): 1480–94.

Whitworth, M., and T. Dowswell. 2009. "Routine Pre-Pregnancy Health Promotion for Improving Pregnancy Outcomes." *Cochrane Database of Systematic Reviews* 2009, Issue 4. Art.: CD007536. DOI: 10.1002/14651858.CD007536.pub2.

Williamson, D.F., T. J. Thompson, R.F. Anda, W.H. Dietz, and V. Felitti. 2002. "Body Weight and Obesity in Adults and Self-Reported Abuse in Childhood." *International Journal of Obesity* 26: 1075–82.

Xu J., E. T. Lee, L. E. Peterson, R. B. Devereux, E. R. Rhoades, J. G. Umans, L. G. Best, W. J. Howard, J. Paranilam, and B. V. Howard. 2012. "Differences in Risk Factors for Coronary Heart Disease among Diabetic and Nondiabetic Individuals from a Population with High Rates of Diabetes: The Strong Heart Study." *Journal of Clinical Endocrinology and Metabolism* 97 (10): 3766–74.

Zephier, E., J. H. Himes, M. Story, et al. 2006. Increasing Prevalences of Overweight and Obesity in Northern Plains American Indian Children." *Archives of Pediatrics & Adolescent Medicine* 160 (1): 34–39.

The Status of HIV/AIDS, Risk Behaviors, Prevention, and Intervention among U.S. American Indian and Alaska Native Populations

Christine Wilson Duclos and Yvonne M. Hamby

In American Indian and Alaska Native (AI/AN)[1] communities HIV/AIDS is a reality even though the numbers of HIV and AIDS diagnoses for AI/ANs seem very low when compared to the total number of HIV/AIDS cases reported. AI/ANs rank third in rates when population size is taken into account (Centers for Disease Control and Prevention 2008a). American Indian males and females have a 40 percent higher rate of HIV/AIDS, respectively, than white males and females (U.S. Department of Health and Human Services 2012).

HIV is an acronym for the human immunodeficiency virus. Acquired immune deficiency syndrome (AIDS) occurs as the result of the destruction of the immune system by HIV. At this time, AIDS has no cure. HIV is transmitted through blood, semen and vaginal secretions during unprotected sexual contact, direct blood contact (including injection drug needles, blood transfusions, accidents, or certain blood products), and mother to baby (before or during birth, or through breast milk).[2] For example, the majority of HIV positive AI/AN women contract HIV through heterosexual intercourse (66 percent), while a significant number (33 percent) are infected through injection drug use (Advocates for Youth 2007). Risk for HIV infection is not increased by race and ethnicity by themselves. However, AI/ANs likely face more challenges that put them at increased risk (e.g. substance use, socioeconomic issues, HIV testing issues, etc.). Thus, the authors hope to enhance your knowledge, abilities, and understanding as they pertain to HIV/AIDS epidemiology and prevention services among American Indians and Alaska Native (AI/ANs) populations.

Planning and implementing programs with AI/AN tribes and nations, tribal agencies, and urban programs requires a specific knowledge and understanding of the history and cultural background of the local tribes and how differing communication styles may impact intended outcomes. This chapter is intended to serve as a basic introduction and overview for individuals or organizations seeking to work with these communities. The primary objectives of this chapter are to:

1. Provide a brief summary of key historical events and policies related to AI/AN communities; and
2. Provide an overview of the social and cultural context in which HIV/AIDS impact AI/AN communities.

HISTORICAL BACKGROUND

In the United States,

> AI/ANs face profound health issues that are exacerbated by poverty and social breakdown. Diabetes and alcoholism are perhaps the most talked about, but while overall numbers for AI/ANs are comparatively small, they are also significantly affected by HIV. As with other communities of color, HIV cases among AI/ANs have increased since the mid-1980s, ranking third in rates of AIDS diagnoses, after African Americans and Hispanics. Yet despite increasing attention paid to health disparities in other racial/ethnic minority populations, Native Americans are often overlooked (Centers for Disease Control and Prevention 2006).

In September 2006, the CDC changed HIV testing guidelines, recommending that all persons between the ages of 13 and 64 be routinely tested for HIV. Persons deemed at high risk should be tested at least every year, while all other persons should be tested at least every three to five years (Center for Disease Control and Prevention 2006). Routine testing is considered cost effective if the prevalence of HIV is 0.1 percent or greater. If the community prevalence is not known, routine testing should be implemented until a prevalence of lower than 0.1 percent can be established., Barriers to expanding HIV screening include perceived cost, staffing/time constraints, and patient acceptance (NASTAD 2007). Many people do not know that low cost or free HIV testing is available. Often providers are under tight time constraints and are reluctant to add to their workload. Patients perceive their risk as low due to monogamy, abstinence, or condom use. Others would prefer not to know their HIV status rather than face psychosocial consequences such as loss of trust in a relationship or disclosure of status in hospital or public health records.

However, the challenges of addressing HIV in the community reach beyond resource allocation or models of testing and prevention. The epidemiologic profile of HIV among AI/ANs manifests from myriad factors, including complex historical events; varying cultural perspectives regarding sexual activity, health, and help-seeking; and coordination of tribal, state, and federal programs.

Historical events with "lasting repercussions mean there are complex issues organizations must understand in their work with AI/AN communities. Historical relationships with the federal government and with the U.S. health-care system have engendered a large degree of mistrust" (NASTAD 2004a). There are four key concepts that are important to understand in relation to these historical events which underpin the difficulty of addressing HIV/AIDS with AI/AN communities (Poupart 2001):

1. Treaty rights:
   - Negotiated between the U.S. government and federally recognized tribes
   - Establishes the unique relationship between tribes and the federal government; the relationship is not based on race or on minority status, but on *legal treaties* between them.
2. Trust responsibility:
   - Establishes the U.S. government's legal *and moral* obligation to uphold promises made to tribes during treaty negotiations.
3. Sovereignty:
   - Provides authority of self-government
   - Establishes government-to-government relations.
4. Historical and intergenerational trauma:
   - "Cumulative emotional and psychological wounding over the life span and across generations, emanating from massive group trauma"
   - Recognizes that "past events shape current reality"
     - Forced removal from traditional lands
     - Infectious disease epidemics
     - Forced attendance at boarding schools
     - Termination of rights
     - Failure to uphold treaty obligations.

Below are the key themes of these historical underpinnings:

- There is a trust responsibility of the federal government toward AI/ANs. The trust responsibility stems from sovereign tribes ceding lands to the U.S. government in exchange for certain protections, including health care, which constitute the "trust." This is the basis for federal funding of health care and education programs for AI/ANs (NASTAD 2004b);
- There have been many breaches of this trust responsibility throughout history, and there are still unresolved issues about tribal sovereignty (Poupart 2001);
- Similar to African Americans' distrust of the federal government stemming from the legacy of slavery and abuses, such as the Tuskegee syphilis study (NASTAD 2004a).

American Indians and Alaska Natives have experienced abuses at the hands of the Bureau of Indian Affairs and the Public Health Service that fuel mistrust of government health programs (NASTAD 2004a). These historical events and underpinnings have important implications for HIV/AIDS prevention and care/treatment programs.

HIV/AIDS ISSUE TODAY

HIV/AIDS among this population is cited to be underreported, resulting in an unclear picture of the true burden. The population, because of small overall numbers, is often put to the "other" category in reporting. In addition, AI/AN people come late into testing and are often racially misidentified (Bertolli et al. 2009). However, some data does exist.

The numbers of HIV and AIDS diagnoses for this group represent less than 1 percent of the total number of HIV/AIDs cases reported to the Center for Disease Control and Prevention (CDC) HIV/AIDS reporting system. However, alarmingly, when population size (per 100,000) is taken into account, the AI/ANs diagnosed with AIDS death rate (inclusive of all death causes) in 2007 was third (3.9) following Hispanic/Latino (6.0) and Black/African American (24.8) rates (Center for Disease Control and Prevention 2008a; 2008b). HIV/AIDS by itself may not be the sole reasons for these higher death rates, which are complicated by many factors including, for example, poverty, ruralness of half the population, the lack of early detection, inadequate health care, inadequate prevention education, and lack of adequate support (Asetoyer 2003).

INCIDENCE, PREVALENCE, AND CHARACTERISTICS

HIV Infection

The data in the figure below tells us that HIV is a problem within this group. Though the numbers of HIV diagnoses for AI/ANs represent only 1 percent of the total number in 2010, when population size is taken into account, they ranked third in rates of HIV diagnosis.

A CDC HIV/AIDS AI/AN specific fact sheet illustrated the transmission categories for both AI/AN adult and adolescent males and females living with HIV/AIDS at the end of 2005. These charts show the gender differences between transmissions: for males the majority is through male-to-male sexual contact and for females it is high-risk heterosexual contact. Approximately 30 percent of transmission in females is through injection drug use, compared to 15 percent of males.

AIDS

Information that is more recent exists for AIDS and HIV infections separately. Again, when taking population size into consideration and not just numbers, the rate of AIDS

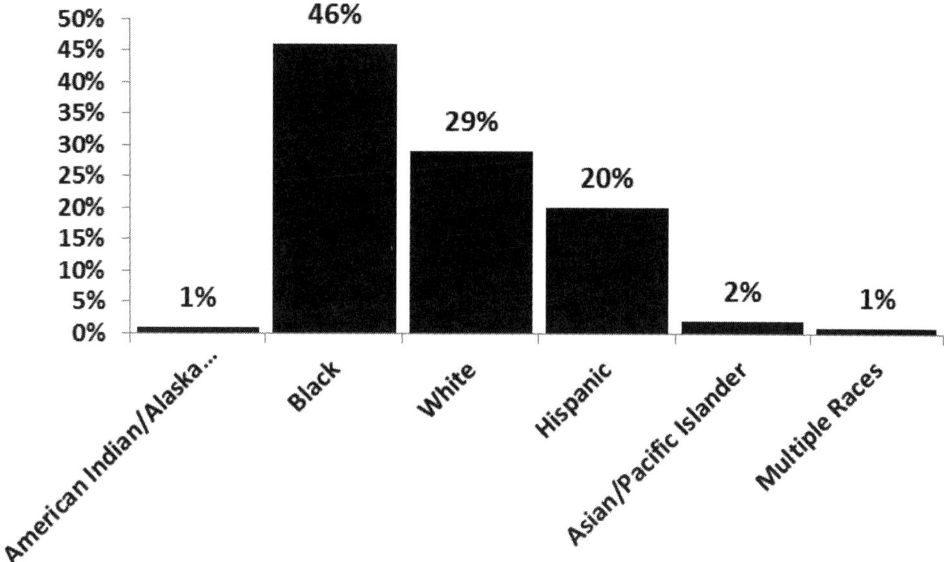

Diagnoses of HIV Infection by Race/Ethnicity in 2010 (Note: Taken from http://www.cdc.gov/hiv/topics/surveillance/basic/htm#hivest accessed November 26, 2012 and based on data from 46 states with long-term, confidential name-based HIV reporting.)

diagnosis for this group has been higher than that for whites since 1995. The AIDS case rate for 2008 was 17.0 or 60 percent higher than that of whites (8.5) (Centers for Disease Control and Prevention 2008d). AI/ANs living with an AIDS diagnosis have increased from 69.7 in 2005 to 73.7 in 2007 (Centers for Disease Control and Prevention 2008e). The transmission category description has not changed and was the same as mentioned in the overall picture. The majority of rural cases reside in the West and South while urban cases were more likely in the Northeast, Midwest, and West. These cases are more likely to be younger than non-AI/AN persons with AIDS, and more likely to be infected as teenagers. While AI/ANs are impacted both in rural, reservation, and urban settings, those impacted are more likely to be residents of rural areas than non-AI/ANs with AIDS (Centers for Disease Control and Prevention 2008a).

HIV Infections

Currently, the estimated diagnosed case rate of HIV infection in 2008 among this group was 11.9 as compared to 8.2 for whites (Centers for Disease Control and Prevention 2008c). Once again, the transmission categories were unchanged from the overall picture. The vast majority of female transmission still occurs through heterosexual contact and injection drug use and of male through male-to-male sexual contact.

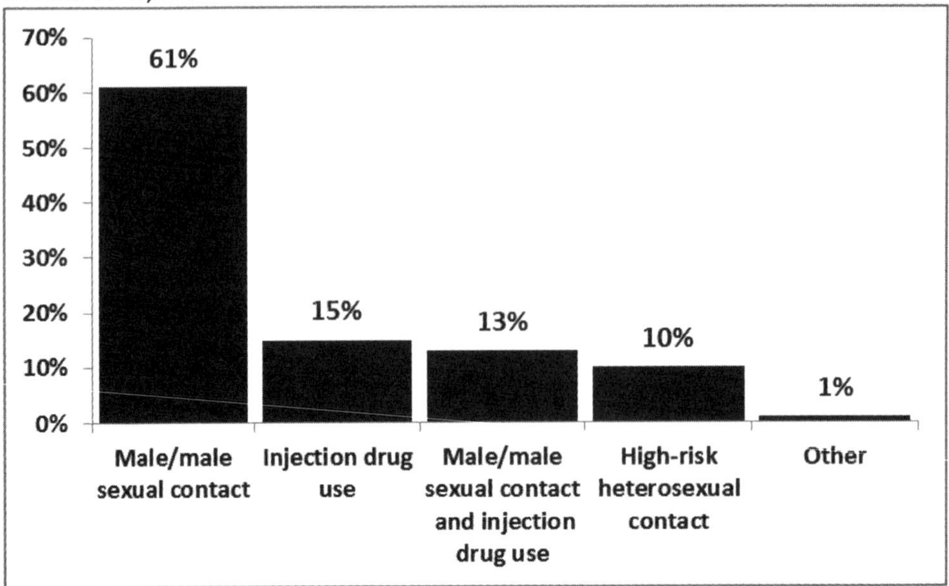

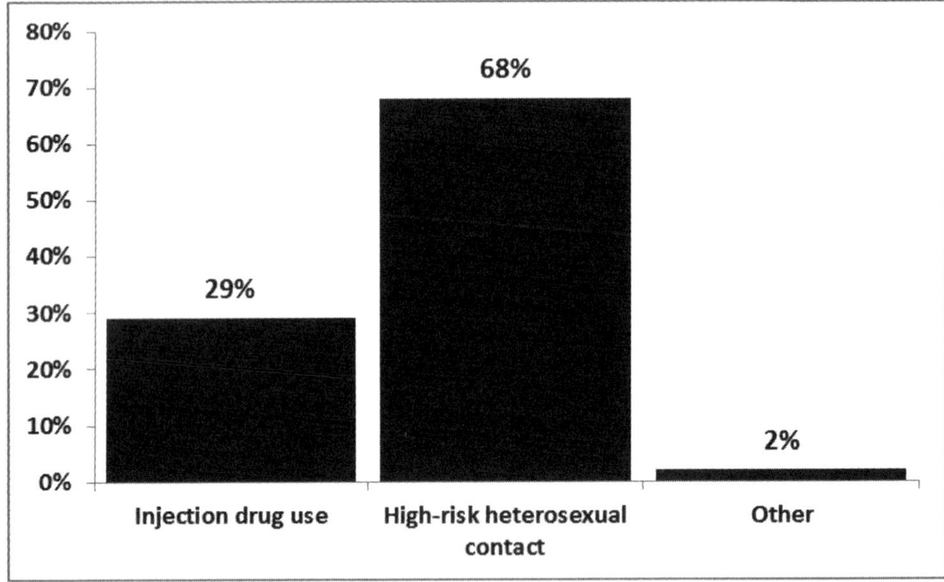

Transmission Categories for AI/ANs Living with HIV/AIDS at the End of 2005 by Gender (Note: Based on data from 33 states with long-term, confidential name-based HIV reporting. Source: Centers for Disease Control and Prevention, 2008)

Table IV.09.1 AI/AN Survival for More Than 12, 24, and 36 Months after Diagnoses of HIV Infection and AIDS during 2000–2004 by Race/Ethnicity

HIV Infection		Proportion Survived in Months		
Race/Ethnicity	**Number**	**>12**	**>24**	**>36**
American Indian/Alaska Native	818	0.91	0.89	0.87
Asian	1,163	0.95	0.93	0.93
Black/African American	91,158	0.93	0.91	0.89
Hispanic/Latino	30,986	0.94	0.92	0.91
Native Hawaiian/Other Pacific Islander	102	0.97	0.95	0.94
White	51,936	0.94	0.92	0.91
Multiple Races	1,686	0.95	0.92	0.90
AIDS		**Proportion Survived in Months**		
Race/Ethnicity	**Number**	**>12**	**>24**	**>36**
American Indian/Alaska Native	862	0.86	0.81	0.77
Asian	1,791	0.90	0.88	0.87
Black/African American	96,366	0.87	0.83	0.80
Hispanic/Latino	34,749	0.90	0.87	0.85
Native Hawaiian/Other Pacific Islander	191	0.90	0.85	0.83
White	55,627	0.89	0.86	0.83
Multiple Races	1,792	0.92	0.88	0.84

Note: 37 states with confidential name-based HIV infection and AIDS reporting.

Source: Centers for Disease Control and Prevention, Division of HIV/AIDS Prevention. 2008b. *HIV Surveillance Report: Diagnoses of HIV Infection and AIDS in the United States and Dependent Areas.* http://www.cdc.gov/hiv/surveillance/resources/report/s2008report/pdf/2008SurveillanceReport.pdf. [accessed Feb.4, 2011].

The 2007 rate of AI/ANs living with a diagnosis of HIV infection was 73.7, slightly lower than that of whites, 80.4. However, the survival rates show an alarming story. This population had the lowest survival percentages of any group diagnosed with HIV infection during 2000–2004 for any time period. Survival rates looked similar for having an AIDS diagnosis. (See table IV.09.1.)

The proportion of diagnosed AIDS cases that initially come to the attention of the CDC's HIV/AIDS surveillance system shows patterns of late HIV testing (Bertolli et al. 2009). AI/ANs wait for testing until they seek care for advanced disease thus underestimating incidence figures. In addition, they seem to experience a faster time course from HIV infection to AIDS than any other racial group in the United States (Kaufman et al. 2007).

It's important to note that current systems are not able to provide HIV/AIDS rates for individual tribes, thus variations in rates among tribal groups may exist

(Bertolli et al. 2009). For small population groups, changes in number of cases may or may not represent stable estimates thus affecting surveillance. This issue creates a dilemma for health administrators and tribal leaders in monitoring any health condition status, including HIV/AIDS, at a local community level (Roubideaux and Dixon 2001).

RISK FACTORS AND RELATED CONDITIONS

We draw heavily for this section on the National Alliance of State and Territorial AIDS Directors (NASTAD) Native American 2004 Report (NASTAD 2004a) and an article by Vernon and Jumper-Thurman (2005). These two sources are cited here with only additional supporting citations and sources added.

Health and Social Conditions

High Rates of Sexually Transmitted Infections (STIs): The same sexual behaviors that cause STIs also cause HIV. Thus, it is not surprising that the association between other STIs with HIV transmission places this group at significant risk (Kaufman et al. 2007). In 2009, the chlamydia rate among AI/ANs was 776.5 cases per 100,000 population (Centers for Disease Control and Prevention 2009). Overall, the rate of AI/AN chlamydia was more than four times that among whites. The gonorrhea rate was 113.3, which was 4.2 times higher than the rate among whites. The disparity between gonorrhea rates for AI/ANs and whites was larger for AI/AN women (4.5 times higher) than for men (3.6 times higher). The disparity in gonorrhea rates was slightly larger in the West and Midwest (4.7 times higher in both regions) than in the Northeast or South (3.5 and 3.0 times higher, respectively). The rate of primary and secondary (P&S) syphilis for this population increased 4.3 percent (from 2.3 to 2.4). Compared with whites, the rate of P&S syphilis was 1.1 times higher. The direct cost of STIs, including HIV, is estimated to be between $9.3 and $15.5 billion dollars, and with a higher STI burden, the associated costs may strain already scarce resources allotted to this population (Kaufman et al. 2007).

Substance Abuse: Substance use including alcohol rates though different among American Indian communities are beyond the national average (Bertolli et al. 2009). The 2009 National Survey on Drug Use and Health (SAMSHA 2010) (one of the few surveys that collect data on this relatively small, but important population) found that while actual alcohol use was lower than the national average "during the past month" for this group, binge drinking and illicit drug use was higher. (See figure IV.09.3 below.)

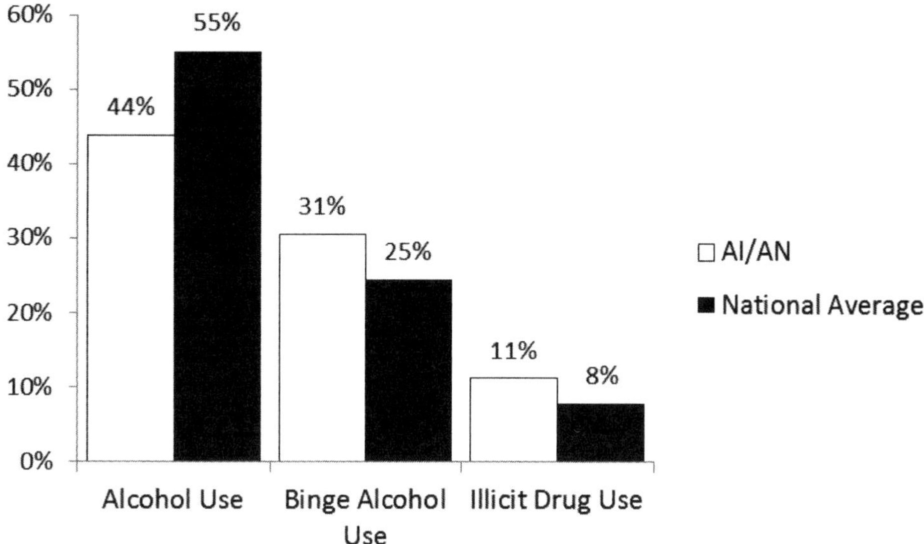

Past Month Substance Use Among AI/AN Aged 18 or Older Compared with the National Average (2004 to 2008) (Note: The difference between AI/AN and the national average is statistically significant at the .05 level. Source: SAMHSA, 2010. Results from the 2009 National Survey on Drug Use and Health. Accessed February 3, 2011. http://oas.samhsa.gov/NSDUH/2k9Results.htm#2.7. The White House Office of National AIDS Policy, 2010. National HIV/AIDS Strategy for the United States. Washington, DC: The White House Office of National AIDS Policy.)

However, Indian Health Service (IHS) reports on their website that alcohol-induced deaths are the sixth leading case of mortality with a ratio of 6.1 to U.S. all races (Indian Health Service 2012). When under the influence of substances, all precautions can be neglected, especially through blackouts. Injectable drug use is a major risk factor for AI/AN women, who are more likely to inject drugs than any other ethnic groups (Vernon 2002a), and for AI/AN men who have sex with men, who were found to have a larger percentage with injection drug use than the general population (Centers for Disease Control and Prevention 2008a). In addition, important to fighting infection, the substances negatively influence the body's absorption of vitamins and minerals.

A 2010 study of 36 HIV-positive Navajos receiving HIV care through the Navajo Area IHS identified factors associated with HIV disease progression (Iralu et al., 2010). It found important differences with incarceration in the last 12 months, household incomes of <$1,000/month, alcohol abuse, and nonuse of traditional medicine. Incarceration and alcohol abuse were interrelated. Incarceration of AI/AN populations is often linked to alcohol-related offenses, and thus the alcohol abuse underlies the statistical significant associations with viral load and T-cell counts used as outcomes more so than the incarceration.

Violence/Domestic Abuse: The high sexual violence rate, which is reported to be 2.5 times the rate for others of the same age, is above that for other racial/ethnic groups in the United States (U.S. Department of Justice 1999). A U.S. Department of Justice report found that 34.1 percent of AI/AN women—or more than one in three—will be raped during their lives, compared with one in five for the United States as a whole (Perry 2004). It happens in intimate relationships, within the family, and at the hands of strangers. While the available data does not provide an accurate portrayal of the extent of sexual violence against these women, it has been reported at least 86 percent of reported cases of rape or sexual assault involved non-Indian men. In contrast, when looking at assaults against non-Indian women, the incidence is committed within an individual's own race. In addition, 50 percent of AI/AN women have reported that they suffered physical injuries in addition to rape, compared to 30 percent of women in general (Deer 2005).

A report by Amnesty International documented many incidents of sexual violence in the three reservation communities studied but concluded that the majority of violence remains unreported (Amnesty International 2007). Perpetrators are often intimate partners, male acquaintances, or husbands. These perpetrators often do so with impunity by the women themselves and by responding authorities. Thus, many women themselves do not report sexual or domestic violence as a result. Reporting barriers include fear of breaches in confidentiality, fear of retaliation, and a lack of confidence that reports will be taken seriously and will result in perpetrators being brought to justice. The report focused its research on response to sexual crimes on tribal lands and in neighboring areas. The experience of those living far from reservation communities or in urban settings is not reflected completely in this report. While the report concluded that it may appear that AI/AN women in the United States may be targeted for acts of violence and even denied access to justice on the basis of their gender and identify, the root causes of discrimination and violence (Amnesty International 2007), such as poverty and socioeconomic marginalization, are complex and interconnected (Office of Justice Programs 1999; Harper and Entrekin 2006).

Sexual violence has been cited to increase the transmission of HIV/AIDS (Krug et al. 2002). Lack of protection during forced sex increases the risk of HIV transmission. Not only does the violence itself create risk, it also impacts the victim's ability to negotiate safer sex. For AI/AN women, this risk factor is perhaps most striking as it is juxtaposed with the traditionally strong and powerful role women have in many AI/AN communities (Vernon 2002).

HIV-RELATED RISK BEHAVIORS AND TESTING

The high rates of sexually transmitted infections (STIs) among AI/ANs, violence, and alcohol and illicit drug abuse discussed above are indicators of the vulnerability of AI/ANs to HIV/AIDS. How do their personal perceptions of risk behaviors impact HIV testing? Lapidus et al. (2006) studied HIV-related risk behaviors (substance use, injection drug use, and risky sexual behavior, etc.) among 218 negative or unknown HIV status urban AI/ANs. They found 72 percent of survey respondents reported some HIV risk behavior, 45 percent potentially high-risk. However, among the participants reporting high-risk behavior, 44 percent rated themselves at no or low risk for HIV infection. Encouragingly, 83 percent of the overall sample had "ever" received an HIV test and 36 percent in the last year. The odds of having received a test were 3.2 times higher (95 percent CI: 1.3-7.6) for those who perceived their personal risk of HIV infection as "high" compared with those who perceived their risk at low or no risk for HIV infection. The odds of having received a test in the past year were not significantly different among those who perceived their risk as "medium" compared with those who perceived themselves to be at low or no risk (OR: 1.0, 95 percent CI:0.5-2.0) (Lapidus et al. 2006 2006).

Reasons for being tested cited most often included "knowing where they stood" (86 percent) and required by court order, or gotten in jail or as part of a drug or alcohol treatment program (25 percent). This latter reason emphasizes the need to link on- and off-reservation correctional detainees and drug and alcohol treatment participants (both inpatient and outpatient) to HIV testing services.

Seventy-four percent of the participants who received an HIV test in the past year reported they delayed seeking testing, with 64 percent delaying for 6 months or more. The most frequent reason for avoiding or delaying testing was "thought I was HIV negative" (67 percent and 41 percent of those who did not test and delayed testing, respectively). Of those who delayed testing 65 percent stated that they were afraid of finding out or did not want to think about being HIV-positive; 25 percent of those who did not test at all gave this same reason. Personal fear of hearing positive results is real, and thus may not be easily addressed in any health promotion efforts.

What about HIV prevention messaging? Eighty-one percent of this same sample had been exposed to *some* HIV prevention messages in the past year. High-risk respondents were somewhat more likely to report receiving information from the Internet than medium or low risk respondents (16 percent vs. 7 percent potentially high and 9 percent lower risk, p=0.18). A lower percent of participants reported receiving some type of counseling session for HIV/STD prevention (17 percent) and did not differ by risk group or testing history. We must note that study recruitment was through anonymous peer-referral sampling with its limitations. What is interesting is that peers referred individuals presumably believing them to be at high risk; however, the individuals themselves did not. However, 75 percent reported to have engaged in alcohol binge drinking and 32 percent in noninjection drug use. This study emphasizes how urban AI/ANs' inaccurate perceptions of risk impacts their subsequent HIV testing (Lapidus et al. 2006).

Cultural Amplifiers

Sexuality: AI/AN communities' acceptance of homosexuality is often overgeneralized. Homophobia exists and varies among tribes (Oropeza 2002). Its presence can impact both the transmission and later detection of the disease. It can prevent two-spirit (gay/lesbian/transgender/bisexual) AI/ANs from seeking prevention and intervention services. The attached stigma and fear of confidentiality, coupled with one's own fear of knowing one's possible positive status, limits testing especially in rural reservation settings and perpetuates disease transmission.

Either way, trauma can be found behind behavioral risk taking.

Historical Trauma: It has been suggested that American Indians, because of "the loss of life, land, and destructive government policies, suffer from a legacy of historical unresolved grief, which shares PTSD symptomatology. Since the losses of American Indians have never been openly acknowledged; many have not undergone the grieving process that facilitates healing" (Brave Heart 2004). It has also been argued that while "some American Indians may experience historical trauma it is also possible that others may experience PTSD symptoms stemming from on-going current losses and/or traumatic experiences" (Levin 2009; Morsette 2007).

Migratory Movement: While many AI/ANs have moved into urban areas seeking better and more confidential care, they return often to the reservations for family gatherings and ceremonies. While not rigorously studied, this migratory movement is feared as a possible factor in the spread of HIV/AIDS.

Structural Amplifiers

Denial of the HIV/AIDS Issue: The denial within these communities that HIV/AIDS is a significant problem because of reports of low numbers usually coincides with the stigma against HIV/AIDS. "Two Spirit" men can be doubly stigmatized for being HIV positive and for their sexuality, marginalizing them further (Rowell and Bouey 1997).

Low Priority: HIV/AIDS is but one of only many problems AI/ANs face. Poverty and unemployment and the related issues of "basic survival" and the high proportion of other health concerns such as alcoholism, diabetes, violence, etc. are often seen as more pressing. With the denial of HIV/AIDS as a problem within these communities, prioritizing the address of HIV/AIDS risk and prevention services is difficult.

Distrust and Internalized Racism: Legacies of colonization, struggle for quality health-care services, breaches of treaty rights, and diminishing tribal sovereignty has impacted trust with the Western-oriented mainstream and Indian Health Service (IHS) system. The 2006 study of urban AI/ANs cited earlier inquired the perceived comfort of HIV testing location. Sixty-four percent of those who had ever tested and indicated comfort with testing at a tribal or urban Indian health center actually went for their last test to a non-Indian clinic (Lapidus et al. 2006).

Assimilation policies and practices has resulted in stereotypes and internalized racism within some AI/AN people. Internalizing negative dominant culture attitudes toward Indian/Native history and ways can lead Indian/Native individuals to abandon the cultural heritage and traditions that can mitigate the effects of trauma and substance use that may put individuals at risk for HIV infection (Waters and Simony 2002).

Western Approaches to Prevention and Treatment: Most HIV prevention and service efforts are based on the Western biomedical model. Duran and Walters examined the strengths and weaknesses of the published literature on prevention and treatment and argued the need for a more "indigenist" etiology paradigm to AI/AN HIV/AIDS risk and protections (Duran and Walters 2004). With a different "worldview," the prevalent biomedical framework may not reach this population.

Concern for Confidentiality: AI/AN communities are close-knit. Thus, serious concerns for protection of confidentiality are warranted as in any other small and isolated community. Many reservation-based people have relatives, friends, or acquaintances working within the local clinic, leading to fear of breaches of confidentiality. This fear then restricts access to local care or forces many to seek care far from home.

Accurate Surveillance: HIV case reporting has challenges in collecting accurate data for this population (Vernon and Jumper-Thurman 2005). First, AI/ANs must get tested. Second, case reporting based on name-based reporting (patient names are forwarded to the Health Department) occurs in 36 of 50 states, and only 25 states have had it in place long enough to provide reliable monitoring. In addition, it has been reported that misidentification of race in the disease surveillance data underestimates what is reported. Bertolli, Lee, and Sullivan (2007) in their study of five states and one county participating in the HIV/AIDS Reporting Systems found that 30 percent of AI/AN individuals were misidentified when data was linked to the Indian Health Service National Patient Information and Reporting System. This misidentification varied by location. AI/AN people were misidentified as white (70 percent), Hispanic (16 percent), black (11 percent), and Asian/Pacific Islander (2 percent). Urban residence at time of diagnosis, degree of AI/AN ancestry, and mode of HIV exposure were significantly associated with this misidentification. The extent of misidentifications has major implications for allocating scare resources to the problem, prevention and service programming, and, most importantly, for an accurate picture of the visibility of HIV/AIDS in this population. We note that since HIV has become a "chronic infection" with the advent of more effective treatment slowing progression to AIDS, AIDS cases alone can no longer accurately reflect trends in HIV infection (Centers for Disease Control and Prevention 2004). Thus, it becomes even more crucial that AI/ANs get tested and their results be reported with accurate race identifiers.

Services and Funding Issues: Although there has been an emphasis on providing resources for minority communities to develop programs and services to address their health care needs by some federal agencies, many Native communities still lack the necessary resources to develop culturally relevant and effective programs. This is due to the political and legal status of the AI/AN communities and the decentralized system of care, which complicates funding, as described above (NASTAD 2004b). However, despite these limitations, the IHS HIV/AIDs program is attempting to implement a comprehensive approach to their HIV/AIDs prevention and treatment program. They are attempting to do this via collaborations both internal and external to the IHS (Indian Health Service, HIV/AIDs Program Goals, accessed on 12/3/12).

The responsibility for AI/AN health care and funding is not widely understood. Health care and prevention services are provided through several ways. First, the IHS provides services through tribally contracted or IHS-operated programs. Members of federally recognized tribes are eligible for these services. Other ways for accessing health care are through private health insurance (e.g. employer/union provided, direct purchase, or military, etc.), public health coverage (e.g., Medicare, Medicaid, VA, CHIP, etc.), or paying out-of-pocket. The breakdown of coverage was shown in an analysis of 2008 data from the U.S. Census Bureau's American Community Survey (ACS). Those who selected the "American Indian and Alaska Native alone" category for race in the ACS indicated that 43.7 percent had private health insurance, 30.4 percent had public health coverage, and 31.6 percent were uninsured (Turner, Boudreaux, and Lynch 2009).

Most of IHS funding goes toward services located on or near a reservation and may not be accessible for many and not at all for those members of state only-recognized tribes. In regards to HIV/AIDS, the IHS has no direct "line-item" for this issue in its budget. Funding appropriated to the IHS through the Hospital and Health Clinics component of Labor, Health and Human Services, and Education Appropriations encompasses treatment and care for multiple diseases. This funding could potentially be used for HIV prevention services if the tribes choose to utilize some of these monies for those services (NASTAD 2004b).

According to the IHS HIV/AIDS program website, funding is acquired from a multitude of sources. The following excerpt is taken directly from the IHS website.

> The HIV/AIDS program receives a portion of funds for HIV/AIDS activities from the U.S. Department of Health and Human Services Office of HIV/AIDS Program and Policy (OHAPP). This is in the form of funds from the Minority AIDS Initiative (MAI), which responds to the epidemic's impact on minority/ethnic populations, including this population. IHS receives its allocation from the HHS Secretary's MAI Fund; however, it is based on multi-agency proposals. These funds are somewhat "discretionary" as opposed to the larger sum of MAI-based funding that goes directly to other HHS agencies. The IHS

> MAI dollars fund initiatives that are linked through MAI to the President's Initiative on HIV/AIDS (Indian Health Service, HIV/AIDS Program, accessed on 12/3/12).

We must note that the IHS does operate a HIV Center of Excellence (HIVCOE). It is a clinically based center for HIV care, treatment, research, and intervention at the Phoenix Indian Medical Center, serving the tribal and IHS facilities in the area. Its goal is to provide the highest quality culturally competent HIV services including clinically based intervention and medically appropriate care and treatment to AI/ANs.

HIV care outside of the IHS would depend on the resources available to the patient. Medicaid and Medicare (M/M) and private insurers likely are the main payers of this care (as they are in any population). The VA is also a likely source of care. For those without M/M or private insurance, then Ryan White eligibility criteria may apply, including the AIDS Drugs Assistance Program (ADAP). AI/ANs are seen as any other applicant at a state ADAP facility, and eligibility is also the same.

This service delivery patchwork of systems, coupled with the complexity within these communities and areas of residence and mistrust of federal systems results in a complex and highly variable approach to HIV/AIDS prevention, care, and treatment. In addition, that direct funding from the CDC and HRSA comes in the form of competitive, often short-term awards contributes to instability and sustainability issues. These confusing, uncoordinated, and incomplete service options result in many not receiving the services they need. In addition, changes in tribal administration and subsequent politic priorities impact service delivery and cannot be underestimated.

AMERICAN INDIAN/ALASKA NATIVE STRENGTHS AND RESILIENCY THAT MAXIMIZE HIV/AIDS PREVENTION EFFORTS

Circle of Life

The "holistic" worldview in many AI/AN traditions is usually depicted as a medicine wheel that focuses on the mental, physical, emotional, and familial community aspects of life. Thus to address the issue of HIV/AIDS in these communities, this holistic strength-based approach must be integrated. The National Native American AIDS Prevention Center along with others uses this "circle of life" concept in their prevention efforts, especially for those living with HIV/AIDS (Lidot 2003). The concept is also extended to the community.

Traditional Healing

Many AI/AN people seek traditional healers in addressing health problems, including HIV/AIDS. This healing helps an individual with overall well-being by aiding coping with stress, which might otherwise lead to risk-taking behaviors, or dealing with a diagnosis of HIV infection or AIDS (Vernon 2002a). Since traditional healers are usually found in reservation settings, migration may occur among urban AI/ANs wishing access to these services. It becomes important for prevention and intervention planning to reach out and not alienate the healers when working in this issue (Iralu et al. 2010; Bouey and Duran 2000).

Respect

Respect is valued, especially the respect of elders and gender relations. For this reason, many programs addressing HIV/AIDS prevention and intervention incorporate elder and women wisdom and help.

Cooperation and Consensual Decision Making

Other key values include cooperation and decision making by consensus. Thus, prevention and intervention activities should include input, agreement, and cooperation of the community. Avoidance of direct, confrontational discussion and a contemplative, listening approach to HIV assessment and problem solving is warranted.

Group Emphasis and Collective Ownership

The idea of collective responsibility rather than individual ownership may differ from the more Western individualistic approach to personal responsibility for health. Some may believe that HIV/AIDS is not a direct result of their own risk-taking behavior. Responsibility then lies within the community and not within the self. Some may even feel that individual testing should be done for the "good" of the community.

CONCLUSION

Competing priorities, lack of resources, and other pressing concerns all affect the capacity of local communities and service agencies to respond to HIV/AIDS appropriately. In addition, HIV/AIDS in Indian Country is situated within a complex web of historical, social, cultural, economic, and health cofactors. Poverty, unemployment, vulnerability to substance abuse and other risk factors, violence, discrimination, distrust, and more all influence the likelihood of HIV/AIDS spread and response. The fact that HIV/AIDS significantly impacts AI/ANs, coupled with their small population size and the unclear picture of the extent of the issue can easily leave this group out of HIV/AIDS prevention and care and treatment. For any appropriate response to be maximally successful, this multifaceted context must be considered as the foundation of an equally multifaceted response.

The United States National HIV/AIDS Strategy (NHAS) has identified "Reducing HIV-Related Disparities and Health Inequities" as one of its three main overarching goals.[3] The strategy has acknowledged that disparities in HIV prevention and care persist among racial/ethnic minorities, as well as among sexual minorities. To address this issue, the NHAS emphasizes the need to move beyond individual-oriented interventions to incorporate and combine community-level approaches. Based on a Social Determinants of Health model (SDH), the strategy provides key recommended actions that if used would likely yield benefits beyond HIV prevention (Centers for Disease Control and Prevention 2010). SDH typically refers to the social and physical environments and health services that are not controllable by the individual but affect the individual's environment. The NHAS-recommended actions included:

- Establishing pilot programs that utilize community models
- Measuring and utilizing community viral load
- Promoting a more holistic approach to health that addresses not only HIV prevention among those at high risk, but also the prevention of HIV-related co-morbidities such as STIs and hepatitis B and C
- Encouraging communities to affirm support for people living with HIV
- Promoting public leadership of people living with HIV
- Strengthening enforcement of civil rights laws.

The SDH approach to HIV prevention and care could have significant impact, especially within the AI/AN population where these determinants have been shown throughout this chapter to be crucial factors for outcomes. Not only does this more holistic approach follow the cultural mores; it could achieve a more balanced portfolio of appropriate prevention and care interventions to complement existing individual, partner, and network approaches used in the prevention and control of HIV/AIDS.

◀ FURTHER INVESTIGATIONS ▶

In their report on improving HIV surveillance, the CDC noted several factors that can impact the effectiveness of the HIV case surveillance system for AI/AN. These included access to HIV services; test-seeking behaviors of individuals and testing practices of providers; case reporting to state systems by providers, laboratories, and facilities; correct identification of AI/AN race; appropriate

data analysis methods; and dissemination of surveillance information back to the community (CDC, DHAP 2012). However, Vernon and Jumper-Thurman (2005) reported HIV case reporting has challenges when collecting accurate data for this population There are several reasons for these challenges. The mistrust of sharing data with state or federal agencies due to the lack of sharing data back with the community; the legal issues related to reporting laws due to sovereignty and treaty rights between AI/AN and the governments; and lastly underreporting due to racial misclassification. Misidentification is supported by such studies as those done by Bertolli, Lee, and Sullivan (2007); Thoroughman, Frederickson, Cameron, Shelby, and Cheek (2002); and others.

Even though there has been much attention paid to disparities among minority groups in the past decade, AI/ANs have not typically been included in these efforts (Rhoades, D.). Dr. Rhoades notes in her commentary that "AI/ANs not only experience disparities in health, they also experience disparities in data." In particular, she recommends that racial misclassification related to AI/AN populations should be included as a data collection issue affecting the reliability of estimates of health care disparities (Rhoades, D.).

As part of the National HIV/AIDs Strategy to encourage improved surveillance among AI/AN populations, the CDC has recommended 15 practices supporting effective HIV surveillance. The recommendations address a few issues related to the improvement of HIV testing and services for AI/AN communities. They included specifics for how to improve testing and making HIV services more culturally appropriate; several addressed challenges related to the collection, reporting, and use of HIV data for AI/AN populations; and four recommendations directed toward improved completeness and accuracy of race/ethnicity in surveillance data (CDC, DHAP 2012).

There are a couple of explanations for racial misclassification. The first is the assumption of the homogeneity of the AI/AN population; in fact, the AI/AN population is heterogeneous, including 565 federally recognized tribes with sovereign status as domestic, dependent nations and with different languages, cultures, and tribal governance structures (Census Profiles); the use of Hispanic surnames to identify race/ethnicity, which means that AI/AN that have Spanish surnames are not counted in the AI/AN racial group in the state surveillance system (Satter 1999; CDC, DHAP 2012); and lastly the provider or other clinic staff using personal observation in completing the race field on lab requisitions and case reports (Satter 1999).

Through their key informant interviews, the CDC identified a predominate standard practice for collection and reporting that negatively impacts the accuracy of race/ethnicity for AI/AN in HIV surveillance reporting:

- Present, in surveillance reports, cases with documented single AI/AN race (AI/AN only without Hispanic ethnicity), and, separately, present AI/AN cases with and without Hispanic ethnicity (CDC, DHAP, 2012).

They also identified four recommended practices that could improve the accuracy of this data:

- **Identify ways to encourage more accurate documentation of race/ethnicity in medical records.**
- **Utilize data sources with self-reported or family-reported race, such as Ryan White program data, to improve the completeness and accuracy of race/ethnicity in surveillance data.**
- **Contact providers for race/ethnicity information when the case report indicates non-AI/AN race and diagnosis has occurred in an IHS-funded or tribally operated facility, or there is other information suggestive of AI/AN race.**
- **Partner with tribes, IHBs, TECs and IHS to identify and correct misidentification of race/ethnicity by periodically linking HIV surveillance data with tribal membership rolls or the IHS patient registration system (CDC, DHAP 2012).**

This issue is crucial to address so that accurate surveillance data can be used for equitable resource allocation decisions, and to inform prevention and intervention public health efforts.

Notes

1. The authors use the term *American Indians and Alaska Natives* and shortened to AI/AN in accord with the 1977 National Congress of American Indians and the National Tribal Chairmen's Association resolution.
2. http://www.aids.org/topics/aids-faqs/how-is-hiv-transmitted/ [accessed March 29, 2012].
3. http://www.whitehouse.gov/administration/eop/onap.

References

Advocates for Youth. 2007. "HIV and Young American Indian/Alaska Native Women." http://www.advocatesforyouth.org/publications/439?task=view [accessed March 29, 2012].

Amnesty International. 2007. *Maze of Injustice: The Failure to Protect Indigenous Women from Sexual Violence in the USA.* New York: Amnesty International.

Asetoyer, Charon, Katharine Cronk, and Samanthi Hewakapuge. 2003. *Indigenous Women's Health Book within the Sacred Circle.* Lake Andes, SD: The Native American Women's Health Education Resource Center.

Bertolli, Jeanne, Lisa M. Lee, and Patrick S. Sullivan. 2007. "Racial Misidentification of American Indians/Alaska Natives in the HIV/AIDS Reporting Systems of Five States and One Urban Health Jurisdiction, U.S. 1984–2002." *Public Health Reports* 122: 382–92.

Bertolli, Jeanne, A. D. McNaghten, Michael Campsmith, Lisa M. Lee, Richard Leman, Ralph T. Bryan, and James W. Buehler. 2009. "Surveillance Systems: Monitoring HIV/AIDS and HIV Risk Behaviors among American Indians and Alaska Natives." *AIDS Education and Prevention.* 16: 218–37.

Bouey, P. D., and Bonnie E. Duran. 2000. "The Ahalaya Case Management Program for HIV-infected American Indians, Alaska Natives, and Native Hawaiians: Quantitative and Qualitative Evaluation of Impacts." *American Indian and Alaska Native Mental Health Research Online* 9 (2).

Brave Heart, Maria Yellow Horse. 2004. "The Historical Trauma Response among Natives and Its Relationship to Substance Abuse." In *Healing and Mental Health for Native Americans: Speaking in Red,* edited by Ethan Nebelkopf and Mary Phillips, 7–18. New York: AltaMira Press.

Census. *Profile America Facts for Features: American Indian and Alaska Native Heritage Month.* http:// www.census.gov/newsroom/releases/pdf/cb11ff-22_ aian.pdf [assessed Dec. 5, 2012].

Centers for Disease Control and Prevention. 2004. *HIV Prevention in the Third Decade: The Changing Epidemic. How Is CDC Responding?* www.cdc.gov [accessed Feb. 11, 2011].

Centers for Disease Control and Prevention. 2006. "Revised Recommendations for HIV Testing of Adults, Adolescents, and Pregnant Women in Health-Care Settings." *MMWR Recommendations and Reports,* 55 (RR14): 1–17. Atlanta: U.S. Department of Health and Human Services, CDC.

Centers for Disease Control and Prevention. 2006. *Sexually Transmitted Disease Surveillance.* Atlanta: U.S. Department of Health and Human Services.

Centers for Disease Control and Prevention. 2008a. *HIV/AIDS among American Indians and Alaska Natives: CDC HIV/AIDS Fact Sheet.* Atlanta: U.S. Department of Health and Humans Services, CDC.

Centers for Disease Control and Prevention. 2008b. *HIV Surveillance Report: Diagnoses of HIV Infection and AIDS in the United States and Dependent Areas.* http://www.cdc.gov/hiv/surveillance/resources/report/s2008report/pdf/2008SurveillanceReport.pdf [accessed Feb. 4, 2011].

Centers for Disease Control and Prevention. 2008c. *HIV Surveillance Report: Diagnoses of HIV Infection and AIDS in the United States and Dependent Areas. Table 3a.* http://www.cdc.gov/hiv/surveillance/resources/report/s2008report/pdf/2008SurveillanceReport.pdf [accessed Feb. 4, 2011].

Centers for Disease Control and Prevention. 2008d. *HIV Surveillance Report: Diagnoses of HIV infection and AIDS in the United States and Dependent Areas. Table 6a.* http://www.cdc.gov/hiv/surveillance/resources/report/s2008report/pdf/2008SurveillanceReport.pdf [accessed Feb. 4, 2011].

Centers for Disease Control and Prevention. 2008e. *HIV Surveillance Report: Diagnoses of HIV infection and AIDS in the United States and Dependent Areas. Table 16a.* http://www.cdc.gov/hiv/surveillance/resources/report/s2008report/pdf/2008SurveillanceReport.pdf [accessed Feb. 4, 2011].

Centers for Disease Control and Prevention. 2009. *STDS in Racial & Ethnic Minorities.* http://www.cdc.gov/std/stats09/minorities.htm.

Centers for Disease Control and Prevention. 2010. *Establishing a Holistic Framework to Reduce Inequities in HIV, Viral Hepatitis, STDs, and Tuberculosis in the United States.* Atlanta: USDHHS, CDC.

Centers for Disease Control and Prevention. 2012. *Improving HIV Surveillance among American Indians and Alaska Natives in the United States.* Atlanta: U.S. Department of Health and Human Services.

Deer, Sarah. 2005. "Sovereignty of the Soul: Exploring the Intersection of Rape Law Reform and Federal Indian Law." *Suffolk U. L. Review.* 455–66.

Duran, Bonnie, and Karina L. Walters. 2004. "HIV/AIDS Prevention In 'Indian Country': Current Practice, Indigenist Etiology Models, and Postcolonial Approaches to Change." *AIDS Education and Prevention* 16: 187–201.

Harper, Shelby Settles, and Christina Marie Entrekin. 2006. *Violence against Native Women: A Guide for Practitioner Action.* Washington, D.C.: Office on Violence against Women and National Center on Full Faith and Credit.

Indian Health Services. n.d "Indian Health Disparities." *IHS Fact Sheets.* http://www.ihs.gov/newsroom/factsheets/disparities [accessed Feb. 5, 2011].

Indian Health Services. n.d. *HIV/AIDs Program, Program Goals.* http://www.ihs.gov/hivaids/index.cfm?module=program [accessed on Dec. 3, 2012].

Iralu, Jonathan, Bonnie Duran, Cynthia R. Pearson, Yizhou Jiang, Kevin Foley, and Melvin Harrison. 2010. "Risk Factors for HIV Disease Progression in a Rural Southwest American Indian Population." *Public Health Reports* 125 (Supplement 4): 43–49.

Kaufman, Carol E., Sara Shelby, Debra J. Mosure, Jeanne Marrazzo, David Wong, Lori De Ravello, Stephanie Craig Rusing, Victoria Warren-Mears, Lisa Neel, Sara Jumping Eagle, Scott Tulloch, Francine Romero, Sarah Patrick, and James E. Cheek. 2007. "Within the Hidden Epidemic: Sexually Transmitted Disease and HIV/AIDS among American Indians and Alaska Natives." *Sexually Transmitted Diseases* 34: 767–77.

Krug, Etienne G., Linda L. Dahlbert, James A. Mercy, Anthony B. Zwi, and Rafael Lozano. 2002. *World Report on Violence and Health.* Switzerland: World Health Organization Publications.

Lapidus, Jodi A., Jeanne Bertolli, Karen McGowan, and Patrick Sullivan. 2006. "HIV-Related Risk Behaviors, Perceptions of Risk: HIV Testing, and Exposure to Prevention Messages and Methods among Urban American Indians and Alaska Natives." *AIDS Education and Prevention* 18: 546–59.

Levin, Aaron. 2009. "How Much Does Historical Trauma Add to Indians' Health Problems?" *Psychiatric News* 44: 9.

Lidot, Tom. 2003. *Visions for Living with HIV in the Circle of Life.* Denver: National Native American AIDS Prevention Center.

Morsette, Aaron, 2007. "Trauma in American Indian Communities,. SAMSA: http://www.giftfromwithin.com/html/amindian.html.

NASTAD. 2004a. *Native Americans and HIV/AIDS: Key Issues and Recommendations for Health Departments.* Washington, D.C.: NASTAD.

NASTAD. 2004b. *Activities to Address HIV/AIDS in Native American Communities.* Washington, D.C.: NASTAD.

NASTAD. 2007. *Report on Findings from an Assessment of Health Department Efforts to Implement HIV Screening in Health Care Settings.* http://www.nastad.org/Docs/Public/Publication/2007626_NASTAD_Screening_Assessment_Report_062607.pdf [accessed Feb. 11, 2011].

Office of Justice Programs, Bureau of Justice Statistics. 1999. *American Indians and Crime.* NCJ 183386, Table 3, p. 3, available at http://www.bjs.gov/content/pub/pdf/aic.pdf.

Oropeza, Laura. 2002. *Clinician's Guide: Working with Native Americans Living with HIV.* Oakland, CA: National Native American AIDS Prevention Center.

Perry, Steven W. 2004. *American Indians and Crime—A BJS Statistical Profile 1992–2002.* Washington, D.C.: Bureau of Justice Statistics, U.S. Department of Justice, Office of Justice Programs.

Poupart, John. 2001. *To Build a Bridge: An Introduction to Working with American Indian Communities.* Minneapolis: American Indian Policy Center.

Rhoades, Dorothy. "Commentary Disparities in Data for American Indians and Alaska Natives." Centers for American Indian and Alaska Native Health Colorado School of Public Health/University of Colorado Anschutz Medical Campus. http://www.ucdenver.edu/academics/colleges/PublicHealth/research/centers/CAIANH/journal/Documents/Volume%20 13/13(1)_Rhoades_Commentary_Disparities_in_Data_70.pdf [accessed on Dec. 4, 2012].

Roubideaux, Yvette, and Mim Dixon. 2001. "Health Surveillance, Research, and Information." In *Promises to Keep,* edited by Mim Dixon and Yvette Roubideaux, 1401–3. Washington, D.C.: American Public Health Association.

Rowell, Ronald, and Paul Bouey. 1997. "Update on HIV/AIDS among American Indian/Alaska Natives." *The IHS Primary Care Provider* 22.

SAMSHA. 2010. *Results from the 2009 National Survey on Drug Use and Health.* http://oas.samhsa.gov/NSDUH/2k9NSDUH/2k9Results.htm#2.7 [accessed Feb. 3, 2011].

Satter, Delight. 1999. "Culturally Competent HIV/AIDS Prevention for American Indians and Alaska Natives." In *Cultural Competence for Providing Technical Assistance, Evaluation and Training For HIV Prevention Programs.* Washington, D.C.: CRP, Inc.

Turner, Joanna, Michel Boudreaux, and Victoria Lynch. 2009. "A Preliminary Evaluation of Health Insurance Coverage in the 2008 American Community Survey." Paper released through the U.S. Census Bureau. http://www.census.gov/hhes/www/hlthins/data/acs/2008/2008ACS_healthins.pdf [accessed Feb. 11, 2011].

Vernon, Irene. 2002a. *Killing Us Quietly: Native Americans and HIV/AIDS.* Lincoln: University of Nebraska Press.

Vernon, Irene. 2002b. "Violence, HIV/AIDS, and Native American Women in the Twenty-first Century." *American Indian Culture and Research Journal* 26: 115–33.

Vernon, Irene, and Pamela Jumper-Thurman. 2005. "The Changing Face of HIV/AIDS among Native Populations." *Journal of Psychoactive Drugs* 37: 247–55.

Waters, Karina L., and Jane Simony. 2002. "Indigenist Stress-Coping Model." *American Journal of Public Health* 92: 520–24.

U.S. Department of Health and Human Services, Office of Minority Health. 2012. http://minorityhealth.hhs.gov/templates/content.aspx?ID=3026 [accessed March 29, 2012].

U.S. Department of Justice. 1999. *American Indians and Crime.* Washington, D.C.: Office of Justice Programs, Bureau of Justice Statistics, U.S. Government Printing Office.

The White House Office of National AIDS Policy. 2010. *National HIV/AIDS Strategy for the United States.* Washington, D.C.: The White House Office of National AIDS Policy.

Wiping the Tears of American Indian and Alaska Native Youth: Suicide Risk and Prevention

Maria Yellow Horse Brave Heart, Doreen M. Bird, Deborah Altschul, and Annette S. Crisanti

> My role and responsibility to keep the children sacred are to remain patient, to trust, to listen to assist, and to be a better parent. . . . I can't blame my parents because they haven't taught me. Now that I know it's my responsibility I know that I'll teach my son and I want my son to teach his children. We can make a better life for the future of our children. . . . (Brave Heart 1999, 119).

Youth suicide is an area of critical concern for American Indians and Alaska Natives (AI/AN). The complex determinants of suicide among AI/AN include historical trauma—the collective, intergenerational wounding emanating from land loss, displacement, and forced separation of children from tribal communities under early federal Indian boarding school policy (Brave Heart 2003). In 1999, the United States Surgeon General issued a *Call to Action to Prevent Suicide,* because rates of suicide in the country were reaching increasingly high levels (U.S. Public Health Service 1999). Decades before that, rates of youth suicides in AI/AN communities were already beginning to reach epidemic levels (Westlake Van Winkle and May 1986; Middlebrook et al. 1998). More recent data show that AI/AN youth have higher rates of suicide, suicide attempts, and suicide ideation compared to other races (Indian Health Service 2008; Dorgan 2010; Mullany, Barlow, Goklish, Larzelere-Hinton, Cwik, Craig, and Walkup 2009; AASTEC 2011). Although most of the current literature reports AI/AN suicide rates that are some of the highest in the country, it is important not to generalize data across all tribal nations. A number of tribes have suicide rates that are lower than those found in the U.S. general population. Moreover, the topic of suicide may be difficult to address in some AI/AN communities. In order to prevent suicide among AI/AN youth we must draw upon indigenous culture and tradition as well as integrate evidence-based knowledge about the causality of suicide, effective prevention, and early intervention strategies that show promise in AI/AN communities as well as in the general population. The introductory quote gives voice to an American Indian parent, a descendant of parents who survived traumatic Indian boarding school experiences, following her participation in a parent-specific version of the Historical Trauma and Unresolved Grief Intervention, a Tribal Best Practice (Brave Heart et al. 2012). AI/AN communities are committed to restoring the sacredness of youth and the traditional sacred responsibility to care for the nation.

This chapter provides an overview of current literature with a focus on distinct issues for youth populations. More specifically, we review traditional AI/AN perspectives of suicide, providing two examples of traditional cultural beliefs and oral histories. Next, we posit an alternative view of suicide through the framework of historical trauma theory. We elucidate the influence of collective intergenerational massive group trauma upon increasing risk factors for suicide, including the destruction of indigenous cultural factors that may have served to limit suicidal behaviors in AI/AN communities. We then review key literature on the context of youth suicidal risk and protective factors in American Indian communities. Next, we present an overview of the research and recommendations regarding treatment options and prevention programming for youth suicide, with a particular focus on American Indian populations when research is available. We then close with a discussion of current controversies surrounding the topic of suicide among AI/AN populations and offer recommendations for prevention. Differing viewpoints found in the literature will be highlighted in order to elicit further discussion.

TRADITIONAL STORIES AND VIEWS OF SUICIDE IN AI/AN CULTURES

Traditionally, many AI/AN cultures are taught to respect life and to view life as being a precious gift from the Creator. However, even before the time of the written documentation of history, oral histories have shared important information regarding the health status of AI/AN peoples. Stories have been passed down through multiple generations and have reached modern-day descendants. One particular story, shared by an unnamed conference participant at the Indian Health Service/Bureau of Indian Affairs/ Bureau of Indian Education/Substance Abuse and Mental Health Services Administration Action Summit for Suicide Prevention on August 2, 2011, talks about suicide in special circumstances under oppression.

> In this story, a group of Indigenous people had suffered years of oppression and colonization by a foreign group of people previously unknown to them. Their people grew weary and tired of what their everyday lives had turned into. Forced assimilation and punishment for attempting to live their own way of life had become unbearable. Sadness and unhappiness was beginning to impact the once peaceful, hardworking and harmonious culture. The Native people wondered why

> this was happening and if it was ever going to end. A group of them decided they did not want to live under these unbearable circumstances any longer. They spoke amongst each other and drew all of their might and courage and locked each other's arms together and walked into the ocean to meet their Creator. Their previous beautiful way of life had been taken away from them. They were not willing to spend another day on Earth living the degrading life that their colonizers were forcing upon them (Interview with conference attendee, August 2, 2011).

Although this story does not intend to glorify suicide, it speaks to the mental anguish and historical trauma suffered by these people at the hands of the domineering society that invaded their lives.

Some tribal communities maintain a traditional teaching that if one commits suicide, her or his spirit cannot enter the Spirit World and will wander. Additionally, burials of those who committed suicide did not involve the full traditional wake and honoring of the deceased. These traditional views and practices may have served to limit the appeal of suicide as an option, making suicide less attractive in terms of fantasies of memorialization and honoring after one's death, particularly for youth. In some tribes, the belongings and often the dwelling place of the deceased would be burned; this, along with specific ceremonies, was believed to facilitate the release of the spirit of the dead person. There were also prescriptions for mourning; bereavement was limited (in some instances to one year), and a traditional grief ceremony was conducted to help the bereaved sufficiently let go of the deceased and move on with their lives (Brave Heart 1995; 1998). If the mourning traditions are not followed, the traditional cultural belief is that the spirit of the deceased will be trapped on earth and not make the transition to the Spirit World. The spirit may also then hover, distract the bereaved relatives, and even attempt to have the living to join them in the Spirit World, causing accidents, fueling suicidal thoughts, and the like, due to the deceased's desire to alleviate the suffering of their surviving relatives (see Brave Heart 2001b). Youth are viewed as particularly vulnerable to the distraction of wandering spirits trapped on earth; in some instances, youth suicide is seen as the preadolescent or adolescent succumbing to the "invitation" of the spirit to join them in the Spirit World.

A further understanding of AI/AN youth suicidal ideation and behavior can be informed by historical trauma theory. With the impact of European colonization and the prohibition against the practice of traditional ceremonies, including burials, wakes, spirit releasing, and mourning resolution ceremonies, communal and open mourning in the tribal cultural tradition eroded, had to be held in secret (under threat of incarceration under the imposed reservation system), or virtually disappeared in some instances. Even after the 1978 American Indian Religious Freedom Act, aspects of tribal burials and other ceremonies remain prohibited or limited. The impairment of indigenous burial and mourning practices, the erosion of traditional protective factors against suicide, and the extent of loss and trauma exposure (U.S. DHHS, IHS 2008a, 2008b; Manson et al. 2005), place AI/AN communities, particularly the youth, at risk for trauma responses, complicated grief, and suicidal behaviors.

CONCEPTUAL FRAMEWORK: HISTORICAL TRAUMA

The historical trauma paradigm frames life span individual trauma within the collective, historical context, which empowers American Indian survivors of both communal and individual trauma by reducing the sense of stigma and isolation. The *historical trauma response* (HTR) is a theoretical concept of a constellation of features that has been observed among massively traumatized populations, including depressive symptoms, psychic numbing, self-destructive behavior, and identification with the dead where vitality in life is seen as a betrayal of ancestors who suffered so much (Brave Heart 1998; 2003). Individual trauma responses are viewed as emerging from genocide, oppression, and racism; this approach diminishes the shame and self-blame that survivors often experience. *Historical unresolved grief,* a component of HTR, is akin to *prolonged or complicated grief* (Shear et al. 2011) but includes the generational collective experience of unresolved grief. Psychoanalytic theorists view suicide as the "affect of mourning" (Pollock 1989). In addition to unresolved grief, the historical trauma response (HTR) includes suicidal ideation and behavior, substance abuse, and other self-destructive behaviors (Brave Heart 2003). Substance abuse, a risk factor for suicide and associated with suicide in the literature on AI/AN youth suicide (May 1987; Mullany et al. 2009), is a complex, multidetermined psychosocial problem. However, within the HT framework, it is viewed as an attempt to numb the pain of trauma, grief, and loss that has occurred across generations and within the life span [self-medication]. Substance abuse may co-occur with depression and PTSD, risk factors for suicide (Kotler et al. 2001; Oquendo 2003). Substance abuse and depression are correlated with PTSD; complicated grief/prolonged grief may co-occur with PTSD and depression (Shear et al. 2011). AI/AN youth suicides have often been observed to occur after an interpersonal loss (e.g., death, breakup of a relationship) and often involve substance abuse, classically alcohol (May 1987). Hence, AI/AN youth suicide can be viewed in the context of historical unresolved grief, the HTR, and current losses superimposed upon the generational collective trauma. Loneliness and abandonment in the life-span, and their placement in the historical background, are also important characteristics for AIs' experiences of depression (O'Nell 1996).

The impact of impairment in traditional, nurturing parenting practices, rooted in boarding schools, may limit protective factors and contribute to risk factors for substance abuse and other self-destructive behaviors, including suicide. Boarding school survivor parents who experienced abuse in boarding schools or traumatic early separation from parental and other familial attachment figures may be emotionally unavailable to their children (Brave Heart 2001a; 2003), thereby increasing suicide risk factors in their children. Internalization of a "good enough" parental figure (Winnicott 1953) is crucial in the capacity to self-soothe in adulthood but also in adolescence to some degree. The lack of this capacity or the internalization of a negative parental figure may lead to unhealthy, risky, self-destructive acting-out behavior such as substance abuse and suicide gestures or attempts. Chronic sadness, depression, and grief, all components of HTR which AI/AN youth may manifest, fuel the risks for suicidal behaviors triggered by current loss and abandonment, superimposed upon intergenerational trauma and unresolved grief. Finally, fantasies of reunification with the deceased loved one may fuel suicide for AI/AN youth experiencing a sense of abandonment and overwhelming grief; the fantasies of seeing and being with lost loved ones among the bereaved has been observed as part of HTR (Brave Heart 1998; 2001a; 2003).

RISK AND PROTECTIVE FACTORS FOR SUICIDAL BEHAVIORS

Risk Factors for Youth Suicide

Much has been written regarding the risk factors for suicidal behaviors among youth in the general population and specifically among AI/AN youth; depression, substance abuse, family problems, relationship problems, knowing someone who has committed suicide, previous attempts of suicide, hopelessness, age, and gender are some of the most common risk factors noted in the literature (Dorgan 2010; May et al. 2005; Johnson and Tomren 1999). Results from a study with White Mountain Apache youth found the most common precipitants to suicide attempts were family or intimate partner conflicts (Mullany et al. 2009). Surveys conducted in the Southwest show that AI students who considered suicide were more likely to drink alcohol, be in a fight, be bullied at school, play video games for three or more hours per day, vomit or take laxatives to lose weight, use marijuana, and have had sex (AASTEC 2011). Many of these risk factors are compounded in AI/AN communities by lack of access to mental health care, lack of adequate funding for Indian Health Services, and high rates of poverty (Dorgan 2010).

Suicide, Trauma, and Alcohol/Drug Abuse Childhood trauma and violent behavior are strong risk factors for suicidal behaviors (Jokinen et al. 2010; Martin 1996). Research consistently shows significantly higher rates of suicide attempts and other self-destructive behaviors among physically and sexually abused children and adolescents in comparison to children and adolescents who have not been abused or those who have been neglected (Martin 1996; Martin et al. 2004; Beautrais 2000). Because of the high prevalence of traumatic experiences among AI/AN youth, it is particularly important for clinicians to be cognizant of the increased risk for suicidal behavior and suicide attempts among these youth.

Although much has been written on the prevalence of trauma among AI/AN tribes, the study by Manson et al. (2005) is, to our knowledge, the first systematic measurement of the prevalence of trauma exposure among two large tribal communities. Data on lifetime exposure to 16 types of trauma were collected through structured interviews among 3,084 tribal members aged 15 to 57 years. Lifetime trauma was frequent among both tribes and higher than that reported among counterparts in the general population. Exposure to at least one event ranged from 62.4 percent to 67.2 percent among AI males and 66.2 percent to 69 percent among females. In contrast, the National Comorbidity Survey, a large psychiatric epidemiological survey of the U.S. population (Kessler et al. 1995) found that lifetime exposure to trauma among U.S. men and women is 60.7 percent and 51.2 percent, respectively. In addition to documenting the magnitude of the problem of trauma among AIs, another significant finding from the study by Manson et al. (2005) was the reported equivalent trauma exposure among women and men. This was contrary to most studies on traumatic exposure, which generally highlight a gender difference, with rates among men consistently higher compared to rates among women (Bromet, Sonnega, and Kessler 1998; Breslau et al. 1998; Breslau et al. 1999; Norris 1992; Creamer, Burgess, and McFarlane 2001). Thus, there appear to be significant differences in exposure to trauma in AI/AN communities. A component of the historical trauma response (Brave Heart 2003), alcohol and other substance abuse have been correlated with several health risks in youth including suicidal behavior, depression, driving under the influence, and unprotected sex (Hawkins, Cummins, and Marlatt 2004). Substance use has been implicated in the disproportionately high suicide mortality rates found among AI/AN youth, especially during adolescence—a period of high stress related to social, physical, cognitive, and academic growth (May et al. 2002) as well as identity formation, peer influences, and developing a sense of belonging.

Screening and Assessment of Youth at Risk for Suicide

In October 2000, the American Academy of Child and Adolescent Psychiatry (AACAP) approved the *Practice Parameter for the Assessment and Treatment of Children and Adolescents with Suicidal Behavior,* which includes guidelines on screening and assessment of youth at risk for suicide. While screening refers to a brief interview to determine the presence of risk factors related to suicidality, assessment is a more thorough evaluation to identify suicidal behavior, lethality or risk of suicide attempt or death, underlying diagnoses, and related risk factors. Research provides some broad indicators or risk factors that have been found to be associated with suicidal behavior and suicide completion. For instance, adolescents who are at greatest risk for suicide include males who are aged 16 years and older, who have a previous suicide attempt and a current mental disorder, especially when complicated by comorbid substance abuse, irritability, agitation, or psychosis (AACAP 2001). Females at greatest risk for suicide are those who have had previous suicide attempts, and mood disorders such as major depression. Youth whose prior suicide attempts used methods other than ingestion or superficial cutting are at higher risk.

Protective Factors

Religious or spiritual practices often speak to a reverence for life and can teach lessons related to protecting one's own existence. Participation in cultural and traditional practices is thought to be a protective factor against involvement in negative behaviors. Spiritual and religious coping are beneficial for preventing suicidal behavioral among survivors of child abuse (Dervic et al. 2006). A traditional notion that can serve as a protective factor for suicide prevention among many tribes is the absence of mind- or mood-altering substances (Brave Heart 2003). Given the prevalence of alcohol use prior to most suicide attempts, traditional cultural restoration and spiritual practices facilitate protective factors for alcohol and other drug abuse prevention (May et al. 2002; Spicer 2001). Work in alcohol and substance use prevention will also inform suicide prevention and help in reducing overall negative health risk behaviors.

Gary, Baker, and Grandbois (2005) found that for AI/AN youth, having caring family relationships, supportive tribal leaders, and positive school experiences can be important protective factors. Knowing this, we can all aim to contribute to increasing these and other protective factors for youth. American Indian youth have unique opportunities to engage with family members and tribal leaders in community and educational settings, at cultural and ceremonial gatherings, and through personal communications with community members. Positive support from community members as well as tribal leaders can have a lasting impact in the lives of youth. Hill (2009) stated that American Indians with a sense of belonging and connection to their community were less likely to report suicidal ideation. This sense of belonging may be reinforced in traditional cultural events and ceremonies, as well as traditional kinship networks.

A recent study conducted in the Southwest surveyed 8,236 American Indian middle- and high-school students with a Youth Risk and Resiliency Survey including data from the Southwest Tribal Youth Project (AASTEC 2011). Of those students who did not consider suicide, more were likely to: a) get higher grades in school, b) participate in extracurricular activities, c) have parents who monitor the youth's whereabouts, and d) confide in parents about problems. AI/AN youth suicide attempters, compared to non-Native youth, had higher thresholds for risk prior to an attempt; the number of protective factors seemed to buffer or reduce suicidal risks (Mackin, Perkins and Furrer 2012). Protective factors from the different levels related to the individual, family, peers, and school environment proved to be important in reducing suicide attempts. Given the high levels of risk factors found in the lives of many AI/AN youth, it is imperative that we focus time on, and direct resources to, activities and programs that aim to increase resilience and protective factors at all levels—individual, family, and community.

PREVENTION AND TREATMENT OF SUICIDAL IDEATION AND BEHAVIOR IN AI/AN YOUTH

As noted earlier, youth suicide is a major concern for many AI/AN communities across the nation. Therefore, knowledge of effective treatment and prevention strategies is critical so that communities can recognize and implement best practices for identifying AI/AN youth at risk for suicide; treating those youth exhibiting suicidal ideation and behavior; assisting parents, siblings, extended family, and other community members who are survivors of suicide; and developing effective community-wide suicide prevention programs.

One example of an evidence-based screening instrument is the Columbia TeenScreen (Shaffer et al. 2004), which identifies youth who are at risk for suicide and who are potentially suffering from mental illness. National studies have found various versions of this tool effective in identifying youth with recent suicidal ideation, past suicide attempts, and other significant problems that were not previously known to school personnel. It has been shown to be a valid suicide screening instrument (Shaffer et al. 2004), and has been recognized as an Evidence-Based Practice by the Substance Abuse and Mental Health Services Administration (SAMHSA) (U.S. DHHS 2010a). The Columbia TeenScreen has been utilized successfully with AI youth, and according to the Indian Health Service (IHS) Community Suicide Prevention website, several tribes and tribal health organizations have received training on the model across the nation. In fact, at the March 2010 hearing of the U.S. Senate Committee on Indian Affairs to discuss the incredibly high number of suicides among AI youth, TeenScreen was identified as having been implemented successfully in many tribes. One important consideration when using the Columbia TeenScreen, and other instruments that screen for suicidality, is the need to ensure that appropriate services are in place to meet the needs of youth who are identified during the screening process. An issue that has arisen in several tribal communities nationwide is that many youth are identified as "at risk" through the screening process and then there is a lack of services to respond to this need. Tribal programs that plan to implement screening programs must first ensure that they have the capacity to meet the needs of youth identified or come up with some alternative options grounded in traditional culture practices that may be sustainable alternatives to formal behavioral health interventions (e.g. elders working with youth, big brothers or sisters mentoring youth, and peer mentoring).

Importantly, the AACAP's guidelines (2001) also note that suicide scales and screens have limited predictive validity. Thus, they can complement, but do not take the place of a thorough assessment. Importantly, information must be gathered from multiple sources; in addition to the youth, parents or guardians, school personnel, and other members of a youth's support network should be included (Shaffer et al. 2001). In tribal communities, this may include extended family, tribal leaders, peers, and other community members.

Treatment of Suicidal Ideation and Behavior

The ACCAP guidelines (2001) indicate that treatment for suicidal ideation and behavior can be provided in multiple settings, such as emergency rooms and inpatient or outpatient settings. The guidelines suggest that if a youth is identified and found to have attempted suicide, he or she should be hospitalized for acute care, which includes a thorough assessment of diagnostic features and social factors that might impact the risk for suicide. An important consideration in tribal communities is access to acute care in highly intensive settings, particularly in rural and isolated tribal communities. Because of the need for intensive treatment, and the limited availability of services, tribes must develop crisis intervention plans to support youth who are vulnerable and at risk for suicide.

The ACCAP guidelines identified the following diagnostic features that signal the need for hospitalization: major depressive disorder with psychotic features, rapid-cycling with irritability and impulsive behavior, psychosis with command hallucinations (e.g. hearing voices telling the person to harm oneself or others), and alcohol or substance abuse (Shaffer et al., 2001). As noted earlier, the etiology of suicidal ideation and behavior may differ across cultures, and therefore it would be important to understand the unique etiology and presentation found in specific tribal communities. This can be done by speaking with elders and cultural leaders prior to implementing a program to understand the norms and values of the community.

Social factors correlated with suicidal ideation and behavior were also identified by the ACCAP, including lack of sufficient environmental supports. Again, these environmental supports will vary by tribal community, and guidance should be sought from elders and/or other cultural leaders as to potential natural supports and community norms surrounding these supports. Environmental supports following release from an emergency room or inpatient setting, available to the general population to varying degrees but rarely in tribal communities, include caregivers who can secure or remove firearms and lethal medications from the home and provide a drug- and alcohol-free milieu. Given the aforementioned historical trauma that is prevalent in many tribal communities, it is important to develop strategies that include youth, families, and other community members and focus on developing plans for limiting access to drugs, alcohol, and firearms, a particularly challenging issue in many AI/AN rural communities.

Partial hospitalization offering intensive multidisciplinary treatment, consistent observation, and support following hospitalization for acutely suicidal youth are rarely available in rural and isolated tribal communities. Instead, tribal communities can consider either residential treatment located outside of the reservation, or intensive outpatient services offered through tribal behavioral health programs or the Indian Health Services. Access to treatment and alternative models using indigenous approaches and resources must be considered when developing programs that serve vulnerable AI/AN youth.

When the youth is no longer at risk for impulsivity and significant supports are identified at home, the AACAP guidelines note that treatment such as psychotherapy and medication management can be provided in outpatient settings. Psychotherapy aims to decrease feelings experienced by suicidal youth (e.g., depression, worthlessness, anger, anxiety, and hopelessness; Kienhorst et al. 1995; Ohring et al. 1996) and improve cognitive and emotional well-being (Kernberg 1994; Spirito 1997). Research has found that clinicians must be available to youth and families during this time of high need and have the ability to: manage crises, relate to youth in honest and consistent ways, be objectively empathetic, and convey a sense of optimism (Katz 1995; Pfeffer 1997; Shaffer et al. 2001). Access to outpatient services is more prevalent in tribal communities, although many tribal behavioral health programs focus on substance abuse rather than the full spectrum of mental health and substance abuse disorders. Therefore, program staff will benefit from training in treatments that best support AI/AN youth experiencing suicidal ideation and behaviors as well as engaging in innovative prevention and intervention models developed to build on traditional cultural protective factors, including AI/AN social support.

According to research gathered by the AACAP, several psychotherapeutic models have been used successfully with youth who are suicidal, including: cognitive behavioral therapy (CBT), interpersonal therapy, dialectical behavioral therapy, psychodynamic psychotherapy, and family therapy (Shaffer et al. 2001). However, very little research has been conducted on these psychotherapeutic approaches to reduce suicide in AI/AN youth, with CBT having the greatest body of literature. In a recent study published by Stanley et al. (2009), 110 depressed adolescents with a recent suicide attempt received CBT–Suicide Prevention (CBT-SP). The clinical utility of CBT-SP was apparent; the model may be useful in prevention for youth with suicidal ideation (Shaffer et al. 2001). The goal of CBT-SP is to develop skills to reduce the negative effects of stressors and decrease suicidal ideation and behaviors. CBT-SP has been successfully adapted for use with AI/AN populations (Bigfoot and Schmidt, 2010). Clearly more research is needed to identify psychotherapeutic approaches that are proven effective in AI/AN communities.

The use of medications to stabilize and treat suicidal youth is a complex issue in tribal communities. Ethno-pharmacology highlights the importance of considering ethnicity when selecting medications and dosage; limited access to child psychiatrists in rural and isolated communities is an issue. Telehealth, provided through Indian Health Services in collaboration with psychiatric outreach centers, is an important modality for connecting youth to needed services that are not present in their home communities. Lithium or mood stabilizers are effective with children and adolescents with co-occurring bipolar disorder and should be prescribed before an antidepressant; Selective Serotonin Reuptake Inhibitors (SSRIs) are effective for youth depression, though youth who are suicidal and prescribed an SSRI should be monitored for increased agitation or suicidality (AACAP 2001). Stimulant medications are also effective, but should only be prescribed for children and adolescents with ADHD. Importantly, these treatment recommendations were based on research conducted with youth in the general population; very little data is available on AI/AN youth specifically (Shaffer et al. 2001).

Treatment for Survivors of Suicide

The AACAP guidelines (2001) also highlight the need for treatment of survivors of suicide, also known as postvention treatment. This is because survivors of suicide are at increased risk for developing major depression, anxiety disorders, suicidal ideation, and PTSD, especially within six months immediately following the suicide (Brent et al. 1996; Pfeffer et al. 1997). This is especially true for individuals with a family or personal history of psychiatric disorder or previous exposure to suicidal behavior. Although intervention is critical in the immediate period following a suicide, long-term support and services are necessary. The goal of treatment is to decrease the likelihood of additional suicide attempts by others who identify the suicidal behavior as an effective way of handling depression or anxiety (Brent and Poling 1997). This is especially important for AI/AN communities, where youth suicide sometimes occur in clusters. Treatment may include grief counseling to assist with mourning and decrease guilt, trauma, and social isolation (Pfeffer 1997). Psycho-education and counseling can be provided in individual meetings, at group sessions with peers, or in conjunction with parents who are also struggling with their own issues. Tribal communities also have unique practices to support youth and families during times of grief and loss. Behavioral health providers working in tribal communities should consult elders and cultural leaders to ensure that families have access to traditional supports when needed. Grief counseling models should be reviewed by elders and cultural leaders to ensure the cultural appropriateness, as very little research exists on the use of these models in AI communities (Gone and Alcántara 2006).

Suicide Prevention Programming

Numerous community-based prevention programs exist, and several have been utilized in AI/AN communities. These initiatives take a public health approach, targeting entire communities, or groups of individuals who regularly come into contact with youth. Examples of suicide prevention activities include crisis hotlines, gatekeeper trainings, primary care screening, peer support, and mental illness recognition and treatment (AACAP 2001). The goals of these activities are identifying of youth who are at risk for suicide early and directing them into treatment immediately. The following are some examples of suicide prevention programs that have been utilized in tribal communities.

Applied Sucide Intervention Skills Training *(ASIST)* is a gatekeeper training suicide intervention program that trains adults who interact with youth (e.g., school staff, coaches, parents/guardians) how to recognize and assess signs of suicide, effectively utilize a suicide intervention model, and connect to existing community resources (Suicide Prevention Council of St. Joseph County 2011). Research indicates that ASIST improves mental health literacy and enhances suicide intervention skills (Pearce, Rickwood, and Beaton 2003). The model provides training to individuals who come into close contact with youth on a daily basis, increasing their capacity to identify youth at risk for suicide. ASIST is the most widely used suicide prevention program in the world (Suicide Prevention Council of St. Joseph County 2011) and it has been used in many tribal communities and is therefore believed to be a practice that is effective for AI/AN youth.

Natural Helpers (NH; see U.S. DHHS 2010b) provides a year-long series of training that begins with an overnight retreat in a setting away from school and focuses on knowledge about suicide prevention and other issues of concern to youth. The goal is to develop helping skills and support team building, self-care, and planning for service projects that that will positively affect the entire school. Through the program, youth gatekeepers learn to recognize suicide risk, respond appropriately, and get help for their peers. A critical piece of the Natural Helpers program is the bonding of students to trusted adults in addition to the bonding of students to students within the group. The core group of natural helpers is intentionally diverse in representing all subgroups in a school. Student participants as well as the Natural Helpers sponsors are chosen by youth in a survey at the beginning of the school year. Nominations ask for peers and adults who are honest, caring, trustworthy and to whom youth could go with a problem. Natural Helpers has been successfully implemented in many schools across the country, including several tribal communities. Participation in Natural Helpers has also been found to increase the development of positive peer relationships and help-seeking behaviors, and improve the school climate to be safe and supportive (Froh 2004). Natural Helpers capitalizes on the strong peer support that occurs during adolescence when peer relationships begin to overshadow relationships that youth have with parents (Furman and Buhrmeister 1992). Research shows that carefully identified peer supports can serve as strong early intervention and prevention supports for a variety of challenges effecting youth, including suicide (Hicks 1992). Peer counseling has also been shown to increase feelings of self-efficacy and self-esteem (Hahn and LeCapitaine 1990). In New Mexico, Natural Helpers has been implemented in many tribal communities, and the peer-to-peer support was identified as key to success.

Project Venture is an experiential youth development program specifically designed for AI youth that engages them in a variety of outdoor activities to encourage investment in their community and the natural world and connection to positive role models. Project Venture utilizes culturally relevant skill-building activities, camping, and community-oriented service learning in order to reach high-risk AI youth (U.S. DHHS 2008c). This model incorporates experiential learning that engages youth at the cognitive, physical, emotional, social, and spiritual levels. It also cultivates the development of healthy behaviors among youth as a strategy to prevent suicide. Research suggests that low self-esteem may play a significant role in risk for suicide among youth (Overholser et al. 1995; Roberts, Roberts, and Chen 1998), and Project Venture aims to cultivate positive self-concept (U.S. DHHS 2008c).

American Indian Life Skills Development Curriculum (AILS) is a middle school- and high-school-based life skills and suicide prevention curriculum with 30, 40-minute sessions given over six weeks covering anger, depression, anxiety, and suicidal thoughts and behaviors. AILS uses a core emphasis on strengths through skills building that goes beyond suicide prevention and identification of warning signs. The curriculum teaches coping strategies to help students learn how to overcome stressful life events and build on their resilience. It encourages engagement of community members and peer helpers in youth suicide prevention while using role-playing to increase youth help-seeking from caring adults (LaFromboise and Fatemi 2011). Posttest survey results indicate decreased hopelessness and increased confidence in ability to manage anger.

The aforementioned programs are just some examples of the therapeutic treatments and programs that have been developed to address suicide prevention in AI communities. Many other prevention programs exist, and can be found on the Indian Health Service American Indian and Alaska Native Suicide Prevention website (http://www/ihs.gov/behavioral/index.cfm?module=bh&option=suicide). Critical to suicide-prevention programming is ensuring a good fit with the values, beliefs, and norms of each unique tribe, and guidance in choosing programs should come from tribal elders and cultural leaders. Also important is ensuring access to needed resources, and community buy-in and investment.

CONCLUSION

Each American Indian and Alaska Native community is unique and represents diverse tribal cultures. Readers should be aware of the heterogeneity of tribal nations and should exercise caution against overgeneralizing. Even more important than the statistics presented in this chapter are the unique and priceless individuals who are touched by and have suffered the agonizing consequences of suicide and suicidal behaviors. There are many other important issues such as suicide risk factors among lesbian, gay, bisexual, and transgendered (LGBT) American Indian and Alaska Native youth that need further attention and research but are beyond the scope of this chapter. American Indian and Alaska Native youth have suffered so much and could use ceremony to aid in the healing process. A term used in the Lakota tradition as “Wiping the Tears” which is a metaphor for grief resolution is relevant in our discussion regarding AI/AN suicide and could be used to set the path toward healing our current and future generations.

Many AI/AN cultures have begun to address the prevention of suicide in their communities while others are not at the place yet to have the difficult discussions around suicide. Cultural barriers and taboos have built walls between AI/AN communities and researchers and others who are traditionalists and maintain the old ways of living. A difficult balance is hard to reach when working with American Indian communities in health disparities research. Should scientists continue to focus on AI/AN problems by working diligently to compile the most accurate data, or should AI/ANs be left to make their own decision to work and deal with these issues in their own way and at their own pace in respect to tribal sovereignty? If the former is chosen, attention must be drawn to the magnitude of research and attention given to the pathology of suicide rather than directing the focus of research on the protective and resilient factors that are inherent in all American Indian and Alaska Native communities.

◀ FURTHER INVESTIGATIONS ▶

Traditional views of suicide and its aftermath may conflict with the dominant culture paradigm in terms of etiology, prevention, intervention, and prevention, which includes management of the aftermath of the death. The imposition of evidence-based practices developed, normed, and researched with non-AI/AN communities are often experienced as another form of colonization and domination. Rather, communities often identify traditional Native practices and healing ceremonies that can effectively address a myriad of physical and behavioral health issues. In this section, we briefly address these issues.

Traditionally, in some tribal communities, a suicide is seen as a barrier to entry into the Spirit World; the person's spirit may wander and be trapped on earth rather than free. In the aftermath of a suicide for a number of tribal communities, rather than the typical ritual of communal mourning after a death, the suicide victim has a small, private burial. The community has the understanding that to approach a completed suicide as one would death by natural causes or accidents, would be to encourage more suicides, particularly among youth. In some tribes, all the belongings of the deceased would be burned, including their dwelling, thought to facilitate the release of the spirit. Although the American Indian Religious Freedom Act was initially passed in 1978 (Pevar 2004) and restored the rights of tribal communities to openly practice many aspects of traditional ceremonies, traditional burial rites still cannot be fully performed, including burning the dwelling of the deceased, for example, or placing the dead on scaffolds, as was the tradition among several Plains tribes. Some view the inability to practice these rites as an impediment to the release of the spirit of the deceased as a causal factor in youth suicide; the wandering spirits distract the living. If the youth is suffering especially following the death of a parental figure, suicidal ideation or impulses may be related to the ancestor spirit coming for them to take them to the Spirit World to alleviate their emotional pain. Ceremonies can address this and have resulted in the cessation of suicidal thoughts and the release of the parent's spirit back to the Spirit World and the lifting of depression (Brave Heart 2001).

Prevention and intervention of youth suicide is also conceptualized differently in a number of tribal communities compared with the general population. One common traditional view is that the restoration of the knowledge and practice of indigenous culture, the Native language and ceremonies, the sacredness of children to be placed at the center of the nation form the path to addressing youth suicide prevention and early intervention. One tension is that, due to the influence of colonization and forced assimilation policies (see Pevar 2004), segments of tribal communities do not embrace traditional values or practices but rather turn to the dominant cultural paradigm for answers

and solutions to youth suicide. We suggest that a blended approach may be best: supporting traditional cultural healing strategies while simultaneously exploring and integrating culturally adapted evidence-based practices guided by elders and spiritual leaders.

References

Albuquerque Area Southwest Tribal Epidemiology Center. 2011. "Healthy Choices, Healthy Students: Mental Health among Native American Youth in New Mexico 2009, 2009 Youth Risk and Resiliency Survey." http://www.aastec.net.

American Academy of Child and Adolescent Psychiatry [AACAP]. 2001. "Practice Parameter for the Assessment and Treatment of Children and Adolescents with Suicidal Behavior." *Journal of the American Academy of Child and Adolescent Psychiatry* 40 (7): 24S–51S.

Beautrais, Annette L. 2000. "Risk Factors for Suicide and Attempted Suicide among Young People." *Australian and New Zealand Journal of Psychiatry* 34 (3): 420–36.

Bigfoot, Dolores Subia, and Susan R. Schmidt. 2010. "Honoring Children, Mending the Circle: Cultural Adaptation of Trauma-Focused Cognitive-Behavioral Therapy for American Indians and Alaska Native Children." *Journal of Clinical Psychology* 66 (8): 847–56.

Brave Heart, Maria Yellow Horse. 1995. "The Return to the Sacred Path: Healing the Historical Trauma Response among the Lakota." *Smith College Studies in Social Work* 68 (3): 287–305.

Brave Heart, Maria Yellow Horse. 1999. "*Oyate Ptayela*: Rebuilding the Lakota Nation through Addressing Historical Trauma among Lakota Parents." *Journal of Human Behavior and the Social Environment* 2(1/2): 109–26.

Brave Heart, Maria Yellow Horse. 2001a. "Clinical Interventions with American Indians." In *Culturally Competent Social Work Practice: Practice Skills, Interventions, and Evaluation,* edited by Rowena Fong and Sharlene Furuto, 285–98. Reading, MA: Longman Publishers.

Brave Heart, Maria Yellow Horse. 2001. "Culturally and Historically Congruent Clinical Social Work Interventions with Native Clients." In *Culturally Competent Social Work Practice: Practice Skills, Interventions, and Evaluation,* edited by Rowena Fong and Sharlene Furuto, 285–98. Reading, MA: Longman Publishers.

Brave Heart, Maria Yellow Horse. 2003. "The Historical Trauma Response among Natives and Its Relationship with Substance Abuse: A Lakota Illustration." *Journal of Psychoactive Drugs* 35 (1): 7–13.

Brave Heart, Maria Yellow Horse, and Lemyra M. DeBruyn. 1998. "The American Indian Holocaust: Healing Historical Unresolved Grief." *American Indian and Alaska Native Mental Health Research Journal of the National Center* 8: 56–78.

Brave Heart, Maria Yellow Horse, Jennifer Elkins, Greg Tafoya, Doreen Bird, and Melina Salvador. 2012. "*Wicasa Was'aka*: Restoring the Traditional Strength of American Indian Males." *American Journal of Public Health* 102 (S2): 177–83.

Brent, David. A., Grace Moritz, Jeff Bridge, Joshua Perper, and Rebecca Canobbio. 1996. "Long-Term Impact of Exposure to Suicide: A Three-Year Controlled Follow-Up." *Journal of the American Academy of Child and Adolescent Psychiatry* 35 (5): 646–53.

Brent, David A., and Kim Poling. (1989) 1997. *Cognitive Therapy Manual for Depressed and Suicidal Youth.* Rev. ed. Pittsburgh, PA: University of Pittsburgh Health System Services for Teens at Risk.

Breslau, Naomi, Howard D. Chilcoat, Ronald. C. Kessler, Edward. L. Peterson, and Victoria. C. Lucia. 1999. "Vulnerability to Assaultive Violence: Further Specification of the Sex Difference in Post-Traumatic Stress Disorder." *Psychological Medicine* 29: 813–21.

Breslau, Naomi, Ronald. C. Kessler, Howard. D. Chilcoat, Lonnie R. Schultz, Glenn C. Davis, and Patricia Andreski. 1998. "Trauma and Posttraumatic Stress Disorder in the Community: The 1995 Detroit Area Survey of Trauma." *Archives of General Psychiatry* 55: 626–70.

Bromet, Evelyn, Amanda Sonnega, and Ronald C. Kessler. 1998. "Risk Factors for DSM-III-R Posttraumatic Stress Disorder: Findings from the National Comorbidity Survey." *American Journal of Epidemiology* 147 (4): 353–61.

Creamer, Mark, Phillip Burgess, and Alexander McFarlane. 2001. "Post-Traumatic Stress Disorder: Findings from the Australian National Survey of Mental Health and Well-Being." *Psychology and Medicine* 31: 1237–47.

Dervic, Kanita., Michael F. Grunebaum, Ainsley K. Burke, John J. Mann, and Maria A. Oquendo. 2006. "Protective Factors against Suicidal Behavior in Depressed Adults Reporting Childhood Abuse." *Journal of Nervous Mental Disorders* 97: 1–4.

Dorgan, Byron L. 2010. "The Tragedy of Native American Youth Suicide." *Psychological Services* 7 (3): 213–18.

Froh, Jeffrey J. 2004. "An Empirical Investigation of a Peer-Helping Program's Effectiveness and Acceptability." *Dissertation Abstracts International: Section B: The Sciences and Engineering* 65 (6B).

Furman, Wyndol, and Duane Buhrmester. 1992. "Age and Sex Differences in Perceptions of Networks of Personal Relationships." *Child Development* 63: 103–15.

Gary, Faye A., Martha Baker, and Donna M. Grandbois. 2005. "Perspectives on Suicide Prevention among American Indian and Alaska Native Children and Adolescents: A Call for Help." *Online Journal of Issues in Nursing* 10 (2): 6. http://www.ncbi.nlm.nih.gov/pubmed/15977979.

Gone, Joseph P., and Carmela Alcántara. 2006. "Traditional Healing and Suicide Prevention in Native American Communities: Research and Policy Considerations." Unpublished report contracted by the Office of Behavioral and Social Sciences Research, National Institutes of Health (Contract No. MI-60823).

Hahn, Jane A., and John E. LeCapitaine. 1990. "The Impact of Peer Counseling upon the Emotional Development, Ego Development, and Self-Concepts of Peer Counselors." *College Student Journal 24* (4): 410–20.

Hawkins, Elizabeth H., Lillian H. Cummins, and Alan G. Marlatt. 2004. "Preventing Substance Abuse in American Indian and Alaska Native Youth: Promising Strategies for Healthier Communities." *Psychological Bulletin* 130 (2): 304–23.

Hicks, Gail F., Barry C. Hicks, and Virginia Bodle. 1992. "Natural Helpers Needs Assessment and Self-Esteem: Pro-Social Foundation for Adolescent Substance Abuse Prevention and Early Intervention." *Journal of Alcohol and Drug Education* 37 (2): 71–82.

Hill, Doris Leal. 2009. "Relationship between Sense of Belonging as Connectedness and Suicide in American Indians." *Archives of Psychiatric Nursing* 23 (1): 65–74.

Indian Health Service, IHS. 2008. "Fact Sheet: Indian Health Disparities." *Indian Health Service Introduction.* Indian Health Service (June).

Indian Health Services [IHS], Bureau of Indian Affairs, Bureau of Indian Education, Substance Abuse and Mental Health Services Administration Action Summit for Suicide Prevention. 2011. "Partnering with Tribes to Protect the Circle of Life." August 1–4, Scottsdale, Arizona.

Johnson, Troy, and Holly Tomren. 1999. "Helplessness, Hopelessness, and Despair: Identifying Precursors to Indian Youth Suicide." *American Indian Culture and Research Journal* 23 (3): 287–301.

Jokinen, Jussi, Kaj Forslund, Ewa Ahnemark, Peter Gustavsson, Peter Nordstrom, Maria Karolinska Asberg. 2010. "Interpersonal Violence Scale Predicts Suicide in Suicide Attempters." *Journal of Clinical Psychiatry* 71 (8): 1025–32.

Katz, Patricia. 1995. "The Psychotherapeutic Treatment of Suicidal Adolescents." *Adolescent Psychiatry* 20: 325–341.

Kernberg, Paulina F. 1994. "Psychological Interventions for the Suicidal Adolescent." *American Journal of Psychotherapy* 48 (1): 52–63.

Kessler Ronald, C., Katherine A. McGonagle, Shanyang Zhao, Christopher B. Nelson, Michael Hughes, Suzann Eshlemann, Hans-Ulrich Wittchen, and Kenneth S. Kendler. 1994. "Lifetime and 12-Month Prevalence of DSM-III-R Disorders in the United States." *Archives of General Psychiatry* 51: 8–19.

Kessler Ronald C., Amanda Sonnega, Evelyn Bromet, Michael Hughes, Christopher B. Nelson. 1995. "Posttraumatic Stress Disorder in the National Comorbidity Study." *Archives of General Psychiatry* 52 (12): 1048–60.

Kienhorst Ineke, C. W. M., Erik J. DeWilde, Rene F. W. Diekstra, and William H. G. Wolters. 1995. "Adolescents' Image of Their Suicide Attempt." *Journal of the American Academy of Child and Adolescent Psychiatry* 34: 623–28.

Kilgariff, Lisa, Mindy Solomon, Mary Zanotti, and Catherine Chambliss. 1999. "High School Peer Helping: A Program Evaluation." *Resources in Education* ERIC/CASS CG028993.

Kotler, Moshe, Iancu, Iulian, Ravit Efroni, Marianne Amir. 2001. "Anger, Impulsivity, Social Support, and Suicide Risk in Patients with Posttraumatic Stress Disorder." *Journal of Nervous & Mental Disease* 189 (3): 162–67.

LaFromboise, Teresa D., and A. Fatemi. 2011. "American Indian Life Skills: A Community Based Intervention for Indigenous Mental Health." In *Child Psycholgy and Mental Health: Cultural and Ethno-Racial Perspectives,* edited by H. Fitzgerald. Santa Barbara, CA: Praeger.

Mackin, Juliette, Tamara Perkins, and Carrie Furrer. 2012. "The Power of Protection: A Population-Based Comparison of Native and Non-Native Youth Suicide Attempters." *American Indian and Alaska Native Mental Health Research* 19 (2): 20–54.

Manson, Spero M., Janette Beals, Suzell A. Klein, Calvin D. Croy, and AISUPERPFP Team. 2005. "Social Epidemiology of Trauma among 2 American Indian Reservations Populations." *American Journal of Public Health* 95 (5): 851–59.

Martin, Graham. 1996. "Reported Family Dynamics, Sexual Abuse and Suicidal Behaviors in Community Adolescents." *Archives of Suicide Research* 2 (3): 183–95.

Martin, Graham, Helen A. Bergen, Angela S. Richardson, Leigh Roeger, and Stephen Allison. 2004. "Sexual Abuse and Suicidality: Gender Differences in a Large Community Sample of Adolescents." *Child Abuse & Neglect* 28 (5): 491–503.

May, Phillip A. 1987. "Suicide and Self-Destruction among American Indian Youths." *American Indian and Alaska Native Mental Health* 1 (1): 52–69.

May, Philip A., Patricia Serna, Lance Hurt, and Lemyra M. DeBruyn. 2005. "Outcome Evaluation of a Public Health Approach to Suicide Prevention in an American Indian Tribal Nation." *American Journal of Public Health* 95 (7): 1238–44.

May, Philip A., Nancy W. Van Winkle, Mary B. Williams, Patricia J. McFeeley, Lemyra M. DeBruyn, and Patricia Serna, 2002. "Alcohol and Suicide Death among American Indians of New Mexico: 1980–1998." *Suicide and Life Threatening Behavior* 32 (3): 240–55.

Middlebrook, Denise L., Pamela L. LeMaster, Janette Beals, J., Douglas K. Novins, and Spero M. Manson. 1998. "Suicide Prevention in American Indian and Alaska Native Communities: A Critical Review of Programs." *National Suicide Prevention Conference.* Reno, Nevada.

Mullany, B., Allison Barlow, Novalene Goklish, Francene Larzelere-Hinton, Mary Cwik, Mariddie Craig, and John T. Walkup. 2009. "Toward Understanding Suicide among Youths: Results from the White Mountain Apache Tribally Mandated Suicide Surveillance System, 2001–2006." *American Journal of Public Health* 99 (10): 1840–48.

Norris, Fran H. 1992. "Epidemiology of Trauma: Frequency and Impact of Different Potentially Traumatic Events of Different Demographic Groups." *Journal of Consulting and Clinical Psychology* 60: 409–18.

Ohring, Richard, Alan Apter, Gideon Ratzoni, Ronit Weizman, Sam Tyano, and Robert Plutchik. 1996. "State and Trait Anxiety in Adolescent Suicide Attempters." *Journal of the American Academy of Child and Adolescent Psychiatry* 35: 154–57.

O'Nell, Theresa D. 1996. *Disciplined Hearts: History, Identity, and Depression in an American Indian Community.* Berkeley: University of California Press.

Oquendo, Maria A., Jeff M. Friend, Batsheva Halberstam, Beth S. Brodsky, Ainsley K. Burke, Michael F. Grunebaum, Kevin M. Malone, J. John Mann. 2003. "Association of Comorbid Posttraumatic Stress Disorder and Major Depression with Greater Risk for Suicidal Behavior." *American Journal of Psychiatry* 160: 580–82.

Overholser, James C., Dalia M. Adams, Kim L. Lehnert, and David C. Brinkman. 1995. "Self-Esteem Deficits and Suicidal Tendencies among Adolescents." *Journal of the American Academy of Child & Adolescent Psychiatry* 34 (7): 919–28.

Pearce, Katie, Debra Rickwood, and Susan Beaton. 2003. "Preliminary Evaluation of a University Based Suicide Intervention Project: Impact on Participants." *Australian e-Journal for the Advancement of Mental Health* 2 (1): 2–11.

Pevar, Stephen L. 2004. *The Rights of Indians and Tribes.* New York: New York University Press, 263–65.

Pfeffer, Cynthia R. 1997. "Childhood Suicidal Behavior: A Developmental Perspective." *Psychiatric Clinic of North America* 20 (3): 551–62.

Pfeffer, Cynthia R, Patricia Martins, Jackie Mann, Mary Sunkenberg, Amy Ice, Joseph Damore, Cornelia Gallo, Ilana Karpenos, and Hong Jiang. 1997. "Child Survivors of Suicide: Psychosocial Characteristics." *Journal of the American Academy of Child and Adolescent Psychiatry* 36 (1): 65–74.

Pollock, George H. 1989. *The Mourning-Liberation Process.* Vol I. Madison, CT: International Universities Press.

Roberts, R. E., C. R. Roberts, and Y. R. Chen. 1998. "Suicidal Thinking among Adolescents with a History of Attempted Suicide." *Journal of American Academic Child Adolescent and Psychiatry* 37 (12): 1294–300.

Shaffer, D., M. Scott, H. Wilcox, C. Maslow, R. Hicks, C. P. Lucas, and S. Greenwald. 2004. "The Columbia Suicide Screen: Validity and Reliability of a Screen for Youth Suicide and Depression." *Journal of American Academic Child Adolescent and Psychiatry* 43 (1): 71–79.

Shaffer, David, Cynthia R. Pfeffer, and the Work Group on Quality Issues: William Bernet, Valerie Arnold, Joseph Beitchman, R. Scott Benson, Oscar Bukstein, Joan Kinlan, Jon McClellan, David Rue, and Jon Shaw American Academy of Child and Adolescent Psychiatry. 2001. "Practice Parameter for the Assessment and Treatment of Children and Adolescents with Suicidal Behavior." *Journal of the American Academy of Child and Adolescent Psychiatry* 40 (7): 24S–51S.

Shear, Katherine M., Naomi Simon, Melanie Wall, Sidney Zisook, Robert Neimeyer, Naihua Duan, Charles Reynolds, et al. 2011. "Complicated Grief and Related Bereavement Issues for DSM-5." *Depression and Anxiety* 28: 103–117.

Spicer, Paul. 2001. "Culture and the Restoration of Self among Former American Indian Drinkers." *Social Science & Medicine* 53 (2): 227–40.

Spirito, Anthony. 1997. "Individual Therapy Techniques with Adolescent Suicide Attempters." *Crisis* 18: 62–64.

Stanley, Barbara, Gregory Brown, David A. Brent, Karen Wells, Kim Poling, John Curry, Betsy D. Kennard, Ann Wagner, Mary F. Cwik, Anat Brunstein Klomek, et al. 2009. "Cognitive-Behavioral Therapy for Suicide Prevention (CBT-SP): Treatment Model, Feasibility, and Acceptability." *Journal of the American Academy of Child & Adolescent Psychiatry* 48 (10): 1005–13.

Suicide Prevention Council of St. Joseph County and Surrounding Areas. 2011. *Applied Suicide Intervention Skills Training (ASIST).* http://www.uhs-in.org/article/3/suicide-prevention.

United States Department of Health and Human Services (U.S. DHHS). 2008. Substance Abuse and Mental Health Administration. National Registry of Evidence-based Programs and Practices. *Project Venture.* http://www.nrepp.samhsa.gov/ViewIntervention.aspx?id=102.

United States Department of Health and Human Services (U.S. DHHS). 2010a. Substance Abuse and Mental Health Services Administration's National Registry of Evidence-based Programs and Practices. *Columbia Teen Screen.* http://nrepp.samhsa.gov/.

United States Department of Health and Human Services (U.S. DHHS). 2010b. Substance Abuse and Mental Health Services Administration's National Registry of Evidence-based Programs and Practices. *Natural Helpers.* Retrieved from http://nrepp.samhsa.gov/.

United States Department of Health and Human Services, Indian Health Services (IHS). 2008a. *Regional Differences in Indian Health, 2002–2003 Edition.* Washington, D.C.: Government Printing Office, March.

United States Department of Health and Human Services, Indian Health Services (IHS). 2008b. *Trends in Indian Health, 2002–2003 Edition.* Washington, D.C.: Government Printing Office, March.

United States Department of Health and Human Services, Indian Health Services (IHS). 2008c. Substance Abuse and Mental Health Administration. National Registry of Evidence-based Programs and Practices. *Project Venture.* http://www.nrepp.samhsa.gov/ViewIntervention.aspx?id=102.

United States Public Health Service. 1999. "The Surgeon General's Call to Action to Prevent Suicide." Washington, D.C.

Westlake Van Winkle, Nancy, and May, Philip, 1986. "Native American Suicide in New Mexico, 1957–1979: A Comparitive Study." *Human Organization* 45 (4): 296–309.

Winnicott, Donald W. 1953. "Transitional Objects and Transitional Phenomena." *International Journal of Psychoanalysis* 34: 89–97.

Selected Bibliography

Section IV

Acton, K. J., N. R. Burrows, L. S. Geiss, and T. Thompson. 2003. "Diabetes Prevalence among American Indians and Alaska Natives and the Overall Population—United States, 1994–2002." *MMWR Weekly* 52 (30): 702–4.

Adams A., and R. Prince. 2010. "Correlates of Physical Activity in Young American Indian Children: Lessons Learned from the Wisconsin Nutrition and Growth Study." *Journal of Public Health Management Practice* 16 (5): 394–400.

Alcántara, Carmela, and Joseph P. Gone. 2007. "Reviewing Suicide in Native American Communities: Situating Risk and Protective Factors within a Transactional–Ecological Framework." *Death Studies* 31: 457–77.

Alchon, Suzanne Austin. 2003. *A Pest in the Land: New World Epidemics in a Global Perspective.* Albuquerque: University of New Mexico Press.

Andre, J. M. 1979. *The Epidemiology of Alcoholism among American Indians and Alaska Natives.* Albuquerque, NM: U.S. Indian Health Services.

Aoun, Suzanne L., and Robert J. Gregory. 1998. "Mental Disorders of Eskimos Seen at a Community Mental Health Center in Western Alaska." *Psychiatric Services* 49: 1485–87.

Arcan C., P. J. Hannan, J. H. Himes, J. A. Fulkerson, B. Holy Rock, M. Smyth, and M. Story. 2012. "American Indian Parents' Assessment of and Concern about Their Kindergarten Child's Weight Status. South Dakota, 2005–2006." Preventing Chronic Disease 2012; 9:110215. DOI. http://dx.doi.org/10.5888/pcd9.110215.

Asetoyer, Charon, Katharine Cronk, and Samanthi Hewakapuge. 2003. *Indigenous Women's Health Book within the Sacred Circle.* Lake Andes, SD: The Native American Women's Health Education Resource Center.

Asturias, Edwin, George R. Brenneman, Kenneth M. Petersen, Mohamed Hashem, and Mathuram Santosham. 2000. "Infectious Diseases." In *American Indian Health: Innovations in Health Care, Promotion, and Policy,* edited by Everett R. Rhoades, 347–69. Baltimore: John Hopkins University Press.

Bachman, Ronet. 1992. *Death and Violence on the Reservation: Homicide, Family Violence, and Suicide in American Indian Population.* New York: Auburn House.

Baldwin, L. M., D. C. Grossman, S. Casey, W. Hollow, J. R. Sugarman, W. L. Freeman, and L. G. Hart. 2002. "Prenatal and Infant Health among Rural and Urban American Indians/Alaska Natives." *American Journal of Public Health* 92 (9): 1491–97.

Baldwin, L. M., W. B. Hollow, S. Casey, E. H. Larson, K. Moore, E. Lewis, C. H. Andrilla, and D. C. Grossman. 2008. "Access to Specialty Health Care for Rural American Indians in Two States." *Journal of Rural Health* 24 (3): 269–278.

Barker, Judith C., and B. Josea Kramer. 1996. "Alcohol Consumption among Older Urban American Indians." *Journal of Studies on Alcohol* 57 (2): 119–124.

Barnes, P. M., P. F. Adams, and E. Powell-Griner. 2005. "Health Characteristics of the American Indian and Alaska Native Adult Population: United States, 1999–2003." *Advance data from Vital and Health Statistics; no. 356.* Hyattsville, MD: National Center for Health Statistics.

Beals, J. "Psychiatric Disorder among American Indian Adolescents: Prevalence in Northern Plains Youth." *Journal of the American Academy of Child and Adolescent Psychiatry,* 1997: 1252–59.

Beals J., D. K. Novins, N. R. Whitesell, P. Spicer, C. M. Mitchell, S. M. Manson, and the AI-SUPERPFP Team. 2005. "Mental Health Disparities: Prevalence of Mental Disorders and Attendant Service Utilization of two American Indian Reservation Populations in a National Context." *American Journal of Psychiatry* 162 1723–32.

Beals, Janette, Spero M. Manson, Christina M. Mitchell, Paul Spicer, and AI-SUPERPFP Team. 2003. "Cultural Specificity and Comparison in Psychiatric Epidemiology: Walking the Tightrope in American Indian Research." *Culture, Medicine and Psychiatry* 27: 259–89.

Beals, Janette, Spero M. Manson, James H. Shore, Matthew Friedman, Marie Ashcraft, John A. Fairbank, and William E. Schlenger. 2002. "The Prevalence of Posttraumatic Stress Disorder among American Indian Vietnam Veterans: Disparities and Context." *Journal of Traumatic Stress* 15: 89–97.

Beals, Janette, Spero M. Manson, Nancy R. Whitesell, Paul Spicer, Douglas K. Novins, and Christina M. Mitchell. 2005. "Prevalence of DSM-IV Disorders and Attendant Help-Seeking in 2 American Indian Reservation Populations." *Archives of General Psychiatry* 62: 99–108.

Beals, Janette, Douglas Novins, Christina Mitchell, James Shore, and Spero Manson. 2002. "Comorbidity between Alcohol Abuse/Dependence and Psychiatric Disorders: Prevalence, Treatment Implications, and New Directions for Research among American Indian Populations." In *Alcohol Use among American Indians and Alaska Natives: Multiple Perspectives on a Complex Problem: Cultural Specificity and Comparison in Psychiatric Epidemiology,* edited by Patricia Mail, Suzanne Heurtin-Roberts, Susan Martin, and Jan Howard. 371–410. Bethesda, MD: U.S. Department of Health and Human Services.

Beals, Janette, Joan Piasecki, Scott Nelson, Monica Jones, Ellen Keane, Paul Dauphinais, Roy Red Shirt, William H. Sack, and Spero M. Manson. 1997. "Psychiatric Disorder among American Indian Adolescents: Prevalence in Northern Plains Youth." *Journal of the American Academy of Child* and *Adolescent Psychiatry* 36: 1252–59.

Beals, Janette, Paul Spicer, Christina M. Mitchell, Douglas K. Novins, Spero M. Manson, and the AI-SUPERPFP Team. 2003. "Racial Disparities in Alcohol Use: Comparison of Two American Indian Reservation Populations with National Data." *American Journal of Public Health* 93 (10): 1683–85.

Beauvais, F. 1996. "Trends in Drug Use among American Indian Students and Dropouts, 1975 to 1994." *American Journal of Public Health* 86: 1594–98.

Beauvais, Fred. 1992. "Comparison of Drug Use Rates for Reservation Indian, Non-Reservation Indian, and Anglo Youth." *American Indian and Alaska Native Mental Health Research* 5: 13–31.

Beauvais, Fred, Pamela J. Jumper-Thurman, H. Helm, B. Plested, and M. Burnside. 2004. "Surveillance of Drug Use among American Indian Adolescents: Patterns over 25 Years." *Journal of Adolescent Health* 34: 493–500.

Bennett, P. H., and W. C. Knowler. 1998. "Randomized Clinical Trial Lifestyle Interventions in Pima Indians: A Pilot Study." *Diabetic Medicine* 15: 66–72.

Bergman, Abraham B., David C. Grossman, Angela M. Erdrich, John C. Todd, and Ralph Forquera. 1999. "A Political History of the Indian Health Service." *Milbank Memorial Quarterly* 77 (4): 571–604.

Bertolli, Jeanne, Lisa M. Lee, and Patrick S. Sullivan. 2007. "Racial Misidentification of American Indians/Alaska Natives in the HIV/AIDS Reporting Systems of Five States and One Urban Health Jurisdiction, U.S. 1984–2002." *Public Health Reports* 122: 382–92.

Bertolli, Jeanne, A. D. McNaghten, Michael Campsmith, Lisa M. Lee, Richard Leman, Ralph T. Bryan, and James W. Buehler. 2009. "Surveillance Systems: Monitoring HIV/AIDS and HIV Risk Behaviors among American Indians and Alaska Natives." *AIDS Education and Prevention* 16: 218–37.

Bhatara, V. S., A. Gupta, and M. Brokenleg. 1999. "The Hiawatha Asylum for Insane Indians: The First Federal Mental Hospital for an Ethnic Group." *The American Journal of Psychiatry* 156: 767.

Bigfoot, Dolores Subia, and Susan R. Schmidt. 2010. "Honoring Children, Mending the Circle: Cultural Adaptation of Trauma-Focused Cognitive-Behavioral Therapy for American Indians and Alaska Native Children." *Journal of Clinical Psychology* 66 (8): 847–56.

Blum, R., B. Harmon, L. Harris, L. Bergeisen, and M. Resnick. 1992. "American Indian-Alaska Native Youth Health." *Journal of the American Medical Association* 267: 1637–44.

Bohn, Diane. 2002. "Lifetime and Current Abuse, Pregnancy Risks, and Outcomes among Native American Women." *Journal of Health Care for the Poor and Underserved* 13: 184–97.

Borowsky, Iris Wagman, Michael D. Resnick, Marjorie Ireland, and Robert W. Blum. 1999. "Suicide Attempts among American Indian and Alaska Native Youth: Risk and Protective Factors." *Archives of Pediatric & Adolescent Medicine* 153: 573–80.

Bouey, P. D., and Bonnie E. Duran. 2000. "The Ahalaya Case Management Program for HIV-infected American Indians, Alaska Natives, and Native Hawaiians: Quantitative and Qualitative Evaluation of Impacts." *American Indian and Alaska Native Mental Health Research Online* 9 (2).

Boyd-Ball, Alison J., Spero M. Manson, Carolyn Noonan, and Janette Beals. 2006. "Traumatic Events and Alcohol Use Disorders among American Indian Adolescents and Young Adults." *Journal of Traumatic Stress* 19: 937–47.

Boyum, William. 1988/1989. "Health Care: An Overview of the Indian Health Service." *American Indian Law Review* 14: 241–67.

Bowekaty, Malcolm B., and Dena S. Davis. 2003. "Cultural Issues in Genetic Research with American Indian and Alaskan Native People." *IRB: Ethics and Human Research* 25 (4): 12–15.

Brave Heart, Maria Yellow Horse. 1995. "The Return to the Sacred Path: Healing the Historical Trauma Response among the Lakota." *Smith College Studies in Social Work* 68 (3): 287–305.

Brave Heart, M. Y., and L. M. DeBruyn. 1998. "The American Indian Holocaust: Healing Historical Unresolved Grief." *American Indian and Alaska Native Mental Health Research Journal of the National Center* 8: 56–78.

Brave Heart, Maria Yellow Horse. 1999. "*Oyate Ptayela*: Rebuilding the Lakota Nation through Addressing Historical Trauma among Lakota Parents." *Journal of Human Behavior and the Social Environment* 2 (1/2): 109–26.

Brave Heart, Maria Yellow Horse. 2001a. "Clinical Interventions with American Indians." In *Culturally Competent Social Work Practice: Practice Skills, Interventions, and Evaluation,* edited by Rowena Fong and Sharlene Furuto, 285–98. Reading, MA: Longman Publishers.

Brave Heart, Maria Yellow Horse. 2001b. "Culturally and Historically Congruent Clinical Social Work Interventions with Native Clients." In *Culturally Competent Social Work Practice: Practice Skills, Interventions, and Evaluation,* edited by Rowena Fong and Sharlene Furuto, 285–98. Reading, MA: Longman Publishers.

Brave Heart, Maria Yellow Horse. 2003. "The Historical Trauma Response among Natives and Its Relationship with Substance Abuse: A Lakota Illustration." *Journal of Psychoactive Drugs* 35 (1): 7–13.

Brave Heart, Maria Yellow Horse. 2004. "The Historical Trauma Response among Natives and Its Relationship to Substance Abuse." In *Healing and Mental Health for Native Americans: Speaking in Red,* edited by Ethan Nebelkopf and Mary Phillips, 7–18. New York: AltaMira Press.

Brave Heart, Maria Yellow Horse, and Lemyra M. DeBruyn. 1998. "The American Indian Holocaust: Healing Historical Unresolved Grief." *American Indian and Alaska Native Mental Health* 8 (2): 60–82.

Brave Heart, Maria Yellow Horse, Jennifer Elkins, Greg Tafoya, Doreen Bird, and Melina Salvador. 2012. "*Wicasa Was'aka*: Restoring the Traditional Strength of American Indian Males." *American Journal of Public Health* 102 (S2): 177–83.

Brenneman, George R., Aaron O. Handler, Stephen Kaufman, and Everett R. Rhoades. 2000. "Health Status and Clinical Indicators." In *American Indian Health: Innovations in Health Care, Promotion, and Policy,* edited by Everett R. Rhoades, 103–21. Baltimore: The John Hopkins University Press.

Brooks, Daniel. 1998. "Environmental Genocide: Native Americans and Toxic Waste." *The American Journal of Economics and Sociology* 57: 105–13.

Brosseau, James. 1994. "Diabetes and Indians: A Clinician's Perspective." In *Diabetes as a Disease of Civilization: The Impact of Culture Change on Indigenous Peoples,* edited by Jennie R. Joe and Robert S. Young, 41–66. New York: Mouton de Gruyter.

Brugge, Doug, Timothy Benally, and Esther Yazzie-Lewis. 2006. *The Navajo People and Uranium Mining.* Albuquerque: University of New Mexico Press.

Brugge, Doug, Jamie deLemos, and Cat Bui. 2007. "The Sequoyah Corporation Fuels Release and the Church Rock Spill: Unpublicized Nuclear Releases in American Indian Communities." *American Journal of Public Health* 97: 1595–1600.

Brugge, Doug, and Rob Goble. 2002. "The History of Uranium Mining and the Navajo People." *American Journal of Public Health* 92: 1410–19.

Buchwald, Dedra, Janette Beals, and Spero M. Manson. 2000. "Use of Traditional Health Practices among Native Americans in a Primary Care Setting." *Medical Care* 38 (12): 1191–99.

Burhansstipanov, Linda, Mark Dignan, Katherine L. Jones, Linda U. Krebs, Paula Marchionda and Judith Salmon Kaur. 2012. "A Comparison of Quality of Life between Native and Non-Native Cancer Survivors." *Journal of Cancer Education* 27 (1): 106–113.

Caballero B., T. Clay, S. M. Davis, B. Ethelbah, B. Holy Rock, T. Lohman, et al. (2003). "Pathways: a School-Based, Randomized Controlled Trial for the Prevention of Obesity in American Indian Schoolchildren." *American Journal of Clinical Nutrition* 78: 1030–38.

Caballero, B., J. H. Hime, T. Lohman, S. M. Davis, J. Stevens, M. Evans, S. Going, and J. Pablo for the Pathways Study Research Group. 2003. "Body Composition and Overweight Prevalence in 1704 Schoolchildren from 7 American Indian Communities." *American Journal of Clinical Nutrition* 78 (2): 308–12.

Calloway, Ewen. 2010. "Native American Settlement Highlights DNA Dilemma." *New Scientist.* http://www.newscientist.com/article/dn18832-native-american-settlement-highlights-dna-dilemma.html [accessed 4 Feb. 2011].

Campbell, Gregory R. 1989a. "The Changing Dimensions of Native American Health: A Critical Understanding of Contemporary Native Health Issues." In *Contemporary Issues in Native American Health,* edited by Gregory R. Campbell, 1–20. *American Indian Culture and Research Journal,* Special Edition. 13 (3 and 4).

Campbell, Gregory R. 2008 "Native American Health Care." In *Encyclopedia of Race Ethnicity, and Society,* Volume 2, edited by Richard T. Schaefer, 949–954. Thousand Oaks, CA: Sage Publications.

Campbell, Gregory R. 2009a "Disease." In *The Encyclopedia of United States Indian Policy and Law,* Volume One, edited by Paul Finkelman and Tim A. Garrison, 262–265. Washington D.C.: Congressional Quarterly Press.

Campbell, Gregory R. 2009b "Indian Health and Health Care." In *The Encyclopedia of United States Indian Policy and Law.* Volume One, edited by Paul Finkelman and Tim A. Garrison, 409–15. Washington D.C.: Congressional Quarterly Press.

Campbell, Gregory R., editor. 1989. *Contemporary Issues in Native American Health. American Indian Culture and Research Journal,* Special Edition. 13 (3 and 4).

Campos-Outcalt, Doug, Jennifer Ellis, Mikel Aickin, Jessie Valencia, Martha Wunsch, and Lois Steele. 1995. "Prevalence of Cardiovascular Disease Risk Factors in a Southwestern Native American Tribe." *Public Health Reports* 110 (6): 742–48.

Cantrell, Betty G. 2001. "Access and Barriers to Food Items and Food Preparation among Plains Indians." *Wicazo Sa Review* 16 (1): 65–74.

Cavanaugh, Casey L., Christopher A. Taylor, Kathryn S. Keim, Jill E. Clutter, and Maureen E. Geraghty. 2008. "Cultural Perceptions of Health and Diabetes among Native Man." *Journal of Health Care for the Poor and Underserved* 19:1029–1043.

Cesario, K.. 2010. "Care of the Native American Woman: Strategies For Practice, Education, and Research. *Journal of Obstetric, Gynecologic, and Neonatal Nursing* 30 (1): 13–19.

Churchill, Ward, and Winona LaDuke. 1992. "Native North America: The Political Economy of Radioactive Colonialism." In *State of Native America: Genocide, Colonization and Resistance,* edited by Annette Jaimes, 241–66. Cambridge, MA: South End Press.

Codru, Neculai, Maria Schymura, Serban Negoita, Robert Rej, and David Carpenter. 2007. "Diabetes in Relation to Serum Levels of Polychlorinated Biphenyls and Chlorinated Pesticides in Adult Native Americans." *Environmental Health Perspectives* 115: 1442–47.

Collins, Robert J., Candace M. Jones, and Robert F. Martin. 2000. "Oral Health," In *American Indian Health: Innovations in Health Care, Promotion, and Policy,* edited by Everett R. Rhoades, 370–88. Baltimore: John Hopkins University Press.

Costello, E. J., E. M. Farmer, A. Angold, B. J. Burns, and A. Erkanli. 1997. "Psychiatric Disorders among American Indian and White Youth in Appalachia: The Great Smoky Mountains Study." *American Journal of Public Health* 87: 827–32.

Daly, Christine Makosky, Anne Kraemer-Diaz, Aimee S. James, Darryl Monteau, Stephanioe Joseph, Joseph Pacheco, Julia White Bull, Angel Cully, Won S. Choi, and K. Allen Greiner. "Breast Cancer Screening Beliefs and Behaviors Among American Indian Women in Kansas and Missouri: A Quantitative Inquiry." *Journal of Cancer Education* 27, no. Suppl. 1 (2012): S32–S40.

Davis, Nancy. 2010. "The Exxon Valdez Oil Spill, Alaska." In *The Long Road to Recovery: Community Responses to Industrial Disaster,* edited by James K. Mitchell, 231–72. New York: United Nations University Press.

Dawson, Susan. 1992. "Navajo Uranium Workers and the Effects of Occupational Illnesses: A Case Study." *Human Organization* 51: 389–97.

Dawson, Susan, and Gary Madsen. 1995. "American Indian Uranium Mill Workers: A Study of the Perceived Effects of Occupational Exposure." *Journal of Health and Social Policy* 7: 19–31.

DeCaprio, Anthony, Glenn Johnson, Alice Tarbell, David Carpenter, Jeffrey Chiarenzelli, Gayle Morse, Azara Santiago-Rivera, and Maria J. Schymura. 2005. "Polychlorinated Biphenyl (PCB) Exposure Assessment by Multivariate Statistical Analysis of Serum Congener Profiles in an Adult Native American Population." *Environmental Research* 98: 284–302.

DeCora, Lorelei. 2001. "The Diabetic Plague in Indian Country: Legacy of Displacement." *Wicazo Sa Review.* 16 (1): 9–15.

DeGonzague, Bernadette, Olivier Receveur, Don Wedell, and Harriet V. Kuhnlein. 1999. "Dietary Intake and Body Mass Index of Adults in Two Ojibwa Communities." *Journal of the American Dietetic Association* 99 (6): 710–716.

DeJong, David H. 2008. "If You Knew The Conditions": A Chronicle of the Indian Medical Service and American Indian Health Care, 1908–1955. Lanham: Lexington Books.

DeJong, David H. 2011. *Plagues, Politics, and Policy: A Chronicle of the Indian Health Service, 1955–2008.* Lanham: Lexington Books.

de Lemos, Jamie L., Doug Brugge, Miranda Cajero, Mallery Downs, John L. Durant, Christine M. George, Sarah Henio-Adeky, Teddy Nez, Thomas Manning, Tommy Rock, Bess Seschillie, Chris Shuey, and Johnnye Lewis. 2009. "Development of Risk Maps to Minimize Uranium Exposures in the Navajo Churchrock Mining District." *Environmental Health* 8: 29–44.

Denham, Melinda, Lawrence Schell, Glenn Deane, Mia Gallo, Julia Ravenscroft and, Anthony DeCaprio. 2005. "Relationship of Lead, Mercury, Mirex, DDE, HCB, and PCBs to Age at Menarche among Akwesasne Mohawk Girls." *Pediatrics* 115:125–34. Accessed May 7, 2011. DOI:10.1542/peds.2004–1161.

Denny C. H., D. Holtzman, and N. Cobb. 2003. "Surveillance for Health Behaviors of American Indians and Alaska Natives: Findings from the Behavioral Risk Factor Surveillance System, 1997–2000." *MMWR Surveillance* 52 (7): 1–13.

Dobyns, Henry F. 1993. "Disease Transfer at Contact," *Annual Review of Anthropology* 22: 273–291.

Dorgan, Byron L. 2010. "The Tragedy of Native American Youth Suicide." *Psychological Services* : 213–18.

Duclos, Christine Wilson, Janette Beals, Douglas K. Novins, Cheryl Martin, Chastity S. Jewett, and Spero M. Manson. 1998. "Prevalence of Common Psychiatric Disorders among American Indian Adolescent Detainees." *Journal of the American Academy of Child and Adolescent Psychiatry* 37: 866–73.

Duran, Bonnie, and Karina L. Walters. 2004. "HIV/AIDS Prevention In 'Indian Country: Current Practice, Indigenist Etiology Models, and Postcolonial Approaches to Change. *AIDS Education and Prevention.* 16: 187–201.

Duran, Bonnie, Margaret Sanders, Betty Skipper, Howard Waitzkin, Lorraine Halinka Malcoe, Susan Paine, and Joel Yager. 2004. "Prevalence and Correlates of Mental Disorders among Native American Women in Primary Care." *American Journal of Public Health* 94: 71–77.

Duran, Eduardo. 2006. Healing the Soul Wound: Counseling with American Indians and Other Native Peoples. Multicultural Foundations of Psychology and Counseling Series. New York, NY, US: Teachers College Press.

Dyer, Christopher. 1993. "Traditional Loss as Secondary Disaster: Long-Term Cultural Impacts of the Exxon Valdez Oil Spill." *Sociological Spectrum* 13: 65–88.

Dyer, Christopher, Duane A. Gill and Steven Picou. 1992. "Social Disruption and the Valdez Oil Spill: Alaskan Natives in a Natural Resource Community." *Sociological Spectrum* 12: 105–26.

Eichstaedt, Peter. 1994. *If You Poison Us: Uranium and Native Americans.* Santa Fe, NM: Red Crane Books.

Evaneshko, Veronica. 1994. "Presenting Complaints in a Navajo Indian Diabetic Population." In *Diabetes as a Disease of Civilization: The Impact of Culture Change on Indigenous Peoples,* edited by Jennie R. Joe and Robert S. Young, 357–377. New York: Mouton de Gruyter.

Everett Jones S., Anderson K., Lowry R., Conner H. (2011). Risks to health among American Indian/Alaska Native high school students in the United States. Preventing Chronic Disease 8(4):A76. http://www.cdc.gov/pcd/issues/2011/jul/10_0193.htm.

Fall, James, Rita Miraglia, William Simeone, Charles Utermohle, and Robert Wolfe. 2001. *Long Term Consequences of the Exxon Valdez Oil Spill for Costal Communities of Southcentral Alaska.* Technical paper #264. Division of Subsistence, Alaskan Department of Fish and Game: Juneau, Alaska. Accessed May 7, 2011. http://www.subsistence.adfg.state.ak.us/TechPap/tp264.pdf.

Ferreira, Marianna L. and Gretchen C. Lang, editors. 2006. *Indigenous Peoples and Diabetes: Community Empowerment and Wellness.* Durham: Carolina Academic Press.

Fitzgerald, Edward, Synian Hwang, Kelley Brix, Brian Bush, and Priscilla Worswick. 1995. "Fish PCB Concentrations and Consumption Patterns among Mohawk Women at Akwesasne." *Journal of Exposure Analysis and Environmental Epidemiology* 5:1–19.

Fitzgerald, Edward, Synian Hwang, George Lambert, Marta Gomez, and Alice Tarbell. 2005. "PCB Exposure and in Vivo CYP1A2 Activity Among Native Americans." *Environmental Health Perspectives* 113:272–7.

Fitzgerald, Edward, Synian Hwang, Marta Gomez, Brian Bush, Bao-Zhu Yang, and Alice Tarbell. 1999. "Local Fish Consumption and Serum PCB Concentrations among Mohawk Men at Akwesasne." *Environmental Research* 80: s97–s103.

Fitzgerald, Edward, Synian Hwang, Marta Gomez, Brian Bush, Bao-Zhu Yang, and Alice Tarbell. 2007. "Environmental and Occupational Exposures and Serum PCB Concentrations and Patterns among Mohawk Men at Akwesasne." *Journal of Exposure Analysis and Environmental Epidemiology* 17: 269–78.

Fitzgerald, Edward, Kelley Brix, Debra Deres, Synian Hwang, Brian Bush, George Lambert and Alice Tarbell. 1996. "Polychlorinated Biphenyl (PCB) and Dichlorodiphenyl Dichloroethylene (DDE) Exposure Among Native American Men from Contaminated Great Lakes Fish and Wildlife." *Toxicology and Industrial Health* 12: 361–68.

Forquera, Ralph. 2001. *Urban Indian Health.* Issue Brief. Menlo Park: The Henry J. Kaiser Family Foundation.

Frank, John W., Roland S. Moore, and Genevieve M. Ames. 2000. "Historical and Cultural Roots of Drinking Problems American Indians." *American Journal of Public Health* 90 (3): 344–51.

Freedenthal, Stacey, and Arlene Rubin Stiffman. 2004. "Suicidal Behavior in Urban American Indian Adolescents: A Comparison with Reservation Youth in a Southwestern State." *Suicide and Life-Threatening Behavior* 34: 160–71.

French, Laurence A. 2000. *Addiction and Native Americans.* Westport, CT: Praeger Press.

Frohmberg, Eric, Robert Goble, Virginia Sanchez, and Dianne Quigley. 2000. "The Assessment of Radiation Exposures in Native American Communities from Nuclear Weapons Testing in Nevada." *Risk Analysis* 20: 101–11.

Galloway, James M. 1996. "Hypertension in Native Americans: Etiology, Association, and Trends." *The Federal Practitioner* May Issue.

Galloway, James M. 2001. "Cardiovascular Disease in Native Americans." *Medicine of the Americas* 2 (2): 109.

Garcia-Smith, Dianna. 1993. "The Gila River Diabetes Prevention Model." In *Diabetes as a Disease of Civilization: The Impact of Culture Change on Indigenous Peoples,* edited by Jennie R. Joe and Robert S. Young, 471–94. New York: Mouton de Gruyter.

Garro, Linda C., and Gretchen C. Lang. 1994. "Explanations of Diabetes" Anishinaabeg and Dakota Deliberate upon a New Illness." In *Diabetes as a Disease of Civilization: The Impact of Culture Change on Indigenous Peoples,* edited by Jennie R. Joe and Robert S. Young, 293–328. New York: Mouton de Gruyter.

Gary, Faye A., Martha Baker, Donna M. Grandbois. 2005. "Perspectives on Suicide Prevention among American Indian and Alaska Native Children and Adolescents: A Call for Help." *Online Journal of Issues in Nursing* 10 (2): 6. http://www.ncbi.nlm.nih.gov/pubmed/15977979.

Gilliland, Frank, William Hunt, Marla Pardilla, and Charles Key. 2000. "Uranium Mining and Lung Cancer among Navajo Men in New Mexico and Arizona, 1969–1993." *Journal of Occupational and Environmental Medicine* 42: 278–83.

Gillum, R.F. 1995. "The Epidemiology of Stroke in Native Americans." *Stroke* 26: 514–21.

Gohdes, D. M. 1986. "Diabetes in American Indians: A Growing Problem." *Diabetes Care* 9 (6): 609–13.

Gohdes, Dorothy M. and Kelly Acton. 2000. "Diabetes Mellitus and Its Complications." In *American Indian Health: Innovations in Health Care, Promotion, and Policy,* edited by Everett R. Rhoades, 221–59. Baltimore: John Hopkins University Press.

Gohdes, Dorothy, Todd S. Harwell, Susan Cummings, Kelly R. Moore, Jane G. Smilie, and Steven D. Helgerson. 2002. "Smoking Cessation and Prevention: An Urgent Public Health Priority for American Indians in the Northern Plains." *Public Health Reports* 117 (3): 281–90.

Going S. B., J. Thompson, S. Cano, D. Stewart, E. Stone, L. Harnack, et al. 2003. "The Effects of the Pathways Obesity Prevention Program on Physical Activity in American Indian Children." *Journal of Preventive Medicine* 37 (1): S62–S69.

Goins, R. Turner, S. Melinda Spencer, Yvette D. Roubideaux, and Spero M. Manson. 2005. "Differences in Functional Disability of Rural American Indian and White Older Adults With Comorbid Diabetes." *Research on Aging* 27 (6): 643–58.

Goncharov, Alexey, Richard Haase, Azara Santiago-Rivera, Gayle Morse, Robert McCaffrey, Robert Rej, and David Carpenter. 2008. "High Serum PCBs are Associated with Elevation of Serum Lipids and Cardiovascular Disease in a Native American Population." *Environmental Research* 106: 226–39.

Goncharov, Alexey, Robert Rej, Serban Negoita, Maria Schymura, Azara Santiago-Rivera, Gayle Morse, the Akwesasne Task Force on the Environment, and David Carpenter. 2009. "Lower Serum Testosterone Associated with Elevated Polychlorinated Biphenyl Concentrations in Native American Men." *Environmental Health Perspectives* 117: 1454–60.

Gone, J. P. 2003. "American Indian Mental Health Service Delivery: Persistent Challenges and Future Prospects." In *Culturally Diverse Mental Health: The Challenges of Research and Resistance,* edited by J. S. Mio and G. Y. Iwamasa. New York City, NY: Brunner-Routledge.

Gone, J. P., and J. E. Trimble. 2012. "American Indian and Alaska Native Mental Health: Diverse Perspectives on Enduring Disparities." *Annual Review of Clinical Psychology* 8: 131–60.

Gone, Joseph. 2007. "'We Never Was Happy Living Like a Whiteman': Mental Health Disparities and the Postcolonial Predicament in American Indian Communities." *American Journal of Community Psychology* 40: 290–300.

Gone, Joseph P. 2004. "Mental Health Services for Native Americans in the 21st Century United States." *Professional Psychology: Research and Practice* 35: 10–18.

Gone, Joseph P. 2008. "'So I Can Be Like a Whiteman': The Cultural Psychology of Space and Place in American Indian Mental Health." *Culture Psychology* 14 (3): 369–99.

Gone, Joseph P., and Carmela Alcántara. 2007. "Identifying Effective Mental Health Interventions for American Indians and Alaska Natives: A Review of the Literature." *Cultural Diversity and Ethnic Minority Psychology* 13: 356–63.

Gould, Kenneth, David Pellow, and Allan Schnaiberg. 2008. *The Treadmill of Production: Injustice and Unsustainability in the Global Economy.* Boulder, CO: Paradigm Publishers.

Gould, Larry. 2006. "Alcoholism, Colonialism, and Crime." In *Native Americans and the Criminal Justice System.* Edited by Jeffrey Ian Ross and Larry Gould, 87–102. Boulder, CO: Paradigm Publishers.

Gowda, Rajeev, and Doug Easterling. 2000. "Voluntary Siting and Equity: The MRS Facility Experience in Native America." *Risk Analysis* 20: 917–30.

Grandbois, Donna. 2005. "Stigma of Mental Illness among American Indian and Alaska Native Nations: Historical and Contemporary Perspectives." *Issues in Mental Health Nursing* 26: 1001–24.

Gurley, Diana, Douglas Novins, Monica Jones, Janette Beals, James Shore, and Spero Manson. 2001. "Comparative Use of Biomedical Services and Traditional Healing Options by American Indian Veterans." *Psychiatric Services* 52: 68–74.

Guyon, Susan. 1973. "The Challenge to the Indian Health Service." *Health Services Reports* 88: 687–691.

Haase, Richard, Robert McCaffrey, Azara Santiago-Rivera, Gayle Morse, and Alice Tarbell. 2009. "Evidence of an Age-Related Threshold Effect of Polychlorinated Biphenyls (PCBs) on Neuropsychological Functioning in a Native American Population." *Environmental Research* 109: 73–85.

Haraldson, Sixten S. R. 1988. "Health and Health Services among the Navajo Indians." *Journal of Community Health* 13: 129–42.

Harris, C. R., B. Albaugh, D. Goldman, and M. A. Enoch. 2003. "Neurocognitive Impairment Due to Chronic Alcohol Consumption in an American Indian Community." *Journal of Studies on Alcohol* 64: 458–466.

Harwell, Todd S., Janet M. McDowall, Kelly Moore, Anne Fagot-Campagna, Steven D. Helgerson, and Dorothy Gohdes. 2001. "Establishing Surveillance for Diabetes in American Indian Youth." *Diabetes Care* 24 (6): 1029–32.

Hawkins, Elizabeth, Lillian H. Cummins and Alan G. Marlatt. 2004. "Preventing Substance Abuse in American Indian and Alaska Native Youth: Promising Strategies for Healthier Communities." *Psychological Bulletin* 130 (2): 305.

Hickey, Martin and Janette Carter. 1994. "Cultural Barriers to Delivering Healthcare: The Non-Indian Provider Perspective." In *Diabetes as a Disease of Civilization: The Impact of Culture Change on Indigenous Peoples,* edited by Jennie R. Joe and Robert S. Young, 453–70. New York: Mouton de Gruyter.

Hill, D. L. 2006. "Sense of Belonging as Connectedness. American Indian Worldview, and Mental Health." *Archives of Psychiatric Nursing* 20 (5): 210–16.

Hill, Doris Leal. 2009. "Relationship Between Sense of Belonging as Connectedness and Suicide in American Indians." *Archives of Psychiatric Nursing* 23 (1): 65–74.

Himes, J. H., K. Ring, J. Gittelsohn, L. Cunningham-Sabo, J. L. Weber, J. Thompson J. et al. 2003. "Impact of the Pathways Intervention on Dietary Intakes of American Indian Schoolchildren." *Preventive Medicine* 37, S55–S61.

Holm, Tom. 1995. "PTSD in Native American Vietnam Veterans: A Reassessment." *Wicazo Sa Review* 11: 83–86.

Holmes, Malcolm D., and Judith A. Antell. 2001. "The Social Construction of American Indian Drinking: Perceptions of American Indian and White Officials." *The Sociological Quarterly* 42 (2): 151–73.

Hooks, Gregory, and Chad Smith. 2004. "The Treadmill of Destruction: National Sacrifice Areas and Native Americans." *American Sociological Review* 69: 558–75.

Howard, B. V., E. T. Lee, L. D. Cowan, et al. 1999. "The Rising Tide of Cardiovascular Disease in Native Americans: The Strong Heart Study." *Circulation* 99: 2389–95.

Howard, Matthew O., R. Dale Walker, Patricia S. Walker, and Everett R. Rhoades. 2000. "Alcoholism and Substance Abuse." In *American Indian Health: Innovations in Health Care, Promotion, and Policy,* edited by Everett R. Rhoades, 281–98. Baltimore: John Hopkins University Press.

Hoy, W., A. Light, and D. Megill. 1994. "Blood Pressure in Navajo Indians and its Association with Type 2 Diabetes and Renal and Cardiovascular Disease." *American Journal of Hypertension* 7: 321–328.

Hoy, W., A. Light, and D. Megill. 1995. "Cardiovascular Disease in Navajo Indians with Type 2 Diabetes." *Public Health Reports* 110: 87–94.

Hwang, Synian, Edward Fitzgerald, and Brian Bush. 1996. "Exposure to PCB's from Hazardous Waste among Mohawk Women and Infants at Akwesasne." *Technology Journal of the Franklin Institute* 333A: 17–23.

Iralu, Jonathan, Bonnie Duran, Cynthia R. Pearson, Yizhou Jiang, Kevin Foley, and Melvin Harrison. 2010. "Risk Factors for HIV Disease Progression in a Rural Southwest American Indian Population." *Public Health Reports* 125: Supplement 4: 43–49.

Janitz A. E., W. E. Moore, A. L. Stephens, K. E. Abbott, and J. E. Eichner. 2012. Weight Status of American Indian and White Elementary School Students Living in the same Rural Environment, Oklahoma, 2005–2009." *Preventing Chronic Disease* 9: 110223. DOI: http://dx.doi.org/10.5888/pcd9.110233.

Jiang, Luohua, Janette Beals, Nancy R. Whitesell, Yvette Roubideaux, and Spero M. Manson. 2009. "Health-Related Quality of Life and Help Seeking among American Indians with Diabetes and Hypertension." *Quality of Life Research* 18 (6): 709–18.

Jilek, W. G . 1974. *Salish Indian Mental Health and Culture Change.* Toronto: Holt, Rinehart and Winston.

Joe, Jennie R. 1994. "Health: Traditional Indian Health Practices and Cultural Views." In *Native American: Portrait of the Peoples,* edited by Duane Champagne, 525–47. Detroit: Visible Ink Press.

Joe, Jennie and Sophie Frishkopf. 2006. "I'm Too Young for This!": Diabetes and American Indian Children." In *Indigenous Peoples and Diabetes: Community Empowerment and Wellness,* edited by Marianna L. Ferreira, and Gretchen C. Lang, 435–58. Durham: Carolina Academic Press.

Johansen, Bruce E. 1999. "Whiteclay, Nebraska: The Town That Booze Built." *Native Americas Journal.* January 28.

Johnson, Emery A., and Everett R. Rhoades. 2000. "The History and Organization of Indian Health Services." In *American Indian Health: Innovations in Health Care, Promotion, and Policy,* edited by Everett R. Rhoades, 74–92. Baltimore: John Hopkins University Press.

Johnson, Jeannette L., and Mark C. Cameron. 2001. "Barriers to Providing Effective Mental Health Services to American Indians." *Mental Health Services Research* 3 (4): 215–3.

Johnson, Jeffrey A., Thomas E. Nowatzki, and Stephen Joel Coons. 1995. "Health-Related Quality of Life of Diabetic Pima Indians." *Medical Care* 34 (2): 97–102.

Johnson, Troy, and Holly Tomren. 1999. "Helplessness, Hopelessness, and Despair: Identifying Precursors to Indian Youth Suicide." *American Indian Culture and Research Journal* 23 (3): 287–301.

Johnston, Susan L. 2002. "Native American Traditional and Alternative Medicine." *Annals of the American Academy of Political and Social Science.* 583 (September): 295–313.

Justice, James. 1989. "Twenty Years of Diabetes on the Warm Springs Indian Reservation, Oregon." In *Contemporary Issues in Native American Health,* edited by Gregory R. Campbell, 49–81. *American Indian Culture and Research Journal,* Special Edition. 13 (3 and 4).

Justice, James W. 1993. "The History of Diabetes in the Desert People." In *Diabetes as a Disease of Civilization: The Impact of Culture Change on Indigenous Peoples,* edited by Jennie R. Joe and Robert S. Young, 69–128. New York: Mouton de Gruyter.

Kaufman, Carol E, Sara Shelby, Debra J. Mosure, Jeanne Marrazzo, David Wong, Lori De Ravello, Stephanie Craig Rusing, Victoria Warren-Mears, Lisa Neel, Sara Jumping Eagle, Scott Tulloch, Francine Romero, Sarah Patrick, and James E. Cheek. 2007. "Within the Hidden Epidemic: Sexually Transmitted Disease and HIV/AIDS Among American Indians and Alaska Natives." *Sexually Transmitted Diseases* 34: 767–77.

Kinney, Andrea, Edward Fitzgerald, Synian Hwang, Brian Bush, and Alice Tarbell. 1997. "Human Exposure to PCBs: Modeling and Assessment of Environmental Concentrations on the Akwesasne Reservation." *Drug Chemistry and Toxicology* 20: 313–28.

Kleinfeld, Judith, and Joseph Bloom. 1977. "Boarding Schools: Effects on the Mental Health of Eskimo Adolescents." *The American Journal of Psychiatry* 134: 411–17.

Kunitz, Stephen J. 1990. "Public Policy and Mortality Among Indigenous Populations of Northern America and Australasia." *Population and Development Review* 16: 647–672.

Kunitz, Stephen J. 1994. *Disease and Social Diversity: The European Impact on the Health of Non-Europeans.* New York: Oxford University Press.

Kunitz, Stephen J. 1996. "The History and Politics of U. S. Health Care Policy for American Indians and Alaskan Natives." *American Journal of Public Health* 86: 1464–73.

Kunitz, Stephen J. 2006. "Life-Course Observations of Alcohol Use among Navajo Indians: Natural History or Careers?" *Medical Anthropology Quarterly* 20 (3): 279–96.

Kunitz, S. J., K. R. Gabriel, J. E. Levy, E. Henderson, K. Lampert, J. McCloskey, G. Quintero, S. Russell, and A. Vince. 1999. "Risk Factors for Conduct Disorder among Navajo Indian Men and Women." *Social Psychiatry and Psychiatric Epidemiology* 34: 180–89.

La Duke, Winona. 1979. "Uranium Mines on Native Land: The New Indian Wars." *The Harvard Crimson.* May 2. http://pubs.usgs.gov/wri/wri994063/. [accessed May 22, 2011].

LaRowe, T. L., D. P. Wubben, K. A. Cronin, S. M. Vannatter, and A. K. Adams. 2007. "Development of a Culturally Appropriate, Home-Based Nutrition and Physical Activity Curriculum for Wisconsin American Indian Families." *Preventing Chronic Disease* 4 (4). http://www.cdc.gov/pcd/issues/2007/oct/07_0018.htm.

LaRowe, T. L., A. K. Adams, J. E. Jobe, K. A. Cronin, S. M. Vannatter, and R. J. Prince. 2010. "Dietary Intakes and Physical Activity among Preschool-Aged Children Living in Rural American Indian Communities before a Family-Based Healthy Lifestyle Intervention." *Journal of the American Dietetic Association* 110: 1049–57.

LaFromboise, Teresa D., and A. Fatemi. 2011. "American Indian Life Skills: A Community Based Intervention for Indigenous Mental Health." In *Child Psycholgy and Mental Health: Cultural and Ethno-Racial Perspectives,* edited by H. Fitzgerald. Santa Barbara, CA: Praeger Publishers.

Lamarine, Roland J. 1988. "Alcohol Abuse among Native Americans." *Journal of Community Health* 13 (3): 143–55.

Lane, Naomi A., Kathleen Evans, Agnes Attakai, Catherine Witte, Maylyn Rriding In-Warne, Kathryne Coe. 2011. "Responding to American Indian Communities: Southwest American Indian Collaborative Network (SAICN) Cancer Educational Activities." *Journal of Health Disparities Research and Practice* 4 (3): 18–33.

Lang, Gretchen C. 1989. "'Making Sense' About Diabetes: Dakota Narratives of Illness." *Medical Anthropology* 11 (3): 305–28.

Lang, Gretchen C. 2006a. "'In Their Tellings': Dakota Narratives about History and the Body." In *Indigenous Peoples and Diabetes: Community Empowerment and Wellness,* edited by Marianna L. Ferreira and Gretchen C. Lang, 53–71. Durham, NC: Carolina Academic Press.

Lang, Gretchen C. 2006b. "Talking about a New Illness with the Dakota: Reflections on Diabetes, Foods, and Culture." In *Indigenous Peoples and Diabetes: Community Empowerment and Wellness,* edited by Marianna L. Ferreira and Gretchen C. Lang, 203–230. Durham, NC: Carolina Academic Press.

Lapidus, Jodi A., Jeanne Bertolli, Karen McGowan, and Patrick Sullivan. 2006. "HIV-Related Risk Behaviors, Perceptions of Risk: HIV Testing, and Exposure to Prevention Messages and Methods Among Urban American Indians and Alaska Natives." *AIDS Education and Prevention* 18: 546–59.

Larsen, Clark S., and George R. Milner. 1994. *In The Wake of Contact: Biological Responses to Conquest.* New York: Wiley-Liss.

Levin, Aaron. 2009. "How Much Does Historical Trauma Add to Indians' Health Problems?" *Psychiatric News* 44: 9.

Levy, Jerold E., and Kunitz, Stephen J. 1974. *Indian Drinking: Navajo Practices and Anglo-American Theories.* New York: John Wiley and Sons.

Lidot, Tom. 2003. *Visions for Living with HIV in the Circle of Life.* Denver, CO: National Native American AIDS Prevention Center.

Lindberg, S. M., A. K. Adams, R. J. Prince. 2012. "Early Predictors of Obesity and Cardiovascular Risk among American Indian Children." *Maternal and Child Health Journal* 16 (9): 1879–86.

Long, Jeffrey C., and Joseph G. Lorenz. 2000. "Genetic Polymorphism and American Indian Origins, Affinities, and Health." In *American Indian Health: Innovations in Health Care, Promotion, and Policy,* edited by Everett R. Rhoades, 122–37. Baltimore: John Hopkins University Press.

Lowe, Lynn P., Cynthia R. Long, Robert B. Wallace, and Thomas K. Welty. 1997. "Epidemiology of Alcohol Use in a Group of Older American Indians." *Annals of Epidemiology* 7 (4): 241–48.

Mackin, Juliette, Tamara Perkins, and Carrie Furrer. 2012. "The Power of Protection: A Population-Based Comparison of Native and Non-Native Youth Suicide Attempters." *American Indian and Alaska Native Mental Health Research* 19 (2): 20–54.

Mahoney, Martin C., Arthur M. Michalek, K. Michael Cummings, John Hanley, and Rae L. Snyder. 1989. "Years of Potential Life Lost among a Native American Population." *Public Health Reports* 104: 279–285.

Mails, Patricia D. 1978. "Hippocrates Was a Medicine Man: The Health Care of Native Americans in the Twentieth Century." *Annals of the American Academy of Political and Social Science* 436: 40–49.

Malcoe, L., R. Lynch, M. Keger, V. Skaggs. 2002. "Lead Sources, Behaviors, and Socioeconomic Factors in Relation to Blood Lead of Native American and White Children." *Environmental Health Perspectives* 110: s2:221–31.

Mancall, P.C. *Deadly Medicine: Indians and Alcohol in Early America.* Ithaca, NY: Cornell University Press, 1995.

Manson, S. M., and D. B. Altschul. 2004. "Cultural Diversity Series: Meeting the Mental Health Needs of American Indians and Alaska Natives." Edited by and National Association of State Mental Health Program Directors National Technical Assistance Center for State Mental Health Planning. Washington, D.C.

Manson, Spero. 2000. "Mental Health Services for American Indians and Alaska Natives: Need, Use, and Barriers to Effective Care." *Canadian Journal of Psychiatry* 45 (7): 617–26.

Manson, Spero, James Shore, and Joseph Bloom. 1985. "The Depressive Experience in American Indian Communities: A Challenge for Psychiatric Theory and Diagnosis." In *Culture and Depression: Studies in the Anthropology and Cross-Cultural Psychiatry of Affect and Disorder,* edited by Arthur Kleinman and Byron J. Good, 331–68. Berkeley: University of California Press.

Manson, Spero M., Janette Beals, Suzell A. Klein, and Calvin D. Croy. 2005. "Social Epidemiology of Trauma among 2 American Indian Reservation Populations." *American Journal of Public Health* 95: 851–59.

Manson, Spero M., Janette Beals, Suzell A. Klein, Calvin D. Croy, and AISUPERPFP Team. 2005. "Social Epidemiology of Trauma among 2 American Indian Reservations Populations." *American Journal of Public Health* 95 (5): 851–59.

Markstrom, Carol, and Perry Charley. 2003. "Psychological Effects of Human Caused Environmental Disasters: Examination of the Navajo and Uranium." *American Indian and Alaska Native Mental Health Research* 11: 19–45.

Martin, Debra L., and Alan H. Goodman. 2000. "Health Conditions Before Columbus: The Paleopathology of Native North America." In *American Indian Health: Innovations in Health Care, Promotion, and Policy,* edited by Everett R. Rhoades, 19–40. Baltimore: John Hopkins University Press.

May, Phillip A. 1987. "Suicide and Self-Destruction among American Indian Youths." *American Indian and Alaska Native Mental Health* 1 (1): 52–69.

May, Phillip A. 1994. "The Epidemiology of Alcohol Abuse among American Indians." *American Indian Culture and Research Journal* 22: 193–226.

May, Phillip A. and Gossage, J. Phillip 2001. "New Data on the Epidemiology of Adult Drinking and Substance Abuse among American Indians of the Northern States: Male and Female Data on Prevalence, Patterns, and Consequences." *American Indian and Alaska Native Mental Health Research* 10: 1–25.

May, Phillip A., McClosky, Joanne, and Gossage, J. Phillip 2002. "Fetal Alcohol Syndrome among American Indians. Epidemiology, Issues, and Research." In *Alcohol Use among American Indians: Multiple Perspectives on a Complex Problem* edited by P. D. Mail, S. Heurtin/Roberts, S. E. Martin, and J. Howard. National Institute on Alcohol Abuse and Alcoholism Research Monograph No. 37. Bethesda, MD: National Institute on Alcohol Abuse and Alcoholism.

May, Philip A., Patricia Serna, Lance Hurt, and Lemyra M. DeBruyn. 2005. "Outcome Evaluation of a Public Health Approach to Suicide Prevention in an American Indian Tribal Nation." *American Journal of Public Health* 95 (7): 1238–44.

May, Philip A., Nancy W. Van Winkle, Mary B. Williams, Patricia J. McFeeley, Lemyra M. DeBruyn, and Patricia Serna, 2002. "Alcohol and Suicide Death Among American Indians of New Mexico: 1980–1998." *Suicide and Life Threatening Behavior* 32 (3): 240–55.

Middlebrook, Denise L., Pamela L. LeMaster, Janette Beals, J., Douglas K. Novins, and Spero M. Manson. 1998. "Suicide Prevention in American Indian and Alaska Native Communities: A Critical Review of Programs." *National Suicide Prevention Conference.* Reno, Nevada.

Mihesuah, Devon A. 2003. "Decolonizing Our Diets by Recovering Our Ancestors' Gardens." *American Indian Quarterly* 27 (3/4): 807–39.

Milburn, Michael P. 2004. "Indigenous Nutrition: Using Traditional Food Knowledge to Solve Contemporary Health Problems." *American Indian Quarterly* 28 (3/4): 411–34.

Miller, Sheldon I., and Lawrence Schoenfeld. 1973. "Grief in the Navajo: Psychodynamics and Culture." *International Journal of Social Psychiatry* 19: 187–91.

Moerman, Daniel E. 2009. *Native American Medicinal Plants: An Ethnobotanical Dictionary.* Portland Timber Press.

Moore, K. 2010. "Youth-Onset Type 2 Diabetes among American Indians and Alaska Natives." *Journal of Public Health Management and Practice* 16 (5): 388–93.

Mullany, B., Allison Barlow, Novalene Goklish, Francene Larzelere-Hinton, Mary Cwik, Mariddie Craig, and John T. Walkup. 2009. "Toward Understanding Suicide among Youths: Results from the White Mountain Apache Tribally Mandated Suicide Surveillance System, 2001–2006." *American Journal of Public Health* 99 (10): 1840–48.

Narayan, K. M. Venkat. 1997. "Diabetes Mellitus in Native Americans: The Problem and Its Implications." *Population Research and Policy Review* 16 (1/2): 169–92.

Nelson, Scott H., George F. McCoy, Maria Stetter, and W. Craig Vanderwagen. 1992. "An Overview of Mental Health Services for American Indians and Alaska Natives in the 1990s." *Hospital and Community Psychiatry* 43: 257–61.

Newman, Joan, Amy Aucompaugh, Lawrence Schell, Melinda Denham, Anthony DeCaprio, Mia Gallo, Julia Ravenscroft, Chin-Cheng Kao, Mary Ellen Rougas Hannover, Dawn David, Agnes Jacobs, Alice Tarbell, Priscilla Worswick, and Akwesasne Task Force on the Environment. 2006. "PCBs and Cognitive Functioning of Mohawk Adolescents." *Neurotoxicology and Teratology* 28: 439–45.

Noren, Jay, David Kindig, and Audrey Sprenger. 1998. "Challenges to Native American Health Care." *Public Health Reports* 113: 22–33.

Novins, Douglas K., Janette Beals, Robert E. Roberts, and Spero M. Manson. 1999. "Factors Associated with Suicide Ideation among American Indian Adolescents: Does Culture Matter?" *Suicide and Life-Threatening Behavior* 29: 332–46.

Novins, Douglas K., Cathleen Patrick Harman, Christina M. Mitchell, and Spero M. Manson. 1996. "Factors Associated with the Receipt of Alcohol Treatment Services among American Indian Adolescents." *Journal of the American Academy of Child and Adolescent Psychiatry* 35: 110–17.

O'Connell, Joan, et al. 2010. "Racial Disparities in Health Status: A Comparison of the Morbidity Among American Indian and U. S. Adult with Diabetes." *Diabetes Care* 33: 1463–70.

O'Connell, Joan M., Novins, Douglas K., Beals, Janette, and Paul Spicer. 2005. "Disparities in Patterns of Alcohol Use among Reservation-Based and Geographically Dispersed American Indian Populations." *Alcoholism: Clinical and Experimental Research* 29 (1): 107–16.

O'Connell M., D. S. Buchwald, G. E. Duncan. 2012. "Food Access and Cost in American Indian Communities in Washington State." *Journal of the American Dietetic Association* 111: 1375–79.

Okoro, Catherine A., Clark H. Denny, Lisa C. Mcguire, Lina S. Balluz, R. Turner Goins, and Ali H. Mokdad. 2007. "Disability among older American Indians and Alaska Natives: Disparities in Prevalence, Health-Risk Behaviors, Obesity, and Chronic Conditions." *Ethnicity and Disease* 17 (4): 686–92.

Olson, Brooke. 2001. "Meeting the Challenges of American Indian Diabetes: Anthropological Perspectives on Prevention and Treatment." In *Medicine Ways: Disease, Health, and Survival Among Native Americans,* edited by Clifford E. Trafzer and Diane Weiner, 163–84. Walnut Creek, CA: AltaMira Press.

O'Nell, Theresa D. 1996. *Disciplined Hearts: History, Identity, and Depression in an American Indian Community.* Berkeley: University of California Press.

Owsley, Douglas W. 1992. "Demography of Prehistoric and Early Historic Northern Plains Populations." In *Disease and Demography in the Americas,* edited by John W. Verano and Douglas H. Ubelaker, 75–86. Washington D. C.: Smithsonian Institution Press.

Paltoo, Dina, and Kenneth Chu. 2004. "Patterns in Cancer Incidence among American Indians/Alaska Natives, United States, 1992–1999." *Public Health Reports* 119: 443–51.

Pearson, Diane. 2000. "Lewis Cass and the Politics of Disease: The Indian Vaccination Act of 1832." *Wicazo Sa Review* 18: 9–35.

Pember, Mary A. 2010. "American Indians Grow Wary of Genetics Research." *Diverse: Issues in Higher Education.* http://diverseeducation.com/article/13905/ [accessed Feb. 4, 2011].

Pfefferbaum, Rose L., Betty Pfefferbaum, Everett R. Rhoades, and Rennard J. Strickland. 1997. "Providing for the Health Care Needs of Native Americans: Policy, Programs, Procedures, and Practices." *American Indian Law Review* 21: 211–58.

Pickering, Kathleen. 2000. "Alternative Economic Strategies in Low-Income Rural Communities: Tanf, Labor Migration, and the Case of the Pine Ridge Indian Reservation*." *Rural Sociology* 65: 148–67.

Polley D. C., M. T. Spicer, A. P. Knight, and B. L. Hartley. 2005. "Intrafamilial Correlates of Overweight and Obesity in African-American and Native-American Grandparents, Parents, and Children in Rural Oklahoma." *Journal of the American Dietetic Association* 105 (2): 262–5.

Poudier, Jennifer. 2007. "The Geneticization of Aboriginal Diabetes and Obesity: Adding Another to the Scene Story of the Thrifty Gene." *Canadian Review of Sociology: Revue Canadienne de Sociologie* 44 (2): 237–261.

Quintero, Gilbert. 2000. "The Lizard in the Green Bottle: 'Aging Out' of Problem Drinking among Navajo Men." *Social Sciences & Medicine* 51: 1031–45.

Quintero, Gilbert. 2001. "Making the Indian: Colonial Knowledge, Alcohol, and Native Americans." *American Indian Culture and Research Journal* 25 (4): 57–71.

Rate R. G., W. C. Knowler, H. G. Morse, et al. 1983. "Diabetes Mellitus in Hopi and Navajo Indians: Prevalence of Microvascular Complications." *Diabetes* 32: 894–99.

Rathore, Minakshi, Pradeep Bhatnagar, D. Mathur, and G. Saxena. 2002. "Burden of Organochlorine Pesticides in Blood and its Effect on Thyroid Hormones in Women." *The Science of the Total Environment* 295: 207–15.

Ravussin, E., M. E. Valencia, J. Esparza, P. H. Bennett, and L. O. Schulz. 1994. "Effects of a Traditional Lifestyle on Obesity in Pima Indians." *Diabetes Care* 17: 1067–1074.

Raymond, Jaime, William Wheeler, and Mary J. Brown. 2011. "Inadequate and Unhealthy Housing, 2007 and 2009." In *CDC Health Disparities and Inequalities Report—United States, 2011.* Supplement, Volume 60, 21–27. Atlanta: Epidemiology and Analysis Program Office, Centers for Disease Control and Prevention.

Reid, R. 2000. "American Indian Health." *Medicine of the Americas* 1: 53–54.

Reid, Raymond, and Everett R. Rhoades. 2000. "Cultural Considerations in Providing Care to American Indians." In *American Indian Health: Innovations in Health Care, Promotion, and Policy,* edited by Everett R. Rhoades, 18–425. Baltimore: John Hopkins University Press.

Rhoades, Dorothy A., Everett R. Rhoades, and Thomas Welty. 2000. "The Rise of Cardiovascular Diseases." In *American Indian Health: Innovations in Health Care, Promotion, and Policy,* edited by Everett R. Rhoades, 151–78. Baltimore: John Hopkins University Press.

Rhoades, Dorothy A., Everett R. Rhoades, Candace M. Jones, and Robert J. Collins. 2000. "Tobacco Use." In *American Indian Health: Innovations in Health Care, Promotion, and Policy,* edited by Everett R. Rhoades, 299–310. Baltimore: John Hopkins University Press.

Rhoades, Everett R., ed. 2000. *American Indian Health: Innovations in Health Care, Promotion, and Policy.* Baltimore: John Hopkins University Press.

Rhoades, Everett R. and Dorothy A. Rhoades. 2000. "Traditional Indian and Modern Medicine." In *American Indian Health: Innovations in Health Care, Promotion, and Policy,* edited by Everett R. Rhoades, 401–17. Baltimore: John Hopkins University Press.

Richards, Timothy J., and Paul M. Patterson. 2006. "Native American Obesity: An Economic Model of the "Thrifty Gene Theory." *American Journal of Agricultural Economics* 88 (3): 542–60.

Ring, Ian, and Ngiare Brown. 2003. "The Health Status of Indigenous Peoples and Others: The Gap Is Narrowing in the United States, Canada, and New Zealand, But a Lot More Is Needed." *BMJ: British Medical Journal* 327 (7412): 404–5.

Rith-Najarian S. J., C. Braunchard, O. Beavlieu, et al. 1998. "Reducing Lower Extremity Amputation due to Diabetes: Application of the Staged Diabetes Management Approach in the Primary Care Setting." *Journal of Family Practice* 47: 127–32.

Robin, Robert W., Jeffrey C. Long, Jolene K. Rasmussen, Bernard Albaugh, and David Goldman. 1998. "Relationship of Binge Drinking to Alcohol Dependence, Other Psychiatric Disorders, and Behavioral Problems in an American Indian Tribe." *Alcoholism: Clinical and Experimental Research* 22: 518–23.

Rodenhauser, Paul. 1994. "Cultural Barriers to Mental Health Care Delivery in Alaska." *The Journal of Mental Health Administration* 21 (1): 60–70.

Roman, Sarah Poff, Lori L. Jervis, and Spero M. Manson. 2012. "Psychology of Older American Indians and Alaska Natives: Strengths and Challenges to Maintaining Mental Health." In *Handbook of Race and Development in Mental Health,* edited by Edward C. Chang, Christina A. Downey, 1270–146. New York: Springer.

Roscoe, Robert, James Deddens, Alberto Salvan, and Teresa Schnorr.1995. "Mortality among Navajo Uranium Miners." *American Journal of Public Health* 85: 535–40.

Rose, Mark E., and Cheryle J. Cherpital. 2011. *Alcohol: Its History, Pharmacology, and Treatment.* Hazelden, MN: Hazelden Foundation.

Rosenberg, Roger N., Ralph W. Richter, Richard C. Risser, Kevin Taubman, Ivette Prado-Farmer, Eleanor Ebalo, Joanne Posey, David Kingfisher, David Dean, Myron F. Weiner, Dorris Svetlik, Perrie Adams, C. Munro Cullum, Frederick V. Schaefer, and Gerard D. Schellenberg. 1996. "Genetic Factors for the Development of Alzheimer Disease in the Cherokee Indian." *Archives of Neurology* 54 (10): 997–1000.

Ross, Luna 1998. *Inventing the Savage.* Austin: University of Texas Press.

Roubidoux, Marilyn A. 2012. "Breast Cancer and Screening in American Indian and Alaska Native Women." *Journal of Cancer Education* 7 (1): 66–72.

Roubideaux, Yvette, and Mim Dixon. 2001. "Health Surveillance, Research, and Information." In *Promises to Keep,* Edited by Mim Dixon and Yvette Roubideaux. Washington, D.C.: American Public Health Association.

Roy, Bernard. 2006. "Diabetes and Identity: Changes in the Food Habits of the Innu—A Critical Look at Health Professionals' Interventions Regarding Diet." In *Indigenous Peoples and Diabetes: Community Empowerment and Wellness,* edited by Marianna L. Ferreira and Gretchen C. Lang, 167–86. Durham, NC: Carolina Academic Press.

Rowell, Ronald, and Paul Bouey. 1997. "Update on HIV/AIDS Among American Indian/Alaska Natives." *The IHS Primary Care Provider* 22.

Rutman S., A. Park, M. Castor, M. Taualii, and R. M. Forquera. 2008. "Urban American Indian and Alaska Native Youth: Youth Risk Behavior Survey 1997–2003." *Maternal and Child Health Journal* 12 (S1): S76–S81.

Sarche, M., and P. Spicer. 2008. "Poverty and Health Disparities for American Indian and Alaska Native Children: Current Knowledge and Future Prospects." *Annals of the New York Academy of Science.* http://www.ncbi.nlm.nih.gov/pmc/articles/PMC2567901/ [accessed Aug. 1, 2012].

Scheper-Hughes, Nancy. 2006. "Forward: Diabetes and Genocide—Beyond the Thrifty Gene." In *Indigenous Peoples and Diabetes: Community Empowerment and Wellness,* edited by Marianna L. Ferreira and Gretchen C. Lang, xvii–xxi. Durham: Carolina Academic Press.

Schell, L. M., and M. V. Gallo. 2012. "Overweight and Obesity among North American Indian Infants, Children, and Youth." *American Journal of Human Biology* 24: 302–13.

Schell, Lawrence, Mia Gallo, Julia Ravenscroft, and Anthony DeCaprio. 2009. "Persistent Organic Pollutants and Anti-Thyroid Peroxidase Levels in Akwesasne Mohawk Young Adults." *Environmental Research* 109: 86–92.

Schell, Lawrence, Mia Gallo, Anthony DeCaprio, Lech Hubicki, Melinda Denham, Julia Ravenscroft, and The Akwesasne Task Force on the Environment. 2004. "Thyroid Function in Relation to Burden of Polychlorinated Biphenyls (PCB's), p,p'-DDE, HCB, Mirex, and Lead among Akwesasne Mohawk Youth: A Preliminary Study." *Environmental Toxicology and Pharmacology* 18: 91–99.

Schell, Lawrence, Lech Hubicki, Anthony DeCaprio, Mia Gallo, Julia Ravenscroft, Alice Tarbell, Agnes Jacobs, Dawn David, Priscilla Worswick, and The Akwesasne Task Force on the Environment. 2003. "Organochlorines, Lead, and Mercury in Akwesasne Mohawk Youth." *Environmental Health Perspective* 111: 954–61.

Scheper-Hughes, Nancy. 2006. "Forward: Diabetes and Genocide—Beyond the Thrifty Gene." In *Indigenous Peoples and Diabetes: Community Empowerment and Wellness,* edited by Marianna L. Ferreira and Gretchen C. Lang, xvii–xxi. Durham: Carolina Academic Press.

Schmidt, Charles W. 2001. "Indi-GENE-ous Conflicts." *Environmental Health Perspectives* 109 (5): A216–A219.

Schulz, L. O. 1999. "Traditional Environment Protects Against Diabetes in Pima Indians." *Healthy Weight Journal* 13 (5): 68–70.

Shields, L., W. Wiese, B. Skipper, B. Charley, L. Banally. 1992. "Navajo Birth Outcomes in the Shiprock Uranium Mining Area." *Health Physics* 63: 542–51.

Shore, J. H., S. M. Manson, J. D. Bloom, G. Keepers, and G. Neligh. 1987. "A Pilot Study of Depression among American Indian Patients with Research Diagnostic Criteria." *American Indian and Alaska Native Mental Health Research* 1: 4–15.

Sievers, M.L. 1977. "Historical Overview of Hypertension among American Indians and Alaska Natives." *Arizona Medicine* XXXIV: 607–10.

Slaton, Elaine. 2000. "Offering Technical Assistance to Native Families: Clues from a Focus Group." Federation of Families for Children's Mental Health.

Smith, Andrea. 2005. *Conquest: Sexual Violence and American Indian Genocide.* Cambridge, MA: South End Press.

Smith-Morris, Carolyn. 2005. "Diagnostic Controversy: Gestational Diabetes and the Meaning of Risk for Pima Indian Women." *Medical Anthropology* 24: 145–177.

Smith-Morris, Carolyn. 2006. *Diabetes among the Pima: Stories of Survival.* Tucson: The University of Arizona Press.

Spicer, Paul. 2001. "Culture and the Restoration of Self among Former American Indian Drinkers." *Social Science and Medicine* 53 (2): 227–40.

Spicer, P., and K. Moore. 2007. "Responding to the Epidemic of American Indian and Alaska Native Childhood Obesity." In *Obesity in America. Volume 2:*

Development and Prevention, edited by Hiram E. Fitzgerald and Vasiliki Mousouli, 143–66. Westport, CT: Praeger Publishers.

Spicer, P., and M. C. Sarche. 2012. "Poverty and Possibility in the Lives of American Indian and Alaska Native Children and Families." In *The Oxford Handbook of Poverty and Child Development,* 480–88. Oxford: Oxford University Press.

Spicer P., D. S. Bigfoot, B. Funderburk, and D. K. Novins. 2012. "Evidence-Based Practice and Early Childhood Intervention in American Indian and Alaska Native Communities." *Zero To Three* 32 (4): 19–24.

Spicer, Paul, Janette Beals, Calvin D. Croy, Christina M. Mitchell, Douglas K. Novins, Laurie Moore, Spero M. Manson, and the AI-SUPERPFP team. 2003. "The Prevalence of DSM-III-R Alcohol Dependence in Two American Indian Populations." *Alcoholism: Clinical and Experimental Research* 27 (11): 1785–97.

Spillane, Nichea S., and Gregory T. Smith. 2007. "A Theory of Reservation-dwelling American Indian Alcohol Use Risk." *Psychological Bulletin* 133 (3): 395–418.

Stillwater, Barbara. 2001. "Major Health Issues among Female Alaska Natives." *Wicazo Sa Review* 16: 113–23.

Stevens J., M. Story, K. Ring, D. M. Murray, C. E. Cornell, Juhaeri, et al. 2003. "The Impact of the Pathways Intervention on Psychosocial Variables Related to Diet and Physical Activity in American Indian Schoolchildren. *Journal of Preventive Medicine* 37 (1): S70–S79.

Story, M., K. M. Kaphingst, R. Robinson-O'Brien, and K. Glanz. 2008. "Creating Healthy Food and Eating Environments: Policy and Environmental Approaches. *Annual Review of Public Health* 29: 253–72.

Story, Mary, Karen F. Strauss, Tim J. Gilbert, and Brenda A. Broussard. 2000. "Nutritional Health and Diet-Related Conditions." In *American Indian Health: Innovations in Health Care, Promotion, and Policy,* edited by Everett R. Rhoades, 201–220. Baltimore: The John Hopkins University Press.

Stringhini, S., A. G. Tabak, T. N. Akbaraly, S. Sabia, M. J. Shipley, M. G. Marmot, E. J. Brunner, G. D. Batty, P. Bovet, M. Kivimäki. 2012. "Contribution of Modifiable Risk Factors to Social Inequalities in Type 2 Diabetes: Prospective Whitehall II Cohort Study." *British Medical Journal* 345: e5452 DOI: 10.1136/bmj.e5452.

Sukdolová, V., S. Negoita, L. Hubicki, A. DeCaprio, D. Carpenter. 2000. "The Assessment of Risk to Acquired Hypothyroidism from Exposure to PCBs: a Study among Akwesasne Mohawk Women." *Central European Journal of Public Health* 8: 167–68.

Sundwall, David. 1987. "Advances in Indian Health Care." *Public Health Reports* 102: 349–51.

Szathmary, Emoke J. E. 1994. "Non-Insulin Dependent Diabetes Mellitus Among Aboriginal North Americans." *Annual Review of Anthropology* 23: 457–484.

Tamashiro, K. L. K. 2012. "Metabolic Syndrome: Links to Social Stress and Socioeconomic Status." *Annals of the New York Academy of Sciences* 1231: 46–55.

Tayal, Upasana. 2003. "Report Shows Health Disparities In American Indians and Alaska Natives." *BMJ: British Medical Journal* 327 (7410): 305.

Taylor, W. C., W. S. C. Poston, L. Jones, and M. K. Kraft. 2006. "Environmental Justice: Obesity, Physical Activity, and Healthy Eating." *Journal of Physical Activity and Health* 3, Suppl 1: S30–S54.

Thomas, S. L., and D. Cook. 2005. Breastfeeding Duration and Prevalence of Overweight among 4- and 5-Year Olds." *The IHS Primary Care Provider* 30 (4): 100–2.

Thornton, Russell. 1986. *We Shall Live Again: The 1870 and 1890 Ghost Dance Movements as Demographic Revitalization.* New York: Cambridge University Press.

Thornton, Russell. 1987. *Indian Holocaust and Survival: A Population History Since 1492.* Norman: University of Oklahoma Press.

Tome-Orne, Lillian. 1994. "Traditional Beliefs and Attitudes about Diabetes among the Navajos and Utes." In *Diabetes as a Disease of Civilization: The Impact of Culture Change on Indigenous Peoples,* edited by Jennie R. Joe and Robert S. Young, 271–91. New York: Mouton de Gruyter.

Townsend, J. A. 1938. "Disease and the Indian." *The Scientific Monthly* 47: 479–495.

Urizar, G. G., and R. F. Munoz. 2011. "Impact of a Prenatal Cognitive-Behavioral Stress Management Intervention on Salivary Cortisol Levels in Low-Income Mothers and Their Infants." *Psychoneuroendocrinology* 36 (10): 1480–94.

Verano, John W., and Douglas H. Ubelaker, ed. 1992. *Disease and Demography in the Americas.* Washington, D. C.: Smithsonian Institution Press.

Vernon, Irene. 2002a. *Killing Us Quietly: Native Americans and HIV/AIDS.* Lincoln: University of Nebraska Press.

Vernon, Irene. 2002b. "Violence, HIV/AIDS, and Native American Women in the Twenty-First Century." *American Indian Culture and Research Journal* 26: 115–33.

Vernon, Irene S., and Roe Bubar. 2001. "Child Sexual Abuse and HIV/Aids in Indian Country." *Wicazo Sa Review* 16: 47–63.

Vernon, Irene, and Pamela Jumper-Thurman. 2005. "The Changing Face of HIV/AIDS Among Native Populations." *Journal of Psychoactive Drugs* 37: 247–55.

Waller, Margaret A., Scott K. Okamoto, Bart W. Miles, and Donna E. Hurdle. 2003. "Resiliency Factors Related to Substance Abuse/Resistance: Perceptions of Native Adolescents of the Southwest." *Journal of Sociology and Social Welfare* 30: 79–94.

Walters, Karina L., and Jane M. Simoni. 2002. "Reconceptualizing Native Women's Health: An Indigenist Stress-Coping Model." *American Journal of Public Health* 92 (4): 520–24.

Warne, Donald, Judith Kaur, and David Perdue. 2012. "American Indian/Alaska Native Cancer Policy: Systemic Approaches to Reducing Cancer Disparities." *Journal of Cancer Education* 27 (1): 18–23.

Weaver, Hilary. 2010. "Native Americans and Cancer Risks: Moving toward Multifaceted Solutions." *Social Work in Public Health* 25: 272–85.

Weibel-Orlando, Joan. 1984. "Substance Abuse among Native American Youth; A Continuing Crisis." *Journal of Drug Issues* 14: 313–33.

Weiner, Diane. 1999. "Ethnogenetics: Interpreting Ideas about Diabetes and Inheritance." *American Indian Culture and Research Journal* 23 (3): 155–84.

Weiner, Diane. 2001. "Interpreting Ideas about Diabetes, Genetics, and Inheritance." *Medicine Ways: Disease, Health, and Survival Among Native Americans,* edited by Clifford E. Trafzer and Diane Weiner, 108–33. Walnut Creek, CA: AltaMira Press.

Weiss, K. M., A. V. Buchanan, R. Valdez, J. H. Moore, and J. Campbell, 1993 "Amerindians and the Price of Modernisation," In *Urban Ecology and Health in the Third World,* edited by L. M. Schell, Malcolm T. Smith, and Alan Bilsborough. Society for the Study of Human Biology Symposium Series, 32. New York: Cambridge University Press, 221–43.

Weiss, Kenneth M., Jan S. Ulbrecht, Peter R. Cavanagh, and Anne V. Buchanan, 1989 "Diabetes Mellitus in American Indians: Characteristics, Origins and Preventive Health Care Implications," *Medical Anthropology* 11 (3): 283–304.

West, K. M., 1974 "Diabetes in American Indians and Other Native Populations of the New World," *Diabetes.* 23: 841–55.

West, K. M. 1978 "Diabetes in American Indians." *Advanced Metabolic Disorders* 9: 29–48.

Westlake Van Winkle, Nancy and May, Philip, 1986. "Native American Suicide in New Mexico, 1957–1979: A Comparative Study." *Human Organization* 45 (4): 296–309.

Whitt, Laurelyn, 2009 *Science, Colonialism, and Indigenous Peoples: The Cultural Politics of Law and Knowledge.* New York: Cambridge University Press.

Whitworth, M. and T. Dowswell. 2009. "Routine Pre-Pregnancy Health Promotion for Improving Pregnancy Outcomes." Cochrane Database of Systematic Reviews 2009, Issue 4. Ar.t: CD007536. DOI: 10.1002/14651858.CD007536.pub2.

Wiedman, Dennis. 2006. "Striving for Healthy Lifestyles: Contributions of Anthropologists to the Challenge of Diabetes in Indigenous Communities." In *Indigenous Peoples and Diabetes: Community Empowerment and Wellness,* edited by Marianna L. Ferreira and Gretchen C. Lang, 511–34. Durham, NC: Carolina Academic Press.

Wiggins, C. L., D. K. Espey, P. A.Wingo, J. S. Kaur, R. T. Wilson, J. Swan, B. A. Miller, M. A. Jim, J. J. Kelly, and A. P. Lanier. 2008. "Cancer among American Indians and Alaska Natives in the United States, 1999–2004." *Cancer* 113: 1142–52.

Wilson, Robert, Carol Graham, Karman G. Booth, and Dorothy Gohdes. 1994. "Community Approaches to Diabetes Prevention." In *Diabetes as a Disease of Civilization: The Impact of Culture Change on Indigenous Peoples,* edited by Jennie R. Joe and Robert S. Young, 495–503. New York: Mouton de Gruyter.

Young, Robert S., and Jennie R. Joe. 2009. "Some Thoughts about the Epidemiology of Alcohol and Drug Use among American Indian/Alaska Native Populations." *Journal of Ethnicity in Substance Abuse* 8: 223–41.

Young, Thomas J. 1992. "Native Americans and Substance Abuse." In *Handbook for Assessing and Treating Addictive Disorders,* edited by Chris Stout, John Levitt, and Douglas Ruben, 203–13. Westport, CT: Greenwood Press.

Young, T. Kue. 1993. "Diabetes Mellitus among Native Americans in Canada and the United States: An Epidemiological Review." *American Journal of Human Biology* 5: 399–413.

Young, T. Kue. 1994. *The Health of Native Americans: Towards a Biocultural Epidemiology.* New York: Oxford University Press.

Young, T. Kue. 1997. "Recent Health Trends in the Native American Population." *Population Research and Policy Review* 16 (1/2): 147–67.

Zechetmayr, M., 1997 "Native Americans: A Neglected Health Care Crisis and a Solution." *Journal of Health and Social Policy* 9 (2): 29–47.

Zephier, E., J. H. Himes, M. Story, et al. 2006. Increasing Prevalences of Overweight and Obesity in Northern Plains American Indian Children." *Archives of Pediatrics & Adolescent Medicine* 160 (1): 34–39.

SECTION V

Work and Society

Introduction to Work and Society in American Indian Communities

Jeffrey Ian Ross

What do human beings do most of the time? Work. Typically, work is boring and unfulfilling, but it is intended to provide the essentials for life. Hopefully, it pays the bills and provides enough for people to afford shelter and put food on the table. In today's society, in order to get well-earning work, one needs appropriate education and training. This is the same for white society, as it is for Native Peoples. The widespread changes associated with moving from a traditional subsistence society, in which American Indians were typically hunters, trappers, fisherman, and to a lesser extent, farmers, to a culture that was disproportionately agrarian to one that focused on manufacturing and is now primarily service-oriented must be appreciated. This dynamic process has been in force from the time of European contact to the present day. Work is related to numerous processes in American Indian communities, including housing, employment, education, economic development, and political participation.

Due to a combination of circumstances, American Indians have faced discrimination in employment-related areas (Anderson 1980; Smith 2011). A considerable amount of legal scholarship has examined this challenge (Baca 2005; Knack and Littlefield 1996). Some of this research has looked at employment-related issues, especially the distribution of American Indians in state and local government bureaucracies (e.g., Hunt, Brinck, Ketcher, and Murphy 2010) and preferential hiring programs for American Indians (e.g. Gamino 1974; Ono 2011).

Numerous critical issues affect the housing of American Indians (e.g., Ingram 1998). Some related studies have examined home ownership by American Indians (e.g., Ingram 1998), while other scholarship has analyzed the relocation of Native tribes (e.g., Lamore-Choate 2002; Moisa 1998). American Indians have faced serious challenges in procuring appropriate housing (Cortelyou 2001). Some scholars have focused on how the federal government has dealt with this problem (Davis 2002).

In order to improve one's economic and social status, achieving a formal education is important to all races, ethnicities, and both genders. A considerable amount of scholarship has been devoted to analyzing the provision and improvement of educational services in American Indian communities (e.g., Deyhle and Swisher 1997; Fuchs and Havighurst 1972; Latham 1989; Lomawaima 1995; Radda, Iwamoto, and Patrick 1998; Huffman 2010; Reyhner 2006, 2010; Reyhner and Hurtado 2008; Reyhner and Eder 2004). The integration of indigenous/culturally appropriate education into the school curriculum has been the focus of an array of studies (Barnhardt 2007; Brayboy and Castagno 2009; Castagno and Brayboy 2008; Coggins, Williams, and Radin 1997). Various initiatives have also examined the failed residential schools experiment (e.g., Adams, 1995; Barrett, 2004) and the critical American Indian dropout rate (e.g., Brandt 1992; Deyhle 1992).

Ever since the westward push, there has been phenomenal competition over the ownership of land and natural resources. American Indians have been at the short end of the stick in these struggles (Banerjee 2009). Some scholarly treatments of this subject are general in nature, while others have looked at specific issues (e.g., Cheyfitz 2000). Some of this research has concentrated on economic development in particular (e.g., Harvard Project on American Indian Economic Development 2008; Riggs 2000).

Given the impoverished nature of many reservations, there has been a big push to achieve sovereignty and implement direct economic development on reservations, while at the same time protecting the natural resources for future generations and not creating environmental hazards (Cornell and Kalt 2007; Smith 2000). In order to improve the economic climate in Indian Country, some reservations have experimented with operating or leasing gambling operations (e.g., Peroff 2006; Schaap 2010).

Finally, since the mid-1960s, American Indians have not remained idle. They have stepped up to the plate and been involved in numerous attempts to achieve increased political participation and power (Cornell 1988; Johnson, Nagel, and Champagne 1997; Johnson 2008; McCool, Olson, and Robinson 2007; McDonald 2010; Nagel 1996; Oeser 2010; Wilkins and Stark 2005; Smith and Warrior 1996). A number of important political texts have advocated increased Indian activism including Vine Deloria's classic *Custer Died for Your Sins: An Indian Manifesto* (1969/1988) and his *Behind the Trail of Broken Treaties: An Indian Declaration of Independence* (1974/1985). One of the biggest issues facing reservations has been increased pressures to achieve sovereignty (Cleveland 2002). Some studies have explored the creation/development of treaties and Native rights (Kannan 2008; Moreton-Robinson 2008; Robyn 2006), and others have reviewed land claims challenges/disputes (Leeds 2006; Von Feigenblatt 2010).

REVIEW OF THE CHAPTERS

In "Contemporary Social Pressures Facing American Indians," Kathleen O'Halleran outlines the historical challenges that Natives have faced surviving against all odds in order to be Native Americans. American Indians have constantly been placed under social pressures. Starting with the colonial period, American Indians were forced to serve the interests of European powers and immigrant colonists.

The romantic image of the Indian was portrayed in Europe and projected onto the American Natives. However, when self-interests collided, the image of the "savage" was cast. As early American settlements marched west of the Mississippi River, Indians were forced onto reservation lands during a period of enforced "acculturation." By the 20th century, assimilation became the dominant trend imposed upon many tribes; reservation lands were dismantled, and tribal members in many territories targeted for white settlements were then forced to "sign the rolls" to accept individual tracts of private property that took apart reservations and collective Native American communities. Tribal languages, dances, customs, and rituals were threatened with extinction as new generations of Native American children were sent off to boarding schools and banned from practicing their Native customs. Simultaneously, in the latter half of the 20th century, some segments of the broader American society co-opted much material and nonmaterial Native American traditions, artifacts, medicine ways, and rituals. Some social critics viewed this as another form of social pressure and dominance. The counterpoint to this has been the long-standing push from within the tribes for tribal sovereignty and self-determination. Today, while tribal members continue to struggle with the multigenerational impacts of poverty and exclusion, tribal identities have in large part remained intact, and many tribes today are actually thriving, while others struggle for self-determination and social space and place. As dominant societies become more diverse, tribal identities today appear to be experiencing a period of strengthening from within. There is a resurgence of interest in elders teaching younger Natives their tribal ways, and new movements are afoot to relearn and save tribal languages. The divide between tribal progressives and traditionalists has become focused on internal self-governance and building strength from within, and now is less dominated by concerns about the onslaught of external social and political pressures.

O'Halleran, in her chapter on housing, states that historically, studies of pre-contact Indian housing have revealed diverse ways of life in collision with colonial traditions. Subsequent U.S. government agendas and policies in ensuing eras dominated the Indian removals and the establishment of reservations, and these policies forced many Native peoples into housing patterns shaped by individual allotments and home ownership. Where and how Native peoples in the United States would peacefully reorganize their tribal communities was supposedly settled a century ago. Yet, their actual living conditions since then have been abysmally underreported. Recent investigations demonstrate that lack of access to safe, affordable, and sufficient housing remains a pervasive threat to the stability of Native people today. In fact, living conditions for Native Americans are among the worst in the nation. In Indian Country, Native peoples are 10 times more likely to live in homes without plumbing than other Americans. The cost of amenities that most Americans take for granted, such as paved streets, electricity, sewers, and landfills, prevents the construction of new homes. High poverty rates also exacerbate housing conditions in Indian Country. Forty percent of Native American housing is substandard, and 33 percent of reservation homes are overcrowded at a rate more than five times the national average. The National American Indian Housing Council (NAIHC) links higher rates of exposure to infectious disease, social problems including domestic violence and alcoholism, child abuse, child neglect, and lower educational attainment to substandard and overcrowded housing on Native lands. Poverty rates, in some pockets of Indian Country as high as 56 percent, present the most significant barriers to affordable home ownership or home rental on Native lands. Isolation and remoteness also prevent access to all but a few lending institutions that have limited loan assets. Subprime lending practices reign over this market niche at a rate of almost 25 percent and are more common than in other areas without dominant Native populations. Legal barriers and complications include an often complex site approval process for housing development. In addition to environmental and archaeological investigations, both Indians and non-Indians involved in such housing transactions are often stymied by the complicated processes and multiple players involved in lending on land held in trust by the U.S. government for Native Americans. Cultural considerations for housing must meet conventional lending and inspection approval processes, as well. At a time when the recovering Native population in the United States has risen from 250,000 in 1950 to more than 2.1 million today, many sources are optimistic that the multiple, negative legacies of land contestation between Native peoples and the rest of the country have run their course. Conversely, the immediacy of the housing crisis in Indian Country belies this sanguinity. Federal and tribal reforms are underway because of renewed investigation into housing conditions for Native peoples. Preliminary findings suggest limited success from the block grants made available to tribal communities through the 1998 Native American Housing Assistance and Self Determination Act; from the public-private partnerships; and most recently, from the innovative development programs organized and coordinated by the tribes themselves. Presently, however, housing remains an issue that is simultaneously very personal and culturally critical to the cohesiveness of Native communities and the sustainability of tribal cultures.

The third chapter in this section, "Improving American Indian Education through Best Practices," is authored by Jon Reyhner. He outlines how historically, schooling for American Indians has focused on "civilizing" them through the teaching of English, Christianity, and the three "Rs," sometimes in boarding schools far removed from the students' homes. While a few individuals questioned this assimilationist approach, it still remains the focus of Indian education today, though now most American Indians speak English and it is no longer seen as appropriate to teach religion in schools. The 1928 Meriam Report questioned putting young children in boarding schools and the cultural insensitivity of the educational system in general. This questioning was renewed in the 1960s with the Civil Rights Movement and coincided with United Nations human rights concerns, which led to a renewed questioning of this assimilationist approach. A National Study of Indian Education and hearings before the Senate Subcommittee on Indian Affairs at that time found serious shortcomings in Indian education. In 1991, the U.S. Secretary of Education's Indian Nations at Risk (INAR) Task Force called for more culturally sensitive education, but the 2009 report of the National Indian Education Study still showed a persistent lag in achievement by American Indian students. The co-chair of the INAR Task Force, Bill Demmert, worked hard to develop strong, culturally based educational approaches; however, the No Child Left Behind Act of 2001 and the current "Race to the Top" program are one-size-fits-all approaches to education that are carrying the day because of the current "revolving-door" leadership in both the Bureau of Indian Education and the Indian programs of the U.S. Department of Education. These have resulted in little progress in the development of any kind of unique culturally and linguistically appropriate educational programs for American Indians. There are two major approaches to the education of ethnic minority students in the United States today. One is a "blame the victim" approach that focuses on a deficit idea that American Indian families and communities are not doing enough to prepare their children for educational success. The second approach is a "blame the oppressor" approach that looks at racism and cultural insensitivity in the U.S. educational system.

Next, Yuka Mizutani, in her chapter "Native American Employment and Unemployment Issues," reviews how Native American people have been a part of a monetary economy since the arrival of the European settlers. In early times, the Natives worked for industries, such as agriculture, railroad construction, and mining. Then, the establishment of boarding schools by the federal government, as well as the urban relocation program from the 1950s to 1980s, greatly impacted Native American peoples' employment situation. These systems pushed more Native American people into the wage laborer status with varying degrees of success. Many Native American laborers have been underpaid, and many of them suffer from unemployment and poverty. In the reservation setting, tribal enterprises, such as casinos and hotels, are the main employers. Even people other than Native Americans are hired by these enterprises. In this chapter, the Native American peoples' current and historical relationships as both employee and employer are described.

This chapter is followed by "Rationally Designed to Further Indian Self-Government: American Indians and Affirmative Action" by D Anthony Clark. He begins by reviewing the importance of the Indian Reorganization Act of 1934, which authorized Indian preference for jobs in the Bureau of Indian Affairs (BIA). Since 1934 and well into the 21st century, Clark suggests, Indian preference in the BIA

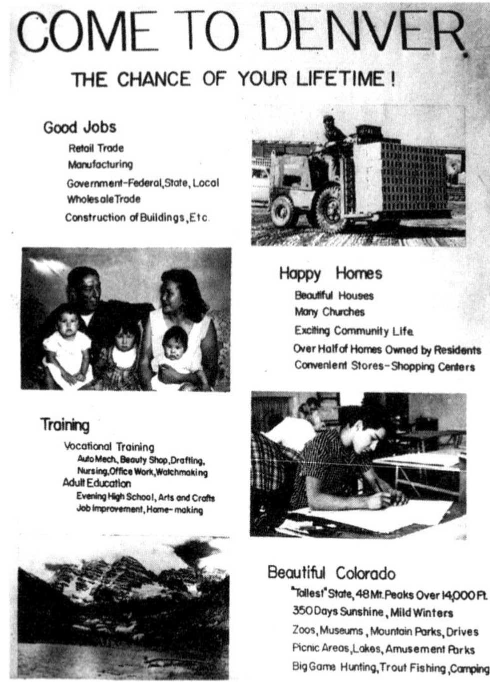

An advertisement designed to encourage Native Americans to leave their reservations and move to urban areas where there would be more opportunities for education and employment in 1953 (Getty Images)

and Indian Health Service combined with affirmative action policies for individual Indians in education, private- and public-sector employment, and housing have made available shared social resources to previously excluded individuals, resulting in the destabilization of tribal sovereigns. In a separate section focused on the contemporary context of attacks on preferential treatment for individual Indians, anti-tribal sovereignty and anti-affirmative action forces, Clark suggests that outlasting these coordinated strikes has had consequences for Indians and others, and he outlines strategies for surviving these assaults on Indian Country. The chapter concludes with a debate on Indian preference.

In "Gambling: A Blessing and a Curse," Bruce Johansen reviews the current status of commercial gambling on American Indian reservations. Through a combination of enabling state and federal legislation, many tribes have staked their economic success and survival to the introduction of gaming operations. A number of examples (i.e., Oneidas, Muckleshoots, and Chukchansi) of this strategy are reviewed. Johansen looks at some of the unintended consequences of the introduction of gaming to reservations, including inequality and conflicts over leadership, as well as the funding of new housing, health centers, and other infrastructure.

Finally in "Time for a New Paradigm for American Indian Policy and Law?" legal scholar James W. Zion suggests that because of the waning utility and breaches of numerous treaties between the U.S. federal government and American Indian tribes, the time has come for radically different laws and policies related to American Indians. Zion traces the history of this challenge back to original documents that established the federal government's role in the lives of the people it first contacted. The chapter begins by outlining the relevance of the Articles of Confederation and the U.S. Constitution, and then focuses on the numerous lobbying organizations that were established to protect American Indians.

CONCLUSION

Only when American Indians can successfully establish more control over their education, employment, housing, economic development, and their resources (natural or otherwise) will they be able to collectively improve their situation. This movement is taking place in the United States, but it is slow and resource intensive. American Indians have made terrific gains over the years, but for most, these are not quick enough.

References

Adams, David. W. 1995. *Education for Extinction: American Indians and the Boarding School Experience, 1875–1928.* Lawrence: University Press of Kansas.

Anderson, K. N. 1980. Indian Employment Preference: Legal Foundations and Limitations." *Tulsa Law Journal* 15: 733–71.

Baca, L. R. 2005. "American Indians, the Racial Surprise in the 1964 Civil Rights Act: They May, More Correctly, Perhaps, Be Denominated a Political Group." *Howard Law Journal* 48 (3): 971–97.

Banerjee, Subhankar. 2009. "Terra Incognita: Communities and Resource Wars." In *The Alaska Native Reader: History, Culture, Politics,* edited by Maria Shaa Tláa Williams, 184–91. Durham, NC: Duke University Press.

Barnhardt, R. 2007. "Creating a Place for Indigenous Knowledge in Education: The Alaska Native Knowledge Network." In *Place-based Education in the Global Age: Local Diversity,* edited by G. Smith and D. A. Gruenewald, 113–33. Hillsdale, NJ: Lawrence Erlbaum Associates.

Barrett, Carole A. 2004. "Boarding and Residential Schools." In *American Indian Culture,* edited by Carole A. Barrett and Harvey J. Markowitz, 138–42. Pasadena, CA: Salem Press, Inc.

Brandt, Elizabeth A. 1992. "The Navajo Area Student Dropout Study: Findings and Implications." *Journal of American Indian Education* 31 (2): 48–63.

Brayboy, Bryan M. J., and Angelina E. Castagno. 2009. Self-determination through Self-Education: Culturally Responsive Schooling for Indigenous Students in the USA." *Teaching Education* 201: 31–53.

Castagno, Angelina E., and Bryan M. J. Brayboy. 2008. "Culturally Responsive Schooling for Indigenous Youth: A Review of the Literature." *Review of Educational Research* 78: 941–93.

Cheyfitz, Eric. 2000. "The Navajo-Hopi Land Dispute: A Brief History." *Interventions* 2 (2): 248–75.

Cleveland, Sarah H. 2002. "Powers Inherent in Sovereignty: Indians, Aliens, Territories, and the Nineteenth Century Origins of Plenary Power over Foreign Affairs." *Texas Law Review* 81 (1): 3–42.

Coggins, Kip, Edith Williams, and Norma Radin. 1997. "The Traditional Tribal Values of Ojibwa Parents and the School Performance of Their Children: An Exploratory Study." *Journal of American Indian Education* 36 (3): 1–15.

Cornell, Stephen. 1988. *The Return of the Native: American Indian Political Resurgence.* New York: Oxford University Press.

Cornell, Stephen, and Joseph P. Kalt. 2007. "Two Approaches to the Development of Native Nations: One Works, the Other Doesn't." In *Rebuilding Native Nations,* edited by Miriam Jorgensen, 3–33. Tucson: University of Arizona Press.

Cortelyou, George H. 2001. "An Attempted Revolution in Native American Housing: The Native American Housing Assistance and Self-Determination Act." *Seton Hall Legislative Journal* 25: 429–66.

Davis, Virginia. 2002. "A Discovery of Sorts: Reexamining the Origins of Federal Indian Housing Obligations." *Harvard Blackletter Law Journal* 18: 211–39.

Deyhle, Donna. 1992. "Constructing Failure and Maintaining Cultural Identity: Navajo and Ute School Leavers." *Journal of American Indian Education* 31 (2): 24–47.

Deyhle, Donna, and Karen Swisher. 1997. "Research in American Indian and Alaska Native Education: From Assimilation to Self-Determination." In *Review of Research in Education,* edited by Michael W. Apple, vol. 22, 113–94. Washington, D.C.: American Educational Research Association.

Fuchs, Estelle, and Robert J. Havighurst. 1972. *To Live on This Earth: American Indian Education.* Garden City, NY: Doubleday.

Gamino, J. 1974. "Bureau of Indian Affairs: Should Indians Be Preferentially Employed?" *American Indian Law Review* 2: 111–18.

Harvard Project on American Indian Economic Development. 2008. *The State of the Native Nations: Conditions under U.S. Policies of Self-Determination.* New York: Oxford University Press.

Huffman, Terry. 2010. *Theoretical Perspectives on American Indian Education: Taking a New Look at Academic Success and the Achievement Gap.* Lanham, MD: AltaMira Press.

Hunt, Valarie H., Brinck Kerr, Linda L. Ketcher, and Jennifer Murphy. 2010. "The Forgotten Minority: An Analysis of American Indian Employment Patterns in State and Local Governments, 1991–2005." The *American Indian Quarterly* 34 (4) (Fall): 409–34.

Ingram, J. M. "Home Ownership in Indian Country." 1998. *Journal of Affordable Housing and Community Development Law* 164 (Winter): 164–86.

Johnson, Troy, Joane Nagel, and Duane Champagne, eds. 1997. *American Indian Activism: Alcatraz to the Longest Walk.* Urbana: University of Illinois Press.

Johnson, Troy R. 2008. *Red Power and Self-Determination: The American Indian Occupation of Alcatraz Island.* New ed. Urbana: University of Illinois Press.

Kannan, Phillip. 2008. "Reinstating Treaty Making with Indian Tribes." *William and Mary Bill of Rights Journal* 16 (5): 809–37.

Knack, Martha C., and Alice Littlefield. 1996. "Native American Labor: Retrieving History, Rethinking Theory." In *Native Americans and Wage Labor: Ethnohistorical Perspectives,* edited by Alice Littlefield and Martha C. Knack, 3–44. Norman: University of Oklahoma Press.

Lamore-Choate, Yvonne. 2002. "My Relocation Experience." In *Urban Voices: The Bay Area American Indian Community,* edited by Susan Lobo, 38–41. Tucson: University of Arizona Press.

Latham, Glenn I. 1989. "Thirteen Most Common Needs of American Indian Education in BIA Schools." *Journal of American Indian Education* 29 (1): 1–11.

Leeds, Stacy. 2006. "Toward Tribal Autonomy of lands." *Natural Resources Journal* 46: 439–61.

Lomawaima, K. Tsianina. 1995. "Educating Native Americans." In *Handbook of Research on Multicultural Education,* edited by James A. Banks and Cherry A. Banks, 331–42. New York: Macmillan.

McCool, D., S. M. Olson, and J. L. Robinson. 2007. *Native Vote: American Indians, the Voting Rights Act, and the Right to Vote.* New York: Cambridge University Press.

McDonald, L. 2010. *American Indians and the Fight for Equal Voting Rights.* Norman: University of Oklahoma Press.

Moisa, Ray. 2002. "Relocation: The Promise and the Lie." In *Urban Voices: The Bay Area American Indian Community,* edited by Susan Lobo, 21–27. Tucson: University of Arizona Press.

Moreton-Robinson, A. 2008. "Writing Off Treaties." In *Transnational Whiteness Matters,* edited by A. Moreton-Robinson, M. Casey, and F. Nicolle, 81–98. Lanham, MD: Lexington Books.

Nagel, Joane. 1996. *American Indian Ethnic Renewal: Red Power and the Resurgence of Identity and Culture.* Oxford: Oxford University Press.

Oeser, M. D. 2010. "Tribal Citizen Participation in State and National Politics: Welcome Wagon or Trojan Horse?" *William Mitchell Law Review* 36: 793–858.

Ono, Azusa. 2011. "The Fight for Indian Employment Preference in the Bureau of Indian Affairs: Red Power Activism in Denver, Colorado, and *Morton v. Mancari.*" *Japanese Journal of American Studies* 22: 171–91.

Peroff, Nicholas C. 2006. "Indian Gaming and the American Indian Criminal Justice System." In *Native Americans and the Criminal Justice System,* edited by Jeffrey Ian Ross and Larry Gould, 179–86. Boulder, CO: Paradigm Publishers.

Radda, Henry T, Dawn Iwamoto, and Carolyn Patrick. 1998. "Collaboration, Research and Change: Motivational Influences on American Indian Students." *Journal of American Indian Education* 17 (2): 2–20.

Reyhner, J. 2006. "Issues Facing New Native Teachers." In *The Power of Native Teachers: Language and Culture in the Classroom,* edited by David Beaulieu and Anna M. Figueira, 63–92. Tempe: Center for Indian Education, Arizona State University.

Reyhner, Jon, and Jeanne Eder. 2004. *American Indian Education: A History.* Norman: University of Oklahoma Press.

Reyhner, Jon, and Denny S. Hurtado. 2008. "Reading First, Literacy, and American Indian/Alaska Native Students." *Journal of American Indian Education* 47 (1): 82–95.

Riggs, Christopher. 2000. "American Indians, Economic Development, and Self-Determination in the 1960s." *Pacific Historical Review* 69 (3): 431–63.

Robyn, Linda. 2006. "Criminalizing of the Treaty Right to Fish." In *Native Americans and the Criminal Justice System,* edited by Jeffrey Ian Ross and Larry Gould, 161–77. Boulder: Paradigm Publishers.

Schaap, James I. 2010. "The Growth of the Native American Gaming Industry: What Has the Past Provided, and What Does the Future Hold?" *The American Indian Quarterly* 34 (3) (Summer): 365–89.

Smith, Dean Howard. 2000. *Modern Tribal Development: Paths to Self-Sufficiency and Cultural Integrity in Indian Country.* Walnut Creek, CA: AltaMira Press.

Smith, K., Jr. 2011. *Labor and Employment in Indian Country.* Boulder, CO: Native American Rights Fund.

Smith, Paul Chaat, and Robert Allen Warrior. 1996. *Like a Hurricane: The Indian Movement from Alcatraz to Wounded Knee.* New York: The New Press.

Von Feigenblatt, Otto F. 2010. "Identity and Culture: A Cultural Interpretation of the Hopi- Navajo Land Dispute." *Vivat Academia* 111: 35–47.

Wilkins, D. E., and H. K. Stark. 2005. "Indian Voters." In *The Unfinished Agenda of the Selma-Montgomery Voting Rights March,* edited by D. N. Byrne, 123–34. Hoboken, NJ: Wiley.

Contemporary Social Pressures Facing American Indians

Kathleen O'Halleran

Historic assaults upon American Indian sovereignty and sustenance, identity, and cultural ways of life by a dominant mainstream society and responses to these insults and injuries have wielded harsh shocks over time and continue to do so. Impacts take form today as social pressures that are bound up in contestations over land as well as challenges to sustenance, cultural identity, and lifeways that confront contemporary American Indians (Evans-Campbell 2008, 316). These assaults take form as social pressures that embody an accumulated legacy shaped of interaction that began with the appearance of Euro-Americans in North America in the 16th century.

Movement of Euro-American settlers ever farther west resulted by 1830 in the Indian Removal Act that sanctioned the exile of American Indians east of the Mississippi to lands in the West. From the 1820s to 1840s, in what became bitterly termed the "Trail of Tears," tribes from the Deep South were forced to march on foot to Indian Territory in Oklahoma. Propelled by the discovery of California gold in 1848, passage of the 1862 Homestead Act, and the construction of the first transcontinental railroad by 1869, white settlement then pushed through and into Indian Territory (Doyle 2007). Tribes from the southwestern U.S. were then expelled from their homelands and marched to confinement camps in what became known as "The Long Walk." Between the 1830s and 1880s, American Indians lost more than 450,000,000 acres of land, and by the 1890s most American Indians had capitulated to reservation life, under the guise of humanitarian reform and policies to "Kill the Indian, and Save the Man" (Waldman 2009, 239). Ensuing late-19th- and early-20th-century policies included political and legal assaults upon Native culture, language, and religious practices (Barrett 2004, 140).

The 1887 General Allotment Act (Dawes Act) allowed the federal government to break up reservation land into 160-acre allotments for each Indian head of household and 80-acre parcels for single Indian adults. Yet, the poor quality of allotted land and hunting restrictions destroyed tribal sustenance practices. The Curtis Act of 1898 abolished Indian Territory in Oklahoma and permitted the federal government to dissolve tribal governments that refused to comply with allotment. The 1924 Indian Citizenship Act led to limits on religious practices, and federal administrative orders also banned Indian dancing and restricted Indians to their reservations. Traditional tribal networks of kinship and familial-based support were disrupted and in many cases the passage of leadership from existing elders to younger generations fractured.

As an American Indian "New Deal" took form as the 1934 Indian Reorganization Act (IRA), some ground was regained: "For the first time, a number of provisions of the IRA provided generally for the consolidation of Indian lands into tribal ownership, or the acquisition of new lands by or for tribes or individual Indians" (Rice 2009, 576). However, the IRA standardized tribal governance through federally driven structural provisions for tribal councils, constitutions, and charters, which failed to reflect traditional American Indian leadership and consensus-style governance (Wunder and Husman 2011).

As political tides turned again, reorganization gave way to anti-Indian policy. In 1949, the Hoover Commission on the Reorganization of Government recommended termination of federal-Indian trust relationship. The aim was to quash all federal-tribal relations and to annul all Indian treaties through the liquidation of all remaining collective Indian land titles and to clear remaining reservation land for purchase and settlement by non-Indians. As a result, 109 Indian tribes were officially terminated and another 1.3 million acres of reservation land lost. The BIA initiated American Indian relocation and urbanization programs to move tribal members off reservations. "In fact, at every 10-year census from 1940–1970, the urban percentage [for American Indians] almost doubled, from seven to 13 to 28 to 45 percent" (Waldman 2009, 48). U.S. House Resolution 108 in 1953 made American Indians ordinary citizens accountable to the laws of the states, and Public Law 280 allowed selected state governments to seize jurisdiction from tribal courts over civil and criminal matters without Native American consent.

Within a few decades, a spirit of American Indian activism emerged from these new, urban Native cultural hearths. The 1964 Civil Rights Act forbade discrimination on the basis of race, national origin, or religion. Causes and legal rights of American Indians and Alaska Natives were advanced by the National Indian Youth Council, the Native American Rights Fund, and the American Indian Movement (AIM). Improvements in American Indian treatment included passage of the Indian Civil Rights Act of 1969 and the Indian Bill of Rights. The tumultuous civil rights era of the 1960s also produced radical American Indian resistance to poor economic and political conditions that reached a crescendo on and off reservations by the end of the decade.

In 1969, American Indians occupied Alcatraz, the abandoned federal penitentiary in San Francisco Harbor. To further publicize American Indian grievances, in 1972, AIM led a "Trail of Broken Treaties" march (a reference to the tragic 1838–39 "Trail of Tears"), where for a week, protestors seized and occupied the offices of the Bureau of Indian Affairs headquarters (Smith and Warrior 1996: 122–23). In 1973, the FBI clashed with a group American Indians and other protestors in an armed siege at Wounded Knee, SD, the same site where approximately 300 Sioux were massacred by the U.S. cavalry in 1890 (Dewing 2000). "The activists of 1973 provided the most sensational evidence yet of the return of Native Americans to the political arena, of their defiant claim of the right once again to make their own choices" (Cornell 1988, 4).

A group of American Indians, part of the Indians of All Tribes Inc., occupying the former prison at Alcatraz Island, stand under a sign they wrote welcoming Indian occupiers to United Indian Property on the dock of Alcatraz Island, San Fransico Bay, California, November 25, 1969. The occupiers are demanding a visit by Secretary of the Interior to discuss possession of the surplus mid-bay property. (AP Photo)

The Indian Self Determination Act of 1970 and subsequent legislation gave more control to tribal governance, greater sovereignty over Indian child welfare and adoption, and tribal operation of some BIA programs including education. Tribal self-determination has remained the official federal policy. As such, this era represents "the longest sustained period in 200 years during which the official U.S. Indian policy has not been designed to inflict systematic human rights abuses on Indians by denying their collective rights as nations and tribes" (Tullberg 2008, 65).

After congressional passage of the 1988 Indian Gaming Regulatory Act (IGRA) and the creation of the National Indian Gaming Commission, more than 220 tribes initiated gaming operations in the hopes of producing viable employment and economic development on their reservations (Waldman 2009, 282). There have been other victories, as well. The American Indian Religious Freedom Act in 1978 and its 1994 amendment strengthened Indian autonomy over worship and ritual ceremonies. In 1990, traditional cultural properties, sacred objects, and burial ground attained designation as protected resources. The Native American Language Act of 1990 and the 1992 U.S. Federal Native Language Act provided for educational self-determination and federal funding for language retention and/or rediscovery (Waldman 2009, 275).

Yet, even amidst self-determination, American Indians and Alaskan Natives have endured a mix of victories and defeats (Wilkinson 2006, 387). Alaska Natives gained mixed ground in 1971 when Congress approved the Alaska Native Claims

Settlement Act (ANCSA). Through ANSCA, the federal government denied Alaskan Native land claims and hunting and fishing rights to 365 million acres of ancestral lands. Instead, ANSCA allocated 44 million acres of public land, and provided a $962 million cash settlement that resulted in a single issue of shares to approximately 80,000 shareholders through 12 regional Alaskan Native corporations and 200 village corporations (Waldman 2009). ANSCA contained a number of flaws. Not only has the corporate model been ill-suited for Alaskan Native communal cultures and wilderness lifestyles, but also in many cases, ANSCA's economic benefits have been drained by lawsuits by village corporations over contested land and resources or have fallen into non-Native hands.

Tribal autonomy over land has become an increasingly contested and critical court issue, often with mixed results (Leeds 2006, 447). Policies that turn upon the issue of land ownership and reservation-member versus non-reservation-members muddy tribal authority and jurisdiction over territorial issues including air, land, and water pollution regulations; tax revenue; economic development; and even child welfare. "Because the federal courts have linked jurisdiction to the status of land, tribes that want to maintain regulatory and adjudicatory jurisdiction over their lands are forced to keep their lands under the supervision of the federal government" (Leeds 2006, 447). As an alternative to this and in the face of high litigation costs, tribes have sometimes opted to surrender some jurisdictional control and enter into agreements instead with state and local entities.

Overall, many social pressures and issues remain to be resolved for American Indians today. The long history of relations between American Indians with a dominant white society leaves a legacy of profound impact today that is also coupled to the contrasting pressures of continuity and change within tribal societies, and the direction of policy has begun once more to threaten tribal sovereignty and sustenance.

CONTEMPORARY SOCIAL PRESSURES

Historic assaults upon American Indian sovereignty and sustenance, identity, and cultural ways of life by a dominant mainstream society and responses to these insults and injuries wielded harsh shocks over time and continue to do so (Ross and Gould 2006). Social pressures are exacerbated by conflicts over land as well as challenges to sustenance and cultural identity that confront contemporary American Indians.

Land: Federal recognition is essential to the tribes' economic survival and sovereignty. Today the United States federal government recognizes 564 American Indian/Alaskan Native tribes that are dispersed on either American Indian reservations or Alaskan Native villages. The (Bureau of Indian Affairs) BIA has also established criteria for recognition of individuals as American Indians based upon one quarter percent of American Indian blood (blood quantum), and/or tribal membership. However, each tribe has its own requirements for membership as well, which may require as much as one-half tribal blood quantum to no blood quantum, instead demanding clearly delineated tribal lineage.

Blood quantum levels and tribal membership requirements must be stipulated in tribal constitutions approved by the BIA before federal tribal recognition can be obtained (Thornton 1996, 105). Not only has this onerous process left dozens of tribes and tribal members still awaiting federal recognition, but it has also stirred controversies among the unenrolled, including some who claim that memberships are trimmed so that the politically powerful could obtain larger portions of tribal benefits and other revenues, based upon "the eugenic notion that Native American identity was tied to blood quantum" (Sturm 2002). Denial of recognized connections to tribal lands and communities are cited as much more historically severe in the aggregate than the pragmatic loss of tribal benefits.

Reservation territories comprise just four percent of the total U.S. land area today. Native villages in Alaska are located on approximately 30 million acres of public land, while 70 million acres are designated as American Indian reservation land or held in trust. Of this total, 14 million acres are owned or controlled by non-Indians (Cornell and Kalt, 2010). In the majority of Native land claims cases, the federal government has made financial settlements with the tribes, in place of restoring land titles (Waldman 2009, 274).

According to the U.S. Census, approximately 3.3 million people in the United States are solely American Indian or solely Alaska Native; though only 1.2 million live in their villages or on their reservations. In other words, 2.1 million—approximately two-thirds of these populations—do not or no longer live on the lands designated for their tribes (Cornell and Kalt 2010). The diffusion of American Indians to urban spaces occupied by other majority populations in many ways dilutes their political power and leads to contested constituency claims. Even though many may live near their reservations, as a result of and given the wax and wane of American Indian policy, American Indian sovereignty status, land claims, and self-determination are not entirely safe: "Like a capricious coin flip, the government and the courts may decide to support either Indian sovereignty or raw political power over Indians, whichever suits their pleasure in a particular dispute" (Tullberg 2008, 68).

Since the 1990s, legislation and rulings have increasingly challenged the tribes' regulatory authority over water rights and water quality, nuclear waste storage, endangered species, hunting and fishing rights, taxation, gaming, tribal expansion of trust lands, protection and preservation of sacred lands, criminal jurisdiction, and even the legal definitions of tribal members and reservations (American Indian Policy Center 2002). Tribal apprehension over such lost ground may have played a role in the 2010 settlement of American Indian tribes' 14-year-long class action lawsuit over missing trust fund monies involving more than 300 tribal governments, an estimated 3,000 tribal accounts, and more than 300,000 individual American

Indian accounts. Total losses were estimated with interest owed to total more than $176 billion (Johansen 2007, 50). Under the Claims Resettlement Act of 2010 (i.e., the Cobell Agreement), American Indians will receive $3.4 billion, roughly 5 percent of their original monetary claim.

The trustee dilemma demonstrates the double bind of needs-based sovereignty that pressures American Indian tribes today. Tribal nations need economic resources to reestablish and stabilize sovereignty, yet these resources derive from their trust relationship with the government. Conversely, their exercise of economic power brings challenges of legitimacy and capacity to tribal sovereignty (Cattalino 2010). "Examples include federally-run, Eurocentric Indian health care, education, social service, and criminal justice systems that have always been and continue to be underfunded and poorly administered, resulting in culturally inappropriate and substandard services" (Waller et al. 2003, 79–94). Social pressures multiply when American Indian attachments to the land and challenges to sovereignty are cast in competition to the pressures of reservation poverty and the need for economic development:

> For so long, "development" and "progress" have been code words for destruction of tribal resources and culture. "Economic development" has been the supposed rationale for the taking of Reservation farmlands, forest lands, and the de-watering of the rivers. The benefit has always gone to the outsiders and newcomers. For some tribal members, "economy" and "culture" are irreconcilable opposites (Confederated Tribes of the Umatilla Indian Reservation 2009, 2).

For many American Indians and Alaska Natives, attachment to place and space are first and foremost cultural and symbolic. Instrumental, goal-oriented, and utilitarian place meanings represent a distant second in terms of attachments, according to such priorities.

Poverty: Poverty rates on American Indian reservations are nearly double the national average and have been reported as high as 30 percent in rural areas, while poverty rates for children under 5 years of age on Indian reservations are almost twice the national average. According to the American Indian Relief Council, 38 to 63 percent of American Indians living on reservations fall below this poverty line and "most rural Indian reservations are similar to conditions found in many underdeveloped nations" (Gonzales 2003, 43). Jobless rates are conservatively reported as 3 times the national average and as high as 80 percent on remote rural reservations (Probst et al. 2004, 1695–703). About half of American Indian students drop out of high school, which limits employment opportunities for large segments of tribal populations, strains tribal social structures, and impacts the stability and sustenance of their families (Orfield et al. 2004).

Poor Infrastructure: On many reservations, essential infrastructure is sorely lacking with respect to housing, telecommunications, utilities, emergency services,

Oglala children play outside a home shared with over a dozen people on the Pine Ridge Reservation in South Dakota on August 9, 2011. (Aaron Huey/National Geographic Society/Corbis)

roads, bridges, and other public works such as flood control. One out of every four tribes is without 9-1-1 service. Twelve percent of American Indian households on reservations have no electricity, and almost twice that many live without natural gas. While 94 percent of mainstream American households have phone service, only 39 percent of households on American Indian reservations do. The "digital divide" between reservation life and mainstream society is even more pronounced. "Only 22 percent of rural Indian households have cable television, 9 percent have personal computers, and less than 1 percent has Internet access" (Gonzales 2003, 48). Almost half of all reservations have no radio stations.

Lack of Adequate Transportation: Studies indicate that half of American Indians are without an automobile, 55 percent cannot access services, and 40 percent have problems securing employment because they lack transportation. Impassable roads are a tremendous socioeconomic barrier and a physical safety issue, also. "For years, a lack of transportation options has held Native Americans captive" (Boyles et al. 2006, 103). Though the BIA has recognized that a minimum of $170 million annually is required to repair and maintain BIA-owned roads and bridges, its actual appropriation requests to Congress represent 15 percent of that amount.

Two-thirds of reservation roads remain unpaved, and bridges broken. "Children are prevented from attending school, sick and injured people are prevented from reaching hospitals, and emergency responders are delayed in providing timely assistance to people in need" (Garcia and Healy 2008, 1–2). While fatal crashes nationwide declined 2.2 percent per year between 2003 and 2008, Indian reservations recorded a 52.5 percent increase in traffic deaths. More American Indian pedestrians per capita were injured and killed in traffic accidents during this period than any other ethnic or racial group in the country (Garcia and Healy 2008).

Poor Health Care: High-carbohydrate, low-nutrition diets, combined with increased inactivity from geographic isolation and unemployment contribute to a diabetes epidemic for American Indians that is 2.5 times the average rate. High dependency on federally subsidized commodities that consist of sugar, lard, flour, and cheese contribute to this outcome. Other major health problems include tuberculosis, at 533 times the national average, and fetal alcohol syndrome, which is 33 times the national average. Acquired Immune Deficiency Syndrome (AIDS) is the eighth leading cause of death for American Indians between the ages of 15 and 34 who live on or near reservations (Vernon 2001). One out of every five American Indians also suffers from significant disabilities (Ni et al. 2009). Only 22 percent of rural American Indians and Alaska Natives have insurance, contributing to infant mortality rates 24 percent higher than the national average (Probst et al. 2004; Hibbard et al. 2008). Overcrowded housing conditions, too few homes, and strained social services also strain the health and well-being of reservation members.

Limited access to Indian Health Services (the federal agency that provides health care to Native American and Alaskan Native peoples) clinics and hospitals in urban areas and a lack of specialty care Indian Health Service centers on rural reservations are significant barriers (Hawkins et al. 2004). Because only 2 percent of the annual budget allocation for IHS pays for urban health-care services, only three major cities in the United States (Anchorage, Phoenix, and Oklahoma City) have IHS hospitals or clinics (Baldwin et al. 2002). This is despite the fact that 66 percent of American Indians now live in urban areas off the reservation. Also, though 65 percent of all rural counties in the nation report insufficient numbers of health-care professionals, this figure jumps to 92 percent for rural counties with majority American Indian and Alaska Native populations (Probst et al. 2004).

Cultural traditions and characteristics surrounding well-being must also be considered. For many tribes, a significant taboo exists in terms of the discussion of harmful or negative health results, which is perceived among some members to even increase the likelihood of poor outcomes (Carrese and Rhodes 2000). Though a number of IHS facilities hire local tribe members as medical staff, the extreme shortage of medical professionals overall—much less those who are culturally competent—widens the sensitivity and effectiveness gap in medical treatment for American Indians. It also impedes their readiness to seek healthcare (Cesario 2001; Baldwin et al. 2002).

Psychosocial health issues linked to poverty include drug abuse, alcoholism, and clinical depression. According to the Indian Health Service, "One in six Indian adolescents has attempted suicide. For Indian youth between five and fourteen years old the suicide rate per capita is twice the national rate, and for those between the ages of fifteen and twenty-four it is nearly three times the national average" (Gonzales 2003, 48). An enduring history of hopelessness and distrust of government-sponsored health care are among the reasons cited as to why American Indians avoid medical treatment (Vernon 2001). One tribal member points out that traditional healing often involves participation in indigenous ritual spaces enacted or performed in designated sacred places but "consultation by community members with 'White psychiatrists' in the local Indian Health Service clinic was an open invitation to 'brainwash me forever so I can be like a Whiteman'" (Gone 2008, 369). Overall, 73 percent of American Indians report that social service agencies are not sensitive to their culture (Ni et al. 2009).

Alcohol and Substance Abuse: Approximately 20 percent of American Indian youth are considered to be at high risk for chronic alcohol abuse and lifelong dependency. These findings are linked to depression, aggression, suicide, academic distress, morbidity, and mortality rates that also disproportionately impact this population subset. In fact, the IHS finds that 3 of the top 10 leading causes of death for American Indian youth—accidents, homicides and suicides—are closely tied to alcohol abuse (Hawkins, Cummins, and Marlatt 2004).

The disenfranchisement of American Indian youth is magnified by the contemporary continuation of the historical legacies of institutionalized racism and oppression. Some psychologists term this impact as "survivor child syndrome." Identification with ancestral grief and the cumulative impact of intergenerational trauma increasingly burdens each subsequent generation (Evans-Campbell 2008). As one young American Indian describes it:

> I have this theory that grief is passed on genetically because it's there and I never knew where it came from. I think we're all inhibited by the sense of responsibility and the sense of guilt . . . we blame ourselves for our loss of tradition. I feel a sense of responsibility to undo the pain of the past. I can't separate myself from the past, the history and the trauma. It [the history] has been paralyzing to us as a group (Brave Heart and DeBruyn 1998, 72).

It is estimated that 22 percent of American Indians suffer from posttraumatic stress disorder (PTSD), while one recent study found that as many as 75 percent of American Indian adolescents in one community alone had PTSD symptoms (Brave Heart and DeBruyn 2003). Though traditional languages, time-honored educational practices, and historic spiritual customs and rituals have been long-honored as a healing balm of resilience for tribal cultures, historical oppression, and loss within these social networks have potentially impacted recovery processes.

Poor Education: Public schools still serve most American Indian students today. Inadequate funding, federal grant and contract regulations, and mandated standards curriculum limit the control tribes have over schooling. Teacher and staff turnover rates exceed 35 percent, and recent policy shifts away from cultural diversity and language retention stymie academic achievement and retention (National Education Association 2005). Statistics for 2009 show that half of American Indian and Alaska Native (AI/AN) fourth graders and 38 percent of AI/AN eighth graders failed to meet basic reading achievement levels. Failures rates for basic competency in math were even higher: 34 percent for fourth graders and 44 percent for eighth graders (United States Department of Education 2009). No statistical improvement has been recorded in math and reading for these students since these national assessments began in 2005 (United States Department of Education 2009). Meanwhile, approximately 49 percent of AI/AN students today drop out of high school, and 29 percent are without high school diplomas (Ogunwole 2006). Students have self-identified the reasons for their own high dropout rates to boredom with school, problems with other students, absenteeism, and academic failure (Reyner 2006).

Higher education for American Indians has historically paralleled experiences with public education. Because of deeply ingrained assimilation and acculturation experiences, 85 percent of tribal students who enroll at public, four-year universities do not graduate. College admission rates are the lowest in the nation for this population, while academic performance and dropout rates are the highest when compared to other ethnic groups (Grande 2004). Only 11 percent of American Indians and Alaska Natives have college degrees (Ogunwale 2006). Too often, educators fail to recognize and respond sensitively to differing degrees of assimilation and cultural variations between tribes. Other key factors often include inadequate involvement with tribal elders, parents, and community members; language barriers; and sharp differences in cultural, pedagogical, and communication strategies between Western and traditional American Indian education (Reyner 2006; Begaye 2004).

The traditional American Indian classroom "existed in the natural form and in contexts wherever children could be found. They learned through experience—by testing, exploring, learning, and trial and error" (Begaye 2004, vii). Tribal family and clan members each took responsibility for lessons within specific learning areas or disciplines, resulting in a balanced, diverse, and robust education. Recent initiatives have emerged for the recovery of AI/AN languages as the cornerstone to building tribal resilience. While approximately 1,200 indigenous languages were spoken in the Americas at the time of European contact, today only about 190 survive at all, while only 20 are still being spoken by parents to their children (Johansen 2007). Just 360,000 tribal members speak their own language. "Most of the culture is expressed in the language. Take language away from the culture and you take away its greetings, its curses, its praises, its laws, its literature, its songs, riddles, proverbs and prayers" (Johansen 2007, 4). After 1990, BIA schools were empowered to use American Indian languages as a medium of instruction (Native American Languages Act 1990). Tribal leaders retain hope that language recovery will rebuild tribal families and their communities (Johansen 2007). The resurgence of interest in AI/AN languages over the past decade appears to be linked to increased interest in reclaiming tribal heritage.

Identity and Identity Loss: Between 1960 and 1990, the number of Americans reporting an American Indian race in the U.S. Census more than tripled, and since then, the number of people claiming American Indian or Alaska Native heritage has risen much more (Cornell and Kalt 2010). The 2000 U.S. Census marked the first time in U.S. history in which citizens could declare themselves as members of more than one race. At that time, 1.9 million people claimed some AI/AN heritage, while 2.4 million identified themselves solely as AI/AN. Actual population growth as determined by births, deaths, and immigration do not account for these phenomenal increases. The present surge in Indian identity choice has multiple causes and ramifications that may not yet be clearly understood, but which are certainly debated and discussed (Dixon, Awe, and Portman 2010, 217–18). Yet with two-thirds of tribal members living in off-reservation urban areas today, the conceptualization of "Indianness" risks distancing itself from cultural hearths on reservations.

Other contested identity claims relate to "bloodmixing." Tribes set their own criteria and definitions for "Indianness" in terms of who they allow tribal roles—and there have been recent controversies. Nearly 3,000 Freedmen (former slaves of the Cherokee) who received tribal citizenship status as part of the federal government's 1866 treaty with the tribe were recently stripped of their Cherokee nation membership in a recent tribal constitutional referendum. Litigation continues in the case (Casteel 2011). Tribal trustee proceeds and federal tribal benefits are often at the heart of such tribal identity contestations.

Conversely, the imposed ascription of identity has been an enduring concern that still marginalizes American Indians and Alaska Natives today. Typically cast as the "noble vanishing Indian," the "hostile Indian," or the "degenerate Indian," such prejudicial images originated from settler attitudes aimed at removing American Indians from the place and space they occupied (Marubbio 2006, 101–39, 201). Another contemporary ascription recycles a less frequent, but historically pervasive victim stereotype of the ethnically conflicted American Indian straddling two different worlds (Marubbio 2006; Aleiss, 2005). Identity pressures materialize from symbolic stereotypes that mirror reflexive, dialectic "fears, desires, politics, conflicts, and structures of power" between the negotiated and renegotiated "selves" and "others" involved in these emerging dynamics of what it means to be and not be American Indian today (Marubbio 2006, 101–39).

CONCLUSION

American Indians and Alaskan Natives today face a myriad of social pressures, both internal and external to the reservation. Forged by an historic accumulation and interplay of events, policies, behaviors, and responses between tribal populations and a dominant white society, these cumulative interactions and situations have metastasized into profound political, environmental, economic, and cultural ills. Prevailing attitudes that have shaped policy decisions and popular opinions during much of this nation's history of interaction with American Indians and Alaskan Natives have elicited a pattern of responses and outcomes that have more often than not been harmful to the survival and well-being of tribes and their members. Over time, these social pressures have taken a myriad of forms, from land contestation, pervasive poverty, poor infrastructure and transportation, and inadequate healthcare to failures in education, alcoholism and substance abuse, and loss of cultural identity.

Amid these ongoing and multiple challenges, American Indians have endured, continuing the struggle for tribal self-determination with each policy pendulum sway. Compared to previous eras, substantial recovery has been demonstrated and claimed over the past half-century and traditional lifeways strengthened on and off tribal reservations. Though they continue to experience vulnerabilities on many fronts, American Indians and Alaskan Natives have survived eras of land removal, land allotment, and collective termination policies. The odds for recovery have been much more favorable in general, as this era of Indian self-determination has progressed. There is demonstrable evidence of progress.

Since 1978, more than 350 bills supporting tribal self-determination and in favor of related socioeconomic reforms have been backed by members of Congress. Due to some of these measures, "per capita income for American Indians on reservations has grown about three times as fast as for the United States as a whole since the early 1990s" (Kalt 2011, para.11). Yet, much more ground must be covered before the litany of problems tribes face is resolved. They are still the poorest of the nation's people, and suffer disproportionately higher rates of joblessness, poor health and suicide, school failure, and substandard living conditions. Representing just 1.5 percent of the nation's population, their political power, and realistically their political destiny is not assured.

Indeed, the question at hand today is whether the current political climate will last long enough for these social pressures and problems to resolve. Though bipartisan political support for self-determination and social policy reform characterized Capitol Hill from 1978 to 1999, there has been a definitive shift away from this position since then, particularly by Republicans who had previously been more likely than their Democratic counterparts to support such measures. A resurgence of politically conservative structural norms and values "along with U.S. court rulings limiting tribal authority over non-members and Republicans' strong showing in recent elections nationally, 'have put these policies of self-determination at considerable risk'" (Kalt 2011, Para. 6). It is likely that progress amid this haunting and all too familiar specter of policy reversal combined with continuing social challenges and pressures will require vigilance, resilience, and ongoing activism by American Indian and Alaskan Native tribes and their supporters for some time to come.

◀ FURTHER INVESTIGATIONS ▶

How might a return to tribal treaty making and the reestablishment of the tribes' sovereignty to the status of equal, independent nations benefit not only the political, social, and economic status of the tribes, but of all Americans? A seemingly innocuous rider to the United States Congressional Appropriations Bill of 1871, referred to as "Section 71," diminished tribal sovereignty and eliminated tribal rights of negotiation for positive change. This measure may have very well been unconstitutional, and as it continues to remain federal policy, threatens not only tribal autonomy, but also the structural, constitutional mechanisms designed to assure liberty for all Americans.

Section 71 held weighty implications that continue to this day. After ratification of the Constitution in 1789 and until 1871, federal Indian policy had been primarily enacted through treaty making. Presidential committees handled the detailed negotiations with each tribe. Final agreements were reviewed by the president and if approved, were sent on to the U.S. Senate for consideration and ratification. In accordance with the Constitution, prior to 1871 the only role the U.S. House played in the treaty process was to approve appropriations relevant to the specific treaties that the president and the Senate had already approved. With the highly politicized "Indian Problem" placing pressure on members of the U.S. House (directly elected by voters in their districts), the majority of its members increasingly resented their lack of input and thus, their power to respond to their constituents' concerns over federal Indian policy. Armed with their only clout, in 1871 House members sent a direct message to the Senate and the president by refusing to approve legislation for the funding needed to carry out new Indian treaties, unless the rider was approved. The Senate abdicated, and the president signed the legislation into law. Thus, after 1871, federal Indian policy was almost entirely legislated by both Houses of Congress. The relevant portion of the Section 71 text states, as follows:

> **[N]o Indian nation or tribe within the territory of the United States shall be acknowledged or recognized as an independent nation, tribe, or power with whom the United States may contract by treaty: *Provided further,* that nothing herein contained shall be construed to invalidate or impair the obligation of any**

> treaty therefore lawfully made and ratified with any such Indian nation or tribe (25 U.S.C. § 71, 1871).

Through this rider, Congress negated the power of the nation's president to make treaties (with the advice and consent of the Senate), as stipulated in Article II, Section 2, Clause 2 of the U.S. Constitution (U.S. Constitution, Art. II, § 2, cl. 2). As the courts, the legislature, and the executive branch have interpreted this rider, Congress stripped the tribes of their sovereign status, and reduced their stature to that of domestic-dependent nations: "Treaties signify sovereignty; a legal prohibition of treaty-making is a denial of it" (Kannan 2008, 811). By reducing the status of the tribes to that of domestic-dependent nations, the 1871 rider set the conditions in motion for the government to legally assume a "guardian-ward" relationship between itself and the tribes.

This policy shift, when combined with constitutional provisions related to congressional appropriations and legislative authority, in effect vested Congress with plenary power over the tribes. In the 1880s, Supreme Court decisions affirmed this notion of congressional plenary power over Indian policy. The 1886 Supreme Court ruling in *United States v. Kagama* states:

> It seems to us that this is within the competency of Congress. These Indian tribes *are* the wards of the nation. They are communities *dependent* on the United States. Dependent largely for their daily food. Dependent for their political rights. . . . From their very weakness and helplessness, so largely due to the course of dealing of the Federal Government with them and the treaties in which it has been promised, there arises the duty of protection, and with it the power (*United States v. Kagama,* 118 U.S., 1886, 375, 383–84).

The Supreme Court in 1903 officially affirmed Congress's authority to abrogate treaties with the tribes. Ensuing late-19th and early-20th-century policies included legally sanctioned political, economic, social, and cultural assaults upon the tribes, as discussed in this report. Over the long term, the 1871 rider stripped the president and the Senate of their abilities to negotiate with the tribes on any key issues. As a result, the tribes became—and remain—dependent upon the capriciousness of policy shifts and partisan sways in Congress to have their social issues addressed and their financial remedies legislated.

To date, the U.S. Supreme Court has not specifically addressed the constitutionality of the 1871 rider. Rather, the nation's high court has increasingly upheld cases that could very well serve to strengthen the premise of Section 71's unconstitutionality. In 2004, U.S. Supreme Court Justice Clarence Thomas opened the door to a consideration of the constitutionality of the 1871 rider. Even though Section 71's constitutionality was not the main thrust of the case brought before the court, Thomas recognized its profound relevance:

> Although this Act is constitutionally suspect (the Constitution vests in the President both the power to make treaties and to recognize foreign governments), it nevertheless reflects the view of the political branches that the tribes had become a purely domestic matter (Thomas, 2004, 218).

The high court has set precedents recently in other cases that, though specifically unrelated to the 1871 rider, are closely connected to questions of its constitutionality. For example, Supreme Court Justice Anthony Kennedy in both *Clinton v. City of New York* (1998) and *United States v. Lara* (2004) observed, "The political freedom guaranteed to citizens by the federal structure is a liberty both distinct from and every bit as important as those freedoms guaranteed by the Bill of Rights. The individual citizen has an enforceable right to those structural guarantees of liberty, a right which the majority ignores" (Kennedy, 2005, 214). Pertinent issues with respect to the constitutionality of Section 71are identified as follows: (1) the enumerated power of the president (and Senate) provided for in the Constitution; (2) the Constitution's checks and balances and separation of powers between the government's legislative and executive branches; (3) and the "structural guarantee" of political liberty that the Constitution's framers sought to secure through the separation of powers and checks and balances that they considered sufficiently vital to specify and allocate into the constitutional document, itself. Section 71 limits, abrogates, and threatens each of these three key instruments of liberty provided for all citizens.

Armed with various and recent, substantive Supreme Court precedents on these three key points in mind, and the Supreme Court's recognition of the profound effects of Section 71, legal leverage is mounting to challenge the 1871 limitations placed upon tribal sovereignty. Such a challenge has much broader implications, as interpreted here, and is needed to preserve the structural liberty anchored by the framers into the very architecture of the Constitution and intended for all Americans.

References

Aleiss, Angela. 2005. *Making the White Man's Indian.* Westport, CT.: Praeger Publishers.

American Indian Policy Center. 2002. *Contemporary Threats to Tribal Sovereignty from the States.* St. Paul, MN: American Indian Policy Center. http://www.airpi.org/research/st98cont_states.html [accessed May 2, 2011].

Baldwin L. M., D. C. Grossman, S. Casey, W. Hollow, J. R. Sugarman, W. L. Freeman, and L. G. Hart. 2002. "Prenatal and Infant Health among Rural and Urban American Indians/Alaska Natives." *American Journal of Public Health* 92 (9): 1491–97.

Baldwin, L. M., W. B. Hollow, S. Casey, E. H. Larson, K. Moore, E. Lewis, C. H. Andrilla, and D. C. Grossman. 2008. "Access to Specialty Health Care for Rural American Indians in Two States." *Journal of Rural Health* 24 (3): 269–78.

Barrett, Carole A. 2004. "Boarding and Residential Schools. In *American Indian Culture,* edited by Carole A. Barrett and Harvey J. Markowitz, 138–42. Pasadena, CA: Salem Press, Inc.

Begaye, Timothy. 2004. Foreword to *Red Pedagogy: Native American Social and Political Thought,* edited by Sandy Grande, vii–viii. Lanham, MD: Rowman & Littlefield.

Boyles, Benjamin, Erin Brinton, Anne Dunning, Angela Mathias, and Mark Sorrell. 2006. "Native American Transit: Current Practices, Needs, Barriers." *Transportation Research Record: Journal of the Transportation Research Board* 1956: 103–10.

Brave Heart, Maria Yellow Horse. 2003. "Historical Trauma Response among Natives and Its Relationship with Substance Abuse: A Lakota Illustration." *Journal of Psychoactive Drug* 3: 7–13.

Brave Heart, Maria Yellow Horse, and Lemyra M. DeBruyn, 1998. "The American Indian Holocaust: Healing Historical Unresolved Grief." *The Journal of the National Center* 8: 72.

Carrese, J. A., and L. A. Rhodes. 2000. "Bridging Cultural Differences in Medical Practice: The Case of Discussing Negative Information with Navajo Patients." *Journal of General Internal Medicine* 15: 92–96.

Casteel, Chris. 2011. "Cherokee Freedmen in Limbo as Legal Cases Move Slowly in Tribal and Federal Courts." *The Daily Oklahoman,* January 21.

http://newsok.com/cherokee-freedmen-in-limbo-as-legal-cases-move-slowly-in-tribal-and-federal-courts/article/3536706 [accessed April 28, 2011].

Cattalino, Jessica R. 2010. "The Double-Bind of American Indian Need-Based Sovereignty." *Cultural Anthropology* 25 (2): 235–62.

Cesario, K. 2010. "Care of the Native American Woman: Strategies for Practice, Education, and Research." *Journal of Obstetric, Gynecologic, and Neonatal Nursing* 30 (1): 13–19.

Cheyfitz, Eric. 2000. "The Navajo-Hopi Land Dispute: A Brief History." *Interventions* 2 (2): 248–75.

Churchill, Ward. 1998. "The Crucible of American Indian Identity: Native Tradition versus Colonial Imposition in Post-Conquest North America." In *Contemporary Native American Cultural Issues,* edited by Duane Champagne, 39–68. Walnut Creek, CA: AltaMira Press.

Cleveland, Sarah H. 2002. "Powers Inherent in Sovereignty: Indians, Aliens, Territories, and the Nineteenth Century Origins of Plenary Power over Foreign Affairs." *Texas Law Review* 81 (1): 3–42.

Clinton v. City of New York, 524 U.S. 417, 449–53 (1998).

Confederated Tribes of the Umatilla Indian Reservation. 2009. *Economic Sovereignty: Overall Economic Development Plan, 2010–2015.* Pendleton, OR: Department of Economic and Community Development.

Cornell, Stephen. 1988. *The Return of the Native: American Indian Political Resurgence.* New York: Oxford University Press.

Cornell, Stephen, and Joseph P Kalt. 2010. "American Indian Self-Determination: The Political Economy of a Policy That Works." Working Paper No. RWP10-043 Harvard University Kennedy School, Boston, MA.

Doyle, Susan Badger. 2007. "Civilians and the Indian Wars in the American West, 1865–90." In *Daily Lives of Civilians in Wartime Modern America: From the Indian*

Wars to Vietnam, edited by David Stephen Heidler and Jeanne Heidler, 1–34. Westport, CT: Greenwood Press.

Dewing, Rolland. 2000. *Wounded Knee II.* Sioux Falls, SD: Pine Hill Press, 1–34.

Dixon, Andrea L., Tarrell Awe, and Agahe Portman. 2011. "The Beauty of Being Native: The Nature of Native American and Alaska Native Identity Development." In *Handbook of Multicultural Counseling,* 3rd ed., edited by Joseph Ponterotto, J. Manuel Casas, Lisa A. Suzuki, and Charles M. Alexander, 217–18. Thousand Oaks, CA: Sage Publications.

Evans-Campbell, Theresa. 2008. "Historical Trauma in American Indian/Native Alaska Communities: A Multi-Level Framework for Exploring Impacts on Individuals, Families, and Communities." *Journal of Interpersonal Violence* 23 (3): 316–38.

Frommer, Frederick. 2001. "Black Hills Are Beyond Price to Sioux Culture: Despite Economic Hardship, Tribe Resists U.S. Efforts to Dissolve an 1868 Treaty for $570 million." *Los Angeles Times,* August 29. http://bellevuecollege.edu/diversitycaucus/aiff/cbe.htm#Black%20Hills [accessed April 29, 2011].

Garcia, Joe, and John C. Healy. 2008. "National Tribal Leadership Paper on Tribal Transportation policy." Paper presented at the National Congress of American Indians and the Intertribal Transportation Association Joint Task Force on Tribal Transportation, Washington, D.C.

Glatzmaier, L., M. Myers, and M. Bordogna. 2000. "American Indians' Construction of Cultural Identity." Paper presented at the annual meeting of the National Association of Native American Studies, Houston, TX.

Gone, Joseph P. 2008. "'So I Can Be Like a Whiteman': The Cultural Psychology of Space and Place in American Indian Mental Health." *Culture Psychology* 14 (3): 369–99.

Gonzales, Angelo A. 2003. "American Indians: Their Contemporary Reality and Future Trajectory." In *Challenges for Rural America in the 21st Century,* edited by David Louis Brown, Louis E., Swanson and Alan W. Barton. University Park: Pennsylvania State University: 43–56.

Grande, Sandy. 2004. *Red Pedagogy: Native American Social and Political Thought.* Lanham, MD: Rowman & Littlefield.

Hawkins, Elizabeth, Lillian H. Cummins, and Alan G. Marlatt. 2004. "Preventing Substance Abuse in American Indian and Alaska Native Youth: Promising Strategies for Healthier Communities. *Psychological Bulletin* 130 (2): 305.

Hibbard, J. H., J. Greene, E. R. Becker, D. W. Roblin, M. Painter, D. Perez, E. Burbank-Schmitt, and M. Tusler. 2008. "Is There a Potential for Reducing Racial and Ethnic Disparities in Health by Increasing Consumer Activation?" *Health Affairs* 27 (5): 1442–53.

Jackson, Deborah Davis. 2002. *Our Elders Lived It: American Indian Identity in the City.* DeKalb: Northern Illinois University Press.

Johansen, Bruce Elliott. 2007. *The Praeger Handbook on Contemporary Issues in Native America.* Santa Barbara, CA: Praeger Publishers.

K, 541 U.S. 193, 214 (2004).

Kalt, Joseph. 2011. "Native Nations: Threatening Self-Rule Policies for American Indians." *Impact* 3 (2). http://www.hks.harvard.edu/news-events/publications/impact-newsletter/archives/winter-2011/threatening-self-rule-policies-for-american-indians [accessed May 1, 2011].

Kannan, Phillip. 2008. "Reinstating Treaty Making with Indian Tribes." *William and Mary Bill of Rights Journal* 16 (5): 809–37.

Langston, Donna Hightower. 2003. "American Indian Women's Activism in the 1960s and 1970s." *Hypatia* 18 (2): 114–32.

Leeds, Stacy. 2006. "Toward Tribal Autonomy of Lands." *Natural Resources Journal* 46: 439–461.

Lobo, Susan, and Kurt Peters, eds. 2001. *American Indians and the Urban Experience.* Walnut Creek, CA: AltaMira Press.

Marubbio, M. Elise. 2006. *Killing the Indian Maiden.* Lexington: University Press of Kentucky.

Native American Languages Act of 1990, 104, 25 U.S.C. 2901–2906, 1990.

National American Indian Housing Council. 2001. *Too Few Rooms: Residential Crowding in Native American Communities and Alaska Native Villages.* Washington, D.C.: National American Indian Housing Council.

National Education Association. 2005. "Indian Student Achievement Today." *Focus on American Indians/Alaska Natives 2004–05.* Washington, D.C.: National Education Association.

Ni, Chung-Fan, Felicia Wilkins-Turner, Valerie Ellien, Corrine Harrington, and Diane E. Liebert. 2009. "Community Needs Assessment of Native Americans and One-Year Follow-Up Evaluation." Paper presented at the Symposium on Special Education and Rehabilitation for the Northeastern Educational Research Association, Las Vegas, NV, Oct. 23.

Ogunwole, Stella U. 2006. *We the People: American Indians and Alaska Natives in the United States.* A special report prepared at the request of the U.S. Census Bureau. Washington, D.C.: Government Printing Office.

Orfield, Gary, Daniel Losen, Johanna Wald, and C. Swanson. 2004. *Losing Our Future: How Minority Youth Are Being Left Behind by the Graduation Rate Crisis.* Cambridge, MA: The Civil Rights Project at Harvard University, Advocates for Children of New York, The Civil Society Institute.

Probst, J. C., Charity G. Moore, Saundra H. Glover, and Michael E. Samuels. 2004. "Person and Place: The Compounding Effects of Race/Ethnicity and Rurality on Health." *American Journal of Public Health* 94 (10): 1695–703.

Resnick, Brendan. 2011. "Genocide of Native Americans: Historical Facts and Historiographical Debates." In *Genocide of Indigenous Peoples: Genocide: A Critical Bibliographic Review.* Vol. 8, edited by Samuel Totten and Richard K. Hitchcock. New Brunswick, NJ: Transaction Publishers, 15–36.

Reyner, Jon. 2006. "American Indian/Alaska Native Education: An Overview." *American Indian Education.* Flagstaff: Northern Arizona University. http://jan.ucc.nau.edu/jar/AIE/Ind_Ed.html [accessed April 10, 2011].

Rice, G. William. 2009. "The Indian Reorganization Act, the Declaration of the Rights of Indigenous Peoples, and a Proposed Carcieri 'Fix': Updating the Trust Land Acquisition Process." *Idaho Law Review* 45 (3): 576–80.

Ross, Jeffrey Ian, and Larry Gould, eds. 2006. *Native Americans and the Criminal Justice System.* Boulder, CO: Paradigm Publishers.

Shoemaker, Nancy. 1999. *American Indian Population Recovery in the Twentieth Century.* Albuquerque: University of New Mexico Press.

Smith, Paul Chaat, and Robert Allen Warrior. 1996. *Like a Hurricane: The Indian Movement from Alcatraz to Wounded Knee.* New York: The New Press.

Sturm, Circe. 2002. *Blood Politics: Race, Culture and Identity in the Cherokee Nation of Oklahoma.* Berkeley: University of California Press.

Thornton, Russell. 1996. "Tribal Membership Requirements and the Demography of 'Old' and 'New' Native Americans." In *Changing Numbers, Changing Needs: American Indian Demography and Public Health,* edited by Gary D. Sandefur, Ronald R. Rindfuss, and Barney Cohen, 103–12. Washington, D.C.: National Academy Press.

Tripp-Reimer, Tony, Eunice Choi, Lisa Skemp Kelley, and Janet C. Enslein. 2001. "Cultural Barriers to Care: Inverting the Problem." *Diabetes Spectrum* 14 (1): 13–22.

Tullberg, Steven. 2008. "Securing Human Rights of American Indians and Other Indigenous Peoples under International Law." In *Bringing Human Rights Home, Vol. 3,* edited by Cynthia Soohoo, Catherine Albisa, and Martha F. Davis. Westport, CT: Praeger Publishers, 53–90.

United States Constitution, Art. II, § 2, cl. 2, 1789.

United States Department of Education. 2009. *National Indian Education Study 2009—Part I.* National Association of Educational Progress. Washington D.C.: Government Printing Office.

United States v. Kagama, 118 U.S. 375, 383–84, 1886.

United States v. Lara, 541 U.S. 193, 2004, 202–218.

Vernon, Irene S. 2001. *Killing Us Quietly: Native Americans and HIV-AIDS.* Lincoln: University of Nebraska Press.

Von Feigenblatt, Otto F. 2010. "Identity and Culture: A Cultural Interpretation of the Hopi- Navajo Land Dispute." *Vivat Academia* 111: 35–47.

Waldman, Carl. 2009. *Atlas of the North American Indian.* New York: Infobase Publishing.

Waller, Margaret A., Scott K. Okamoto, Bart W. Miles, and Donna E. Hurdle. 2003. "Resiliency Factors Related to Substance Abuse/Resistance: Perceptions of Native Adolescents of the Southwest." *Journal of Sociology & Social Welfare* 30: 79–94.

Wilkinson, Charles. 2006. "Peoples Distinct from Others: The Making of Modern Indian Law." *Utah Law Review* 50 (127): 379–96.

Wunder, John R., and John P. Husman. 2011. *Native Americans and the Law: History the Years before the Constitution, 1492–1787.* http://law.jrank.org/pages/18859/Native-Americans-Law-History.html [accessed April 8, 2011].

Housing Pressures Facing American Indians

Kathleen O'Halleran

Despite diverse historical eras, little ground has actually been gained over time in resolving pervasive Indian housing pressures. As a result, American Indian and Alaska Native populations today face a dire housing crisis on reservation lands and in tribal villages.

Through the so-called "Indian Commerce Clause," the United States Constitution provided only the federal government with the power to enter into treaties with American Indian tribes. Thus, the first 40 years of United States-American Indian relations was an era of "treaties among equals" between the federal government and the tribes. Any prospect of peaceful coexistence between the two was dashed with an 1823 Supreme Court ruling. In *Johnson v. McIntosh,* the court determined that the United States had inherited the same right of discovery and dominion over American Indians that Christian European nations had invoked and previously established over the land during the era of conquest and colonization. "Consequently, the indigenous peoples lost the right to complete sovereignty, although they . . . retained the right to occupy and use the land. The United States, however, retained title to the land they inherited" (U.S. Commission on Civil Rights 2003, 2). For American Indians, loss of secure land title soon equated to loss of security in their homes.

The 1830 Indian Removal Act formalized the resettlement of tribes west of the Mississippi River, which by the mid-19th century "resulted in the formal establishment of the reservation system in the 1850s" (Davis 2002, 216). In many treaties, the federal government pledged to supply tribal housing or the allocation of funds for housing (Davis 2002, 217). Some treaties stipulated that the U.S. government supply housing allowances or pay annual housing annuities drawn from a percentage of the proceeds of Indian land sales. Many agreements incorporated federally supplied sawmills and carpenters (Davis 2002, 219–20). Indian agent reports during this period reflect loose interpretation and implementation. Sometimes, "agents paid Indians to build their own houses, while others expected Indians to provide the labor with the government providing the materials"; others stipulated that houses be built only "on the allotments of those who have proven the most worthy and industrious" and that American Indians "not live in houses until they have first learned manual labor" (Davis 2002, 221). Even before 1880, complaints surfaced that government houses were ramshackle or falling apart (National American Indian Housing Council 2001, 7).

Critics of the reservation system as a failed mechanism for "civilizing" American Indians joined forces with those who resented the program for removing land from white settlement. In 1887, these pressures took form as the General Allotment Act (Dawes Act) and the Curtis Act of 1898. American Indians were to "abandon their tribal relations and take lands in severalty as the cornerstone of their complete success"; each to embrace a "homestead of his own with assistance by the government to build houses and fences and open farms" (Davis 2002, 224). The tribes lost more than 90 million acres (two-thirds) of their reservation land that was in turn opened, sold, or leased to white settlers and to timber and mining interests (National Congress of American Indians 2009, 2). "Reformers . . . turned to federal policy to fracture these extended indigenous families into male-dominant, nuclear families, modeled after middle-class, Anglo-American households" (Stremlau 2005, 265). At the federal Bureau of Indian Affairs (BIA), individual superintendents devised their own plans for housing assistance. Most houses consisted of whatever building materials were available, and entailed "one or two rooms, few windows, dirt floors, no running water, and no electricity" (Davis 2002, 225; National American Indian Housing Council 2001, 7).

Just over 19,000 houses were constructed for American Indians by 1900; a profoundly inadequate number even for an all-time low American Indian population of 237,000 (Shoemaker 1999). Poor healthcare, sanitation, and nutrition, combined with crowded and substandard housing contributed to high morbidity rates among American Indians due to tuberculosis, dysentery, pneumonia, and other infectious diseases (National American Indian Housing Council 2001, 7). Alaska Native populations, still designated as members of a U.S. territory, were not yet recognized as tribes (National American Indian Housing Council 2001, 7). In many cases, sole dependency on welfare and on missionaries was a pragmatic reality for Alaska Native populations until well into the 20th century.

The Allotment program was replaced in 1934 when Congress passed the Wheeler-Howard Act (known as the Indian Reorganization Act) that allowed tribes to reassemble through the adoption of constitutions, charters, and elections. Enacted during Franklin D. Roosevelt's administration (1933–1945), the IRA authorized annual federal funding to purchase land for those American Indians who had none and put mechanisms in place allowing individual tracts of allotted land to revert to tribal land status. The IRA also authorized a $2.5 million revolving loan fund to be leveraged for sawmills, housing improvements, and community development construction needs (Collier 1935, 1–2). In 1936, Roosevelt's Emergency Relief Appropriations Act earmarked work relief funds to build and renovate American Indian housing. This was the first program *solely* dedicated to American Indian Housing issues.

In the mid 1950s it was not unusual to find log cabins with a tent beside it being used as homes by Indians on the Pine Ridge reservation in southwest South Dakota. This cabin is in better condition than many cabins, with a tar paper instead of a dirt roof, and it has two rooms. The reservation is the second largest in the country—55 by 75 miles of arid plains. (Associated Press)

Indian "New Deal" programs ended after 1941 when a new conservative policy direction known as "termination" emerged (Davis 2002, 228–30). This broad movement planned to eliminate federal supervision by abolishing the trustee relationship and all inherited treaty rights of American Indians in exchange for per capita cash payments (Handler 2009, 261). Tribes themselves had to provide the resources needed for housing and all other social services or leverage credit through the sparsely funded federal Revolving Loan Program. The BIA launched an urban relocation program, "to assist [Indians] to move to new communities and establish themselves" (Davis 2002, 231). Around 200,000 American Indians moved to urban areas under this program, more than twice the number forced to relocate under the 1830 Indian Removal Act (Langston 2003, 116). A synchronized policy of "encouraged assimilation" was similarly employed for Native populations in Alaska (National American Indian Housing Council 2001, 8). By the early 1960s, a PHA report found American Indian housing to be "'a rural slum of shacks and one-room huts,' where many residences had dirt floors and lacked such amenities as running water, electricity, safe methods of heating, and sanitary facilities. Abandoned cars, tarpaper shacks, and tents served as homes for some families" (Riggs 2000, 432–35).

However, new urban American Indian cultural hearths were buoyed by an ensuing 1960s era of rising radicalism (Stanley and Thomas 1978, 111). In 1961, American Indians from 90 tribal nations gathered for a conference in Chicago endorsed by the National Congress of American Indians (NCAI). There, they drafted the Declaration of Indian Purpose, which condemned unsanitary and inadequate housing conditions endured by American Indians, termed the situation a "serious emergency condition requiring immediate consideration and action," and challenged the federal government to reform the program in order to provide affordable, safe, and sanitary housing (National Anthropological Archives 1961, 5). The political tide turned once more. The Housing Act of 1937 was broadened in 1961 to include housing needs on American Indian reservations. This policy reorientation allowed tribes for the first time to create Indian Housing Authorities (IHAs). The 1964 Economic Opportunity Act and subsequent creation of the Office of Economic Opportunity provided that grants and other funding be channeled directly to tribal governments and not just state and federal agencies (Wilkinson 2006, 128). In 1971, Nixon signed into law the Alaska Native Claims Act (ANCA) in an effort to resolve the question of Alaska Native land entitlement. In a complicated and onerous process that significantly reduced the amount of land and hunting and fishing rights claims of Alaskan Natives, ANCA authorized the establishment of regional and village corporations and the conveyance of corporate stock in order to settle these claims (Jones 1981, 1).

The benchmark reform during this era was the 1975 Indian Self-Determination and Education Assistance Act that strengthened the federal government's trust responsibilities to the tribes and simultaneously allowed more tribal autonomy over the management of their own affairs (Canby 2004, 29–31). This cleared the way for tribes to absorb administrative responsibilities for programs including housing that had been previously controlled by the BIA and other federal agencies. However, by this time tribal populations were beginning to experience significant population growth, placing further pressure on existing substandard and overcrowded housing and poor infrastructure on reservations (National American Indian Housing Council 2001, 9).

Closely situated cluster rental housing, built on reservations during this era, soon became known by American Indians as "reservation ghettos." According to a South Dakota Pine Ridge Reservation tribal member, "Government houses just tore the families apart. We talk so much about our way of life, the 'Indian-ness' in us . . . but we don't have that when they put us in these cluster homes" (Housing Assistance Council 2008, 99). Yet another unfavorable policy shift was President Ronald Reagan's austerity policy of New Federalism (Kotlowski 2008, 617). American Indian Housing Programs through U.S. Department of Housing and

Urban Development (HUD) were quite nearly terminated in 1982, when the Reagan budget called for only one more year of appropriations to be followed by program closeout. Funding cuts hit tribal housing programs especially hard (Muhammad 2009).

Policy tides shifted more favorably toward funding for tribal housing in the 1990s. The 1992 Housing and Community Development Act created the Section 184 Indian Housing Loan Guarantee Program to stimulate mortgage lending on tribal lands by providing loan guarantees to private sector lenders. In 1993, the U.S. Department of Interior and the State of Alaska also recognized Alaska Native villages as entitled to the same rights granted to American Indian tribes and individuals (National American Indian Housing Council 2001, 7). In the late 1990s, President Bill Clinton signed into law the Native American Housing Assistance and Self-Determination Act (NAHASDA), which remains the primary source of housing assistance for the tribes today.

CONTEMPORARY HOUSING PRESSURES

NAHASDA has marked perhaps the most sweeping reform in American Indian and Alaska Native Housing to date (Cortelyou 2001, 429). Under NAHASDA, tribes may apply for six types of funding ranging from direct housing assistance, development, housing services, and housing management services to crime prevention and safety and model activities (National American Indian Housing Council 2001, 54). NAHASDA "eliminated nine of the 14 separate Native American housing assistance programs and replaced them with a single block grant" (National American Indian Housing Council 2001, 54). The act also includes a mandatory Title VI set-aside, providing federally guarantees to private mortgage lenders for tribal members or housing entities that cannot otherwise obtain loans.

The Section 184 Indian Home Loan Guarantee program created through the 1992 Housing and Community Development Act represents another major piece of existing HUD-related funding for American Indian housing (U.S. Commission on Civil Rights 2003, 60). Annual funding ranges from $5–$6 million annually and provides mortgage financing to tribal members that make too much money to qualify for low-income programs. American Indian tribes and Alaska Native communities also continue to rely heavily upon the Indian Community Development Block Grant Program to meet housing and other critical project needs in their communities. Each year, a minimum of 1 percent of national CDBG competitive grant funds is set aside for tribal communities for infrastructure, housing, and/or economic development (U.S. Commission on Civil Rights 2003, 61).

Funding for NAHASDA is theoretically noncompetitive, though grants are awarded based upon an allocation formula that measures seven weighted criteria.

This includes "factors such as population, overcrowding, extent of poverty, and burden of household's housing costs" (U.S. Commission on Civil Rights 2003, 54). Tribal participation in the NAHASDA program has marked an improvement over past efforts (Cortelyou 2001, 447–64). Yet, these results must be placed in perspective to the many factors that continue to impair tribal housing today.

Arbitrary Policy Prescriptions—Capricious about-faces in policy direction appear distinctly unique on the American Indian and Alaskan Native political and social landscape. Today, funding trends reveal large disparities between HUD's discretionary budget authority and spending on HUD's American Indian Alaska Native programs. At best, "the level of need far exceeds the amount of funding. As a result, tribal housing entities are only able to maintain the status quo, and cannot offer significant improvement to overall living conditions" (U.S. Commission on Civil Rights 2003, 55). Recent data suggests that at least 200,000–250,000 additional housing units are needed to meet immediate housing needs on tribal lands (Youmans 2002, 4).

Meanwhile, sharp declines have occurred overall in federal funding. Current Title VI funding has endured a 60–70 percent funding decline since program inception (U.S. Department of Housing and Urban Development 2010, 1–5). The U.S. Commission on Civil Rights recommends an increase in federal spending on tribal housing to $1.1 billion annually, as opposed to the average $645 million in block grant funds allocated annually for American Indian-Alaska Native (AI/AN) housing needs. Overall, at HUD from 1998 to 2004, "after adjusting for inflation, the agency's budget authority actually increased 46.5 percent . . . and Native American funding decreased 1.3 percent" (U.S. Commission on Civil Rights 2003, 55). Federal Section 184 mortgage loan guarantee funding has also declined, "reducing the amount of loans supported and lessening the opportunity for home ownership" by American Indians (U.S. Commission on Civil Rights 2003, 13). The sizes of annual funding allocations are also often problematic.

Smaller tribes often must bank funds for several years for their planned housing projects, primarily because they receive lesser grant amounts (U.S. Government Accountability Office 2010, 10–11, 19). In fiscal year 2008, 102 of the 359 tribal grantees received less than $250,000 each. According to a 2010 Government Accounting Office (GAO) report, in such cases, fewer homes are built and renovated, particularly through smaller tribal housing authorities (U.S. Government Accountability Office 2010, 10–11). How grant monies are spent represents another barrier to progress. On average, actual construction and renovation constitutes just 40 percent of NAHASDA block grant funding, while the 60 percent remaining pays for operating subsidies that include training, travel for training, staffing costs, and administrative expenses (U.S. Commission on Civil Rights 2003, 59). Clearly, NAHASDA is not sufficient to solve current tribal housing needs.

Population Pressures and Overcrowding—Over the past several decades, the AI/AN population in the United States has grown at least twice as rapidly as the overall U.S. population. In 1950, the AI/AN population stood at 357,000. By 1990, approximately two million people reported their race as only American Indian or Alaska Native. According to the National American Indian Housing Council, "while roughly a third of the population gain appears to be due to increased self-identification as AI/AN, especially in the more urbanized states, the remaining two-thirds, almost quadrupling in thirty years, appears to be due to natural population increases" (National American Indian Housing Council 2001, 9). In 2000, this figure grew still more, to 2.4 million. By 2010, the AI/AN-only population had grown to 2.93 million members. Though representing just 1 percent of the total U.S. population, the "only AI/AN" population group grew by 18.4 percent between 2000 and 2010 and is one of the fastest growing ethnic groups in the United States, second only to Hispanics (U.S. Census Bureau 2010, 7).

Based upon U.S. Census criterion that defines overcrowding as more than 1.01 persons per room, approximately 33 percent of American Indian reservation households and 40 percent of Alaska Native village households are overcrowded, compared to just 4.9 percent overcrowding for all U.S. households. Extended families and often many different families share one housing unit, and overcrowding has been reported in 70 percent of Inupiat village homes on the northern Alaskan coast. In one village, researchers with the National American Indian Housing Council (NAIHC) found approximately 700 people living in 150 homes and one 20-unit, low-income apartment building (National American Indian Housing Council 2001, 10). Five family members occupied one 15 foot by 15 foot room house:

> The door does not close properly, windows do not fit tightly, and drafts blow through the house. The roof leaks badly when it rains, or when there is snow on the roof, often dripping through the electrical fixtures. During the winter, the house is so cold the windows frost over—even with the small oil heater turned up high, and with the hot plates turned on and the electric heater on (National American Indian Housing Council 2001, 12).

The NAIHC found several cases of 25–30 people living in a three-bedroom home, and 15 people living in a one-room house (National American Indian Housing Council 2001, 22).

Forty to 47 percent of the housing structures on American Indian reservations are substandard, compared to a 6.5 percent substandard housing rate for the nation as a whole (Youmans 2002, 4). Between 10 and 16 percent of all reservation households lack adequate plumbing; "a rate that is ten times the national average" (Housing Assistance Council 2008, 97). On the Navajo reservation—the nation's largest—over 50 percent of the homes lack adequate plumbing. The majority of homes use wood fires to heat their homes. Thirty-seven to 40 percent of reservation homes have no electricity.

Less than half of all reservation homes are connected to a public sewer system, and one out of every five tribal households have to find another way to dispose of their sewage. "This often results in 'honey-bucket' methods in which household waste and sewage are collected into large receptacles that are later dumped into lagoons . . . Settlements that use this system often suffer serious contamination and severe bacterial and viral infection. . . . [T]his system also results in the poisoning of crops" (U.S. Commission on Civil Rights 2003, 52). Twenty-nine percent of reservation homes also lack basic kitchen facilities, compared to just 1 percent of the total U.S. population (Taylor and Kalt 2005, 39).

Overall, the geographic remoteness of tribal reservations, distances from urban areas and metropolitan centers, and private ownership of trust land produce regional variations in housing availability and quality. "For example, in Alaska, Arizona, and New Mexico, the rate of overcrowding and substandard housing is more than 60 percent" (U.S. Commission on Civil Rights 2003, 52). In the Plains region today, there are ten Lakota and Dakota reservations that are located within the nation's poorest counties. With unemployment rates as high as 85 percent in these areas, most tribal members cannot meet home loan requirements for consistent income.

House rental on reservations is often the only remaining option. However, a number of older housing units constructed through HUD in the 1960s were designed as transitional housing with an anticipated life cycle of just five years. Many of these deteriorated one-bedroom homes are still occupied today, sometimes as many as 12–20 tribal members reside in one unit. NAIC researchers describe one such home:

> There is very little insulation in the house and the winds rip through it, even with plastic over the windows. In the winter, the single wood stove and the oven going full blast in the kitchen cannot keep the house warm. The roof over the bedroom is near collapsing. Floors in the bedroom, kitchen and front room are caving in. The electrical wiring is disintegrating. The bathroom fixtures spray water across the room (National American Indian Housing Council 2001, 28).

Despite these conditions, the average wait time for housing may be as long as three and a half years, more than double the national average off reservation (Housing Assistance Council 2008, 98).

Turning family members away from the door is traditionally inappropriate, as well. "They very rarely have anywhere to turn for shelter besides the home of another family member. . . . Hence, the stray family members are taken in and given a place to stay, and the homes become overcrowded" (National American Indian Housing Council 2004, 82). Despite these conditions, overcrowding is not the first housing problem that American Indians and Alaskan Natives, themselves, cite. Poverty is their main concern.

Socioeconomic Challenges—Nearly 1.3 million American Indians and Alaska Natives make less than $10,000 per year (U.S. Census Bureau 2009, 441). One out of every five homeowners and one out of every three renters on tribal lands are cost-burdened, meaning that they spend more than 30 percent of their monthly income on housing (Housing Assistance Council 2004, 100). Approximately 28.4 percent of the AI/AN population live in poverty, which is more than double the national population's poverty rate of 12.4 percent. "In 2003, more than twice as many Native American families as white families with children under 18 lived in poverty. In 2007, the poverty rate for all Native Americans was almost three times as high as the rate among non-Hispanic whites" (Muhammad 2009, 18–21). According to a 2009 Institute for Policy Studies report, *Challenges to Native American Advancement: The Recession and Native America,* despite progress in reducing the poverty rate on reservations between 1987 and 2007, at that same rate of decline it would take another 50 years for the AI/AN poverty rate just to drop to the level recorded today by the U.S. population as a whole (Muhammad 2009, 21).

At 25.6 percent, the jobless rate for American Indians and Alaska Natives on reservation and trust land is also more than twice the national average, though on some reservations unemployment runs as high as 75 to 85 percent. For example, the median income on the South Dakota Pine Ridge Oglala Sioux Reservation is $2,600; the unemployment rate is 84 percent and 66 percent of the Pine Ridge population lives below the poverty rate (Youmans 2002, 4). Given the rate of increase in real AI/AN per capita income since 1970, "it would take around 104 years for Native Americans on reservations to attain a per capita income equal to just one-half that of the average U.S. resident" (Muhammad 2009, 17). A disproportionate percentage of AI/AN members are underemployed in short-term, seasonal jobs, including jobs in tourism, the timber industry, construction, maintenance, repair, extraction, and firefighting that do not provide sufficient income or consistent income needed to qualify for home ownership (National American Indian Housing Council 2004, 23). Collectively, these same sectors constitute between 30 and 40 percent of American Indian businesses, and both the construction and timber industries were hard hit by the steep and abrupt drop in housing markets that triggered the 2007 recession (Muhammad 2009, 27).

Poor credit ratings frequently develop from the lack of year-round employment for tribal populations. Oftentimes, although tribal members may be employed for two or four months out of the year, they may also find themselves jobless for three or four months out of the year. "As a result, bills and loans become harder to pay off, and poor credit ratings developed. Even those who have steady jobs due to recent tribal advancements find they are still ineligible for credit because of prior financial missteps" (National American Indian Housing Council 2004, 13). A related issue is that fulltime employment often places tribal members in an even more precarious position. "While a new job might provide community members with newfound sources of income, it may also disqualify them from access to certain federal housing initiatives. Yet, this new income is generally not enough to allow a tribal family to move out of their existing home" (National American Indian Housing Council 2004, 11).

Threats to housing stability are closely tied to ongoing economic vulnerability. Many tribal members remark that worries over paying bills and feeding their families take precedence over other issues such as substandard housing or overcrowding at home. Concerns are also mounting over rising homelessness:

> Individuals and whole families are observed living in cars and tents for months at a time. . . . "[T]here are some guys who sleep in a tool shed with lawnmowers and equipment. There were two guys living in a pigsty—they say it's warm. Every year there are one or two people that freeze to death sleeping in abandoned cars and unheated sheds (National American Indian Housing Council 2001, 30).

While American Indians and Alaska Natives constitute only one percent of the total U.S. population, it is estimated that they comprise 8 percent of all homeless people in the United States (Manson 2004, 13). This represents a disproportionately high percentage of homelessness among American Indian and Alaska Native populations.

HUD ranks American Indians and Alaska Natives as the fourth highest percentage of all races/ethnicities that are homeless. African Americans comprise the largest homeless population among all races and ethnicities, accounting for an estimated 53.8 percent designated as homeless persons within families and 42.3 percent designated as homeless in emergency shelters. White non-Hispanic/Latino populations represent the second largest racial/ethnic homeless population, comprising 36.3 percent of the U.S. homeless population in emergency shelters and 20.5 percent of those designated as homeless persons within families in the United States. Hispanic/Latino populations make up the third largest racial/ethnic category of homeless in the United States, comprising 12.9 percent of the U.S. homeless population in emergency shelters and 14.1 percent of those designated as homeless persons within families in the United States. Asian and Pacific Islander populations combined account for approximately 1.5 percent of U.S. homeless populations in emergency shelters and 2.5 percent of homeless persons within families in the U.S. (Office of Community Planning and Development 2009, 154).

Many AI/AN homeless populations live temporarily with other family members in already overcrowded conditions, especially on reservations. Home ownership is problematic across many dimensions. While incomes are too low and jobless rates soar to 75 percent, in many areas the cost of building a home is conversely quite high. "The expense of building in Native American communities is high because of geographic isolation, distance from urban centers, lack of infrastructure, and harsh climates that limit the construction season" (U.S. Commission on Civil Rights 2003, 62). In one Inupiat village, for example, a 945 square foot home where nine family members reside today cost approximately $190,000 to construct in 1997 (National American Indian Housing Council 2001, 11).

Shortfalls in Tribal Access and Capacity—Links between self-determination, tribal economic development, and adequate housing on tribal lands represent a close-knit and unique dynamic. As observed by the National American Indian Housing Council, "The relationship is not one that can be summarized in just a few words. It requires much deeper analysis into the cultural, political and geographic factors . . . and should not merely be taken at face value" (National American Indian Housing Council 2004, 4).

For example, physical location can wield a positive or negative impact on economic development for AI/AN reservations and villages, and thus, on the capacity of the tribe as a whole to maintain a stable housing base (National American Indian Housing Council 2004, 7). The closer a tribe is situated to an urban center or metropolitan area, the more likely it is to prosper, and the closer it is situated to a major interstate or thoroughfare, the greater the likelihood of economic success. Unfortunately, the majority of tribes and trust lands are located in remote rural areas, with limited infrastructure, "in communities smaller than 4,000" (Snipp 1991, 88).

Also, the absence of physical infrastructure including paved roads, electricity, plumbing, sewer facilities, and landfills impair not only housing development, but also the location of new business ventures. Thus, not only are fewer jobs available, but the type of jobs available are also affected: "Economic development efforts do little to improve the quantity or quality of jobs in sparsely settled rural areas where Indians tend to reside. Jobs are not equally allocated across urban and rural labor markets. Rural labor markets disproportionately depend on low-skill, labor-intensive routine industries and consumer services" (Tootle 1993, 103).

Gaming revenues represent a boon for some tribes. According to the National Indian Gaming Commission (NIGC), in 2010 236 gaming tribes generated approximately $26.5 billion in gaming revenue. As the NIGC reports, "In 2010, 55 percent of Indian gaming operations reported gaming revenue of less than $25 million. Of these operations, approximately 62 percent generated less than $10 million" (Tirado 2011, para. 3). Tribes with gaming operations near cities and along highways fare the best. According to another report, more than 37 percent of gaming profits have been generated by just 4 percent of participating tribes. In addition, the NIGC reports that more than half of all tribal gaming operations reported a revenue decrease in 2010, due more than likely to the nationwide recession. Moreover, gaming profits do not necessarily translate into per capita benefits/income for tribal members. Thus, despite gaming, overall income for tribal members has remained virtually unchanged.

Tensions exist between the immediate need of tribal citizens for cash flow against the need for investing resources in services and infrastructure for jobs, education, health care, and housing. For these reasons, according to the National Indian Gaming Association, by 2006 only 25 percent of Native nations with gaming operations were making per capita distributions to tribal members (Cornell et al. 2007, 4). In the decade prior, "between 1995 and 2005 . . . for every $4.625 million the gaming industry generated during those 10 years, real median household income for Native Americans increased by only $1" (Muhammad 2009, 25). The per capita gaming revenue issue has become increasingly divisive and politicized among tribal legislators and tribal elected officials. One key problem encountered thus far with per capita payments has been that the establishment of a set amount for tribal members reduces funding available for tribal services and operations during periods of economic slowdown, as evidenced by the recent recession (Cornell et al. 2007, 12).

In addition, it is estimated that only 40 percent of those employed in tribal gaming enterprises are actually tribal members. In the United States, most successful gaming enterprises are located in or near urban centers and alongside major highways, but few tribes have such choice locations. Moreover, not all tribes or tribal members favor gaming as the leverage point for economic development. Some view gaming as a primary source of promising support that could benefit tribal members in multiple ways. For others, the link between self-determination and economic development must be tempered by traditions and cultural considerations. Factionalism over the nature and pace of economic development can produce friction and entropy that impairs tribal sustainability and individual well-being (Cornell and Kalt 2006).

For much of the 20th century, the federal government encouraged economic development on tribal lands that was (and in many cases, still is) geared toward single-project job creation. "[I]t is short-term and non-strategic; it lets persons or organizations other than the Indian nation set the development agenda; it views development as primarily an economic problem; it views indigenous culture as an obstacle to development; and it encourages narrowly defined and often self-serving leadership" (Cornell and Kalt 2006, 3). Underlying barriers to economic development on reservations, such as infrastructure, transportation, child care, education, and job skills training were typically ignored. Without addressing such underlying issues, only a small percentage of these jobs-driven development initiatives survive beyond their first cycle. Meanwhile, this approach has long nurtured a warped, development-dependency pathology:

> All of this means that there are enormous incentives for tribal politicians to retain control of scarce resources and use them to stay in office. . . . It reduces politics to a battle between factions trying to gain or keep control of tribal

Leon Brave Heart a 22-year-old Ogala Sioux tribe member by his old trailer he calls home, is facing a bleak future without federal college grants due to budget cuts, on the Pine Ridge Indian reservation. (Time & Life Pictures/Getty Images)

> government resources. . . . People vote for whomever they think will send more resources in their direction. Leadership becomes almost meaningless under these conditions: the nation isn't really going anywhere; it's just shoving resources around among factions (Cornell and Kalt 2006, 8).

Tribes seeking to eliminate the standard, federal project approach and to instead nurture sustainable economic development have been faced with the challenge of disrupting these ingrained patterns.

A lengthy study by the Harvard Project on American Indian Economic Development at Harvard University and the Native Nations Institute for Leadership, Management, and Policy at the University of Arizona finds the emergent alternative—aptly named the nation-building, or assets-based approach—is much more successful with economic development when tribal members push for the separation of economic enterprise and investment from tribal governments accustomed to political opportunism (Cornell and Kalt 2002, 3). Many tribal members—particularly young adults that are disappointed with the lack of employment and housing, and who are disillusioned with political corruption—leave the reservation system behind. Such exoduses exacerbate even pragmatic housing constraints that include inadequate staff resources, limited expertise, and high administrative turnover. The preparation of grants and of burdensome grant reports are frequently reported by smaller grantees as factors that limit their abilities to seek additional NAHASDA funding for housing (U.S. Government Accountability Office 2010, 30). Tribes must annually submit an Indian Housing Plan and an Annual Performance Report to HUD that demonstrates compliance with NAHASDA provisions. During implementation, if NAHASDA regulations are not followed, HUD may reduce or terminate future tribal participation in the program. Difficulties meeting these requirements have delayed or reduced funding for some tribes. "Each year, there have been allocated funds that have not been distributed to eligible tribes" (U.S. Commission on Civil Rights 2003, 58).

Legal Hurdles, High-Cost Lending, and Discrimination—Significant disparity exists between the number of conventional home loans approved for reservation housing and home loans granted elsewhere in the United States. Title ambiguity, poor credit, and discrimination hamper home ownership on reservations. Most tribal lands are actually owned by the federal government and held in trust for American Indians. Tribes in turn typically parcel out these lands in order to provide 50- to 99-year residential leases to tribal members. "Generally, trust lands cannot be leased without the approval of the federal Bureau of Indian Affairs (BIA), a process that can take months or years. . . . Nor can Indian tribes or individuals sell trust land, because the BIA holds title" (Kolluri and Rengert 2000, 1). Banks and mortgage companies are most comfortable when land is put up as collateral for home loans. The trust status of reservation land causes many banks to balk. "Banks often follow the path of least resistance and turn down mortgage applications or drag out processing so long that Indians do not even bother asking for a loan" (Claiborne 1998, A3). Tribal land tenure practices can also complicate mortgage processes.

For example, on the Pine Ridge Indian Reservation in South Dakota, Lakota land ownership is shared through family lineage structures. "This results in . . . fractionalized land ownership—a condition known as individual interest. Before any individual who shares land with others in this type of ownership can build a house . . . s/he has to get permission from all other owners before subdividing the parcel" (Housing Assistance Council 2002, 102). Because of pervasive poverty, high unemployment, and sheer geographic constraints that prevent conventional banks from locating on or near reservations, access to credit is limited on reservations (Housing Assistance Council 2002, 107). A severe shortage of financial institutions on or near tribal lands also contributes to subprime lending practices. When traveling beyond the reservation, tribal members confront additional barriers to fair lending: "The private sector's perceived risk, due in large part to their inexperience in working in Indian Country, is a major barrier to mortgage financing on Native lands" (Kolluri and Rengert 2000, 4).

Subprime lending practices are almost 25 percent more likely to prevail in counties where American Indian and Alaska Native populations prevail than in other rural areas. While access to home loans dominated fair lending policy issues until the mid-1990s, price discrimination is at the forefront of policy concern today for American Indians and Alaska Natives. According to a survey on predatory lending conducted by the NAIC and the National Community Reinvestment Coalition (NCRC), approximately 53 percent of American Indian reservation officials believe that home mortgage lenders discriminate based upon race, particularly in the form of higher interest rates charged to American Indians, when they qualified for lower interest loans. "Abusive manufactured home lending was also the most frequently mentioned predatory practice" (National Community Reinvestment Coalition 2003, 3). More than one-third of reservation officials also reported that first-time American Indian homebuyers were frequent targets of subprime lending practices. The NCRC/NAIC study found that on average in the United States, subprime and manufactured home loans were made to American Indians at more than double the rate made to whites (National Community Reinvestment Coalition 2003, 5). Thirty-five percent of reservation officials also reported that they either knew of someone who had their home foreclosed upon due to predatory lending, or had suffered such foreclosures, themselves.

CONCLUSION

Housing problems today on American Indian and Alaska Native lands stem from systemic historic pressures shaped and exacerbated by shifts in the politics and culture of the American nation and its own views regarding its treatment of and responsibility to its own indigenous populations.

American Indian settlements have weathered no less than five major federal policy reversals that have repeatedly shifted the very foundations of Indian housing policies and their outcomes for Indian people. As the United States Commission on Civil Rights has observed, "The . . . federal funding of Native American programs is tethered to and built upon a past in which federal and obligation to Native Americans was clearly established" (U.S. Commission on Civil Rights 2003, 1–2). Though such provisions for housing and sustainable livelihoods have played an essential historical role since the 1800s in Indian settlement policies, "the federal government has never successfully provided housing assistance to Indian tribes" (Davis 2002, 211). These legacies, coupled with phenomenal AI/AN population growth since 1950, have exacerbated poverty for tribal populations and produced significant housing problems on reservation lands and in tribal villages.

Substandard conditions and overcrowded housing conditions predominate, causing a myriad of related problems including "increases in infectious diseases, lower educational attainment among children, and social problems like alcoholism, domestic violence, and child abuse and neglect" (Housing Assistance Council 2006, 1). Lack of water, sewer, electrical and other essential housing infrastructure, needs for cooking, heating and cooling, and basic plumbing represent dramatic shortcomings in meeting the most basic living standards for many reservation populations. Housing costs and socioeconomic barriers to housing availability aggravate already crowded conditions for American Indian and Alaska Native communities, and contribute to rising homelessness on tribal lands. Despite 50 years of policy initiatives aimed at American Indian and Alaska Native self-determination, significant barriers to tribal autonomy find physical form in the worst housing conditions in our nation that exist on tribal lands today. “Although current federal policies support self-determination, the lingering effects of past injustices remain” (U.S. Commission on Civil Rights 2003, 5).

U.S. federal policy regarding American Indian and Alaska Native populations today is characterized as the era of self-determination. However, self-determination is best understood as a work in progress—a conceptual framework that continues to evolve in terms of policy formation, that has also been hampered by various cycles of funding and program setbacks over the past fifty years. While NAHASDA has demonstrated the most significant policy improvement over past federal Indian housing funding programs, moribund funding of this program since 2004 has significantly stymied housing rehabilitation, home construction, and the development of needed infrastructure, particularly for smaller tribes that make up the majority of housing authorities across the nation. Inadequate access to mortgage loan financing, subprime lending, and discrimination against tribal borrowers continues to hamper efforts to improve housing conditions for American Indians and Alaska Natives.

Overall, while direct federal funding, loan guarantees, and other program supports for housing must remain an important component of the government’s trust relationship with tribal entities, it appears that actual progress toward self-determination with respect to housing will require new, innovative strategies and initiatives if tribal housing problems are to be solved. Tribal gaming enterprises are not sufficient for most reservations to provide either the needed funding for housing, or the employment opportunities needed to support tribal incomes and housing costs on reservations. Improving economic development opportunities on tribal lands and developing partnerships with private, nonprofit, community, and government entities will likely occur only if tribal governments themselves take a leadership role in these initiatives. Some tribes are beginning to take these steps. However, amid grinding poverty dependency on waning federal assistance and unforgiving living conditions, housing pressures remains dire today for American Indians and Alaska Natives.

◀ FURTHER INVESTIGATIONS ▶

The trustee status that the U.S. federal government has assumed with the nation’s tribes embodies a complex relationship that has historically and persistently caused immense complication and harm to American Indian and Alaskan native (AI/AN) populations on both a collective and an individual basis. This is particularly true as it has concerned AI/ANs’ capacity to make

a sustainable, productive living, and to live securely in their own homes on their reservation. Yet paradoxically, dismantling this trustee relationship could potentially cause even more harm to the tribes and to tribal individuals. Bound up in this paradox is the mounting controversy over blood quantum requirements for tribal membership (which guarantees trust status eligibility), the potential erosion of tribal land bases, and threats to tribal jurisdiction on reservation lands.

As discussed in this report, under the General Allotment Act (also known as the Dawes Act) of 1887, the government became the arbitrator of individual tracts of reservation land that were divided among American Indians in parcels ranging from 40 to 160 acres. At this juncture, the federal government assumed the role of trustee, holding these property parcels "in trust" for a period of 25 years or such time as the individual tribal members had demonstrated their "ability" to integrate into the dominant society. In the meantime, the federal government was to manage proceeds from productive use of the land from agricultural, mining, drilling, timber sales, manufacturing, or other enterprises, and send tribal members the proceeds/royalties each month. By 1930, over 80 percent of reservation land had been declared surplus and sold to outsiders, and 90 percent of the American Indians that had received title to their allotted lands had either sold them, or lost them. Most profoundly, and wielding enduring impacts, was the stipulation under allotment policy that Indian land ownership and non-Indian land ownership be treated differently. Non-Indians that had purchased the so-called "surplus" reservation land, or who had acquired land from Indians that had sold or lost them, could sell their land unfettered because they retained fee simple title and ownership to their property. American Indians could not do so, because the federal government held their titles in trust. American Indians thus held only the right to use the land. They could neither lease it, nor sell it until at least 25 years had passed, and/or when the federal government had ended its trustee status.

Lack of clear ownership presented (and continues to present) significant obstacles to the abilities of American Indians to construct homes on their properties, and clearly, tribes as a whole suffered from the inability to stimulate or manage economic growth. Capital and profit flowed outward away from the reservations, as tribal autonomy eroded and lands and natural resources became controlled by corporate and non-Indian interests. Poor housing conditions, overcrowding, and related health problems mounted, as did chronic economic underdevelopment, lack of educational facilities, substandard infrastructure required for basic subsistence, and the survival-driven outmigration of tribal members over the ensuing decades to urban centers. The legacies of allotment also mounted into a grinding poverty and growing dependency by American Indians upon the federal government for assistance, while $176 billion dollars in trust royalty payments to tribal members that had accumulated since allotment simply "disappeared" or were misappropriated. With an agreed-upon trust settlement amount of merely 5 percent of this amount, it is unlikely that tribal dependencies will end any time soon.

Ironically, the General Allotment Act was meant to "get the federal government out of the Indian business," and to limit the amount of time the federal government would serve as trustee (Leeds, 200, 440). Yet, it has generated the opposite effect, as it and legislation subsequent to it continue to generate reverberating barriers and paradoxes that harm tribes' movement toward self-determination and which continue to limit individual tribal members' abilities to cope with property-related income and housing issues. Despite efforts at reform with passage of the 1934 Indian Reorganization Act (IRA) and related legislation, millions of acres allotted to both individual tribal members and tribes remain in federal trusteeship today. When the IRA was passed, numerous properties were still under the 25-year trust requirement. Under the provisions of the IRA, the length of that trust status was lengthened into perpetuity. This had the effect of stopping the clock "on trust allotments that would have otherwise expired to become fee lands" (Leeds, 2006, 445). Moreover, the IRA provided the federal government with the power to designate even more tribal lands as trust property. Effectively, since the allotment period, the government has taken a 180 degree about-face in terms of its role with the tribes and the scope of its relationship with the tribes. The federal government could not be more embedded than it is today in sustaining tribal dependency, particularly with respect to the most fundamental needs and rights of secure property and property-based income.

The government's sweeping role as trustee today includes its mandatory control over not only property sales, but also mineral leases, probate, and all other potential property conveyances, and "good faith" management of the trust property income that tribes and their members may obtain. For all intents and purposes, the trustee relationship erodes tribal autonomy and self-determination over property and as a result, impairs sustenance and viable housing. Firstly, by sustaining in perpetuity federal control over tribal lands, the government not only continues to hold power over the tribes, but also sequesters control over the lucrative proceeds these properties generate, all the while perpetuating the need for more and more funds to administer tribal trust properties. Secondly, the trustee system, which restricts trust property from alienation or other encumbrances, simultaneously shields this same trust property from taxation and external jurisdictional authority. Thus paradoxically, it is in the tribes' best fiduciary and political interest to retain as much land as possible in federal trust status indefinitely. Thirdly, trust lands predominantly define the tribes' remaining territorial land base. If these were to be redesignated as fee-simple properties and sold to non-Indian interests, tribal territorial land bases would be significantly and permanently reduced. Finally, as trustee laws stand, tribes retain jurisdictional, regulatory, and adjudicative authority over property that is held on their or their members behalf in federal trust, whereas land on reservations held as fee simple are, at best, subject to shared jurisdictional authority with the states they are located in. When tribal jurisdictional issues are called into question in the courts, so are tribal property status issues.

Tribal jurisdiction is only assured when property is placed in federal trust.

Collectively, these limitations and provisions translate into untenable options for tribes and their populations. On the one hand, they may keep their lands in federal trust, and accept the limitations imposed upon them as to alienability (and even the ability to obtain a home loan), as well as management (or mismanagement) of trust proceeds. Or, they may take their chances and choose to abdicate federal trust status for their lands, while risking the loss of jurisdictional and regulatory control over tribal properties and the loss of tribal land bases, as well as the imposition of taxes. Neither option provides a true benefit to tribal autonomy and self-determination, or to meeting the needs of individual tribal members to secure and sustain their properties and homes. Yet, as the law stands, tribes have no choice but to either accept dependent federal status, or to accept the specter of losing more reservation land, while subjecting themselves to the burden of tax debt and state control. Entrenched in past, flawed beliefs and prejudices of American Indian incompetency and inadequacy, such limited options should be held suspect today and reexamined with respect to their intents, purposes, and outcomes.

References

Canby, William C., Jr. 2004. *American Indian Law in a Nutshell.* St. Paul, MN: West Publishing Company.

Claiborne, William. 1998. "On Indian Reservations, Little Hope for Home Loans." *Washington Post,* Nov 25. http://www.washingtonpost.com/wprv/national/frompost/nov98/homeloan25.htm [accessed May 1, 2011].

Collier, John. 1935. "Commissioner of Indian Affairs Defends the Indian New Deal." In *Collier, "Annual Report": Bureau of Indian Affairs.* Washington, D.C.: Government Printing Office.

Cornell, Stephen, Miriam Jorgensen, Stephanie Carroll-Rainie, Ian Record, Ryan Seelau, and Rachel Rose-Starks, 2007. *Per Capita Distributions of American Indian Tribal Revenues: A Preliminary Discussion of Policy Considerations.* Tucson: Udall Center for Studies in Public Policy, Native Nations Institute for Leadership, University of Arizona.

Cornell, Stephen, and Joseph P. Kalt. 2006. *Two Approaches to Economic Development on American Indian Reservations: One Works, the Other Doesn't.* Tucson: Harvard Project on American Indian Economic Development and the Native Nations Institute for Leadership, Management, and Policy on behalf of the Arizona Board of Regents University of Arizona Press: 1–26.

Cortelyou, George H. 2001. "An Attempted Revolution in Native American Housing: The Native American Housing Assistance and Self-Determination Act." *Seton Hall Legislative Journal* 25: 429–66.

Davis, Virginia. 2002. "A Discovery of Sorts: Reexamining the Origins of Federal Indian Housing Obligations." *Harvard Blackletter Law Journal* 18: 211–39.

Handler, Mathew. 2009. "Tribal Law and Disorder: A Look at a System of Broken Justice in Indian Country and the Steps Needed to Fix It." *Brooklyn Law Review* 75: 261–303.

Housing Assistance Council. 2006. *Housing on Native American Lands.* Washington, D.C.: Housing Assistance Council.

Housing Assistance Council. 2008. *Taking Stock: Rural People, Poverty and Housing for the 21st Century: Native American Lands.* Washington, D.C.: Housing Assistance Council. http://216.92.48.246/pressreleasesview.php?id=115 [accessed April 15, 2011].

Indian Tribal Lands: Barriers, Progress, and the Promise of New Initiatives." *Fannie Mae Foundation Housing Facts and Findings* 2 (3), 2000. http://www.fanniemaefoundation.org/programs/hff/v2i3-indian.shtml [May 1, 2011].

Jones, Richard S. 1981. *Alaska Native Claims Settlement Act of 1971 (Public Law 92–203): History and Analysis Together with Subsequent Amendments.* Report No. 81–127 GOV Anchorage: University of Alaska Anchorage Institute of Social and Economic Research.

Kotlowski, Dean J. 2008. "From Backlash to Bingo: Ronald Reagan and Federal Indian Policy." *Historical Review* 77 (4): 617–52.

Langston, Donna Hightower. 2003. "American Indian Women's Activism in the 1960s and 1970s." *Hypatia* 18 (2): 114–32.

Leeds, Stacey L. 2006. "Moving Toward Exclusive Tribal Autonomy over Lands and Natural Resources." *Natural Resources Journal* 46, 440–463.

Manson, Spero M. 2004. "Meeting the Mental Health Needs of American Indians and Alaska Natives." *Cultural Diversity Series: Meeting the Mental Health Needs of American Indians and Alaska Natives.* Alexandria, VA: National Association of State Mental Health Program Directors [NASMHPD] Office of Technical Assistance.

Muhammad, Dedrick. 2009. *Challenges to Native American Advancement: The Recession and Native America.* Washington, D.C.: Institute for Policy Studies.

National American Indian Housing Council. 2001. *Too Few Rooms: Residential Crowding in Native American Communities and Alaska Native Villages.* Washington, D.C.: National American Indian Housing Council.

National American Indian Housing Council. 2004. *Sustaining Indian Housing: An Evaluation of Tribal Economic Development and Its Impact on Housing in Four Case Studies.* Washington, D.C.: National American Indian Housing Council.

National Anthropological Archives. 1961. American Indian Chicago Conference Charter Convention Series XI, box 148/5. *National Congress of American Indian Papers.* Washington, D.C.: National Anthropological Archives, Smithsonian Institution.

National Congress of American Indians. 2009. *Testimony of the National Congress of American Indians on the Supreme Court Decision in Carcieri v. Salazar and Executive Branch Authority to Acquire Trust Lands for Indian Tribes.* Washington, D.C.: United States Senate Committee on Indian Affairs. http://indian.senate.gov/public/_files/Allentestimony.pdf [accessed March 15, 2011].

NCRC and NAIHC. 2003. *High Cost Lending on Indian Reservations—Watch Out if You Are Buying a Home.* Washington, D.C.: National Community Reinvestment Coalition & National American Indian Housing Council. http://www.naihc.net/uploads/research/2003%20NCRC%20Pred%20Lending%20REPORT.pdf [accessed April 20, 2011].

Office of Community Planning and Development. 2009. *The 2008 Annual Homeless Assessment Report to Congress.* Washington, D.C.: United States Department of Housing and Urban Development. http://www.huduser.org/publications/pdf/4thHomelessAssessmentReport.pdf [accessed May 10, 2012].

Riggs, Christopher. 2000. "American Indians, Economic Development, and Self-Determination in the 1960s." *Pacific Historical Review* 69 (3): 431–63.

Robbins, Rebecca. 1989. "The Forgotten American: A Foundation for Contemporary American Indian Self-Determination." Paper presented at the Western Social Sciences Association Annual Conference, Albuquerque, New Mexico, April 28.

Shoemaker, Nancy. 1999. *American Indian Population Recovery in the Twentieth Century.* Albuquerque: University of New Mexico Press.

Shuravloff, Marty. 2011. Prepared statement of the Honorable Marty Shuravloff, Chairman, National American Indian Housing Council. Presented to the United States Senate Committee on Indian Affairs Oversight Hearing to Examine Tribal Programs and Initiatives Proposed in the FY2011 Budget Request. Washington, D.C., March 15. http://www.indian.senate.gov/public/_files/58128.pdf.

Snipp, C. Mathew. 1991. *American Indians: The First of This Land.* New York: The Russell Sage Foundation.

Stanley, Sam, and Robert K. Thomas. 1978. "Current Demographic and Social Trends among North American Indians." *The Annals of the American Academy of Political and Social Science* 436 (1): 111–20.

Stremlau, Rose. 2005. "'To Domesticate and Civilize Wild Indians': Allotment and the Campaign to Reform Indian Families: 1875–1887." *Journal of Family History* 30 (3): 265–86.

Taylor, Jonathan B., and Joseph P. Kalt. 2005. *Cabazon, the Indian Gaming Regulatory Act, and the Socioeconomic Consequences of American Indian Governmental Gaming: A Ten-Year Review.* Cambridge, MA: The Harvard Project on American Indian Economic Development, Malcolm Weiner Center for Social Policy. http://www.indiangaming.org/info/pr/databook/Databook-HPAIED_Gaming_Study.pdf [accessed Feb. 22, 2011].

Tirado, Michelle, 2010. "Indian Gaming Revenues Stable, NIGC Reports. *American Indian Chamber of Commerce of New Mexico.* http://www.americanindianreport.com/wordpress/2011/07/indian-gaming-revenues-stable-nigc-reports/ [accessed May 10, 2012].

Tootle, Deborah M. 1993. *American Indians: Economic Opportunities and Development.* Washington, D.C.: United States Department of Agriculture, Economic Research Service. http://www.ers.usda.gov/publications/aer731/aer731i.pdf [accessed April 15, 2011].

U.S. Census Bureau. 2009. "American Indian, Alaska Native Tables from the Statistical Abstract of the United States: 2004–2005." *Statistical Abstract of the United States.* Washington, D.C.: United States Census Bureau.

U.S. Census Bureau. 2010. "Overview of Race and Hispanic Origin: 2010." *U.S. Census Briefs.* Washington, D.C.: United States Census Bureau.

U.S. Commission on Civil Rights. 2003. *A Quiet Crisis: Federal Funding and Unmet Needs in Indian Country.* Washington, D.C.: United States Commission on Civil Rights.

U.S. Department of Housing and Urban Development. 1996. *Assessment of American Indian Housing Needs and Programs: Final Report.* Washington, D.C.: United States Department of Housing and Urban Development.

U.S. Department of Housing and Urban Development. 2010. *Notice of Funding Availability (NOFA) for HUD's Fiscal Year 2010 Indian Community Development Block Grant Program.* Washington, D.C. United States Department of Housing and Urban Development, Docket No. FR-5415-N-08. http://archives.hud.gov/funding/2010/icdbgsec.pdf [accessed April 28, 2011].

U.S. Department of Housing and Urban Development. 2011. "Public and Indian Housing: Native American Housing Block Grants 2011 Summary Statement and Initiatives." *2011 CFO Reports*. Washington, D.C.: United States Department of Housing and Urban Development. http://www.hud.gov/offices/cfo/reports/2011/cjs/nahb-grants2011.pdf [accessed April 19, 2011].

U.S. Government Accountability Office. 2010. *Native American Housing: Tribes Generally View Block Grant Program as Effective, but Tracking of Infrastructure Plans and Investments Needs Improvement.* Washington, D.C.: United States Government Accountability Office, GAO-10-326.

Wilkinson, Charles. 2006. *Blood Struggle: The Rise of Modern Indian Nations.* Boston: Norton.

Youmans, Roberta. 2002. "Native American Housing Needs and Proposed Recommendations." Background paper presented to the Federal Housing Finance Board Millennial Housing Commission, Washington, D.C., April 2.

Improving American Indian Education through Best Practices

Jon Reyhner

Establishing best practices in education, let alone American Indian education, is a daunting task. As Ellen Lagemann (2000) pointed out in her study *An Elusive Science: The Troubling History of Educational Research,* educational research is not simple. One cannot assign students and teachers to different "treatments" and expect results that can be replicated in other classrooms and schools in the same way one can plant seeds in various soils under various conditions to find out under what situation plants grow best. Similarly, the medical model of randomized double-blind studies with lots of subjects, considered the "gold standard" of empirical research, is pretty much impossible in schools.

Factors external to classrooms—especially living in poverty and parents' education level—all bear on educational outcomes regardless of teacher quality, curriculum, and instruction. The U.S. Census 2010 American Community Survey found 35 percent of American Indian students living in poverty and 20 percent growing up in families where the head of the household does not have a high school diploma (*KIDS COUNT* 2012). Even new "value added" approaches currently being promoted to evaluate teachers that look at fall–spring test scores to track student gains fail to take into account factors external to schools and classrooms, including the many students that can transfer in and out of a single classroom during the school year in some schools.

An example of the use of research gone awry is the report of the congressionally authorized National Reading Panel (NRP) whose findings were used to design the Reading First provisions of the No Child Left Behind (NCLB) Act of 2001. This panel looked only at research that involved pitting one reading program against another and ignored ethnographic studies where researchers actually observed classroom interaction as well as the role of motivation in getting students to become better readers (Reyhner and Hurtado 2008). The panel also did not include correlation studies, the type of studies that gave the first indications that cigarette smoking caused major health problems and indicate the effect growing up in poverty has on test scores of children (Berliner and Biddle 1995; Berliner 2005). Former International Reading Association president Richard Allington (2002) documents how the NRP and the Reading First advocates got off track by emphasizing the importance of teaching phonics (how to sound out words aloud) in reading instruction and downplaying the importance of knowing what those words mean.

In sharp contrast to the emphasis on teaching phonics that resulted from NRP's report based on research that did not focus on ethnic minority students are those of a well-funded long-term study of the schooling of Native Hawaiian students who historically have not done well in assimilationist English-only schools (Tharp 1982). After trying a phonics approach to teaching reading for two years with very limited results, the Kamehameha Early Education Program (KEEP) researchers changed to a culturally compatible reading comprehension focus that brought student reading test scores to at or near national averages (Tharp and Gallimore 1988; Jordan 1984).

Brayboy and Castagno (2009) note that while some U.S. schools showed some increase in test scores after adopting Reading First approaches, others showed a decline in scores as well as a decline in culturally relevant education. As Lagemann notes, "publishers, test makers, and reformers of every color and stripe can 'sell' their wares without prior piloting or evaluation" (2000, 238). Despite weak research that also almost never focused on American Indian students, teachers are being asked to sign "fidelity" oaths that they will not waiver from implementing detailed scripted "teacher-proof" reading programs that emphasize direct instruction and allow little or no deviation to take into account local needs. Pogrow (2000) documents how a reading program that was designed using the results of various research studies, despite that research backing, can fail to produce the claimed results.

Generally, the NCLB Act has been problematic for Indian Country beyond its Reading First and other provisions. Based on hearings across the United States, the National Indian Education Association (NIEA) documented in 2005 the pressures educators face under the law to provide English-only instruction geared toward high-stakes tests. The NIEA reported NCLB is "narrowing the broad public purposes of schools" with its emphasis on teaching and testing reading and math at the expense of also teaching music, literature, art, history, and Native studies (NIEA 2005, 6). NCLB's emphasis on high-stakes testing in a few academic areas draws attention away from improving the social, mental, and physical well-being of Native children. Testimony at the NIEA hearings indicated that NCLB promotes a "one-size-fits-all" curriculum that makes it difficult for teachers to "connect education to the lives of students in their communities," with the result that schooling is "increasingly boring and disconnected from student lives" (NIEA 2005, 6). Rather than reducing the achievement gap, NCLB increased student dropout rates while driving teachers from the profession (NIEA 2005, 6). An Arizona State University study funded by the U.S. Department of Education similarly documented NCLB-related pressures on new Native teachers to use "rigid prescribed" teaching methods and "canned" commercial curricula because school administrators are worried about their school being labeled "underperforming" under NCLB (Reyhner 2006, Reyhner and Hurtado 2008).

THE ASSIMILATIONIST HISTORY OF AMERICAN INDIAN EDUCATION

Historically schooling for American Indians has focused on "civilizing" them through the teaching of English, Christianity, and the three "Rs," sometimes in boarding schools far removed from the students' homes (Adams 1995; Reyhner and Eder 2004). Although some individuals questioned this culturally assimilationist approach, it remains in many ways the focus of Indian education today, though now most American Indians speak English and it is no longer seen as appropriate to teach religion in public and government-funded Indian schools. Criticism of the U.S. government's handling of American Indians through its Indian Office is not new and was intense in the 1920s. To counter this criticism an independent study of the Indian Office was undertaken by the Brookings Institution at Johns Hopkins University under the direction of Louis Meriam and published in 1928. The education section of this study criticized putting young children in boarding schools and the cultural insensitivity of the schooling they received there (Institute 1928). This questioning of the assimilationist approach was renewed in the 1960s when the civil rights movement and the United Nations focused concerns on human rights. The comprehensive National Study of Indian Education (see Fuchs and Havighurst 1972) done from 1967 to 1971 and report of hearings across the country before the U.S. Senate (1969) Subcommittee on Indian Affairs titled *Indian Education: A National Tragedy, A National Challenge* at that time found serious shortcomings in Indian education. Based on the National Study, Fuchs and Havighurst concluded

> Many Indian children live in homes and communities where the cultural expectations are different and discontinuous from the expectations held by schoolteachers and school authorities. The average Indian family teaches its children valuable attitudes and skills, but conditions of poverty, isolation, nonparticipation in the urban-industrial society, and language difference are conducive to lower performance on the usual measurements of academic achievement (1972, 299).

Despite the findings of various studies going back to the Meriam Report that pointed to a problem of cultural discontinuity between home and school, assimilationist English-only education continues in the center of U.S. Indian policy. Former U.S. secretary of education Dr. Terrel H. Bell stated in 1988, "Regardless of students' cultural and ethnic background, if they are to hope for access to the full range of options available in our society, the language of their education must be English; no other language will suffice" (as quoted in Latham 1989, 8). Glen Latham went on to write "should a tribe decide that English will be taught as a second language, or that the tribal language will be the language of instruction through grades two or three, it must be understood that such a decision has cultural, social, and economic

Omaha boys in cadet uniforms at the U.S. government-administered Carlisle Indian School in Carlisle, Pennsylvania, circa 1880. The Carlisle school was the nation's first off-reservation boarding school, where students were required to abandon their native clothing and hairstyles to assimilate into white culture. (National Archives)

consequences" (Latham 1989, 8–9). In 2003, Arizona Superintendent of Public Instruction Tom Horne remarked as he was sworn into office,

> for students who come to school not speaking English, the first priority is that they must learn English as fast as possible. Then there is no limit to their ability, as individuals, to achieve academic excellence. . . . I will keep my campaign promise to enforce the initiative, under which English immersion is to take the place of bilingual [sic].

The U.S. Secretary of Education's Indian Nations at Risk (INAR) Task Force, which ironically Bell cochaired, called in 1991 for more culturally sensitive education. In the introduction to the Task Force's final report, Bell and cochair Dr. William Demmert, Jr. (Tinglit/Sioux) state, "The Task Force believes that a well-educated American Indian and Alaska Native citizenry and a renewal of the language and cultural base of the American Native community will strengthen self-determination and economic well-being and will allow the Native community to contribute to building a stronger nation" (INAR, iv).

This linkage between language, culture, and community health can be seen in a study by Hallett, Chandler, and LaLonde (2007) examining data from 150 First Nations communities in British Columbia. They found that communities with less conversational knowledge of their native language had suicide rates six times greater than those with more knowledge.

STUDIES SUPPORTING CULTURALLY RELEVANT EDUCATION

One of the most well-known studies of cultural conflict being played out in classrooms is Susan Phillip's (1983) research on American Indian students from the Warm Springs Reservation in Oregon. She concluded that for Indian students to have more academic success, teachers need to be much more aware of the differing communication patterns of different cultures. One could hypothesize that American Indian teachers from the same community as their students would not have these problems, but that is not always the case. As Littlebear (1992) points out, sometimes those teachers assimilated into the mainstream culture in order to be successful and need to be reintegrated into their Native culture if they return home to teach.

Cleary and Peacock (1998) interviewed 60 indigenous and non-indigenous teachers of American Indian students plus 50 other teachers in Australia and Costa Rica and found that traditional culture played a positive role in developing academically successful Indian students. They summed up their findings with a quote from one of the teachers they interviewed, "The key to producing successful American Indian students in our modern educational system . . . is to first ground these students in their American Indian belief and value systems" (101). Based on their study, they emphasized,

> The need to build trust; to connect with the community; to establish cultural relevance in the curriculum; to tap intrinsic motivation for learning; to use humor; to establish family support; to provide situations that yield small successes; to make personal connections with students; to use highly engaging, activity-based learning and in some cases, cooperative learning; to provide role models; to be flexible, fair, and consistent; and to provide real audience and purpose for student work (13).

There are two major approaches to the education of ethnic minority students in the United States today. One is to "blame the victim," which focuses on a deficit idea that families and communities (in this case American Indians) are not doing enough to prepare their children for educational success. The second is "blame the oppressor," which looks at racism and cultural insensitivity in the U.S. educational system. The amount of research done over the years on American Indian students attempting to determine why they either fail or succeed academically is extensive. Deyhle and Swisher (1997) reviewed over a half century of this research and pointed out the poor quality of much of it, finding that research before the 1960s tended to measure American Indian and Alaska Native students using yardsticks, especially intelligence and achievement tests, largely designed for "white" mainstream Euro-Americans. The result was that Indian students were reported to be suffering from cultural and intellectual deficits. In other words, they were considered less "civilized" and less intelligent than white Americans were. However, in the National Study of Indian Education carried out from 1967 to 1971, the Goodenough Draw-A-Man [IQ] Test was given to 867 Indian and Eskimo children ages 6 to 8.5 from 25 schools. Their scores were "well above the national average for Caucasians" (Fuchs and Havighurst 1972, 120). Today, it is seen that if you give an IQ test in standard English to a child that does not speak standard English, to a large measure you are determining standard English-language competence, not intelligence.

Deyhle and Swisher concluded that educational research often viewed Indian cultures as deficient, which "has tended to buttress the assimilatory model by locating deficiencies in Indian students and families" (1997,116). They found that researchers generally ignored the effects of discrimination and echoed the then popular idea that cultural assimilation into mainstream white America was the solution to the "Indian problem" in general and low academic achievement of Indian students in particular. This approach was exemplified by the motto "Tradition is the Enemy of Progress" of a southwestern boarding school that Wilcomb Washburn (1971, 218), director of the American Studies Program at the Smithsonian, recalled seeing in 1952. Another research review by Lomawaima (1995) concluded that studies either overgeneralized, ignoring the diversity among indigenous Americans, or were too specific to one particular tribe.

Alan Peshkin (1997) tackled the question of why American Indian students' academic achievement is below national averages, even in Indian-controlled schools with a high proportion of Indian teachers. Over a period of three years he completed a "thick" ethnographic study of a boarding school serving New Mexico's Pueblo Indians. The school sought to prepare students for college, but academic success was limited. Students participate with sustained effort and enthusiasm in basketball, but "regrettably, I saw no academic counterpart to this stellar athletic performance" (5). He observed that,

> In class, students generally were well-behaved and respectful. They were not rude, loud, or disruptive. More often they were indifferent. . . . teachers could not get students to work hard consistently, to turn in assignments, to participate in class, or to take seriously . . . their classroom performance. (5)

Peshkin found the school staffed with well-educated teachers, and it had the highest percentage of Indian teachers of any high school in New Mexico and parents who valued education. To explain the lack of academic success, Peshkin expanded the cultural discontinuity (two worlds) theory of academic failure (see e.g., Henze and Vanett, 1993). He found "student malaise" originating from an ambivalent attitude of Pueblo Indians toward schooling. After 400 years of contact with European colonists, the Pueblos were deeply suspicious of anything "white." Schools—even Indian-controlled ones with Indian administrators and Indian teachers—remained alien "white" institutions, "places to become white." In contrast to the individualism of mainstream American culture, Pueblo communities taught their children to fit into the group—to stand in versus to stand out. "Schooling is necessary to become competent in the very world that Pueblo people perceive as rejecting them" (107).

The work of anthropologist John Ogbu (1995) sheds light on the situation Peshkin encountered in New Mexcio. Ogbu found evidence that for American Indians and other groups that he classifies as "involuntary minorities," school learning tends to be equated with the learning of the culture and language of white Americans. In other words, learning the cultural and language frames of reference of their enemies and oppressors (587). Ogbu (1983) found minority status to be determined by power relationships that subordinate the minority group, which may or may not be a numerical minority, under a dominant group. The reality, or even the perception, of continuous long-term discrimination could lead to the development of an oppositional identity to the point where "what is depicted as the culture of native peoples represents the absolute opposite of what is thought of as "Western" culture—it is the *Whiteman's shadow*" (Simard 1990, 333, italics in original). So if schools are for whites, they are not for Indians by definition. To counteract this oppositional school identity, it is imperative that a school's curriculum reflects and validates the culture of a student's home and community (Cummins 2009).

One study that documents that the retention of traditional cultural traits do not hurt students' chances for academic success is by Willeto (1999), a Navajo researcher, who reviewed past research and presents findings drawn from a random sample of 451 Navajo high-school students from eleven different Navajo Nation schools. She compared student achievement with students' orientation toward traditional Navajo culture as measured by participation in Navajo ritual activities and cultural conventions as well as Navajo language use. She found no support "for the argument that traditionalism had a negative effect on academic success of Navajo young people" (13). Her findings confirmed previous studies with similar results, including Rindone (1988) and Brandt (1992).

Coggins, Williams, and Radin's study (1997) of 19 Ojibwa families measured traditional orientation by looking at eight characteristics that their literature review identified as core values of a majority of American Indians. These values were sharing, other-centered, harmony with nature, noninterference (in the lives of other people, including one's children), patience, circular time, nonconfrontive, and broad view of family (extended families). They concluded, "the overall picture presented [by their research] is encouraging for those who have argued the importance of maintaining cultural identity among American Indians" (13). Cummins (2000), reviewing the literature on minority education, found that students with a strong sense of cultural and personal identity were more likely to have academic success.

Radda, Iwamoto, and Patrick (1998) surveyed 1,171 students in grades 5 through 12 attending an urban public school district, including 81 American Indians. Indian students reported being retained at three times the rate of non-Indians and a preference for cooperative group over competitive individual activities. They tended to shy away from being praised in front of their peers and those expressing a positive attitude for completing high school were less interested in external "token" type rewards. Similarly to what Deyhle (1992) found, Radda et al. determined that,

> The students also perceive that the intention to complete high school has little to do with employability. There is a disconnection between the intention to complete school and the common perception that it will affect ability to work or get a job. This suggests, as does other data in the study, that the relevance of completing school in relation to employment and type of employment is lacking. These results support the importance of school being personally relevant to the student, the impact the parents can have in reinforcing that relevance, and the work teachers can do to connect schoolwork to the student's life (15).

The National Center for Education Statistics noted that Indian students were less likely than other students to report that "discipline is fair," "the teaching is good," "teachers are interested in students," and "teachers really listen to me" than other racial or ethnic groups (1990, 43). Deyhle, in a seven-year study of Navajo and Ute students, found that they "complained bitterly that their teachers did not care about them or help them in school" (1989, 39). She found, "a little less than half of the Navajo and almost two-thirds of the Ute [students] felt school was not important for what they wanted to do in life" (1989, 42). Students who "experienced minimal individual attention or personal contact with their teachers" interpreted this neglect as "teacher dislike and rejection," and they "spoke of the boredom of remedial classes, the repetition of the same exercises and uninteresting subjects" (Deyhle 1989, 39, 44).

Both Deyhle's (1989, 1992) study and the Navajo Dropout Study (Brandt 1992) found that students gave "boredom" as their major reason for dropping out. Deyhle found that Navajo students perceived school as a cold and unrewarding place with an irrelevant curriculum and uncaring teachers. High-school students typically had instruction that involved being told to read the textbook and answer the questions at the end of the chapter. Because the Navajo and Ute students read on average two grade levels behind their non-Indian peers, such textbook-oriented teaching was especially problematic.

Canada's experience with Indian and Native students has both parallels and differences to that of the United States. One of these parallels is a history of academic failure and attempts to turn that failure around. In a study of 10 schools in north, central, and eastern Canada, from the islands of Hudson Bay to the coast of Newfoundland identified as having exemplary success with indigenous students, the researchers concluded:

> All schools worked to provide culturally relevant learning experiences and affirm students' pride in their identity. Aboriginal language immersion programs were present in about half the schools and in some this was the language of instruction until Grade 6. Most offered local cultural classes—some of which were accredited, and the remainder infused cultural content across the core curriculum. In all schools, the importance of the traditions and culture was affirmed by displays, ceremonies, excursions on the land, and the use of elders and local resource people (Fulford 2007, 12).

A previous Canadian study of successful schools for indigenous students noted, "the fully independent band-operated model provides Aboriginal communities with the greatest control of their educational systems" (Bell 2004, 295). The researchers in that study found that band-operated (locally run) schools could better integrate the delivery of education from Pre-K to postsecondary into an overall community plan.

The Alaska Native/Rural Education Consortium, representing over 50 organizations impacting education in rural Alaska, established the Alaska Rural Systemic Initiative (ARSI) in 1994. After 10 years, data gathered from the 20 rural school districts (compared to 24 other rural Alaskan districts) indicates that its educational reform strategy fostering interconnectivity and complementarity between the formal education system and the indigenous communities being served in rural Alaska had produced an increase in student achievement scores, a decrease in the dropout rate, an increase in the number of rural students attending college, and an increase in the number of Native students choosing to pursue studies in STEM (science, technology, engineering, and math) fields. Figure V.04.1 below shows how the ARSI worked to integrate Native and Western knowledge systems (Barnhardt 2007).

HUMAN RIGHTS AND LANGUAGE IMMERSION

On September 13, 2007, the United Nations adopted the *Declaration on the Rights of Indigenous Peoples.* In contrast to the focus on individual rights that is a Euro-American cultural heritage, this new declaration focuses on the group rights of indigenous peoples to maintain and pass on their languages and cultures to their

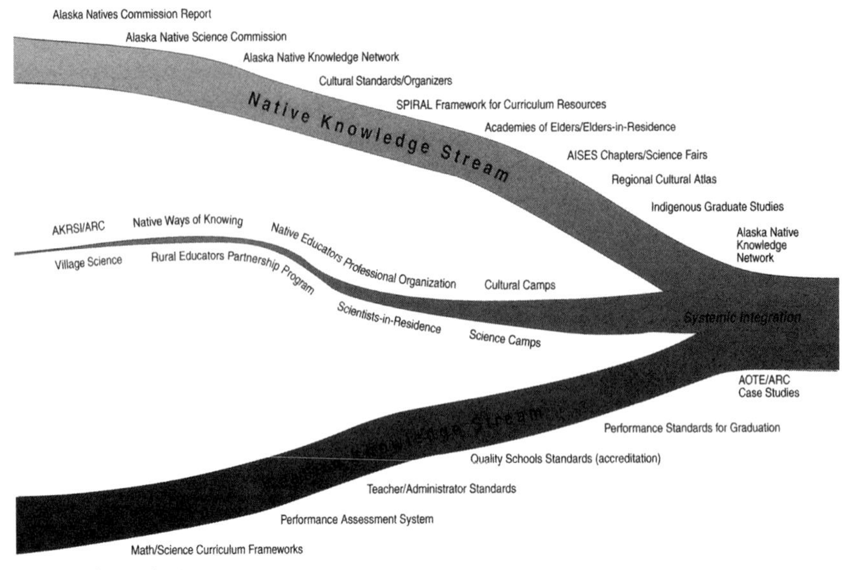

Native and Western Knowledge Systems are integrated through the ARSI (Courtesy of the Alaska Native Knowledge Network)

children. Only four countries voted against this declaration, including the United States of America. However, since then all four have reversed their positions. On December 16, 2010, President Barack Obama declared,

> And as you know, in April, we announced that we were reviewing our position on the U.N. Declaration on the Rights of Indigenous Peoples. And today I can announce that the United States is lending its support to this declaration.
>
> The aspirations it affirms—including the respect for the institutions and rich cultures of Native peoples—are one we must always seek to fulfill. And we're releasing a more detailed statement about U.S. support for the declaration and our ongoing work in Indian Country. But I want to be clear: What matters far more than words—what matters far more than any resolution or declaration—are actions to match those words. . . . That's the standard I expect my administration to be held to (Obama 2010, n.p.).

Article 13-1 of the declaration reads "Indigenous peoples have the right to revitalize, use, develop and transmit to future generations their histories, languages, oral traditions, philosophies, writing systems and literatures, and to designate and retain their own names for communities, places and persons"; and Article 14-1 reads "Indigenous peoples have the right to establish and control their educational systems and institutions providing education in their own languages, in a manner appropriate to their cultural methods of teaching and learning."

In their 2008 review of educational research on culturally responsive schooling for indigenous youth that emphasizes Tribal Critical Race Theory and human rights, Castagno and Brayboy argue that "The increased emphasis on standardization and high-stakes accountability under the No Child Left Behind Act of 2001 seems to have resulted in less, rather than more, culturally responsive educational efforts and more, rather than no, Indigenous children left behind in our school systems" (942). They note the two dominant models of indigenous education discussed in the United States, "the assimilative model and the culturally responsive model" and conclude that "the research is quite clear: there is no evidence that the assimilative model improves academic success; there is growing evidence that the culturally responsive model does, in fact, improve academic success for American Indian/Alaska Native children" (2009, 31). However, they found that "None of the research suggest that Indigenous youth should learn tribal cultures and languages at the expense of learning mainstream culture, English, and the typical 'academic' subjects generally taught in schools" (37).

Huffman (2010) discards older "cultural deficit" explanations used to explain the academic performance of American Indian students and examines newer theories that look at cultural discontinuity between home and school. His review of research supports the idea that American Indian students entering off-reservation colleges with strong tribal identities can draw strength from those identities, enabling them to persevere and be successful students. A "both/and" bilingual bicultural educational approach is advocated that supports American Indian languages and cultures while also teaching the English language and about the United States and the increasingly globalized world we all live in today.

CONCLUSION

The *National Indian Education Study 2011* (National 2012) documents a persistent gap in achievement by American Indian Students that the No Child Left Behind Act of 2001 has been unable to close. NCLB has received extensive criticism for its focus on high-stakes testing and punitive measures against failing students, teachers, and schools. Students are to be retained in grade if they do not reach arbitrary proficiency levels on high-stakes tests, their teachers and principals are to be fired, and their schools are to be restructured. There is little indication that this one-size-fits all draconian approach is producing the desired effects.

While NCLB and President Barak Obama's "Race to the Top" initiative are trying to close the academic achievement gap by focusing on teacher quality and testing, a small but growing effort is looking to heal the wounds of colonialism that leads to alcohol and drug abuse, high suicide rates, and dysfunctional communities by revitalizing indigenous languages and cultures. One of the most promising efforts are the indigenous language immersion schools, mostly small, that are taking mostly English-speaking young Native Hawaiian, Native Alaskan, and American Indian children and immersing them all day in their heritage language and culture and only bringing in English instruction in limited ways or after fifth grade as with Hawaiian immersion schools. Reyhner (2010) argues that these schools, unlike those conforming to NCLB requirements, are in line with the United Nations 2007 Declaration on the Rights of Indigenous Peoples and are healing the wounds of colonialism, helping students persist educationally and providing students with a strong sense of identity that helps them resist the negative effects of the materialistic and hedonistic modern culture that increasingly permeates the mass media in the United States and elsewhere in the world.

FURTHER INVESTIGATIONS

One can either blame teachers, students, and their families for the lower than average academic performance of American Indian and many other ethnic minorities in the United States, or one can blame "white" America for not doing enough to eliminate poverty and to allow for culturally appropriate education for ethnic minorities.

BLAME THE VICTIM

"Blame the victim" supporters tend to see America as providing a "level playing field" where all have an equal chance, and they focus on the importance of individual effort of students to "pull themselves up by their bootstraps" and be successful. They point to how Asian immigrant students and some other ethnic and racial minority groups have been very successful in the United States and question why others cannot be equally successful under existing conditions. If students are not successful, it is because their families suffer from a cultural deficit and refuse to assimilate and/or are lazier and less intelligent than those who are more successful. Efforts by those who blame the victim to help failing students include passing English-only educational laws, as has been done in California, Arizona, and Massachusetts, and promoting a national "one-size-fits-all" core curriculum standards and punitive high-stakes tests with little or no allowances for regional and cultural differences across the United States. Scholars in well-funded conservative "think tanks" put out a steady stream of studies supporting this agenda, and anyone disagreeing with them can be accused of working to disunite America and promoting "class warfare." For example, in a monograph published by the Hoover Institution at Stanford University, Peter Duignan (1998) writes,

> **I reiterate that assimilation through English-only should be the United States' national object—not bilingualization and the ethnicization of America. I observe**

with pleasure that assimilation and intermarriage are ongoing processes. I am pleased that ethnic separatists at U.S. universities have not had much success in converting to their own viewpoints those popular masses for whom the ethnic elites profess to speak.

BLAME THE OPPRESSOR

The "blame the oppressor" supporters see an unlevel playing field where those with power and wealth pass it on from generation to generation and tilt opportunities toward their children, often sending them to expensive private schools and Ivy League universities while children of the poor attend less-well-funded schools and colleges with less-well-prepared teachers who lack adequate teaching supplies (Kozol 1991). At these schools students receive an education that emphasizes rote memory rather than critical thinking and which at best ignores and at worse devalues the cultures and languages of American Indian and other ethnic minorities. Tribal critical race theorists (see e.g., Brayboy 2005) see a hegemonic power structure in the United States supporting tax cuts for the wealthy and budget cuts for social and educational programs for American Indians and other ethnic and racial minorities. Advocates for American Indians tend to call for contextualized place-, community-, and culture-based education that would eliminate the cultural discontinuity between home and school that can hurt Indian students' chances for success (see e.g., Reyhner, Gilbert, and Lockard 2011). Critical race theorists and their allies, many of them liberal university faculty, put out a steady stream of studies documenting the inequality of education received by different social classes in the United States as well as the increasing gap between the rich and poor in America.

References

Adams, David. W. 1995. *Education for Extinction: American Indians and the Boarding School Experience, 1875-1928.* Lawrence: University Press of Kansas.

Allington, Richard L. 2002. *Big Brother and the National Reading Curriculum: How Ideology Trumped Evidence.* Portsmouth, NH: Heinemann.

Barnhardt, R. 2007. "Creating a Place for Indigenous Knowledge in Education: The Alaska Native Knowledge Network." In *Place-based Education in the Global Age: Local Diversity,* edited by G. Smith and D. A. Gruenewald, 113–53. Hillsdale, NJ: Lawrence Erlbaum Associates.

Bell, David. 2004. *Sharing Our Success: Ten Case Studies in Aboriginal Schooling.* Kelowna, BC, Canada: Society for the Advancement of Excellence in Education. http://www.academia.edu/3481931/Sharing_our_success_More_case_studies_in_Aboriginal_schooling [accessed June 7, 2013].

Berliner, David. C. 2005. "Our Impoverished View of Educational Reform." *Teachers College Record* 108 (6): 949–95.

Berliner, David C., and Bruce J. Biddle. 1995. *The Manufactured Crisis: Myths, Fraud and the Attack On America's Public Schools.* Reading, MA: Addison-Wesley.

Brandt, Elizabeth A. 1992. "The Navajo Area Student Dropout Study: Findings and Implications." *Journal of American Indian Education* 31 (2): 48–63.

Brayboy, Bryan M. J. 2005. "Toward a Tribal Critical Race Theory in Education." *Urban Review* 37 (5): 425–46.

Brayboy, Bryan M. J., and Angelina E. Castagno. 2009. "Self-Determination through Self-education: Culturally Responsive Schooling for Indigenous Students in the USA." *Teaching Education* 201: 31–53.

Castagno, Angelina E., and Bryan M. J. Brayboy. 2008. "Culturally Responsive Schooling for Indigenous Youth: A Review of the Literature." *Review of Educational Research* 78: 941–93.

Cleary, Linda Miller, and Thomas D. Peacock. 1998. *Collected Wisdom: American Indian Education.* Boston: Allyn and Bacon.

Coggins, Kip, Edith Williams, and Norma Radin. 1997. "The Traditional Tribal Values of Ojibwa Parents and the School Performance of Their Children: An Exploratory Study." *Journal of American Indian Education* 36 (3): 1–15.

Cummins, Jim. 2000. *Language, Power and Pedagogy: Bilingual Children in the Crossfire.* Clevedon, UK: Multilingual Matters.

Cummins, Jim. 2009. "Pedagogies of Choice: Challenging Coercive Relations of Power in Classrooms and Communities." *International Journal of Bilingual Education and Bilingualism* 12 (3): 261–71.

Deyhle, Donna. 1992. "Constructing Failure and Maintaining Cultural Identity: Navajo and Ute School Leavers." *Journal of American Indian Education* 31 (2): 24–47.

Deyhle, Donna. 1989. "Pushouts and Pullouts: Navajo and Ute School Leavers." *Journal of Navajo Education* 6 (2): 36–51.

Deyhle, Donna, and Karen Swisher. 1997. "Research in American Indian and Alaska Native Education: From Assimilation to Self-Determination." In *Review of Research in Education,* edited by Michael W. Apple, Vol. 22, 113–94. Washington, D.C.: American Educational Research Association.

Duignan, Peter J. 1998. *Bilingual Education: A Critique.* Palo Alto, CA: Hoover Institution. http://www.hoover.org/publications/monographs/27198.

Fuchs, Estelle, and Robert J. Havighurst. 1972. *To Live on This Earth: American Indian Education.* Garden City, NY: Doubleday.

Fulford, George. 2007. *Sharing Our Success: More Case Studies in Aboriginal Schooling.* Kelowna, BC, Canada: Society for the Advancement of Excellence in Education. http://www.academia.edu/3481931/Sharing_our_success_More_case_studies_in_Aboriginal_schooling [accessed June 7, 2013].

Hallett, D., M. J. Chandler, and C. E. Lalonde. 2007. "Aboriginal Language Knowledge and Youth Suicide." *Cognitive Development* 22: 392–99.

Henze, Rosemary C., and Lauren Vanett. 1993. "To Walk In Two Worlds—Or More? Challenging a Common Metaphor of Native Education." *Anthropology and Education Quarterly* 24 (2): 116–34.

Horne, Tom. 2003, January 6. *Remarks at Time of Swearing into Office.* http://129.219.247.59/attachments/77562/content/2003%20Inauguration.pdf%E2%80%8E [accessed June 7, 2013].

Huffman, Terry. 2010. *Theoretical Perspectives on American Indian Education: Taking a New Look at Academic Success and the Achievement Gap.* Lanham, MD: AltaMira.

INAR–Indian Nations at Risk Task Force. 1991. *Indian Nations at Risk: An Educational Strategy for Action.* Washington, D.C.: U.S. Department of Education.

Jordan, Cathy. 1984. "Cultural Compatibility and the Education Of Hawaiian Children: Implications for Mainland Educators." *Educational Research Quarterly* 8 (4): 59–71.

KIDS COUNT Data Book. 2012. Baltimore, MD: Annie E. Casey Foundation.

Kozol, Jonathan 1991. *Savage Inequalities.* New York: Crown.

Lagemann, Ellen Condliffe. 2000. *An Elusive Science: The Troubling History of Education Research.* Chicago: University of Chicago Press.

Latham, Glenn I. 1989. "Thirteen Most Common Needs of American Indian Education in BIA Schools." *Journal of American Indian Education* 29 (1): 1–11.

Littlebear, Dick [Richard]. 1992. "Getting Teachers and Parents to Work Together." In *Teaching American Indian Students,* edited by Jon Reyhner, 104–11. Norman: University of Oklahoma.

Lomawaima, K. Tsianina. 1995. "Educating Native Americans." In *Handbook of Research on Multicultural Education,* edited by James A. Banks and Cherry A. Banks, 331–42. New York: Macmillan.

National Center for Education Statistics. 1990. *National Education Longitudinal Study of 1988: A Profile of the American Eighth Grader* (NCES 90-458). Washington, D.C.: Author.

National Center for Education Statistics. 2012. *National Indian Education Study 2011.* http://nces.ed.gov/nationsreportcard/pdf/studies/2012466.pdf [retrieved July 17, 2012].

NIEA–National Indian Education Association. 2005. *Preliminary Report on No Child Left Behind in Indian Country.* Washington, D.C.: Author.

Obama, Barak. 2010. Remarks by the President at the White House Tribal Nations Conference, December 16. http://www.whitehouse.gov/the-press-office/2010/12/16/remarks-president-white-house-tribal-nations-conference [accessed June 7, 2013].

Ogbu, John U. 1983. "Minority Status and Schooling in Plural Societies." *Comparative Education Review* 17 (2): 169–90.

Ogbu, John U. 1995. "Understanding Cultural Diversity and Learning." In *Handbook of Research on Multicultural Education,* edited by James A. Banks and Cherry A. Banks, 582–93. New York: Macmillan.

Peshkin, Alan. 1997. *Places of Memory: Whiteman's Schools and Native American Communities.* Mahwah, NJ: Lawrence Erlbaum.

Philips, Susan Urmston. 1993/1983. *The Invisible Culture: Communication in Classroom and Community on the Warm Springs Indian Reservation.* Prospect Heights, IL: Waveland.

Pogrow, Stanley. 2000. "Success for All Does Not Produce Success for Students." *Phi Delta Kappan* 82 (1): 67–80.

Radda, Henry T, Dawn Iwamoto, and Carolyn Patrick. 1998. "Collaboration, Research and Change: Motivational Influences on American Indian Students." *Journal of American Indian Education* 17 (2): 2–20.

Reyhner, J. 2006. "Issues Facing New Native Teachers." In *The Power of Native Teachers: Language and Culture in the Classroom,* edited by David Beaulieu and Anna M. Figueira, 63–92. Tempe: Center for Indian Education, Arizona State University.

Reyhner, Jon. 2010. "Indigenous Language Immersion Schools for Strong Indigenous Identities." *Heritage Language Journal* 7 (2): 138–52.

Reyhner, Jon, and Jeanne Eder. 2004. *American Indian Education: A History.* Norman: University of Oklahoma Press.

Reyhner, Jon, and Denny S. Hurtado. 2008. "Reading First, Literacy, and American Indian/Alaska Native Students." *Journal of American Indian Education* 47 (1): 82–95.

Reyhner, Jon, Willard S. Gilbert, and Louise Lockard, eds. 2011. *Honoring Our Heritage: Culturally Appropriate Approaches for Teaching Indigenous Students.* Flagstaff: Northern Arizona University. http://jan.ucc.nau.edu/~jar/HOH [accessed June 7, 2013].

Ridone, Pauline. 1988. "Achievement Motivation and Academic Achievement of Native American Students." *Journal of American Indian Education* 28 (1): 1–7.

Simard, Jean-Jacques. 1990. "White Ghosts, Red Shadows: The Reduction of North American Indians." In *The Invented Indian: Cultural Fictions and Government Policies,* edited by James A. Clifton, 333–69. New Brunswick, NJ: Transaction Publishers.

Tharp, Roland G. 1982. "The Effective Instruction of Comprehension: Results and Description of the Kamehameha Early Education Program." *Reading Research Quarterly* 17: 503–27.

Tharp, Roland G., and Gallimore, Ronald. 1988. *Rousing Minds to Life: Teaching, Learning, and Schooling in Social Context.* Cambridge: Cambridge University Press.

United Nations. 2007. Declaration on the Rights of Indigenous Peoples. General Assembly Resolution 61/295 on September 13, 2007. http://www.un.org/esa/socdev/unpfii/documents/DRIPS_en.pdf [accessed June 7, 2013].

U.S. Senate. 1969. *Indian Education: A National Tragedy, a National Challenge.* 1969 Report of the Committee on Labor and Public Welfare, 91st Congress, 1st Session, Report No. 91-501. Washington, D.C.: U.S. Government Printing Office.

Washburn, Wilcomb E. 1971. *Red Man's Land/White Man's Law: A Study of the Past and Present of the American Indian.* New York: Charles Scribner's Sons.

Willeto, Angela A. 1999. "Navajo Culture and Family Influences on Academic Success: Traditionalism Is Not a Significant Predictor of Achievement among Young Navajos." *Journal of American Indian Education* 38 (2): 1–21.

Native American Employment and Unemployment Issues

Yuka Mizutani

Before the arrival of European settlers, Native American people (i.e., American Indians and Alaska Natives in this context) had relied on a subsistence style of living (i.e., fishing, hunting, and farming) to conduct their lives. Also, Native American societies had managed and maintained natural resources on their lands, and conducted economic activities in their own ways (Smith 2000, 31; O' Neill 2004, 13). After their arrival, European settlers took lands away from Native Americans. To Native American people, losing land meant losing ways to access "a steady supply of renewable inputs into the production of various goods such as food, clothing, shelter, hunting materials, and the like" (Smith 2000, 29). At the same time, the idea of capitalism was brought by settlers, which changed the economic system on the American continent (Champagne 2007, 45–62). Therefore, in modern society, most Native American people work in various industries to gain monetary income. In addition, federally led Native American relocation programs have encouraged them to move to cities and become employed. Yet various historical and modern problems are creating a "pattern of poverty" (Cornell and Kalt 2007, 6) that "tears at their social fabrics and culture" (Cornell and Kalt 2007, 5).

RESEARCH

Very little scholarly research specifically focused on the employment of Native American people has been conducted. Knack and Littlefield conducted research about Native American people employed as wage laborers, writing that "studies of North American Indian economic life have largely ignored the participation of indigenous people in wage labor" (1996, 3). According to Knack and Littlefield, there are two main reasons behind the ignorance about Native American employment. First, researchers have been more concentrated on discussions regarding Indian policy than economic activities (1996, 3.) Second is "the restrictive definition of Native American economics as an issue of natural resources, specifically land" (1996, 4). Hunt et al. attempted to analyze employment of Native American people by state and local governments, and wrote "there are no studies in the political science and public administration literatures that focus primarily on American

Indian employment" (2010, 409). These authors also suggested that "studies in the extant literature suffer from some notable shortcomings" (Hunt et al. 2010 415).

NATIVE AMERICAN TRADITIONAL WORK

For some Native American peoples, natural resources are important parts of their economy. Wilma Mankiller (1945–2010), a Cherokee woman who led the tribe from 1985 to 1995, remembers her family living in a rural part of the Cherokee Nation in Oklahoma. She wrote that they "raised large vegetable gardens and harvested plant foods from the woods, such as wild onions, greens, mushrooms, and berries" (Mankiller 1993, 34). She also wrote about her family hunting groundhog, wild pig, and squirrel, as well as catching various kinds of bird and fish to supplement their diet (1993, 34). Although Mankiller recalls that her family sold strawberries and peanuts for cash (1993, 34), most of their activities were not associated with cash. This type of work may not appear in statistics as employment, but it certainly contributes to the economy of the community.

Fishing and hunting are also an important part of the current Native American economy. At the same time, getting natural resources can be more of a cultural and ritual

Inupiat Eskimo Fred Weyiouanna drags a seal he just shot and harponed onto his boat, during the traditional spring hunt, June 15, 2005 on the Chukchi Sea near Shishmaref, Alaska. Located on the small island of Sarichef off the coast of Alaska near the Artic circle, Shishmaref, population 591, is a century old Inupiat Eskimo village whose economy depends partly on subsistence fishing and hunting. (Getty Images)

matter than just getting food or selling for monetary income. For example, some Alaska Native peoples hunt whale, as well as other wild animals such as caribou. According to Banerjee, an Inupiat community called Kaktovik catches up to three whales each September (2009, 190). "After each whale is brought to shore, the entire community, elders, adults, and children, gather first to give thanks to the whale and the creator for providing food for their community, and then participate in the butchering and sharing of the muktuk (whale blubber and skin) and other parts of the whale" (Banerjee 2009, 190). This is an example of how the Native American economy functions. In the words of Champagne, "sharing and redistribution is generally preferred to accumulation for reinvestment in the marketplace" (2007, 321). In the case of the Kaktovik, catching whales as a community and sharing it among community members is their way of economic activity, which is different from that of the U.S. dominant society. In fact, Robyn points out, Native American ways of conducting economic activities are balanced, and such sustainable use of natural resources can benefit many non–Native American people as well (Robyn 2006, 176–77).

Other examples of non–employment-based work characteristic of Native American people include berry picking; hide tanning; beading; and competing in dance, song, and drumming at powwows for prize money (O'Nell 1996, 103–4).

OCCUPATION AND INCOME

As stated above, a subsistence style of living with natural resources and a tradition of sharing are important parts of Native American culture. However, in modern society, Native American people are more likely to be engaged in industries not related to natural resources. According to the U.S. Census 2000, among total Native American workers, only 1.3 percent (national average 0.7 percent) work in the field of farming, fishing, and forestry (Ogunwole 2006, 10). Other Native American people today are employed in various fields. Table V.05.1 shows that fewer Native American people are employed in management or professional jobs than the national average. As for distribution of people among different occupations, only a slight difference is seen among different Native American peoples (Ogunwole 2006, 10; see table 1).

As for wages, when working full time and year-round, the average income of Native American men is about US$28,900 (national average $37,100) and of women $22,800 (national average $27,200; Ogunwole 2006, 11). In other words, the average income of both Native American men and women is lower than the national average. Moreover, 25.7 percent of Native American people live under the poverty level, which is almost double the national average (Ogunwole 2006, 12).

In addition, considering only the Native American people on reservations, the per capita income becomes as low as $7,942 a year (U.S. Senate, Committee on Indian Affairs 2010, 3). Thus, Native American people on reservations earn much less than Native American people in general.

Table V.05.1 Native American Peoples and Types of Occupation

Name of people	Management, professional, and related	Service	Sales and office	Farming, fishing, and forestry	Construction, extraction, and maintenance	Production, transportation, and material moving
National Average (non-Native American)	33.6	14.9	26.7	0.7	9.4	14.6
Average of American Indian and Alaska Native	24.3	20.6	24.0	1.3	12.9	16.8
Apache	23.7	21.4	24.6	1.8	13.0	15.5
Cherokee	26.9	18.0	24.3	0.9	12.8	17.2
Chippewa	24.9	24.5	23.1	0.8	12.0	14.5
Choctaw	28.6	17.6	24.4	1.4	12.1	15.9
Creek	28.3	16.6	26.6	1.1	12.0	15.4
Iroquois	26.8	19.1	22.8	0.7	11.7	18.9
Lumbee	21.5	15.2	16.6	1.0	20.0	25.6
Navajo	22.2	20.1	24.4	0.6	16.9	15.8
Pueblo	26.9	21.8	27.3	0.6	11.0	12.4
Sioux	26.0	23.8	24.5	1.0	10.5	14.2
Alaskan Athabaskan	26.4	22.1	27.4	0.5	11.7	11.9
Aleut	22.2	20.7	26.7	5.4	10.5	14.4
Eskimo	27.3	22.3	26.7	1.0	10.6	12.2
Tlingit-Haida	25.6	20.0	27.2	3.0	10.1	14.2

Source: Ogunwole, Stella U. 2006. *We the People: American Indians and Alaska Natives in the United States: Census 2000 Special Reports.* U.S. Census Bureau, U.S. Department of Commerce.

UNEMPLOYMENT RATE

The Native American unemployment rate is high, especially in reservations. In 2009, the unemployment rate of Native Americans in general was 12.4 percent (U.S. Senate, Committee on Indian Affairs 2010, 3). The unemployment rate on reservations at the same time was 21.9 percent (U.S. Senate, Committee on Indian Affairs 2010, 3). Nationally, the unemployment rate at the same time was 5.7 percent (U.S. Senate, Committee on Indian Affairs 2010, 3). The unemployment rate of Native American people on reservations in 2009 was 3.8 times higher than the national average.

Native American unemployment rates on reservations are almost the same as during the Great Depression. In 1933 (unemployment rate regardless of race was 25 percent, which is only 3.1 percent higher than the unemployment rate of Native Americans on reservations in 2009 (U.S. Senate, Committee on Indian Affairs 2010, 3). Moreover, on some reservations the unemployment problem is even more serious. On the Colville Reservation in Washington State, the unemployment rate was 50 percent in 2010 (U.S. Senate, Committee on Indian Affairs 2010, 7). Clearly, employment of Native American people is in a critical situation.

One of the factors causing Native American unemployment is a fundamental difference between the dominant U.S. belief and those of Native American peoples on economy. Champagne points out that "Native Americans have not been quick to accept capitalist enterprise, either at present or historically" (2007, 47) because "native communities . . . do not wish to sacrifice culture, preferred institutional relations, and their internal social relations in favor of economic development" (2007, 58). In other words, the low employment rate among Native American nations is occasioned by their choice, yet the capitalism the dominant society brought forced them into this situation.

EMPLOYMENT ON RESERVATIONS

An additional reason for the lower employment rates on reservations is partially related to their unique environment. Schaap has pointed out that many Native American reservations and other tribally owned lands are in rural or isolated locations, where it is hard to develop economies since "access to markets is one of the most important components of economy building, and much tribal land is simply too isolated to attract consumers" (2010, 367). Massey conducted research about employment at the Wind River Indian Reservation in Wyoming, and found a similar situation. He wrote that this reservation is "an environment with almost no manufacturing and assembly operations, few private-sector service jobs, and few jobs requiring professional and technical expertise" (2004, 797). What is available there is "only marginal agricultural employment" (2004, 801). Massey also pointed out the shortage of job opportunities and "poor fit between available human capital and job requirements" (2004, 800). The same conditions would apply to many other reservations and tribally owned lands throughout the United States.

According to Massey, jobs on reservations are typically found at schools; health clinics; local government; and in maintaining and repairing roads, houses, and other tribal facilities (2004, 801). The variety of jobs is limited, as is the number of jobs. As a result, regardless of the job seeker's levels of education and skills, finding a job on the reservation becomes extremely difficult

(Massey 2004, 801). Moreover, Massey noted "a lack of confidence on the part of young people to find and retain gainful employment and personal doubts that hinder their initiative to apply what they have learned in school" (2004, 802). It is obvious that shortage of employment is negatively affecting the self-esteem of young people on reservations, which further worsens Native American unemployment.

Messages about the issue of unemployment and education are conveyed in a fictional movie, *The Brave,* directed by Johnny Depp in 1997 and based on a novel of the same title by Gregory McDonald. The main character, Rafael, lives in a small Native American (tribe not specified) rural community. He has not been employed for years. Occasionally, he gets money from robbery. In addition, Rafael and other community members collect scrap metal and useful electrical appliances from the dump next to the community. With his wife and two children, Rafael lives in a tiny old mobile home, just as other people in the community do. There is no school. There is electricity, but no running water and other basic infrastructure. One day, Rafael takes a bus to get to a city, in search of a job. The job available for him is being murdered for a snuff film. Rafael receives an advance on the film contract. He goes home with the money and spends it on his family and community members. After one week, he needs to get back to the studio to "complete his job." Before leaving the community, Rafael tells his son Frankie that Frankie needs better living conditions and education in order to be successful in the future.

As a fictional movie, some exaggeration is included in the story. For example, snuff films are unlikely to happen in the real world. However, some aspects introduced in this movie represent real problems Native Americans face. Just like the community in the movie, 12 percent of Native American homes are without running water and 13 percent are without electricity (DeMarban 2011, n.p). In 2000, 14.8 percent of Native American people lived in overcrowded houses, and the rate is 2.5 times higher than the U.S. average (Indian Health Service 2005, 17). In terms of education, 29.1 percent of the Native American population receive less than a high school education (national average 19.6 percent), and 11.5 percent complete four years of college (national average 24.4 percent; Ogunwole 2006, 17). When the number is limited to reservations and tribally owned land, 33.1 percent of people do not finish high school, and only 8.1 percent receive a college degree (Ogunwole 2006, 17). In the movie *The Brave,* Rafael was worried that his son Frankie would end up undereducated and unemployed like himself.

PROGRAMS FOR NATIVE AMERICAN EMPLOYMENT

However, leaving a rural community for the city is not the only solution to the need for an education or a job. Many Native American cultures and beliefs are deeply related to their lands. Also, spending time with family members and elders is important to keep many Native American cultures alive. Today, there are many programs offered by the federal government and nonprofit organizations to assist Native American people in receiving education and training, in order to be employed within Native American communities. As of 2009, eight federally funded programs specifically for Native Americans and Native Hawaiians are provided by various departments (U.S. Government Accountability Office 2011, 65).

To enhance the employment of Native American people, the Bureau of Indian Affairs in the Department of the Interior runs programs related to employment of federally recognized tribes. Under the Indian Employment, Training and Related Services Act of 1992 (Public Law 102-477), BIA' s Division of Workforce Development in Indian Energy and Economic Development serves 50,000 Native American clients a year and has distributed more than $100 million (Division of Workforce Development 2011). This act was later amended by the Omnibus Indian Advancement Act of 2000 (Public Law 106-568) in order to integrate Native American employment-related programs across various departments of the federal government.

For example, the Department of Labor conducts programs to provide job training and employment to Native Americans. Section 166 of the Workforce Investment Act (WIA) of 1998, entitled Native American Programs, explain services provided for Native American people. According to this section, the federal government provides grants for "Indian tribes, tribal organizations, Alaska Native entities, Indian-controlled organizations serving Indians, or Native Hawaiian organizations" (WIA §166 1998) to "meet the needs of Indians or Native Hawaiians preparing to enter, reenter, or retain unsubsidized employment" (WIA §166 1998). This definition shows that more people can apply for the WIA' s program than for the BIA' s. In 2011, over $52.1 million were provided to 180 tribes and organizations. In addition, $12.3 million were provided to 136 tribes and organizations for the WIA Youth Program (U.S. Department of Labor 2011).

Other programs are run by the Department of Health and Human Services (DHHS), in collaboration with Native American tribes. For example, with tribal work grants from the DHHS and funding from other organizations, Cook Inlet Tribal Council in Alaska conducts its Healthcare Training Program, which provides the tribe's member opportunities to get nursing licenses (Cook Inlet Tribal Council 2011).

In addition, the Department of Education conducts Native American and Native Hawaiian specific programs related to employment. These include Vocational Rehabilitation Services Projects for American Indians with Disabilities, Career and Technical Education—Indians Set-Aside, Native Hawaiian Career and Technical Education, and Tribally Controlled Postsecondary Career and Technical Institutions (U.S. Government Accountability Office 2011, 6).

NATIVE AMERICAN EDUCATION AND EMPLOYMENT

Historically, job training has been emphasized in Native American education in general, and instructors have encouraged their students to engage in labor work. However, such a policy has brought both positive and negative impacts on Native American peoples.

In 1839, a manual labor school for Native American youth was built in the Methodist Shawnee mission in Kansas. The school provided agricultural and domestic skills, as well as English language skills, to both male and female students on the reservation. Officials in the federal government at this time thought that to Native American students, schools teaching manual labor were more valuable than grammar schools (Prucha 1984, 101). Then, industrial off-reservation Indian schools started to be promoted in the 1880s. The number of this type of school increased to 25, with 7,430 students, by 1890 (Prucha 1984, 280). In addition, there were 81 boarding schools on reservations at the same time. Boarding schools also started focusing on industrial training (Prucha 1984, 280).

The preference in Indian education for vocational training continued in the 1900s, 1910s, and 1920s. In the Course of Study promulgated in 1901, half of the time in Indian schools was expected to be spent on industrial and domestic works (Prucha 1984, 284). In the Course of Study of 1922, vocational education was divided into two years of junior vocational phase and four years of senior vocational phase. Although the time for vocational training in the junior phase was reduced, it was enhanced in the senior phase by adding new courses such as gas engines and auto mechanics (Prucha 1984, 285).

When the Indian New Deal started in 1935, at first BIA director John Collier was critical about Native American education heavily focused on job training. Collier and his staff tried to change this policy by either closing Indian boarding schools or turning them into community day schools (Prucha 1984, 329). However, soon they changed their minds and supported Native American education with vocational training. This was because they came to believe that some job training was essential for Native American students for their survival (Prucha 1984, 329–30).

The outbreak of World War II caused a huge budget cut in Native American education. Due to the budget cut, as well as increased demand for labor, both teachers and students left schools and worked in the military or industries related to war (Prucha 1984, 330; Parman 1994, 107). The Indian Citizenship Act of 1924 had enabled all Native Americans to be able to join the military. Therefore, more Native American people fought in WWII than in WWI (Parman 1994, 111). It is recorded that 24,521 Native American men (Parman 1994, 111) and about 800 Native American women (Parman 1994, 110) served in the military. In 1943, approximately 12,000 Native American women worked in the war industry (Parman 1994, 110). Even a separate

Native American military unit was discussed. In fact, a unit consisting of all Navajo people was made by the Selective Service Act of 1940 (Parman 1994, 112).

RELOCATION PROGRAM AND NATIVE AMERICAN EMPLOYMENT

After the war period, vocational training started to be provided in conjunction with the program to relocate Native Americans from reservations to urban areas. From the 1950s to the 1970s, the U.S. federal government tried to help Native American people to get wage work by implementing the Indian Relocation Act of 1956 (Public Law 959). Between 1952 and 1972, more than 100,000 Native American people participated in this program to work in urban areas, although many of them later returned to their rural communities (Nagel 1996, 120). The BIA established relocation offices to assist Native American relocatees in large cities, such as Chicago, Los Angeles, Denver, San Francisco, San Jose, and St. Louis, starting in 1956. In 1958, the number of these offices increased to 12; however, only 8 of them (4 in California, in addition to Chicago, Cleveland, Denver, and Dallas) remained by 1960 (Prucha 1984, 355).

The Indian Relocation Act of 1956 provided three types of services: on the job training programs, adult vocational training programs, and Direct Employment Programs (Fixico 2000, 16–17). On the job training for Native American individuals provided 24 months of training on or near the reservation, in order to increase their possibilities of being employed in cities (Fixico 2000, 16–17). Adult vocational training was for Native Americans between 18 and 35 years old with families, and participants were trained for certain manual skills. The direct employment program provided job information, as well as employment on the reservation. In this program, BIA program workers made arrangements between potential Native American relocatees and employers in urban areas. Then, Native Americans were given a one-way ticket to BIA' s relocation centers in cities to settle and work (Fixico 2000, 17).

The Indian Relocation Act of 1956 was reformed a year later, and the Indian Vocational Training Act of 1957 (Public Law 959) was established. By this act, vocational training centers were established to provide job training in 125 occupations for Native American workers, along with accredited schools in 26 states (Fixico 2000, 17). In these centers and schools, Native American relocatees acquired skills and knowledge useful for employment especially in an urban setting.

Lamore-Chaote was one Native American relocatee to the San Francisco area, originally from the Fort Yuma Indian Reservation in California at the Arizona state line. She wrote how she felt when she got a job at the University of California at

Berkeley as a secretary: "around 10 am my counselor from BIA called and told me I got the job and to report to work that same day. . . . It was like a dream; one day I' m in school and the next I' m working at one of the most prestigious universities in the country, in one of the first Native American studies programs in the nation" (Lamore-Chaote 2002, 40). She continued: "My years at the Native American studies office were very exciting and rewarding—I couldn't' have dreamed up a more exciting job" and "it gave me a chance to experience some wonderful things in my life" (2002, 41).

However, such experiences didn't happen to everyone who participated in the relocation program. Most Native American relocatees were employed in seasonal railroad and agricultural work, which was temporary and paid less than other jobs (Fixico 2000, 12). Also, Fixico argues that "American Indians have been restricted to blue-collar types of jobs because of the old myth that Indians work best with their hands," and such ideas prevented Native American people from becoming leaders and administrators (2000, 77). This tendency seems to be continuing until today, as shown in the "Occupation and Income" section of this article: in 2000, the rate of Native American people working in management and professional jobs was 9.1 percent lower than the national average (Ogunwole 2006, 10).

Additionally, Fixico reported that Native American relocatees who acquired English skills had higher income than the ones who didn't (Fixico 2000, 49). At the time of the relocation period, many Native American relocatees spoke various Native American languages. In 1970, 26 percent of the urban Native American people in the San Francisco Bay Area spoke in Native American languages rather than English (Fixico 2000, 49). The policy of encouraging Native American people to use English rather than their own languages possibly impacted on the loss of Native American languages since then.

Currently, there are various opinions on the relocation program. Johnson wrote, "many relocatees, discouraged, disillusioned, and with no other place to turn, returned to their reservations" (Johnson 2008, 12). At the same time, according to Johnson, relocatees "chose to remain in urban areas and hang onto their dream of a better life, a better future to pass on to their children, an easier life with running water, indoor toilets, automobiles, telephones, employment, educational opportunities, and material goods not obtainable on most reservations" (2008, 13). Moisa has pointed out that some relocatees were lost in the totally foreign environment, and "some Indian leaders believe the program hurt tribal government by draining off the supply of young potential tribal leaders" (2001, 26). Yet some relocatees later went back to their homelands and helped people there with skills acquired at urban areas; some relocatees adapted to urban lives and kept living in the cities (Moisa 2001, 26).

Native American relocatees who remained in cities constructed a new united identity as Native American beyond differences among various Native American cultures. It became a base for the American Indian Movement (AIM). When Alcatraz Island was occupied as a part of AIM, Indians of All Tribes, the group led the occupation and issued a proclamation for Native American rights. In the proclamation, the topic of Native American employment was taken up, among many other issues. Indians of All Tribes asked for "a great Indian Training School . . . to teach our people how to make a living in the world, improve our standards of living, and end hunger and unemployment among all our peoples" (Eagle 1997, 63).

FUTURE OF NATIVE AMERICAN EMPLOYMENT

Although many Native American individuals are unemployed, now many Native American tribes are job suppliers, especially in the field of gaming. In the past few decades, Native American tribes started to establish and run bingo operations to gain funding to support the tribal economy (Schaap 2010, 365). In 1987, in the court case California v. Cabazon Band of Mission Indians, the U.S. Supreme Court recognized Native American rights to run casinos (Schaap 2010, 365). Then, the Indian Gaming Regulatory Act was established in 1988. The act prescribed that "all the revenues from gaming activities be used to promote the economic development and welfare of these tribes" (Shaap 2010, 366). Many consumers prefer Native American tribal casinos near urban areas to Las Vegas, because "when airplane fares and other costs of transportation are high, some gaming consumers prefer to drive to a relatively close Indian casino instead of to large gaming establishments that are farther away" (Schaap 2010, 367).

As a result, the Native American gaming industry grew rapidly. In 2008, 233 Native American tribes ran 411 casinos, and 636,000 jobs (284,000 direct Indian gaming, 102,000 indirectly related to Indian gaming, and 208,000 Indian gaming and government projects) were created (Schaap 2010, 369). Considering the high unemployment rate among Native Americans, especially on tribally owned lands, the number of jobs created by the casino industry was huge. The created positions provide employment opportunities for non-Native American people in local areas, too (Schaap 2010, 383).

Besides gaming, an increasing number of other kinds of enterprises are being established and operated by Native American people, as a tribe or as individuals. According to the U.S. Census, in 2007, 237,286 Native American–owned businesses were being operated, which is a 17.9 percent increase from 2002 (U.S. Census Bureau). These Native American–owned firms employed 184,416 persons in 2007 (U.S. Census Bureau). By state, California holds the largest number of these firms (13.5 percent of total Native American–owned firms), and Oklahoma (8.9 percent) and Texas (8.0 percent) follow (U.S. Census Bureau).

Types of Native American–owned businesses in the 1970s and 1980s were mainly small grocery stores, gas stations, repair stations, and arts and crafts stores (Champagne 2007, 54). Today, diversity and uniqueness are seen in terms of types of Native American–owned business. Following are some examples. In 2011, the Cherokee Nation established a company to produce outfits for babies and youth. The company's products are not traditional outfits. They are baby bodysuits and T-shirts available anywhere. However, traditional Cherokee images and symbols are printed on them (Indian Country Today Media Network 2011a). Another example is Yocha Dele Wintun Nation in California, which started a business to grow olive trees and produce olive oil on tribally owned land (Indian Country Today Media Network 2011b). These businesses can increase the number of jobs available to Native Americans while contributing to their cultural maintenance and environmental protection. They can benefit the construction of a healthier social and cultural environment for the next generation, while bringing money to Native American people.

Although the number of Native American people working as managers and professionals is still small, it is steadily increasing. Consequently, today, Native American business specialists are supporting Native American enterprises, and creating employment opportunities for Native American people. There are organizations to help set up these companies. For example, the National Center for American Indian Enterprise Development (NCAIED) was established by Native American community leaders in Los Angeles in 1969 (later the headquarters moved to Mesa, Arizona). According to NCAIED's website, they "have worked with approximately 80 percent of the tribes and assisted over 25,000 Indian Enterprises while training over 10,000 tribal members in various aspects of business development" and their clients have "obtain[ed] over $4.5 billion in contracts and financing" (2011).

According to the U.S. of Commerce Minority Business Development Agency (MBDA), there are various Native American–owned enterprises (see table V.05.2).

Table V.05.2 American Indian & Alaska Native–Owned Firms' Top Industry Sectors, 2007

All Other Industry Sectors	29.0%
Construction	15.9%
Health Care and Social Assistance	10.6%
Professional, Scientific, and Technical Services	10.1%
Administration, Support, Waste Management and Remediation Services	9.6%
Retail Trade	8.4%
Arts, Entertainment, and Recreation	5.7%
Transportation and Warehousing	5.5%
Real Estate, Rental and Leasing	5.2%

Source: MBDA; United States Department of Commerce, Minority Business Development Agency. 2007. "American Indian & Alaska Native Owned Business Growth and Global Reach."

Among 236,967 firms owned by Native American people, 23,704 companies have employees, and these companies employ 184,416 people (MBDA 2007). More employment opportunities for Native American people can be created when enterprises owned by Native American tribes and individuals are enhanced and supported.

CONCLUSION

In a book about the relationship between Native Americans and European settlers on the Rosebud Reservation of the Oglala Sioux Tribe, South Dakota, Biolsi mentioned the high unemployment and poverty rate (2007, xviii). He added, "as many Indian people would insist, the poverty story may deflect attention from other justice issues" (2007, xix–xxi). As an example, Biolsi pointed to ignorance of sovereignty, which was indirectly causing Native American unemployment and poverty. Biolsi thinks ignorance of sovereignty is a result of colonization (2008, xxi).

As previously mentioned, federal policy on Native American education has aimed to train Native American people for simple types of manual labor. The assumption that Native American people do well in such jobs, rather than showing their leadership, professions, and talents, may be understood as a part of the legacy of colonization, just as Biolsi said.

Many issues are contained in the topic of Native American employment, such as Native American education and land tenure. The combination of these issues is producing "the cycle of employment and unemployment" (Massey 2004, 788). There are many potential ways to stop this negative cycle. Strengthening of sovereignty and enhancement of Native American–owned business would be some of many choices.

◀ FURTHER INVESTIGATIONS ▶

Because of their historical legacy and modern-day elements, Native Americans have unique challenges with respect to employment opportunities compared to those of people from other ethnic groups.

1. **Effects from Native American education and relocation programs**
   The high rate of unemployment among Native American people is a result of limited educational opportunities and the practice of relocation designed by the federal government. Although the education provided for Native American people has improved for some, and the relocation program has ended, the problems that resulted remain today. The federal government needs to provide opportunities for Native American young people to know what types of jobs are available in addition to low-paid blue-collar jobs. Moreover, supplemental educational funds and supports are necessary to provide better education for descendants of the urban relocatees, in order for them to be able to work as professionals.

2. **High unemployment rate in reservations**
   The unemployment rate is higher in reservations. Also, there are few employment opportunities available in reservations. It is necessary to create places to work in reservations. Tribes are expected to establish new companies and stores on reservation lands. Additionally, creative venture companies should be run by Native American individuals. Multiple federal and nonfederal programs support Native American small businesses owners. In order to increase the number of Native American business owners, more support may be required to help Native American students attending colleges and MBA programs. Also, the federal government, together with tribal governments, needs to establish new regulations to support Native- and non-Native–owned companies operating in reservations.
3. **Needs for diversification of economical resource**
   In terms of economic development, the gaming industry is popular among Native American nations. During the current economic recession, relying solely on the gaming industry may be risky. Native American tribes would be more stable economically if industries available in their areas become more diverse. Although natural resources are available in most reservations, with modern technologies, it is possible to start various types of business, including IT-related companies and organic agriculture. The federal government needs to provide support to improve infrastructure in reservations, so Native American tribes can start running such businesses to create more employment opportunities for their members.

References

Banerjee, Subhankar. 2009. "Terra Incognita: Communities and Resource Wars." In *The Alaska Native Reader: History, Culture, Politics,* edited by Maria Shaa Tláa Williams, 184–91. Durham, NC: Duke University Press.

Biolsi, Thomas. 2007. *Deadliest Enemies: Law and Race Relations On and Off Rosebud Reservation.* New ed. Minneapolis: University of Minnesota Press.

Champagne, Duane. 2007. *Social Change and Cultural Continuity among Native Nations.* Lanham, MD: AltaMira Press.

"Cherokee Nation Launches Kids and Baby Clothing Line." 2011. *Indian Country Today Media Network,* July 22 [accessed online Oct. 25, 2011].

Cook Inlet Tribal Council. n.d. "Finding Jobs: Healthcare Training." http://www.citci.com/content/healthcare-training [accessed July 25, 2011].

Cornell, Stephen, and Joseph P. Kalt. 2007. "Two Approaches to the Development of Native Nations: One Works, the Other Doesn't." In *Rebuilding Native Nations,* edited by Miriam Jorgensen, 3–33. Tucson: University of Arizona Press.

DeMarban, Alex. 2011. "Tribes and Obama: Rating the President's Progress on Native American Policy." *First Alaskans Magazine* Feb./March [accessed online Oct. 1, 2011].

Depp, Johnny. 1997. *The Brave.* Majestic Films International.

Division of Workforce Development, Indian Energy and Economic Development, Bureau of Indian Affairs, U.S. Department of the Interior. Workforce Development. http://www.bia.gov/WhoWeAre/AS-IA/IEED/DWD/index.htm [accessed May 24,, 2013].

Eagle, Adam Fortunate. 1997. "Urban Indians and the Occupation of Alcatraz Island." In *American Indian Activism: Alcatraz to the Longest Walk,* edited by Troy Johnson, Joane Nagel, and Duane Champagne, 53–73. Urbana: University of Illinois Press.

Fixico, Donald L. 2000. *The Urban Indian Experience in America.* Albuquerque: University of New Mexico Press.

Hunt, Valarie H., Brinck Kerr, Linda L. Ketcher, and Jennifer Murphy. 2010. "The Forgotten Minority: An Analysis of American Indian Employment Patterns in State and Local Governments, 1991-2005." The *American Indian Quarterly* 34 (4) (Fall): 409–34.

Indian Health Service, U.S. Department of Health and Human Services. 2005. *The First 50 Years of the Indian Health Service: Caring & Curing.*

Johnson, Troy R. 2008. *Red Power and Self-Determination: The American Indian Occupation of Alcatraz Island.* New ed. Urbana: University of Illinois Press.

Knack, Martha C., and Alice Littlefield. 1996. "Native American Labor: Retrieving History, Rethinking Theory." In *Native Americans and Wage Labor: Ethnohistorical Perspectives,* 3–44. Norman: University of Oklahoma Press.

Lamore-Choate, Yvonne. 2002. "My Relocation Experience." In *Urban Voices: The Bay Area American Indian Community,* edited by Susan Lobo, 38–41. Tucson: University of Arizona Press.

Lobo, Susan, and Kurt Peters, eds. 2001. *American Indians and the Urban Experience.* Walnut Creek, CA: AltaMira Press.

Mankiller, Wima. 1993. *A Chief and Her People: An Autobiography by the Principal Chief of the Cherokee Nation.* New York: St. Martin's.

McDonald, Gregory. 1991. *The Brave.* Fort Lee, NJ: Barricade Books.

Massey, Garth. 2004. "Making Sense of Work on the Wind River Indian Reservation." *The American Indian Quarterly* 28 (3) and 28 (4): 786–816.

Moisa, Ray. 2002. "Relocation: The Promise and the Lie." In *Urban Voices: The Bay Area American Indian Community,* edited by Susan Lobo, 21–28. Tucson: University of Arizona Press.

Nagel, Joane. 1996. *American Indian Ethnic Renewal: Red Power and the Resurgence of Identity and Culture.* Oxford: Oxford University Press.

National Center for American Indian Enterprise Development. 2010. "History of the Organization" [accessed online, July 29, 2011].

O' Neill, Colleen. 2004. "Rethinking Modernity and the Discourse of Development in American Indian History, an Introduction." In *Native American Pathways: American Indian Culture and Economic Development in the Twentieth Century,* edited by Brian Hosmer and Colleen O' Neill, 1–24. Boulder, CO: University Press of Colorado.

O' Nell, Theresa DeLeane. 1996. *Disciplined Hearts: History, Identity, and Depression in an American Indian Community.* Berkeley: University of California Press.

Ogunwole, Stella U. 2006. *We the People: American Indians and Alaska Natives in the United States: Census 2000 Special Reports.* U.S. Census Bureau, United States Department of Commerce.

Omnibus Indian Advancement Act of 2000 (Public Law 106-568).

Parman, Donald L. 1994. *Indian and the American West in the Twentieth Century.* Bloomington: Indiana University Press.

Prucha, Francis Paul. 1984. *The Great Father: The United States Government and the American Indians.* Abridged ed. Lincoln: University of Nebraska Press.

Robyn, Linda. 2006. "Criminalizing of the Treaty Right to Fish." In *Native Americans and the Criminal Justice System,* edited by Jeffrey Ian Ross and Larry Gould, 161–77. Boulder, CO: Paradigm Publishers.

Schaap, James I. 2010. "The Growth of the Native American Gaming Industry: What Has the Past Provided, and What Does the Future Hold?" *The American Indian Quarterly* 34 (3) (Summer): 365–89.

Smith, Dean Howard. 2000. *Modern Tribal Development: Paths to Self-Sufficiency and Cultural Integrity in Indian Country.* Walnut Creek, CA: AltaMira Press.

U.S. Census Bureau. 2011. *Survey of Business Owners and Alaska Native-Owned Firms: 2007.* June 7. http://www.census.gov/econ/sbo/get07sof.html?14 [accessed Oct. 3, 2011].

U.S. Department of Commerce, Minority Business Development Agency (MBDA). 2007. *American Indian & Alaska Native Owned Business Growth and Global Reach.*

U.S. Department of Labor. Employment and Training Administration. 2011. "TEGL 34-10—Notice of Program Year (PY) 2011 Final Youth and Adult Allotments for the WIA Section 166 Program." June 16. http://wdr.doleta.gov/directives/attach/TEGL/TEGL34-10.pdf [accessed July 20, 2011].

U.S. Government Accountability Office. 2011. *Multiple Employment and Training Programs: Providing Information on Colocating Services and Consolidating Administrative Structures Could Promote Efficiencies.* Report to Congressional Requesters. January.

U.S. Senate, Committee on Indian Affairs. 2005. Oversight Hearing on "Unemployment on Indian Reservations at 50%: The Urgent Need to Create Jobs in Indian Country." Written Testimony of the National Congress of American Indians.

Workforce Investment Act of 1998 (Public Law 105–220). Section 166. 1998.

"The Yocha Dehe Return Focus to Their Land through an Olive Oil Enterprise—and More." 2011b. *Indian Country Today Media Network,* June 13.

"Rationally Designed to Further Indian Self-Government": American Indians and Affirmative Action

D Anthony Clark

Because the Negro labored, he was considered a draft animal. Because the Indian occupied large areas of land, he was considered a wild animal.

—Vine Deloria Jr. (1969, 252)

News media, scholarly presses, and legal journals have dedicated considerable time and many volumes to affirmative action (for a synthesis, see Leiter and Leiter 2011). Seemingly commonsensical, the term *affirmative action* in fact signifies a variety of public and private policies and strategies tied to ending racial discrimination in public life. Sympathetic scholars draw largely from the African American experience to distinguish affirmative action optimistically in terms of racial justice. Sociologists Nijole Benokraitis and Joe Feagin (1978), for instance, defined it as aggressive actions which remove barriers to education and employment. Philosopher Gertrude Ezorsky (1991) depicted affirmative action as both a remedy for institutional racism and commitment to right historical wrongs. Other scholars understand it in terms of democratic aspirations and struggle. Black studies scholar Gerald Horne (1992, 2), for instance, characterized affirmative action as "a core component of the ongoing struggle for democracy." Similarly, critical race scholars Charles Lawrence III and Mari Matsuda (1997, 1) "see affirmative action as a gain for all, an affirmation of democratic values."

The prevailing narrative of affirmative that has African American and Latina/o actors on center stage ignores American Indians. Federal law distinguishes American Indians from other racialized minorities as having a political status (Baca 2005; Fletcher 2008; Pevar 2012). Representing hundreds of distinct communities (566 as of August 2012), American Indians are the only racialized group that negotiated treaties as sovereigns—often exchanging land to preserve some measure of autonomy from the aggressively expanding United States. The U.S. Senate ratified hundreds of these agreements. There were hundreds more that the Senate did not approve. It amended many to the point that American Indian tribes rejected them.

There were countless additional agreements between tribes and the federal and state governments, other nation-states (e.g., France and Spain), the Republic of Texas and Confederate states, and even railroad companies. Vine Deloria Jr. and Raymond DeMallie (1999) identified a wide range of unratified treaties, agreements, and conventions between 1775 and 1979. Many treaties and agreements negotiated between the United States and tribes included terms for education, often in exchange for ceding land to public or private interests (see, for instance, Deloria 1974). Thus, rather than understanding it only in terms of racial justice or democratic aspirations, affirmative action for American Indians and tribes also comes into view as a political struggle to self-determine connections with the United States and uphold the terms of earlier agreements.

AIMS OF THIS CHAPTER

The purpose of this chapter is to provide an overview and examination intended to raise an awareness of the distinguishing features of affirmative action and the rights of American Indians and tribes. For tribes, the U.S. political economy of affirmative action originates in intergenerational transfers of land and attempted destruction of tribal political economies, and, as a result, wealth and power to the United States and non-Native Americans. Drawing from a synthesis and summary of existing research and available data, my aim is to urge consideration of the steps taken by American Indians to make use of the U.S. political economy of affirmative action as one means of exercising and expanding their rights both as domestic dependent nations and as U.S. citizens who happen to be Indians.

For theoretical grounding, my analysis of U.S. political economy of affirmative action draws in part from historical materialism. Framed with York University professor emeritus Ellen Wood's "political Marxism," the U.S. political economy of affirmative action comes into view as one aspect of material production and production relations that are political in the sense that are contested "as relations of domination, as rights of property, as the power to organize and govern production and appropriation." She suggests that "the object of this theoretical stance is practical, to illuminate the terrain of struggle by viewing modes of production not as abstract structures but as they actually confront people who must act in relation to them" (1995, 25). Extending Wood's theoretical stance with the conceptual concerns of white supremacy and settler colonialism, in this chapter I frame the U.S. political economy of affirmative action as one site of contestation over what constitutes both racial justice and the rights of American Indian tribes.

WHITE SUPREMACY AND SETTLER COLONIALISM

Centering American Indians in analyses of the U.S. political economy of affirmative action, scholarly perspectives on white supremacy and settler colonialism are critical (Smith 2012). Indeed, the racial formation of the white "race" is foundational to the development of modern capitalism in the British colonization of the Atlantic seaboard before 1790 and the territorial expansion of United States afterward (Martinot 2010; Omi and Winant 1994). White supremacy provided the rationale under industrialized and corporatized capital for purposefully allocating economic and educational advantages unevenly between whites and differently racialized communities (Roediger 1999; 2006). While in the political context of 21st century financialized global capital these advantages still are not uniformly dispersed among all whites, as a number of scholars have argued, a "white" norm nonetheless has currency as material and psychological wages under the class and race logics of white supremacy. Thus, white supremacy is foundational to the *racialization* of a stratified social order of asymmetrical access to wealth and power. As the tangible returns of white supremacy are inseparable from the substantial compensations of property, settler colonialism is foundational to them as well (see, for instance, Moreton-Robinson 2008; Wolfe 2011). In the name of "Manifest Destiny," white settler material production and racialized production relations replaced indigenous production relations and justified the common sense of liquidating Indians from their wellsprings of wealth and power—land and its biospheric features that support all life. Not much has changed. In "Who Owns the Land?" Jess Gilbert and colleagues (2002) determined that at the end of the 20th century whites owned 97 percent of value in all privately owned agricultural land and 98 percent in all acreage.

RACIALIZATION & RACIAL CATEGORIES

In order to better understand this analysis, two terms must be understood: racialization and racial categories. *Racialization* is a basic concept in critical studies of race (see, for instance, Murji and Solomos 2005) that explains the role of race and racism as organizing principles in political economies. As the epigraph from Vine Deloria Jr. intimates, the racialization of African Americans as domesticated beasts and Indians as untamed creatures during the national eras of both slavery (1790–1865) and Indian dispossession (1790–present) rationalizes nation building in political and economic terms. In its relationship to the wild animals it named "Indians," the nation needs exploitable land; thus, in the drama of white supremacy's ascendency and continuance, Indians perform the vital role of getting out of the way of progress.

Thus understood as products of history, *categories of racial difference* shape relations between "us" and "them." As such, racial categories provide conviction to the view that whites as "us" are more entitled to the bulk of society's resources because it was "our" ancestors' considerable intellect and substantial risk that built the nation. This "white racial frame" (Feagin 2010) vindicates the prevailing material inequalities by situating them in fixed traits of phenotypic or cultural differences for "them." Thus, racial categories for "them" are most productively understood as constructs that legitimize white supremacy's rewards.

Racial categories also provide means to counter the white racial frame. Broad designations such as "people of color" and "American Indian" in this sense are best understood as identities from which minoritized human beings and their allies come together to create the conditions necessary for safer, more self-determining futures (Sheth 2009). As imposed through violence, the racialized designation *Indian* may alternatively both undermine antiracism struggles (Trudell 2005; Yellow Bird 1999) and validate collective action to repossess what was taken. Thus, without ignoring this assessment of "the Indian" as problematic, I draw upon the term in this chapter to shed light on two critical points. First, "the Indian" summons a long history of collective action against injustice and, thus, continued resistance to the miserable material conditions made for Indians by white supremacy and settler colonialism (Porter 2006). Second, *Indian* is the term used in treaties and the Commerce Clause of the U.S. Constitution; it offers a necessary basis from which to make legal claims in federal courts and on the world stage (Baca 2005).

EMPLOYMENT, EDUCATION, AND THE POLITICAL STATUS OF INDIAN TRIBES

Two distinct threads distinguish the U.S. political economy of affirmative action for Indians from other racialized communities: Indian preference law in employment (25 U.S.C. § 472) and a patchwork of approaches to remedy wrongs in the historically white traditions of higher education. When framed either as rights of tribes or civil rights, employment and education do not stand alone. There are other battlefields in the larger struggle for tribal self-determination and racial justice. Understood in a context of white supremacy and settler colonialism, for instance, the matter of fair housing for Indians and tribes, like equal opportunity in employment and education, is tied to the form of tribal self-government dictated by Congress (Public Law 104-330). Thus, U.S. affirmative action for Indians and tribes alike must be understood in the broader context of the consolidation of federal power and legislative concessions to Indians' insistence on self-determining political relationships with the United States (Ingram 1998). The United States and Indian tribes long have pursued treaty-based relations as sovereigns. In the domains of both employment and education, the focal point of this chapter, Indians have sought redress from racial harassment in a struggle for simply exercising what constitutes U.S. citizenship. Thus, histories of federal Indian control law and racial harassment both figure in the U.S. political economy of affirmative action.

Indian Preference

The U.S. Congress in 1934 codified "Indian preference," an affirmative employment policy ostensibly designed to strengthen tribal self-governance. Indian preference in federal employment today applies only to two cabinet-level agencies: the Department of Interior's Office of the Special Trustee for American Indians and the Bureau of Indian Affairs, primary administrator of federal trust responsibilities and principal custodian in the ward-guardian relationship, and the Department of Health and Human Services' Indian Health Service (IHS). Under the terms of Tribal Employment Rights ordinances (TERO), many tribal governments

Navajo nurses inspect slides in the laboratory class in the first nursing school program for Native American students in the hospital on the Navajo reservation at Ganado, Arizona, July 14, 1947. The school was set up by Dr. Clarence G. Salsbury in partnership with Sage Memorial Hospital in Ganado. (AP Photo)

administer their own tribal employment preference policies in tribal-sector businesses and construction projects (Smith 2011) and in Public Law 93-638 contracts (25 U.S.C. § 450), which shift the administration of tribal affairs from the BIA to tribal governments themselves.

Contemporary Indian preference law attaches to a broad range of employment practices in the federal and tribal governments alike. According to several acts of Congress and affirmed in federal case law since 1974, its purpose is to facilitate tribal self-governance and economic self-sufficiency on U.S. terms by increasingly drawing Indians and tribes into market capitalism and careers enjoyed by the professional middle class (e.g., attorneys, business administration). More than 300 sections in Chapter 25 of the *Code of Federal Regulations* control the administration of Indian preference. Thus written, Indian preference applies to employment in everything from tribal judicial systems to the federal civilian workforce to contracts awarded by the Federal Highway Administration to state highway agencies and their contractors and subcontractors for projects on or near Indian reservations. Hundreds of Indian tribes work from tribal employment rights ordinances (TEROS), which allow for the enforcement of employment preference in contracts with private-sector companies conducting business on or near Indian Country.

Because Congress codified it, Indian preference law is inseparable from federal control over the political terms of tribal self-governance. Congress first forged Indian preference in 1834, directing U.S. diplomats to employ Indian interpreters in treaty negotiations and other federal dealings with Indians and tribes. Under pressure from tribal delegations to the nation's capital and Indian graduates of federal government schools, Congress mandated Indian preference in a series of laws between 1882 and 1903 for BIA clerical staff, laborers, and teachers (Cahill 2011). These statutes required Indians to qualify for BIA jobs under the educational requirements of civil service standards, which, because of their not having the opportunity to acquire the necessary educational credentials, excluded most Indians from federal employment. In response to stubborn lobbying from nongovernmental groups and the representatives of tribal governments, Congress made small appropriations in the Indian Reorganization Act of 1934 (25 U.S.C. § 472) for vocational education tied to an Indian employment preference that exempted Indians from civil service requirements. As part of subsequent legislation, Congress expanded Indian preference law to tribal government practices in hiring, subcontracting, and vending.

Compelling adherence to Indian preference in federal employment is an outcome of Indians' persistence in exposing abuses of law (Ono 2011). Indian employees at BIA offices in New Mexico and Utah, for instance, filed a series of complaints in 1969. An internal investigation found that while Indians made up 53 percent of all BIA employees, supervisors segregated them in entry-level, low-paying positions. In practice after 1934 senior-level administrators rationed Indian preference, using it only for reappointments and making entry-level appointments; they refused to use it to make promotions and lateral moves (Anderson 1980), which were available primarily to whites. Thus, under pressure from Indian employees seeking redress and confirmation of their allegations from the BIA's internal investigation, Secretary of the Interior Rogers C. B. Morton in 1972 issued guidelines to force actual results in BIA employment of qualified Indians.

Secretary Morton defended his concessions to Indian employees in the U.S. Supreme Court's first affirmative action case. White BIA employees from New Mexico in a class-action suit claimed that the secretary's guidelines deprived them of property rights without due process. The U.S. Supreme Court in Morton v. Mancari (417 U.S. 535) struck down a district court finding in favor of the white employees. Writing the opinion for a unanimous Court in 1974, Justice Harry Blackman held that "Indian preference is reasonable and rationally designed to further Indian self-government." It does not, he held, "constitute 'racial discrimination' or even 'racial' preference." He indicated that filling jobs and promoting employees was "granted to Indians not as a discrete racial group, but, rather, as members of quasi-sovereign tribal entities." Thus, the Supreme Court affirmed that fostering the ward (Indian)-guardian (U.S.) relation is a matter of the domestic-dependent political status of Indian tribes (Fletcher 2008).

Today only the BIA and IHS employ substantial percentages of Indians in the federal civilian workforce. Indian preference means that Indian applicants may fill vacancies only when qualified. If there are no qualified Indian applicants, administrators are required by law to select from qualified non-Native Americans. According to the National Academy of Public Administration, Indians comprised 90 percent of the BIA's permanent workforce at the end of the 20th century. According to the IHS, 68 percent of its employees in 2001 were Indians. In the opening decade of the twenty-first century, Indians occupied almost all senior-level positions in the headquarters, regional offices, service units, and program offices of both federal agencies.

Within the entire federal civilian workforce, Indians virtually disappear. According to the *Congressional Record* in July 1970, less than 2 percent of all federal jobs were filled by Indian employees (cited in Gamino 1974); in 2010, according to the U.S. Office of Personnel Management, Indians were 1.8 percent of two million federal employees. According to a study of federal salaries requested by Congress in 2006, Indians remained as segregated as they had been 40 years earlier. Noting that the number of Indian employees in 2006 was "so small that a trend [could] hardly be detected," the non-partisan Congressional Budget Office (CBO) reported that Indians represented less than 1 percent of all senior-pay levels in the entire federal civilian workforce. With an average annual salary of $52,752, the CBO reported, Indians were the lowest paid federal civilian employees. Whites in 2006 were the highest paid at $90,000.

Enduring Hostility to Indian Preference

Contextualizing criticisms of Indian preference in unemployment data is critical. Chronic and intergenerational unemployment among all Indians in the 21st century poses a colossal challenge for tribal governments and Congress alike. Indians in 2010 represent about one-half of 1 percent of the nation's total civilian labor force of 140 million workers. The BIA in 2005 found an unemployment rate of 49 percent in Indian Country. In South Dakota and Louisiana, the unemployment rate among Indians in 2005 was 83 and 93 percent, respectively. Using a methodology that includes Indians living outside of Indian Country, the Economic Policy Institute (EPI) reported a gap of 6.1 percent between white (9.2 percent) and Indian (15.3 percent) unemployment during the first half of 2010 at the height of an economic recession. In Alaska, according to the EPI, unemployment among Indians was 21.3 percent in 2010. Thus, even with statutory Indian preference in federal and tribal employment that has been affirmed by federal court case law since 1974, 80 years after the Indian Reorganization Act, considerable unemployment in rural and urban Indian and Alaska Native communities nonetheless lingers unresolved during both good economic times and bad.

In the context of massive unemployment among Indians, Indian employment preference law nonetheless is under attack. In Niagara County of western New York, for instance, where the collapse of industrialized capital and corporate outsourcing has devastated majority-white communities and families, the Seneca Nation of Indians in 2009 was upgrading a golf course and country club on tribally acquired property. A county administrator called the tribal government's preference statute and BIA endorsement of it "socially repugnant." The business manager of a private-sector union called the tribal law "unfair." These opponents ignored the contradictory evidence published in a local newspaper. The tribe employed 3,500 workers, 60 percent of whom were white residents of Niagara County. Less than 6 percent of these employees were Indians.

Higher Education

Interpreting concessions from historically-white colleges and universities to allegations of racial bias is complicated. The responsiveness of states and private colleges and universities may be related to the proximity of tribal governments and Indian advocacy groups to governors, state legislators, and university administrators. They may be tied to media reporting that understands the political status of Indian tribes and their rights under federal law. Creating the conditions necessary to make higher education available to Indians and tribes also may be linked to local protest movements against racist symbols and traditions. Thus, we must understand that higher education concessions to Indians and tribes are time-specific and local.

Nongovernmental organizations track affirmative action measures taken by state governments. As part of its Indian Education Legal Support Project, for instance, Native American Rights Fund (NARF) staff attorney Melody McCoy identified 24 states in 2005 that mandated higher education grants or scholarships, recruitment, or tuition waivers for Indians who were accepted to enroll in community colleges and public universities. Of these 24 states, 9 have cooperative agreements with tribal governments. Thus, state-mandated affirmative action programs for Indians and tribes vary widely; they are tied as much and perhaps more to a wide variety of unique local circumstances than to federal mandates.

Among the 24 states singled out by NARF is Michigan's Indian Tuition Waiver Program. While its legal authority today is codified in Public Act 174, as Martin Reinhardt (with Tippeconnic, 2010) detailed, Michigan legislators have not made appropriations for this purpose without ongoing pressure from Indians themselves. What became Public Act 174 (The Waiver of Tuition for North American Indians Act) in 1976, according to Reinhardt, was not a benevolent undertaking by non-Native American Michigan legislators. Rather, the Michigan law was a legislative response to a shrewd political strategy in which Indians alleged that the state flagrantly ignored treaty rights. In 1934, without participation from tribal governments, the state and federal governments alone negotiated an agreement in which Michigan accepted land held in trust for Indians by the United States in exchange for assuming the federal government's obligation to fund treaty-negotiated Indian education (Reinhardt and Tippeconnic 2010). What sovereign (federal, tribal, state) was responsible for what aspects of the education of Indians in Michigan remained unresolved.

Michigan's Indian tuition waiver was a watered-down, precarious response to the education provisions of 16 different treaties ratified by the U.S. Senate between 1817 and 1864. One of these treaties, the Treaty of Fort Meigs in 1817, for instance, traded land for continued access to St. Anne Catholic religious services and the incorporation of the University of Michigania near Detroit. Michigan acquired the land and rights to the Catholic university in 1934 and moved it to Ann Arbor where the University of Michigan is today. After Michigan banned racially conscious affirmative action in 2006 and following a successful outcome by the 12 federally recognized Michigan tribes to convince lawmakers that their legal status is political not racial, Indian applicants to colleges and universities since 2010 nonetheless must evidence one-fourth Indian blood quantum or prove citizenship in one of 565 federally-recognized tribes. They must meet state residency requirements and be accepted into one of Michigan's community colleges or universities. The State of Michigan Department of Civil Rights processes applications; students' tribes must verify them. As an outcome of amending the law in 2006, the citizens of state-recognized tribes no longer are eligible for the tuition waiver. Thus, the Michigan example suggests that tribal governments must hold political power to pressure state governments; it also reveals the limits of federal Indian control law as the means to deliver racial justice in historically white institutions of higher education.

Situating the Michigan example as concessions to tribes working from treaty law, Illinois comes into view as a case of redressing racial bias without the participation of tribal governments. State of Illinois Compiled Statutes disperses Indians into a broad category of difference that may eliminate deliberate strategies for recruiting them in the state's colleges and universities. The Illinois law places responsibility for addressing underrepresentation in higher education admissions on campus administrators who may delegate responsibility to marginalized committees whose reports they then ignore. The University of Illinois at Urbana-Champaign, for instance, elected in 2007 not to implement Project 200, an affirmative action measure developed by the American Indians Studies faculty for the Chancellor's campus-wide Diversity Committee. Illinois Project 200 included a tuition-waiver for Indians from tribes that, under extreme duress, were removed from the state between 1817 and 1833. It also outlined a five-year plan for graduating 200 tribally recognized Indian students modeled after earlier programs at the university that had increased the enrollment of African American and Latina/o students.

Lingering Antagonism to Affirmative Action in Higher Education

Political and judicial attacks on affirmative action gains made through the protest traditions among racialized communities, including Indians, have left their future seeming bleak. Between 1996, with Proposition 209 in California, through *Grutter v. Bollinger* (539 U.S. 306) in 2003, and *Fisher v. the University of Texas* (570 U.S.), legal hits to equal consideration, opportunity, and results in law school admissions led to re-segregating law schools at UCLA, the University of Texas, and the University of Michigan (Lawrence 2001).

This should not suggest that Indians and their allies have been lackadaisical as they look ahead to achieving racial justice in education. Their actions take form largely as defensive maneuvers. In Michigan, for instance, Indians from 12 federally recognized tribes and their allies blocked attacks from legislators like Tea Party-favorite Dave Agema (R-Grand Rapids), who drew upon racial bias in 2008 to argue that Michigan's anti-affirmative action ballot initiative Proposal 2 mandated an end to the Indian tuition waiver; the waiver, he suggested, was not a treaty right (*Grand Rapids Press,* June 16, 2008). The staff of the Grand Valley State University newspaper followed Agema's lead in an editorial entitled "Waive it Goodbye." While the tuition waiver remains in Michigan law for now, there is no guarantee that Michigan legislators will not continue searching for ways to undermine it.

ELECTORAL PARTICIPATION AS AFFIRMATIVE ACTION

Before turning to my closing thoughts, I present a brief note about Indian electoral participation. Individual Indians are represented in Congress only as citizens of states and inhabitants of congressional districts. Tribes currently are not represented. In a context of pervasive racial bias as an obstacle to electoral politics for Indians (McCool, Olsen, and Robinson 2007; McDonald 2010), there are tribal rights at issue in electoral participation that are intimately tied up in the U.S. political economy of affirmative action. Thus, there are two views on this matter. On the one hand, ACLU attorney Laughlin McDonald (2010) and David Wilkins and Heidi Kiiwetinepinesiik Stark (2005) defend electoral participation. National Congress of American Indians president Joe A. Garcia went so far in 2007 to suggest that "Increasing civic participation among American Indian and Alaska Native communities is imperative to protecting sovereignty and ensuring Native issues are addressed on every level of government." John Marshall Law School professor Michael D. Oeser (2010), on the other hand, argues that "reservation citizens are embracing the demise of tribal governments if they continue to participate in federal and state elections." Academic lawyer and president of the Seneca Nation Robert Porter (1999; 2002; 2006) condemns participation, asserting that doing so undercuts struggles to restore tribal sovereignty. Thus, electoral politics offers an immediate means to participate in defending against both attacks on Indian and tribal employment preference and assaults on treaty-based rights to education such as those in Michigan. However, continued participation in this political economy may undermine longer-term visions of tribal autonomy.

CONCLUSION

> *The utmost good faith shall always be observed toward the Indians; their land and property shall never be taken from them without their consent.*
>
> —Northwest Ordinance (1787)

> *Affirmative action by the Congress of the United States to define Indian tribes as smaller nations . . . would freeze the present Indian lands within the context of national boundaries rather than reservation boundaries.*
>
> —Vine Deloria Jr. (1985, 252)

As the United States wrestled land away from Indians, it distributed the wealth it acquired to whites. Generations in the making, a racial wealth gap in the 21st century separates whites from all racialized minorities. According to the Insight

Center for Community Economic Development, families of color in 2009 owned only 16 cents for every dollar owned by the average white family. Drawing from Census 2010 data, the Pew Research Center (2011) found that the 2007 recession erased decades of small gains made by racialized communities, including Indians; the racial wealth gap between whites and "not white" minorities was wider after 2007 than it had been in 1995.

The political status of Indians and tribes distinguishes them from other exploited racialized minorities. Standing for the accumulation of wealth and power disproportionately in the hands of whites while diminishing tribal governments to domestic-dependent status, the United States stripped tribes of their stewardship over their places. Pollution, miserable water rights, and other debilitating policies only make terrible conditions in those places worse. Consequently, human conditions have deteriorated. According to the U.S. Census Bureau (2011), more than one of every four Indians and Alaska Natives live in poverty (28.4 percent), which is almost twice that experienced by the overall U.S. population. Thirteen percent of Indians and Alaska Natives have undergraduate degrees or higher; this compares to 20 percent of the overall population.

Thus, the U.S. political economy of affirmative action in its current formulation fails to buffer Indians from crushing hardships. It invites Indians to participate in reproducing the relation of white wealth and Indian poverty; thus, even as they make minimal concessions to Indians and tribes, whites in the 21st century continue to thrive from Indian dispossession. For Indians and tribes, affirmative action after 80 years plainly has not yet righted historical wrongs. Something much more transformative clearly is necessary.

◀ FURTHER INVESTIGATIONS ▶

> **[I] would never have had a career as a college professor or a public voice as a native scholar without legalized affirmative actions on the part of the government and the law that forced the institutions of this country to act affirmatively.**
>
> **—Professor Elizabeth Cook-Lynn (2007, 223)**

Reflecting on her academic career in *New Indians, Old Wars* (2007) Isianti/Ihanktowan Dakota author, critic, and poet Elizabeth Cook-Lynn singles out affirmative action for comment. Self-disclosing as a beneficiary of affirmative action, she portrayed it as a "vision of grace, the hope of a transcendent time when people like [me] would be welcomed as American Indians into America's modern debates concerning society and knowledge" (1996, xi). From her first book of poetry in 1977 through *New Indians, Old Wars* and *From the Notebooks of Elizabeth Cook-Lynn* in 2007 and in dozens of articles, chapters, essays, and commentary, as well as in her role as founding editor of *Wicazo Sa Review*

and public lecturer and speaker, Cook-Lynn added substantially to discussions regarding politics, environmental justice, historical narrative, land reparations, purpose for American Indian Studies, racism, and tribal sovereignty.

Cook-Lynn was not alone. In taking advantage of gateways to the world of white-male privilege during the 1950s and 1960s, the first generation of Indian scholars employed in universities experienced a variety of familiar challenges and difficulties. Indian scholars since have shined light generally on widely sanctioned ignorance, discrimination, and systemic marginalization (Cook-Lynn 2000; Deloria 2004; Valandra 2003). Commenting on whites who forcefully opposed affirmative action during his long career at Western Washington University, the University of Arizona, and the University of Colorado at Boulder, intellectual giant Vine Deloria Jr. wrote that attacks on affirmative action in employment carry "the tacit assumption that no minorities could ever be employed without special treatment and that all jobs should automatically go to whites without any questions whatsoever" (1999, 256).

Anticipating racial justice from the U.S. political economy of affirmative action alone, as Deloria suggests, seems doubtful. Viewpoints on affirmative action evidence two pathways forward, one with the public sector reproducing federal Indian control law or another that imagines a restoration of political power in the tribal sector. Nowhere is this debate more evident than in a lively exchange between academic lawyers Sam Deloria and Robert Laurence. What follows is the essence of exchange between Deloria and Laurence excerpted from the *Arkansas Law Review* (1991, 1108–11).

Sam Deloria: There is no reason to expect that those persons identified as "Indians" by a government—federal or tribal—will be more "Indian" than those who only identify themselves as "Indians." Think of Audrey Martinez [Santa Clara Pueblo v. Martinez, 436 U.S. 49 (1978)].

Robert Laurence: Audrey Martinez, while a full-blooded Indian, is the member of no Indian tribe. . . . Audrey Martinez, while unenrolled, is surely an Indian for some purposes. Like affirmative action? It's hard to imagine a reason for affirmative action that would not be satisfied by Audrey's presence: she speaks an Indian language, practices an Indian religion, has Indian parents and children, looks like an Indian, if that's important to you.

Deloria: [T]hat depends on exactly why the institution wants to have an Indian around. . . . It's not hard at all to imagine an affirmative action program in which she would not be considered an Indian. *Morton v. Mancari* dealt with such a program. . . . You have to be more careful in your observation about Audrey Martinez's eligibility: it may be hard for you to imagine a reason for having affirmative action that would exclude her, but it's not hard to imagine the existence of an affirmative action program, like *Mancari,* based on membership. Besides, a program that uses an objective criterion like membership will be easier to administer.

Laurence: Granted, and I guess I'd expect the government to use its own definition of Indian when administering its own affirmative action plans.

Deloria: Ah ha! It's for that reason that we are not, in this conversation, going to be able to finesse the underlying rationales for affirmative action, as you will soon see. I assume, though, that no one would suggest that administrative convenience is, in and of itself, an underlying rationale.

Laurence: O.K. Suppose the law school asks your difficult "why-do-you-want-an-Indian" question and decides that it is to diversify the student body, to make it less white, less wealthy, less homogeneous. "Cultural pluralism" is the going phrase. Would that be appropriate?

Deloria: Who's to say?

Laurence: I don't know. You. Me. The courts. Truth.

Deloria: Look. There are two basic reasons for affirmative action. One: a mostly white institution wishes to diversify itself. Two: pay-backs. The first is essentially for the benefit of the white institution; it is saying, in essence, that it would be for the benefit of its present, mostly white students that they be educated in the presence of non-whites. The second may be for the benefit of the mostly white institution-to assuage well-known white liberal guilt—but mostly it is reparations for past wrongs. Now here is what is, for me, a nearly fundamental principle: to the degree that an institution is taking affirmative action steps to service itself, its definition of "Indian" might control, but to the extent that it's trying to pay-back the Indians for past wrongs, then to that same extent the Indians have an important say in how the program is structured and whom it serves.

Thus, the exchange between academic lawyers Deloria and Laurence captures a fundamental source of tension in the U.S. political economy of affirmative action. Distinguishing "two basic reasons for affirmative action" as formulating public policy with implications for Indians, Deloria makes it a matter of whose material, psychological, and social interests are served. By calling into question which Indians benefit from public policy and what is the political

controlling authority for who is Indian—the public sector or tribal sector—the back-and-forth between Deloria and Laurence illustrates the political tug of war over determining what should determine the future for brain-power in Indian Country and why.

References

Anderson, K. N. 1980. "Indian Employment Preference: Legal Foundations and Limitations." *Tulsa Law Journal* 15: 733–71.

Baca, L. R. 2005. "American Indians, the Racial Surprise in the 1964 Civil Rights Act: They May, More Correctly, Perhaps, Be Denominated a Political Group." *Howard Law Journal* 48 (3): 971–97.

Benokraitis, N. V., and J. R. Feagin. 1978. *Affirmative Action and Equal Opportunity: Action, Inaction, Reaction.* Boulder, CO: Westview Press.

Cahill, Cathleen. 2011. *Federal Fathers and Mothers: A Social History of the United States Indian Service, 1869–1933.* Chapel Hill: University of North Carolina Press.

Carr, L. G. 1997. *"Color-Blind" Racism.* Thousand Oaks, CA: SAGE Publications.

Cook-Lynn, E. 1996. *Why I Can't Read Wallace Stegner and Other Essays: A Tribal Voice.* Madison: University of Wisconsin Press.

Cook-Lynn, E. 2000. "How Scholarship Defames the Native Voice . . . And Why." *Wicazo Sa Review* 15: 79–92.

Cook-Lynn, E. *New Indians, Old Wars.* 2007. Urbana: University of Illinois Press.

Deloria, P. S., and R. Laurence. 1991. "What's an Indian? A Conversation about Law School Admissions, Indian Tribal Sovereignty and Affirmative Action." *Arkansas Law Review* 44: 1107–35.

Deloria Jr., V. (1969) 1988. *Custer Died for Your Sins: An Indian Manifesto.* Reprint, Norman: University of Oklahoma Press.

Deloria Jr., V. (1974) 1985. *Behind the Trail of Broken Treaties: An Indian Declaration of Independence.* Reprint, Austin: University of Texas Press.

Deloria Jr., V. 1974. "Federal Treaty Responsibility for Indian Education." In *Indian Education Confronts the Seventies, Vol. 4: Technical Problems in Indian Education,* edited by V. Deloria, Jr., 188–227. Tsaile, AZ: Navajo Community College.

Deloria Jr., V. 1999. "More Others." In *Spirit and Reason: The Vine Deloria Jr. Reader,* edited by B. Deloria, K. Foehner, and S. Scinta, 249–56. Golden, CO: Fulcrum Publishing.

Deloria Jr., V. 2004. "Marginal and Submarginal." In *Indigenizing the Academy: Transforming Scholarship and Empowering Communities,* edited by D. A. Mihesuah and A. C. Wilson, 16–30. Lincoln: University of Nebraska Press.

Deloria, V., and R. J. DeMallie. 1999. *Documents of American Indian Diplomacy: Treaties, Agreements, and Conventions, 1775–1979.* Norman: University of Oklahoma Press.

Ezorsky, G. 1991. *Racism and Justice: The Case for Affirmative Action.* Ithaca, NY: Cornell University Press.

Feagin, Joe R. 2010. *The White Racial Frame: Centuries of Racial Framing and Counter-Framing.* New York: Routledge.

Fletcher, M. L. M. 2008. "The Original Understanding of the Political Status of Indian Tribes." *St. John's Law Review* 82: 153–81.

Gamino, J. 1974. "Bureau of Indian Affairs: Should Indians Be Preferentially Employed?" *American Indian Law Review* 2: 111–18.

Gilbert, J., S. D. Wood, and G. Sharp. 2002. "Who Owns the Land? Agricultural Land Ownership by Race/Ethnicity." *Rural America* 17: 55–62.

Horne, G. 1992. *Reversing Discrimination: The Case for Affirmative Action.* New York: International Publishers.

Ingram, J. M. 1998. "Home Ownership in Indian Country." *Journal of Affordable Housing and Community Development Law* 164 (Winter): 164–86.

Lawrence, C. M. 2001. "Two Views of the River: A Critique of the Liberal Defense of Affirmative Action. *Columbia Law Review* 101 (May): 928–75.

Lawrence, C. M., and M. J. Matsuda. 1997. *We Won't Go Back: Making the Case for Affirmative Action.* Boston: Houghton Mifflin.

Leiter, W. M., and S. Leiter. 2011. *Affirmative Action in Antidiscrimination Law and Policy: An Overview and Synthesis.* Albany: State University of New York Press.

McCool, D., S. M. Olson, and J. L. Robinson. 2007. *Native Vote: American Indians, the Voting Rights Act, and the Right to Vote.* New York: Cambridge University Press.

McDonald, L. 2010. *American Indians and the Fight for Equal Voting Rights.* Norman: University of Oklahoma Press.

Martinot, S. 2010. *The Machinery of Whiteness: Studies in the Structure of Racialization.* Philadelphia: Temple University Press.

Moreton-Robinson, A. 2008. "Writing Off Treaties." In *Transnational Whiteness Matters,* edited by A. Moreton-Robinson, M. Casey, and F. Nicolle, 81–96. Lanham, MD: Lexington Books.

Murji, K., and J. Solomos. 2005. *Racialization: Studies in Theory and Practice.* New York: Oxford University Press, 2005.

Oeser, M. D. 2010. "Tribal Citizen Participation in State and National Politics: Welcome Wagon or Trojan Horse?" *William Mitchell Law Review* 36: 793–858.

Omi, M., and H. Winant. 1994. *Racial Formation in the United States from the 1960s to the 1990s.* New York: Routledge.

Ono, Azusa. 2011. "The Fight for Indian Employment Preference in the Bureau of Indian Affairs: Red Power Activism in Denver, Colorado, and *Morton v. Mancari.*" *Japanese Journal of American Studies* 22: 171–91.

Pevar, S. L. 2012. *The Rights of Indians and Tribes.* New York: Oxford University Press.

Porter, R. B. 1999. "The Demise of the Ongwehoweh and the Rise of the Native Americans: Redressing the Genocidal Act of Forcing American Citizenship upon Indigenous Peoples." *Harvard BlackLetter Law Journal* 15: 107–227.

Porter, R. B. 2002. "Two Kinds of Indians, Two Kinds of Indian Nation Sovereignty." *Kansas Journal of Law and Public Policy* 11: 629–56.

Porter, R. O. 2006. "Tribal Disobedience." *Texas Journal on Civil Liberties & Civil Rights* 11: 137–83.

Reinhardt, M. J., and J. W. Tippeconnic III. 2010. "The Treaty Basis of Michigan Indian Education." *Indigenous Policy Journal* 21 (3): 1–35.

Roediger, David R. 1999. *The Wages of Whiteness: Race and the Making of America's Working Class.* New York: Verso.

Roediger, David R. 2006. *Working toward Whiteness: How America's Immigrants Became White.* New York: Basic Books.

Sheth, F. A. 2009. *Toward a Political Philosophy of Race.* Albany: State University of New York Press.

Smith, A. 2012. "Indigeneity, Settler Colonialism, White Supremacy." In *Racial Formation in the Twenty-First Century,* edited by D. HoSang, O. LaBennett, and L. Pulid, 66–90. Berkeley: University of California Press.

Smith, K., Jr. 2011. *Labor and Employment in Indian Country.* Boulder, CO: Native American Rights Fund.

Trudell, J. 2005. "Half of Anything." M.A. thesis, University of Washington. Dir. Jonathan Tomhave.

Valandra, E. C. 2003. "Remember 9–11! White Belligerence in the Academy." *American Indian Quarterly* 27: 420–28.

Wilkins, D. E., and H. K. Stark. 2005. "Indian Voters." In *The Unfinished Agenda of the Selma-Montgomery Voting Rights March,* edited by D. N. Byrne, 123–34. Hoboken, NJ: Wiley.

Wolfe, P. 2011. "After the Frontier: Separation and Absorption in U.S. Indian Policy." *Settler Colonial Studies* 1: 13–50.

Wood, E. M. 1995. *Democracy against Capitalism: Renewing Historical Materialism.* New York: Cambridge University Press.

Yellow Bird, M. 1999. "What We Want to Be Called: Indigenous Peoples' Perspectives on Racial and Ethnic Identity Labels." *American Indian Quarterly* 23: 1–21.

Gambling: A Blessing and a Curse

Bruce E. Johansen

One of the most important—and, often, most vexing—questions in Indian Country today concerns the creation of reservation economic bases that produce necessary cash income while being culturally appropriate and sustainable. Casinos, the reservation cash cow *du jour*, sometimes produce mountains of money as they transform parts of reservations into annexes of the non-Indian economy, with all of their imported artifices and vices.

Dean Howard Smith, writing in *Modern Tribal Development* (2000), creates a theoretical context in which he seeks reservation economic development consistent with "the cultural integrity and sovereignty of the Native American nations . . . leading to cultural integrity, self-determination, and self-sufficiency." Instead of being assimilated into an industrial capitalistic system, Smith believes that Native American traditions can be used to design "a new type of system that incorporates competitive behavior, social compatibility and adaptation, and environmental concerns" (Smith, 2000, 77). On some reservations, casino gambling has aided the recovery of infrastructure in a culturally appropriate manner. On others, it has led to raw conflict and even death.

Gaming has provided cash flow of unprecedented proportions that has been used in many ways. For example, the Muckleshoots (south of Seattle) were down to their last half acre of commonly owned land in 1970. Following recovery of their fishing rights, capital was invested in a bingo hall, then a casino, which has enabled purchase of land, construction of housing, establishment of a school system, and acquisition of other businesses. Similar efforts are underway in other parts of Indian Country.

Even during the worst economic times in the United States since the Great Depression, revenues from Native American gambling operations remained stable between 2009 and 2010, according to the National Indian Gaming Commission, with gross revenues at $26.5 billion in 2010 (Tirado, March 3 and July 11, 2011). Based on 422 financial statements from 236 tribes and nations with gaming venues, during 2000, Native American gaming operations in 29 states earned more than double the $10.6 billion they did in 2000.[1]

In 2010, 55 percent of Indian gaming operations reported gaming revenue of less than $25 million. Of these operations, approximately 62 percent generated less than $10 million (Tirado 2011b). A large proportion of revenues were generated by a small number of casinos with large operations in or near large non-Native population centers. Examples include the Pequots' Foxwoods and Mohegan Sun in Connecticut, the New York Oneidas' Turning Stone, and the Muckleshoot Casino, near Seattle, many of which generate $1 million or more in gross revenues per day.

Commercial Indian gaming began with the Florida Seminoles in 1979. By the 1980s, the Cabazon, near Riverside, California, offered bingo and card games. Their operations were upheld by the U.S. Supreme Court in *California v. Cabazon Band of Mission Indians*. In 1988, the Indian Gaming Regulatory Act brought many more Native nations into gaming.

Native peoples cooperate on gaming. The nonprofit National Indian Gaming Association (NIGA) was created in 1985 to promote the use of gaming for self-sufficiency in the interest of Native sovereignty. The group works with the federal government, but it is not a government agency. Establishment of the NIGA pre-dated, by a few years, passage of federal legislation upon which Native American gaming has been built since the late 1980s. Over the years, the NIGA has grown so that it provides advocacy (e.g. lobbying) on behalf of gaming tribes, as well as technical assistance. The group's headquarters is located in Washington, D.C.

The largest of casinos are truly spectacular. By the year 2000, the Foxwoods complex was drawing about 50,000 people on an average day. The Foxwoods Resort Casino complex included five casinos housing more than 300,000 square feet of gaming space, 5,842 slot machines, 370 gaming tables, a 3,000-seat high-stakes bingo parlor with $1 million jackpots, a 200-seat sportsbook, A keno lounge, and pull-tabs. Table games included baccarat, mini-baccarat, big six wheels, blackjack, Caribbean stud poker, craps, pai gow, pai gow tiles, red dog, roulette, and a number of others. The Foxwoods casino complex also includes four hotels ranging in size from 280 to 800 rooms and suites each. In addition to gaming space and its four hotels, Foxwoods also offers 23 shopping areas, 24 food-and-beverage outlets, and a movie-theater complex, as well as the Mashantucket Pequot museum, and a Fox Grand Theater with Las Vegas-style entertainment.

Foxwoods has quickly become an integral pillar of Connecticut's economy and a multimillion-dollar contributor to Connecticut charities. The Pequots' casino even put up cash one year to help the state balance its budget. By the year 2000, the Foxwoods casino complex was paying the state of Connecticut more than $189 million a year. The Foxwoods and the Mohegan Sun casinos combined paid the state of Connecticut 20 percent of their slot-machine profits, more than $318 million during the 1999–2000 fiscal year. The Mashantucket Pequots also became the State of Connecticut's largest single taxpayer, and, with 13,000 jobs, one of its larger employers. The casino employed a staff of lawyers and its own permanent lobbying office in Washington, D.C. These three have been selected to provide a national sampling.

Aerial view of the Foxwoods Resort Casino on the Mashantucket Pequot Indian Reservation in Ledyard, Connecticuit. Awash in cash from the vast casino, the Pequots are thriving in the world of high finance, snapping up scores of properties in Connecticut and Rhode Island, opening its own shipbuilding business and socializing with politicians, including former President Clinton. (Associated Press)

FACTIONAL CONFLICT AMONG THE NEW YORK ONEIDAS

In 1983, the New York Oneidas' landholdings were down to 32 acres east of Syracuse, with almost no economic infrastructure. Three decades later, the New York Oneidas own a large casino, the Turning Stone, which has incubated a number of other business ventures. Many of the roughly 1,000 Oneidas who reside in the area have received substantial material benefits.

Amid the prosperity, however, a substantial dissident movement exists among Oneidas who assert that Ray Halbritter, who calls himself the "nation representative" of the New York Oneidas, was never voted into such an office. This group, centered in the Shenandoah extended family (that includes notable singer Joanne Shenandoah and her husband Doug George-Kanentiio) believe that the New York Oneidas under Halbritter have established a business, called it a nation, and acquired the requisite approvals from New York State and the U.S. federal government to use this status to open the Turning Stone. The dissidents' tribal benefits were eliminated after they took part in a "march for democracy" (to protest Halbritter's autocratic actions). To regain their benefits, those who had "lost their voice" were told that they would have to sign papers agreeing not to criticize Halbritter's government, not to speak to the press, and to pledge allegiance to Halbritter and his men's council.

The New York Oneidas' men's council (a body unheard of in traditional matrilineal Iroquois law or tradition) also issued a zoning code to "beautify" the Oneida Nation. This code enabled the Oneidas' 54-member police force (patrolling a 32-acre reservation) to "legally" evict from their homes Oneidas who opposed Halbritter's role as leader of the New York Oneidas, which was solidified by the acquisition of a number of other businesses, a phalanx of public-relations spin-doctors, several dozen lawyers, and ownership of *Indian Country Today,* a national Native American newspaper.

The story of the New York Oneidas is a particularly raw example of conflicts that beset many Native American nations that have attempted to address problems of persistent poverty and economic marginalization by opening casinos. Supporters of the casinos see them as a source of financial support, or "the new buffalo," while opponents look at them as a form of internal colonization, an imposition of European-descended economic institutions and values upon Native American peoples.

In few areas is the conflict as sharp as among the Haudenosaunee, or Iroquois Confederacy, where New York state governor George Pataki at one point announced plans to open as many as six new Native-sponsored casinos in an attempt to jump-start a state economy badly damaged by the attacks of September 11, 2001. On various Internet sites and chat rooms, supporters of Halbritter accuse the Shenandoah family of supporting anti-treaty groups, while opponents of the Oneidas' corporate structure routinely call Halbritter "the king" and "the despot."

The recent experience of the Oneidas of New York raises several significant questions for Indian Country as a whole. Is the Oneida model of an economic powerhouse key to defining the future of Native American sovereignty in the opening years of the 21st century, as many of its supporters believe? Materially, the New York Oneidas gained a great deal in a quarter century, including repurchase of 16,000 acres of land by the end of 2002. Have these gains been offset by an atmosphere of stifling totalitarianism and a devastating loss of traditional bearings, as many Oneida dissidents attest? This conflict also has an important bearing on the pending solution of an Oneida land claim that is more than two centuries old.

The burgeoning business climate has been attended by some controversy from Oneidas who assert that the New York Oneidas have built a business empire on an illegitimate claim to a political base that does not exist in treaty, law, or Iroquois custom. Two reporters writing for the *New York Times* characterized the situation in Oneida: "The root of the Oneida story is a bitter dispute between the traditionalist aunt who resuscitated the Oneidas and her modernist nephew who built the casino" (Chen and LeDuff 2001, A-29). The *Times*' first error in this piece was its characterization of the conflict as a family squabble. It's more than that. Factually, the *Times* did worse in this piece; before a correction was published, its report

Turning Stone Casino has been an inexhaustible jackpot for the Oneida Indian Nation, transforming the once poverty-stricken, land-poor tribe into a major economic and political force in central New York. (Associated Press)

placed the Onondagas' reservation "near Buffalo," when it is south of Syracuse, New York, roughly 150 miles away (Chen and LeDuff 2001, A-29).

The family conflict is a single, albeit superficial, dimension of the Oneidas' story. Maisie Shenandoah, a Wolf Clan mother among the Oneidas, spoke out against her nephew Ray Halbritter. She called Halbritter "an overfed despot with a taste for Italian suits, ruling from a white palace near the New York State Thruway"—an office at the Turning Stone casino that overlooks the championship-caliber Shenandoah Golf Course. "He's a petty tyrant," she said (Chen and LeDuff 2001, A-29; Shenandoah 2001).

Halbritter does not apologize for having helped to create an economic juggernaut that has helped to build housing, a health clinic, and other programs, as well as per capita payments for individual Oneidas (from which Maisie Shenandoah and others who oppose his methods have been excluded). According to Christiansen Capital Advisors, a Manhattan consulting company that maintains a database of gambling statistics, the Turning Stone Casino Resort in Verona took in an estimated $167 million in annual revenue by 2001, with a profit margin as high as 50 percent (Chen and LeDuff 2001, A-29). From these profits, each enrolled Oneida member (except the dissidents) was receiving a quarterly check of $1,100 late in the year 2001.

Many Haudenosaunee (Iroquois) traditionalists believe that Halbritter is operating under self-assumed authority, in defiant opposition to the structure of the thousand-year-old confederacy, as well as the 200-year-old beliefs of the Seneca prophet Handsome Lake, who abhorred four things that he said would doom his people: whiskey, the *Bible,* the fiddle, and gambling (Shenandoah 2001). Rick Hill Sr., a Tuscarora leader, has warned that gambling has translated into the three G's—greed, guns, and grief. From Seneca promoters of new casinos, cut-rate cigarettes, and gasoline without off-reservation taxes to Mohawks who "buttleg" untaxed smokes across the border with Canada ("Buttleg" is a play on words for smuggling of "butts," or cigarettes.) Hill has said that young Iroquois are being seduced. "They all want to be the next Halbritter," he said derisively (Chen and LeDuff 2001, A-29).

In the meantime, Halbritter seems to regard the confederacy mainly as a toothless (and largely moneyless) debating society. "Our revenue has enabled us to take control of our own destiny more than any political or theoretical speech can make," he has said. "While people meet and make speeches, we're actually doing things" (Chen and LeDuff 2001, A-29). In May 1993 the Haudenosaunee (Iroquois Confederacy) Grand Council at Onondaga refused to recognize Halbritter's authority as a representative of the New York Oneidas.

Oneida traditional Diane Shenandoah countered: "Without a trial or hearing we have been found to be guilty by the 'men's council' of conspiring with the Confederacy, meeting with Wisconsin-based Oneidas and being in the company of unnamed, but apparently dangerous, 'Canadians.' Halbritter has taken away our benefits while denying us, at risk of arrest, access to our Oneida facilities, including the Longhouse. He has punished Oneidas for speaking to the press, enacted ordinances which are unknown to residents and passed laws which he can change on a whim" (Shenandoah 2001).

By the year 2000, the men's council had enacted a housing code, and then began using its provisions to evict several of the corporate structure's most severe critics from their homes. Most of them lived in trailer homes on the "32 acres." The housing code and bulldozing of homes was presented not as an attempt to silence his opponents, but as a way to "beautify" the reservation.

Most of the 22 families who were living on the 32-acre territory in the spring of 2000 agreed to inspections. Every home entered by the Oneida Nation Police was condemned and subsequently bulldozed. By the fall of 2001, only seven families remained (Schenandoah 2001). Many of the homes previously demolished were in excellent condition, according to their owners (Oneida Nation Clanmother 2001).

One of the traditionalists, Danielle Schenandoah Patterson, a single mother of three children who was 31 years of age in 2002, flatly refused to move. Faced with an Oneida Nation condemnation order, Patterson had been trying to repair her home on her meager income, doing beadwork. The Oneida Nation had refused to comply with a 1998 Madison court order to garnish the paycheck of her ex-husband, who was an Oneida Nation employee, because of Patterson's political views. Patterson is among the Oneidas who were stripped of their "rights" as Oneidas because they opposed Halbritter's management of the Oneida Nation ("Oneida Nation Clanmother" 2001). According to Schenandoah, "When we tried using our own resources to improve our homes we were threatened with arrest by the Oneida Nation Police for violation of ordinances unknown to us" (Schenandoah, 2001). After her strenuous protests, Schenandoah's trailer was demolished.

INFRASTRUCTURE CONSTRUCTION AT MUCKLESHOOT: "THIS CASINO REPRESENTS HOPE"

By the 1980s, Muckleshoot leaders decided that their overriding priority on their reservation near Seattle was finding a way to alleviate grinding poverty. Thus, a decision was made to take up gambling. Gilbert King George, tribal chairman and cultural leader during the 1980s, said: "My people have no other alternative but to support economic development. . . . It will be a great challenge to lead my people out of poverty" (LaBranche 1984, D-1). Fishing runs were declining due to urbanization and the fact that the land-locked Muckleshoots got their shot at the salmon only after many other fishing people have had a chance to catch fish that were migrating to their spawning grounds from the open ocean. The same urbanization that had destroyed many of the salmon runs (and saddened many Muckleshoots) also brought a financial boost: gaming drew players from the large and growing non-Indian urban population of Puget Sound. The literal avalanche of income from the casino enabled the purchase of land, creation of businesses, and a wide array of social services. The Muckleshoots saw it coming, and made a plan, which is still unfolding.

The 3,500 acres remaining within the Muckleshoots' jurisdiction became more valuable with the spread of suburbs south of Seattle and north of Tacoma. What became even more valuable was a location near an Interstate highway in the midst of an urban area of more than two million people. The Muckleshoot Casino, the closest such venue to Seattle itself, quickly became one of the most profitable in the United States.

Gambling per se is not new to the Muckleshoots. The scale of the games, and use of the revenues to rebuild their nation is an innovation, however. The Muckleshoots (near Seattle) are not moralistic about gambling, and generally resented attempts by 19th-century missionaries to ban their sla-hal (stick game) social gaming as sinful. The games sometimes grew so large that they redistributed wealth, another rub with the missionaries. Sla-hal games are described by today's participants as social events: "We sing, drum, shake rattles, and use hand motions. We laugh, mimic, tease, and just all-out have a great time. Sla-hal has been around for a long time, and is for people to get together and have fun. We visit with relatives and friends we haven't seen for a long time. It's a gathering time to share laughter, love, stories, and fun" (Sla-hal 2010).

Modern commercial gaming has an assigned role at Muckleshoot. Matt Conner wrote in *Indian Gaming Business,* a publication of the National Indian Gaming Association:

> While business programs often support cultural activities, the tribe does not expect casino or bingo hall patrons to come away from their gaming experience with a deep-seated knowledge of Muckleshoot history and culture. "The tribe has used, and will continue to use, the resources from its gaming operations to support, directly and indirectly, many cultural and traditional activities," said John Daniels [chairman of the tribal council]. "However, the tribe operates its gaming facilities as a business, not a cultural facility, with all proceeds going to support the tribal government. Through the tribal government, support for cultural and traditional activities is maintained. While some neighbors expressed concern prior to each facility's opening, skeptics have become believers that the tribe would exceed its promise to be a good and responsible neighbor" (Conner 2002, 12).

Early in the 1990s, the Muckleshoot government purchased 25 acres within reservation boundaries for a casino adjacent to the bingo hall. Soon thereafter, in 1993, Washington governor Mike Lowry signed the compact with the Muckleshoots that is required by a federal law (the Indian Gaming Regulatory Act of 1988), which initially covered only table games. Slot machines, video poker, and other games were added later. The Muckleshoot government's annual report for the year 1994, issued January 26, 1995, was nearly giddy with anticipation for the future. "The tribe is on the fast track to a brighter future. Strap yourself in because it's going to be an exciting and dizzying ride" (*Annual Report* 1995, n.p.).

The Muckleshoots signed the gaming compact with mixed feelings, described in a contemporary newspaper account: "This compact does not represent the best interests of our tribe. It limits our sovereign rights; we're not accepting this agreement because we believe it's wise, which we do not, but because we are desperate. We simply cannot afford further delays and expenses of litigation" (*Valley Daily News* 1993, n.p.).

The casino opened April 28, 1995, in a large, temporary tent. Construction of the permanent casino building required a year and a half, with funding from Capitol Gaming, which received a percentage of the revenue. The tent, which operated through the spring and summer of 1995, became so crowded that the gaming floor developed a human gridlock. On weekends, many people waited as long as an hour to get in the door. Within a few weeks after the casino moved out of its tent, it was the busiest gaming facility in the State of Washington.

The casino's permanent home opened formally September 8, 1996, with a prayer dedicating it to a better life for Muckleshoot children. "I feel like I've waited all my life for this," said chairwoman Virginia Cross, of the Muckleshoot Tribe. "We are not rich, but we are no longer starving" (Wallace 1995, B-1). "To me and all Muckleshoots," Cross said. "This casino represents hope" (*Valley Daily News* n.d., A-12). Cross added that, "Unlike some tribes, who have seen a lot of their casino revenues scatter to the winds, every dollar generated by this casino will go to provide a better future for all Muckleshoots" (Archbold n.d. A-12).

Within six months of its opening in April, 1996, the casino was beginning to bear financial fruit: Muckleshoot employment rose by 150 jobs (in a tribe that at the time enrolled 1,400 members). The casino at the beginning was grossing about $2.75 million a month before operating expenses. In 15 years that figure would be roughly estimated at $30 million a month ("Casino a Big Winner" 1995, n.p.; "Muckleshoot Revenues Soar" 1996, n.p.).

With the casino in its first year of operation, netting about $18 million annually, Gregg Paisley, the Muckleshoots' director of economic development, met with John Daniels Jr., Virginia Cross, and others, who created a plan, "to build," as the Seattle *Daily Journal of Commerce* phrased it, "a personalized, multi-tiered approach to improve the lives of tribal members" ("Casino a Big Winner 1995" n.p.). "It would really offer a lot of people a chance to get to work. . . . We're improving things for our children and our children's children. We're thinking generations ahead," Cross said. Cross set the tone when she said that the Muckleshoots had begun to "close out a long chapter of financial dependence and move into a proud and prosperous period of true self-determination" (Archbold 1997, A-7).

By 1997, a 16-officer Muckleshoot police department had begun operating, plans were underway for a 23,000-seat amphitheatre, and a 65-unit housing project was rising. The tribe had pledged to put one-eighth (12.5 percent) of casino profits into housing. That was $2.2 million (a figure that has risen substantially since), compared to the $60,000 per year that it had been receiving for housing from the federal government (Tribal Leaders 1996, n.p.). A new tribal administration building (the Philip Starr Building) was under construction, and fishing, hunting, and wildlife programs were being enhanced with more than $1 million a year. The Muckleshoots also were diversifying into businesses other than gambling, such as seafood processing and sales, horse racing, and resorts. Shortly after the casino opened, the Muckleshoots began returning up to 2 percent of profits to the city of Auburn, State Patrol, and local fire departments to cover costs of police, fire, court, and other services, an average of $300,000 to $500,000 each three months.

After seven years, the initial $10 million that the Muckleshoots' spent on the casino had proved to be a very good investment. The casino grew in several steps. In 2000, the casino, which began in the 13,000-square-foot tent (63,000 square feet in its first permanent building) expanded to more than 145,000 square feet

(3.3 acres) with a $20 million renovation. A new restaurant was added with a family theme and seating capacity of 490 people. In 2009, 46,662 more square feet were added to the casino, connecting two existing buildings, adding a family buffet, sweet shop, and gift shop, plus gambling venues (*Annual Report* 2009, 49). By 2010, the rambling edifice was more than a third of a mile long. Employment rose from 400 in 1995 to 1,200 in 2001 and 1,800 in 2005, and 2,100 a year later, as the Muckleshoots became the second-largest employer in South King County, behind only the Boeing Company.

The advent of casino gambling fundamentally changed Muckleshoot economic development. During the 1970s, the Muckleshoots had relied on federal grants and contracts. Administrators or consultants wrote proposals to provide reservation services, a procedure that had grown out of the 1960s War on Poverty through programs maintained largely by the U.S. Office of Economic Opportunity (OEO) which, for the first time, had provided local communities with resources to develop economic projects. Many Native governments had received OEO funds to combat unemployment, and to utilize reservation resources for various purposes, such as construction of fishing boats.

Without its own income, resources were difficult to obtain without collateral to back bank loans. Reservation land or resources (defined as federal trust property) was unacceptable because it could not be foreclosed. Gaming revenue provided independent cash income that met standards as collateral. The Muckleshoots already had used this tactic in a very small way by taxing fishing catches, and with a small shop that sold cigarettes free of state taxes, another factor that fed animosity between Washington's state authorities and Native peoples. The State of Washington contended in 1995 that it was losing $52 million a year on untaxed Indian cigarettes (Westneat and Simon 1995).

The casino's income stream enabled the Muckleshoots to start (or buy) other businesses, including, by 2010, the high-end Snoqualmie Inn in the Cascades and the Emerald Downs racetrack, the biggest horse-racing establishment in the Pacific Northwest. The Muckleshoots by 2008 also had become a minority investor in the Four Seasons Hotel and Residences in downtown Seattle, as well as owner of the Salish Lodge near Snoqualmie Falls (bought for $62.5 million in 2007). Once the casino began to provide jobs, unemployment compensation fell and taxes paid increased.

Even with gaming's success at Muckleshoot, some of the elders evoke caution. Stanley Moses, who served on the tribal council for many years, said in 2011 that while he likes the fact that gaming income has contributed to Muckleshoot self-reliance, he worries that political winds could shift at the state level. With a scramble in recessionary times for revenue, the state could allow gaming by non-Indians. "It may not be around forever," he cautioned in 2011 (Moses 2011). The tribe's emphasis on a diversity of income sources must continue, he said.

DISENROLLMENT AND CASINO "PER CAPS:" THE CHUKCHANSI OF CALIFORNIA

After many decades of struggling to restore population loss caused by disease, alcoholism, and deprivation of land and resources, some Native American tribes have elected to reduce their membership by evicting proportionately large numbers of people through "disenrollment." This has provoked several bitter disputes in Indian Country. Native American reservation governments, under the Indian Reorganization Act of 1934, maintain membership rolls and determine membership criteria, usually a measure of "blood quantum." Tribes and nations may set their own quantum. A typical (but hardly universal) standard is one-quarter.

Each tribe sets its own membership standards; personal issues and politics sometimes play a role in enrollment decisions.

Casino profits, distributed as "per caps" (payments to individuals, or per capita) can be a factor, as among the Oneidas (above), as well as the Chukchansi in California.

Carmen George described the irony of Chukchansi disenrollment in The *Sierra Star*:

> Written on a beam holding up Chukchansi Gold Resort & Casino are the names of the Chukchansi elders, like a symbol they would always stand as their tribe's foundation—and that from them everything else has come: children, grandchildren, great-grandchildren, and now also, a casino. This winter, many of those names have been erased from the tribe's history books. It is a practice among many gaming tribes that some scholars are calling "paper genocide" (George, November 17, 2011).

Opponents of these disenrollments argue that old family differences have combined with competition for casino "per capita" payments. However, Reggie Lewis, chairman of the Chukchansi tribal council, said he had based the disenrollments on a statement dated 1915 alleging that some descendants were incorrectly classified as Chukchansi.

Laura Wass, director of the Central California American Indian Movement, said about 400 to 500 Chukchansis had been disenrolled by November 2011. "I call it a cultural genocide," said one Chukchansi woman. "There are very few of us left and now they are weeding them out. It seems like we are all related; it's one big family tree, and it's not going to be like that anymore. Like my son said, it's going to be a stick now, not a tree, with just one family" (George, November 17, 2011).

According to the Chukchansi Constitution, a person is a legal Chukchansi tribal member if they are a "distribute" —related to the Wyatt or Ramirez family granted power by the government in the 1980s to help reform the tribe—an "allottee" related to a descendant given one of the original Chukchansi allotment lands in the 1800s—or a "petitioner," a Chukchansi "who falls under neither category, but is a lineal descendant of a Chukchansi ancestor, and who petitioned for membership into the tribe no later than two years following the constitution's ratification in the late 1980s." According to the council, disenrolled members failed these tests (George, November 24. 2011).

Under disenrollment, a former tribal member loses casino "per caps," (about $280 a month in 2011 at Chukchansi), as well as benefits for social services through the Bureau of Indian Affairs. Fewer members means higher casino per caps for those still enrolled. Lewis said the tribe had about 1,500 members as of September 2011 (George, November 24, 2011). Disenrollments are allowed without appeal because "The Indian Civil Rights Act really [has] no enforceability and because of that, tribal leaders and governments can violate that law but aren't held accountable for it," said John Gomez, president of the American Indian Rights and Resources Organization. "What has been created, or what exists now, is an era or time that very much mirrors that time when individual Indians asked the United States to protect them from tribal governments that were violating their civil rights" (George, November 17, 2011).

Ruby Cordero, 87 years of age in 2011, who was born and raised in the area, speaks Chukchansi. She was among the Chukchansis' "Original 60," and an elder. Even so, she was disenrolled in September 2011, after hearings at the Picayune Rancheria of the Chukchansi Indians. Cordero was a descendant of Jack Roan, who had held one of the first Chukchansi allotments. Roan was listed in a 1919 tribal census as son of a Chukchansi mother and a partially Miwok father of mixed blood.

Two weeks after Codero and her family were disenrolled, about 200 more people were kicked off the rolls. Many of them traced their ancestry to the last Chukchansi chief, Chief Hawa, and his daughter Princess Malliot, who with her Swedish husband once owned a ranch on the location of today's Chukchansi reservation.

"Twenty years down the line there is not going to be a tribe unless they promote incest," said one Chukchansi elder. "The elders are angry because of the things that have been done to our people. How shameful is it that we are now eliminating our own people? How sick are we? Is money so great that we can not see past the greenback?" (George, November 24, 2011).

◀ FURTHER INVESTIGATIONS ▶

Although federal law provides a single legal template for Native American gaming enterprises, the response of each Native tribe or nation has been different. This chapter has attempted to sketch a range of local examples across the United States.

Without question, commercial gaming has provided a minority of American Indian tribes and nations with unprecedented wealth. Native American gaming

tends to do well in tribes with little in-fighting, such as the Muckleshoots, who decide to use their new revenues for a collective purpose (rebuilding infrastructure in this case). The Muckleshoots and other western Washington tribes have done such a good job of economic development that state authorities have agreed to restrict some forms of commercial gambling to reservations within the state, so that development can continue.

Gaming does best when a Native tribe or nation is located near a major population center (Seattle, Tacoma, and surrounding suburbs in this case), providing a ready market. The same has been true to an even greater extent for the Pequots in Connecticut, whose casinos draw gamblers from the New York City, Boston, and Providence areas, as well as their suburbs. Conversely, the worst risk-reward ratio for Indian gaming occurs in the impoverished rural areas of the Great Plains (such as Pine Ridge in South Dakota) that need the revenue the most. Some large Native nations (one example is the Navajo) have decided not to engage in gaming at all.

Gaming has been most contentious in areas such as Oneida, where an existing political context embeds it in an atmosphere of conflict that extends, in this case, about two hundred years ago, when the prophet Handsome Lake instructed his followers to resist the temptation to wager. Today, conflict follows the lines of traditional people who follow Handsome Lake's instructions, against others, who are predisposed toward gaming's monetary rewards.

Even Native peoples with substantial gaming income have come to realize that it could be temporary. An effort is underway among the most financially sagacious to invest in sustainable businesses, and to buy back land. Many peoples with gaming income also must walk a fine cultural line between revival of infrastructure, tradition, and land base, and a new form of capitalistic assimilation. The Native gaming boom is barely two decades old. No one should write its history in too hasty a manner.

Native American gaming will thus continue to be a source of revenue for development as well as conflict—an opportunity as well as a challenge.

Note

1. These figures include class II or class III gaming. Class II includes bingo, lotto, pull-tabs, punch boards, and card games that are legal under various state laws. Class III includes casino table games such as craps and roulette, card games (poker and blackjack).

References

Annual Report to the Muckleshoot Community. 1995. Auburn, WA: The Muckleshoot Tribe, January 26.

Annual Report, 2009: Muckleshoot Indian Tribe. 2009. Auburn, WA: Muckleshoot Indian Tribe, January 19.

Archbold, Mike. 1997. "Muckleshoots Buying Back Their Reservation Land." *South* [King] *County Journal,* February 4, A-7.

Archbold, Miike. [no title] *Valley Daily News,* n.d., A-12.

Bilodeau, Mike. 2002. "Homer to be Demolished Soon." *Oneida Daily Dispatch,* September 7. http://www.zwire.com/site/news.cfm?newsid=5279651&BRD=1709&PAG=461&dept_id=68844&rfi=6.

Bilodeau, Mike. 2002. "Patterson's Mobile Home Leveled." *Oneida Daily Dispatch,* October 24. http://www.zwire.com/site/news.cfm?newsid=5803138&BRD=1709&PAG=461&dept_id=68844&rfi=6.

"Casino a Big Winner Coming and Going." 1995. *Daily Journal of Commerce* [Seattle], October 31, n.p.

Chen, David W., and Charlie LeDuff. 2001. "Bad Blood in Battle over Casinos; Issue Divides Tribes and Families as Expansion Looms." *New York Times,* October 28, A-29.

Coin, Glenn. 2001. "Nation Offers Rental House as Option." *Syracuse Post-Standard,* December 19. http://www.syracuse.com/news/syrnewspapers/index.ssf?/newsstories/20011219_rnnatio.html.

Connor, Matt. 2002. "The Good Neighbor: The Muckleshoot Tribe's Gaming Enterprises Have Helped Foster Good Will with Local Communities." *Muckleshoot Monthly,* September 15, 3, 12. [Reprinted from *Indian Gaming Business,* a publication of the National Indian Gaming Association.]

Corbett, R. Patrick. 2002. "Casino, Vernon Downs: The Gambling Connection. Harness Track Hopes to Cash in on Turning Stone's Success." Utica *Observer-Dispatch,* October 27. http://uticaod.com/archive/2002/10/27/news/8195.html.

George, Carmen. 2011. "Chukchansi Tribal Members Disenrolled." *Sierra Star,* November 17. http://www.sierrastar.com/2011/11/17/56912/chukchansi-tribal-members-disenrolled.html.

George, Carmen. 2011. "Tribal Disenrollment Effort Continues." *Sierra Star,* November 24. http://www.standupca.org/tribes/Picayune%20Rancheria/tribal-disenrollment-effort-continues.

Johansen, Bruce E. 2002. "The New York Oneidas: A Case Study in the Mismatch of Cultural Tradition and Economic Development." *American Indian Culture & Research Journal* 26 (3): 25–46.

Johansen, Bruce E. 2004. "The New York Oneidas: A Business Called a Nation." In *Enduring Legacies: Native American Treaties and Contemporary Controversies,* edited by Bruce E. Johansen, 95–134 . Westport, CT: Praeger Publishers, 2004.

LaBranche, Janet. 1984. [No title.] *New Journal Globe News,* March 14, D-1.

Moses, Stanley. 2011. Interview, at Muckleshoot, August 16.

"Muckleshoot Revenues Soar with Gambling." 1996. *Portland Oregonian,* January 21, n.p. (in LEXIS).

"Oneida Nation Clanmother Assaulted by Oneida Nation Police." 2001. In Personal Communication, Barbara Gray (Kanatiyosh). November 17, from Oneida Indian Territory, Oneida, New York. http://207.126.116.12/culture/native_news/m19480.html.

Richey, Warren. 1985. "Unregulated High-stakes Gambling Grows on American Indian Reservations." *Christian Science Monitor,* March 25, 1 (in LEXIS).

Schenandoah, Diane. 2001. "Oneida Struggle Not a 'Family Dispute.'" Oneidas for Democracy, December. www.oneidasfordemocracy.com.

Sla-hal participant. 2010. Interview, Muckleshoot reservation, July 17.

Smith, Dean Howard. 2000. *Modern Tribal Development: Paths to Self-Sufficiency and Cultural Integrity in Indian Country.* Walnut Creek, CA: AltaMira Press.

Tirado, Michelle. 2011A. "Indian Gaming Revenues Slide for the First Time." *American Indian Report: Fallmouth Institute's Online Magazine,* March 11. http://www.americanindianreport.com/wordpress/2011/03/indian-gaming-revenues-slide-for-the-first-time/.

Tirado, Michelle. 2011B. "Indian Gaming Revenues Stable, NIGC Report." *American Indian Report: Fallmouth Institute's Online Magazine.* July 20. http://www.americanindianreport.com/wordpress/2011/07/indian-gaming-revenues-stable-nigc-reports/.

"Tribal Leaders Pave Way for Brighter Future." *Valley Daily News* (Kent, WA), January 10, 1996, n.p. *Valley Daily News,* 1993, A-12, n.p.

Wallace, James. "Muckleshoots Betting on Casino to Better Their Lot." Seattle *Post-Intelligencer,* September 9, 1995, B-1.

Westneat, Danny, and Jim Simon. 1995. "Move to Tax Casino Profits Angers Native Americans." Seattle *Times,* November 19.

Time for a New Paradigm for American Indian Policy and Law?

James W. Zion[1]

The Constitution of the United States gives the United States Congress the leading role to make American Indian affairs policy by default—the Indian Commerce Clause gives it the authority to "regulate commerce" with Indian tribes, and the Treaty Clause gives the United States Senate the authority to ratify treaties (Pevar 2012). It is silent about treaties with "whom," but the United States Supreme Court once clarified the fact that Indian treaties are included and that they have equal dignity with treaties with foreign nations (and international human rights covenants today) (Kannan 2008).[2] The United States Senate's Committee on Indian Affairs guides the course of legislation dealing with Indians. While the House can initiate Indian legislation, the Senate committee still has the lead role. The President of the United States carries out the policy through his subordinates—they include the Secretary of the Interior and Assistant Secretary for Indian Affairs (head of the Bureau of Indian Affairs) and sometimes the Attorney General of the United States (on law enforcement issues). The guiding theme of Indian policy for the past 40 years since President Nixon's landmark address on the subject has been "self-determination." We need to revisit what it means in light of contemporary events.

The Senate Committee on Indian Affairs held an oversight hearing on Indian policy on June 23, 2011, on "The Indian Reorganization Act—75 Years Later: Renewing our Commitment to Restore Tribal Homelands and Promote Self-Determination." The witnesses called to address the hearing subject repeated tired clichés, prompting this call for a new paradigm, and they did not address new or concrete policy points to give guidance for any real commitment to restore homelands or promote self-determination. We need to examine what *self-determination* means under contemporary circumstances and revisit the commitment in the 1934 Act to the restoration of treaty boundaries. The observation of the 75th year that the 1934 statute has been in place is a good time to do a reassessment of contemporary Indian policy. The Indian Reorganization Act was the first comprehensive attempt by Congress to establish the framework for relationships between the central government of the United States and Indian nations within its boundaries. The current paradigm of relation and relationships between the central government and Indian tribes is based on original treaty arrangements, but that foundation of

American Indians sit near a construction site in Chicago, September 25, 1975. Chicago is one of several cities with populations of over 10,000 of the Native Americans who have come to urban areas, leaving behind both the troubles and the security of the reservation. They still face problems: many are without jobs, and lack adequate housing and health care. (AP Photo/Charles Knoblock)

tribal government and autonomy exists within a new reality that 75 percent or more of all American Indians do not live on an Indian reservation and they do not enjoy the benefits of federal programs that are based on the treaty and reservation model (Zion and Yazzie 1997). The basic question is whether legislation for Indian programs is designed to benefit Indians or whether the reality is that they benefit only those individuals who lead "recognized" Indian tribes. Most American Indians do not get benefits from programs that are managed by Indian governments under self-determination legislation.

Past policies toward Indians living on reservations created social, political, and economic conditions that led Indians to leave to live in near-reservation communities (called "bordertowns") or nearby urban areas. They also left to join the American mainstream or to enjoy its benefits while maintaining strong family ties and returning home often (Fixico 2000; Lobo and Peters 2001). They retain identities as "Indians." They are "urban Indians," and American Indian policy left them out. While a great deal of the West and Native Alaska is rural, with isolated Indian lands, on-reservation poverty and economic conditions drive individuals to near-reservation communities or major urban areas, and there are Indian ghettoes in such place.

This chapter is an attempt to address the new reality that most American Indians live off-reservation; they are largely left out of programs for Indians and marginalized in state or federal "pass-through" programs that accidentally include Indians; and it is time to elaborate a new paradigm for the "History of Indian-White Relations."[3] This chapter is largely the story of urban Indians and their hopes and aspirations, their advocacy for rights on the international level, and the resulting declaration of indigenous rights that recognizes individuals before groups (while recognizing important collective and group rights). The organization that speaks for their interests and expresses their views is the National Indian Youth Council.[4] It was founded by young Indians in 1961 to express their voice; it is the second-oldest national Indian organization in the United States; it coined the term "Red Power" during the civil rights movement in the United States in the 1960s; and it commemorates its 50th anniversary as we observe the 75th of the Indian Reorganization Act. The NIYC is the focus of this discussion of the contemporary situation with Indian policy and how its work points to the need for a new paradigm for Indian policy. This chapter will focus on the 1934 statute, how it has been brought forward in national American Indian policy to date, recent developments (and particularly those in the international arena), and how a new policy, based on a concept of "Indian civil society," might update American Indian policy is a more positive and productive manner.

This addresses the thrust of policy development leading up to the Indian Reorganization Act of 1934; subsequent statutory developments to date; the emergence of a new Indian civil society (exemplified by the National Indian Youth Council and a grassroots movement in the Navajo Nation—the tribe with the largest land base and second highest population); the Declaration on the Rights of Indigenous Peoples; and policy factors for a new paradigm in a concluding section.

PROMPTS FOR INDIAN POLICY DEVELOPMENT

Different realities shaped the development of Indian policy at various stages in American history. Initial Indian policy was established by the English crown in an attempt to maintain stability on the North American continent while the English sorted out what they were going to do on the mainland of Europe. The first Indian policy document was the Royal Proclamation of 1763. It attempted to stabilize Indian-white relations in North America after the defeat of the French and avoid having to maintain a military presence in America that England could not afford. The proclamation formally recognized Indian nations as "nations" to be dealt with as political entities, initiated the policy we see in the U.S. Constitution that the central government makes Indian policy, and drew a line down the "fall line" of the chain of mountains on the east coast of what would become the new United States to keep Britons on the east side and Indians on the west. Whitehall (the popular term for the government of Great Britain) followed up on the proclamation by creating the office of "Commissioner of Indian Affairs" (that still exists today in the American title of "Commissioner of Indian Affairs" that is now called the "Assistant Secretary of the Interior—Indian Affairs"), adopting a treaty policy to deal with land acquisitions and maintaining peace, and generally creating the model of Indian separateness and independence ("sovereignty") that is still the central focus of policies toward Indians today. What was not acknowledged is that the core of English Indian policy was in fact Spanish Indian policy that was developed over the course of over 250 years of Spanish trial-and-error policy development in the Americas before the British adopted it.

Initial American policy adopted the British model wholesale, with the addition of the political reality at the time of the Revolution—and one that persists today. The Articles of Confederation that were drafted in 1776 and 1777 and used as the working model for revolutionary government through their adoption in 1781 were based on an assumption that there were thirteen separate sovereigns in North America (Quebec was still under the thumb of England) and that there should be a confederation of them, with a very weak central government. Article IX gave the revolutionary congress the "sole and exclusive right and power" of "regulating the trade and managing all affairs with the Indians, not members of any of the States, provided that the legislative right of any State within its own limits be not infringed or violated." It was Congress, and not a president or a general, that was legally responsible for making Indian policy, and this provision continued the British policy that the central government would make Indian treaties. The new element for revolutionary America was the prohibition that central policy would not infringe upon, or violate, the "right of any State." That "states' rights" problem has consistently plagued Indian policy for over 230 years.

The Constitution that replaced the Articles in 1789 tinkered with the Indian policy of the Articles by clarifying the sole authority of the federal government to deal with Indians. Article I, Section 2 dealt with that by providing that when representatives in the House and direct taxes were allocated, Indians would be excluded from the count—if they were not taxed (meaning that they had not submitted to the authority of the States); Article I, Section 8 gave the national Congress the power "To regulate Commerce with foreign Nations, and among the several States, and with the Indian Tribes"; and Article II, Section 2 provided that among the powers of the president would be that "He shall have Power, by and with the Advice and Consent of the Senate, to make Treaties, provided that two thirds of the Senators present concur." The "Indians not taxed" clause recognized the separate-ness and separate authority of Indian tribes; only Congress would "regulate" commerce" with "the Indian tribes,"[5] and the Treaty Clause includes Indian treaties.

The Treaty Clause was the most important provision on Indian policy in the early days of the Republic for very pragmatic reasons. The English attempted to bypass colonial governments and attempts by local interests to deal with Indians by having a royal Indian commissioner deal with them outside the framework of relations of the colonies with the crown, keeping Indians and non-Indians separate and by making treaties—designed to avoid the expenditure of monies needed to fight the French and others on the Continent. Washington's military advisor, Henry Knox, advised that the better approach to defense in dealing with Indians was to make treaties with them and to control expansion through a regular course of treaty dealing. The central government had difficulties restraining settlement and expansion to the west in an orderly manner, so it was necessary to site treaty making in a central authority and reinforce the "sovereign" character of Indians, organized as "tribes."[6] A close reading of the Constitution's provisions on "Indians" shows that it referred to Indians both within and outside the established colonies (and particularly Indians in the Canada of the time and the cross-mountain Ohio and Mississippi river systems) and groups of Indians. Indian "tribes" were a creation of settler government because someone had to sign the treaties that could be the pretext for military action, if need be.

Although the Constitution clarified roles and authority as between the central government and the States, early conflicts over that authority introduced a new element to policy-making with or about Indians—the courts. Andrew Jackson, former general in the War of 1812, and seventh president of the United States, confronted the central government in Georgia over who made Indian policy in that State and that led to three U.S. Supreme Court decisions, known in Indian law culture as the "Marshall Trilogy,"[7] that reinforced the authority of the central government and put Indians and their sovereignties largely under the control of the federal courts. The developments of the early period of the Republic established the longstanding processes of treaty-making, the creation of territories[8] by Act of Congress, "hands-off" statutes such as the "Non-Intercourse" laws (that prohibited separate state and individual arrangements with Indians and reinforced central executive authority in dealing with Indians),[9] and westward expansion controlled by Congress and the president.

Despite that, the states' rights problem persisted in Indian Policy (as well as being part of other issues, such as slavery, the creation of new states with the same powers as the original ones, and periodic schemes to nullify central government initiatives or powers). One of the problem areas that is not mentioned in "Indian-White Relations" is who the representatives and senators of the various states really represent in Congress. They do not represent Indians. That is, politicians who are elected to the House and Senate of Congress represent the states (and of course special interests—many of which have interests aligned against those of Indians), and there are no representatives for Indians or their tribes. Curiously,

Indian legislation is not bilateral, despite the history of recognition of Indian tribes as separate sovereigns and treaty-making with Indian sovereigns. No matter what politicians may claim, senators and representatives represent the interests of the states, and not Indians. There are some outstanding instances of state jealousy and control in Indian policy reflected in clashes between the two houses of Congress: the end of treaty making in 1871; the assertion of federal criminal jurisdiction in Indian Country; the inclusion of the House of Representatives in the making of Indian policy so that the Senate or Senate Indian Affairs Committee does not dominate; and the statutory definition of the term *Indian Country* for federal jurisdiction. Congress enacted a statute to abolish making treaties in Indian tribes in 1871 because the House of Representatives was left out of the treaty-making process; when the U.S. Supreme Court ruled that state law does not apply in Indian areas, Congress adopted the Major Crimes Act in 1885 to prosecute people accused of crimes in Indian Country in federal court (with the crimes defined in state law),[10] requiring that any appropriation of monies for Indians be based on legislation defining the objects of appropriation so that the House controls the purse strings when it originates appropriations (as provided in the Constitution); and the very definition of "Indian Country."[11]

Tempered central authority in a milieu of states' rights, the inability of Congress to truly exercise its authority to fix Indian policy because of state jealousy over control of policy in state interests, the dominance of the judicial system in developing and defining the relationship and powers, and a lack of consistency in recognizing Indian "sovereignty" typified the making of Indian policy through the end of the 19th century. By then the United States pushed west to the Pacific Ocean, attempted to pacify Indians in a series of treaties, established then reduced reservations, and created the mess that the Indian Reorganization Act was meant to resolve in the early 20th century. The initial foundations of Indian policy were largely military and expansionist, and they were largely set by central government leaders (including judges) and tempered by politics based on states' rights. The "reformers" entered the picture early on and achieved formal status, starting in 1883.

"FRIENDS OF THE INDIAN" AND INDIAN POLICY

One of the more curious events in the development of the unilateral nature of American Indian policy, that created a precedent for today, is the meetings of "reformers" at the Lake Mohonk Resort in New York from 1883 through 1916 (Sattuck and Norgren 1991). They were the Indian Rights Association, or "Friends of the Indian," a group that organized in Philadelphia in 1882 and remained active through 1994. It influenced Indian policy development in the latter part of the nineteenth century and introduced a new element to Indian policy development of involving the private—humanitarian—element. Clerics, tycoons, society ladies, and individuals who were sincerely concerned about the condition of Indians (but who knew little about them) met to discuss Indian policy initiatives and how to influence federal government officials to implement them.

Early on in the 20th century, it became apparent that the "Reservation Policy" of confining Indians to reservations under the tutelage of non-Native Indian agents did not work. Hubert Work, the Interior Secretary under President Calvin Coolidge (a noted reformer himself), commissioned the Institute for Government Research (which later became the Brookings Institution) to undertake a "survey" of Indian affairs in 1926. The survey brief, financed by the Rockefeller Foundation, was that "The investigation would cover nearly all reservations and would deal with educational, industrial, social, and medical activities of the BIA, as well as with Indian property rights and economic conditions." The 1928 report, *The Problem of Indian Administration* (or "Meriam Report" after Lewis Meriam, leader of the survey team) offered a comprehensive (and liberal—for the time) analysis and recommendations, but as it often is with such reports, it went nowhere.

On March 4, 1933, President Franklin D. Roosevelt went about the massive task of helping the United States recover from a great depression. One of the obvious areas of reform was Indian policy, and Roosevelt chose John Collier, a social reformer who got interested in Indian issues while visiting a friend in Taos, New Mexico. That led him to advocacy to repeal a failed "land reform" law passed in 1887, criticism of incompetent and corrupt Bureau of Indian Affairs officials, and prompting the Meriam Report. Collier was appointed as the Commissioner of Indian Affairs[12] and he introduced the law we now know as the Indian Reorganization Act as his first order of business (Philp 1977).

The states' rights movement, particularly represented by Democrat Burton K. Wheeler of Montana, derailed many of Collier's ideas, but the core concept that survived in the Indian Reorganization Act of 1934 (popularly known as the "IRA") was Indian tribal self-government. It was set up in an unusual way. Indian tribes were to have the option of organizing or not, with a section that set out the specific powers of Indian tribal governments if they did organize under the act, and an offhand mention of powers if they did not. That is, the section that set out the powers of organized tribes began with proviso language that "In addition to all powers vested in any Indian tribe or tribal council *by existing law,* the constitution adopted by said tribe shall also vest in such tribe the following rights and powers" (with a listing; emphasis supplied). What were those "existing powers"?

Collier had a subtle agenda: he recruited a bright lawyer, Felix S. Cohen, who was part of the "legal realist" movement of the time to set up the legalistics for Indian policy reform, and one of the little time bombs that was in the IRA was the term *existing law.* Shortly after the president signed the new law Collier asked for a legal opinion on what tribal powers under existing law happened to be, and that led

John Collier, Indian Affairs Commissioner, with Blackfeet chiefs in Rapid City, South Dakota, in 1934. (Library of Congress)

to a comprehensive legal opinion by the Interior Department solicitor, and a later text by Felix S. Cohen, on what those powers were. The existing powers the two works outlined were largely based on collections of decisional law by the federal courts.

Moving forward quickly, Congress became disillusioned with even the new reform, proposing to end the existence of Indian tribes after adopting a comprehensive scheme to pay Indians for their lands and be done with them, starting during World War II, and postwar initiatives to simply terminate Indian tribes. That was almost completed when the civil rights movement sparked in the 1960s.

RED POWER

Indian tribes had little political power to counter moves to abolish their existence by extinguishing aboriginal land rights and abolishing tribal governments. While such termination policies and laws were being implemented, there was a lot of frustration that grew in American society because of legacies of slavery, control of statehouses by a propertied white elite, and the suppression of minorities. Indians had their own grievances, so as African Americans organized and pushed for their rights, Indians joined an emerging civil rights movement (Cornell 1988;

Smith and Warrior 1996). One of the postwar policies of the Bureau of Indian Affairs was to relocate Indians to urban areas for employment training and placement, and there were improvements in Indian education that allowed Indians to enter college in meaningful numbers. Young Indians also got involved in the civil rights movement, and in 1961, a group of college students founded the National Indian Youth Council. One of the elements of termination policies was the abolition of treaty rights, but rather than do so directly, Congress took that move indirectly—in a 1953 statute to shift jurisdiction to the states that included a list of states where tribes and their members were put directly under state jurisdiction. One of the states was Washington, and it set about abolishing individual and tribal Indian rights to fish. The National Indian Youth Council (NIYC) undertook a noisy and visible campaign to confront the state in "fish-ins," involved Marlon Brando and Hunter S. Thompson, and coined the term *Red Power* in the process. The NIYC was active throughout the 1960s, but its high point was in the (peaceful) occupation of the Bureau of Indian Affairs Building in 1968.[13]

There is no documentation to show a connection between the Red Power movement and the seemingly liberal policy of President Richard M. Nixon to declare and implement a new "self-determination" policy for Indians to end termination and prompt a new era of Indian policy. Nixon set a bold policy on Indians at the height of the civil rights movement, but we do not know why he chose to address Indian grievances. Nixon set the tone in a special message to Congress on July 8, 1970, that called for Indian "self-determination," and that call for policy change culminated in the Indian Self-Determination and Education Assistance Act of January 4, 1975.

This chapter focuses on the essential element of the Indian Reorganization Act—the "powers of Indians" language was vital to establish the scope of powers of Indian tribes. While such powers were, and are, challenged in the courts and Congress, they were fairly established by January of 1975 when the Self-Determination Act became law. When the House of Representatives demanded that Indian programs be reduced in scope in an authorization statute called the "Snyder Act" of 1921 it codified the federal obligation to Indians in terms of federal programs and appropriations. One of the problems that helped lead to the Nixon policy of self-determination was that direct service policies were expensive, duplicative, and mismanaged. The thinking of the Self-Determination Act (popularly known as the "PL 637" program, after the public law citation to the law) was that there should be a statutory mandate that the federal programs and their funding should be handled by Indian tribes under grants and contracts. That shifted federal program management, as defined by federal statutes and agency regulations, to the tribes. It did not do two important things—it did not fund tribal governmental infrastructure along lines chosen by tribes, in some kind of fair allocation of funds that also satisfied federal obligations to Indians, and it did not fully recognize tribal powers. Essential government services have never been funded adequately, in accordance with the obligation the United States has to Indians who gave up a lot in treaties. The Self-Determination Act is, at the end of the day, simply a devolution of federal program statutory authority to tribes and not a meaningful recognition of tribal "sovereignty." That is the current policy, with some discussion of reforms that actually aren't.

INDIANS GO TO THE UNITED NATIONS

It is difficult to assign a date to Indian efforts to advocate for international human rights in the United Nations, but indigenous representatives (Maori and Mohawk) did attend the Versailles Peace Conference in Paris in 1919 to demand that indigenous rights be recognized. Starting sometime around the time the NIYC occupied the Bureau of Indian Affairs building in Washington in 1968, there were efforts to get United Nations attention, and in 1971 the Economic and Social Council of that body commissioned a study of patterns of discrimination against indigenous peoples around the globe. The report prompted the creation of the Working Group on Indigenous Populations with mandates to review national developments for the protection of the human rights and freedoms of indigenous peoples, and to develop international standards to protect those rights. The Working Group began drafting the text of a proposed declaration of indigenous human rights in 1985, and a text was settled in July of 1993. It was submitted to the Commission on Human Rights in 1994, and it in turn created a Working Group to review and offer a final draft of the Declaration on the Rights of Indigenous Peoples. One was offered, and the General Assembly of the United Nations adopted the Declaration on the Rights of Indigenous Peoples on September 13, 2007. Four of the major "settler" nations (i.e., modern states peopled by immigrants from Europe in indigenous lands), the United States, Canada, Australia, and New Zealand, voted against adoption of the declaration and announced they would be "persistent objectors" to its implementation.[14]

The declaration is a comprehensive statement of basic indigenous human rights, and it was elaborated and adopted by the United Nations with significant indigenous input. Unlike policies developed by military commanders, politicians, and non-Native "reformers," the declaration is the first modern statement of human rights made with indigenous participation. The indigenous caucus that fought for the declaration in discussions of the Working Group in Geneva had something else in mind as the document of preference, but the current declaration is a start (Daes 1994–1995). It should be seen as the start of a reappraisal of United States Indian policy, based on international human rights principles. The United States has given its (grudging) acceptance of the declaration, and the Senate Indian Affairs Committee had a meaningless oversight hearing on it in 2011.

CONCLUSION: A NEW STATEMENT OF RIGHTS IN U.S. DOMESTIC LAW

The Declaration on the Rights of Indigenous Peoples is the basis for a new paradigm: Indian policies of the past were driven by military necessity and the struggle between certain elements in the states and the central authority. Indian tribes and Indian policy were the pawns of westward expansion and conflicts over the occupation of lands to the north and south of the United States that drove through the middle to the Pacific. Prominent statesmen and generals started it out and the voices of non-Indian "humanitarians" joined toward the close of the 19th century. Professional reformers took charge in the 20th century, but even they could not ward off the proponents of states' rights.

The United States did everything in its power to block or frustrate the adoption of a declaration on the rights of indigenous peoples.[15] It voted against the declaration in the General Assembly and persisted in its objections until recently. The intentions of the United States to continue blocking the notion of international indigenous human rights are plain.

While there are many substantive provisions in the declaration that are worthy of implementation in national U.S. legislation, what is more important is the tone the document represents. Past Indian policy excluded Indians from meaningful participation in the process, and there were no good governance principles to guide the process. They are recognized in the United Nations Development Programme (to implement the international human right to development; spelling in the original) and five principles of good governance, namely (1) legitimacy and voice (with effective participation), (2) direction (in the sense of having a strategic vision), (3) performance (meaning responsiveness to serve all and serving stakeholders with effectiveness and efficiency), (4) accountability (including transparency and information-sharing), and (5) fairness (meaning equity and opportunities for all and adherence to the rule of law). All five concepts are important to any democratic paradigm for a new policy, but perhaps the most important notions are legitimacy, voice, and participation in the concept of "civil society" and strict adherence to the "rule of law."

There is no current consensus definition of the term *civil society,* but it speaks to voluntary collective action by institutions that are separate and apart from the state, and such institutions are diverse—ranging from well-organized interest groups to simple nongovernmental organizations and nonprofits and to what we know as the "grass roots." They promote the issue of "voice" and inclusion and assert needs to be fulfilled—in ways they expect out of notions of equity, decency, and democracy. They want recognition of civil society to demand adherence to the rule of law.

A refusal to adhere to the rule of law is at the core of Indian dissatisfaction with Indian policy. Why is it that contemporary advocates of Indian issues look to the elders for guidance, and while many of them do not understand (or wish to) the strange ways of non-Indian society, they uniformly insist upon strict adherence to their treaties—the elders understand the notion of the rule of law—and the understanding that treaties work when parties keep their word. Indians went to the United Nations because the United States did not keep its treaty promises, so now Indians demand notification, including meaningful participation as full members of civil society, and they demand adherence to the rule of law where the rule is human rights, as stated in the declaration.

The declaration is not a statement of rights of indigenous states or governments. While indigenous peoples have the right to form indigenous governments and adopt their own laws, and such forms of governance and statements of substantive law are to be recognized and enforced, the objects of the statements of rights in the declaration are in fact individuals. They are the Indian individuals who may or may not live on a reservation. They are the 75 percent+ of the American Indian population who, largely, fully support treaty rights in documents executed by tribal leaders and who support the viability of their home reservations. The treaties were with Indians, and the object of historic Indian legislation is Indians. The United States is attempting to use the Indian Reorganization Act and the Self-Determination Act to quietly push Indians off the table in Congress. That is why a new policy is necessary and why a new and nongovernmental paradigm for Indian policy is necessary today.

The new paradigm incorporates the past by asking for a reinterpretation of indigenous treaty texts as international documents, made between western colonial states and indigenous states, that embody an interpretation of state interdependence and respect and a sense of mutuality for the preservation of Indian culture, and a new respect for human rights in an instrument (the Declaration on the Rights of Indigenous Peoples) that recognizes indigenous peoples as groupings of individuals who possess individual rights but who live in arrangements that require the recognition of collective rights. The desired paradigm recognizes Indian tribes and tribal governments, but it also recognizes the reality of a growing civil society of local and global groups, and individual self-determination based in traditional thought that is represented by institutions of "self-determination" with central government recognition. The treaty paradigm gave way to the democratic model that John Collier envisioned, but today the paradigm must be grounded in international human rights discourse and recognition of the place of the individual in indigenous society.

◀ FURTHER INVESTIGATIONS ▶

1. **In your opinion does the geographic dispersion of American Indians, including their movement from reservations to Borderlands to major urban centers minimize their collective efficacy to achieve their goals for basic civil and human rights? How has the Red Power movement improved their ability to assert their demands to the federal government?**

2. American Indians have struggled against the federal government in terms of seeking agreements and treaties. Many of these treaties have not been honored or at least lip service has been given to them. Do you think it is appropriate that American Indians needed to go beyond the United States to bodies like the United Nations to call attention to, protect, and expand their rights at home?

Notes

1. Pinpoint citation to references will not be used in this chapter because it addresses broad historic trends rather than fine points. The bibliography lists the major works that were used as sources. I thank the leadership and friends of the National Indian Youth Council for suggesting the theme of this chapter and its policy conclusions, including Fay Givens (who prompted the idea of going to a meeting of the U.S. Special Rapporteur on Indigenous Rights), Kay McGowan (part of that conversation), Cecelia Belone (NIYC President), Dr. Shirley Hill Witt (NIYC board member and original founder), and Norman Ration (executive director). My mistakes are not their fault.
2. This statement requires a pinpoint citation because the State Department refuses to recognize that this is the law. The decision is United States v. Forty-Three Gallons of Whiskey, 92 U.S. 188 (1876).
3. The Smithsonian Institute published a series of handbooks on American Indians, and the one that gives the best overview of "Indian-White Relations" (i.e., the relationship of the European overlords and the subjected peoples of this land) was edited by noted historian Wilcomb E. Washburn and published in 1988. The most readily available text on Indian law is an occasionally updated work by Felix S. Cohen, the "father" of American Indian law, and the most perceptive work is likely one by Indian academic and think tank head Robert A. Williams. See the bibliography for the citation to these three works.
4. The website citation of the organization is http: www.niyc-alb.org. It is a former membership organization that is now headed by a board of directors and mostly funded under a federal employment training program.
5. The "Indian Commerce Clause" is usually interpreted to give Congress a sole and exclusive right to "regulate Indians" rather than "regulate commerce" *with* them. An originalist interpretation of the clause would lead to far different conclusions than the approach that was developed in court decisions well after the Constitution was adopted.
6. Indian "tribes," as it is with Indian "chiefs," are European colonial concepts and not necessarily reflective of Indian political arrangements. The Spanish needed "chiefs" (*caciques*) to use as pawns for control, and likewise the other European powers needed a mental construct to justify colonial expansion in dealings with some sort of Indian "authority."
7. The "Marshall Trilogy" is a lawyer term to describe three U.S. Supreme Court decisions that established basic American Indian Affairs Law policies. There are many dreary law journal articles that continuously dissect them that need not be cited. It is sufficient to say that the U.S. Supreme Court intervened in the making of Indian policy during a foundational period of the history of the Republic, and the Court persists in making definitive new statements because of the negligence of Congress in doing so.

That neglect is precisely a product of the persistence of the "States Rights" problem in American federalism.

8. One of the curious things about the organic laws that created the territories, beginning with the Northwest Ordinance of 1787, was the "Utmost Good Faith" provision that required fair dealings with Indians and likely restated a 1537 papal bull on the treatment of Indians, *Sublimus Dei.* That provision was also put in the Louisiana Territory and Oregon Territory ordinances and, curiously, it has never been effectively used or interpreted as a source of Indian rights—as was the likely intent of its author (said to be Thomas Jefferson). An "organic" law is one that deals with the establishment and basic organization of a territory.
9. The "Non-Intercourse" laws were a series of statutes that declared the authority of the federal government to deal with Indians and prohibited and nullified dealings by the states and entrepreneurs. The usual practice was that a developer of the time would make deals with selected Indian "chiefs" and have them sign deeds and other evidences of land title. Whiskey and other inducements were common (as is still done today). The purposes of the statutes were to prohibit dealings by persons other than federal officials and to nullify any such dealings.
10. Congress has not been able to get away from the straitjacket of the law by recognizing tribal authority to prosecute crime—likely because of state fears of shifting too much power to tribes. That has led to systemic patterns of violence against Indian women and a lack of effective law enforcement that may approach anarchy.
11. This, too, created problems because of United States Supreme Court rulings that sharply cut back on the scope of the definition and ignored the plain language of the statute on tribal jurisdiction in land areas defined in the statute. It is clear that Indian reservations and lands set aside for individual Indians are and should be "Indian Country." What is unclear is what "dependent Indian communities" are. They were original Indian settlement areas that were not included in a treaty "reservation" of Indian land, and some such communities remain. A major issue in a confused area in New Mexico, the "Checkerboard Area," is the ability of Navajos to prohibit uranium mining in their backyard. Also unaddressed is the land status of lands that Indian tribes buy outright (fee simple). Are they "Indian Country" or not?
12. Note the continuity of that office from British policy.
13. The author of this essay was the student legal advisor during the occupation—that ended to join a large confrontation with police at the nearby Agriculture Department building.
14. While the declaration is not "binding" as a statement of international law under UN procedure, it may in fact state binding principles of international customary law. There is a "persistent objector" doctrine of international treaty law that it might be possible to block human rights by imply objecting to them.
15. The author was present at several sessions on the declaration in Geneva, Switzerland.

References

Cornell, Stephen. 1988. *The Return of the Native: American Indian Political Resurgence.* New York: Oxford University Press.

Daes, Erica-Irene A. 1994–1995. "Equality of Indigenous Peoples under the Auspices of the United Nations—Draft Declaration on the Rights of Indigenous Peoples, *St. Thomas Law Review* 7: 493–519.

Fixico, Donald L. 2000. *The Urban Indian Experience in America.* Albuquerque: University of New Mexico Press.

Kannan, Phillip. 2008. "Reinstating Treaty Making with Indian Tribes." *William and Mary Bill of Rights Journal* 16 (5): 809–37.

Lobo, Susan, and Kurt Peters, eds. 2001. *American Indians and the Urban Experience.* Walnut Creek, California: AltaMira Press.

Pevar, S. L. 2012. *The Rights of Indians and Tribes.* New York: Oxford University Press.

Philp, Kenneth R. 1977. *John Collier's Crusade for Indian Reform: 1920–1954.* Tucson: University of Arizona Press.

Shattuck, Petra T., and Jill Norgren. 1991. *Partial Justice: Federal Indian Law in a Liberal Constitutional System.* New York: Oxford University Press.

Smith, Paul Chaat, and Robert Allen Warrior. 1996. *Like a Hurricane: The Indian Movement from Alcatraz to Wounded Knee.* New York: The New Press.

Zion, J., and R. Yazzie. 1997. "Indigenous Law in North America in the Wake of Conquest." *Boston College International and Comparative Law Review* 20 (1): 55–84.

Selected Bibliography

Section V

Anderson, K. N. 1980. "Indian Employment Preference: Legal Foundations and Limitations." *Tulsa Law Journal* 15: 733–71.

Baca, L. R. 2005. "American Indians, the Racial Surprise in the 1964 Civil Rights Act: They May, More Correctly, Perhaps, Be Denominated a Political Group." *Howard Law Journal* 48 (3): 971–97.

Banerjee, Subhankar. 2009. "Terra Incognita: Communities and Resource Wars." In *The Alaska Native Reader: History, Culture, Politics,* edited by Maria Shaa Tláa Williams, 184–91. Durham, NC: Duke University Press.

Barnhardt, R. 2007. Creating a Place for Indigenous Knowledge in Education: The Alaska Native Knowledge Network." In *Place-based Education in the Global Age: Local Diversity,* edited by G. Smith and D. A. Gruenewald, 113–33. Hillsdale, NJ: Lawrence Erlbaum Associates.

Barrett, Carole A. 2004. "Boarding and Residential Schools." In *American Indian Culture,* edited by Carole A. Barrett and Harvey J. Markowitz, 138–42. Pasadena, CA: Salem Press, Inc.

Begaye, Timothy. 2004. Foreword to *Red Pedagogy: Native American Social and Political Thought,* edited by Sandy Grande, vii–viii. Lanham, MD: Rowman & Littlefield.

Biolsi, Thomas. 2007. *Deadliest Enemies: Law and Race Relations On and Off Rosebud Reservation.* New ed. Minneapolis: University of Minnesota Press.

Boyles, Benjamin, Erin Brinton, Anne Dunning, Angela Mathias, and Mark Sorrell. 2006. "Native American Transit: Current Practices, Needs, Barriers." *Transportation Research Record: Journal of the Transportation Research Board* 1956: 103–10.

Brandt, Elizabeth A. 1992. "The Navajo Area Student Dropout Study: Findings and Implications." *Journal of American Indian Education* 31 (2): 48–63.

Brayboy, Bryan M. J., and Angelina E. Castagno. 2009. "Self-Determination through Self-Education: Culturally Responsive Schooling for Indigenous Students in the USA." *Teaching Education* 201: 31–53.

Cahill, Cathleen. 2011. *Federal Fathers and Mothers: A Social History of the United States Indian Service, 1869-1933.* Chapel Hill: University of North Carolina Press.

Castagno, Angelina E., and Bryan M. J. Brayboy. 2008. "Culturally Responsive Schooling for Indigenous Youth: A Review of the Literature." *Review of Educational Research* 78: 941–93.

Champagne, Duane. 2007. *Social Change and Cultural Continuity among Native Nations.* Lanham, MD: AltaMira Press.

Cheyfitz, Eric. 2000. "The Navajo-Hopi Land Dispute: A Brief History." *Interventions* 2 (2): 248–75.

Cleveland, Sarah H. 2002. "Powers Inherent in Sovereignty: Indians, Aliens, Territories, and the Nineteenth Century Origins of Plenary Power over Foreign Affairs." *Texas Law Review* 81 (1): 3–42.

Cleary, Linda Miller, and Thomas D. Peacock. 1998. *Collected Wisdom: American Indian Education.* Boston: Allyn and Bacon.

Coggins, Kip, Edith Williams, and Norma Radin. 1997. "The Traditional Tribal Values of Ojibwa Parents and the School Performance of Their Children: An Exploratory Study." *Journal of American Indian Education* 36 (3): 1–15.

Cornell, Stephen. 1988. *The Return of the Native: American Indian Political Resurgence.* New York: Oxford University Press.

Cornell, Stephen, and Joseph P. Kalt. 2007. "Two Approaches to the Development of Native Nations: One Works, the Other Doesn't." In *Rebuilding Native Nations,* edited by Miriam Jorgensen, 3–33. Tucson: University of Arizona Press.

Cortelyou, George H. 2001. "An Attempted Revolution in Native American Housing: The Native American Housing Assistance and Self-Determination Act." *Seton Hall Legislative Journal* 25: 429–66.

Davis, Virginia. 2002. "A Discovery of Sorts: Reexamining the Origins of Federal Indian Housing Obligations." *Harvard Blackletter Law Journal* 18: 211–39.

Deloria, P. S., and R. Laurence. 1991. "What's an Indian? A Conversation about Law School Admissions, Indian Tribal Sovereignty and Affirmative Action." *Arkansas Law Review* 44: 1107–35.

Deloria Jr., V. (1974) 1985. *Behind the Trail of Broken Treaties: An Indian Declaration of Independence.* Reprint, Austin: University of Texas Press.

Deloria Jr., V. 1974. "Federal Treaty Responsibility for Indian Education." In *Indian Education Confronts the Seventies, Vol. 4: Technical Problems in Indian Education,* edited by V. Deloria, Jr., 188–227. Tsaile, AZ: Navajo Community College.

Deloria Jr., V. (1969) 1988. *Custer Died for Your Sins: An Indian Manifesto.* Reprint, Norman: University of Oklahoma Press.

Deloria Jr., V. 1999. "More Others." In *Spirit and Reason: The Vine Deloria Jr. Reader,* edited by V. Deloria, K. Foehner, S. Scinta, and B. Deloria, 249–56. Golden, CO: Fulcrum Publishing.

Deloria Jr., V. 2004. "Marginal and Submarginal." In *Indigenizing the Academy: Transforming Scholarship and Empowering Communities,* edited by D. A. Mihesuah and A. C. Wilson, 17–30. Lincoln: University of Nebraska Press.

Deyhle, Donna. 1992. "Constructing Failure and Maintaining Cultural Identity: Navajo and Ute School Leavers." *Journal of American Indian Education* 31 (2): 24–47.

Deyhle, Donna, and Karen Swisher. 1997. "Research in American Indian and Alaska Native education: From Assimilation to Self-Determination." In *Review of Research in Education,* edited by Michael W. Apple, vol. 22, 113–94. Washington, D.C.: American Educational Research Association.

Doyle, Susan Badger. 2007. "Civilians and the Indian Wars in the American West, 1865-90." In *Daily Lives of Civilians in Wartime Modern America: From the Indian Wars to Vietnam,* edited by David Stephen Heidler and Jeanne Heidler, 1–34. Westport, CT: Greenwood Press.

Eagle, Adam Fortunate. 1997. "Urban Indians and the Occupation of Alcatraz Island." *American Indian Activism: Alcatraz to the Longest Walk.* Eds. Troy Johnson, Joane Nagel, and Duane Champagne. eds. Urbana: University of Illinois Press.

Fixico, Donald L. 2000. *The Urban Indian Experience in America.* Albuquerque: University of New Mexico Press.

Fletcher, M. L. M. 2008. "The Original Understanding of the Political Status of Indian Tribes." *St. John's Law Review* 82: 153–81.

Fuchs, Estelle, and Robert J. Havighurst. 1972. *To Live on This Earth: American Indian Education.* Garden City, NY: Doubleday.

Gamino, J. 1974. "Bureau of Indian Affairs: Should Indians Be Preferentially Employed?" *American Indian Law Review* 2: 111–18.

Grande, Sandy. 2004. *Red Pedagogy: Native American Social and Political Thought.* Lanham, MD: Rowman & Littlefield.

Hallett, D., Chandler, M. J., and Lalonde, C. E. 2007. "Aboriginal Language Knowledge and Youth Suicide." *Cognitive Development* 22: 392–99.

Harvard Project on American Indian Economic Development. 2008. *The State of the Native Nations: Conditions under U.S. Policies of Self-Determination.* New York: Oxford University Press

Henze, Rosemary C., and Lauren Vanett. 1993. "To Walk in Two Worlds—Or More? Challenging a Common Metaphor of Native Education." *Anthropology and Education Quarterly* 24 (2): 116–34.

Huffman, Terry. 2010. *Theoretical Perspectives on American Indian Education: Taking a New Look at Academic Success and the Achievement Gap.* Lanham, MD: AltaMira Press.

Hunt, Valarie H., Brinck Kerr, Linda L. Ketcher, and Jennifer Murphy. 2010. "The Forgotten Minority: An Analysis of American Indian Employment Patterns in State and Local Governments, 1991-2005." The *American Indian Quarterly* 34 (4) (Fall):409–34.

Indian Health Service, United States Department of Health and Human Services. 2005. *The First 50 Years of the Indian Health Service: Caring & Curing.*

Ingram, J. M. "Home Ownership in Indian Country." 1998. *Journal of Affordable Housing and Community Development Law* 164 (Winter): 164–86.

Jackson, Deborah Davis. 2002. *Our Elders Lived It: American Indian Identity in the City.* DeKalb: Northern Illinois University Press.

Johansen, Bruce. 2007. *Praeger Handbook on Contemporary Issues in Native America.* Santa Barbara, CA.: Praeger Publishers.

Johnson, Troy R. 2008. *Red Power and Self-Determination: The American Indian Occupation of Alcatraz Island.* New ed. Urbana: University of Illinois Press.

Johnson, Troy, Joane Nagel, and Duane Champagne, eds. 1997. *American Indian Activism: Alcatraz to the Longest Walk.* Urbana: University of Illinois Press.

Jorgensen, Miriam. ed. 2007. *Rebuilding Native Nations.* Tucson: The University of Arizona Press.

Kannan, Phillip. 2008. "Reinstating Treaty Making with Indian Tribes." *William and Mary Bill of Rights Journal* 16 (5): 809–37.

Kotlowski, Dean J. 2008. "From Backlash to Bingo: Ronald Reagan and Federal Indian Policy." *Historical Review* 77 (4): 617–52.

Knack, Martha C., and Alice Littlefield. 1996. "Native American Labor: Retrieving History, Rethinking Theory." In *Native Americans and Wage Labor: Ethnohistorical Perspectives,* edited by Alice Littlefield and Martha C. Knack, 3–44. Norman: University of Oklahoma Press.

Latham, Glenn I. 1989. "Thirteen Most Common Needs of American Indian Education in BIA Schools." *Journal of American Indian Education* 29 (1): 1–11.

Lamore-Choate, Yvonne. 2002. "My Relocation Experience." In *Urban Voices: The Bay Area American Indian Community,* edited by Susan Lobo, 38–41. Tucson: University of Arizona Press.

Langston, Donna Hightower. 2003. "American Indian Women's Activism in the 1960s and 1970s." *Hypatia* 18 (2): 114–32.

Leeds, Stacy. 2006. "Toward Tribal Autonomy of Lands." *Natural Resources Journal* 46: 439–61.

Lobo, Susan, and Kurt Peters, eds. 2001. *American Indians and the Urban Experience.* Walnut Creek, California: AltaMira Press.

Lomawaima, K. Tsianina. 1995. "Educating Native Americans." In *Handbook of Research on Multicultural Education,* edited by James A. Banks and Cherry A. Banks, 331–42. New York: Macmillan.

McCool, D., S. M. Olson, and J. L. Robinson. 2007. *Native Vote: American Indians, the Voting Rights Act, and the Right to Vote.* New York: Cambridge University Press.

McDonald, L. 2010. *American Indians and the Fight for Equal Voting Rights.* Norman: University of Oklahoma Press.

Moisa, Ray. 2002. "Relocation: The Promise and the Lie." In *Urban Voices: The Bay Area American Indian Community,* edited by Susan Lobo, 21–27. Tucson: University of Arizona Press.

Moreton-Robinson, A. 2008. "Writing Off Treaties." In *Transnational Whiteness Matters,* edited by A. Moreton-Robinson, M. Casey, and F. Nicolle, 81–98. Lanham, MD: Lexington Books.

Nagel, Joane. 1996. *American Indian Ethnic Renewal: Red Power and the Resurgence of Identity and Culture.* Oxford: Oxford University Press.

Oeser, M. D. 2010. "Tribal Citizen Participation in State and National Politics: Welcome Wagon or Trojan Horse?" *William Mitchell Law Review* 36: 793–858.

O' Neill, Colleen. 2004. "Rethinking Modernity and the Discourse of Development in American Indian History, an Introduction." In *Native American Pathways: American Indian Culture and Economic Development in the Twentieth Century,* edited by Brian Hosmer and Colleen O' Neill, 1–26. Boulder: University Press of Colorado.

Ono, Azusa. 2011. "The Fight for Indian Employment Preference in the Bureau of Indian Affairs: Red Power Activism in Denver, Colorado, and *Morton v. Mancari.*" *Japanese Journal of American Studies* 22: 171–91.

Peroff, Nicholas C. 2006. "Indian Gaming and the American Indian Criminal Justice System." In *Native Americans and the Criminal Justice System,* edited by Jeffrey Ian Ross and Larry Gould, 179–86. Boulder, CO: Paradigm Publishers.

Peshkin, Alan. 1997. *Places of Memory: Whiteman's Schools and Native American Communities.* Mahwah, NJ: Lawrence Erlbaum.

Pevar, S. L. 2012. *The Rights of Indians and Tribes.* New York: Oxford University Press.

Pickering, K. 2000. "Alternative Economic Strategies in Low-Income Rural Communities: TANF, Labor Migration, and the Case of the Pine Ridge Indian Reservation." *Rural Sociology* 65: 148–67.

Radda, Henry T., Dawn Iwamoto, and Carolyn Patrick. 1998. "Collaboration, Research and Change: Motivational Influences on American Indian Students." *Journal of American Indian Education* 17 (2): 2–20.

Reyhner, J. 2006. "Issues Facing New Native Teachers." In *The Power of Native Teachers: Language and Culture in the Classroom,* edited by David Beaulieu and Anna M. Figueira, 63–92. Tempe: Center for Indian Education, Arizona State University.

Reyhner, Jon. 2010. "Indigenous Language Immersion Schools for Strong Indigenous Identities." *Heritage Language Journal* 7 (2): 138–52.

Reyhner, Jon, and Jeanne Eder. 2004. *American Indian Education: A History.* Norman: University of Oklahoma Press.

Reyhner, Jon, and Denny S. Hurtado. 2008. "Reading First, Literacy, and American Indian/Alaska Native Students." *Journal of American Indian Education* 47 (1): 82–95.

Reyhner, Jon, Willard S. Gilbert, and Louise Lockard, eds. 2011. *Honoring Our Heritage: Culturally Appropriate Approaches for Teaching Indigenous Students.* Flagstaff: Northern Arizona University. http://jan.ucc.nau.edu/~jar/HOH.

Ridone, Pauline. 1988. "Achievement Motivation and Academic Achievement of Native American Students." *Journal of American Indian Education* 28 (1): 1–7.

Riggs, Christopher. 2000. "American Indians, Economic Development, and Self-Determination in the 1960s." *Pacific Historical Review* 69 (3): 431–63.

Robyn, Linda. 2006. "Criminalizing of the Treaty Right to Fish." In *Native Americans and the Criminal Justice System,* edited by Jeffrey Ian Ross and Larry Gould, 161–77. Boulder: Paradigm Publishers.

Schaap, James I. 2010. "The Growth of the Native American Gaming Industry: What Has the Past Provided, and What Does the Future Hold?" *The American Indian Quarterly* 34 (3) (Summer): 365–89.

Shoemaker, Nancy. 1999. *American Indian Population Recovery in the Twentieth Century.* Albuquerque: University of New Mexico Press.

Smith, Dean Howard. 2000. *Modern Tribal Development: Paths to Self-Sufficiency and Cultural Integrity in Indian Country.* Walnut Creek, CA: AltaMira Press.

Smith, K., Jr. 2011. *Labor and Employment in Indian Country.* Boulder, CO: Native American Rights Fund.

Smith, Paul Chaat, and Robert Allen Warrior. 1996. *Like a Hurricane: The Indian Movement from Alcatraz to Wounded Knee.* New York: The New Press.

Stremlau, Rose. 2005. "'To Domesticate and Civilize Wild Indians': Allotment and the Campaign to Reform Indian Families: 1875-1887." *Journal of Family History* 30 (3): 265–86.

Tharp, Roland G. 1982. "The Effective Instruction of Comprehension: Results and Description of the Kamehameha Early Education Program." *Reading Research Quarterly* 17: 503–27.

Tootle, Deborah M. 1993. *American Indians: Economic Opportunities and Development.* Washington, D.C.: United States Department of Agriculture, Economic Research Service. http://www.ers.usda.gov/publications/aer731/aer731i.pdf [retrieved April 15, 2011].

Thornton, Russell. 1997. "Tribal Membership Requirements and the Demography of 'old' and 'New' Native Americans." *Population Research and Policy Review* 16 (1-2): 33–42.

Tullberg, Steven. 2008. "Securing Human Rights of American Indians and Other Indigenous Peoples under international law." In *Bringing Human Rights Home, Vol. 1,* edited by Cynthia Soohoo, Catherine Albisa, Martha F. Davis. Westport, CT: Praeger Publishers.

U.S. Senate. 1969. *Indian Education: A National Tragedy, a National Challenge.* 1969 Report of the Committee on Labor and Public Welfare, 91st Congress, 1st Session, Report No. 91-501. Washington, D.C.: U.S. Government Printing Office.

Von Feigenblatt, Otto F. 2010. "Identity and Culture: A Cultural Interpretation of the Hopi- Navajo Land Dispute." *Vivat Academia* 111: 35–47.

Washburn, Wilcomb E. 1971. *Red Man's Land/White Man's Law: A Study of the Past and Present of the American Indian.* New York: Charles Scribner's Sons.

Willeto, Angela A. 1999. "Navajo Culture and Family Influences on Academic Success: Traditionalism Is Not a Significant Predictor of Achievement among Young Navajos." *Journal of American Indian Education* 38 (2): 1–21.

Wilkins, D. E., and H. K. Stark. 2005. "Indian Voters." In *The Unfinished Agenda of the Selma-Montgomery Voting Rights March,* edited by D. N. Byrne, 123–34. Hoboken, NJ: Wiley.

Wilkinson, Charles. 2006. "Peoples Distinct from Others: The Making of Modern Indian Law." *Utah Law Review* 379–96.

Wolfe, P. 2011. "After the Frontier: Separation and Absorption in U.S. Indian Policy." *Settler Colonial Studies* 1: 13–50.

Glossary

American Indians: Used as a synonym for Native Americans. Typically a person/group who is recognized as one of the indigenous persons of the United States.

Blood Quantum: A measure of Indian identity used by tribes to determine how Indian they are. Each tribe has their own formula to qualify as a member. Blood quantum has important implications for the kinds of rights/benefits an individual may have.

Bureau of Indian Affairs (BIA): Division of the United States Department of Interior responsible for supervising the land held in trust by the federal government on behalf of American Indians and Alaskan Natives.

First Nations: A term used to describe the indigenous peoples of Canada.

First Peoples: Label given in Canada to Native Canadians, the Inuit, and Métis.

Indian Country: A legal term that refers to land under the control of American Indians. Typically, this refers to reservations.

Indian Health Service: A division of the United States Department of Public Health. It provides medical and public health services to federally recognized Indian tribes and Alaskan Natives.

Indian Territory: Land set aside by the United States government that was to be occupied by American Indians. This was done through the policy and practice of Indian removal that occurred during the 18th and 19th centuries.

Indigenous: Individuals who occupied a geographical territory before the arrival of Europeans (e.g., Aborigines in Australia, Maori in New Zealand, Inuit in Canada, etc.).

Lineal descent: Means a direct descendent.

Native Americans: used as a synonym for American Indians. Typically a person/group who is recognized as one of the indigenous persons of the United States.

Removal: Official policy of the U.S. government to remove Natives from areas where there was conflict between Natives and white settlers.

Reservation: Distinct geographic territory set aside by the federal government for American Indians/First Nations peoples.

Primary Documents

CRIME AND CRIMINAL JUSTICE

CULTURE

FAMILY

HEALTH

WORK AND SOCIETY

Crime and Criminal Justice

PUBLIC LAW 83–280 (1953)

Source: Public Law 83–280 (1953) (18 U.S.C. § 1162, 28 U.S.C. § 1360). http://www.tribal-institute.org/lists/pl_280.htm.

18 U.S.C. § 1162. State Jurisdiction over offenses committed by or against Indians in the Indian country

(a) Each of the States or Territories listed in the following table shall have jurisdiction over offenses committed by or against Indians in the areas of Indian country listed opposite the name of the State or Territory to the same extent that such State or Territory has jurisdiction over offenses committed elsewhere within the State or Territory, and the criminal laws of such State or Territory shall have the same force and effect within such Indian country as they have elsewhere within the State or Territory:

State or Territory of	Indian country affected
Alaska	All Indian country within the State, except that on Annette Islands, the Metlakatla Indian community may exercise jurisdiction over offenses committed by Indians in the same manner in which such jurisdiction may be exercised by Indian tribes in Indian country over which State jurisdiction has not been extended.
California	All Indian country within the State.
Minnesota	All Indian country within the State, except the Red Lake Reservation.
Nebraska	All Indian country within the State.
Oregon	All Indian country within the State, except the Warm Springs Reservation.
Wisconsin	All Indian country within the State.

(b) Nothing in this section shall authorize the alienation, encumbrance, or taxation of any real or personal property, including water rights, belonging to any Indian or any Indian tribe, band, or community that is held in trust by the United States or is subject to a restriction against alienation imposed by the United States; or shall authorize regulation of the use of such property in a manner inconsistent with any Federal treaty, agreement, or statute or with any regulation made pursuant thereto; or shall deprive any Indian or any Indian tribe, band, or community of any right, privilege, or immunity afforded under Federal treaty, agreement, or statute with respect to hunting, trapping, or fishing or the control, licensing, or regulation thereof.

(c) The provisions of sections 1152 and 1153 of this chapter shall not be applicable within the areas of Indian country listed in subsection (a) of this section as areas over which the several States have exclusive jurisdiction.

28 U.S.C. § 1360. State Civil Jurisdiction in Actions to which Indians are parties

(a) Each of the States listed in the following table shall have jurisdiction over civil causes of action between Indians or to which Indians are parties which arise in the areas of Indian country listed opposite the name of the State to the same extent that such State has jurisdiction over other civil causes of action, and those civil laws of such State that are of general application to private persons or private property shall have the same force and effect within such Indian country as they have elsewhere within the State:

State of	Indian country affected
Alaska	All Indian country within the State.
California	All Indian country within the State.
Minnesota	All Indian country within the State, except the Red Lake Reservation.
Nebraska	All Indian country within the State
Oregon	All Indian country within the State, except the Warm Springs Reservation.
Wisconsin	All Indian country within the State.

(b) Nothing in this section shall authorize the alienation, encumbrance, or taxation of any real or personal property, including water rights, belonging to any Indian or any Indian tribe, band, or community that is held in trust by the United States or is subject to a restriction against alienation imposed by the United States; or shall authorize regulation of the use of such property in a manner inconsistent with any Federal treaty, agreement, or statute or with any regulation made pursuant thereto; or shall confer jurisdiction upon the State to adjudicate, in probate proceedings or otherwise, the ownership or right to possession of such property or any interest therein.

(c) Any tribal ordinance or custom heretofore or hereafter adopted by an Indian tribe, band, or community in the exercise of any authority which it may possess shall, if not inconsistent with any applicable civil law of the State, be given full force and effect in the determination of civil causes of action pursuant to this section.

25 U.S.C. § 1321. Assumption by State of Criminal Jurisdiction

(a) *Consent of United States; force and effect of criminal laws*

The consent of the United States is hereby given to any State not having jurisdiction over criminal offenses committed by or against Indians in the areas of Indian country situated within such State to assume, with the consent of the Indian tribe occupying the particular Indian country or part thereof which could be affected by such assumption, such measure of jurisdiction over any or all of such offenses committed within such Indian country or any part thereof as may be determined by such State to the same extent that such State has jurisdiction over any such offense committed elsewhere within the State, and the criminal laws of such State shall have the same force and effect within such Indian country or part thereof as they have elsewhere within that State.

(b) *Alienation, encumbrance, taxation, and use of property; hunting, trapping, or fishing*

Nothing in this section shall authorize the alienation, encumbrance, or taxation of any real or personal property, including water rights, belonging to any Indian or any Indian tribe, band, or community that is held in trust by the United States or is subject to a restriction against alienation imposed by the United States; or shall authorize regulation of the use of such property in a manner inconsistent with any Federal treaty, agreement, or statute or with any regulation made pursuant thereto; or shall deprive any Indian or any Indian tribe, band, or community of any right, privilege, or immunity afforded under Federal treaty, agreement, or statute with respect to hunting, trapping, or fishing or the control, licensing, or regulation thereof.

25 U.S.C. § 1322. Assumption by State of Civil Jurisdiction

(a) *Consent of United States; force and effect of civil laws*

The consent of the United States is hereby given to any State not having jurisdiction over civil causes of action between Indians or to which Indians are parties which arise in the areas of Indian country situated within such State to assume, with the consent of the tribe occupying the particular Indian country or part thereof which would be affected by such assumption, such measure of jurisdiction over any or all such civil causes of action arising within such Indian country or any part thereof as may be determined by such State to the same extent that such State has jurisdiction over other civil causes of action, and those civil laws of such State that are of general application to private persons or private property shall have the same force and effect within such Indian country or part thereof as they have elsewhere within that State.

(b) *Alienation, encumbrance, taxation, use, and probate of property*

Nothing in this section shall authorize the alienation, encumbrance, or taxation of any real or personal property, including water rights, belonging to any Indian or any Indian tribe, band, or community that is held in trust by the United States or is subject to a restriction against alienation imposed by the United States; or shall authorize regulation of the use of such property in a manner inconsistent with any Federal treaty, agreement, or statute, or with any regulation made pursuant thereto; or shall confer jurisdiction upon the State to adjudicate, in probate proceedings or otherwise, the ownership or right to possession of such property or any interest therein.

(c) *Force and effect of tribal ordinances or customs*

Any tribal ordinance or custom heretofore or hereafter adopted by an Indian tribe, band, or community in the exercise of any authority which it may possess shall, if not inconsistent with any applicable civil law of the State, be given full force and effect in the determination of civil causes of action pursuant to this section.

25 U.S.C. § 1323. Retrocession of Jurisdiction by State

(a) *Acceptance by United States*

The United States is authorized to accept a retrocession by any State of all or any measure of the criminal or civil jurisdiction, or both, acquired by such State pursuant to the provisions of section 1162 of title 18, section 1360 of title 28, or section 7 of the Act of August 15, 1953 (67 Stat. 588), as it was in effect prior to its repeal by subsection (b) of this section.

(b) *Repeal of statutory provisions*

Section 7 of the Act of August 15, 1953 (67 Stat. 588), is hereby repealed, but such repeal shall not affect any cession of jurisdiction made pursuant to such section prior to its repeal.

25 U.S.C. § 1324. Amendment of State Constitutions or Statutes to Remove Legal Impediment; Effective Date

Notwithstanding the provisions of any enabling Act for the admission of a State, the consent of the United States is hereby given to the people of any State to amend, where necessary, their State constitution or existing statutes, as the case may be, to remove any legal impediment to the assumption of civil or criminal jurisdiction in accordance with the provisions of this subchapter. The provisions of this subchapter shall not become effective with respect to such assumption of jurisdiction by any such State until the people thereof have appropriately amended their State constitution or statutes, as the case may be.

25 U.S.C. § 1325. Abatement of Actions

(a) *Pending actions or proceedings; effect of cession*

No action or proceeding pending before any court or agency of the United States immediately prior to any cession of jurisdiction by the United States pursuant to this subchapter shall abate by reason of that cession. For the purposes of any such action or proceeding, such cession shall take effect on the day following the date of final determination of such action or proceeding.

(b) *Criminal actions; effect of cession*

No cession made by the United States under this subchapter shall deprive any court of the United States of jurisdiction to hear, determine, render judgment, or impose sentence in any criminal action instituted against any person for any offense committed before the effective date of such cession, if the offense charged in such action was cognizable under any law of the United States at the time of the commission of such offense. For the purposes of any such criminal action, such cession shall take effect on the day following the date of final determination of such action.

25 U.S.C. § 1326. Special Election

State jurisdiction acquired pursuant to this subchapter with respect to criminal offenses or civil causes of action, or with respect to both, shall be applicable in Indian country only where the enrolled Indians within the affected area of such Indian country accept such jurisdiction by a majority vote of the adult Indians voting at a special election held for that purpose. The Secretary of the Interior shall call such special election under such rules and regulations as he may prescribe, when requested to do so by the tribal council or other governing body, or by 20 per centum of such enrolled adults.

INDIAN CIVIL RIGHTS ACT (1968)

This federal legislation, enacted with the Omnibus Civil Rights Act of 1968 on April 11, 1968, specifically delineated the civil rights of Indians as protected by the U.S. Constitution and recognized by the federal government. The act also extended certain provisions of the Constitution to Indian tribes. Below is an excerpt of the act.

Source: Indian Civil Rights Act (1968) (25 U.S.C. 1301–03). at http://www.tribal-institute.org/lists/icra1968.htm.

Title II. Rights of Indians

Section 210. Definitions

For purposes of this title, the term:

(1) "Indian tribe" means any tribe, band, or other group of Indians subject to the jurisdiction of the United States and recognized as possessing powers of self-government;

(2) "powers of self-government" means and includes all governmental powers possessed by an Indian tribe, executive, legislative, and judicial, and all offices, bodies, and tribunals by and through which they are executed, including courts of Indian offenses; and

(3) "Indian court" means any Indian tribal court or court of Indian offense.

Section 202. Indian Rights

No Indian tribe in exercising powers of self-government shall:

(1) make or enforce any law prohibiting the free exercise of religion, or abridging the freedom of speech, or of the press, or the right of the people peaceably to assemble and to petition for a redress of grievances:

(2) violate the right of the people to be secure in their persons, houses, papers and effects against unreasonable search and seizures, nor issue warrants, but upon probable cause, supported by oath or affirmation, and particularly describing the place to be searched and the person or thing to be seized;

(3) subject any person of the same offense to be twice put in jeopardy;

(4) compel any person in any criminal case to be a witness against himself;

(5) take any private property for a public use without just compensation;

(6) deny to any person in a criminal proceeding the right to a speedy and public trial, to be informed of the nature and cause of the accusation, to be confronted with the witnesses against him, to have compulsory process for obtaining witnesses in his favor, and at his own expense to have the assistance of counsel for his defense;

(7) require excessive bail, impose excessive fines, inflict cruel and unusual punishments, and in no event impose for conviction of any one offense any penalty or punishment greater than imprisonment for a term of six months or a fine of $500, or both;

(8) deny to any person within its jurisdiction the equal protection of its laws or deprive any person of liberty or property without due process of law:

(9) pass any bill of attainder or ex post facto law; or

(10) deny to any person accused of an offense punishable by imprisonment the right, upon request, to a trial by jury of not less than six persons.

Section 203. Habeas Corpus

The privilege of the writ of habits corpus shall be available to any person, in a court of the United States, to test the legality of his detention by order of an Indian tribe.

Title III. Model Code Governing Courts of Indian Offenses

Section 301.

The Secretary of the Interior is authorized and directed to recommend to the Congress, on or before July 1, 1968, a model code to govern the administration of justice by courts of Indian offenses on Indian reservations. Such code shall include provisions which will (1) assure that any individual being tried for an offense by a court of Indian offenses shall have the same rights, privileges, and immunities under the United States Constitution as would be guaranteed any citizen of the United States being tried in a Federal court for any similar offense, (2) assure that any individual being tried for an offense by a court of Indian offenses will be advised and made aware of his rights under the United States Constitution, and under any tribal constitution applicable to such individual, (3) establish proper qualifications for the office of judge of the court of Indian offenses, and (4) provide for the establishing of educational classes for the training of judges of courts of Indian offenses. In carrying out the provisions of this title, the Secretary of the Interior shall consult with the Indians, Indian tribes, and interested agencies of the United States.

Section 302.

There is hereby authorized to be appropriated such sum as may be necessary to carry out the provisions of this title.

Title IV. Jurisdiction Over Criminal and Civil Actions

Section 401. Assumption by State

(a) The consent of the United States is hereby given to any State not having jurisdiction over criminal offenses committed by or against Indians in the areas of Indian country situated within such State to assume, with the consent of the Indian tribe occupying the particular Indian country or part thereof which could be affected by such assumption, such measure of jurisdiction over any or all of such offenses committed within such Indian country or any part thereof as may be determined by such State to the same extent that such State has jurisdiction over any such offense committed elsewhere within the State, and the criminal laws of such State shall have the same force and effect within such Indian country or part thereof as they have elsewhere within that State.

(b) Nothing in this section shall authorize the alienation, encumbrance, or taxation of any real or personal property, including water rights, belonging to any Indian or any Indian Tribe, band, or community that is held in trust by the United States or is subject to a restriction against alienation imposed by the United States; or shall authorize regulation of the use of such property in a manner inconsistent with any Federal treaty, agreement, or statute or with any regulation made pursuant thereto; or shall deprive any Indian or any Indian tribe, band or community of any right, privilege, or immunity afforded under Federal treaty, agreement, or statute with respect to hunting, trapping, or fishing or the control, licensing, or regulation thereof.

Section 402. Assumption by State of Civil Jurisdiction

(a) The consent of the United States is hereby given to any State not having jurisdiction over civil causes of action between Indians or to which Indians are parties which arise in the areas of Indian country situated within such State to assume, with the consent of the tribe occupying the particular Indian country or part thereof which would be affected by such assumption, such measure of jurisdiction over any or all such civil causes of action arising within such Indian country or any part thereof as may be determined by such State to the same extent that such State has jurisdiction over other civil causes of action, and those civil laws of such State that are of general application to private persons or private property shall have the same force and effect within such Indian country or part thereof as they have elsewhere within that State.

(b) Nothing in this section shall authorize the alienation, encumbrance, or taxation of any real or personal property, including water rights, belonging to any Indian or any Indian tribe, band, or community that is held in trust by the United States or is subject to a restriction against alienation imposed by the United States: or shall authorize regulation of the use of such property in a manner inconsistent with any Federal treaty, agreement, or statute, or with any regulation made pursuant thereto: or shall confer jurisdiction upon the State to adjudicate, in probate proceedings or otherwise, the ownership or right to possession of such property or any interest therein.

(c) Any tribal ordinance or custom heretofore or hereafter adopted by an Indian tribe, band, or community in the exercise of any authority which it may possess shall, if not inconsistent with any applicable civil law of the State, be given full force and effect in the determination of civil causes of action pursuant to this section.

Section 403. Retrocession of Jurisdiction by State

(a) The United States is authorized to accept a retrocession by any State of all or any measure of the criminal or civil jurisdiction, or both, acquired by such State pursuant to the provisions of section 1162 of title 18 of the United States Code, section 1360 of title 28 of the United States Code, or section 7 of the Act of August 15, 1953 (by Stat. 588), as it was in effect prior to its repeal by subsection (b) of this section.

(b) Section 7 of the Act of August 15, 1953 (67 Stat. 588), is hereby repealed, but such repeal shall not affect any cession of jurisdiction made pursuant to such section prior to its repeal.

Section 404. Consent to Amend State Laws

Notwithstanding the provisions of any enabling Act for the admission of a State, the consent of the United States is hereby given to the people of any State to amend, where necessary, their State constitution of existing statutes, as the case may be, to remove any legal impediment to the assumption of civil or criminal jurisdiction in accordance with the provisions of this title. The provisions of this title shall not become effective with respect to such assumption of jurisdiction by any such State until the people thereof have appropriately amended their State constitution or statutes, as the case may be.

Section 405. Actions Not to Abate

(a) No action or proceeding pending before any court of agency of the United States immediately prior to any cession of jurisdiction by the United States pursuant to this title shall abate by reason of that cession. For the purposes of any such action or proceeding, such cession shall take effect on the day following the date of final determination of such action or proceeding.

(b) No cession made by the United States under this title shall deprive any court of the United States of jurisdiction to hear, determine, render judgment, or impose sentence in any criminal caution instituted against any person for any offense committed before the effective date of such cession, if the offense charged in such action was cognizable under any law of the United States at the time of the commission of such offense. For the purposes of any such criminal action, such cession shall take effect on the day following the day of final determination of such action.

Section 406. Special Election

State jurisdiction acquired pursuant to this title with respect to criminal offenses or civil causes of action, or with respect to both, shall be applicable in Indian country only where the enrolled Indians within the affected area of such Indian country accept such jurisdiction by a majority vote of the adult Indians voting at a special election held for that purpose. The Secretary of the Interior shall call such special election under such rules and regulations as he may prescribe, when requested to do so by the tribal council or other governing body, or by 20 per centum of such enrolled adults.

Title V. Offenses Within Indian Country

Section 501. Amendment

Section 1153 of title 18 of the United States Code is amended by inserting immediately after "weapon," the following: "assault resulting in serious bodily injury,".

Title VI. Employment of Legal Counsel

Section 601. Approval

Notwithstanding any other provision of law, if any application made by an Indian, Indian tribe, Indian council, or any band or group of Indians under any law requiring the approval of the

Secretary of the Interior or the Commissioner of Indian Affairs of contracts or agreements relating to the employment of legal counsel (including the choice of counsel and the fixing of fees) by any such Indians, tribe, council, band, or group is neither granted nor denied within ninety days following the making of such application, such approval shall be deemed to have been granted.

Title VII. Materials Relating to Constitutional Rights of Indians

Section 701. Secretary of Interior to Prepare

(a) In order that the constitutional rights of Indians might be fully protected, the Secretary of the Interior is authorized and directed to:

(1) have the document entitled "Indian Affairs, Laws and Treaties" (Senate Document Numbered 319, volumes 1 and 2, Fifty-eighth Congress), revised and extended to include all treaties, laws, Executive orders, and regulations relating to Indian affairs in force on September 1, 1967, and to have such revised document printed at the Government Printing Office;

(2) have revised and republished the treatise entitled "Federal Indian Law"; and

(3) have prepared, to the extent determined by the Secretary of the Interior to be feasible, an accurate compilation of the official opinions, published and unpublished, of the Solicitor of the Department of the Interior relating to Indian affairs rendered by the Solicitor prior to September 1, 1967, and to have such compilation printed as a Government publication at the Government Printing Office.

(b) With respect to the document entitled "Indian Affairs, Laws and Treaties: as revised and extended in accordance with paragraph (1) of subsection (a), and the compilation prepared in accordance with paragraph (3) of such subsection, the Secretary of the Interior shall take such action as may be necessary to keep such document and compilation current on an annual basis.

(c) There is authorized to be appropriated for carrying out the provisions of this title, with respect to the preparation by not including printing, such sum as may be necessary. . . .

KEEBLE V. UNITED STATES (1973)

In Keeble v. United States, the U.S. Supreme Court ruled that a Native American on trial under the Indian Major Crimes Act could have his jury consider a lesser charge, one not inscribed in the list of crimes covered by the act. Justice William Brennan wrote the Court's opinion for a six-person majority.

Source: Keeble v. United States, 412 U.S. 205 (1973). http://caselaw.lp.findlaw.com/scripts/getcase.pl?court=us&vol=412&invol=205.

MR. JUSTICE BRENNAN delivered the opinion of the Court.

The Major Crimes Act of 1885 authorizes the prosecution in federal court of an Indian charged with the commission on an Indian reservation of certain specifically enumerated offenses. This case requires us to decide whether an Indian prosecuted under the Act is entitled to a jury instruction on a lesser included offense where that lesser offense is not one of the crimes enumerated in the Act.

At the close of petitioner's trial for assault with intent to commit serious bodily injury, the United States District Court for the District of South Dakota refused to instruct the jury, as petitioner requested, that they might convict him of simple assault. The court reasoned that since simple assault is not an offense enumerated in the Act, it is exclusively "a matter for the tribe." . . . A panel of the United States Court of Appeals for the Eighth Circuit, one judge dissenting, upheld that determination on the strength of the court's earlier decision in *Kills Crow v. United States* (1971). . . . Following a remand to the District Court for a hearing on an unrelated issue, the case returned to the Court of Appeals and the conviction was affirmed. . . . We granted certiorari limited to the question of the validity of denying the requested instruction . . . , and we reverse.

The events that led to the death of petitioner's brother-in-law, Robert Pomani, and hence to this criminal prosecution, took place on the South Dakota Reservation of the Crow Creek Sioux Tribe. Petitioner and the deceased, both Indians of that Tribe, spent the evening of March 6, 1971, drinking and quarreling over petitioner's alleged mistreatment of his wife, Pomani's sister. The argument soon became violent, and it ended only when petitioner, having beaten Pomani severely and left him bleeding from the head and face, went to bed. The next morning he discovered Pomani's lifeless body on the ground a short distance from the house where the beating had occurred. He reported the death to an official of the Department of the Interior serving as Captain of the Tribal Police at Fort Thompson, South Dakota. An autopsy revealed that Pomani died because of exposure to excessive cold, although the beating was a contributing factor. Petitioner was convicted of assault with intent to inflict great bodily injury, and sentenced to five years' imprisonment.

Although the lesser included offense doctrine developed at common law to assist the prosecution in cases where the evidence failed to establish some element of the offense originally charged, it is now beyond dispute that the defendant is entitled to an instruction on a lesser included offense if the evidence would permit a jury rationally to find him guilty of the lesser offense and acquit him of the greater. The Federal Rules of Criminal Procedure deal with lesser included offenses, . . . and the defendant's right to such an instruction has been recognized in numerous decisions of this Court. See, e. g., *Sansone v. United States* (1965); *Berra v. United States* (1956); *Stevenson v. United States* (1896).

In defending the trial court's refusal to offer the requested instruction, the Government does not dispute this general proposition, nor does it argue that a lesser offense instruction was incompatible with the evidence presented at trial. Compare *Sansone v. United States* . . . ; *Sparf v. United States* (1895). On the contrary, the Government explicitly concedes that any non-Indian who had committed this same act on this same reservation and requested this same instruction would have been entitled to the jury charge that petitioner was refused. . . . The Government does maintain, however, that the Major Crimes Act precludes the District Court from offering a lesser offense instruction on behalf of an Indian, such as the petitioner before us. Specifically, the Government contends that the Act represents a carefully limited intrusion of federal power into the otherwise exclusive jurisdiction of the Indian tribes to punish Indians for crimes committed on Indian land. To grant an instruction on the lesser offense of simple assault would, in the Government's view, infringe the tribe's residual jurisdiction in a manner inconsistent with the Act. Under the Government's approach, in other words, the interests of an individual Indian defendant in obtaining a jury instruction on a lesser offense must fall before the congressionally sanctioned interests of the tribe in preserving its inherent jurisdiction. Since that conclusion is compelled neither by the language, nor the purposes, nor the history of the Act, we cannot agree.

The Major Crimes Act was passed by Congress in direct response to the decision of this Court in *Ex parte Crow Dog* (1883). The Court held there that a federal court lacked jurisdiction to try an Indian for the murder of another Indian, a chief of the Brule Sioux named Spotted Tail, in Indian country. Although recognizing the power of Congress to confer such jurisdiction on the federal courts, the Court reasoned that, in the absence of explicit congressional direction, the Indian tribe retained exclusive jurisdiction to punish the offense. Compare *Talton v. Mayes* (1896); *Worcester v. Georgia* (1832).

The prompt congressional response conferring jurisdiction on the federal courts to punish certain offenses reflected a view that tribal remedies were either non-existent or incompatible with principles that Congress thought should be controlling. Representative Cutcheon, sponsor of the Act, described the events that followed the reversal by this Court of Crow Dog's conviction:

Thus Crow Dog went free. He returned to his reservation, feeling, as the Commissioner says, a great deal more important than any of the chiefs of his tribe. The result was that another murder grew out of that a murder committed by Spotted Tail, Jr., upon White Thunder. And so these things must go on unless we adopt proper legislation on the subject.

It is an infamy upon our civilization, a disgrace to this nation, that there should be anywhere within its boundaries a body of people who can, with absolute impunity, commit the crime of murder, there being no tribunal before which they can be brought for punishment. Under our present law there is no penalty that can be inflicted except according to the custom of the tribe, which is simply that the "blood-avenger" that is, the next of kin to the person murdered shall pursue the one who has been guilty of the crime and commit a new murder upon him. . . .

If . . . an Indian commits a crime against an Indian on an Indian reservation there is now no law to punish the offense except, as I have said, the law of the tribe, which is just no law at all. . . .

The Secretary of the Interior, who supported the Act, struck a similar note:

If offenses of this character [the killing of Spotted Tail] can not be tried in the courts of the United States, there is no tribunal in which the crime of murder can be punished. Minor offenses may be punished through the agency of the "court of Indian offenses," but it will hardly do to leave the punishment of the crime of murder to a tribunal that exists only by the consent of the Indians of the reservation. If the murderer is left to be punished according to the old Indian custom, it becomes the duty of the next of kin to avenge the death of his relative by either killing the murderer or some one of his kinsmen. . . .

In short, Congress extended federal jurisdiction to crimes committed by Indians on Indian land out of a conviction that many Indians would "be civilized a great deal sooner by being put under [federal criminal] laws and taught to regard life and the personal property of others." . . . That is emphatically not to say, however, that Congress intended to deprive Indian defendants of procedural rights guaranteed to other defendants, or to make it easier to convict an Indian than any other defendant. Indeed, the Act expressly provides that Indians charged under its provisions "shall be tried in the same courts, and in the same manner, as are all other persons committing any of the above crimes within the exclusive jurisdiction of the United States." . . . In the face of that explicit statutory direction, we can hardly conclude that Congress intended to disqualify Indians from the benefits of a lesser offense instruction, when those benefits are made available to any non-Indian charged with the same offense.

Moreover, it is no answer to petitioner's demand for a jury instruction on a lesser offense to argue that a defendant may be better off without such an instruction. True, if the prosecution has not established beyond a reasonable doubt every element of the offense charged, and if no lesser offense instruction is offered, the jury must, as a theoretical matter, return a verdict of acquittal. But a defendant is entitled to a lesser offense instruction in this context or any other precisely because he should not be exposed to the substantial risk that the jury's practice will diverge from theory. Where one of the elements of the offense charged remains in doubt, but the defendant is plainly guilty of some offense, the jury is likely to resolve its doubts in favor of conviction. In the case before us, for example, an intent to commit serious bodily injury is a necessary element of the crime with which petitioner was charged, but not of the crime of simple assault. Since the nature of petitioner's intent was very much in dispute at trial, the jury could rationally have convicted him of simple assault if that option had been presented. But the jury was presented with only two options: convicting the defendant of assault with intent to commit great bodily injury, or acquitting him outright. We cannot say that the availability of a third option convicting the defendant of simple assault could not have resulted in a different verdict. Indeed, while we have never explicitly held that the Due Process Clause of the Fifth Amendment guarantees the right of a defendant to have the jury instructed on a lesser included offense, it is nevertheless clear that a construction of the Major Crimes Act to preclude such an instruction would raise difficult constitutional questions. In view of our interpretation of the Act, those are questions that we need not face.

Finally, we emphasize that our decision today neither expands the reach of the Major Crimes Act nor permits the Government to infringe the residual jurisdiction of a tribe by bringing prosecutions in federal court that are not authorized by statute. We hold only that where an Indian is prosecuted in federal court under the provisions of the Act, the Act does not require that he be deprived of the protection afforded by an instruction on a lesser included offense, assuming of course that the evidence warrants such an instruction. No interest of a tribe is jeopardized by this decision. Accordingly, the judgment of the Court of Appeals is reversed and the case is remanded for further proceedings consistent with this opinion.

Reversed and remanded.

TABLE: Violent and Property Crime Reports by Tribal Law Enforcement Agencies to the FBI's UCR Program (2008–2010)

Offense	2008–2010	2008	2009	2010
Total	71,623	24,923	22,637	24,063
Violent	17,394	6,212	5,650	5,532
Murder and non-negligent manslaughter	444	172	139	133
Forcible rape	2,613	879	882	852
Robbery	869	296	293	280
Aggravated assault	13,468	4,865	4,336	4,267
Property	54,229	18,711	16,987	18,531
Burglary	14,286	4,692	4,604	4,990
Larceny-theft	29,744	10,168	9,081	10,495
Motor vehicle theft	7,338	2,664	2,446	2,228
Arson*	2,861	1,187	856	818

*Law enforcement agencies do not submit reports for arson to the FBI's UCR Program unless they have the full 12 months of arson data for that year.

Source: FBI, Crime in the United States, 2008–2010.

Culture

AMERICAN INDIAN RELIGIOUS FREEDOM ACT (1978)

Enacted on August 11, 1978, the American Indian Religious Freedom Act offers safeguards for Native Americans' traditional religious practices and religions. After the U.S. Supreme Court ruled in Department of Human Services of Oregon v. Smith *(1990) and* Oregon v. Black *(1988) that this law did not allow Native Americans to use the illegal drug peyote in their religious services, Congress amended the act in 1994 to extend such protection.*

Source: American Indian Religious Freedom Act (1978). Public Law 95–341. Available at http://www.blm.gov/pgdata/etc/medialib/blm/wo/Planning_and_Renewable_Resources/coop_agencies/cr_publications.Par.77059.File.dat/78airfa.pdf

---

Resolved by the Senate and House of Representatives of the United States of America in Congress assembled,

That henceforth it shall be the policy of the United States to protect and preserve for American Indians their inherent fight of freedom to believe, express and exercise the traditional religions of the American Indian, Eskimo, Aleut, and Native Hawaiians, including but not limited to access to sites, use and possession of sacred objects, and the freedom to worship through ceremonials and traditional rites.

An Act To emend the American Indian Religious Freedom Act to provide for the traditional use of peyote by Indians for religious purposes, and for other purposes.

Be it enacted by the Senate and House of Representatives of the United States of America in Congress assembled,

SECTION 1. SHORT TITLE. This Act may be cited as the "American Indian Religious Freedom Act Amendments of 1994".

SECTION 2. TRADITIONAL INDIAN RELIGIOUS USE OF THE PEYOTE SACRAMENT. The Act of August 11, 1978 (42 U.S.C. 1996), commonly referred to as the "American Indian Religious Freedom Act", is amended by adding at the end thereof the following new section:

SECTION 3.

a. The Congress finds and declares that

1. for many Indian people, the traditional ceremonial use of the peyote cactus as a religious sacrament has for centuries been integral to a way of life, and significant in perpetuating Indian tribes and cultures;

2. since 1965, this ceremonial use of peyote by Indians has been protected by Federal regulation;

3. while at least 28 States have enacted laws which are similar to, or are in conformance with, the Federal regulation which protects the ceremonial use of peyote by Indian religious practitioners, 22 States have not done so, and this lack of uniformity has created hardship for Indian people who participate in such religious ceremonies;

4. the Supreme Court of the United States, in the case of *Employment Division v. Smith,* 494 U.S. 872 (1990), held that the First Amendment does not protect Indian practitioners who use peyote in Indian religious ceremonies, and also raised uncertainty whether this religious practice would be protected under the compelling State interest standard; and

5. the lack of adequate and clear legal protection for the religious use of peyote by Indians may serve to stigmatize and marginalize Indian tribes and cultures, and increase the risk that they will be exposed to discriminatory treatment.

b. 1. Notwithstanding any other provision of law, the use, possession, or transportation of peyote by an Indian for bona fide traditional ceremonial purposes in connection with the practice of a traditional Indian religion is lawful, and shall not be prohibited by the United States or any State. No Indian shall be penalized or discriminated against on the basis of such use, possession or transportation, including, but not limited to, denial of otherwise applicable benefits under public assistance programs.

2. This section does not prohibit such reasonable regulation and registration by the Drug Enforcement Administration of those persons who cultivate, harvest, or distribute peyote as may be consistent with the purposes of this Act.

3. This section does not prohibit application of the provisions of section 481.111 of Vernon's Texas Health and Safety Code Annotated, in effect on the date of enactment of this section, insofar as those provisions pertain to the cultivation, harvest, and distribution of peyote.

4. Nothing in this section shall prohibit any Federal department or agency, in carrying out its statutory responsibilities and functions, from promulgating regulations establishing reasonable limitations on the use or ingestion of peyote prior to or during the performance of duties by sworn law enforcement officers or personnel directly involved in public transportation or any other safety-sensitive positions where the performance of such duties may be adversely affected by such use or ingestion. Such regulations shall be adopted only after consultation with representatives of traditional Indian religions for which the sacramental use of peyote is integral to their practice. Any regulation promulgated pursuant to this section shall be subject to the balancing test set forth in section 3 of the Religious Freedom Restoration Act (Public Law 103–141; 42 U.S.C.2000bb-1).

5. This section shall not be construed as requiring prison authorities to permit, nor shall it be construed to prohibit prison authorities from permitting, access to peyote by Indians while incarcerated within Federal or State prison facilities.

6. Subject to the provisions of the Religious Freedom Restoration Act (Public Law 103–141; 42 U.S.C. 2000bb-1), this section shall not be construed to prohibit States from enacting or enforcing reasonable traffic safety laws or regulations.

7. Subject to the provisions of the Religious Freedom Restoration Act (Public Law 103–141; 42 USC 2000bb-1), this section does not prohibit the Secretary of Defense from promulgating regulations establishing reasonable limitations on the use, possession, transportation, or distribution of peyote to promote military readiness, safety, or compliance with international law or laws of other countries. Such regulations shall be adopted only after consultation with representatives of traditional Indian religions for which the sacramental use of peyote is integral to their practice.

c. For purposes of this section—

1. the term 'Indian' means a member of an Indian tribe;

2. the term 'Indian tribe' means any tribe, band, nation, pueblo, or other organized group or community of Indians, including any Alaska Native village (as defined in, or established pursuant to, the Alaska Native Claims Settlement Act (43 U.S.C. 1601 et seq.), which is recognized as eligible for the special programs and services provided by the United States to Indians because of their status as Indians;

3. the term 'Indian religion' means any religion—A. which is practiced by Indians; and B. the origin and interpretation of which is from within a traditional Indian culture or community; and

4. the term 'State' means any State of the United States and any political subdivision thereof.

d. Nothing in this section shall be construed as abrogating, diminishing, or otherwise affecting—

1. the inherent rights of any Indian tribe;

2. the rights, express or implicit, of any Indian tribe which exist under treaties, Executive orders, and laws of the United States;

3. the inherent right of Indians to practice their religions; and

4. the right of Indians to practice their religions under any Federal or State law.

NATIVE AMERICAN LANGUAGES ACT (1992)

Throughout much of U.S. history the federal government promoted the assimilation of Native Americans. One of the primary methods of assimilation was to do away with Native languages in favor of Native Americans adopting English. By the 1980s, in the new multicultural environment affecting American politics and education, Congress passed the Native American Languages Act (1990) to promote the preservation of Native languages. In 1992, President George H. W. Bush amended the 1990 act by signing the Native American Languages Act (1992), which ensured additional funding for tribes and Native American organizations to establish Native language programs, compile oral histories, and construct educational facilities.

Source: Native American Languages Act (1992). 102nd Congress (1991–1992). S.2044.ENR. Available at http://thomas.loc.gov/cgi-bin/query/z?c102:S.2044.ENR.

S.2044 – To assist Native Americans in assuring the survival and continuing vitality of (Enrolled Bill [Final as Passed Both House and Senate] - ENR)

One Hundred Second Congress of the United States of America

AT THE SECOND SESSION

Begun and held at the City of Washington on Friday, the third day of January,

one thousand nine hundred and ninety-two

An Act To assist Native Americans in assuring the survival and continuing vitality of their languages.

Be it enacted by the Senate and House of Representatives of the United States of America in Congress assembled,

Section 1. Short Title.

This Act, other than section 4, may be cited as the `Native American Languages Act of 1992'.

Sec. 2. Grant Program.

The Native American Programs Act of 1974 (42 U.S.C. 2991 et seq.) is amended by inserting before section 804 the following:

Sec. 803C. Grant Program to Ensure the Survival and Continuing Vitality of Native American Languages.

(a) AUTHORITY TO AWARD GRANTS- The Secretary shall award a grant to any agency or organization that is–

(1) eligible for financial assistance under section 803(a); and

(2) selected under subsection (c);

to be used to assist Native Americans in ensuring the survival and continuing vitality of Native American languages.

(b) PURPOSES FOR WHICH GRANTS MAY BE USED- The purposes for which each grant awarded under subsection (a) may be used include, but are not limited to–

(1) the establishment and support of a community Native American language project to bring older and younger Native Americans together to facilitate and encourage the transfer of Native American language skills from one generation to another;

(2) the establishment of a project to train Native Americans to teach a Native American language to others or to enable them to serve as interpreters or translators of such language;

(3) the development, printing, and dissemination of materials to be used for the teaching and enhancement of a Native American language;

(4) the establishment or support of a project to train Native Americans to produce or participate in a television or radio program to be broadcast in a Native American language;

(5) the compilation, transcription, and analysis of oral testimony to record and preserve a Native American language; and

(6) the purchase of equipment (including audio and video recording equipment, computers, and software) required to conduct a Native American language project.

(c) APPLICATIONS For the purpose of making grants under subsection (a), the Secretary shall select applicants from among agencies and organizations described in such subsection on the basis of applications submitted to the Secretary at such time, in such form, and containing such information as the Secretary shall require, but each application shall include at a minimum–

(1) a detailed description of the current status of the Native American language to be addressed by the project for which a grant under subsection (a) is requested, including a description of existing programs and projects, if any, in support of such language;

(2) a detailed description of the project for which such grant is requested;

(3) a statement of objectives that are consonant with the purpose described in subsection (a);

(4) a detailed description of a plan to be carried out by the applicant to evaluate such project, consonant with the purpose for which such grant is made;

(5) if appropriate, an identification of opportunities for the replication of such project or the modification of such project for use by other Native Americans; and

(6) a plan for the preservation of the products of the Native American language project for the benefit of future generations of Native Americans and other interested persons.

(d) PARTICIPATING ORGANIZATIONS– If a tribal organization or other eligible applicant decides that the objectives of its proposed Native American language project would be accomplished more effectively through a partnership arrangement with a school, college, or university, the applicant shall identify such school, college, or university as a participating organization in the application submitted under subsection (c).

(e) LIMITATIONS ON FUNDING–

(1) SHARE- Notwithstanding any other provision of this title, a grant made under subsection (a) may not be expended to pay more than 80 percent of the cost of the project that is assisted by such grant. Not less than 20 percent of such cost–

(A) shall be in cash or in kind, fairly evaluated, including plant, equipment, or services; and

(B)(i) may be provided from any private or non-Federal source; and

(ii) may include funds (including interest) distributed to a tribe–

(I) by the Federal Government pursuant to the satisfaction of a claim made under Federal law;

(II) from funds collected and administered by the Federal Government on behalf of such tribe or its constituent members; or

(III) by the Federal Government for general tribal administration or tribal development under a formula or subject to a tribal budgeting priority system, such as, but not limited to, funds involved in the settlement of land or other judgment claims, severance or other royalty payments, or payments under the Indian Self-Determination Act (25 U.S.C. 450f et seq.) or tribal budget priority system.

(2) DURATION– The Secretary may make grants made under subsection (a) on a 1-year, 2-year, or 3-year basis.

(f) ADMINISTRATION- (1) The Secretary shall carry out this section through the Administration for Native Americans.

(2)(A) Not later than 180 days after the effective date of this section, the Secretary shall appoint a panel of experts for the purpose of assisting the Secretary to review–

(i) applications submitted under subsection (a);

(ii) evaluations carried out to comply with subsection (c)(4); and

(iii) the preservation of products required by subsection (c)(5).

(B) Such panel shall include, but not be limited to–

(i) a designee of the Institute of American Indian and Alaska Native Culture and Arts Development;

(ii) a designee of the regional centers funded under section 5135 of the Elementary and Secondary Education Act of 1965 (20 U.S.C. 3215);

(iii) representatives of national, tribal, and regional organizations that focus on Native American language, or Native American cultural, research, development, or training; and

(iv) other individuals who are recognized for their expertise in the area of Native American language.

Recommendations for appointment to such panel shall be solicited from Indian tribes and tribal organizations.

(C) The duties of such panel include–

(i) making recommendations regarding the development and implementation of regulations, policies, procedures, and rules of general applicability with respect to the administration of this section;

(ii) reviewing applications received under subsection (c);

(iii) providing to the Secretary a list of recommendations for the approval of such applications–

(I) in accordance with regulations issued by the Secretary; and

(II) the relative need for the project; and

(iv) reviewing evaluations submitted to comply with subsection (c)(4).

(D)(i) Subject to clause (ii), a copy of the products of the Native American language project for which a grant is made under subsection (a)–

(I) shall be transmitted to the Institute of American Indian and Alaska Native Culture and Arts Development; and

(II) may be transmitted, in the discretion of the grantee, to national and regional repositories of similar material;

for preservation and use consonant with their respective responsibilities under other Federal law.

(ii) Based on the Federal recognition of the sovereign authority of Indian tribes over all aspects of their cultures and language and except as provided in clause (iii), an Indian tribe may make a determination–

(I) not to transmit copies of such products under clause (i) or not to permit the redistribution of such copies; or

(II) to restrict in any manner the use or redistribution of such copies after transmission under such clause.

(iii) Clause (ii) shall not be construed to authorize Indian tribes–

(I) to limit the access of the Secretary to such products for purposes of administering this section or evaluating such products; or

(II) to sell such products, or copies of such products, for profit to the entities referred to in clause (i).

Sec. 3. Authorization of Appropriations.

Section 816 of the Native American Programs Act of 1974 (42 U.S.C. 2992d) is amended–

(1) by inserting `803C' after `803A' each place it appears; and

(2) by adding at the end the following:

(f) There are authorized to be appropriated to carry out section 803C, $2,000,000 for fiscal year 1993 and such sums as may be necessary for fiscal years 1994, 1995, 1996, and 1997.'.

Sec. 4. Native Americans Educational Assistance Act.

(a) SHORT TITLE- This section may be cited as the `Native Americans Educational Assistance Act'.

(b) AGREEMENT TO CARRY OUT DEMONSTRATION PROJECT- The Secretary of the Interior is authorized to enter into an agreement with a nonprofit captioning agency engaged in manufacturing and distributing captioning decoders, for the purpose of carrying out a demonstration project to determine the effectiveness of captioned educational materials as an educational tool in schools operated by the Bureau of Indian Affairs.

(c) REPORT- Prior to the expiration of the 12-month period following the date of the agreement entered into pursuant to subsection (b), the Secretary of the Interior shall report to the Congress the results of the demonstration project carried out pursuant to such agreement, together with recommendations of the Secretary.

(d) AUTHORIZATION- There are authorized to be appropriated such sums as may be necessary to carry out this section.

Speaker of the House of Representatives.

Vice President of the United States and

President of the Senate.

RELIGIOUS FREEDOM RESTORATION ACT (1993)

In Employment Division, Department of Human Resources of Oregon v. Smith (1990), the U.S. Supreme Court ruled that general criminal laws (in this case a law prohibiting drug use) that have an adverse impact on religious adherents are not necessarily unconstitutional. The Religious Freedom Restoration Act (RFRA) of 1993 was designed to overturn that decision. The act required governments to establish a compelling interest in cases where laws substantially burdened the free exercise of religion. The RFRA stalled at first, because of concerns that it would be used to challenge state restrictions on abortion, but those fears were quelled, and Congress subsequently approved the act. However, in City of Boerne, Texas v. Flores (1997), the U.S. Supreme Court struck down the RFRA, ruling that it exceeded congressional powers under Section 5 of the Fourteenth Amendment, or the enforcement provision.

Source: Religious Freedom Restoration Act (1993), Public Law 103–141, 107 Stat. 1488. http://uscode.house.gov/download/pls/42C21B.txt.

An Act to protect the free exercise of religion.

Be it enacted by the Senate and House of Representatives of the United States of America in Congress assembled,

Section 1. Short Title.

This Act may be cited as the "Religious Freedom Restoration Act of 1993".

Sec. 2. Congressional Findings and Declaration of Purposes.

(a) Finances.—The Congress finds that—

(1) the framers of the Constitution, recognizing free exercise of religion as an unalienable right, secured its protection in the First Amendment to the Constitution;

(2) laws "neutral" toward religion may burden religious exercise as surely as laws intended to interfere with religious exercise;

(3) governments should not substantially burden religious exercise without compelling justification;

(4) in Employment Division v. Smith (1990) the Supreme Court virtually eliminated the requirement that the government justify burdens on religious exercise imposed by laws neutral toward religion; and

(5) the compelling interest test as set forth in prior Federal court rulings is a workable test for striking sensible balances between religious liberty and competing prior governmental interests.

(b) PURPOSES.—The purposes of this Act are—

(1) to restore the compelling interest test as set forth in Sherbert v. Verner (1963) and Wisconsin v. Yoder (1972) and to guarantee its application in all cases where free exercise of religion is substantially burdened; and

(2) to provide a claim or defense to persons whose religious exercise is substantially burdened by government.

Sec. 3. Free Exercise of Religion Protected.

(a) IN GENERAL.—Government shall not substantially burden a person's exercise of religion even if the burden results from a rule of general applicability, except as provided in subsection (b).

(b) EXCEPTION.—Government may substantially burden a person's exercise of religion only if it demonstrates that application of the burden to the person—

(1) is in furtherance of a compelling governmental interest; and

(2) is the least restrictive means of furthering that compelling governmental interest.

(c) JUDICIAL RELIEF.—A person, whose religious exercise has been burdened in violation of this section may assert that violation as a claim or defense in a judicial proceeding and obtain appropriate relief against a government. Standing to assert a claim or defense under this section shall be governed by the general rules of standing under article HI of the Constitution.

Sec. 4. Attorneys Fees.

(a) Section 722 of the Revised Statutes (42 U.S.C. 1988) is amended by inserting "the Religious Freedom Restoration Act of 1993," before title VI of the Civil Rights Act of 1964.

(b) ADMINISTRATIVE PROCEEDINGS.—Section 504(b)(1)(C) of title 5, United States Code, is amended—

(l) by striking "and" at the end of clause (ii);

(2) by striking the semicolon at the end of clause (iii) and inserting "and"; and

(3) by inserting "(iv) the Religious Freedom Restoration Act of 1993;" after clause (iii).

Sec. 5. Definitions.

As used in this Act.

(1) the term "government" includes a branch, department, agency, instrumentality, and official (or other person acting under color of law) of the United States, a State, or a subdivision of a State;

(2) the term "State" includes the District of Columbia, the Commonwealth of Puerto Rico, and each territory and possession of the United States;

(3) the term "demonstrates" means meets the burdens of going forward with the evidence and of persuasion; and

(4) the term "exercise of religion" means the exercise of religion under the First Amendment to the Constitution.

Sec. 6. Applicability.

(a) IN GENERAL. This Act applies to all Federal and State law, and the implementation of that law, whether statutory or otherwise, and whether adopted before or after the enactment of this Act.

(b) RULES OF CONSTRUCTION. Federal statutory law adopted after the date of the enactment of this Act is subject to this Act unless such law explicitly excludes such application by reference to this Act.

(c) RELIGIOUS BELIEF UNAFFECTED. Nothing in this Act shall be construed to authorize any government to burden any religious belief

Sec. 7. Establishment Clause Unaffected.

Nothing in this Act shall be construed to affect, interpret, or in any way address that portion of the First Amendment prohibition laws respecting the establishment of religion (referred to in this section as the "Establishment Clause"). Granting government funding, benefits, or exemptions, to the extent permissible under the Establishment Clause, shall not constitute a violation of this Act.

Approved November 16, 1993.

Family

INDIAN CHILD WELFARE ACT OF 1978

Source: Indian Child Welfare Act of 1978 (25 U.S.C. §§ 1901–63). Public Law 95–608. https://www.childwelfare.gov/systemwide/laws_policies/federal/index.cfm?event=federalLegislation.viewLegis&id=3

Congressional findings

Recognizing the special relationship between the United States and the Indian tribes and their members and the Federal responsibility to Indian people, the Congress finds–

1. that clause 3, section 8, article I of the United States Constitution provides that "The Congress shall have Power * * * To regulate Commerce * * * with Indian tribes and, through this and other constitutional authority, Congress has plenary power over Indian affairs;
2. that Congress, through statutes, treaties, and the general course of dealing with Indian tribes, has assumed the responsibility for the protection and preservation of Indian tribes and their resources;
3. that there is no resource that is more vital to the continued existence and integrity of Indian tribes than their children and that the United States has a direct interest, as trustee, in protecting Indian children who are members of or are eligible for membership in an Indian tribe;
4. that an alarmingly high percentage of Indian families are broken up by the removal, often unwarranted, of their children from them by nontribal public and private agencies and that an alarmingly high percentage of such children are placed in non-Indian foster and adoptive homes and institutions; and
5. that the States, exercising their recognized jurisdiction over Indian child custody proceedings through administrative and judicial bodies, have often failed to recognize the essential tribal relations of Indian people and the cultural and social standards prevailing in Indian communities and families. (Pub. L. 95–608, § 2, Nov. 8, 1978, 92 Stat. 3069.) Short Title Section 1 of Pub. L. 95–608 provided: "That this Act [enacting this chapter] may be cited as the `Indian Child Welfare Act of 1978'."

§ 1902. *Congressional declaration of policy*

The Congress hereby declares that it is the policy of this Nation to protect the best interests of Indian children and to promote the stability and security of Indian tribes and families by the establishment of minimum Federal standards for the removal of Indian children from their families and the placement of such children in foster or adoptive homes which will reflect the unique values of Indian culture, and by providing for assistance to Indian tribes in the operation of child and family service programs. (Pub. L. 95–608, § 3, Nov. 8, 1978, 92 Stat. 3069.)

§ 1903. *Definitions*

For the purposes of this chapter, except as may be specifically provided otherwise, the term–

1. "child custody proceeding" shall mean and include–
   i. "foster care placement" which shall mean any action removing an Indian child from its parent or Indian custodian for temporary placement in a foster home or institution or the home of a guardian or conservator where the parent or Indian custodian cannot have the child returned upon demand, but where parental rights have not been terminated;

ii. "termination of parental rights" which shall mean any action resulting in the termination of the parent-child relationship;

iii. "preadoptive placement" which shall mean the temporary placement of an Indian child in a foster home or institution after the termination of parental rights, but prior to or in lieu of adoptive placement; and

iv. "adoptive placement" which shall mean the permanent placement of an Indian child for adoption, including any action resulting in a final decree of adoption. Such term or terms shall not include a placement based upon an act which, if committed by an adult, would be deemed a crime or upon an award, in a divorce proceeding, of custody to one of the parents.

2. "extended family member" shall be as defined by the law or custom of the Indian child's tribe or, in the absence of such law or custom, shall be a person who has reached the age of eighteen and who is the Indian child's grandparent, aunt or uncle, brother or sister, brother-in-law or sister-in-law, niece or nephew, first or second cousin, or stepparent;
3. "Indian" means any person who is a member of an Indian tribe, or who is an Alaska Native and a member of a Regional Corporation as defined in 1606 of title 43;
4. "Indian child" means any unmarried person who is under age eighteen and is either (a) a member of an Indian tribe or (b) is eligible for membership in an Indian tribe and is the biological child of a member of an Indian tribe;
5. "Indian child's tribe" means (a) the Indian tribe in which an Indian child is a member or eligible for membership or (b), in the case of an Indian child who is a member of or eligible for membership in more than one tribe, the Indian tribe with which the Indian child has the more significant contacts;
6. "Indian custodian" means any Indian person who has legal custody of an Indian child under tribal law or custom or under State law or to whom temporary physical care, custody, and control has been transferred by the parent of such child;
7. "Indian organization" means any group, association, partnership, corporation, or other legal entity owned or controlled by Indians, or a majority of whose members are Indians;
8. "Indian tribe" means any Indian tribe, band, nation, or other organized group or community of Indians recognized as eligible for the services provided to Indians by the Secretary because of their status as Indians, including any Alaska Native village as defined in section 1602(c) of title 43;
9. "parent" means any biological parent or parents of an Indian child or any Indian person who has lawfully adopted an Indian child, including adoptions under tribal law or custom. It does not include the unwed father where paternity has not been acknowledged or established;
10. "reservation" means Indian country as defined in section 1151 of title 18 and any lands, not covered under such section, title to which is either held by the United States in trust for the benefit of any Indian tribe or individual or held by any Indian tribe or individual subject to a restriction by the United States against alienation;
11. "Secretary" means the Secretary of the Interior; and (12) "tribal court" means a court with jurisdiction over child custody proceedings and which is either a Court of Indian Offenses, a court established and operated under the code or custom of an Indian tribe, or any other administrative body of a tribe which is vested with authority over child custody proceedings. (Pub. L. 95–608, § 4, Nov. 8, 1978, 92 Stat. 3069.) This section is referred to in sections 1727, 3202, 3653, 4302 of this title; title 12 section 4702; title 26 section 168.

§ 1911. *Indian tribe jurisdiction over Indian child custody proceedings*

a. Exclusive jurisdiction

An Indian tribe shall have jurisdiction exclusive as to any State over any child custody proceeding involving an Indian child who resides or is domiciled within the reservation of such tribe, except where such jurisdiction is otherwise vested in the State by existing Federal law. Where an Indian child is a ward of a tribal court, the Indian tribe shall retain exclusive jurisdiction, notwithstanding the residence or domicile of the child.

b. Transfer of proceedings; declination by tribal court

In any State court proceeding for the foster care placement of, or termination of parental rights to, an Indian child not domiciled or residing within the reservation of the Indian child's tribe, the court, in the absence of good cause to the contrary, shall transfer such proceeding to the jurisdiction of the tribe, absent objection by either parent, upon the petition of either parent or the Indian custodian or the Indian child's tribe: Provided, That such transfer shall be subject to declination by the tribal court of such tribe.

c. State court proceedings; intervention

In any State court proceeding for the foster care placement of, or termination of parental rights to, an Indian child, the Indian custodian of the child and the Indian child's tribe shall have a right to intervene at any point in the proceeding.

d. Full faith and credit to public acts, records, and judicial proceedings of Indian tribes

The United States, every State, every territory or possession of the United States, and every Indian tribe shall give full faith and credit to the public acts, records, and judicial proceedings of any Indian tribe applicable to Indian child custody proceedings to the same extent that such entities give full faith and credit to the public acts, records, and judicial proceedings of any other entity. (Pub. L. 95–608, title I, § 101, Nov. 8, 1978, 92 Stat. 3071.) Section Referred to in Other Sections This section is referred to in sections 1914, 1918, 1923 of this title.

§ 1912. *Pending court proceedings*

a. Notice; time for commencement of proceedings; additional time for preparation

In any involuntary proceeding in a State court, where the court knows or has reason to know that an Indian child is involved, the party seeking the foster care placement of, or termination of parental rights to, an Indian child shall notify the parent or Indian custodian and the Indian child's tribe, by registered mail with return receipt requested, of the pending proceedings and of their right of intervention. If the identity or location of the parent or Indian custodian and the tribe cannot be determined, such notice shall be given to the Secretary in like manner, who shall have fifteen days after receipt to provide the requisite notice to the parent or Indian custodian and the tribe. No foster care placement or termination of parental rights proceeding shall be held until at least ten days after receipt of notice by the parent or Indian custodian and the tribe or the Secretary: Provided, That the parent or Indian custodian or the tribe shall, upon request, be granted up to twenty additional days to prepare for such proceeding.

b. Appointment of counsel

In any case in which the court determines indigency, the parent or Indian custodian shall have the right to court-appointed counsel in any removal, placement, or termination proceeding. The court may, in its discretion, appoint counsel for the child upon a finding that such appointment is in the best interest of the child. Where State law makes no provision for appointment of counsel in such proceedings, the court shall promptly notify the Secretary upon appointment of counsel, and the Secretary, upon certification of the presiding judge, shall pay reasonable fees and expenses out of funds which may be appropriated pursuant to section 13 of this title.

c. Examination of reports or other documents

Each party to a foster care placement or termination of parental rights proceeding under State law involving an Indian child shall have the right to examine all reports or other documents filed with the court upon which any decision with respect to such action may be based.

d. Remedial services and rehabilitative programs; preventive measures

Any party seeking to effect a foster care placement of, or termination of parental rights to, an Indian child under State law shall satisfy the court that active efforts have been made to provide remedial services and rehabilitative programs designed to prevent the breakup of the Indian family and that these efforts have proved unsuccessful.

e. Foster care placement orders; evidence; determination of damage to child

No foster care placement may be ordered in such proceeding in the absence of a determination, supported by clear and convincing evidence, including testimony of qualified expert witnesses, that the continued custody of the child by the parent or Indian custodian is likely to result in serious emotional or physical damage to the child.

f. Parental rights termination orders; evidence; determination of damage to child

No termination of parental rights may be ordered in such proceeding in the absence of a determination, supported by evidence beyond a reasonable doubt, including testimony of qualified expert witnesses, that the continued custody of the child by the parent or Indian custodian is likely to result in serious emotional or physical damage to the child. (Pub. L. 95–608, title I, § 102, Nov. 8, 1978, 92 Stat. 3071.) Section Referred to in Other Sections This section is referred to in sections 1914, 1916 of this title.

§ 1913. *Parental rights; voluntary termination*

a. Consent; record; certification matters; invalid consents

Where any parent or Indian custodian voluntarily consents to a foster care placement or to termination of parental rights, such consent shall not be valid unless executed in writing and recorded before a judge of a court of competent jurisdiction and accompanied by the presiding judge's certificate that the terms and consequences of the consent were fully explained in detail and were fully understood by the parent or Indian custodian. The court shall also certify that either the parent or Indian custodian fully understood the explanation in English or that it was interpreted into a language that the parent or Indian custodian understood. Any consent given prior to, or within ten days after, birth of the Indian child shall not be valid.

b. Foster care placement; withdrawal of consent

Any parent or Indian custodian may withdraw consent to a foster care placement under State law at any time and, upon such withdrawal, the child shall be returned to the parent or Indian custodian.

c. Voluntary termination of parental rights or adoptive placement; withdrawal of consent; return of custody

In any voluntary proceeding for termination of parental rights to, or adoptive placement of, an Indian child, the consent of the parent may be withdrawn for any reason at any time prior to the entry of a final decree of termination or adoption, as the case may be, and the child shall be returned to the parent.

d. Collateral attack; vacation of decree and return of custody; limitations

After the entry of a final decree of adoption of an Indian child in any State court, the parent may withdraw consent thereto upon the grounds that consent was obtained through fraud or duress and may petition the court to vacate such decree. Upon a finding that such consent was obtained through fraud or duress, the court shall vacate such decree and return the child to the parent. No adoption which has been effective for at least two years may be invalidated under the provisions of this subsection unless otherwise permitted under State law. (Pub. L. 95–608, title I, § 103, Nov. 8, 1978, 92 Stat. 3072.) Section Referred to in Other Sections This section is referred to in section 1914 of this title.

§ 1914. *Petition to court of competent jurisdiction to invalidate action upon showing of certain violations*

Any Indian child who is the subject of any action for foster care placement or termination of parental rights under State law, any parent or Indian custodian from whose custody such child was removed, and the Indian child's tribe may petition any court of competent jurisdiction to invalidate such action upon a showing that such action violated any provision of sections 1911, 1912, and 1913 of this title. (Pub. L. 95–608, title I, § 104, Nov. 8, 1978, 92 Stat. 3072.)

§ 1915. *Placement of Indian children*

a. Adoptive placements; preferences

In any adoptive placement of an Indian child under State law, a preference shall be given, in the absence of good cause to the contrary, to a placement with (1) a member of the child's extended family; (2) other members of the Indian child's tribe; or (3) other Indian families.

b. Foster care or preadoptive placements; criteria; preferences

Any child accepted for foster care or preadoptive placement shall be placed in the least restrictive setting which most approximates a family and in which his special needs, if any, may be met. The child shall also be placed within reasonable proximity to his or her home, taking into account any special needs of the child. In any foster care or preadoptive placement, a preference shall be given, in the absence of good cause to the contrary, to a placement with–

i. a member of the Indian child's extended family;
ii. a foster home licensed, approved, or specified by the Indian child's tribe;
iii. an Indian foster home licensed or approved by an authorized non-Indian licensing authority; or
iv. an institution for children approved by an Indian tribe or operated by an Indian organization which has a program suitable to meet the Indian child's needs.

c. Tribal resolution for different order of preference; personal preference considered; anonymity in application of preferences

In the case of a placement under subsection (a) or (b) of this section, if the Indian child's tribe shall establish a different order of preference by resolution, the agency or court effecting the placement shall follow such order so long as the placement is the least restrictive setting appropriate to the particular needs of the child, as provided in subsection (b) of this section. Where appropriate, the preference of the Indian child or parent shall be considered: Provided, That where a consenting parent evidences a desire for anonymity, the court or agency shall give weight to such desire in applying the preferences.

d. Social and cultural standards applicable

The standards to be applied in meeting the preference requirements of this section shall be the prevailing social and cultural standards of the Indian community in which the parent or extended family resides or with which the parent or extended family members maintain social and cultural ties. (e) Record of placement; availability. A record of each such placement, under State law, of an Indian child shall be maintained by the State in which the placement was made, evidencing the efforts to comply with the order of preference specified in this section. Such record shall be made available at any time upon the request of the Secretary or the Indian child's tribe. (Pub. L. 95–608, title I, § 105, Nov. 8, 1978, 92 Stat. 3073.)

§ 1916. *Return of custody*

a. Petition; best interests of child

Notwithstanding State law to the contrary, whenever a final decree of adoption of an Indian child has been vacated or set aside or the adoptive parents voluntarily consent to the termination of their parental rights to the child, a biological parent or prior Indian custodian may petition for return of custody and the court shall grant such petition unless there is a showing, in a proceeding subject to the provisions of section 1912 of this title, that such return of custody is not in the best interests of the child.

b. Removal from foster care home; placement procedure

Whenever an Indian child is removed from a foster care home or institution for the purpose of further foster care, preadoptive, or adoptive placement, such placement shall be in accordance with the provisions of this chapter, except in the case where an Indian child is being returned to the parent or Indian custodian from whose custody the child was originally removed. (Pub. L. 95–608, title I, § 106, Nov. 8, 1978, 92 Stat. 3073.)

§ 1917. ***Tribal affiliation information and other information for protection of rights from tribal relationship; application of subject of adoptive placement; disclosure by court***

Upon application by an Indian individual who has reached the age of eighteen and who was the subject of an adoptive placement, the court which entered the final decree shall inform such individual of the tribal affiliation, if any, of the individual's biological parents and provide such other information as may be necessary to protect any rights flowing from the individual's tribal relationship. (Pub. L. 95–608, title I, § 107, Nov. 8, 1978, 92 Stat. 3073.)

§ 1918. ***Reassumption of jurisdiction over child custody proceedings***

a. Petition; suitable plan; approval by Secretary

Any Indian tribe which became subject to State jurisdiction pursuant to the provisions of the Act of August 15, 1953 (67 Stat. 588), as amended by title IV of the Act of April 11, 1968 (82 Stat. 73, 78), or pursuant to any other Federal law, may reassume jurisdiction over child custody proceedings. Before any Indian tribe may reassume jurisdiction over Indian child custody proceedings, such tribe shall present to the Secretary for approval a petition to reassume such jurisdiction which includes a suitable plan to exercise such jurisdiction.

b. Criteria applicable to consideration by Secretary; partial retrocession

1. In considering the petition and feasibility of the plan of a tribe under subsection (a) of this section, the Secretary may consider, among other things:

   i. whether or not the tribe maintains a membership roll or alternative provision for clearly identifying the persons who will be affected by the reassumption of jurisdiction by the tribe;

   ii. the size of the reservation or former reservation area which will be affected by retrocession and reassumption of jurisdiction by the tribe;

   iii. the population base of the tribe, or distribution of the population in homogeneous communities or geographic areas; and (iv) the feasibility of the plan in cases of multitribal occupation of a single reservation or geographic area.

2. In those cases where the Secretary determines that the jurisdictional provisions of section 1911(a) of this title are not feasible, he is authorized to accept partial retrocession which will enable tribes to exercise referral jurisdiction as provided in section 1911(b) of this title, or, where appropriate, will allow them to exercise exclusive jurisdiction as provided in section 1911(a) of this title over limited community or geographic areas without regard for the reservation status of the area affected.

c. Approval of petition; publication in Federal Register; notice; reassumption period; correction of causes for disapproval

If the Secretary approves any petition under subsection (a) of this section, the Secretary shall publish notice of such approval in the Federal Register and shall notify the affected State or States of such approval. The Indian tribe concerned shall reassume jurisdiction sixty days after publication in the Federal Register of notice of approval. If the Secretary disapproves any petition under subsection (a) of this section, the Secretary shall provide such technical assistance as may be necessary to enable the tribe to correct any deficiency which the Secretary identified as a cause for disapproval.

d. Pending actions or proceedings unaffected

Assumption of jurisdiction under this section shall not affect any action or proceeding over which a court has already assumed jurisdiction, except as may be provided pursuant to any agreement under section 1919 of this title. (Pub. L. 95–608, title I, § 108, Nov. 8, 1978, 92 Stat. 3074.)

References in Text

Act of August 15, 1953, referred to in sub§ (a), is act Aug. 15, 1953, ch. 505, 67 Stat. 588, as amended, which enacted section 1162 of Title 18, Crimes and Criminal Procedure, section 1360 of Title 28, Judiciary and Judicial Procedure, and provisions set out as notes under section 1360 of Title 28. For complete classification of this Act to the Code, see Tables.

Section Referred to in Other Sections

This section is referred to in sections 1727, 1923 of this title.

§ 1919. ***Agreements between States and Indian tribes***

a. Subject coverage

States and Indian tribes are authorized to enter into agreements with each other respecting care and custody of Indian children and jurisdiction over child custody proceedings, including agreements which may provide for orderly transfer of jurisdiction on a case-by-case basis and agreements which provide for concurrent jurisdiction between States and Indian tribes.

b. Revocation; notice; actions or proceedings unaffected

Such agreements may be revoked by either party upon one hundred and eighty days' written notice to the other party. Such revocation shall not affect any action or proceeding over which a court has already assumed jurisdiction, unless the agreement provides otherwise. (Pub. L. 95–608, title I, § 109, Nov. 8, 1978, 92 Stat. 3074.)

Section Referred to in Other Sections

This section is referred to in sections 1918, 1923 of this title.

§ 1920. ***Improper removal of child from custody; declination of jurisdiction; forthwith return of child: danger exception***

Where any petitioner in an Indian child custody proceeding before a State court has improperly removed the child from custody of the parent or Indian custodian or has improperly retained custody after a visit or other temporary relinquishment of custody, the court shall decline jurisdiction over such petition and shall forthwith return the child to his parent or Indian custodian unless returning the child to his parent or custodian would subject the child to a substantial and immediate danger or threat of such danger.

§ 1921. ***Higher State or Federal standard applicable to protect rights of parent or Indian custodian of Indian child***

In any case where State or Federal law applicable to a child custody proceeding under State or Federal law provides a higher standard of protection to the rights of the parent or Indian custodian of an Indian child than the rights provided under this subchapter, the State or Federal court shall apply the State or Federal standard.

§ 1922. ***Emergency removal or placement of child; termination; appropriate action***

Nothing in this subchapter shall be construed to prevent the emergency removal of an Indian child who is a resident of or is domiciled on a reservation, but temporarily located off the reservation, from his parent or Indian custodian or the emergency placement of such child in a foster home or institution, under applicable State law, in order to prevent imminent physical damage or harm to the child. The State authority, official, or agency involved shall insure that the emergency removal or placement terminates immediately when such removal or placement is no longer necessary to prevent imminent physical damage or harm to the child and shall expeditiously initiate a child custody proceeding subject to the provisions of this subchapter, transfer the child to the jurisdiction of the appropriate Indian tribe, or restore the child to the parent or Indian custodian, as may be appropriate.

§ 1923. ***Effective date***

None of the provisions of this subchapter, except sections 1911(a), 1918, and 1919 of this title, shall affect a proceeding under State law for foster care placement, termination of parental rights, preadoptive placement, or adoptive placement which was initiated or completed prior to one hundred and eighty days after November 8, 1978, but shall apply to any subsequent proceeding in the same matter or subsequent proceedings affecting the custody or placement of the same child.

§ 1931. ***Grants for on or near reservation programs and child welfare codes***

a. Statement of purpose; scope of programs

The Secretary is authorized to make grants to Indian tribes and organizations in the establishment and operation of Indian child and family service programs on or near reservations and in the preparation and implementation of child welfare codes. The objective of every Indian child and family service program shall be to prevent the breakup of Indian families and, in particular, to insure that the permanent removal of an Indian child from the custody of his parent or Indian custodian shall be a last resort. Such child and family service programs may include, but are not limited to–

1. a system for licensing or otherwise regulating Indian foster and adoptive homes;
2. the operation and maintenance of facilities for the counseling and treatment of Indian families and for the temporary custody of Indian children;
3 family assistance, including homemaker and home counselors, day care, afterschool care, and employment, recreational activities, and respite care;
4. home improvement programs;
5. the employment of professional and other trained personnel to assist the tribal court in the disposition of domestic relations and child welfare matters;
6. education and training of Indians, including tribal court judges and staff, in skills relating to child and family assistance and service programs;
7. a subsidy program under which Indian adoptive children may be provided support comparable to that for which they would be eligible as foster children, taking into account the appropriate State standards of support for maintenance and medical needs; and
8. guidance, legal representation, and advice to Indian families involved in tribal, State, or Federal child custody proceedings.

b. Non-Federal matching funds for related Social Security or other Federal financial assistance programs; assistance for such programs unaffected; State licensing or approval for qualification for assistance under federally assisted program

Funds appropriated for use by the Secretary in accordance with this section may be utilized as non-Federal matching share in connection with funds provided under titles IV-B and XX of the Social Security Act [42 U.S.C. 620 et seq., 1397 et seq.] or under any other Federal financial assistance programs which contribute to the purpose for which such funds are authorized to be appropriated for use under this chapter. The provision or possibility of assistance under this chapter shall not be a basis for the denial or reduction of any assistance otherwise authorized under titles IV-B and XX of the Social Security Act or any other federally assisted program. For purposes of qualifying for assistance under a federally assisted program, licensing or approval of foster or adoptive homes or institutions by an Indian tribe shall be deemed equivalent to licensing or approval by a State.

References in Text

The Social Security Act, referred to in sub§ (b), is act Aug. 14, 1935, ch. 531, 49 Stat. 620, as amended. Titles IV-B and XX of the Social Security Act are classified generally to part B (§ 620 et seq.) of subchapter IV and subchapter XX (§ 1397 et seq.) of chapter 7 of Title 42, The Public Health and Welfare. For complete classification of this Act to the Code, see section 1305 of Title 42 and Tables.

§ 1932. ***Grants for off-reservation programs for additional services***

The Secretary is also authorized to make grants to Indian organizations to establish and operate off-reservation Indian child and family service programs which may include, but are not limited to–

1. a system for regulating, maintaining, and supporting Indian foster and adoptive homes, including a subsidy program under which Indian adoptive children may be provided support comparable to that for which they would be eligible as Indian foster children, taking into account the appropriate State standards of support for maintenance and medical needs;

2. the operation and maintenance of facilities and services for counseling and treatment of Indian families and Indian foster and adoptive children;
3. family assistance, including homemaker and home counselors, day care, afterschool care, and employment, recreational activities, and respite care; and
4. guidance, legal representation, and advice to Indian families involved in child custody proceedings. (Pub. L. 95–608, title II, § 202, Nov. 8, 1978, 92 Stat. 3076.)

Section Referred to in Other Sections

This section is referred to in section 1934 of this title.

§ 1933. *Funds for on and off reservation programs*

a. Appropriated funds for similar programs of Department of Health and Human Services; appropriation in advance for payments in the establishment, operation, and funding of Indian child and family service programs, both on and off reservation, the Secretary may enter into agreements with the Secretary of Health and Human Services, and the latter Secretary is hereby authorized for such purposes to use funds appropriated for similar programs of the Department of Health and Human Services: Provided, That authority to make payments pursuant to such agreements shall be effective only to the extent and in such amounts as may be provided in advance by appropriation Acts.

b. Appropriation authorization under section 13 of this title Funds for the purposes of this chapter may be appropriated pursuant to the provisions of section 13 of this title. (Pub. L. 95–608, title II, § 203, Nov. 8, 1978, 92 Stat. 3076; Pub. L. 96–88, title V, § 509(b), Oct. 17, 1979, 93 Stat. 695.)

Change of Name

"Secretary of Health and Human Services" and "Department of Health and Human Services" substituted for "Secretary of Health, Education, and Welfare" and "Department of Health, Education, and Welfare", respectively, in sub§ (a) pursuant to section 509(b) of Pub. L. 96–88, which is classified to section 3508(b) of Title 20, Education.

Section Referred to in Other Sections

This section is referred to in section 1934 of this title.

§ 1934. *"Indian" defined for certain purposes*

For the purposes of sections 1932 and 1933 of this title, the term "Indian" shall include persons defined in section 1603(c) of this title.

§ 1951. *Information availability to and disclosure by Secretary*

a. Copy of final decree or order; other information; anonymity affidavit; exemption from Freedom of Information Act

2. Any State court entering a final decree or order in any Indian child adoptive placement after November 8, 1978, shall provide the Secretary with a copy of such decree or order together with such other information as may be necessary to show–

1. the name and tribal affiliation of the child;
2. the names and addresses of the biological parents;
3. the names and addresses of the adoptive parents; and
4. the identity of any agency having files or information relating to such adoptive placement. Where the court records contain an affidavit of the biological parent or parents that their identity remain confidential, the court shall include such affidavit with the other information. The Secretary shall insure that the confidentiality of such information is maintained and such information shall not be subject to the Freedom of Information Act (5 U.S.C. 552), as amended.

c. Disclosure of information for enrollment of Indian child in tribe or for determination of member rights or benefits; certification of entitlement to enrollment Upon the request of the adopted Indian child over the age of eighteen, the adoptive or foster parents of an Indian child, or an Indian tribe, the Secretary shall disclose such information as may be necessary for the enrollment of an Indian child in the tribe in which the child may be eligible for enrollment or for determining any rights or benefits associated with that membership. Where the documents relating to such child contain an affidavit from the biological parent or parents requesting anonymity, the Secretary shall certify to the Indian child's tribe, where the information warrants, that the child's parentage and other circumstances of birth entitle the child to enrollment under the criteria established by such tribe.

§ 1952. ***Rules and regulations***

Within one hundred and eighty days after November 8, 1978, the Secretary shall promulgate such rules and regulations as may be necessary to carry out the provisions of this chapter.

Locally convenient day schools

a. Sense of Congress

It is the sense of Congress that the absence of locally convenient day schools may contribute to the breakup of Indian families.

b. Report to Congress; contents, etc.

The Secretary is authorized and directed to prepare, in consultation with appropriate agencies in the Department of Health and Human Services, a report on the feasibility of providing Indian children with schools located near their homes, and to submit such report to the Select Committee on Indian Affairs of the United States Senate and the Committee on Interior and Insular Affairs of the United States House of Representatives within two years from November 8, 1978. In developing this report the Secretary shall give particular consideration to the provision of educational facilities for children in the elementary grades. (Pub. L. 95–608, title IV, § 401, Nov. 8, 1978, 92 Stat. 3078; Pub. L. 96–88, title V, § 509(b), Oct. 17, 1979, 93 Stat. 695.)

c. Change of Name

"Department of Health and Human Services" substituted for "Department of Health, Education, and Welfare" in sub§ (b), pursuant to section 509(b) of Pub. L. 96–88 which is classified to section 3508(b) of Title 20, Education.

Select Committee on Indian Affairs of the Senate redesignated Committee on Indian Affairs of the Senate by section 25 of Senate Resolution No. 71, Feb. 25, 1993, One Hundred Third Congress.

Committee on Interior and Insular Affairs of the House of Representatives changed to Committee on Natural Resources of the House of Representatives on Jan. 5, 1993, by House Resolution No. 5, One Hundred Third Congress.

Committee on Natural Resources of House of Representatives treated as referring to Committee on Resources of House of Representatives by section 1(a) of Pub. L. 104–14, set out as a note preceding section 21 of Title 2, The Congress.

§ 1962. ***Copies to the States***

Within sixty days after November 8, 1978, the Secretary shall send to the Governor, chief justice of the highest court of appeal, and the attorney general of each State a copy of this chapter, together with committee reports and an explanation of the provisions of this chapter.

§ 1963. ***Severability***

If any provision of this chapter or the applicability thereof is held invalid, the remaining provisions of this chapter shall not be affected thereby.

SAFETY FOR INDIAN WOMEN IN THE VIOLENCE AGAINST WOMEN ACT (2005)

In 2005 the Violence Against Women Act (VAWA) was reauthorized with an added provision—Title IX, Safety for Indian Women. The VAWA was originally passed as Title IV of The Violent Crime Control and Law Enforcement Act (1994), and it was reauthorized in 2000 and in

2005. The Safety for Indian Women provision in the 2005 reauthorization brought the high rates of violence against indigenous women to the forefront, when Congress found that Native American women suffer the highest occurrences of domestic violence, sexual assault, and murder. The Act proposes to decrease these rates and to increase the authority of tribal governments to protect women and to prosecute offenders. Below is Title IX, excerpted from the VAWA (2005).

Source: Safety for Indian Women in the Violence Against Women Act (2005). Public Law 162. http://www.gpo.gov/fdsys/pkg/PLAW-109publ162/html/PLAW-109publ162.htm

---

H.R. 3402

One Hundred Ninth Congress
of the
United States of America

AT THE FIRST SESSION

Begun and held at the City of Washington on Tuesday, the fourth day of January, two thousand and five

An Act

To authorize appropriations for the Department of Justice for fiscal years 2006 through 2009, and for other purposes.

Be it enacted by the Senate and House of Representatives of the United States of America in Congress assembled,

Section 1. Short Title.

This Act may be cited as the "Violence Against Women and Department of Justice Reauthorization Act of 2005".

H.R. 3402–118

TITLE IX—SAFETY FOR INDIAN WOMEN

Sec. 901. Findings.

Congress finds that—

(1) 1 out of every 3 Indian (including Alaska Native) women are raped in their lifetimes;

(2) Indian women experience 7 sexual assaults per 1,000, compared with 4 per 1,000 among Black Americans, 3 per 1,000 among Caucasians, 2 per 1,000 among Hispanic women, and 1 per 1,000 among Asian women;

(3) Indian women experience the violent crime of battering at a rate of 23.2 per 1,000, compared with 8 per 1,000 among Caucasian women;

(4) during the period 1979 through 1992, homicide was the third leading cause of death of Indian females aged 15

H.R. 3402—119

to 34, and 75 percent were killed by family members or acquaintances;

(5) Indian tribes require additional criminal justice and victim services resources to respond to violent assaults against women; and

(6) the unique legal relationship of the United States to Indian tribes creates a Federal trust responsibility to assist tribal governments in safeguarding the lives of Indian women.

Sec. 902. Purposes.

The purposes of this title are—

(1) to decrease the incidence of violent crimes against Indian women;

(2) to strengthen the capacity of Indian tribes to exercise their sovereign authority to respond to violent crimes committed against Indian women; and

(3) to ensure that perpetrators of violent crimes committed against Indian women are held accountable for their criminal behavior.

Sec. 903. Consultation.

(a) IN GENERAL.—The Attorney General shall conduct annual consultations with Indian tribal governments concerning the Federal administration of tribal funds and programs established under this Act, the Violence Against Women Act of 1994 (title IV of Public Law 103–322; 108 Stat. 1902) and the Violence Against Women Act of 2000 (division B of Public Law 106–386; 114 Stat.1491).

(b) RECOMMENDATIONS.—During consultations under subsection (a), the Secretary of the Department of Health and Human Services and the Attorney General shall solicit recommendations from Indian tribes concerning—

(1) administering tribal funds and programs;

(2) enhancing the safety of Indian women from domestic violence, dating violence, sexual assault, and stalking; and

(3) strengthening the Federal response to such violent crimes.

Sec. 904. Analysis And Research On Violence Against

Indian Women.

(a) NATIONAL BASELINE STUDY.—

(1) IN GENERAL.—The National Institute of Justice, in consultation with the Office on Violence Against Women, shall conduct a national baseline study to examine violence against Indian women in Indian country.

(2) SCOPE.—

(A) IN GENERAL.—The study shall examine violence committed against Indian women, including—

(i) domestic violence;

(ii) dating violence;

(iii) sexual assault;

(iv) stalking; and

(v) murder.

(B) EVALUATION.—The study shall evaluate the effectiveness of Federal, State, tribal, and local responses to the violations described in subparagraph (A) committed against Indian women.

H. R. 3402—120

(C) RECOMMENDATIONS.—The study shall propose recommendations to improve the effectiveness of Federal, State, tribal, and local responses to the violation described in subparagraph (A) committed against Indian women. (3) TASK FORCE.—

(A) IN GENERAL.—The Attorney General, acting through the Director of the Office on Violence Against Women, shall establish a task force to assist in the development and implementation of the study under paragraph (1) and guide implementation of the recommendation in paragraph (2) C).

(B) MEMBERS.—The Director shall appoint to the task force representatives from—

(i) national tribal domestic violence and sexual assault nonprofit organizations;

(ii) tribal governments; and

(iii) the national tribal organizations.

(4) REPORT.—Not later than 2 years after the date of enactment of this Act, the Attorney General shall submit to the Committee on Indian Affairs of the Senate, the Committee on the Judiciary

of the Senate, and the Committee on the Judiciary of the House of Representatives a report that describes the study.

(5) AUTHORIZATION OF APPROPRIATIONS.—There is authorized to be appropriated to carry out this section $1,000,000 for each of fiscal years 2007 and 2008, to remain available until expended.

(b) INJURY STUDY.—

(1) IN GENERAL.—The Secretary of Health and Human Services, acting through the Indian Health Service and the Centers for Disease Control and Prevention, shall conduct a study to obtain a national projection of—

(A) the incidence of injuries and homicides resulting from domestic violence, dating violence, sexual assault, or stalking committed against American Indian and Alaska Native women; and

(B) the cost of providing health care for the injuries described in subparagraph (A).

(2) REPORT.—Not later than 2 years after the date of enactment of this Act, the Secretary of Health and Human Services shall submit to the Committee on Indian Affairs of the Senate, the Committee on the Judiciary of the Senate, and the Committee on the Judiciary of the House of Representatives a report that describes the findings made in the study and recommends health care strategies for reducing the incidence and cost of the injuries described in paragraph (1).

(3) AUTHORIZATION OF APPROPRIATIONS.—There is authorized to be appropriated to carry out this section $500,000 for each of fiscal years 2007 and 2008, to remain available until expended.

Sec. 905. Tracking Of Violence Against Indian Women.

(a) ACCESS TO FEDERAL CRIMINAL INFORMATION DATABASES.—

Section 534 of title 28, United States Code, is amended—

(1) by redesignating subsection (d) as subsection (e); and

(2) by inserting after subsection (c) the following:

H. R. 3402—121

"(d) INDIAN LAW ENFORCEMENT AGENCIES.—The Attorney General shall permit Indian law enforcement agencies, in cases of domestic violence, dating violence, sexual assault, and stalking, to enter information into Federal criminal information databases and to obtain information from the databases."

(b) TRIBAL REGISTRY.—

(1) ESTABLISHMENT.—The Attorney General shall contract with any interested Indian tribe, tribal organization, or tribal nonprofit organization to develop and maintain—

(A) a national tribal sex offender registry; and

(B) a tribal protection order registry containing civil and criminal orders of protection issued by Indian tribes and participating jurisdictions.

(2) AUTHORIZATION OF APPROPRIATIONS.—There is authorized to be appropriated to carry out this section $1,000,000 for each of fiscal years 2007 through 2011, to remain available until expended.

Sec. 906. Grants To Indian Tribal Governments.

(a) IN GENERAL.—Part T of title I of the Omnibus Crime Control and Safe Streets Act of 1968 (42 U.S.C. 3796gg et seq.) is amended by adding at the end the following:

Sec. 2007. Grants To Indian Tribal Governments.

"(a) GRANTS.—The Attorney General may make grants to Indian tribal governments and tribal organizations to—

"(1) develop and enhance effective governmental strategies to curtail violent crimes against and increase the safety of Indian women consistent with tribal law and custom;

"(2) increase tribal capacity to respond to domestic violence, dating violence, sexual assault, and stalking crimes against Indian women;

"(3) strengthen tribal justice interventions including tribal law enforcement, prosecution, courts, probation, correctional facilities;

"(4) enhance services to Indian women victimized by domestic violence, dating violence, sexual assault, and stalking;

"(5) work in cooperation with the community to develop education and prevention strategies directed toward issues of domestic violence, dating violence, and stalking programs and to address the needs of children exposed to domestic violence;

"(6) provide programs for supervised visitation and safe visitation exchange of children in situations involving domestic violence, sexual assault, or stalking committed by one parent against the other with appropriate security measures, policies, and procedures to protect the safety of victims and their children; and

"(7) provide transitional housing for victims of domestic violence, dating violence, sexual assault, or stalking, including rental or utilities payments assistance and assistance with related expenses such as security deposits and other costs incidental to relocation to transitional housing, and support services to enable a victim of domestic violence, dating violence, sexual assault, or stalking to locate and secure permanent housing and integrate into a community.

"(b) COLLABORATION.—All applicants under this section shall demonstrate their proposal was developed in consultation with a nonprofit, nongovernmental Indian victim services program,

H. R. 3402—122

including sexual assault and domestic violence victim services providers in the tribal or local community, or a nonprofit tribal domestic violence and sexual assault coalition to the extent that they exist. In the absence of such a demonstration, the applicant may meet the requirement of this subsection through consultation with women in the community to be served.

"(c) NONEXCLUSIVITY.—The Federal share of a grant made under this section may not exceed 90 percent of the total costs of the project described in the application submitted, except that the Attorney General may grant a waiver of this match requirement on the basis of demonstrated financial hardship. Funds appropriated for the activities of any agency of an Indian tribal government or of the Bureau of Indian Affairs performing law enforcement functions on any Indian lands may be used to provide the non-Federal share of the cost of programs or projects funded under this section.".

(b) AUTHORIZATION OF FUNDS FROM GRANTS TO COMBAT VIOLENT CRIMES AGAINST WOMEN.—Section 2007(b)(1) of the Omnibus Crime Control and Safe Streets Act of 1968 (42 U.S.C. 3796gg–

1(b)(1)) is amended to read as follows:

"(1) Ten percent shall be available for grants under the program authorized in section 2007. The requirements of this part shall not apply to funds allocated for such program.".

(c) AUTHORIZATION OF FUNDS FROM GRANTS TO ENCOURAGE STATE POLICIES AND ENFORCEMENT OF PROTECTION ORDERS PROGRAM.—

Section 2101 of the Omnibus Crime Control and Safe Streets Act of 1968 (42 U.S.C. 3796hh) is amended by striking subsection (e) and inserting the following:

"(e) Not less than 10 percent of the total amount available under this section for each fiscal year shall be available for grants under the program authorized in section 2007. The requirements of this part shall not apply to funds allocated for such program.".

(d) AUTHORIZATION OF FUNDS FROM RURAL DOMESTIC VIOLENCE AND CHILD ABUSE ENFORCEMENT ASSISTANCE GRANTS.—Subsection 40295(c) of the Violence Against Women Act of 1994 (42 U.S.C. 13971(c)(3)) is amended by striking paragraph (3) and inserting the following:

"(3) Not less than 10 percent of the total amount available under this section for each fiscal year shall be available for grants under the program authorized in section 2007 of the Omnibus Crime Control and Safe Streets Act of 1968. The requirements of this paragraph shall not apply to funds allocated for such program.".

(e) AUTHORIZATION OF FUNDS FROM THE SAFE HAVENS FOR CHILDREN PROGRAM.—Section 1301 of the Violence Against Women Act of 2000 (42 U.S.C. 10420) is amended by striking subsection (f) and inserting the following:

"(f) Not less than 10 percent of the total amount available under this section for each fiscal year shall be available for grants under the program authorized in section 2007 of the Omnibus Crime Control and Safe Streets Act of 1968. The requirements of this subsection shall not apply to funds allocated for such program.".

(f) AUTHORIZATION OF FUNDS FROM THE TRANSITIONAL HOUSING ASSISTANCE GRANTS FOR CHILD VICTIMS OF DOMESTIC VIOLENCE, STALKING, OR SEXUAL ASSAULT PROGRAM.—

Section 40299(g) of the

H. R. 3402—123

Violence Against Women Act of 1994 (42 U.S.C. 13975(g)) is amended by adding at the end the following:

"(4) TRIBAL PROGRAM.—Not less than 10 percent of the total amount available under this section for each fiscal year shall be available for grants under the program authorized in section 2007 of the Omnibus Crime Control and Safe Streets Act of 1968. The requirements of this paragraph shall not apply to funds allocated for such program.".

(g) AUTHORIZATION OF FUNDS FROM THE LEGAL ASSISTANCE FOR VICTIMS IMPROVEMENTS PROGRAM.—Section 1201(f) of the Violence Against Women Act of 2000 (42 U.S.C. 3796gg–6) is amended by adding at the end the following:

"(4) Not less than 10 percent of the total amount available under this section for each fiscal year shall be available for grants under the program authorized in section 2007 of the Omnibus Crime Control and Safe Streets Act of 1968. The requirements of this paragraph shall not apply to funds allocated for such program.".

Sec. 907. Tribal Deputy in the Office on Violence Against Women.

Part T of title I of the Omnibus Crime Control and Safe Streets Act of 1968 (42 U.S.C. 3796gg et seq.), as amended by section 906, is amended by adding at the end the following:

"Sec. 2008. Tribal Deputy.

"(a) ESTABLISHMENT.—There is established in the Office on Violence Against Women a Deputy Director for Tribal Affairs.

"(b) DUTIES.—

"(1) IN GENERAL.—The Deputy Director shall under the guidance and authority of the Director of the Office on Violence Against Women—

"(A) oversee and manage the administration of grants to and contracts with Indian tribes, tribal courts, tribal organizations, or tribal nonprofit organizations;

"(B) ensure that, if a grant under this Act or a contract pursuant to such a grant is made to an organization to perform services that benefit more than 1 Indian tribe, the approval of each Indian tribe to be benefitted shall be a prerequisite to the making of the grant or letting of the contract;

"(C) coordinate development of Federal policy, protocols, and guidelines on matters relating to violence against Indian women;

"(D) advise the Director of the Office on Violence Against Women concerning policies, legislation, implementation of laws, and other issues relating to violence against Indian women;

"(E) represent the Office on Violence Against Women In the annual consultations under section 903;

"(F) provide technical assistance, coordination, and support to other offices and bureaus in the Department of Justice to develop policy and to enforce Federal laws relating to violence against Indian women, including through litigation of civil and criminal actions relating to those laws;

H. R. 3402—124

"(G) maintain a liaison with the judicial branches of Federal, State, and tribal governments on matters relating to violence against Indian women;

"(H) support enforcement of tribal protection orders and implementation of full faith and credit educational projects and comity agreements between Indian tribes and States; and

"(I) ensure that adequate tribal technical assistance is made available to Indian tribes, tribal courts, tribal organizations, and tribal nonprofit organizations for all programs relating to violence against Indian women.

"(c) AUTHORITY.—

"(1) IN GENERAL.—The Deputy Director shall ensure that a portion of the tribal set-aside funds from any grant awarded under this Act, the Violence Against Women Act of 1994 (title IV of Public Law 103–322; 108 Stat. 1902), or the Violence Against Women Act of 2000 (division B of Public Law 106–386; 114 Stat. 1491) is used to enhance the capacity of Indian tribes to address the safety of Indian women.

"(2) ACCOUNTABILITY.—The Deputy Director shall ensure that some portion of the tribal set-aside funds from any grant made under this part is used to hold offenders accountable through—

"(A) enhancement of the response of Indian tribes to crimes of domestic violence, dating violence, sexual assault, and stalking against Indian women, including legal services for victims and Indian-specific offender programs;

"(B) development and maintenance of tribal domestic violence shelters or programs for battered Indian women, including sexual assault services, that are based upon the unique circumstances of the Indian women to be served;

"(C) development of tribal educational awareness programs and materials;

"(D) support for customary tribal activities to strengthen the intolerance of an Indian tribe to violence against Indian women; and

"(E) development, implementation, and maintenance of tribal electronic databases for tribal protection order registries.".

SEC. 908. ENHANCED CRIMINAL LAW RESOURCES.

(a) FIREARMS POSSESSION PROHIBITIONS.—Section 921(33)(A)(i) of title 18, United States Code, is amended to read: "(i) is a misdemeanor under Federal, State, or Tribal law; and".

(b) LAW ENFORCEMENT AUTHORITY.—Section 4(3) of the Indian Law Enforcement Reform Act (25 U.S.C. 2803(3) is amended—

(1) in subparagraph (A), by striking "or";

(2) in subparagraph (B), by striking the semicolon and inserting ", or"; and

(3) by adding at the end the following:

"(C) the offense is a misdemeanor crime of domestic violence, dating violence, stalking, or violation of a protection order and has, as an element, the use or attempted use of physical force, or the threatened use of a deadly weapon, committed by a current or former spouse, parent, or guardian of the victim, by a person with whom the

H. R. 3402—125

victim shares a child in common, by a person who is cohabitating with or has cohabited with the victim as a spouse, parent, or guardian, or by a person similarly situated to a spouse, parent or guardian of the victim, and the employee has reasonable grounds to believe that the person to be arrested has committed, or is committing the crime;".

SEC. 909. DOMESTIC ASSAULT BY AN HABITUAL OFFENDER.

Chapter 7 of title 18, United States Code, is amended by adding at the end the following:

"§ 117. Domestic assault by an habitual offender

"(a) IN GENERAL.—Any person who commits a domestic assault within the special maritime and territorial jurisdiction of the United States or Indian country and who has a final conviction on at least 2 separate prior occasions in Federal, State, or Indian tribal court proceedings for offenses that would be, if subject to Federal jurisdiction—

"(1) any assault, sexual abuse, or serious violent felony against a spouse or intimate partner; or

"(2) an offense under chapter 110A, shall be fined under this title, imprisoned for a term of not more than 5 years, or both, except that if substantial bodily injury results from violation under this section, the offender shall be imprisoned for a term of not more than 10 years.

"(b) DOMESTIC ASSAULT DEFINED.—In this section, the term 'domestic assault' means an assault committed by a current or former spouse, parent, child, or guardian of the victim, by a person with whom the victim shares a child in common, by a person who is cohabitating with or has cohabitated with the victim as a spouse, parent, child, or guardian, or by a person similarly situated to a spouse, parent, child, or guardian of the victim.".

Health

INDIAN HEALTH CARE IMPROVEMENT ACT (1976)

The Indian Health Care Improvement Act (IHCIA), that provides health care to American Indians and Alaska Natives, was made permanent in 2010 when President Obama signed the bill into law as part of the Patient Protection and Affordable Care Act.

Source: Indian Health Care Improvement Act (1976) Public Law 94–437 (90 Stat. 1400). http://www.ssa.gov/OP_Home/comp2/F094–437.html

* * * * * * *

DEFINITIONS

Sec. 4. [25 U.S.C. 1603] For purposes of this Act—

(a) "Secretary", unless otherwise designated, means the Secretary of Health and Human Services.

(b) "Service" means the Indian Health Service.

(c) "Indians" or "Indian", unless otherwise designated, means any person who is a member of an Indian tribe, as defined in subsection (d) hereof, except that, for the purpose of sections 102 and 103, such terms shall mean any individual who (1), irrespective of whether he or she lives on or near a reservation, is a member of a tribe, band, or other organized group of Indians, including those tribes, bands, or groups terminated since 1940 and those recognized now or in the future by the State in which they reside, or who is a descendant, in the first or second degree, of any such member, or (2) is an Eskimo or Aleut or other Alaska Native, or (3) is considered by the Secretary of the Interior to be an Indian for any purpose, or (4) is determined to be an Indian under regulations promulgated by the Secretary.

(d) "Indian tribe" means any Indian tribe, band, nation, or other organized group or community, including any Alaska Native village or group or regional or village corporation as defined in or established pursuant to the Alaska Native Claims Settlement Act (85 Stat. 688), which is recognized as eligible for the special programs and services provided by the United States to Indians because of their status as Indians.

(e) "Tribal organization" means the elected governing body of any Indian tribe or any legally established organization of Indians which is controlled by one or more such bodies or by a board of directors elected or selected by one or more such bodies (or elected by the Indian population to be served by such organization) and which includes the maximum participation of Indians in all phases of its activities.

(f) "Urban Indian" means any individual who resides in an urban center, as defined in subsection (g) hereof, and who meets one or more of the four criteria in subsection (c)(1) through (4) of this section.

(g) "Urban center" means any community which has a sufficient urban Indian population with unmet health needs to warrant assistance under title V, as determined by the Secretary.

(h) "Urban Indian organization" means a nonprofit corporate body situated in an urban center, governed by an urban Indian controlled board of directors, and providing for the maximum participation of all interested Indian groups and individuals, which body is capable of legally cooperating with other public and private entities for the purpose of performing the activities described in section 503(a).

(i) "Area office" means an administrative entity including a program office, within the Indian Health Service through which services and funds are provided to the service units within a defined geographic area.

(j) "Service unit" means—

(1) an administrative entity within the Indian Health Service, or

(2) a tribe or tribal organization operating health care programs or facilities with funds from the Service under the Indian Self-Determination Act,

through which services are provided, directly or by contract, to the eligible Indian population within a defined geographic area.

(k) "Health promotion" includes—

(1) cessation of tobacco smoking,

(2) reduction in the misuse of alcohol and drugs,

(3) improvement of nutrition,

(4) improvement in physical fitness,

(5) family planning,

(6) control of stress, and

(7) pregnancy and infant care (including prevention of fetal alcohol syndrome).

(l) "Disease prevention" includes—

(1) immunizations,

(2) control of high blood pressure,

(3) control of sexually transmittable diseases,

(4) prevention and control of diabetes,

(5) control of toxic agents,

(6) occupational safety and health,

(7) accident prevention,

(8) fluoridation of water, and

(9) control of infectious agents.

(m) "Service area" means the geographical area served by each area office.

(n) "Health profession" means family medicine, internal medicine, pediatrics, geriatric medicine, obstetrics and gynecology, podiatric medicine, nursing, public health nursing, dentistry, psychiatry, osteopathy, optometry, pharmacy, psychology, public health, social work, marriage and family therapy, chiropractic medicine, environmental health and engineering, and allied health professions.

(o) "Substance abuse" includes inhalant abuse.

(p) "FAE" means fetal alcohol effect.

(q) "FAS" means fetal alcohol syndrome.

TABLE: Age-Adjusted Percentages of Persons 18 Years of Age and Over with Diabetes (2004–2008)

	American Indian/ Alaska Native	White	American Indian/ Alaska Native/ White Ratio
Men and Women	17.5	6.6	2.7
Men	18.2	7.2	2.5
Women	16.2	6.2	2.6

Source: CDC 2010. Health Characteristics of the American Indian and Alaska Native Adult Population: United States, 2004–2008.

TABLE: Age-Adjusted Percentage of Persons 18 Years of Age and Over Who are Overweight but Not Obese, 2010. (Persons are considered overweight if they have a Body Mass Index [BMI] of 25 or greater.) National Health Interview Survey (NHIS) (2004–2008)

American Indian/Alaska Native	Non-Hispanic White	American Indian/Alaska Native/ Non-Hispanic White Ratio
29.6	33.7	0.9

Source: CDC 2012. Summary Health Statistics for U.S. Adults: 2010. Table 31. http://www.cdc.gov/nchs/data/series/sr_10/sr10_252.pdf [PDF | 3MB]

TABLE: Age-Adjusted Percentage of Persons 18 Years of Age and Over Who are Obese (2004–2006)

	American Indian/ Alaska Native	White	American Indian/ Alaska Native/ White Ratio
Men & Women	39.4	24.3	1.6
Men	38.7	25.5	1.5
Women	39.7	23.0	1.7

Source: CDC 2010. Health Characteristics of the American Indian and Alaska Native Adult Population: United States, 2004–2008. Table 2. http://www.cdc.gov/nchs/data/ad/ad356.pdf [PDF | 304KB]

TABLE: Age-Adjusted Percentage of Persons 18 Years of Age and Over Who are Obese (2010)

American Indian/ Alaska Native	Non-Hispanic White	American Indian/ Alaska Native/ Non-Hispanic White Ratio
39.6	26.1	1.5

Source: CDC 2012. Summary Health Statistics for U.S. Adults: 2010. Table 31. http://www.cdc.gov/nchs/data/series/sr_10/sr10_252.pdf [PDF |3MB]

Work and Society

INDIAN SELF-DETERMINATION AND EDUCATION ASSISTANCE ACT (1975)

Congress passed the Indian Self-Determination and Education Assistance Act (1975), also known as ISDEAA, in response to the Native American activism of the 1970s that called for the "self-determination" of Native nations in the management of federal programs. Signed into law by President Gerald Ford, the ISDEAA, excerpted below, established a new relationship between federal agencies and tribal authorities by permitting tribal governments to negotiate and contract directly with the Bureau of Indian Affairs (BIA) and the Department of Health, Education, and Welfare (HEW) for services. This landmark law also gave Native Americans the right to choose and to administer directly the government programs impacting their communities.

Source: Indian Self-Determination and Education Assistance Act (1975). Public Law 93–638, 88 Stat. 2203. http://www.justice.gov/olc/isdafin.htm

---

Be it enacted by the Senate and House of Representatives of the United States of America in Congress assembled, (25 U.S.C. 450 note) That this Act may be cited as the "Indian Self-Determination and Education Assistance Act".

CONGRESSIONAL FINDINGS SEC. 2. 25 U.S.C. 450 (a) The Congress, after careful review of the Federal Government's historical and special legal relationship with, and resulting responsibilities to, American Indian people, finds that—(1) the prolonged Federal domination of Indian service programs has served to retard rather than enhance the progress of Indian people and their communities by depriving Indians of the full opportunity to develop leadership skills crucial to the realization of self-government, and has denied to the Indian people an effective voice in the planning and implementation of programs for the benefit of Indians which are responsive to the true needs of Indian communities; and (2) the Indian people will never surrender their desire to control their relationships both among themselves and with non-Indian governments, organizations, and persons.

(b) The Congress further finds that—(1) true self-determination in any society of people is dependent upon an educational process which will insure the development of qualified people to fulfill meaningful leadership roles; (2) the Federal responsibility for and assistance to education of Indian children has not effected the desired level of educational achievement or created the diverse opportunities and personal satisfaction which education can and should provide; and (3) parental and community control of the educational process is of crucial importance to the Indian people.

DECLARATION OF POLICY SEC. 3. 25 U.S.C. 450a (a) The Congress hereby recognizes the obligation of the United States to respond to the strong expression of the Indian people for self-determination by assuring maximum Indian participation in the direction of educational as well as other Federal services to Indian communities so as to render such services more responsive to the needs and desires of those communities.

(b) The Congress declares its commitment to the maintenance of the Federal Government's unique and continuing relationship with, and responsibility to, individual Indian tribes and to the Indian people as a whole through the establishment of a meaningful Indian self-determination policy which will permit an orderly transition from the Federal domination of programs for, and services to, Indians to effective and meaningful participation by the Indian people in the planning, conduct, and administration of those programs and services. In accordance with this policy, the United States is committed to supporting and assisting Indian tribes in the development of strong and stable tribal governments, capable of administering quality programs and developing the economies of their respective communities.

(c) The Congress declares that a major national goal of the United States is to provide the quantity and quality of educational services and opportunities which will permit Indian children to compete and excel in the life areas of their choice, and to achieve the measure of self-determination essential to their social and economic well-being. ...

WAGE AND LABOR STANDARDS ...

(b) Any contract, subcontract, grant, or subgrant pursuant to this Act, the Act of April 16, 1934 (48 Stat. 596), as amended, or any other Act authorizing Federal contracts with or grants to Indian organizations or for the benefit of Indians, shall require that to the greatest extent feasible—

(1) preferences and opportunities for training and employment in connection with the administration of such contracts or grants shall be given to Indians; and

(2) preference in the award of subcontracts and subgrants in connection with the administration of such contracts or grants shall be given to Indian organizations and to Indian-owned economic enterprises as defined in section 3 of the Indian Financing Act of 1974 (88 Stat. 77).

(c) Notwithstanding subsections (a) and (b), with respect to any self-determination contract, or portion of a self-determination contract, that is intended to benefit one tribe, the tribal employment or contract preference laws adopted by such tribe shall govern with respect to the administration of the contract or portion of the contract. ...

CALIFORNIA V. CABAZON BAND OF MISSION INDIANS (1987)

In this case, the U.S. Supreme Court upheld the right of Native Americans on reservations to conduct gambling free of state control, despite the fact that California claims civil and criminal jurisdiction under Public Law 280. In California, according to a number of court rulings, state criminal jurisdiction is concurrent with that of Native American governments. This case arose after California asserted a right to regulate gambling (including card games and bingo) on the reservations of the Cabazon and Morongo bands of Mission Indians.

Source: California v. Cabazon Band of Mission Indians (1987), 480 U.S. 202. http://supreme.justia.com/cases/federal/us/480/202/case.html

---

Justice White (for the Court):

The Cabazon and Morongo Bands of Mission Indians, federally recognized Indian Tribes, occupy reservations in Riverside County, California. [Footnote 1. . . . The Cabazon Band has 25 enrolled members and the Morongo Band . . . approximately 730. . . . Each Band, pursuant to an ordinance approved by the [U.S.] Secretary of the Interior, conducts bingo games on its reservation. The Cabazon Band has also opened a card club at which draw poker and other card games are played. The games are open to the public and are played predominantly by non-Indians coming onto the reservations. The games are a major source of employment for tribal members, and the profits are the Tribes' sole source of income. The State of California seeks to apply to the two Tribes [a California Penal Code provision that] . . . does not entirely prohibit the playing of bingo but permits it [only] when the games are operated and staffed by members of designated charitable organizations who may not be paid for their services. Profits must be kept in special accounts and used only for charitable purposes; prizes may not exceed $250 per game. Asserting that the bingo games on the two reservations violated each of these restrictions, California insisted that the Tribes comply with state law. Riverside County also sought to apply its local [o]rdinance . . . regulating bingo, as well as its [o]rdinance . . . prohibiting the playing of draw poker and the other card games. . . .

[The Ninth Circuit U.S. Court of Appeals], applying what it thought to be the civil/criminal dichotomy [of] Bryan[,] . . . [has drawn] a distinction between state "criminal/prohibitory" laws and state "civil/regulatory" laws: [I]f the intent of a state law is generally to prohibit certain conduct, it falls within Public Law 280's grant of criminal jurisdiction, but if the state law generally permits the conduct at issue, subject to regulation, it must be classified as civil/regulatory and Public Law 280 does not authorize its enforcement on an Indian reservation. The shorthand test is whether the conduct at issue violates the State's public policy. Inquiring into the nature of [the California bingo statute], the Court of Appeals held that it was regulatory rather than prohibitory. . . .

We are persuaded that the prohibitory/regulatory distinction is consistent with Bryan's construction of Public Law 280. It is not a bright-line rule [and] . . . an argument of some weight may be made that the bingo statute is prohibitory rather than regulatory. But . . . we are reluctant to disagree with [the Court of Appeals'] view of the nature and intent of the state law at issue here. . . .

. . . This case . . . involves a state burden on tribal Indians in the context of their dealings with non-Indians since the question is whether the State may prevent the Tribes from making available high stakes bingo games to non-Indians coming from outside the reservations. . . . [S]tate authority . . . "is preempted . . . if it interferes . . . with federal and tribal interests reflected in federal law, unless the state interests at stake are sufficient to justify the assertion of state authority." [*New Mexico v. Mescalero Apache Tribe* 1983, 333–334] The inquiry is to proceed in light of traditional notions of Indian sovereignty and the congressional goal of Indian self-government, including its "overriding goal" of encouraging tribal self-sufficiency and economic development. [*Mescalero* 1983, 334–335]

These are important federal interests. They were reaffirmed by [President Ronald Reagan's] 1983 Statement on Indian Policy. More specifically, the Department of the Interior, which has the primary responsibility for carrying out the Federal Government's trust obligations to Indian tribes, [and also the Department of Health and Human Services and the Department of Housing and Urban Development,] ha[ve] sought to implement these policies by promoting tribal bingo enterprises. . . .

These policies and actions, which demonstrate the Government's approval and active promotion of tribal bingo enterprises, are of particular relevance in this case. The Cabazon and Morongo Reservations contain no natural resources which can be exploited. The tribal games at present provide the sole source of revenues for the operation of the tribal governments and the provision of tribal services. They are also the major sources of employment on the reservations. Self-determination and economic development are not within reach if the Tribes cannot raise revenues and provide employment for their members. The Tribes' interests obviously parallel the federal interests. . . .

The [other] interest asserted by the State to justify the imposition of its bingo laws on the Tribes is in preventing the infiltration of the tribal games by organized crime. To the extent that the State seeks to prevent any and all bingo games from being played on tribal lands while permitting regulated, off-reservation games, this asserted interest is irrelevant. . . . The State insists that the high stakes offered at tribal games are attractive to organized crime, whereas the controlled games authorized under California law are not. This is surely a legitimate concern, but we are unconvinced that it is sufficient. . . . California does not allege any present criminal involvement in the Cabazon and Morongo enterprises. . . . [F]ar from any action being taken [by the Federal Government] evidencing this concern[,]. . . the prevailing federal policy continues to support these tribal enterprises, including those of the Tribes involved in this case.

We conclude that the State's interest in preventing the infiltration of the tribal bingo enterprises by organized crime does not justify state regulation of [those] enterprises in light of the compelling federal and tribal interests supporting them.

Further Reading

Light, Steven Andrew, and Kathryn R. L. Rand. *Indian Gaming and Tribal Sovereignty: The Casino Compromise.* Lawrence: University Press of Kansas, 2005; Pritzker, Barry M. *Native Americans: An Encyclopedia of History, Culture and Peoples.* 2 vols. Santa Barbara, CA: ABC-CLIO, 1998; Williams, Robert A., Jr. *The American Indian in Western Legal Thought: The*

INDIAN GAMING REGULATORY ACT (1988)

Enacted on October 17, 1988, the key portion of this law was the establishment of the National Indian Gaming Commission, which oversaw the rapid and widespread expansion of casinos on Indian lands all across the United States in the late 1980s and 1990s. The U.S. Supreme Court upheld the constitutionality of the act in Seminole Tribe of Florida v. Florida *(1996).*

Source: Indian Gaming Regulatory Act (1988) Public Law 100–497, 25 U.S.C. 2701. http://www.nigc.gov/Laws_Regulations/Indian_Gaming_Regulatory_Act.aspx.

Section 2701. Findings

The Congress finds that—

(1) numerous Indian tribes have become engaged in or have licensed gaming activities on Indian lands as a means of generating tribal governmental revenue;

(2) Federal courts have held that section 81 of this title requires Secretarial review of management contracts dealing with Indian gaming, but does not provide standards for approval of such contracts;

(3) existing Federal law does not provide clear standards or regulations for the conduct of gaming on Indian lands;

(4) a principal goal of Federal Indian policy is to promote tribal economic development, tribal self-sufficiency, and strong tribal government; and

(5) Indian tribes have the exclusive right to regulate gaming activity on Indian lands if the gaming activity is not specifically prohibited by Federal law and is conducted within a State which does not, as a matter of criminal law and public policy, prohibit such gaming activity.

Section 2702. Declaration of policy

The purpose of this chapter is—

(1) to provide a statutory basis for the operation of gaming by Indian tribes as a means of promoting tribal economic development, self-sufficiency, and strong tribal governments;

(2) to provide a statutory basis for the regulation of gaming by an Indian tribe adequate to shield it from organized crime and other corrupting influences, to ensure that the Indian tribe is the primary beneficiary of the gaming operation, and to assure that gaming is conducted fairly and honestly by both the operator and players; and

(3) to declare that the establishment of independent Federal regulatory authority for gaming on Indian lands, the establishment of Federal standards for gaming on Indian lands, and the establishment of a National Indian Gaming Commission are necessary to meet congressional concerns regarding gaming and to protect such gaming as a means of generating tribal revenue.

Section 2703. Definitions

For purposes of this chapter—

(1) The term "Attorney General" means the Attorney General of the United States.

(2) The term "Chairman" means the Chairman of the National Indian Gaming Commission.

(3) The term "Commission" means the National Indian Gaming Commission established pursuant to section 2704 of this title.

(4) The term "Indian lands" means—

(A) all lands within the limits of any Indian reservation; and

(B) any lands title to which is either held in trust by the United States for the benefit of any Indian tribe or individual or held by any Indian tribe or individual subject to restriction by the United States against alienation and over which an Indian tribe exercises governmental power.

(5) The term "Indian tribe" means any Indian tribe, band, nation, or other organized group or community of Indians which—

(A) is recognized as eligible by the Secretary for the special programs and services provided by the United States to Indians because of their status as Indians, and

(B) is recognized as possessing powers of self-government.

(6) The term "class I gaming" means social games solely for prizes of minimal value or traditional forms of Indian gaming engaged in by individuals as a part of, or in connection with, tribal ceremonies or celebrations.

(7)(A) The term "class II gaming" means—

(i) the game of chance commonly known as bingo (whether or not electronic, computer, or other technologic aids are used in connection therewith)—

(I) which is played for prizes, including monetary prizes, with cards bearing numbers or other designations,

(II) in which the holder of the card covers such numbers or designations when objects, similarly numbered or designated, are drawn or electronically determined, and

(III) in which the game is won by the first person covering a previously designated arrangement of numbers or designations on such cards, including (if played in the same location) pull-tabs, lotto, punch boards, tip jars, instant bingo, and other games similar to bingo, and

(ii) card games that—

(I) are explicitly authorized by the laws of the State, or

(II) are not explicitly prohibited by the laws of the State and are played at any location in the State, but only if such card games are played in conformity with those laws and regulations (if any) of the State regarding hours or periods of operation of such card games or limitations on wagers or pot sizes in such card games.

(B) The term "class II gaming" does not include—

(i) any banking card games, including baccarat, chemin de fer, or blackjack (21), or

(ii) electronic or electromechanical facsimiles of any game of chance or slot machines of any kind.

(C) Notwithstanding any other provision of this paragraph, the term "class II gaming" includes those card games played in the State of Michigan, the State of North Dakota, the State of South Dakota, or the State of Washington, that were actually operated in such State by an Indian tribe on or before May 1, 1988, but only to the extent of the nature and scope of the card games that were actually operated by an Indian tribe in such State on or before such date, as determined by the Chairman.

(D) Notwithstanding any other provision of this paragraph, the term "class II gaming" includes, during the 1-year period beginning on October 17, 1988, any gaming described in subparagraph (B)(ii) that was legally operated on Indian lands on or before May 1, 1988, if the Indian tribe having jurisdiction over the lands on which such gaming was operated requests the State, by no later than the date that is 30 days after October 17, 1988, to negotiate a Tribal-State compact under section 2710(d)(3) of this title.

(E) Notwithstanding any other provision of this paragraph, the term "class II gaming" includes, during the 1-year period beginning on December 17, 1991, any gaming described in subparagraph (B)(ii) that was legally operated on Indian lands in the State of Wisconsin on or before May 1, 1988, if the Indian tribe having jurisdiction over the lands on which such gaming was operated requested the State, by no later than November 16, 1988, to negotiate a Tribal-State compact under section 2710(d)(3) of this title.

(F) If, during the 1-year period described in subparagraph (E), there is a final judicial determination that the gaming described in subparagraph (E) is not legal as a matter of State law, then such gaming on such Indian land shall cease to operate on the date next following the date of such judicial decision.

(8) The term "class III gaming" means all forms of gaming that are not class I gaming or class II gaming.

(9) The term "net revenues" means gross revenues of an Indian gaming activity less amounts paid out as, or paid for, prizes and total operating expenses, excluding management fees.

(10) The term "Secretary" means the Secretary of the Interior.

Section 2704. National Indian Gaming Commission

(a) Establishment. There is established within the Department of the Interior a Commission to be known as the National Indian Gaming Commission.

(b) Composition; investigation; term of office; removal.

(1) The Commission shall be composed of three full-time members who shall be appointed as follows:

(A) a Chairman, who shall be appointed by the President with the advice and consent of the Senate; and

(B) two associate members who shall be appointed by the Secretary of the Interior.

(2)(A) The Attorney General shall conduct a background investigation on any person considered for appointment to the Commission.

(B) The Secretary shall publish in the Federal Register the name and other information the Secretary deems pertinent regarding a nominee for membership on the Commission and shall allow a period of not less than thirty days for receipt of public comment.

(3) Not more than two members of the Commission shall be of the same political party. At least two members of the Commission shall be enrolled members of any Indian tribe.

(4)(A) Except as provided in subparagraph (B), the term of office of the members of the Commission shall be three years.

(B) Of the initial members of the Commission—

(i) two members, including the Chairman, shall have a term of office of three years; and

(ii) one member shall have a term of office of one year.

(5) No individual shall be eligible for any appointment to, or to continue service on, the Commission, who—

(A) has been convicted of a felony or gaming offense;

(B) has any financial interest in, or management responsibility for, any gaming activity; or

(C) has a financial interest in, or management responsibility for, any management contract approved pursuant to section 2711 of this title.

(6) A Commissioner may only be removed from office before the expiration of the term of office of the member by the President (or, in the case of associate member, by the Secretary) for neglect of duty, or malfeasance in office, or for other good cause shown.

(c) Vacancies. Vacancies occurring on the Commission shall be filled in the same manner as the original appointment. A member may serve after the expiration of his term of office until his successor has been appointed, unless the member has been removed for cause under subsection (b)(6) of this section.

(d) Quorum. Two members of the Commission, at least one of which is the Chairman or Vice Chairman, shall constitute a quorum.

(e) Vice Chairman. The Commission shall select, by majority vote, one of the members of the Commission to serve as Vice Chairman. The Vice Chairman shall serve as Chairman during meetings of the Commission in the absence of the Chairman.

(f) Meetings. The Commission shall meet at the call of the Chairman or a majority of its members, but shall meet at least once every 4 months.

(g) Compensation.

(1) The Chairman of the Commission shall be paid at a rate equal to that of level IV of the Executive Schedule under section 5315 of title 5.

(2) The associate members of the Commission shall each be paid at a rate equal to that of level V of the Executive Schedule under section 5316 of title 5.

(3) All members of the Commission shall be reimbursed in accordance with title 5 for travel, subsistence, and other necessary expenses incurred by them in the performance of their duties.

Section 2705. Powers of Chairman

(a) The Chairman, on behalf of the Commission, shall have power, subject to an appeal to the Commission, to—

(1) issue orders of temporary closure of gaming activities as provided in section 2713(b) of this title;

(2) levy and collect civil fines as provided in section 2713(a) of this title;

(3) approve tribal ordinances or resolutions regulating class II gaming and class III gaming as provided in section 2710 of this title; and

(4) approve management contracts for class II gaming and class III gaming as provided in sections 2710(d)(9) and 2711 of this title.

(b) The Chairman shall have such other powers as may be delegated by the Commission.

Section 2706. Powers of Commission

(a) Budget approval; civil fines; fees; subpoenas; permanent orders The Commission shall have the power, not subject to delegation—

(1) upon the recommendation of the Chairman, to approve the annual budget of the Commission as provided in section 2717 of this title;

(2) to adopt regulations for the assessment and collection of civil fines as provided in section 2713(a) of this title;

(3) by an affirmative vote of not less than 2 members, to establish the rate of fees as provided in section 2717 of this title;

(4) by an affirmative vote of not less than 2 members, to authorize the Chairman to issue subpoenas as provided in section 2715 of this title; and

(5) by an affirmative vote of not less than 2 members and after a full hearing, to make permanent a temporary order of the Chairman closing a gaming activity as provided in section 2713(b)(2) of this title.

(b) Monitoring; inspection of premises; investigations; access to records; mail; contracts; hearings; oaths; regulations. The Commission—

(1) shall monitor class II gaming conducted on Indian lands on a continuing basis;

(2) shall inspect and examine all premises located on Indian lands on which class II gaming is conducted;

(3) shall conduct or cause to be conducted such background investigations as may be necessary;

(4) may demand access to and inspect, examine, photocopy, and audit all papers, books, and records respecting gross revenues of class II gaming conducted on Indian lands and any other matters necessary to carry out the duties of the Commission under this chapter;

(5) may use the United States mail in the same manner and under the same conditions as any department or agency of the United States;

(6) may procure supplies, services, and property by contract in accordance with applicable Federal laws and regulations;

(7) may enter into contracts with Federal, State, tribal and private entities for activities necessary to the discharge of the duties of the Commission and, to the extent feasible, contract the enforcement of the Commission's regulations with the Indian tribes;

(8) may hold such hearings, sit and act at such times and places, take such testimony, and receive such evidence as the Commission deems appropriate;

(9) may administer oaths or affirmations to witnesses appearing before the Commission; and

(10) shall promulgate such regulations and guidelines as it deems appropriate to implement the provisions of this chapter.

(c) Report. The Commission shall submit a report with minority views, if any, to the Congress on December 31, 1989, and every two years thereafter. The report shall include information on—

(1) whether the associate commissioners should continue as full or part-time officials;

(2) funding, including income and expenses, of the Commission;

(3) recommendations for amendments to the chapter; and

(4) any other matter considered appropriate by the Commission.

Section 2707. Commission staffing

(a) General Counsel. The Chairman shall appoint a General Counsel to the Commission who shall be paid at the annual rate of basic pay payable for GS-18 of the General Schedule under section 5332 of title 5.

(b) Staff. The Chairman shall appoint and supervise other staff of the Commission without regard to the provisions of title 5 governing appointments in the competitive service. Such staff shall be paid without regard to the provisions of chapter 51 and subchapter III of chapter 53 of such title relating to classification and General Schedule pay rates, except that no individual so appointed may receive pay in excess of the annual rate of basic pay payable for GS-17 of the General Schedule under section 5332 of that title.

(c) Temporary services. The Chairman may procure temporary and intermittent services under section 3109(b) of title 5, but at rates for individuals not to exceed the daily equivalent of the maximum annual rate of basic pay payable for GS-18 of the General Schedule.

(d) Federal agency personnel. Upon the request of the Chairman, the head of any Federal agency is authorized to detail any of the personnel of such agency to the Commission to assist the Commission in carrying out its duties under this chapter, unless otherwise prohibited by law.

(e) Administrative support services. The Secretary or Administrator of General Services shall provide to the Commission on a reimbursable basis such administrative support services as the Commission may request.

Section 2708. Commission; access to information

The Commission may secure from any department or agency of the United States information necessary to enable it to carry out this chapter. Upon the request of the Chairman, the head of such department or agency shall furnish such information to the Commission, unless otherwise prohibited by law.

Section 2709. Interim authority to regulate gaming

Notwithstanding any other provision of this chapter, the Secretary shall continue to exercise those authorities vested in the Secretary on the day before October 17, 1988, relating to supervision of Indian gaming until such time as the Commission is organized and prescribes regulations. The Secretary shall provide staff and support assistance to facilitate an orderly transition to regulation of Indian gaming by the Commission.

Section 2710. Tribal gaming ordinances

(a) Jurisdiction over class I and class II gaming activity.

(1) Class I gaming on Indian lands is within the exclusive jurisdiction of the Indian tribes and shall not be subject to the provisions of this chapter.

(2) Any class II gaming on Indian lands shall continue to be within the jurisdiction of the Indian tribes, but shall be subject to the provisions of this chapter.

(b) Regulation of class II gaming activity; net revenue allocation; audits; contracts.

(1) An Indian tribe may engage in, or license and regulate, class II gaming on Indian lands within such tribe's jurisdiction, if—

(A) such Indian gaming is located within a State that permits such gaming for any purpose by any person, organization or entity (and such gaming is not otherwise specifically prohibited on Indian lands by Federal law), and

(B) the governing body of the Indian tribe adopts an ordinance or resolution which is approved by the Chairman. A separate license issued by the Indian tribe shall be required for each place, facility, or location on Indian lands at which class II gaming is conducted.

(2) The Chairman shall approve any tribal ordinance or resolution concerning the conduct, or regulation of class II gaming on the Indian lands within the tribe's jurisdiction if such ordinance or resolution provides that—

(A) except as provided in paragraph (4), the Indian tribe will have the sole proprietary interest and responsibility for the conduct of any gaming activity;

(B) net revenues from any tribal gaming are not to be used for purposes other than—

(i) to fund tribal government operations or programs;

(ii) to provide for the general welfare of the Indian tribe and its members;

(iii) to promote tribal economic development;

(iv) to donate to charitable organizations; or

(v) to help fund operations of local government agencies;

(C) annual outside audits of the gaming, which may be encompassed within existing independent tribal audit systems, will be provided by the Indian tribe to the Commission;

(D) all contracts for supplies, services, or concessions for a contract amount in excess of $25,000 annually (except contracts for professional legal or accounting services) relating to such gaming shall be subject to such independent audits;

(E) the construction and maintenance of the gaming facility, and the operation of that gaming is conducted in a manner which adequately protects the environment and the public health and safety; and

(F) there is an adequate system which—

(i) ensures that background investigations are conducted on the primary management officials and key employees of the gaming enterprise and that oversight of such officials and their management is conducted on an ongoing basis; and

(ii) includes—

(I) tribal licenses for primary management officials and key employees of the gaming enterprise with prompt notification to the Commission of the issuance of such licenses;

(II) a standard whereby any person whose prior activities, criminal record, if any, or reputation, habits and associations pose a threat to the public interest or to the effective regulation of gaming, or create or enhance the dangers of unsuitable, unfair, or illegal practices and methods and activities in the conduct of gaming shall not be eligible for employment; and

(III) notification by the Indian tribe to the Commission of the results of such background check before the issuance of any of such licenses.

(3) Net revenues from any class II gaming activities conducted or licensed by any Indian tribe may be used to make per capita payments to members of the Indian tribe only if—

(A) the Indian tribe has prepared a plan to allocate revenues to uses authorized by paragraph (2)(B);

(B) the plan is approved by the Secretary as adequate, particularly with respect to uses described in clause (i) or (iii) of paragraph (2)(B);

(C) the interests of minors and other legally incompetent persons who are entitled to receive any of the per capita payments are protected and preserved and the per capita payments are disbursed to the parents or legal guardian of such minors or legal incompetents in such amounts as may be necessary for the health, education, or welfare, of the minor or other legally incompetent person under a plan approved by the Secretary and the governing body of the Indian tribe; and

(D) the per capita payments are subject to Federal taxation and tribes notify members of such tax liability when payments are made.

(4)(A) A tribal ordinance or resolution may provide for the licensing or regulation of class II gaming activities owned by any person or entity other than the Indian tribe and conducted on Indian lands, only if the tribal licensing requirements include the requirements described in the subclauses of subparagraph (B)(i) and are at least as restrictive as those established by State law governing similar gaming within the jurisdiction of the State within which such Indian lands are located. No person or entity, other than the Indian tribe, shall be eligible to receive a tribal license to own a class II gaming activity conducted on Indian lands within the jurisdiction of the Indian tribe if such person or entity would not be eligible to receive a State license to conduct the same activity within the jurisdiction of the State.

(B)(i) The provisions of subparagraph (A) of this paragraph and the provisions of subparagraphs (A) and (B) of paragraph (2) shall not bar the continued operation of an individually owned class II gaming operation that was operating on September 1, 1986, if—

(I) such gaming operation is licensed and regulated by an Indian tribe pursuant to an ordinance reviewed and approved by the Commission in accordance with section 2712 of this title,

(II) income to the Indian tribe from such gaming is used only for the purposes described in paragraph (2)(B) of this subsection,

(III) not less than 60 percent of the net revenues is income to the Indian tribe, and

(IV) the owner of such gaming operation pays an appropriate assessment to the National Indian Gaming Commission under section 2717(a)(1) of this title for regulation of such gaming.

(ii) The exemption from the application of this subsection provided under this subparagraph may not be transferred to any person or entity and shall remain in effect only so long as the gaming activity remains within the same nature and scope as operated on October 17, 1988.

(iii) Within sixty days of October 17, 1988, the Secretary shall prepare a list of each individually owned gaming operation to which clause (i) applies and shall publish such list in the Federal Register.

(c) Issuance of gaming license; certificate of self-regulation.

(1) The Commission may consult with appropriate law enforcement officials concerning gaming licenses issued by an Indian tribe and shall have thirty days to notify the Indian tribe of any objections to issuance of such license.

(2) If, after the issuance of a gaming license by an Indian tribe, reliable information is received from the Commission indicating that a primary management official or key employee does not meet the standard established under subsection (b)(2)(F)(ii)(II) of this section, the Indian tribe shall suspend such license and, after notice and hearing, may revoke such license.

(3) Any Indian tribe which operates a class II gaming activity and which—

(A) has continuously conducted such activity for a period of not less than three years, including at least one year after October 17, 1988; and

(B) has otherwise complied with the provisions of this section

(4) The Commission shall issue a certificate of self-regulation if it determines from available information, and after a hearing if requested by the tribe, that the tribe has—

(A) conducted its gaming activity in a manner which—

(i) has resulted in an effective and honest accounting of all revenues;

(ii) has resulted in a reputation for safe, fair, and honest operation of the activity; and

(iii) has been generally free of evidence of criminal or dishonest activity;

(B) adopted and is implementing adequate systems for—

(i) accounting for all revenues from the activity;

(ii) investigation, licensing, and monitoring of all employees of the gaming activity; and

(iii) investigation, enforcement and prosecution of violations of its gaming ordinance and regulations; and

(C) conducted the operation on a fiscally and economically sound basis.

(5) During any year in which a tribe has a certificate for self-regulation—

(A) the tribe shall not be subject to the provisions of paragraphs (1), (2), (3), and (4) of section 2706(b) of this title;

(B) the tribe shall continue to submit an annual independent audit as required by subsection (b)(2)(C) of this section and shall submit to the Commission a complete resume on all employees hired and licensed by the tribe subsequent to the issuance of a certificate of self-regulation; and

(C) the Commission may not assess a fee on such activity pursuant to section 2717 of this title in excess of one quarter of 1 per centum of the gross revenue.

(6) The Commission may, for just cause and after an opportunity for a hearing, remove a certificate of self-regulation by majority vote of its members.

(d) Class III gaming activities; authorization; revocation; Tribal-State compact.

(1) Class III gaming activities shall be lawful on Indian lands only if such activities are—

(A) authorized by an ordinance or resolution that—

(i) is adopted by the governing body of the Indian tribe having jurisdiction over such lands,

(ii) meets the requirements of subsection (b) of this section, and

(iii) is approved by the Chairman,

(B) located in a State that permits such gaming for any purpose by any person, organization, or entity, and

(C) conducted in conformance with a Tribal-State compact entered into by the Indian tribe and the State under paragraph (3) that is in effect.

(2)(A) If any Indian tribe proposes to engage in, or to authorize any person or entity to engage in, a class III gaming activity on Indian lands of the Indian tribe, the governing body of the Indian tribe shall adopt and submit to the Chairman an ordinance or resolution that meets the requirements of subsection (b) of this section.

(B) The Chairman shall approve any ordinance or resolution described in subparagraph (A), unless the Chairman specifically determines that—

(i) the ordinance or resolution was not adopted in compliance with the governing documents of the Indian tribe, or

(ii) the tribal governing body was significantly and unduly influenced in the adoption of such ordinance or resolution by any person identified in section 2711(e)(1)(D) of this title. Upon the approval of such an ordinance or resolution, the Chairman shall publish in the Federal Register such ordinance or resolution and the order of approval.

(C) Effective with the publication under subparagraph (B) of an ordinance or resolution adopted by the governing body of an Indian tribe that has been approved by the Chairman under subparagraph (B), class III gaming activity on the Indian lands of the Indian tribe shall be fully subject to the terms and conditions of the Tribal-State compact entered into under paragraph (3) by the Indian tribe that is in effect.

(D)(i) The governing body of an Indian tribe, in its sole discretion and without the approval of the Chairman, may adopt an ordinance or resolution revoking any prior ordinance or resolution that authorized class III gaming on the Indian lands of the Indian tribe. Such revocation shall render class III gaming illegal on the Indian lands of such Indian tribe.

(ii) The Indian tribe shall submit any revocation ordinance or resolution described in clause (i) to the Chairman. The Chairman shall publish such ordinance or resolution in the Federal Register and the revocation provided by such ordinance or resolution shall take effect on the date of such publication.

(iii) Notwithstanding any other provision of this subsection—

(I) any person or entity operating a class III gaming activity pursuant to this paragraph on the date on which an ordinance or resolution described in clause (i) that revokes authorization for such class III gaming activity is published in the Federal Register may, during the 1-year period beginning on the date on which such revocation ordinance or resolution is published under clause (ii), continue to operate such activity in conformance with the Tribal-State compact entered into under paragraph (3) that is in effect, and

(II) any civil action that arises before, and any crime that is committed before, the close of such 1-year period shall not be affected by such revocation ordinance or resolution.

(3)(A) Any Indian tribe having jurisdiction over the Indian lands upon which a class III gaming activity is being conducted, or is to be conducted, shall request the State in which such lands are located to enter into negotiations for the purpose of entering into a Tribal-State compact governing the conduct of gaming activities. Upon receiving such a request, the State shall negotiate with the Indian tribe in good faith to enter into such a compact.

(B) Any State and any Indian tribe may enter into a Tribal-State compact governing gaming activities on the Indian lands of the Indian tribe, but such compact shall take effect only when notice of approval by the Secretary of such compact has been published by the Secretary in the Federal Register.

(C) Any Tribal-State compact negotiated under subparagraph (A) may include provisions relating to—

(i) the application of the criminal and civil laws and regulations of the Indian tribe or the State that are directly related to, and necessary for, the licensing and regulation of such activity;

(ii) the allocation of criminal and civil jurisdiction between the State and the Indian tribe necessary for the enforcement of such laws and regulations;

(iii) the assessment by the State of such activities in such amounts as are necessary to defray the costs of regulating such activity;

(iv) taxation by the Indian tribe of such activity in amounts comparable to amounts assessed by the State for comparable activities;

(v) remedies for breach of contract;

(vi) standards for the operation of such activity and maintenance of the gaming facility, including licensing; and

(vii) any other subjects that are directly related to the operation of gaming activities.

(4) Except for any assessments that may be agreed to under paragraph (3)(C)(iii) of this subsection, nothing in this section shall be interpreted as conferring upon a State or any of its political subdivisions authority to impose any tax, fee, charge, or other assessment upon an Indian tribe or upon any other person or entity authorized by an Indian tribe to engage in a class III activity. No State may refuse to enter into the negotiations described in paragraph (3)(A) based upon the lack of authority in such State, or its political subdivisions, to impose such a tax, fee, charge, or other assessment.

(5) Nothing in this subsection shall impair the right of an Indian tribe to regulate class III gaming on its Indian lands concurrently with the State, except to the extent that such regulation is inconsistent with, or less stringent than, the State laws and regulations made applicable by any Tribal-State compact entered into by the Indian tribe under paragraph (3) that is in effect.

(6) The provisions of section 1175 of title 15 shall not apply to any gaming conducted under a Tribal-State compact that—

(A) is entered into under paragraph (3) by a State in which gambling devices are legal, and

(B) is in effect.

(7)(A) The United States district courts shall have jurisdiction over—

(i) any cause of action initiated by an Indian tribe arising from the failure of a State to enter into negotiations with the Indian tribe for the purpose of entering into a Tribal-State compact under paragraph (3) or to conduct such negotiations in good faith,

(ii) any cause of action initiated by a State or Indian tribe to enjoin a class III gaming activity located on Indian lands and conducted in violation of any Tribal-State compact entered into under paragraph (3) that is in effect, and

(iii) any cause of action initiated by the Secretary to enforce the procedures prescribed under subparagraph (B)(vii).

(B)(i) An Indian tribe may initiate a cause of action described in subparagraph (A)(i) only after the close of the 180-day period beginning on the date on which the Indian tribe requested the State to enter into negotiations under paragraph (3)(A).

(ii) In any action described in subparagraph (A)(i), upon the introduction of evidence by an Indian tribe that—

(I) a Tribal-State compact has not been entered into under paragraph (3), and

(II) the State did not respond to the request of the Indian tribe to negotiate such a compact or did not respond to such request in good faith, the burden of proof shall be upon the State to prove that the State has negotiated with the Indian tribe in good faith to conclude a Tribal-State compact governing the conduct of gaming activities.

(iii) If, in any action described in subparagraph (A)(i), the court finds that the State has failed to negotiate in good faith with the Indian tribe to conclude a Tribal-State compact governing the conduct of gaming activities, the court shall order the State and the Indian Tribe to conclude such a compact within a 60-day period. In determining in such an action whether a State has negotiated in good faith, the court—

(I) may take into account the public interest, public safety, criminality, financial integrity, and adverse economic impacts on existing gaming activities, and

(II) shall consider any demand by the State for direct taxation of the Indian tribe or of any Indian lands as evidence that the State has not negotiated in good faith.

(iv) If a State and an Indian tribe fail to conclude a Tribal-State compact governing the conduct of gaming activities on the Indian lands subject to the jurisdiction of such Indian tribe within the 60-day period provided in the order of a court issued under clause (iii), the Indian tribe and the State shall each submit to a mediator appointed by the court a proposed compact that represents their last best offer for a compact. The mediator shall select from the two proposed compacts the one which best comports with the terms of this chapter and any other applicable Federal law and with the findings and order of the court.

(v) The mediator appointed by the court under clause (iv) shall submit to the State and the Indian tribe the compact selected by the mediator under clause (iv).

(vi) If a State consents to a proposed compact during the 60-day period beginning on the date on which the proposed compact is submitted by the mediator to the State under clause (v), the proposed compact shall be treated as a Tribal-State compact entered into under paragraph (3).

(vii) If the State does not consent during the 60-day period described in clause (vi) to a proposed compact submitted by a mediator under clause (v), the mediator shall notify the Secretary and the Secretary shall prescribe, in consultation with the Indian tribe, procedures—

(I) which are consistent with the proposed compact selected by the mediator under clause (iv), the provisions of this chapter, and the relevant provisions of the laws of the State, and

(II) under which class III gaming may be conducted on the Indian lands over which the Indian tribe has jurisdiction.

(8)(A) The Secretary is authorized to approve any Tribal-State compact entered into between an Indian tribe and a State governing gaming on Indian lands of such Indian tribe.

(B) The Secretary may disapprove a compact described in subparagraph (A) only if such compact violates—

(i) any provision of this chapter,

(ii) any other provision of Federal law that does not relate to jurisdiction over gaming on Indian lands, or

(iii) the trust obligations of the United States to Indians.

(C) If the Secretary does not approve or disapprove a compact described in subparagraph (A) before the date that is 45 days after the date on which the compact is submitted to the Secretary for approval, the compact shall be considered to have been approved by the Secretary, but only to the extent the compact is consistent with the provisions of this chapter.

(D) The Secretary shall publish in the Federal Register notice of any Tribal-State compact that is approved, or considered to have been approved, under this paragraph.

(9) An Indian tribe may enter into a management contract for the operation of a class III gaming activity if such contract has been submitted to, and approved by, the Chairman. The Chairman's review and approval of such contract shall be governed by the provisions of subsections (b), (c), (d), (f), (g), and (h) of section 2711 of this title.

(e) Approval of ordinances. For purposes of this section, by not later than the date that is 90 days after the date on which any tribal gaming ordinance or resolution is submitted to the Chairman, the Chairman shall approve such ordinance or resolution if it meets the requirements of this section. Any such ordinance or resolution not acted upon at the end of that 90-day period shall be considered to have been approved by the Chairman, but only to the extent such ordinance or resolution is consistent with the provisions of this chapter.

Section 2711. Management contracts

(a) Class II gaming activity; information on operators.

(1) Subject to the approval of the Chairman, an Indian tribe may enter into a management contract for the operation and management of a class II gaming activity that the Indian tribe may engage in under section 2710(b)(1) of this title, but, before approving such contract, the Chairman shall require and obtain the following information:

(A) the name, address, and other additional pertinent background information on each person or entity (including individuals comprising such entity) having a direct financial interest in, or management responsibility for, such contract, and, in the case of a corporation, those individuals who serve on the board of directors of such corporation and each of its stockholders who hold (directly or indirectly) 10 percent or more of its issued and outstanding stock;

(B) a description of any previous experience that each person listed pursuant to subparagraph (A) has had with other gaming contracts with Indian tribes or with the gaming industry generally, including specifically the name and address of any licensing or regulatory agency with which such person has had a contract relating to gaming; and

(C) a complete financial statement of each person listed pursuant to subparagraph (A).

(2) Any person listed pursuant to paragraph (1)(A) shall be required to respond to such written or oral questions that the Chairman may propound in accordance with his responsibilities under this section.

(3) For purposes of this chapter, any reference to the management contract described in paragraph (1) shall be considered to include all collateral agreements to such contract that relate to the gaming activity.

(b) Approval. The Chairman may approve any management contract entered into pursuant to this section only if he determines that it provides at least—

(1) for adequate accounting procedures that are maintained, and for verifiable financial reports that are prepared, by or for the tribal governing body on a monthly basis;

(2) for access to the daily operations of the gaming to appropriate tribal officials who shall also have a right to verify the daily gross revenues and income made from any such tribal gaming activity;

(3) for a minimum guaranteed payment to the Indian tribe that has preference over the retirement of development and construction costs;

(4) for an agreed ceiling for the repayment of development and construction costs;

(5) for a contract term not to exceed five years, except that, upon the request of an Indian tribe, the Chairman may authorize a contract term that exceeds five years but does not exceed seven years if the Chairman is satisfied that the capital investment required, and the income projections, for the particular gaming activity require the additional time; and

(6) for grounds and mechanisms for terminating such contract, but actual contract termination shall not require the approval of the Commission.

(c) Fee based on percentage of net revenues.

(1) The Chairman may approve a management contract providing for a fee based upon a percentage of the net revenues of a tribal gaming activity if the Chairman determines that such percentage fee is reasonable in light of surrounding circumstances. Except as otherwise provided in this subsection, such fee shall not exceed 30 percent of the net revenues.

(2) Upon the request of an Indian tribe, the Chairman may approve a management contract providing for a fee based upon a percentage of the net revenues of a tribal gaming activity that exceeds 30 percent but not 40 percent of the net revenues if the Chairman is satisfied that the capital investment required, and income projections, for such tribal gaming activity require the additional fee requested by the Indian tribe.

(d) Period for approval; extension. By no later than the date that is 180 days after the date on which a management contract is submitted to the Chairman for approval, the Chairman shall approve or disapprove such contract on its merits. The Chairman may extend the 180-day period by not more than 90 days if the Chairman notifies the Indian tribe in writing of the reason for the extension. The Indian tribe may bring an action in a United States district court to compel action by the Chairman if a contract has not been approved or disapproved within the period required by this subsection.

(e) Disapproval. The Chairman shall not approve any contract if the Chairman determines that—

(1) any person listed pursuant to subsection (a)(1)(A) of this section—

(A) is an elected member of the governing body of the Indian tribe which is the party to the management contract;

(B) has been or subsequently is convicted of any felony or gaming offense;

(C) has knowingly and willfully provided materially important false statements or information to the Commission or the Indian tribe pursuant to this chapter or has refused to respond to questions propounded pursuant to subsection (a)(2) of this section; or

(D) has been determined to be a person whose prior activities, criminal record if any, or reputation, habits, and associations pose a threat to the public interest or to the effective regulation and control of gaming, or create or enhance the dangers of unsuitable, unfair, or illegal practices, methods, and activities in the conduct of gaming or the carrying on of the business and financial arrangements incidental thereto;

(2) the management contractor has, or has attempted to, unduly interfere or influence for its gain or advantage any decision or process of tribal government relating to the gaming activity;

(3) the management contractor has deliberately or substantially failed to comply with the terms of the management contract or the tribal gaming ordinance or resolution adopted and approved pursuant to this chapter; or

(4) a trustee, exercising the skill and diligence that a trustee is commonly held to, would not approve the contract.

(f) Modification or voiding. The Chairman, after notice and hearing, shall have the authority to require appropriate contract modifications or may void any contract if he subsequently determines that any of the provisions of this section have been violated.

(g) Interest in land. No management contract for the operation and management of a gaming activity regulated by this chapter shall transfer or, in any other manner, convey any interest in land or other real property, unless specific statutory authority exists and unless clearly specified in writing in said contract.

(h) Authority. The authority of the Secretary under section 81 of this title, relating to management contracts regulated pursuant to this chapter, is hereby transferred to the Commission.

(i) Investigation fee. The Commission shall require a potential contractor to pay a fee to cover the cost of the investigation necessary to reach a determination required in subsection (e) of this section.

Section 2712. Review of existing ordinances and contracts

(a) Notification to submit. As soon as practicable after the organization of the Commission, the Chairman shall notify each Indian tribe or management contractor who, prior to October 17, 1988, adopted an ordinance or resolution authorizing class II gaming or class III gaming or entered into a management contract, that such ordinance, resolution, or contract, including all collateral agreements relating to the gaming activity, must be submitted for his review within 60 days of such notification. Any activity conducted under such ordinance, resolution, contract, or agreement shall be valid under this chapter, or any amendment made by this chapter, unless disapproved under this section.

(b) Approval or modification of ordinance or resolution.

(1) By no later than the date that is 90 days after the date on which an ordinance or resolution authorizing class II gaming or class III gaming is submitted to the Chairman pursuant to subsection (a) of this section, the Chairman shall review such ordinance or resolution to determine if it conforms to the requirements of section 2710(b) of this title.

(2) If the Chairman determines that an ordinance or resolution submitted under subsection (a) of this section conforms to the requirements of section 2710(b) of this title, the Chairman shall approve it.

(3) If the Chairman determines that an ordinance or resolution submitted under subsection (a) of this section does not conform to the requirements of section 2710(b) of this title, the Chairman shall provide written notification of necessary modifications to the Indian tribe which shall have not more than 120 days to bring such ordinance or resolution into compliance.

(c) Approval or modification of management contract.

(1) Within 180 days after the submission of a management contract, including all collateral agreements, pursuant to subsection (a) of this section, the Chairman shall subject such contract to the requirements and process of section 2711 of this title.

(2) If the Chairman determines that a management contract submitted under subsection (a) of this section, and the management contractor under such contract, meet the requirements of section 2711 of this title, the Chairman shall approve the management contract.

(3) If the Chairman determines that a contract submitted under subsection (a) of this section, or the management contractor under a contract submitted under subsection (a) of this section, does not meet the requirements of section 2711 of this title, the Chairman shall provide written notification to the parties to such contract of necessary modifications and the parties shall have not more than 120 days to come into compliance. If a management contract has been approved by the Secretary prior to October 17, 1988, the parties shall have not more than 180 days after notification of necessary modifications to come into compliance.

Section 2713. Civil penalties

(a) Authority; amount; appeal; written complaint.

(1) Subject to such regulations as may be prescribed by the Commission, the Chairman shall have authority to levy and collect appropriate civil fines, not to exceed $25,000 per violation, against the tribal operator of an Indian game or a management contractor engaged in gaming for any violation of any provision of this chapter, any regulation prescribed by the Commission pursuant to this chapter, or tribal regulations, ordinances, or resolutions approved under section 2710 or 2712 of this title.

(2) The Commission shall, by regulation, provide an opportunity for an appeal and hearing before the Commission on fines levied and collected by the Chairman.

(3) Whenever the Commission has reason to believe that the tribal operator of an Indian game or a management contractor is engaged in activities regulated by this chapter, by regulations prescribed under this chapter, or by tribal regulations, ordinances, or resolutions, approved under section 2710 or 2712 of this title, that may result in the imposition of a fine under subsection (a)(1) of this section, the permanent closure of such game, or the modification or termination of any management contract, the Commission shall provide such tribal operator or management contractor with a written complaint stating the acts or omissions which form the basis for such belief and the action or choice of action being considered by the Commission. The allegation shall be set forth in common and concise language and must specify the statutory or regulatory provisions alleged to have been violated, but may not consist merely of allegations stated in statutory or regulatory language.

(b) Temporary closure; hearing.

(1) The Chairman shall have power to order temporary closure of an Indian game for substantial violation of the provisions of this chapter, of regulations prescribed by the Commission pursuant to this chapter, or of tribal regulations, ordinances, or resolutions approved under section 2710 or 2712 of this title.

(2) Not later than thirty days after the issuance by the Chairman of an order of temporary closure, the Indian tribe or management contractor involved shall have a right to a hearing before the Commission to determine whether such order should be made permanent or dissolved. Not later than sixty days following such hearing, the Commission shall, by a vote of not less than two of its members, decide whether to order a permanent closure of the gaming operation.

(c) Appeal from final decision. A decision of the Commission to give final approval of a fine levied by the Chairman or to order a permanent closure pursuant to this section shall be appealable to the appropriate Federal district court pursuant to chapter 7 of title 5.

(d) Regulatory authority under tribal law. Nothing in this chapter precludes an Indian tribe from exercising regulatory authority provided under tribal law over a gaming establishment within the Indian tribe's jurisdiction if such regulation is not inconsistent with this chapter or with any rules or regulations adopted by the Commission.

Section 2714. Judicial review

Decisions made by the Commission pursuant to sections 2710, 2711, 2712, and 2713 of this title shall be final agency decisions for purposes of appeal to the appropriate Federal district court pursuant to chapter 7 of title 5.

Section 2715. Subpoena and deposition authority

(a) Attendance, testimony, production of papers, etc. By a vote of not less than two members, the Commission shall have the power to require by subpoena the attendance and testimony of witnesses and the production of all books, papers, and documents relating to any matter under consideration or investigation. Witnesses so summoned shall be paid the same fees and mileage that are paid witnesses in the courts of the United States.

(b) Geographical location. The attendance of witnesses and the production of books, papers, and documents, may be required from any place in the United States at any designated place of hearing. The Commission may request the Secretary to request the Attorney General to bring an action to enforce any subpoena under this section.

(c) Refusal of subpoena; court order; contempt. Any court of the United States within the jurisdiction of which an inquiry is carried on may, in case of contumacy or refusal to obey a subpoena for any reason, issue an order requiring such person to appear before the Commission (and produce books, papers, or documents as so ordered) and give evidence concerning the matter in question and any failure to obey such order of the court may be punished by such court as a contempt thereof.

(d) Depositions; notice. A Commissioner may order testimony to be taken by deposition in any proceeding or investigation pending before the Commission at any stage of such proceeding or investigation. Such depositions may be taken before any person designated by the Commission and having power to administer oaths. Reasonable notice must first be given to the Commission in writing by the party or his attorney proposing to take such deposition, and, in cases in which a Commissioner proposes to take a deposition, reasonable notice must be given. The notice shall state the name of the witness and the time and place of the taking of his deposition. Any person may be compelled to appear and depose, and to produce books, papers, or documents, in the same manner as witnesses may be compelled to appear and testify and produce like documentary evidence before the Commission, as hereinbefore provided.

(e) Oath or affirmation required. Every person deposing as herein provided shall be cautioned and shall be required to swear (or affirm, if he so requests) to testify to the whole truth, and shall be carefully examined. His testimony shall be reduced to writing by the person taking the deposition, or under his direction, and shall, after it has been reduced to writing, be subscribed by the deponent. All depositions shall be promptly filed with the Commission.

(f) Witness fees. Witnesses whose depositions are taken as authorized in this section, and the persons taking the same, shall severally be entitled to the same fees as are paid for like services in the courts of the United States.

Section 2716. Investigative powers

(a) Confidential information. Except as provided in subsection (b) of this section, the Commission shall preserve any and all information received pursuant to this chapter as confidential pursuant to the provisions of paragraphs (4) and (7) of section 552(b) of title 5.

(b) Provision to law enforcement officials. The Commission shall, when such information indicates a violation of Federal, State, or tribal statutes, ordinances, or resolutions, provide such information to the appropriate law enforcement officials.

(c) Attorney General. The Attorney General shall investigate activities associated with gaming authorized by this chapter which may be a violation of Federal law.

Section 2717. Commission funding

(a)(1) The Commission shall establish a schedule of fees to be paid to the Commission annually by each gaming operation that conducts a class II or class III gaming activity that is regulated by this chapter.

(2)(A) The rate of the fees imposed under the schedule established under paragraph (1) shall be—

(i) no more than 2.5 percent of the first $1,500,000, and

(ii) no more than 5 percent of amounts in excess of the first $1,500,000, of the gross revenues from each activity regulated by this chapter.

(B) The total amount of all fees imposed during any fiscal year under the schedule established under paragraph (1) shall not exceed $8,000,000.

(3) The Commission, by a vote of not less than two of its members, shall annually adopt the rate of the fees authorized by this section which shall be payable to the Commission on a quarterly basis.

(4) Failure to pay the fees imposed under the schedule established under paragraph (1) shall, subject to the regulations of the Commission, be grounds for revocation of the approval of the Chairman of any license, ordinance, or resolution required under this chapter for the operation of gaming.

(5) To the extent that revenue derived from fees imposed under the schedule established under paragraph (1) are not expended or committed at the close of any fiscal year, such surplus funds shall be credited to each gaming activity on a pro rata basis against such fees imposed for the succeeding year.

(6) For purposes of this section, gross revenues shall constitute the annual total amount of money wagered, less any amounts paid out as prizes or paid for prizes awarded and less allowance for amortization of capital expenditures for structures.

(b)(1) The Commission, in coordination with the Secretary and in conjunction with the fiscal year of the United States, shall adopt an annual budget for the expenses and operation of the Commission.

(2) The budget of the Commission may include a request for appropriations, as authorized by section 2718 of this title, in an amount equal the amount of funds derived from assessments authorized by subsection (a) of this section for the fiscal year preceding the fiscal year for which the appropriation request is made.

(3) The request for appropriations pursuant to paragraph (2) shall be subject to the approval of the Secretary and shall be included as a part of the budget request of the Department of the Interior.

Section 2717a. Availability of class II gaming activity fees to carry out duties of Commission

In fiscal year 1990 and thereafter, fees collected pursuant to and as limited by section 2717 of this title shall be available to carry out the duties of the Commission, to remain available until expended.

Section 2718. Authorization of appropriations

(a) Subject to section 2717 of this title, there are authorized to be appropriated, for fiscal year 1998, and for each fiscal year thereafter, an amount equal to the amount of funds derived from the assessments authorized by section 2717(a) of this title.

(b) Notwithstanding section 2717 of this title, there are authorized to be appropriated to fund the operation of the Commission, $2,000,000 for fiscal year 1998, and $2,000,000 for each fiscal year thereafter. The amounts authorized to be appropriated in the preceding sentence shall be in addition to the amounts authorized to be appropriated under subsection (a) of this section.

Section 2719. Gaming on lands acquired after October 17, 1988

(a) Prohibition on lands acquired in trust by Secretary. Except as provided in subsection (b) of this section, gaming regulated by this chapter shall not be conducted on lands acquired by the Secretary in trust for the benefit of an Indian tribe after October 17, 1988, unless—

(1) such lands are located within or contiguous to the boundaries of the reservation of the Indian tribe on October 17, 1988; or

(2) the Indian tribe has no reservation on October 17, 1988, and—

(A) such lands are located in Oklahoma and—

(i) are within the boundaries of the Indian tribe's former reservation, as defined by the Secretary, or

(ii) are contiguous to other land held in trust or restricted status by the United States for the Indian tribe in Oklahoma; or

(B) such lands are located in a State other than Oklahoma and are within the Indian tribe's last recognized reservation within the State or States within which such Indian tribe is presently located.

(b) Exceptions.

(1) Subsection (a) of this section will not apply when—

(A) the Secretary, after consultation with the Indian tribe and appropriate State and local officials, including officials of other nearby Indian tribes, determines that a gaming establishment on newly acquired lands would be in the best interest of the Indian tribe and its members, and would not be detrimental to the surrounding community, but only if the Governor of the State in which the gaming activity is to be conducted concurs in the Secretary's determination; or

(B) lands are taken into trust as part of—

(i) a settlement of a land claim,

(ii) the initial reservation of an Indian tribe acknowledged by the Secretary under the Federal acknowledgment process, or

(iii) the restoration of lands for an Indian tribe that is restored to Federal recognition.

(2) Subsection (a) of this section shall not apply to—

(A) any lands involved in the trust petition of the St. Croix Chippewa Indians of Wisconsin that is the subject of the action filed in the United States District Court for the District of Columbia entitled St. Croix Chippewa Indians of Wisconsin v. United States, Civ. No. 86–2278, or

(B) the interests of the Miccosukee Tribe of Indians of Florida in approximately 25 contiguous acres of land, more or less, in Dade County, Florida, located within one mile of the intersection of State Road Numbered 27 (also known as Krome Avenue) and the Tamiami Trail.

(3) Upon request of the governing body of the Miccosukee Tribe of Indians of Florida, the Secretary shall, notwithstanding any other provision of law, accept the transfer by such Tribe to the Secretary of the interests of such Tribe in the lands described in paragraph (2)(B) and the Secretary shall declare that such interests are held in trust by the Secretary for the benefit of such Tribe and that such interests are part of the reservation of such Tribe under sections 465 and 467 of this title, subject to any encumbrances and rights that are held at the time of such transfer by any person or entity other than such Tribe. The Secretary shall publish in the Federal Register the legal description of any lands that are declared held in trust by the Secretary under this paragraph.

(c) Authority of Secretary not affected. Nothing in this section shall affect or diminish the authority and responsibility of the Secretary to take land into trust.

(d) Application of title 26.

(1) The provisions of title 26 (including sections 1441, 3402(q), 6041, and 6050I, and chapter 35 of such title) concerning the reporting and withholding of taxes with respect to the winnings from gaming or wagering operations shall apply to Indian gaming operations conducted pursuant to this chapter, or under a Tribal-State compact entered into under section 2710(d)(3) of this title that is in effect, in the same manner as such provisions apply to State gaming and wagering operations.

(2) The provisions of this subsection shall apply notwithstanding any other provision of law enacted before, on, or after October 17, 1988, unless such other provision of law specifically cites this subsection.

Section 2720. Dissemination of information

Consistent with the requirements of this chapter, sections 1301, 1302, 1303 and 1304 of title 18 shall not apply to any gaming conducted by an Indian tribe pursuant to this chapter.

Section 2721. Severability

In the event that any section or provision of this chapter, or amendment made by this chapter, is held invalid, it is the intent of Congress that the remaining sections or provisions of this chapter, and amendments made by this chapter, shall continue in full force and effect.

SEMINOLE TRIBE OF FLORIDA V. FLORIDA (1996)

Chief Justice William Rehnquist authored the five to four decision for the U.S. Supreme Court in Seminole Tribe of Florida v. Florida, *which interpreted the Eleventh Amendment of the Constitution to prohibit a suit brought by the Seminole tribe of Florida. The tribe accused the state of refusing to negotiate in good faith on a plan that would allow Indian gaming in the state under provisions of the Indian Gaming Regulatory Act of 1988. The congressional law allowed tribes to sue states that did not so negotiate in good faith.*

Source: Seminole Tribe of Florida v. Florida (1996), 517 U.S. 44. http://www.law.cornell.edu/supct/html/historics/USSC_CR_0517_0044_ZO.html

---

CHIEF JUSTICE REHNQUIST delivered the opinion of the Court.

The Indian Gaming Regulatory Act provides that an Indian tribe may conduct certain gaming activities only in conformance with a valid compact between the tribe and the State in which the gaming activities are located. The Act, passed by Congress under the Indian Commerce Clause, U.S. Const., Art. I, 10, cl. 3, imposes upon the States a duty to negotiate in good faith with an Indian tribe toward the formation of a compact, 2710(d)(3)(A), and authorizes a tribe to bring suit in federal court against a State in order to compel performance of that duty, 2710(d)(7). We hold that notwithstanding Congress' clear intent to abrogate the States' sovereign immunity, the Indian

Commerce Clause does not grant Congress that power, and therefore 2710(d)(7) cannot grant jurisdiction over a State that does not consent to be sued. We further hold that the doctrine of *Ex parte Young* (1908), may not be used to enforce 2710(d)(3) against a state official.

Congress passed the Indian Gaming Regulatory Act in 1988 in order to provide a statutory basis for the operation and regulation of gaming by Indian tribes. The Act divides gaming on Indian lands into three classes I, II, and III and provides a different regulatory scheme for each class. Class III gaming the type with which we are here concerned is defined as "all forms of gaming that are not class I gaming or class II gaming," and includes such things as slot machines, casino games, banking card games, dog racing, and lotteries. It is the most heavily regulated of the three classes. The Act provides that class III gaming is lawful only where it is: (1) authorized by an ordinance or resolution that (a) is adopted by the governing body of the Indian tribe, (b) satisfies certain statutorily prescribed requirements, and (c) is approved by the National Indian Gaming Commission; (2) located in a State that permits such gaming for any purpose by any person, organization, or entity; and (3) "conducted in conformance with a Tribal-State compact entered into by the Indian tribe and the State under paragraph (3) that is in effect."

The "paragraph (3)" to which the last prerequisite of 2710(d)(1) refers is 2710(d)(3), which describes the permissible scope of a Tribal-State compact, see 2710(d)(3)(C), and provides that the compact is effective "only when notice of approval by the Secretary [of the Interior] of such compact has been published by the Secretary in the Federal Register." More significant for our purposes, however, is that 2710(d)(3) describes the process by which a State and an Indian tribe begin negotiations toward a Tribal-State compact:

(A) Any Indian tribe having jurisdiction over the Indian lands upon which a class III gaming activity is being conducted, or is to be conducted, shall request the State in which such lands are located to enter into negotiations for the purpose of entering into a Tribal-State compact governing the conduct of gaming activities. Upon receiving such a request, the State shall negotiate with the Indian tribe in good faith to enter into such a compact.

The State's obligation to "negotiate with the Indian tribe in good faith," is made judicially enforceable by 2710(d)(7)(A)(i) and (B)(i):

(A) The United States district courts shall have jurisdiction over (i) any cause of action initiated by an Indian tribe arising from the failure of a State to enter into negotiations with the Indian tribe for the purpose of entering into a Tribal-State compact under paragraph (3) or to conduct such negotiations in good faith. . . .

(B)(i) An Indian tribe may initiate a cause of action described in subparagraph (A)(i) only after the close of the 180-day period beginning on the date on which the Indian tribe requested the State to enter into negotiations under paragraph (3)(A).

Sections 2710(d)(7)(B)(ii)-(vii) describe an elaborate remedial scheme designed to ensure the formation of a Tribal-State compact. A tribe that brings an action under 2710(d)(7)(A)(i) must show that no Tribal-State compact has been entered and that the State failed to respond in good faith to the tribe's request to negotiate; at that point, the burden then shifts to the State to prove that it did in fact negotiate in good faith. If the district court concludes that the State has failed to negotiate in good faith toward the formation of a Tribal-State compact, then it "shall order the State and Indian tribe to conclude such a compact within a 60-day period." If no compact has been concluded 60 days after the court's order, then "the Indian tribe and the State shall each submit to a mediator appointed by the court a proposed compact that represents their last best offer for a compact." The mediator chooses from between the two proposed compacts the one "which best comports with the terms of [the Act] and any other applicable Federal law and with the findings and order of the court," and submits it to the State and the Indian tribe. If the State consents to the proposed compact within 60 days of its submission by the mediator, then the proposed compact is "treated as a Tribal-State compact entered into under paragraph (3)." If, however, the State does not consent within that 60-day period, then the Act provides that the mediator "shall notify the Secretary [of the Interior]" and that the Secretary "shall prescribe . . . procedures . . . under which class III gaming may be conducted on the Indian lands over which the Indian tribe has jurisdiction."

In September 1991, the Seminole Tribe of Indians, petitioner, sued the State of Florida and its Governor, Lawton Chiles, respondents. Invoking jurisdiction under 25 U.S.C. 2710(d)(7)(A), as well as 28 U.S.C. 1331 and 1362, petitioner alleged that respondents had "refused to enter into any negotiation for inclusion of [certain gaming activities] in a tribal-state compact," thereby violating the "requirement of good faith negotiation" contained in 2710(d)(3). Respondents moved to dismiss the complaint, arguing that the suit violated the State's sovereign immunity from suit in federal court. The District Court denied respondents' motion, and the respondents took an interlocutory appeal of that decision. See *Puerto Rico Aqueduct and Sewer Authority v. Metcalf & Eddy, Inc.* (1993) (collateral order doctrine allows immediate appellate review of order denying claim of Eleventh Amendment immunity).

The Court of Appeals for the Eleventh Circuit reversed the decision of the District Court, holding that the Eleventh Amendment barred petitioner's suit against respondents. The court agreed with the District Court that Congress in 2710(d)(7) intended to abrogate the States' sovereign immunity, and also agreed that the Act had been passed pursuant to Congress' power under the Indian Commerce Clause, U.S. Const., Art. I, 8, cl. 3. The court disagreed with the District Court, however, that the Indian Commerce Clause grants Congress the power to abrogate a State's Eleventh Amendment immunity from suit, and concluded therefore that it had no jurisdiction over petitioner's suit against Florida. The court further held that *Ex parte Young* (1908), does not permit an Indian tribe to force good faith negotiations by suing the Governor of a State. Finding that it lacked subject-matter jurisdiction, the Eleventh Circuit remanded to the District Court with directions to dismiss petitioner's suit.

Petitioner sought our review of the Eleventh Circuit's decision, and we granted certiorari, in order to consider two questions: (1) Does the Eleventh Amendment prevent Congress from authorizing suits by Indian tribes against States for prospective injunctive relief to enforce legislation enacted pursuant to the Indian Commerce Clause?; and (2) Does the doctrine of *Ex parte Young* permit suits against a State's governor for prospective injunctive relief to enforce the good faith bargaining requirement of the Act? We answer the first question in the affirmative, the second in the negative, and we therefore affirm the Eleventh Circuit's dismissal of petitioner's suit.

The Eleventh Amendment provides: "The Judicial power of the United States shall not be construed to extend to any suit in law or equity, commenced or prosecuted against one of the United States by Citizens of another State, or by Citizens or Subjects of any Foreign State."

Although the text of the Amendment would appear to restrict only the Article III diversity jurisdiction of the federal courts, "we have understood the Eleventh Amendment to stand not so much for what it says, but for the presupposition . . . which it confirms." That presupposition, first observed over a century ago in *Hans v. Louisiana* (1890), has two parts: first, that each State is a sovereign entity in our federal system; and second, that "'[i]t is inherent in the nature of sovereignty not to be amenable to the suit of an individual without its consent.'" . . . See also *Puerto Rico Aqueduct and Sewer Authority* ("The Amendment is rooted in a recognition that the States, although a union, maintain certain attributes of sovereignty, including sovereign immunity"). For over a century we have reaffirmed that federal jurisdiction over suits against unconsenting States "was not contemplated by the Constitution when establishing the judicial power of the United States."

Here, petitioner has sued the State of Florida and it is undisputed that Florida has not consented to the suit. See *Blatchford* (States by entering into the Constitution did not consent to suit by Indian tribes). Petitioner nevertheless contends that its suit is not barred by state sovereign immunity. First, it argues that Congress through the Act abrogated the States' sovereign immunity. Alternatively, petitioner maintains that its suit against the Governor may go forward under *Ex parte Young*. We consider each of those arguments in turn.

Petitioner argues that Congress through the Act abrogated the States' immunity from suit. In order to determine whether Congress has abrogated the States' sovereign immunity, we ask two questions: first, whether Congress has "unequivocally expresse[d] its intent to abrogate the immunity," *Green v. Mansour* (1985); and second, whether Congress has acted "pursuant to a valid exercise of power."

Congress' intent to abrogate the States' immunity from suit must be obvious from "a clear legislative statement." This rule arises from a recognition of the important role played by the Eleventh Amendment and the broader principles that it reflects. See *Atascadero State Hospital v. Scanlon* (1985); *Quern v. Jordan* (1979). In *Atascadero,* we held that "[a] general authorization for suit in federal court is not the kind of unequivocal statutory language sufficient to abrogate the Eleventh Amendment." [S]ee also *Blatchford* ("The fact that Congress grants jurisdiction to hear a claim does not suffice to show Congress has abrogated all defenses to that claim"). Rather, as we said in *Dellmuth v. Muth* (1989),

To temper Congress' acknowledged powers of abrogation with due concern for the Eleventh Amendment's role as an essential component of our constitutional structure, we have applied a simple but stringent test: "Congress may abrogate the States' constitutionally secured immunity from suit in federal court only by making its intention unmistakably clear in the language of the statute."

See also *Welch v. Texas Dept. of Highways and Public Transp.* (1987) (plurality opinion).

Here, we agree with the parties, with the Eleventh Circuit in the decision below, and with virtually every other court that has confronted the question that Congress has in 2710(d)(7) provided an "unmistakably clear" statement of its intent to abrogate. Section 2710(d)(7)(A)(i) vests jurisdiction in "[t]he United States district courts . . . over any cause of action . . . arising from the failure of a State to enter into negotiations . . . or to conduct such negotiations in good faith." Any conceivable doubt as to the identity of the defendant in an action under 2710(d)(7)(A)(i) is dispelled when one looks to the various provisions of 2710(d)(7)(B), which describe the remedial scheme available to a tribe that files suit under 2710(d)(7)(A)(i). Section 2710(d)(7)(B)(ii)(II) provides that if a suing tribe meets its burden of proof, then the "burden of proof shall be upon the State. . . ."; 2710(d)(7)(B)(iii) states that if the court "finds that the State has failed to negotiate in good faith . . . , the court shall order the State . . ."; 2710(d)(7)(B)(iv) provides that "the State shall . . . submit to a mediator appointed by the court" and subsection (B)(v) of 2710(d)(7) states that the mediator "shall submit to the State." Sections 2710(d)(7)(B)(vi) and (vii) also refer to the "State" in a context that makes it clear that the State is the defendant to the suit brought by an Indian tribe under 2710(d)(7)(A)(i). In sum, we think that the numerous references to the "State" in the text of 2710(d)(7)(B) make it indubitable that Congress intended through the Act to abrogate the States' sovereign immunity from suit.

Having concluded that Congress clearly intended to abrogate the States' sovereign immunity through 2710(d)(7), we turn now to consider whether the Act was passed "pursuant to a valid exercise of power." Before we address that question here, however, we think it necessary first to define the scope of our inquiry.

Petitioner suggests that one consideration weighing in favor of finding the power to abrogate here is that the Act authorizes only prospective injunctive relief rather than retroactive monetary relief. But we have often made it clear that the relief sought by a plaintiff suing a State is irrelevant to the question whether the suit is barred by the Eleventh Amendment. See, e.g., *Cory v. White* (1982) ("It would be a novel proposition indeed that the Eleventh Amendment does not bar a suit to enjoin the State itself simply because no money judgment is sought"). We think it follows a fortiori from this proposition that the type of relief sought is irrelevant to whether Congress has power to abrogate States' immunity. The Eleventh Amendment does not exist solely in order to "preven[t] federal court judgments that must be paid out of a State's treasury," *Hess v. Port Authority Trans-Hudson Corporation* (1994); it also serves to avoid "the indignity of subjecting a State to the coercive process of judicial tribunals at the instance of private parties," *Puerto Rico Aqueduct and Sewer Authority.*

Similarly, petitioner argues that the abrogation power is validly exercised here because the Act grants the States a power that they would not otherwise have, viz., some measure of authority over gaming on Indian lands. It is true enough that the Act extends to the States a power withheld from them by the Constitution. See *California v. Cabazon Band of Mission Indians* (1987). Nevertheless, we do not see how that consideration is relevant to the question whether Congress may abrogate state sovereign immunity. The Eleventh Amendment immunity may not be lifted by

Congress unilaterally deciding that it will be replaced by grant of some other authority. Cf. *Atascadero* ("[T]he mere receipt of federal funds cannot establish that a State has consented to suit in federal court").

Thus our inquiry into whether Congress has the power to abrogate unilaterally the States' immunity from suit is narrowly focused on one question: Was the Act in question passed pursuant to a constitutional provision granting Congress the power to abrogate? See, e.g., *Fitzpatrick v. Bitzer* (1976). Previously, in conducting that inquiry, we have found authority to abrogate under only two provisions of the Constitution. In *Fitzpatrick,* we recognized that the Fourteenth Amendment, by expanding federal power at the expense of state autonomy, had fundamentally altered the balance of state and federal power struck by the Constitution. We noted that 1 of the Fourteenth Amendment contained prohibitions expressly directed at the States and that 5 of the Amendment expressly provided that "The Congress shall have the power to enforce, by appropriate legislation, the provisions of this article." We held that through the Fourteenth Amendment, federal power extended to intrude upon the province of the Eleventh Amendment and therefore that 5 of the Fourteenth Amendment allowed Congress to abrogate the immunity from suit guaranteed by that Amendment.

In only one other case has congressional abrogation of the States' Eleventh Amendment immunity been upheld. In *Pennsylvania v. Union Gas Co.* (1989), a plurality of the Court found that the Interstate Commerce Clause, Art. I, 8, cl. 3, granted Congress the power to abrogate state sovereign immunity, stating that the power to regulate interstate commerce would be "incomplete without the authority to render States liable in damages." Justice White added the fifth vote necessary to the result in that case, but wrote separately in order to express that he "[did] not agree with much of [the plurality's] reasoning." (White, J., concurring in judgment in part and dissenting in part).

In arguing that Congress through the Act abrogated the States' sovereign immunity, petitioner does not challenge the Eleventh Circuit's conclusion that the Act was passed pursuant to neither the Fourteenth Amendment nor the Interstate Commerce Clause. Instead, accepting the lower court's conclusion that the Act was passed pursuant to Congress' power under the Indian Commerce Clause, petitioner now asks us to consider whether that clause grants Congress the power to abrogate the States' sovereign immunity.

Petitioner begins with the plurality decision in *Union Gas* and contends that "[t]here is no principled basis for finding that congressional power under the Indian Commerce Clause is less than that conferred by the Interstate Commerce Clause." Noting that the Union Gas plurality found the power to abrogate from the "plenary" character of the grant of authority over interstate commerce, petitioner emphasizes that the Interstate Commerce Clause leaves the States with some power to regulate, see, e.g., *West Lynn Creamery, Inc. v. Healy* (1994), whereas the Indian Commerce Clause makes "Indian relations . . . the exclusive province of federal law." *County of Oneida v. Oneida Indian Nation of N. Y.* (1985). Contending that the Indian Commerce Clause vests the Federal Government with "the duty of protect[ing]" the tribes from "local ill feeling" and "the people of the States," *United States v. Kagama* (1886), petitioner argues that the abrogation power is necessary "to protect the tribes from state action denying federally guaranteed rights."

Respondents dispute the petitioner's analogy between the Indian Commerce Clause and the Interstate Commerce Clause. They note that we have recognized that "the Interstate Commerce and Indian Commerce Clauses have very different applications," *Cotton Petroleum Corp. v. New Mexico* (1989), and from that they argue that the two provisions are "wholly dissimilar." Respondents contend that the Interstate Commerce Clause grants the power of abrogation only because Congress' authority to regulate interstate commerce would be "incomplete" without that "necessary" power. The Indian Commerce Clause is distinguishable, respondents contend, because it gives Congress complete authority over the Indian tribes. Therefore, the abrogation power is not "necessary" to the Congress' exercise of its power under the Indian Commerce Clause.

Both parties make their arguments from the plurality decision in *Union Gas,* and we, too, begin there. We think it clear that Justice Brennan's opinion finds Congress' power to abrogate under the Interstate Commerce Clause from the States' cession of their sovereignty when they gave Congress plenary power to regulate interstate commerce. See *Union Gas* ("The important point . . . is that the provision both expands federal power and contracts state power"). Respondents' focus elsewhere is misplaced. While the plurality decision states that Congress' power under the Interstate Commerce Clause would be incomplete without the power to abrogate, that statement is made solely in order to emphasize the broad scope of Congress' authority over interstate commerce. Moreover, respondents' rationale would mean that where Congress has less authority, and the States have more, Congress' means for exercising that power must be greater. We read the plurality opinion to provide just the opposite. Indeed, it was in those circumstances where Congress exercised complete authority that Justice Brennan thought the power to abrogate most necessary. ("Since the States may not legislate at all in [the aforementioned] situations, a conclusion that Congress may not create a cause of action for money damages against the States would mean that no one could do so. And in many situations, it is only money damages that will carry out Congress' legitimate objectives under the Commerce Clause").

Following the rationale of the *Union Gas* plurality, our inquiry is limited to determining whether the Indian Commerce Clause, like the Interstate Commerce Clause, is a grant of authority to the Federal Government at the expense of the States. The answer to that question is obvious. If anything, the Indian Commerce Clause accomplishes a greater transfer of power from the States to the Federal Government than does the Interstate Commerce Clause. This is clear enough from the fact that the States still exercise some authority over interstate trade but have been divested of virtually all authority over Indian commerce and Indian tribes. Under the rationale of *Union Gas,* if the States' partial cession of authority over a particular area includes cession of the immunity from suit, then their virtually total cession of authority over a different area must also include cession of the immunity from suit. . . . We agree with the petitioner that the plurality opinion in *Union Gas* allows no principled distinction in favor of the States to be drawn between the Indian Commerce Clause and the Interstate Commerce Clause.

Respondents argue, however, that we need not conclude that the Indian Commerce Clause grants the power to abrogate the States' sovereign immunity. Instead, they contend that if we find the rationale of the *Union Gas* plurality to extend to the Indian Commerce Clause, then "*Union Gas* should be reconsidered and [*SEMINOLE TRIBE OF FLORIDA v. FLORIDA* (1996)] overruled." Generally, the principle of stare decisis, and the interests that it serves, viz., "the evenhanded, predictable, and consistent development of legal principles, . . . reliance on judicial decisions, and . . . the actual and perceived integrity of the judicial process," *Payne v. Tennessee* (1991), counsel strongly against reconsideration of our precedent. Nevertheless, we always have treated stare decisis as a "principle of policy," and not as an "inexorable command." "[W]hen governing decisions are unworkable or are badly reasoned, 'this Court has never felt constrained to follow precedent.'" Our willingness to reconsider our earlier decisions has been "particularly true in constitutional cases, because in such cases 'correction through legislative action is practically impossible.'"

The Court in *Union Gas* reached a result without an expressed rationale agreed upon by a majority of the Court. We have already seen that Justice Brennan's opinion received the support of only three other Justices. . . . Of the other five, Justice White, who provided the fifth vote for the result, wrote separately in order to indicate his disagreement with the majority's rationale (White, J., concurring in judgment and dissenting in part), and four Justices joined together in a dissent that rejected the plurality's rationale. . . . Since it was issued, *Union Gas* has created confusion among the lower courts that have sought to understand and apply the deeply fractured decision. See, e.g., *Chavez v. Arte Publico Press* ("Justice White's concurrence must be taken on its face to disavow" the plurality's theory); (Justice White's "vague concurrence renders the continuing validity of *Union Gas* in doubt").

The plurality's rationale also deviated sharply from our established federalism jurisprudence and essentially eviscerated our decision in *Hans.* See *Union Gas* ("If *Hans* means only that federal-question suits for money damages against the States cannot be brought in federal court unless Congress clearly says so, it means nothing at all") (SCALIA, J., dissenting). It was well established in 1989 when Union Gas was decided that the Eleventh Amendment stood for the constitutional principle that state sovereign immunity limited the federal courts' jurisdiction under Article III. The text of the Amendment itself is clear enough on this point: "The Judicial power of the United States shall not be construed to extend to any suit. . . ." And our decisions since *Hans* had been equally clear that the Eleventh Amendment reflects "the fundamental principle of sovereign immunity [that] limits the grant of judicial authority in Article III," *Pennhurst State School and Hospital v. Halderman* (1984); see *Union Gas* ("'[T]he entire judicial power granted by the Constitution does not embrace authority to entertain a suit brought by private parties against a State without consent given . . . '"). As the dissent in *Union Gas* recognized, the plurality's conclusion that Congress could under Article I expand the scope of the federal courts' jurisdiction under Article III"contradict[ed] our unvarying approach to Article III as setting forth the exclusive catalog of permissible federal court jurisdiction."

Never before the decision in *Union Gas* had we suggested that the bounds of Article III could be expanded by Congress operating pursuant to any constitutional provision other than the Fourteenth Amendment. Indeed, it had seemed fundamental that Congress could not expand the jurisdiction of the federal courts beyond the bounds of Article III. The plurality's citation of prior decisions for support was based upon what we believe to be a misreading of precedent. See *Union Gas* (SCALIA, J., dissenting). The plurality claimed support for its decision from a case holding the unremarkable, and completely unrelated, proposition that the States may waive their sovereign immunity. . . .

The plurality's extended reliance upon our decision in *Fitzpatrick v. Bitzer* (1976), that Congress could under the Fourteenth Amendment abrogate the States' sovereign immunity was also, we believe, misplaced. Fitzpatrick was based upon a rationale wholly inapplicable to the Interstate Commerce Clause, viz., that the Fourteenth Amendment, adopted well after the adoption of the Eleventh Amendment and the ratification of the Constitution, operated to alter the pre-existing balance between state and federal power achieved by Article III and the Eleventh Amendment. Id., at 454. As the dissent in Union Gas made clear, Fitzpatrick cannot be read to justify "limitation of the principle embodied in the Eleventh Amendment through appeal to antecedent provisions of the Constitution."

In the five years since it was decided, *Union Gas* has proven to be a solitary departure from established law. See *Puerto Rico Aqueduct and Sewer Authority v. Metcalf & Eddy, Inc.* (1993). Reconsidering the decision in *Union Gas,* we conclude that none of the policies underlying stare decisis require our continuing adherence to its holding. The decision has, since its issuance, been of questionable precedential value, largely because a majority of the Court expressly disagreed with the rationale of the plurality. See *Nichols v. United States* (1994) (the "degree of confusion following a splintered decision . . . is itself a reason for reexamining that decision"). The case involved the interpretation of the Constitution and therefore may be altered only by constitutional amendment or revision by this Court. Finally, both the result in *Union Gas* and the plurality's rationale depart from our established understanding of the Eleventh Amendment and undermine the accepted function of Article III. We feel bound to conclude that *Union Gas* was wrongly decided and that it should be, and now is, overruled.

The dissent makes no effort to defend the decision in Union Gas, see post at 2, but nonetheless would find congressional power to abrogate in this case. Contending that our decision is a novel extension of the Eleventh Amendment, the dissent chides us for "attend[ing]" to dicta. We adhere in this case, however, not to mere *obiter dicta,* but rather to the well-established rationale upon which the Court based the results of its earlier decisions. When an opinion issues for the Court, it is not only the result but also those portions of the opinion necessary to that result by which we are bound. Cf. *Burnham v. Superior Court of Cal., County of Marin* (1990) (exclusive basis of a judgment is not dicta) (plurality); *Allegheny County v. American Civil Liberties Union, Greater Pittsburgh Chapter* (1989) ("As a general rule, the principle of stare decisis directs us to adhere not only to the holdings of our prior cases, but also to their explications of the governing rules of law.") (KENNEDY, J., concurring and dissenting); *Sheet Metal Workers v. EEOC* (1986) ("Although technically dicta, . . . an important part of the Court's rationale for the result that it reache[s] . . . is entitled to greater weight . . .") (O'CONNOR, J., concurring). For over a century, we have grounded our decisions in the oft-repeated understanding of state sovereign immunity as an essential part of the Eleventh Amendment. In *Principality of Monaco v. Mississippi* (1934), the Court held that the Eleventh Amendment barred a suit brought against a State by a foreign state. Chief Justice Hughes wrote for a unanimous Court:

[N]either the literal sweep of the words of Clause one of 2 of Article III, nor the absence of restriction in the letter of the Eleventh Amendment, permits the conclusion that in all controversies of the sort described in Clause one, and omitted from the words of the Eleventh Amendment, a State may be sued without her consent. Thus Clause one specifically provides that the judicial power shall extend "to all Cases, in Law and Equity, arising under this Constitution, the Laws of the United States, and Treaties made, or which shall be made, under their Authority." But, although a case may arise under the Constitution and laws of the United States, the judicial power does not extend to it if the suit is sought to be prosecuted against a State, without her consent, by one of her own citizens. . . .

Manifestly, we cannot rest with a mere literal application of the words of 2 of Article III, or assume that the letter of the Eleventh Amendment exhausts the restrictions upon suits against non-consenting States. Behind the words of the constitutional provisions are postulates which limit and control. There is the essential postulate that the controversies, as contemplated, shall be found to be of a justiciable character. There is also the postulate that States of the Union, still possessing attributes of sovereignty, shall be immune from suits, without their consent, save where there has been a "surrender of this immunity in the plan of the convention."

. . . It is true that we have not had occasion previously to apply established Eleventh Amendment principles to the question whether Congress has the power to abrogate state sovereign immunity (save in *Union Gas*). But consideration of that question must proceed with fidelity to this century-old doctrine.

The dissent, to the contrary, disregards our case law in favor of a theory cobbled together from law review articles and its own version of historical events. The dissent cites not a single decision since *Hans* (other than *Union Gas*) that supports its view of state sovereign immunity, instead relying upon the now-discredited decision in *Chisholm v. Georgia* (1793). Its undocumented and highly speculative extralegal explanation of the decision in *Hans* is a disservice to the Court's traditional method of adjudication.

The dissent mischaracterizes the *Hans* opinion. That decision found its roots not solely in the common law of England, but in the much more fundamental "'jurisprudence in all civilized nations.'" . . . The dissent's proposition that the common law of England, where adopted by the States, was open to change by the legislature, is wholly unexceptionable and largely beside the point: that common law provided the substantive rules of law rather than jurisdiction. Cf. *Monaco* (state sovereign immunity, like the requirement that there be a "justiciable" controversy, is a constitutionally grounded limit on federal jurisdiction). It also is noteworthy that the principle of state sovereign immunity stands distinct from other principles of the common law in that only the former prompted a specific constitutional amendment.

Hans with a much closer vantage point than the dissent recognized that the decision in *Chisholm* was contrary to the well-understood meaning of the Constitution. The dissent's conclusion that the decision in *Chisholm* was "reasonable," certainly would have struck the Framers of the Eleventh Amendment as quite odd: that decision created "such a shock of surprise that the Eleventh Amendment was at once proposed and adopted." The dissent's lengthy analysis of the text of the Eleventh Amendment is directed at a straw man we long have recognized that blind reliance upon the text of the Eleventh Amendment is "to strain the Constitution and the law to a construction never imagined or dreamed of." The text dealt in terms only with the problem presented by the decision in *Chisholm;* in light of the fact that the federal courts did not have federal question jurisdiction at the time the Amendment was passed (and would not have it until 1875), it seems unlikely that much thought was given to the prospect of federal question jurisdiction over the States.

That same consideration causes the dissent's criticism of the views of Marshall, Madison, and Hamilton to ring hollow. The dissent cites statements made by those three influential Framers, the most natural reading of which would preclude all federal jurisdiction over an unconsenting State. Struggling against this reading, however, the dissent finds significant the absence of any contention that sovereign immunity would affect the new federal-question jurisdiction. But the lack of any statute vesting general federal question jurisdiction in the federal courts until much later makes the dissent's demand for greater specificity about a then-dormant jurisdiction overly exacting.

In putting forward a new theory of state sovereign immunity, the dissent develops its own vision of the political system created by the Framers, concluding with the statement that "[t]he Framer's principal objectives in rejecting English theories of unitary sovereignty . . . would have been impeded if a new concept of sovereign immunity had taken its place in federal question cases, and would have been substantially thwarted if that new immunity had been held untouchable by any congressional effort to abrogate it." This sweeping statement ignores the fact that the Nation survived for nearly two centuries without the question of the existence of such power ever being presented to this Court. And Congress itself waited nearly a century before even conferring federal question jurisdiction on the lower federal courts.

In overruling *Union Gas* today, we reconfirm that the background principle of state sovereign immunity embodied in the Eleventh Amendment is not so ephemeral as to dissipate when the subject of the suit is an area, like the regulation of Indian commerce, that is under the exclusive control of the Federal Government. Even when the Constitution vests in Congress complete law-making authority over a particular area, the Eleventh Amendment prevents congressional authorization of suits by private parties against unconsenting States. The Eleventh Amendment restricts the judicial power under Article III, and Article I cannot be used to circumvent the constitutional limitations placed upon federal jurisdiction. Petitioner's suit against the State of Florida must be dismissed for a lack of jurisdiction.

Petitioner argues that we may exercise jurisdiction over its suit to enforce 2710(d)(3) against the Governor notwithstanding the jurisdictional bar of the Eleventh Amendment. Petitioner notes that since our decision in *Ex parte Young* (1908), we often have found federal jurisdiction over a suit against a state official when that suit seeks only prospective injunctive relief in order to "end a continuing violation of federal law." The situation presented here, however, is sufficiently different from that giving rise to the traditional *Ex parte Young* action so as to preclude the availability of that doctrine.

Here, the "continuing violation of federal law" alleged by petitioner is the Governor's failure to bring the State into compliance with 2710(d)(3). But the duty to negotiate imposed upon the State by that statutory provision does not stand alone. Rather, as we have seen, Congress passed 2710(d)(3) in conjunction with the carefully crafted and intricate remedial scheme set forth in 2710(d)(7).

Where Congress has created a remedial scheme for the enforcement of a particular federal right, we have, in suits against federal officers, refused to supplement that scheme with one created by the judiciary. *Schweiker v. Chilicky* (1988) ("When the design of a Government program suggests that Congress has provided what it considers adequate remedial mechanisms for constitutional violations that may occur in the course of its administration, we have not created additional . . . remedies"). Here, of course, the question is not whether a remedy should be created, but instead is whether the Eleventh Amendment bar should be lifted, as it was in *Ex parte Young,* in order to allow a suit against a state officer. Nevertheless, we think that the same general principle applies: therefore, where Congress has prescribed a detailed remedial scheme for the enforcement against a State of a statutorily created right, a court should hesitate before casting aside those limitations and permitting an action against a state officer based upon *Ex parte Young.*

Here, Congress intended 2710(d)(3) to be enforced against the State in an action brought under 2710(d)(7); the intricate procedures set forth in that provision show that Congress intended therein not only to define, but also significantly to limit, the duty imposed by 2710(d)(3). For example, where the court finds that the State has failed to negotiate in good faith, the only remedy prescribed is an order directing the State and the Indian tribe to conclude a compact within 60 days. And if the parties disregard the court's order and fail to conclude a compact within the 60-day period, the only sanction is that each party then must submit a proposed compact to a mediator who selects the one which best embodies the terms of the Act. Finally, if the State fails to accept the compact selected by the mediator, the only sanction against it is that the mediator shall notify the Secretary of the Interior who then must prescribe regulations governing Class III gaming on the tribal lands at issue. By contrast with this quite modest set of sanctions, an action brought against a state official under *Ex parte Young* would expose that official to the full remedial powers of a federal court, including, presumably, contempt sanctions. If 2710(d)(3) could be enforced in a suit under *Ex parte Young,* 2710(d)(7) would have been superfluous; it is difficult to see why an Indian tribe would suffer through the intricate scheme of 2710(d)(7) when more complete and more immediate relief would be available under *Ex parte Young.*

Here, of course, we have found that Congress does not have authority under the Constitution to make the State suable in federal court under 2710(d)(7). Nevertheless, the fact that Congress chose to impose upon the State a liability which is significantly more limited than would be the liability imposed upon the state officer under *Ex parte Young* strongly indicates that Congress had no wish to create the latter under 2710(d)(3). Nor are we free to rewrite the statutory scheme in order to approximate what we think Congress might have wanted had it known that 2710(d)(7) was beyond its authority. If that effort is to be made, it should be made by Congress, and not by the federal courts. We hold that *Ex parte Young* is inapplicable to petitioner's suit against the Governor of Florida, and therefore that suit is barred by the Eleventh Amendment and must be dismissed for a lack of jurisdiction.

The Eleventh Amendment prohibits Congress from making the State of Florida capable of being sued in federal court. The narrow exception to the Eleventh Amendment provided by the *Ex parte Young* doctrine cannot be used to enforce 2710(d)(3) because Congress enacted a remedial scheme, 2710(d)(7), specifically designed for the enforcement of that right. The Eleventh Circuit's dismissal of petitioner's suit is hereby affirmed.

It is so ordered.

TABLE: American Indians and Alaska Natives Reporting Tribal Affiliation by Race (2010)

	AIAN*				
		As the only race		Two or more races	
Tribal affiliation	Total number	Number	Percent	Number	Percent
Total AIAN* population	5,220,579	2,932,248	56%	2,288,331	44%
10 largest tribes	2,249,792	1,202,320	53%	1,048,590	47%
Cherokee	819,105	286,687	35%	532,418	65%
Navajo	332,129	285,631	86%	46,498	14%
Choctaw	195,764	103,755	53%	92,000	47%
Mexican American Indian	175,494	121,091	69%	54,403	31%
Chippewa	170,742	112,690	66%	58,052	34%
Sioux	170,110	112,273	66%	57,837	34%
Apache	111,810	63,732	57%	49,196	44%
Blackfeet	105,304	27,379	26%	77,925	74%
Creek	88,332	48,583	55%	39,749	45%
Iroquois	81,002	40,501	50%	40,501	50%

*American Indian and Alaska Native.

Source: U.S. Census Bureau (2012). The American Indian and Alaska Native Population: 2010.Retrieved from http://www.census.gov/prod/cen2010/briefs/c2010br-10.pdf

About the Editor

JEFFREY IAN ROSS, PhD, is a Professor in the School of Criminal Justice and a Fellow of the Center for International and Comparative Law at the University of Baltimore. He has researched, written, and lectured on corrections, policing, political crime (esp., terrorism and state crime), violence (esp. criminal, political, and religious), cybercrime, extreme/abnormal criminal behavior, and crime and justice in Indian Communities for over two decades. Ross's work has appeared in many academic journals and books, as well as popular media. He is the author, coauthor, editor, or coeditor of several books including *Native Americans and the Criminal Justice System* (Paradigm Publishers, 2006). Ross has been a consultant on a number of Indian Country grants funded by the federal government. He has also served as a peer reviewer for projects that these agencies have funded or are considering funding. Ross taught at American University, as part of their Washington Internships for Native Students (WINS) program. He has worked and lived in Indian Country. His website is www.jeffreyianross.com.

About the Contributors

DEBORAH ALTSCHUL is a psychologist who is Director of Research and Deputy Director of the University of New Mexico Department of Psychiatry's Center for Rural and Community Behavioral Health. Her research focuses on examining the connection between behavioral health disparities, cultural competency, consumer outcomes, and evidence-based practice. Dr. Altschul works closely with New Mexico's behavioral health authority on health disparities research aimed at impacting public policy. She also currently works with several tribal communities researching and evaluating the impact of mental health service infrastructure development. Prior to working in New Mexico, Dr. Altschul was on faculty at the University of Hawai'i Mental Health Services Research, Evaluation, and Training Program, where she was involved in public mental health–related research, including a study examining the impact of cultural adaptation on evidence-based practice implementation. She also led the Consumer Assessment Team, aimed at involving individuals with serious mental illnesses in study design, data collection, analysis, interpretation, and report writing. Dr. Altschul completed a mental health disparities research postdoctoral fellowship with the National Association of State Mental Health Program Directors, a predoctoral internship at the University of Florida, and her doctoral studies at the University of Georgia.

OWEN ANDERSON, PhD is Associate Professor in the New College at Arizona State University. He has researched, written, and lectured on the philosophy of religion, religion in America, and applied ethics. He has published in these areas with leading academic journals. His most current book is titled *The Natural Moral Law* (Cambridge UP, 2012). Dr. Anderson has also been a frequent guest on Phoenix area radio shows discussing the application of philosophy to contemporary issues. He has been invited to participate in debates and has written Op-Ed articles for the *Arizona Republic.*

WILLIAM G. ARCHAMBEAULT, PhD is Professor and former Department Chair at Minot State University, Minot, ND. He retired from LSU in Baton Rouge, LA, after more than 28 years with the rank of Professor. He served as a faculty member in the School of Social Work and the Department of Criminal Justice where he also served as Department Chair. His research and publications for the past two decades focused on various aspects of crime, justice, and corrections in Indian County and the applications of traditional tribal methods of healing in corrections. Previously, he published in the broader areas of corrections; criminal justice administration, management, and technology; and international criminal justice. He is a graduate of Florida State University and Indiana State University. He is mixed-blood Lakota, Ojibwa, and French ancestry; trained in some Ojibwa traditional healing ways; including being a Sun Dancer and sweat lodge leader.

LANA O. BEASLEY, PhD received her PhD in Clinical Child Psychology from the University of Kansas in 2008. Currently, she is Assistant Professor of Psychology at Oklahoma State University and Assistant Professor of Research at the University of Oklahoma Health Sciences Center. She conducts research in the area of child maltreatment. Specifically, she is interested in research on child abuse prevention and is currently working on a project examining a child maltreatment prevention program. She is also interested in research involving American Indians, the cultural adaptation of treatments, the family environment of children exposed to maltreatment, and research focusing on foster children. Dr. Beasley is a member of the Choctaw Nation.

MARCELLINO BERARDO, PhD is a linguist and language teacher at the Applied English Center at the University of Kansas. His research interests include language revitalization, issues in language teaching and learning, and language documentation and description. He has worked with speakers of many different American Indian languages to describe, document, and teach aspects of their language. Specific interests in language pedagogy include the comparison of teaching widely spoken languages with teaching endangered languages. He has given many presentations and workshops on language revitalization and is the author and coauthor of a number of articles on documenting and revitalizing Native American languages.

DOREEN M. BIRD, MPH, is from Santo Domingo Pueblo, New Mexico. She works as a Community-Based Research Specialist at the University of New Mexico Health Sciences Center, Department of Psychiatry, Center for Rural and Community Behavioral Health. She received her bachelor's degree in Psychology, master's degree in Public Health, and has been trained as a National Institute of Mental Health research fellow. She has focused her research on mental and behavioral health issues among American Indian populations since 2004. Ms. Bird's current work includes: a NIH-funded Community-Based Participatory Research project that addresses mental health intervention, prevention, and early detection among American Indian adolescents and their families in a southwest tribal community; the state of New Mexico's Suicide Prevention Clearinghouse for Native Americans; and community outreach, trainings, and presentations on topics such as suicide prevention, cultural competency, cultural identity, and guiding principles in research. Ms. Bird enjoys mentoring Native American youth into higher education and health careers. Ms. Bird is the proud mother of six children and maintains a Native-centered approach in her daily life.

DOLORES SUBIA BIGFOOT, PhD is trained as a child psychologist, and an associate professor directing the Native American Programs at the Center on Child Abuse and Neglect at OUHSC. Funded since 1994 by the Children's Bureau, she has directed Project Making Medicine and from 2003 she has directed the Indian Country Child Trauma Center where she was instrumental in the cultural adapted interventions of evidence based treatments. Under her guidance, four EBTs were adapted for American Indian and Alaska Native families in Indian Country titled the Honoring Children Series. One of the four is Honoring Children, Making Relatives, a cultural adaptation of Parent-Child Interaction Therapy, for use with AI/AN children and their families. It incorporates AI/AN teachings, practices, rituals, traditions, and cultural orientation while maintaining the guiding principles and theory of PCIT. Dr. Bigfoot has over 15 published articles and chapters, including the lead author of the recent publication, "Adapting Evidence-Based Treatments for Use with American Indians and Native Alaskan Children and Youth." Dr. Bigfoot has served as PI on thirteen federally funded projects. Another distinction has been her service on the SAMHSA/CMHS National Advisory Council, National Network to Eliminate Health Disparities, and on the working groups for the Indian Health Service and the National Indian Child Welfare Association. She was selected to attend the White House conference on children's mental health, and is Past President of the Society of Indian Psychologists. She serves as an advisor to the home visitation tribal grantees and the NRC4 Tribes both funded by the Children's Bureau; these address various concerns dealing with child welfare issues with American Indian and Alaska Native tribal grantees. Dr. Bigfoot has over 30 years of experience and is knowledgeable about the concerns of implementation and adaptation of evidenced based practices being introduced into Indian Country. She is an enrolled member of the Caddo Nation of Oklahoma.

DOROTHY BRACEY, PhD is Professor Emeritus of Anthropology at John Jay College of Criminal Justice and Professor Emeritus of Criminal Justice at the Graduate Center, City University of New York. She has been Visiting Professor at Sam Houston State University, the American University, the South Australia Institute of Technology, and the University of Illinois at Chicago. She has a BA from the College of William and Mary, a PhD from Harvard University, and a Master of Studies in Law from Yale Law School. She is the author of "Criminalizing Culture: An Anthropologist Looks at Native Americans and the U.S. Legal System" as well as articles on "Tribal Policing" and "Federal Policing on Indian Lands" in the *Encyclopedia of Law Enforcement.* Her most recent book is *Exploring Law and Culture* (Waveland Press, 2005). Professor Bracey is a member of the Board of Managers of the School for Advanced Research (SAR), is treasurer of the Foundation for the Institute for American Indian Arts (IAIA), and has served on the board of the Cancer Institute of New Mexico Foundation. She currently lives in Santa Fe, New Mexico.

MARIA YELLOW HORSE BRAVE HEART, PhD (Hunkpapa/Oglala Lakota) is Associate Professor of Psychiatry/Director of Native American and Disparities Research at the University of New Mexico, Center for Rural and Community Behavioral Health. Prior academic appointments include Associate Professor at Columbia University and the University of Denver. Dr. Brave Heart was president/cofounder of the Takini Network, based in Rapid City, South Dakota, a Native collective devoted to community healing from intergenerational massive group trauma among Indigenous Peoples. Currently, she is president of the Takini Institute. Dr. Brave Heart developed historical trauma and unresolved grief theory and interventions, conducting close to 300 presentations and trainings for tribes across the country and Canada. In 1992, she developed the *Historical Trauma and Unresolved Grief Intervention,* a Tribal Best Practice. Dr. Brave Heart developed and directed the international Models for Healing Indigenous Survivors of Historical Trauma: A Multicultural Dialogue among Allies Conference from 2001 to 2004. Currently, Dr. Brave Heart is Principal Investigator of the Tribal Preventive and Early Mental Health Intervention Project funded by NIH's National Institute for Minority Health and Health Disparities.

GREGORY R. CAMPBELL, PhD is Professor of Anthropology at the University of Montana, Missoula. Professor Campbell is author of numerous articles and edited volumes about the Native American experience in America, with special research interests in health, demography, political economy, ethnicity, and heritage issues. He is an author and the editor of *Many Americas: Critical Perspectives on Race, Racism, and Ethnicity* (Kendall/Hunt, 2001), served as associate editor for the Native American and Indigenous section in the *Encyclopedia of Race and Racism* (Gale Cengage Learning, 2008), and has authored numerous articles about Native American health and demography. He has conducted ethnographic field research among various Native communities of the Great Plains and Southwest.

D ANTHONY CLARK, PhD is a historian of race, and a member of the faculty of Interdisciplinary and Liberal Studies at Arizona State University, who has articles and reviews published in the *American Journal of Sociology, American Quarterly, American Studies, Black Scholar, Cultural Critique, Journal of Diversity in Higher Education,* and *Wicazo Sa Review.* He has chapters in *Across the Great Divide* (2001), *Beyond Red Power* (2007), *Indigenizing the Academy* (2004), and *Making of the American West* (2007). He has a coedited a thematic issue of *American Indian Quarterly* entitled *Resisting Exile in "The Land of the Free"* (2008). His major project is *Roots of Red Power: American Indians Lobbying Congress, Courts, and Public Opinion, 1871–1934* . He is past president of the Mid-America American Studies Association.

ANNETTE S. CRISANTI, PhD is Research Associate Professor in the Center for Rural and Community Behavioral Health, Department of Psychiatry, School of Medicine, University of New Mexico. Her academic training is in Epidemiology, specializing in Psychiatric Epidemiology. Dr. Crisanti's research and program evaluation interests aim to improve public mental health-care services and address health disparities in rural areas for persons with serious mental illness and/or co-occurring substance use disorders, particularly for those with trauma histories and those involved in the criminal justice system. She has researched, written, and lectured primarily on research methodology, mental health first aid, alternatives to incarceration, the employment and training of peer researchers and evaluators, evidence-based practices in mental health services, and trauma-informed systems of care, including trauma-specific services. She has published over 20 articles in peer-reviewed journals and has a lengthy and extensive presentation history at national and international conferences.

CHRISTINE WILSON DUCLOS, PhD, MPH is a behavioral scientist and Senior Consultant with JSI Research and Training Institute, Inc., Clinical Assistant Professor of Family Medicine at the University of Colorado Denver (UCD), and affiliated faculty member with the UCD Health and Behavioral Sciences Program. Dr. Duclos has over 30 years' experience in health care as a practitioner, researcher, and consultant. Her expertise includes behavioral health risk and its consequences within American Indian and Alaska Native populations, especially how it intersections with juvenile and adult criminal justice systems. She is author and coauthor on numerous publications in this area. Recently, she was a technical advisor for a HIV integration project funded by the CDC for integrating HIV prevention and intervention services within health clinics serving AI/ANs. Dr. Duclos is or has been PI and/or consultant on numerous Indian Country grants funded by Centers for Disease Control, National Institute of Justice, Office of Justice Programs, Office of Juvenile Justice and Delinquency Prevention, Indian Health Services, and the Substance Abuse and Mental Health Services Administration. As a peer reviewer for these same agencies, she evaluated funded projects as well as those that were being considered for funding.

M. GEORGE EICHENBERG, PhD has worked in private security, municipal policing, and juvenile corrections, accumulating a total of 15 years of field practice in criminal justice, mostly in rural areas. He received a bachelor's of science in Criminal Justice from the University of Texas at Tyler, Texas, and a master's of science in Criminal Justice Management and a PhD in Criminal Justice from Sam Houston State University in Huntsville, Texas. He taught at Wayne State College of Nebraska, a state college with three First Nations in its service area and worked on programs for the benefit of these nations. He returned to Texas after six years at Wayne State and currently is Professor of Criminal Justice at Tarleton State University in Stephenville, Texas.

LAURA L. FINLEY earned her PhD in Sociology from Western Michigan University in 2002. She is currently Assistant Professor of Sociology and Criminology at

Barry University. Dr. Finley is the author or coauthor of 11 books and has 2 in production. She has also authored numerous book chapters and journal articles. In addition to her academic work, Dr. Finley is a community peace activist, with active involvement in local, national, and international groups. She regularly presents on topics related to peace and social justice. In addition, Dr. Finley is board chair of No More Tears, a nonprofit that provides individualized assistance to victims of domestic violence and their children, as well as cochair of the South Florida Diversity Alliance. Dr. Finley also serves on the board of the Humanity Project, Floridians for Alternatives to the Death Penalty, and is K-12 Educational Liaison for the Peace and Justice Studies Association. Additionally, Dr. Finley helps organize the College Brides Walk, a South Florida event that raises awareness about dating and domestic violence.

ADRIENNE FRENG is Associate Professor in the Department of Criminal Justice at the University of Wyoming. She received a BA in Psychology and Sociology from Black Hills State University, and an MA and PhD in Sociology from the University of Nebraska-Lincoln. In the course of her career, Dr. Freng has examined several issues as they relate to American Indian populations, including education, the portrayal in crime news, and gangs. She has also worked as part of a national evaluation of gang prevention programs from 1997 to 2001 and then again from 2006 to 2011. Her publication record includes numerous articles and a book dealing with program evaluation; methodological issues; and delinquency, gang, and violence issues. Her research interests include juvenile delinquency, gangs, and race and crime issues, and specifically as they relate to American Indian populations.

YVONNE M. HAMBY, MPH has a strong background in research, evaluation, and functional program areas, such as prevention programming. With 13 years of experience in working in community-level evaluation and with diverse groups including American Indian Tribes and organizations, she has gained extensive, firsthand knowledge in all stages of social science research, including developing protocols, collecting and analyzing data, writing up and presenting results to multiple audiences, and coordinating the activities of a research team. This experience has allowed Ms. Hamby to gain invaluable insight into the many facets of community services research and delivery, which enables her to provide innovative solutions to improve the health of underserved populations. One of her principal strengths is her ability to infuse evaluation projects with a cultural perspective. While such a pursuit entails becoming a part of communities with whom she works, she recognizes that the process ultimately belongs to them. Most recently, she collaborated with the Centers for Disease Control and Prevention and Indian Health Service to contribute to the article "An On-going Burden: Chlamydial Infections among Young American Indian Women" for the *Maternal Child Health Journal* 12 (2008): S25–29.

SIDNEY L. HARRING, PhD, LLB has degrees in both law and sociology from the University of Wisconsin. He is currently Law Foundation of Saskatchewan Chair in Law and Public Policy at the University of Saskatchewan College of Law. Much of his work has been in the area of American Indian law and indigenous rights. He has worked in 10 countries and held 3 Fulbright professorships (i.e., Malaysia, Namibia, and Sweden). He is the author of three books and fifty articles and chapters in the area of police, crime, Indian law, and indigenous rights, including Crow Dog's Case.

TRACY HIRATA-EDDS earned her PhD in Child Language from the University of Kansas. She was a Peace Corps Volunteer teacher and a Fulbright Scholar teacher trainer in Nepal. Her professional interests include endangered language revitalization, documentation, immersion schools, teacher training, assessment design, language learning, and children's first and second language development. She partners with Native communities for language and culture maintenance and revitalization, including working closely with Cherokee Nation, serving as an advisor to their immersion school and conducting NIH- and NSF-funded research related to language learning, teaching, and revitalization issues. She has published articles in *Language Learning, Bilingual Research Journal, International Journal of Applied Linguistics, International Journal of Bilingual Education and Bilingualism,* and *Cultural Survival Quarterly,* and chapters in *Immersion Education: Practices, Policies, Possibilities*; *One Voice, Many Voices: 6th Annual Stabilizing Indigenous Languages Conference Proceedings*; and *The Five-Minute Linguist: Bite-Sized Essays on Language and Languages.* Additionally, she supports revitalization efforts by providing workshops and teacher trainings with Oklahoma's Breath of Life, Oklahoma Native Language Association, and the Institute for Collaborative Language Research.

LORI L. JERVIS, PhD is Associate Professor in Anthropology and the Center for Applied Social Research at the University of Oklahoma. She is a cultural and medical anthropologist who has worked on Native issues for 16 years. Much of her work focuses on the intersection of culture, gerontology, and psychiatry, with specific research projects on cognitive and psychiatric issues in tribal nursing homes, cognitive impairment and family caregiving among Native elders, and elder mistreatment (abuse, neglect, and financial exploitation). These projects have been funded by the Administration on Aging and the National Institute on Aging. Dr. Jervis was invited to speak on the culturally valid cognitive assessment of American Indians at the International Conference on Alzheimer's Disease, and presented in expert meetings on elder mistreatment and abuse at the National Academies of Science. She is the immediate president-elect of the Association of Anthropology and Gerontology.

BRUCE E. JOHANSEN, PhD is Jacob J. Isaacson Professor in Communication and Native American Studies at the University of Nebraska at Omaha. He has authored or edited 38 books, the most recent of which is *The Encyclopedia of the American Indian Movement* (Greenwood, 2013). In addition to writing in Native American Studies, Johansen also has written widely in environmental studies, including several volumes on global warming (latest: *The Encyclopedia of Global Warming Science and Technology,* Greenwood, 2009) and toxic chemicals (*The Dirty Dozen,* Praeger, 2003). Johansen also has written occasionally in national newspapers and magazines, including *The New Yorker, The Progressive,* the *New York Times,* the *Washington Post,* and several others. Johansen, who has taught at UNO since 1982, is presently at work on histories of Seattle's El Centro de la Raza and the Muckleshoot Indian Tribe, as well as a two-volume encyclopedia of Native American culture for Greenwood. He lives in Omaha with his wife, Pat Keiffer, and an extended family.

MICHAEL J. LYNCH, PhD is Professor in the Department of Criminology, and Associated Faculty Member of the School of Global Sustainability at the University of South Florida. His research examines economic, racial, and social inequality related to radical criminology, racial bias in criminal justice processes, corporate crime, green criminology, environmental crime, and environmental justice. His recent books include: *Radical-Marxist Criminology* (2011, with P. B. Stretesky), *Racial Divide: Race, Ethnicity and Criminal Justice* (2008, with E. B. Patterson and K. K Childs), *Environmental Law, Crime and Justice* (2008 with R. G. Burns and P. B. Stretesky), *Big Prisons, Big Dreams: Crime and the Failure of the US Prison System* (2007), and *Primer in Radical Criminology* (2006, 4th edition, with R. J. Michalowski).

FAVIAN ALEJANDRO MARTÍN earned his doctorate from the Criminology and Criminal Justice Program at Old Dominion University in Norfolk, VA. He is currently an Assistant Professor in the Department of Sociology, Anthropology, and Criminal Justice at Arcadia University in Glenside, Pennsylvania. His research interests are in the areas of race/ethnicity and crime, immigration and crime, and social justice. Martin's dissertation investigated the perceptions of crime, violence, and justice among tribal police officers working in Indian Country. He has published work in journals such as *Journal of Criminal Justice, International Criminal Justice Review, Criminal Justice Policy Review,* and *Journal of Criminal Justice Education.*

YUKA MIZUTANI, PhD is Assistant Professor in the Center for Global Discovery at Sophia University, Japan. She has been focusing on issues related to the Pascua Yaqui people in Arizona, and urban Native American societies in the United States. Her interests include the federal recognition process, borderland issues, image creation, and Native American modern life and society. Yuka is the author of *Senjumin Pascua Yaqui no Beikoku Hennyu* (*Integration of the Pascua Yaqui into the United States,* Hokkaido University Press, 2012, in Japanese) which won a prize from the Japan Consortium for Area Studies in 2012. In addition to publishing articles, she works for museum exhibits in Japan to introduce Native American culture, history, and modern life.

KATHLEEN O'HALLERAN resides in northwest Arizona where she consults and writes on issues of social justice, environmental concerns, cultural problems and pressures, and geopolitics. She most recently taught at Northwestern Oklahoma State University. Following an award-winning journalism career, O'Halleran studied History of the American West, Anthropology, and Environmental History at Northern Arizona University and then obtained degrees in Sustainability Education at Arizona's Prescott College. O'Halleran's research efforts aim toward sustaining local and indigenous communities amid change. Toward that end, she serves as a policy advisor and consultant on a local, national, and international scale in the field of Sustainability and Sustainable Education, and has worked on behalf of indigenous communities in Arizona, Oklahoma, New York, Iraq, and Columbia. Research contributions include: (1) The Historical Terrain of the 1868 Battle of the Washita: An Analysis of Cultural Framing, Social Reformation and New Voices from the Margins: Sod House Museum, OK., 2011; (2) The Columbia Group: Education in Emergencies and Post-Crisis Transition Programme, Inter-Agency Network for Education in Emergencies: UNHCR, Geneva, Switzerland, 2010; (3) Achieving Sustainable Development. United Nations Development Group Report: Millennium Development Goals United Nations ECOSOC/UNDP, (2008, Feb.–March). New York, NY.

BARBARA PERRY is Professor and Associate Dean of Social Science and Humanities at the University of Ontario Institute of Technology. She has written extensively in the area of hate crime, including five books on the topic; among them: *In the Name of Hate: Understanding Hate Crime* (Taylor & Francis, 2001) and *Silent Victims: Hate Crime against Native Americans* (University of Arizona, 2008). She is also general editor of a five-volume set on hate crime (Praeger), and editor of Volume 3: *Victims of Hate Crime* of that set. Dr. Perry continues to work in the area of hate crime, and has begun to make contributions to the limited scholarship on hate crime in Canada. Here, she is particularly interested in anti-Muslim violence and hate crime against Aboriginal people. Currently, she is conducting innovative research on the community impacts of hate crime.

LIZETTE PETER, PhD is Associate Professor in the Department of Curriculum and Teaching and an affiliated faculty member of the Indigenous Studies program at the University of Kansas. She teaches courses in second-language acquisition and pedagogy, mostly pertaining to critical issues surrounding the teaching of English to speakers of other languages in U.S. and international settings. Her primary research interest, however, is the revitalization of languages that have been displaced by English and other colonizing languages in the United States and around the world. In particular, her research and writing to date have documented the linguistic and sociolinguistic nature of acquiring Cherokee by children in the Cherokee Language Immersion School in Tahlequah, Oklahoma, since its inception in 2001. She is the author and coauthor of a number of articles and book chapters on Cherokee language revitalization and currently serves on the editorial board for the *Journal of Immersion and Content-Based Education.*

JON REYHNER is Professor of Education at Northern Arizona University. He also taught at Montana State University-Billings. Before that, he taught junior high school for four years in the Navajo Nation and was a school administrator for 10 years in Indian schools in Arizona, Montana, and New Mexico. He served as a commissioned author for the U.S. government's Indian Nations at Risk Task Force and coauthored a research review for the government's American Indian/Alaska Native Research Group. He has written extensively on American Indian education and Indigenous language revitalization, including editing *Teaching American Indian Students* (University of Oklahoma, 1992), coediting *Honoring Our Heritage: Culturally Appropriate Approaches for Teaching Indigenous Students* (Northern Arizona University, 2011), and coauthoring *Language and Literacy Teaching for Indigenous Education* (Multilingual Matters, 2002) and *American Indian Education: A History* (University of Oklahoma, 2004). He cochaired the Fourth and Eighth Annual Stabilizing Indigenous Languages Symposia at Northern Arizona University in 1997 and 2001. He currently coordinates the Symposia Steering Committee. He has also edited a column on issues in indigenous education for the magazine of the National Association for Bilingual Education for over 20 years. He maintains an American Indian Education website at http://nau.edu/aie and a Teaching Indigenous Languages web site at http://nau.edu/til.

KAREN SCHAUMANN-BELTRÁN is Service Learning Director, Honors Program Co-Director and Assistant Professor of Sociology at Schoolcraft College in Livonia, Michigan. She has contributed to Roberto Rodreguizs's X Column in "Thirteen Steps to Heaven for Ramona," and wrote "The First Americans" for LaVoz Latina. She is currently in the process of writing an oral and tribal history with Passamaquoddy elder David Francis. Her work as an applied sociologist and anti-poverty activist is included in Cheryl Joseph's (ed.) *Putting Sociology to Work* and *Our Social World,* by Jeanne Ballantine and Keith Roberts (second ed., Sage, 2011). As a member of the Michigan Coalition against Racism in Sports and the Media, she has participated in educating the public about the negative effects of using Native American mascots, team names, and logos in sports and the media. She hosted the State of Michigan Museum and Library "Statehood Day" on behalf of the Nokomis Learning Center (Okemos, Michigan), and sings traditional Native songs with the Miskwaasining Nagamojig (Swamp Singers) and the Ogichidaa Kwe (warrior women) women's hand drum groups. Her dedication to maintaining traditional and social Native songs and culture stems from her grandmother's influence and early instruction on the traditions of the Passamaquoddy Nation.

WILLIAM SCONZERT-HALL earned his MA in Applied Linguistic Anthropology from the University of Oklahoma. His main area of interest concerns indigenous language revitalization and language policy. He has also worked on a research project on Native elder mistreatment (abuse, neglect, and financial exploitation).

PAUL SPICER is an anthropologist and developmentalist who specializes in research on health and human development in American Indian communities. Dr. Spicer is Professor of Anthropology at the University of Oklahoma, where he also serves as codirector of the Center for Applied Social Research. He began his career at the American Indian and Alaska Native Programs at the University of Colorado in 1995, moving to the University of Oklahoma in 2008. In addition to his research on alcoholism, he has lead research in the health and development of American Indian and Alaska Native children, which includes his research on childhood and family obesity. Dr. Spicer has served as Principal Investigator on 8 grants from the National Institutes of Health, two grants from the Robert Wood Johnson Foundation, and was founding director of the American Indian and Alaska Native Head Start Research Center, which was funded by the Administration on Children and Families. He is the author of over 50 contributions in peer-reviewed journals in addition to 10 chapters in edited volumes. Dr. Spicer currently serves on the Secretary's Advisory Committee for the Evaluation of the Maternal, Infant, and Early Childhood Home Visiting Program, the Board of Zero To Three: The National Center for Infants, Toddlers, and Families, and is president of the Oklahoma Association for Infant Mental Health.

PAUL D. STEELE, PhD is Professor of Sociology and Criminology and Director of the Center for Justice Studies at Morehead State University. He is emeritus Professor of Sociology at the University of New Mexico, where he was appointed by the Governor as Director of the New Mexico Criminal Justice Analysis Center. He also served as Director of Research at the Vera Institute of Justice in New York City. Steele is a Distinguished Visiting Scholar at Cornell University, fellow of the Institute for Behavioral Research at the University of Georgia, and is a member of the Oxford Roundtable. He has completed research on the sexual victimization of children and case outcomes on nine southwestern reservations. He has also conducted research on traditional and Eurocentric models of alcohol, mental health, and drug abuse treatment in Indian Country, and evaluated mental health and social service programs for Natives residing in urban communities. Steele was invited to testify before the U.S. Senate's Indian Affairs Subcommittee concerning the reauthorization of the Indian Child Protection and Family Violence Prevention Act, and has served as a member of the advisory board for American Indian/Alaska Native Child Abuse Intervention of the National Children's Alliance and the Native American Children's Alliance.

PAUL B. STRETESKY, PhD is Professor of Criminology in the School of Public Affairs at the University of Colorado-Denver. He publishes and teaches in the areas of environmental crime and justice. He is coauthor (with Michael J. Lynch and Ronald Burns) of *Environmental Crime, Law, and Justice* (LFB, 2009) and *Treadmill of Crime: Political Economy and Green Criminology* (with Michael A. Long and Michael J. Lynch, Routledge, 2013). He is also coeditor (with Michael J. Lynch) of Ashgate's book series entitled *Green Criminology.* He has published numerous book chapters and articles on issues related to the environment in journals such as *Social Problems, Criminology, Archives of Pediatrics and Adolescent Medicine,* and *Social Science Research.*

STAN WEEBER, PhD (University of North Texas, 2000) is Professor of Sociology and Criminal Justice at McNeese State University in Lake Charles, Louisiana. His interests in sociology include ethnic minorities, political sociology, collective behavior/social movements, sociological theory, sociology of disaster, and crime/deviance. He has authored or edited 21 books, including *Political Crime in the United States* (Praeger, 1978) and *Militias in the New Millennium* (University Press of America, 2004). His sociological work has appeared in *The American Sociologist, The Sociological Quarterly,* the *Journal of Public Management and Social Policy, International Review of Modern Sociology,* the *Canadian Review of Sociology and Anthropology,* the *Contemporary Law and Justice Journal,* the *Journal of Popular Culture,* the *Journal of Law, Politics, and Societies,* the *Journal of Global Analysis, Humanity and Society,* and several other journals. In addition, Dr. Weeber serves on the editorial boards of numerous international sociology journals and has served as a reviewer for the *American Sociological Review.* In 2010, he participated in the Oxford Roundtable on Social Justice, a social issues think tank at Oxford University. That same year, he won the McNeese State President's Award for Outstanding Scholarship. During the 2012–2013 academic year he is serving as the Mr. and Mrs. William D. Blake Professor of Criminal Justice at McNeese State University.

L. EDWARD WELLS is Professor Emeritus in Criminal Justice Sciences at Illinois State University where he has been a faculty member since 1986. His research interests are focused on theoretical models of crime and social control, with a special interest on crime, policing, and social control processes that occur in non-metropolitan and rural settings. He is a coauthor (with Ralph Weisheit and David Falcone) of *Crime and Policing in Rural and Small Town America* (Waveland Press, 2006) and coeditor (with Joseph Rankin) of *Social Control and Self-Control Theories in Crime and Delinquency* (Ashgate Press, 2011). Recent scholarship focused on American Indian policing includes the article "Tribal Policing on American Indian Reservations" in *Policing: An International Journal of Police Strategies and Management* (vol. 34, 2008) and the chapter "Policing Subordinate Sovereignties:

Policing in Democratic Societies" in *Comparative and International Policing, Justice, and Transnational Crime* (ed. Sesha Kethineni, Carolina Press, 2010).

DIANE J. WILLIS is Professor Emeritus, Department of Pediatrics, University of Oklahoma Health Sciences Center. She has been president of Divisions of the American Psychological Association 12 and 37 and of 53 and 54 when they were sections. She was also president of the American Orthopsychiatric Association. She was awarded the Distinguished Professional Contribution to Clinical Psychology by Division 12, the Nicholas Hobbs award by Division 37, Indian Woman of the Year by the Oklahoma Federation of Indian Woman, and is a Fellow of the American Psychological Association. Dr. Willis was founding editor of the *Journal of Pediatric Psychology.* For 25 years, Dr. Willis directed the psychological services at the Child Study Center, Department of Pediatrics, University of Oklahoma Health Sciences Center and began the first Behavioral Clinic, Attention Deficit Hyperactivity Disorders Clinic, and Drug/Alcohol Infant Clinic in the state. Dr. Willis took early retirement after being approached by the American Indian Programs Branch in Washington, D.C., and the American Indian Institute at Oklahoma University to help Indian tribes establish their Early Head Start programs. She is a member of the Kiowa tribe. Willis is the coeditor of four books, one on the prevention of child maltreatment, and the author of over 55 published articles.

JAMES W. ZION is an Indian law practitioner and "scholar on the run" who practices law in the Navajo Nation and has been writing on Indian justice issues for more than 30 years. He is an adjunct professor in the Department of Criminal Justice of Northern Arizona University and has published a great deal on Navajo peacemaking, Indian customary law, and the human rights of indigenous peoples. He is the international counsel for the National Indian Youth Council.

Index